MIDRASH
AND LECTION IN
MATTHEW

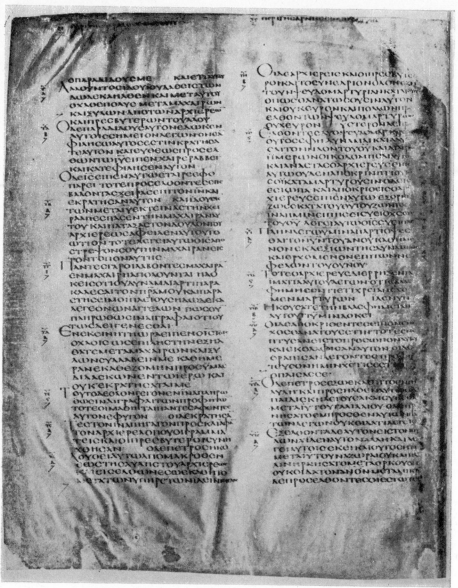

CODEX ALEXANDRINUS, f.27 verso (Matt. 26. 46–73)

At the top of each column is written the title of the relevant lection:

ξε ΠΕΡΙΤΗΣΠΑΡΑΔΟΣΕΩΣΤΟΥ͞Ι͞Υ
65. Of the Betrayal of Jesus

ξϛ ΠΕΡΙΤΗΣΑΡΝΗΣΕΩΣ(ΠΕΤΡΟΥ)
66. Of Peter's Denial

The end of the reading is marked with a 7 close to the left margin (5th line left; 14 lines from bottom right). The paragraphs, marked with capitals and numbers, are the Eusebian canons, and are irrelevant for reading purposes. See pp. 180–1.

MIDRASH AND LECTION IN MATTHEW

M. D. GOULDER

The Speaker's
Lectures in Biblical Studies
1969–71

LONDON **SPCK**

First published in Great Britain in 1974
Second impression 1977
S.P.C.K.
Holy Trinity Church
Marylebone Road
London NW1 4DU

Reproduced and printed by photolithography and bound in
Great Britain at The Pitman Press, Bath

ISBN 0 281 02713 7

In Memory of
AUSTIN FARRER

CONTENTS

viii   *Contents*

ABBREVIATIONS

AAGA	Matthew Black, *An Aramaic Approach to the Gospel and Acts*. 3e, Oxford 1967
Allen	W. C. Allen, *A Critical and Exegetical Commentary on the Gospel according to St Matthew*. Edinburgh 1912
ANCL	Ante-Nicene Christian Library
Arak	Arakhin
B . . .	Babylonian Talmud
Bauer	W. Bauer, *A Greek–English Lexicon of the New Testament and other early Christian Literature*. Tr. and ed. W. F. Arndt and F. W. Gingrich. 4e., Cambridge 1952
Bekh	Bekhoroth
Ber.	Berakhoth
BFBS	British and Foreign Bible Society
BJRL	*Bulletin of John Rylands Library*
BRPOS	J. Mann, *The Bible as Read and Preached in the Old Synagogue*. Vol. I. Cincinnati 1940.
BZNW	*Beihefte zur Zeitschrift für neutestamentliche Wissenschaft*
Dem.	Demai
e.	edition
Erub.	Erubin
E.T.	English Translation
EWJ	J. Jeremias, *The Eucharistic Words of Jesus*. E.T., London 1966
FG	B. H. Streeter, *The Four Gospels*. London 1924
Git.	Gittin
Hag.	Hagigah
HTR	*Harvard Theological Review*
HUCA	*Hebrew Union College Annual*
J . . .	Jerusalem Talmud

JBL	*Journal of Biblical Literature*
JEH	*Journal of Ecclesiastical History*
JJS	*Journal of Jewish Studies*
Jon.	Jonathan
JPN	J. Jeremias, *Jesus' Promise to the Nations*. E.T., London, 1958
JQR	*Jewish Quarterly Review*
JTS	*Journal of Theological Studies*
Kel.	Kelim
Ket.	Ketuboth
Kidd.	Kiddushin
Kil.	Kilaim
Lohmeyer	E. Lohmeyer, *Das Evangelium des Matthäus*. Ed. W. Schmauch. 3e., Gottingen 1962.
LXX	The Septuagint, the Greek translation of the O.T. and Apocrypha
M . . .	Mishnah
Maas. Shen.	Maaser Sheni
McNeile	A. H. McNeile, *The Gospel according to St Matthew*. London 1915
Meg.	Megillah
Mek.	Mekilta
Mid.	Midrash
MM	B. Gerhardsson. *Memory and Manuscript*. Uppsala 1964
Ned.	Nedarim
Nestle–Aland	*Novum Testamentum Graece*. 25e., 1963
NTD	*Neue Testament Deutsch*
NTRJ	D. Daube, *New Testament and Rabbinic Judaism*. London 1956
NTS	*New Testament Studies*
Origins	G. D. Kilpatrick, *The Origins of the Gospel according to St Matthew*. Oxford 1946
Pes.	Pesahim
Pes. R.	Pesiqta Rabbati

PJ	J. Jeremias, *The Parables of Jesus.* 6e., 1962; 2e., E.T., London 1963
PJ(e.1)	signifies the first edition
Proc. B.A.	*Proceedings of the British Academy*
PSR	A. Feldman, *The Parables and Similes of the Rabbis.* Cambridge 1927
R.	Rabbi
. . . R.	Rabbah
RB	*Revue Biblique*
R.H.	Rosh haShanah
S–B	H. L. Strack and P. Billerbeck, *Kommentar zum N.T. aus Talmud und Midrash.* Vol. i. 4e., Munich 1926
Sanh.	Sanhedrin
SBT	Studies in Biblical Theology
Setting	W. D. Davies, *Setting of the Sermon on the Mount.* Cambridge 1964
Shab.	Shabbath
Sheb.	Shebuoth
Shek.	Shekalim
SJ	T. W. Manson. *The Sayings of Jesus.* London 1937
SNTS	Studiorum Novi Testamenti Societas
Sot.	Sotah
SSM	K. Stendahl, *The School of St Matthew.* Uppsala 1954
Suk.	Sukkah
T . . .	Tosephta
Taan.	Ta'anit
Targ.	Targum
TIM	G. Barth in *Tradition and Interpretation in Matthew.* Ed. G. Bornkamm, G. Barth, and H. J. Held. E.T., London 1963
TWNT	*Theologisches Wörterbuch zum Neuen Testament* Ed. G. Kittel and G. Friedrich. Vols. 1–9. Stuttgart 1933.
UOTSM	R. H. Gundry. *The Use of the O.T. in St. Matthew's Gospel.* Leiden 1967
WG	G. Strecker, *Der Weg der Gerechtigkeit.* Bonn 1966
WI	W. Trilling, *Das Wahe Israel.* 3e., Munich 1964
ZNW	*Zeitschrift für die neutestamentliche Wissenschaft*

ACKNOWLEDGEMENTS

Scripture quotations from the Revised Standard Version of the Bible, copyrighted 1946 and 1952 by the Division of Christian Education of the Churches of Christ in the United States of America, are used by permission.

Scripture quotations followed by (AT) are in the author's translation.

Thanks are due to the Cambridge University Press for permission to quote from *Parables and Similes of the Rabbis*, by A. Feldman.

PREFACE

This book is substantially the Speaker's Lectures in Biblical Studies, delivered in the Hilary Terms of 1969–71 at Trinity College, Oxford. The lectures were given under the title, 'St Matthew's Materials—a pan–Marcan Hypothesis'. I had developed a conclusion reached originally on the Lord's Prayer into a comprehensive view of the First Gospel: as the work of a Christian 'scribe' who had only Mark before him—no Q, no M, and very little oral tradition—and who expounded Mark in standard Jewish ways. This hypothesis was accepted by the Electors as the basis for the lectures, and in the first year I set out what I understand to be the Matthaean manner, here presented in chapters 1–6, 8. I intended to devote the whole of the second and third years to applying the picture thus gained to the text of the Gospel without more ado.

While the characteristics of the evangelist, thus worked out, seemed to explain much of the detail of the Gospel, I was relying on Dr Farrer's theory of parallelism with the Hexateuch to account for the salient features of its structure. But during the winter of 1968–69 a very much more satisfactory theory occurred to me. First I found what seemed to be a Hexateuchal structure to the Chronicler's work. Then in response to questions after the first lectures I followed up lectionary suggestions made by Dr Carrington; and became convinced that a lectionary hypothesis for Matthew, on a different scheme from Carrington's, would account for many details of the Gospel, and for the general structure, better than Farrer's literary theory (9). By the summer I had elaborated a similar theory for the Chronicler (10), and for Mark (9, appendix B). The same general approach later seemed to me to be valid for Luke too (21), and to be the solution to the riddle of the Lucan order, and the end of the Q hypothesis. I therefore opened the second year's lectures with this new material, and wrote the remainder in the light of it. I began the third year with an examination of the *a priori* arguments which underlie all discussions of the evidential questions, and have now transferred this discussion to its logical place at chapter 7. The book thus divides into two halves, the first on the evangelist, the second on his Gospel: and it proposes two new theories to account for the latter, my original midrashic theory, and my later lectionary theory. Hence the new title.

Although the book divides in two in this way, it is not an introduction and commentary in the normal sense. Part 1 does not recapitulate the tradition of the Fathers, for example, and those parts of the Gospel which are generally conceded to be Marcan are hardly commented on. The first Part aims to forge the tools with which the Gospel is to be interpreted in the second. In a broad sense the book is a commentary —I might dare to say a more thorough-going commentary than any such more narrowly conceived: not (of course) in its scholarship, but in the nature of its theory. All other theories view Matthew as an editor because they assume multiple sources: I assume one source, and offer an explanation of the rest of the book in the light of the evangelist's character. What is not so explicable must be credited to non-Marcan tradition, but it is not much. Part 1 is thus not an optional foreword: with the possible exception of chapter 10 it is essential to following the argument of Part 2.

As I am not writing a commentary of the normal kind, I have discussed only matters germane to my thesis. I have confined discussion of other scholars' views to the footnotes as far as possible, and then only when they support or conflict with my own view: even so there are many relevant writings which I have had to pass over, as well as very many which I shall have overlooked. I have followed the Nestle–Aland text (*Synopsis Quattuor Evangeliorum* (Stuttgart 1967) for the Gospels; *N.T. Graece* (25e., 1963) for the remainder) without discussion, except where either I—or on occasion other scholars— disagree with it, or the variants shed light on the exposition. For the Hebrew of the OT I have followed *Biblia Hebraica* (14e., 1966), and for the LXX Rahlfs' 8th edition (1965), though for the latter I have quoted Mss. in the case of variants. The English translation used is (except in chapter 4) the RSV, which is used by permission: where I have deserted this, either for the sense or the rhythm of the Greek, I have marked the text AT (author's translation).

I am very grateful to the Electors for trusting me, a little-known student of the Bible, with an august Lecturership, to argue a highly unorthodox thesis. My thanks are due to Trinity College for kindly putting the Danson Room at my disposal; and especially to the Reverend Leslie Houlden, who has helped me with comments on a number of the lectures, and with great generosity in many ways. I am grateful to Professor H. D. F. Sparks, Dr H. Chadwick, and Canon C. P. M. Jones, who came to many of the lectures, and asked helpful and courteous questions; to my daughter Catharine for compiling the Bibliography; and to my own University, and the Hort Memorial and Bethune–Baker Funds at Cambridge, for grants towards the cost of publication. But above all I owe the seminal

ideas, and the opportunity to deliver them, to Austin Farrer, my
tutor and mentor, who taught me to look at Matthew as an author,
and at his Gospel as revelation, and who died three weeks before the
first lecture was given.

Birmingham, March 1971   MICHAEL GOULDER

PART I

The Matthaean
Manner

1

A SCRIBE DISCIPLED

If it were asked, 'Which book in the Old Testament had a history of composition most like St Matthew's Gospel?', I suppose that most of us would answer, 'Why, one of the historical books, perhaps the Books of Kings.' The answer seems obvious. The Deuteronomic historian had no doubt a basic written record in the form of annals of kings just as Matthew had the written Mark. He had further material in the form of tradition from the prophetic schools, perhaps fixed, in written form, like the historical matter in Isaiah and Jeremiah, perhaps nearly fixed in the community memory; just as Matthew had either a fixed written Q and M, or material in viscous state preserved in the Christian community. The historian edited and interpreted this material in the light of a theology which had developed from the time of the events he chronicles; just as Matthew edited and interpreted the Gospel traditions in the light of the theology of his community.

Such, perhaps, would be the normal pattern of answer to the question I have suggested. It is not, however, the only answer, for an equally valid analogy might be the Books of Chronicles. It would, of course, be foolish to try to draw a hard line between the method of composition of the two works, but we are conscious of some difference of *genre* between them. The Chroniclers may have had ancient traditions stretching back up the centuries which are not preserved in Samuel and Kings. But undeniably a good deal of their work has been creative. The addresses put into the mouths of prophets at different points in the narrative are Levitical sermons largely aimed at the listener.[1] Many details have been changed, elaborated, or omitted because events which had seemed harmless to the author of Kings seemed to be monstrous impossibilities to the Chroniclers. Samuel must have been a Levite, not an Ephraimite;[2] and Obed-Edom the Gittite, at whose house the Ark lodged on one fateful occasion, is promoted to an Israelite, to a Levite, and to be the ancestor of a whole order of doorkeepers of the house of the Lord.[3] Numbers are regularly multiplied, the armies of Judah do better in battle, and numerous other tendencies can be noticed. Without wishing to involve ourselves in a controversial question we may fairly claim that the Books of Chronicles are substantially a midrashic expansion of Kings, with an

[1] G. Von Rad, 'The Levitical Sermon in I and II Chronicles', in *The Problem of the Hexateuch and Other Essays* (E.T., Edinburgh 1966), pp. 267–80.
[2] 1 Chron. 6.28.   [3] 1 Chron. 15.18; 16.4,38.

unresolved modicum of independent tradition—midrashic, that is an embroidery somewhat in the rabbinic manner, aimed at doctrinal reconciliation, and at edification.[4]

The purpose of this book is to explore the possibility that the Gospel according to St Matthew was written on the Chronicles model rather than the Kings model. I shall take it for granted that Matthew had Mark in front of him, and shall ask at each point whether we can provide an adequate account of any new material on the hypothesis that Matthew had very little non-Marcan tradition, written or oral. Or, to put it in other words, I shall consider the grounds for thinking that Matthew was writing a midrashic expansion of Mark: that the new teaching is his teaching, that the new poetry is his poetry, that the new parables are his parables. As with the Chronicler, I think we shall have to concede a modicum of non-Marcan material—so much anyhow as we can get from the Epistles of St Paul. But my thesis is a radical one, if it has nothing else to commend it.

Perhaps I should give a brief illustration of method. One of the few passages in Mark not reproduced in Matthew is the parable of the Seed Growing Secretly. In the place in the Marcan order where we might have expected it there is a somewhat similar parable, the Tares. Holtzmann[5] suggested seventy years ago that the Tares was a development of the Seed Growing Secretly—it has the same point, the same background, and in some remarkable details the same language. Other matters not noted by Holtzmann confirm this—the grander scale, the increased allegory, the interest in angels and hell, and so on, all of which are very Matthaean characteristics. It seems very likely, then, that Matthew expanded the Marcan parable himself. Similarly the little Doorkeeper parable in Mark 13 is omitted by Matthew, but in its place we find a succession of parables, the Burglar, the Faithful and Unfaithful Servants, the Bridesmaids, and the Talents; all of which have a similar theme—'Watch'—and furthermore all of which draw on one detail or another of Mark's Doorkeeper: one the watches of the night, one the master going away, and so on. Now Professor Kilpatrick suggests,[6] entirely properly as I should think, that through use in church, preaching and so on, these parables gathered in a cluster and pushed out the little Marcan Doorkeeper: but Dr Kilpatrick also thinks, and here perhaps more questionably, that the parables were ready to Matthew's hand in Q and M. Again, a close look at the

---

[4] Cf. G. Vermes, 'Bible and Midrash: Early Old Testament Exegesis', *The Cambridge History of the Bible* (Cambridge 1970) I, pp. 199–231.

[5] H. J. Holtzmann, *Hand-Kommentar zum NT* (3e., Tübingen 1901), p. 248.

[6] G. D. Kilpatrick, *The Origins of the Gospel according to St. Matthew* [*Origins*] (Oxford 1946), p. 89.

parables reveals a large amount of Matthaean interest, habit of writing, doctrine as well as language; and a simpler solution might seem to be that Matthew has done the expanding himself. Please note that I am not saying that Matthew made them up from nothing, out of his head. I am saying that they are so typical of him that *he* must have composed them, and that we are lucky enough to have in our Mark the matrix from which he worked.

Now once we have got used to the shock of such a suggestion, it must, I think, have a certain attraction. This is partly in virtue of its simplicity, a virtue which I will not press on you—much. How Matthew was written is an historical question, and historical questions are commonly found to have complex solutions: nevertheless the omission from our reconstruction of a number of hypothetical entities cannot but be considered an advantage. We are better without putative documents which have disappeared, and whose contents are disputed and heterogeneous; and without supposed traditions which would appear to demand the attention of all Christians, and yet are apparently unknown to Paul and Mark. There will be more to say on this matter in a moment, but at least in priority of agenda we may ask that attention be given to the more simple answer before we turn to the more complex.

Much of the attraction of the midrashic theory, however, is that it seems that the book has its origin in educated Jewish–Christian circles. Von Dobschütz proposed in 1928 that Matthew was a converted rabbi,[7] and although this thesis has been criticized in recent years, the evidence is weighty that he was on the right lines: not quite that Matthew was a rabbi, but that he was a scribe, a provincial schoolmaster. The greater part of this chapter will be given to examining the Gospel's attitude to the scribes, and to the Jewish legal system. This will lead us, in the second chapter, to examine the Gospel from the angle of what we might expect of a Christian scribe. One of the principal scribal activities is midrash, and Matthew is often stated to contain midrash, for example in the first two chapters. But very little attention has been given to the thorough-going application of the concept of midrash to the Gospel. We will trace in outline the development of typical midrashic handling of a given inspired text, from the Chronicler's handling of Samuel–Kings to the Jubileeist's and the Testamentalist's handling of Genesis, from the Targums to the rabbis' treatment of the Pentateuch and Lamentations in the Midrash Rabbah; and notice some of the traits which recur in Matthew, and often in Matthew alone of the Gospels. This will be found to suggest

[7] E. von Dobschütz, 'Matthäus als Rabbi und Katechet', *ZNW* 27 (1928), pp. 328–48.

that Matthew is much more a free reworking of Mark, and much less an edited compendium of traditions, than has been commonly supposed.

By this point we shall have amassed a short list of midrashic tendencies visible in Matthew—that is, habits of mind common to him and the Jewish writers of the millennium in which he stands at the middle point. In the next four chapters we shall examine the Gospel for various other tendencies. Many of these are non-controversial. Some are linguistic; others are traits of thought rather than of language, as for example the Gospel's penchant for large figures and the grand scale, in a way that is quite distinct from the thought of the other evangelists. Some of this is new, but it is only an extension of the linguistic argument worked out by Hawkins[8] and now basic to all discussion. Matthew has δικαιοσύνη seven times, Luke once, Mark never; therefore the word is Matthaean, and probably introduced by the evangelist. Matthew has the grand scale in about fifteen contexts, Luke once, Mark never; therefore the grand scale is Matthaean, and probably introduced by the evangelist. Other traits are theological, and here again the path is *multis ante tritum pedibus*. We shall break new ground chiefly in two directions, both of which have been opened up by English studies over the last generation, and which have not been exploited, so far as I know, in Gospel criticism. A word may be in place to introduce these two areas here, since such originality as this book can boast is to be found largely at this point.

The first is the use of imagination. Detailed and fascinating studies have been made of the imagery of Shakespeare and his contemporaries. When describing a scene at sea, say, Bacon is out there with the sailors in the boat, while Shakespeare watches from the land; Marlowe has far more celestial imagery than either of the others, and so on.[9] Now an examination of the Gospels reveals a similar contrast. We find in M and Q alike a host of colourful images: there are for example 38 uses of animal imagery between them where Mark and L have only a handful. On the other hand the imagination behind the L matter is of a strong and differentiated kind. This is one line of evidence which will add up to a strong suggestion that there is a Matthaean imagination at work in M and Q. But further, we can see from the redactional handling of Mark the strongly antithetical bent of the evangelist's mind. This antithetical approach is clearly visible in the Q and M material, pairing a female illustration to a male, a marine to a land image, an agricultural to a pastoral figure, and so on; a habit of mind which is rare in the other three evangelists. To such an

[8] Sir J. C. Hawkins, *Horae Synopticae* (2e., Oxford 1909).
[9] C. Spurgeon, *Shakespeare's Imagery* (Cambridge 1935), pp. 25f, chart II.

extent is St Matthew's mind, as I see it, antithetical, that it is possible to see time and again how he develops his theme. The imaginative evidence is very strong.

The second new area into which we shall move is that of sentence-form, or rhythm. The gauging of rhythms is notoriously a difficult and subjective matter, but in the Gospels the rhythms are strongly marked, and it is possible to isolate a number of basic rhythms of a clearly definable kind. These rhythms stand out in the Greek, and go well beyond the analysis of Burney,[10] who, in common with most commentators on rhythm, concentrated on the presumed Aramaic rhythms. Having established these basic rhythms, it is easy to pick out the various elaborations of them. The evidence thus obtained will be found to point in the same direction. Mark contains some poetry, but the rhythms are rough, and the complex patterns are rare. Q and M are both heavily rhythmical, with polished basic rhythms, and highly elaborate antithetical patterns built therefrom. Where Matthew takes over Marcan poetry he commonly polishes it. Conversely, the poetry in Luke is almost all Q matter. Where there are L rhythms they are usually formed by parallel to antecedent Q rhythms. Often the Lucan version spoils the rhythm. The simplest conclusion to this study would seem to be that Matthew was free to impose his own strong antithetical rhythms on his material, at the least, and Luke those typical of him.

Other areas which we will consider are Matthaean language; characteristic use of scripture; and Matthaean doctrinal innovations, which we shall find almost always paralleled in the rabbis, or in the Christian rabbi Paul, whose writings are much more closely related to Matthew than is often supposed. A further major innovation, the relationship of the Gospel to the Jewish Festal Year, I pass over for the moment.

In this way we shall have established, I hope, a fair number of categories which may be held to constitute, in a rough way, the Matthaean manner. It will then be open to us, in Part II to go through the Gospel paragraph by paragraph, asking ourselves: Do the Matthaean tendencies which we have established account for this paragraph completely, granted the possibility that the Gospel may be a midrashic expansion of Mark? Is it Matthaean in doctrine, in language, in rhythm, in manner, etc.? There must come a point at which we are driven in theory to say: If this passage is Matthaean in so many respects, in what way is it not Matthaean? And if no obvious answer is forthcoming, the presumption must be that we have a piece of Matthew's own writing. But surely, it may be objected, you are not saying that the evangelist made it up out of his head? Surely he must

[10] C. F. Burney, *The Poetry of Our Lord* (Oxford 1925).

have had something from the tradition before him at each point? Surely he didn't dream up the whole Sermon on the Mount? Precisely so. The Sermon, like every other M and Q paragraph, comes to Matthew in essence from tradition. He has not written an historical novel. It is only that it seems to me that this tradition can be traced in almost every case to the tradition we have in Mark. His Gospel is a midrashic expansion of Mark.

The task we are undertaking is a formidable one. We shall look at each point for a matrix from Mark from which the paragraph may have grown, and for a reason why this matrix might have been taken at this point. We shall ask whether a natural reading of the passage makes sense of it in the context given. If the matrices suggested, or the motive suggested, or the sense suggested, are unconvincing, then for that passage our theory will not work. Once past these initial hurdles there remains the task of applying our categories, and asking how far an adequate explanation of the passage has been obtained without recourse to the hypothesis of a non-Marcan tradition. The argument is necessarily cumulative, and there will be points to weigh in every paragraph.

Nor is this all: for any thesis about Matthew involves a thesis about Luke. As I am exploring the possibility that the Q material is Matthew's own embroidery of Mark, naturally I do not accept the Q hypothesis. This is no great penance, for the minor agreements of Matthew and Luke against Mark have made the theory in any simple form untenable:[11] but it lays upon us two further duties. First, in each Q passage, we must consider whether the Lucan version appears to be a secondary handling of Matthew; for if ever the Lucan version seems to be the earlier, for that passage my hypothesis is invalid. Second, I must give an account of the reordering by Luke of the Marcan and Matthaean material; and this I shall do, in the form of a lectionary scheme for Luke, in a final chapter.

There is thus a daunting series of labours before my infant Hercules. I am involved in challenging three time-honoured theories: the Q

[11] The minor agreements have always been an embarrassment to the Q theory, and have had to be explained as instances of textual corruption. B. H. Streeter, for example, gave 37 pages (pp. 295–331) of *The Four Gospels* [*FG*] (London 1924) to such explanations, and much work has been done on them since. But W. R. Farmer, in *The Synoptic Problem* (London 1965), and others, have shown that the minor agreements include not merely words and phrases but omissions and inversions, which may total as many as seven in a single pericope such as the Paralytic or the Wicked Husbandmen, and constitute a formidable problem. As long as (*a*) Matthew seemed to be an editor of traditions, and not a writer of midrash, and (*b*) there was no rational interpretation of the Lucan order, a common tradition, Q, was the best available hypothesis. Now we have another hypothesis, which can explain the minor agreements: Luke had read Matthew.

solution to the Synoptic Problem; the hypothesis of Aramaic originals behind the Q and M matter; and, so far as it affects Matthew, the form-critical theory. No mean task: but the new considerations, midrashic and lectionary, which I am adducing, combine to put a powerful weapon in our hands, and the conclusion to which I am impelled is that virtually the whole Gospel can be adequately explained in this way. We shall not need to spare many sops to Cerberus.

In a sense all that we are doing is to take a step further the study undertaken by Kilpatrick in his still classic *Origins of the Gospel according to St Matthew*. Kilpatrick accepted the traditional editorial status for the evangelist, and found that the linguistic evidence pointed to a far more extensive redactoral activity than had been suspected. The milieu that suggested itself for the editor was a liturgical one. It was clear that the traditional material had developed through use in church—probably a Syrian church—in the 70s and 80s. Two basic arguments could be applied. Where there was evident redactoral activity, we had evidence of the position of the evangelist's church— if the Lord forbids the apostles to get gold in their purses in place of the Marcan brass, it is because the Matthaean church is more middle-class. Secondly, a count of vocabulary even in non-Marcan passages enabled us to see the evangelist at work, as with δικαιοσύνη instanced above. Both of these arguments are basic to our own study, and almost everything which Kilpatrick concludes from them seems to me irrefutable. But a difficult problem emerges from the analysis. How can we reconcile the apparently free, smoothly-running flow of the book, the activity of whose editor has been so convincingly described, with the harsh fact assumed that the material of the Gospel came to him in pre-cast units? We are able to suggest an advance beyond Kilpatrick, in part because the confidence felt in the Q solution has waned in the last two decades, and in part because other arguments than the linguistic one can now be applied in the same basic two ways. My Matthew is still a bishop of a Syrian church, though I will posit him a little earlier than Kilpatrick, say in the second half of the eighth decade. With his Jewish background in mind I am crediting him with the possibility of a more pervasive liturgical activity. The main difference between us is that writing later I am able to make fewer assumptions, and to deploy more sophisticated tools; but the method is taught me by him.

The *sôphēr*, or scribe, like his English counterpart the secretary, has come down in the world over the centuries. Once the highest civil office in the land, he has come to be a mere copyist. The Chronicler looked back with reverence to Ezra as the Scribe *par excellence*, and the first of the succession of great schools of Judaism were remembered as the Sopherim. In all probability the Chroniclers were themselves *sôph^erîm*, scholars of scripture interpreting the divine message to their contemporaries from their Levitical background. The mists of history part with more clarity with ben Sirach, to reveal an accomplished scribe of about 200 B.C. about his business; and it is hard not to believe that the portrait of the *grammateus/sôphēr* of *c.* 38 is an idealized view of the author. Learned and at leisure, he surveys with patronizing complacency the restricted life of the workers. His wideranging studies qualify him to speak in the council, and to take the lead in the assembly, to judge, to understand the principles of the law, to bring out the rights of a case. He has sought out the wisdom of scripture—law, prophecy, and *m^eshālîm*: his understanding is rooted in the divine wisdom, and is unshakeable. Honoured by the great at home and abroad, he can pray and praise God in public; he expounds the scripture in synagogue and in his *Bêth-Midrāsh*, and pours out like rain his words of wisdom. His book gives us a full and sympathetic picture of the class which, more than any other, made Judaism what it was, with its glory and its limitations.

The *sôphēr* of rabbinic times is a less splendid figure.[12] Writing, *sāphar*, has become more widely disseminated, and is in demand: the *sôphēr* is the man who can write, and teach others to write, the schoolmaster. It is true that we hear still of distinguished scribes—Naqqai the Scribe about A.D. 120,[13] R. Hamnuna the Scribe, his disciple,[14] R. Hanina ben Hama,[15] a disciple of the following generation, who was able to correct the Patriarch himself on the reading of Ezek. 7.16. These were scholars of the front rank who were experts on the text of scripture, and who trained disciples: but as increasingly expertise in the text of scripture came to be assumed of all, it is not surprising that the title scribe, in this honorific sense, fades away.[16] The normal use of the word, already early in the first century, was for the ordinary schoolmaster, who was a common figure throughout Palestine and in Jewish communities abroad.[17] Primary education was not universal,

[12] J. Jeremias, *TWNT*, art. γραμματεύς.

[13] B. Gerhardsson, *Memory and Manuscript* [*MM*] (Uppsala 1964), p. 51; J. Maas. Shen. v. 2; Lam. R. 3.7, etc.

[14] J Taan. IV. 2; Eccl. R. 7.7.

[15] As for n. 13: see also Rashi ad B Taan. 27b.

[16] Moses and Aaron are still the *sôph^erîm* of Israel in Targ. Jon. Num. 21. 19; Targ. Cant. 1. 2; and the school of Hillel is so spoken of in J Ber. I. 7 and B R.H. 19a. The term is honorific in B Sot. 15a, but = schoolteachers ibid. 49a. See Gerhardsson, *MM*, pp. 56–66.

[17] J Meg. III. 1; B Ket. 105a; B Git. 58a; Lam. R. Proem 12.

though it was to become virtually so by the third century.[18] There were still the ignorant *'ammê hā'ārets*, but for the children of the godly and the ambitious education was a necessity. The primary school was called the *Bêth Sēpher*, the Book-House, and the syllabus was the Bible. Inevitably this involved the schoolmaster in much labour of copying the Book, at first on tablets, later on scrolls, for the children to read: for reading (*qārā'*) was the end of this education, and what was to be read was the *Miqrā'*, the written version of scripture. Hence the teacher's natural title of *sôphēr*: however much, in practice, learning tended to be by rote, written texts had to be available, which only he could write with the necessary accuracy. He thus combined in his professional qualification the ability to copy accurately, a good knowledge of the Torah and a working knowledge of the Prophets and Writings, and a familiarity with the *Targûm*, the standard Aramaic translation; as well as any more down-to-earth pedagogical gifts.[19]

The *sôphēr* made his living by teaching and copying scripture: but of necessity his influence was large in the Sabbath worship too. In the early period of which we are speaking few villages had a separate school: the *Bêth Sēpher* was the Synagogue. In towns where a separate *Bêth Sēpher* existed, often the secondary school was the synagogue.[20] The service consisted of two lections, one from the Law, one from the 'prophets', both read: the Targum, which was recited from memory; and the Sermon: all interspersed with prayers, psalms, and so on. The schoolteacher often had the task of preparing in advance both the readers and the reciters of Targum.[21] It was the task of the village elders, the rulers of the synagogue, to order the worship, but the mantle of authority must frequently have fallen on the *sôphēr* as the most educated man in the village. Sermons were only to a limited extent free exercises of exposition. What was passed on was *midrāsh*, the oral lore of the community, interpretations, applications, instructions on use in everyday life, edificatory parables, anecdotes, and the like; the community's commentary on scripture, amassed century upon century, deposited in fixed form in the Mishnah and Homiletic Midrash of the second century, and in the Midrash and Talmud from the fifth onwards, but known by heart for generations before then. The task of the preacher was formidable, for he must interpret in line with this tradition—indeed he should know this by heart too; and

[18] On Jewish Education see N. Morris, *The Jewish School* (1937); N. Drazin, *History of Jewish Education from 515 B.C. to 220 C.E.* (1940); E. Ebner, *Elementary Education in Ancient Israel* (1956).

[19] M Shab. 1. 3; T Shab. I. 12; Gerhardsson, *MM*, p. 69.

[20] G. F. Moore, *Judaism* (Cambridge, Mass. 1927) I, p. 318; Gerhardsson, *MM*, p. 75.

[21] Gerhardsson, *MM*, pp. 67–70.

questions of application to everyday life (*H^alākāh*) above all he must
get right. The need was therefore keenly felt for the best exposition
that the village could get, and small wonder if the hard-pressed scribe
found himself frequently called upon for this task also. 'Larger synagogues had a paid attendant (a sort of super-verger), the Ḥazzan. In
smaller communities the Ḥazzan often had to fulfil a variety of other
offices. When there were not readers enough at the service, he had
to fill out the number;[22] he might also have to lead in prayer.[23] The
people of Simonias asked the patriarch Judah to give them a man
who could serve them as preacher, judge, Ḥazzan, sopher, teacher of
traditional law and whatever else they needed; and he sent them Levi
ben-Sisi.[24] Especially frequent was the combination of Ḥazzan and
Sopher.'[25] The demand for, and the short supply of, competent
preachers is widely testified in the Gospels and Acts.

To meet the demand for competent exposition of the Oral Torah
there existed colleges of varying academic standing, which provided
the structure for all secondary education in Judaism.[26] Eventually
these were widespread, but during the pre-Tannaitic period we have
no evidence of them in any considerable numbers. Perhaps ben Sirach
ran one, the first reference we have to a Beth-haMidrash,[27] but it is
clear that this is a fairly aristocratic establishment. Schools gathered
round famous teachers, the School of Hillel and the School of Shammai in the life of Jesus; and Josephus mentions a number of similar
establishments.[28] Later we hear of fairly low-level Mishnah schools,
which were not recognized by authority,[29] but the impetus towards
expansion of general education in the Oral Torah came after A.D. 70,
and it is probable that there was no formal means available in the
country villages or outside Palestine till then. Paul came, for example,
from Tarsus to attend a Beth-haMidrash at Jerusalem, and no doubt
many a local scribe in the country or abroad had to do on what he had
picked up at second-hand. The rabbinic way of thinking would be
entirely familiar to him, but he could not be expected to be a master
of the ever-developing system of case-law (*Mishnāh*), or of the 'sea of
the Talmud', the commentary on scripture and Mishnah, whose
compressed form fills shelves of our libraries. No doubt this was very
reprehensible from an official point of view, and the Pharisaic movement existed to make matters better: but, so far as our knowledge
goes, Pharisaism did not provide the structure to remedy it effectively
till the Jamnia period.

[22] B Meg. 25b; cf. T Meg. IV. 21.   [23] J Ber. 12d, middle.
[24] J Yebamot 13a; cf. J Sheb. 36d   [25] Moore, *Judaism* I, pp. 289ff.
[26] Gerhardsson, *MM*, pp. 89ff.   [27] Ecclus. 51.23.
[28] *Bell. Jud.* 33.2; *Ant.* 17.6.2.   [29] Gerhardsson, *MM*, pp. 85ff, 91.

Now there seems to be a strong case to suggest that Matthew was a *sôphēr* of this kind himself.[30] This case is formed partly from the references to scribes in his Gospel, both in the redactional and in the new material sections, partly from his attitude to the Torah, both oral and written, including considerable knowledge of the Oral Torah, both accurate and inaccurate; and partly, and most significantly, from the scribal method which is both used and referred to in numerous subtle ways. All three approaches represent a strong contrast with the other two Synoptic Gospels. Matthew does not, of course, think of himself as a humble provincial copyist–schoolmaster, a mere scribe as opposed to the rabbis or Learned Ones (*Hᵃkhāmîm*): in his eyes he is the Christian inheritor of the noble title borne by a line of servants of God from Ezra to Ben Sirach and Hillel and Shammai, but betrayed by their Pharisaic descendants.

The word γραμματεύς occurs 21 times in Mark, of which 19 instances are hostile. In the earliest Gospel there is no escaping the fact that the scribes are the villains of the tale; local *sôphᵉrîm* and Jerusalem *sôphᵉrîm* alike, they lead disaffection, initiate controversy, have a name for hypocrisy, plot and largely engineer the Lord's Passion, as he knew they would. Of these 19 hostile references, 6 are retained by Matthew at points where they were perhaps inevitable: the controversies over the Paralytic (9.3) and over washing (15.1), the first and third Passion prophecies (16.21 and 20.18), and in the Passion, for the examination of Jesus (26.57) and the connected mocking (27.41). On the other hand six of the Marcan references to scribes are dropped: one for stylistic reasons (15.2), one each at the controversies over the Epileptic (17.14), the Question of Authority (21.23), and David's Son (22.42), one in the plotting of the Passion (21.13), and one at the handing over to Pilate (27.1). A further six are glossed or altered. Jesus' authoritative teaching, not as the scribes (Mark 1.22), becomes 'not as their scribes' (7.29). The scribes of the Pharisees who questioned Jesus' eating with sinners (Mark 2.16) become 'the Pharisees' (9.11), as do the scribes from Jerusalem who blasphemed over Beelzebul (12.24); though they are permitted to make their entry later, and much less damagingly, in the same scene, to ask for a sign (12.38). Both in the initiation of the Passion (26.3) and in the sending of the crowd (26.47) the scribes are replaced by 'the elders of the people'. Each omission or gloss either lessens the blackness of the scribal image, or contrasts 'their' scribes with (presumably) 'ours'.

But although Matthew thus consistently rescues the reputation of the *sôphᵉrîm* as such, the presence of an active scribal movement at

[30] cf. Jeremias, art. cit., 'Das erste Evangelium, insbesondere sein Schriftbeweis, zeigt ihn [sc. the Christian scribe] uns an der Arbeit', p. 472.

the heart of the Jamnia reform involves him in an ambivalence. Scribes as such are fine people, but the persecuting scribes of Judaism are a monstrosity. The good scribe of Mark 12.28ff, who asked of the first commandment and was not far from the kingdom, evokes a Matthaean reaction. 'Their' scribes are as far as one can be from the kingdom (5.20). If they asked questions of the Lord, it was to tempt him (Matthew adds πειράζων αὐτόν); if the Lord commended one of them, it would be wise to suppress the fact (he omits Mark 12.32–34b); in fact to save misunderstanding it would be good not to call him a scribe at all (he substitutes the higher-powered νομικός). This is even clearer with the Marcan command, 'Beware of the scribes, . . .' (Mark 12.38), which Matthew uses as an opportunity to expound his attitude to the scribes in full, with new material (23). Scribes in principle are a divine institution, placed by God on Moses' throne to hand on the Torah, and to be obeyed to the last iota; but Pharisaism has corrupted the order with its leaven of hypocrisy (16.6,12), saying and doing not. By Scribes-and-Pharisees he means Pharisaic Scribes: ordinary run-of-the-mill Pharisees did not sit on Moses' seat.[31] It is they who have thus betrayed their holy calling, and on them falls the curse of the New Law: seven times here, and in their exclusion from the Kingdom at the beginning of the Lord's teaching (5.20). This is made amply plain by the peroration: 'Therefore I send you prophets and wise men (ḥᵃkhāmîm) and scribes . . .' The renegade Pharisaic scribes now persecute their Christian successors.[32]

There are four other instances of the word in Matthew. At 2.4 the scribes are the learned in scripture who are able to advise Herod of the prophesied birthplace of Messiah. At 8.19 a scribe asks to join Jesus' company, and is warned of the hard road—there is no hint of insincerity in the scribe, and most commentators remark that the man is apparently accepted. 13.52 provides the text for this chapter. The scribe who has been discipled to the kingdom of heaven is like a householder bringing out of his treasure-chest things new and old. He is the master of the Torah that was in circulation before him; he has the resource to embroider this further himself for his people's needs. I shall expound this text with special reference to the context

---

[31] So D. R. A. Hare, *The Theme of Jewish Persecution of Christians in the Gospel according to St. Matthew* (Cambridge 1967), p. 81; A. H. McNeile, *The Gospel according to St. Matthew* [McNeile] (London 1915), ad loc.

[32] R. Hummel, *Die Auseinandersetzung zwischen Kirche und Judentum im Matthäusevangelium* (Munich 1963), is correct in saying that Matthew identifies the scribes with the Pharisaic party, and neglects Sadducaic scribes: so reflecting the post-70 situation (p. 14). He also says, less happily (p. 17), that scribes are neutral for Matthew, a name for Jewish authority. But in general his survey of Jewish parties in Matthew is excellent.

in which it stands, Matthew's development of the Marcan parables and *māshāl* sayings. Finally at 21.15 the high-priests and scribes reproach Jesus for the children's Hosannas: the inclusion of the scribes here probably turns on the contrast between νήπιοι and σόφοι (11.25).

A consistent picture seems thus to emerge both in the redactoral and the new material. Matthew's sympathy for the scribes is shown plainly in his omission or change of their name in two-thirds of the hostile Marcan references. He leaves them in when they are essential to a legal controversy, and in the two Passion-prophecies, and nowhere else; whenever he can, and in all serious matters like the Beelzebul blasphemy or the Passion plot, he quietly exonerates them. He draws a line between good Christian scribes and bad Jewish scribes. The new material displays only a clearer focusing of the same picture. Scribes are learned and authoritative teachers of the Church, even from Judaism; the tragedy is the chasm between their teaching and their practice, which keeps them from the Kingdom. In the meantime some of them wish to become disciples, and when they do, have great gifts to contribute in teaching and under persecution. It is hard to think that so regular a picture is without significance.

The attitude to the Torah in the Gospel seems to be in every way consonant with this. We should expect a Christian provincial scribe to be loyal and enthusiastic about the Law, written and oral, and to glory in it as fulfilled in Christ. We should expect equally to find him embarrassed by the radical position taken towards the Law, especially the ceremonial law and the oral traditions, which he found evidenced in Mark. And that is exactly what we do find, both in the redactoral and in the new matter.

This is a well-ploughed field, and it must suffice here to mention briefly the main passages which support such a conclusion, with selected illustrations. The matter is not uncontroversial, and it will be necessary to answer in a moment some recent arguments by G. Strecker and P. Nepper-Christensen; but the line we are taking has much in common with that of G. Barth,[33] and older standard works.

No Gospel has so many citations of scripture: every move geographically, every new development of policy, and many other incidentals evoke the triumphant, 'All this came to pass that it might be fulfilled which was spoken . . .'. All of this is unquestionably the work of the evangelist. The fulfilment of scripture is a theme common to all NT authors, but to none was it as dear as to Matthew. The word

---

[33] Barth's essay, 'Matthew's Understanding of the Law', is classic. It is published in *Tradition and Interpretation in Matthew* [*TIM*] (1960), ed. G. Bornkamm, G. Barth and H. J. Held (E.T., London 1963), pp. 58–164.

νόμος occurs eight times in Matthew as against never in Mark, and has been intruded three times into Marcan contexts (12.5; 22.36,40). Where Mark says that Moses ordained the Fifth Commandment, Matthew writes, 'God commanded . . .' (15.3). The inviolability of the Law is proclaimed forcefully in the new material. Jesus came not to abolish the Law, but to fulfil it (5.17) a word with several meanings, but of plainly positive intention. It means first to put into action what had been foretold in word, like the LXX πληροῦν, the Hebrew *mālē*: fulfilling in action both those prophecies of the future, of the type, 'A virgin shall conceive . . .' (LXX), and also those foreshadowings of the future in the stories in the Law, of the type of the word to Moses, 'They are dead who sought thy life' (LXX). For the *laws* of the Old Testament it is intended to express unlimited approval, and deepening, perhaps with the thought of the Aramaic *qayyēm*, as is shown by prefacing these words to the Antitheses of the Sermon.[34] If the later Antitheses wander a little from this high statement of belief, it is not without reason, as we shall see. In the meantime, the scribe's love for his Hebrew text comes to the fore. Not one *yôdh*, the smallest letter, not one *qōts*, the flourish with which the scribe formed his letters,[35] nothing shall fail of fulfilment till the end of time.[36] Every commandment must be kept, even the very least, and woe betide whoever breaks the smallest even, still more the false prophet who teaches them to be dispensable. Their performance, and their faithful teaching, will bring rewards in the Age to Come; and the listeners had better excel the Pharisees and their scribes. We can hear the rabbis behind every sentence here: 'God spake [to the Torah]—Solomon and a thousand like him will pass away, but I will not permit the smallest stroke of thee to pass away.'[37] 'Heaven and earth have measures, but the Law has none: heaven and earth will have an end, but the Law will not.'[38]

No distinction is drawn between the ceremonial law and the moral. Inserted into the Marcan warning to pray that their flight should not be in winter is the redactoral addition 'nor on a sabbath' (24.20). New material at 5.23 envisages offerings at the Temple, which are also assumed in 'Give not the holy thing to the dogs' (AT). The Temple Tax is to be paid as heretofore. No distinction is drawn between the written law and the oral in the new matter. All the Oral Torah delivered by the Pharisaic scribes comes from Moses' throne, and is valid. The

---

[34] So G. Dalman retranslates, *Jesus-Jeshua*, p. 57. See G. Barth, *TIM*, pp. 67ff for discussion.

[35] H. L. Strack and P. Billerbeck [S-B], *Kommentar zum N.T. aus Talmud und Midrash* I, p. 248.

[36] See p. 284 below.   [37] J Sanh. II. 20c; see S–B I, pp. 244ff.

[38] Gen. R. 10.1; Moore, *Judaism* I, p. 270.

tithing of herbs is good, and ought not to be left undone: the fault of the Pharisees and their scribes is their failure to keep the weightier matters (23.23). Prayer, alms, and fasting, the backbone of rabbinic piety, are enjoined. Temple vows, phylacteries and hems, the washing of vessels inside and out, sackcloth and ashes, and the whole gamut of Pharisaic piety are familiar to author and congregation. And the indispensability of an incumbent of the throne of Moses is never forgotten: the Matthaean Christ sets Peter and the Twelve in his place to bind and to loose for the Church.

Such a thoroughgoing adherence to the Torah would be entirely typical of a scribe; but a Christian scribe was bound to be brought into tension and inconsistency by the irreversible tradition of Jesus' radical attitude towards both Written and Oral Torah. The three matters on which Jesus had especially declared against orthodoxy were in the matters of the Sabbath, of Divorce, and of Ritual Cleanness. In Mark the Sabbath is virtually abrogated by Jesus' justification of his disciples in the cornfield, and by his Sabbath healings; divorce and remarriage are labelled adultery; and the washing and dietary laws are repealed. This tradition could not but be an embarrassment to the Christian scribe, and Matthew simply does his best to gloss the relevant stories so as to minimize the radicalism. We have inconsistency here, but it is an inconsistency that every NT writer is involved in. They all believed in scripture, and the Lord in his lifetime, and the Spirit since, had led them into paths that were at variance with scripture. Mark leaves the two positions starkly side by side: Matthew attempts to paper over the cracks.

The Cornfield is the most offensive pericope on the Sabbath issue. Mark says baldly, 'His disciples began to pluck ears of grain'—sheer deliberate Sabbath-breaking, which Jesus justified. Matthew adds, 'his disciples *were hungry*, and they began . . .'—ah, but the Sabbath-breaking was not unprovoked: they were in need. The issue is thus muddied from the first verse. Secondly, he adds to the Marcan example of David's overruling of the shewbread law a second example of his own showing that the Sabbath-law is overridden by the priests in the Temple: the example is a true one,[39] and shows the evangelist's familiarity with the Oral Torah. It is more relevant than the inadequate Marcan example because it shows that sometimes the Sabbath-law may be overruled, and it serves Matthew's purpose because it shows this within the scribal system.[40] Thirdly, he invokes Hosea, 'I desire mercy, and not sacrifice', by which he means exactly what the prophet meant: religion is first a matter of the heart. Finally, he omits the

---

[39] B Shab. 132b (three times), and often; S–B I, pp. 620ff.
[40] See below, p. 328, n. 50.

uncomfortable epigram in which the Lord had laid the way open to
the complete abrogation of the Sabbath: 'The Sabbath was made for
man, not man for the Sabbath.' It is no mean effort to get over so
uncomfortable a moment. The Sabbath is saved, and the conditions
of need which justify its breaking in the Church are left suitably vague.
In the next pericope, the Withered Hand, the same issue crops up, and
an attempt is made to provide a general ruling. Mark: 'They watched
him, to see whether he would heal him on the Sabbath'; Matthew:
'They asked him, is it lawful to heal on the sabbath?' And at the close
a ruling is provided, which surely will give offence to none: 'So it is
lawful to do good on the sabbath' (12.12). The context shows Jesus'
mind (and Matthew's): *agape* always takes priority. The wording is
not framed to encourage Sabbath-breaking.[41] Here, as in the Cornfield, Matthew inserts an appeal to Sabbath-breaking as permitted in
the Oral Torah, the sheep that may be rescued from the pit. From our
point of view it is unfortunate that he gets the Oral Torah wrong in
this instance,[42] but from his point of view the example is perfect: it
shows that Sabbath-breaking in the name of mercy was accepted in
principle under the Oral Torah. You can have a radical Jesus and the
authority of the Law at the same time.

The same glossing is notorious in the two Divorce pericopes, where
the radical Jesus disappears in qualifying phrases, and emerges as a
rabbi of the school of Shammai. The Marcan Jesus set Gen. 2 against
Deut. 24, and concluded that what God had joined man should not
divide. He saved the Deuteronomic permission of divorce as a provision for 'your hardness of heart'; but his conclusion for his disciples
had been uncompromising, 'Whoever divorces his wife and marries
another, commits adultery against her', and *vice versa* for the wife.
Matthew, at 19.1ff, immediately makes plain his knowledge of
rabbinic controversy: 'Is it lawful to divorce one's wife *for any cause*?'
The last phrase, Matthew's addition, represents the view of the school
of Hillel.[43] But Jesus' answer in Matthew merely rejects this lax
approach in favour of the sterner, and more original sense. Divorce
is wrong for a man, except on grounds of sexual fault, μὴ ἐπὶ πορνείᾳ;
divorce for a woman is not mentioned, as also in the rabbinic tradition.
The version in 5.32 puts the same attitude in a briefer compass: divorce
is forbidden except in the case of sexual fault, παρεκτὸς λόγου πορνείας.
There is something more than this which can be usefully said, and
which we will come to in due course, but here is the bones of the matter.

[41] Cf. Barth, *TIM*, pp. 79f, 91f. Exceptions were made to sabbath-law for war
and visitation of the sick and sad before Matthew in Judaism, S–B I, p. 630.
[42] B Shab. 128b, etc. See S–B I, pp. 629ff.
[43] S–B I, pp. 312ff, 801.

Matthew saves Deuteronomy, but the cost in this case is high, the loss of Jesus' authentic radicality, and his approximation to the teaching of the Shammaites.

The hardest problem of all is set by the Mark 7 controversy on ritual cleanness, since here Jesus is represented not merely as attacking the parity of the oral with the written Law, but also as abrogating the dietary laws in Leviticus. Matthew makes the best he can of a bad job. His first trouble is that Mark begins with the scribes' criticism of the disciples for eating without washing, and has Jesus immediately open up on them with the quotation from Isa. 29, which he interprets as an attack on human tradition as against divine law. This plainly implies that the Oral Torah is merely human tradition, which Matthew does not believe. He therefore transfers Isaiah and the comment to the end of the paragraph, and brings forward the Korban illustration, which he exaggerates. Mark had, 'You no longer permit him to do anything for his father'; Matthew has, 'You say . . . He *need* not honour his father'. The version then runs in plain contradiction of the divinely given Fifth Commandment, and is therefore void, and the Isaiah citation can then follow harmlessly. We are all agreed that if hypocritical Pharisees legislate in contradiction of Sinai, we are not bound, and they will be rooted out. But this does not affect our general confidence in the authority of the Oral Torah. Matthew's second worry is the clarity of Jesus' words in Mark, 'There is nothing outside a man which by going into him can defile him', and the final, 'Thus he declared all foods clean' (Mark 7.15,19). The second and more obviously offensive he leaves out. The first he turns into a sermon on what goes into and comes out of the mouth, which he mentions four times, although it does not fit with the Marcan catalogue of sins at the end, which do not all proceed from the mouth. The sermon, as Barth remarks,[44] might well come from Johanan ben Zakkai, or we might add, St James. It is perfectly easy to understand every word in a comparative sense. Ritual uncleanness is as nothing compared with moral uncleanness (15.11): behold how great evils come out of the mouth, my brethren—it is these, not eating with unwashen hands, which really defile a man (15.20). The ceremonial laws cannot actually be saved: but the emphasis—'Excuse me, inner cleanliness comes first'—suffices to distract both reader and writer from their repeal. The oral Law emerges intact.

Matthew's greatest theological achievement is his reconciliation of the radical position of Mark with the continued validity of the full Torah. We have seen this applied redactionally in the story of the Withered Hand: it is lawful to do good on the Sabbath Day, i.e. when

[44] *TIM*, p. 90.

agape is in conflict with Torah, *agape* comes first. The Lord has said
in Mark that the love of God, and of our neighbour, were the two
Great Commandments, and Matthew adds that all the Law and the
Prophets hang (*tālāh*) on them. The setting up of summary sentences
(*kᵉlālôt*) from which the rest can be said to hang was a widely testified
rabbinic habit.[45] But what Matthew is doing is setting up a summary
of the spirit of the Torah *against which the rest can be judged*. This the
rabbis did not, and here we may feel he is following his master. Hillel
gave his negative version of the Golden Rule, and added, 'This is the
whole Torah. The rest is only commentary.[46] But Hillel's intention
was merely to give a convenient summary, not that anyone should
cite his words against the Torah: Matthew, as a good scribe, here of
the Hillel school, puts the Golden Rule in the mouth of Jesus, and
continues, 'This is the Law and the Prophets', but he means the words
in a dynamic sense. Urgent need in the service of God in the Temple,
urgent need of man with a dried up arm, overrule the Sabbath. Christ
fulfils the Law in his commandments by drawing out of it the two
basic principles, which sometimes deepen and broaden the laws of the
older Torah, and sometimes overturn them. There is no contradiction
between 'I have come not to abolish them but to fulfil them', and the
Antitheses following. The principle of loving your neighbour draws
out of the Sixth Commandment the corollary that hatred is wrong;
out of the Seventh that lust is wrong. Love of God gives to all speech
the sanctity of an oath, so that oaths become superfluous. Love
replaces 'An eye for an eye' with mercy, and the hating of one's
enemy, which is so often indirectly commanded and implied in the
OT, with indiscriminate care for all men as brothers. The later Antitheses overturn provisions of scripture, but Matthew still knows that
the Lord was fulfilling scripture as he did so; for his *kᵉlāl*, his Golden
Rule, gave a touchstone on which the rest could be assessed. The
Pharisees' refusal so to assess makes their teaching hypocrisy (16.12).

Matthew's inconsistency is that he dare not apply his principle in
a thoroughgoing way. When it comes to washing, dietary laws, or
divorce, he wants to have the best of both worlds, and compromises.
No doubt he did not realize the magnitude of the difference between
his use of the summary, and Hillel's. It is I, not he, who has set the
distinction on paper. He still thought, like a scribe, that not one jot
could perish from the Law. It was not until his poetry has taken him
beyond the first two 'deepening' Antitheses that whole sentences
begin to perish from the Law. By then it is too late to notice that the
meaning of πληροῦν has shifted: from the deepening of individual

---

[45] Sifra on Lev. xix. 18 (Aqiba); B Shab. 31a (Hillel); Gerhardsson, *MM*, p. 138.
[46] B Shab. 31a.

laws to the plumbing of the whole Law and the reversal of individual laws.[47] It is, of course, a naive mistake to suppose that wherever we have inconsistency we have a different source. Matthew is inconsistent in lots of ways, and on an issue as large as this inconsistency is exactly what we should expect with the confrontation of two irreconcilable principles. The point is that the same inconsistency comes in the redactoral and in the new material.

It has been important to establish that Matthew's attitude to the Torah is fully consistent with what we might expect of a Christian scribe, because it is this point which is normally raised when the matter is put in question whether Matthew is a Jewish Christian book. G. Strecker, for example, raises a series of objections in the first chapter of *Der Weg der Gerechtigkeit* [*WG*],[48] of which this is the most considerable. He mentions five further difficulties:

(*a*) Matthew makes an error on the Oral Torah at 12.11 (the passage just referred to), and misunderstands the parallelism in the Zechariah quotation about the ass and the colt;[49]

(*b*) he deletes almost all the Aramaic loan-words in Mark (Abba, Rabbouni, Talitha Cumi, Ephphatha; Corban, Boanerges, and the title Rabbi several times); he retains only Beelzebul, Cananaios, Golgotha; and introduces Mamonas, raqa, and korbanas. This seems unlikely, *prima facie*, for a Jewish Christian author;[50]

(*c*) he cites two Semitisms, εὐθέως or εὐθύς, and ἄρχεσθαι in its weak sense, which Matthew shows a tendency to drop from his Marcan original;[51]

(*d*) he maintains that the citations show a knowledge of Hebrew only in the pre-Matthaean stage;[52]

(*e*) he finds an inconsistency in the Gospel's attitude to the universalist debate, which he thinks resolvable only if a universalist evangelist is handling particularist matter.[53]

Points (*d*) and (*e*) will require more extended treatment, which we will postpone.[54]

1. 12.11 seems certainly to be an error. Jesus asks the Pharisees which of them would not pull a sheep out of a pit on the Sabbath Day:

---

[47] See p. 328 below.
[48] Bonn 1966.
[49] Strecker, *WG*, pp. 18f.
[50] ibid., p. 20ff.
[51] ibid., p. 20.
[52] ibid., pp. 21ff.
[53] ibid., pp. 30ff.
[54] For the citations see pp. 124–36 below and ad loc. For the universalist–particularist tension see pp. 339–44 below. These two matters are the bases of P. Nepper-Christensen's similar conclusion in *Das Matthäusevangelium—ein judenchristliches Evangelium?* (Aarhus 1958).

but in fact the Talmud permitted the owner to feed an animal in such
a case in the pit, or even, with some rabbis, to help the animal to
release itself, but he might not lift it out in person.[55] Strecker mentions
further instances in 21 and 27 where the Gospel seems to show ignorance of the Temple laws—Judas, for example, would not have been
allowed to go, as a non-priest, into the Temple building. Another
example, which Strecker does not mention, would be the tithing of
mint, which so far as our documents go was not a Pharisaic practice,
though anice and cummin were liable to tithing.

Strecker is arguing against von Dobschütz' formulation of the
Jewish theory of origin for Matthew, that the evangelist was a converted rabbi. These objections are unquestionably fatal to the theory
in that form, for no rabbi, that is a *ḥākhām*, a learned teacher and
formulator of Torah, would have been so ignorant. But for the milieu
which we are supposing for the evangelist, the community schoolmaster in a town in southern Syria, say, such mistakes would be not
only natural, but likely. The *sôphēr's* qualification was to know the
scriptures: he would be bound to have some acquaintance with the
Oral Torah, but he would be extremely unlikely, even in his Jewish
days, to have been accurate on minutiae. Further, if we suppose that
he has been a Christian out of contact with the synagogue for a decade,
he would have every opportunity of losing touch with actual Jewish
teaching.

On the question of parallelism, it is Strecker who is mistaken.
Matthew cites Zech. 9.9 ending, '. . . riding upon an ass, and
upon a colt the foal of a beast of burden' (AT); and he has the disciples
bring a foal with the ass, as against Mark who has the ass only; and
they put their clothes on them, and Jesus rides on them. It seems a
trifle naive to suggest that Matthew could not see that this was Hebrew
poetry, and that the parallelism was of form and not of substance.
Even Gentile Christians such as Luke knew about parallelism—he
writes very good psalms himself; and any choirboy knows the same.
Matthew treats it literally because he has the midrashic mind. Scripture is endlessly rich. Every word of it is meaningful.[56] There are
seventy faces to scripture. Often the Hebrew will reveal hidden depths
which are concealed in the Greek version. Here the Hebrew has the
doubled preposition '*al*, 'on an ass and on a colt', which is missing in

---

[55] B Shab. 128b; cf. S–B 629.

[56] Almost any page of rabbinic writing will furnish examples of this. Lev. R.
37.4 may stand as an example, 'As regards Jephthah, limb after limb fell off his
body, and was buried separately, as is proved by the text, "And was buried in
the cities of Gilead" [Judg. 12.7]. It does not say "In the city of Gilead", but
"In the cities". This teaches that limb after limb fell off his body, and he was
buried in many places.' Cf. Paul's 'seed' and 'seeds' in Gal. 3.16.

the Greek. He translates the Hebrew, and takes it to mean what it says. Nothing more Jewish could be asked. Strecker himself refers to a similar use in the Fourth Gospel, 'They parted my garments among them, and upon my vesture did they cast lots' (John 19.24). John has the soldiers divide the clothes into four, and dice for the seamless coat, thus taking the two halves of the parallelism literally. Strecker says this is because the Fourth Gospel is from a Gentile background too, a highly dubious comment. The First and Fourth Gospels are of the four, the ones most deeply rooted in Judaism and it is in keeping with this that they seek for further meaning within the outward form of poetry.

2. The translation of the majority of the Marcan Aramaic loan-words tells the same story. The profession of the scribe was in part to render the Hebrew into the vernacular: to give a Targum, first in the school and often in the synagogue. Thus it is to be expected that Matthew will have translated Abba, Rabbouni, and Korban into their Greek equivalents, My Father, Lord, a gift, just as he renders κεντουρίων into ἑκατόνταρχος. Talitha cumi, Ephphatha, and Boanerges are abbreviated out of the story. The names he leaves in. He leaves Mark's Beelzebul because of the play on the word, the master of the house, which only comes over in the Hebrew; he leaves the semi-Graecised Καναναῖος, which Luke later correctly renders, 'the Zealot', just as he puts in the semi-Graecised Ἰσκαριωτής for Mark's Iscarioth. He leaves Golgotha, with Mark's translation, and the liturgical Hosanna: Mamonas, Korbanas, and Emmanuel are names he introduces, the latter two with their meanings. The only name he regularly renders is Satan, for which there were equivalents to hand, in ὁ διάβολος (the accuser), or ὁ πονηρός (the evil one).

It is not clear that any argument can be drawn from the use of rabbi. Matthew once retains it in the Marcan context, once drops it, and once changes it to κύριε; he also introduces it in the new matter, 'You are not to be called Rabbi' (23.7ff). This certainly is no evidence for non-Jewish provenance: rather, it would be hard to see a reason in such a background for any interest in being called rabbi.

3. The argument from omitted Semitisms is very curious. Mark has εὐθέως/εὐθύς 45 times, Matthew only 18 times; and behind them may lie the Aramaic *miyyadh*:[57] but even if this is so, we can all think of a reason why Matthew should wish to cut down the Marcan use. The pleonastic ἄρχομαι, which Mark has 26 times and Matthew 13, is no doubt due to the Aramaic use of *shārî*. But then Matthew tends to

[57] G. Dalman, *The Words of Jesus* (E.T., Edinburgh 1902), p. 28; Strecker, *WG*, p. 20.

abbreviate the Marcan account, and one of the most obvious pleon-
asms to cut is ἄρχομαι in such sentences as, 'He began to teach them'.
As he introduces the word seven times in the new matter, as well as
retaining it six times in the Marcan matter, this seems a more likely
explanation than his revulsion from Semitisms. Luke, who did come
from a Hellenistic background, has far the most instances of pleonastic ἄρχομαι. On the other hand the Semitisms that flood the First
Gospel are proverbial: εἷς instead of the normal τις,[58] a certain, from
the Aramaic *hadh;* καὶ ἰδού, and lo, for the Hebrew *w^ehēn*; ἐν τοῖς
οὐρανοῖς, in the heavens, instead of the normal singular, from
bashshāmayim, to name but a few of the most famous. The battle
which we shall have to fight later is rather to resist the false conclusion
that Matthew has in many places inherited material translated from
Aramaic, or translated it himself.

So much then, for the moment, for Strecker. But the weight of the
case that Matthew was a scribe, lies not so much in his familiarity
with Jewish Torah or with sayings of the rabbis, which might be due
to matter he took over, or even with his scribal theology, though this
is sufficiently striking, as with the thoroughly rabbinic manner in
which he sets out his book. Jewish studies have uncovered many
particulars of the rabbinic method, and time and again it is in Matthew
rather than in Mark and Luke that we find the echoes. I will cite many
examples of this over particular passages, but the following are sufficient to show the basically scribal cast of Matthew's mind.

1. Hillel[59] set out about A.D. 30 a list of seven principles of interpretation of scripture. Of these the first and most famous is the principle
of Light-and-Heavy, *qal wahômēr*, which approximates to our *a fortiori*
arguing. This type of argument is common in Matthew, as, for
example, 'If you then, who are evil, know how to give good gifts to
your children, how much more . . .' (7.11); or, 'Of how much more
value is a man than a sheep!' (12.12). It is not found in Mark, and
occurs mainly in Q passages in Luke; the only obvious instances in L
are at Luke 16.10–12.

2. A second of Hillel's rules is that of Principle and Cases[60]
(*'ābh w^ethôl^edôt*, Father and Descendants). We find this in the prin-

---

[58] εἷς is in fact found in classical Greek in the sense of τις: Eur. *Bacc.* 917;
Ar. *Av.* 1292; cf. Thuc. 4.50; Plat. *Legg.* 855D. But it is common in the LXX,
and is unquestionably a Semitism in the N.T.

[59] Hillel's norms of interpretation are set out conveniently in E. E. Ellis, *Paul's
Use of the Old Testament* (Edinburgh 1957), p. 41. See also D. Daube, *New
Testament and Rabbinic Judaism* [*NTRJ*] (London 1956), Pt II.

[60] Daube, *NTRJ*, pp. 63–6.

ciple set out at the beginning of the Sermon, 'I have come not to abolish [the commandments] but to fulfil them', of which six examples are then given in the Antitheses, 'You have heard . . . but I say to you . . .'; or in the principle at 6.1, 'Beware of practising your piety before men in order to be seen by them', which is then exemplified in the teaching on Almsgiving, Prayer, and Fasting. It would be difficult to claim with confidence any examples of such systematic ordering in the wandering discourses of Mark and Luke.

3. A third of Hillel's principles was the $k^e l\bar{a}l$ or summary[61] to which we have already referred: once a general summary can be made of a position then particular cases can be assessed on that basis. We have mentioned the summary at 7.12, the Golden Rule, which expressed in other words the two Great Commandments from which all else hang. Apart from the Great Commandments, this is unknown in Mark and Luke: and in that context it is Matthew who adds, 'On these two Commandments depend all the law and the prophets'.[62]

4. A rabbinic habit was to give names[63] to the particular sections ($p^a r\bar{a}sh\hat{o}t$) of the Old Testament to which they were referring. Thus Jesus refers in Mark to 'the passage about the Bush' (ἐπὶ τῆς βάτου) or Lev. R. I. 8 refers to the section at the end of Exodus as 'The Sum of Things' ($p^a r\bar{a}sh\bar{a}h\ p^e k\bar{u}dh\hat{e}$). Matthew alone gives similar names to some of the paragraphs in the Gospel: 'the parable of the Sower' (13.18), 'the parable of the weeds of the field' (13.36).

5. Most typical of all perhaps is the rabbinic habit of glossing interpretations. We have watched Matthew at this already with Mark's Cornfield and Withered Hand and other passages. Had history gone differently we might have read in the Mishnah Divorce Tractate, 'Mark said in the name of the Apostle Peter, Whoever divorces his wife and marries another commits adultery. R. Matthew said, Except in the case of sexual offence. The Sages said, R. Matthew judged rightly.' This habit of glossing is exceedingly frequent in Matthew. We are so used to Lucan scholars drawing conclusions from the redactoral changes in Luke that we easily forget how little doctrinal glossing there is in Luke. Compared to Matthew Luke treats the Marcan source with very great respect.

[61] Gerhardsson, *MM*, pp. 136ff.
[62] cf. Hillel's, 'What you do not like to have done to you, do not do to your fellow. This is the whole of the Law; the rest is the explanation of it. Go, learn it'. (B Shab. 31a). Gerhardsson, *MM*, p. 138; Daube, *NTRJ*, p. 250.
[63] Gerhardsson, *MM*, pp. 143ff, 153ff, *simanim*.

6. The rabbis frequently used parables to illuminate their teaching. Cant. R. I. 1.6 preserves a famous saying, 'Each [idea] finds confirmation in a verse of scripture, each in a *māshāl*, and each in a figure of speech.' We shall have much to say in the third chapter about rabbinic parables, and we shall try to show that the parables are Matthew's own. Chapter 13 is one instance of the ideas of Mark finding confirmation in scripture (Isa. 6 and Ps. 78) and in parables, *m^eshālîm*: 21—22 and 24—25 would be others.

7. Rabbinic sermons were of two types. The so-called *Y^elamm^edēnû* (Let-our-rabbi teach-us) sermons start off with a problem of religious behaviour (*h^alākāh*) from which the preacher leads round to his text. There is something of this kind in Mark 10, where the rich man's asking about eternal life leads into the sermon on discipleship. Matthew has this, and the more marked example in 18 where the disciples ask who is greatest in the kingdom of heaven, and the discourse on Church Order follows. The other kind of sermon began with a formal Proem. We shall cite proems similar to the Beatitudes which serve this function in the Sermon on the Mount, and there is a proem in 23.2–10. The only parallel in the other two Synoptics would be the Beatitudes and Woes in the Sermon on the Plain. Another common feature of rabbinic sermons is a peroration.[64] There are strong perorations to several of Matthew's sermons: the Two Ways—Two Trees—Two Builders to the Sermon on the Mount; the Righteous Blood—Jerusalem Jerusalem to 23; the Great Assize to the Apocalypse (24—25). There is nothing of this force to be found in Mark or Luke.

8. The rabbis often used illustrations in threes,[65] and were often very repetitive. So Matthew expounds the Sixth Commandment: not to be angry; and if angry to make it up before offering sacrifice; and to make peace with your creditor quickly. Or he expounds the three pious duties, and very repetitively. We shall find plenty of instances of this—also on occasion in Mark and Luke, but regularly in Matthew.

9. Dr Daube says that in judgements of Halakah *example* from scripture was useful, but *precept* from scripture or Oral Torah was vital.[66] Thus Mark has the example of David with the Shewbread to justify the disciples' plucking the ears of corn, but this would not suffice for their justification, since there is no express permission given.

---

[64] J. Mann, *The Bible as Read and Preached in the Old Synagogue* [*BRPOS*] (Cincinnati 1940), p. 27, 'The Sermon (Seder 1) is concluded with a peroration as to the respective lot of the sinner and the well-deserved'; cf. p. 34.
[65] Mann, *BRPOS*, p. 25n: 'Illustration of such a statement by three examples is frequent in Midr. Yalkut and elsewhere.'
[66] Daube, *NTRJ*, pp. 67–89.

Matthew supplies a reference to the teaching that the priests may profane the sabbath with impunity in the Temple. Similarly in the Divorce pericope in 19 Matthew inserts what Mark omits, the clause from Genesis, 'and be joined to his wife', which supplies the authority for the Lord's judgement.

10. The Mishnah is divided into Tractates, as the rabbis grouped the teaching of various topics together. So Matthew groups together logia on discipleship in the Sermon, from all over Mark; or on the Apostles' mission from Mark 6, 9, and 13. He puts the parables of the growth of the kingdom together in 13, concentrates the miracles in 8—9, and generally makes his book a tidy construction where it is easier to find things than in the rag-bags of the other two, as we can all witness.

11. The rabbis so reverenced scripture that they could draw on different readings, or versions, to expound their teaching. K. Stendahl[67] and R. H. Gundry[68] conclude that Matthew used the LXX and the Hebrew, and perhaps other versions as well: sometimes all in the same citation.

12. The Proems to rabbinic sermons begin with a text and work back to the text:[69] Matthew's favourite *inclusio* is a rabbinic habit, and one rarely if ever to be found in the other two synoptists.

[67] K. Stendahl, *The School of St. Matthew* [*SSM*] (Uppsala 1954).
[68] R. H. Gundry, *The Use of the O.T. in St. Matthew's Gospel* [*UOTSM*] (Leiden 1967).
[69] Mann, *BRPOS*, p. 27: 'In this manner the circle was completed by returning to the starting point, viz. the commencement of the Sermon.'

2
THE MIDRASHIC METHOD

Rabbinic activity is classically divided into two, Mishnah and Midrash. Mishnah is the making and codification of laws in interpretation of the written Law. It is derived from *shānāh*, to repeat, and means the repetition, that which has to be known by heart, and not written down, the δευτέρωσις in Greek. There is very little trace of this activity in the New Testament: δευτέρωσις does not occur. Perhaps the *Haustafeln* are an echo of the practice. But then casuistry was a pursuit foreign to life in the Spirit, and the Church was lacking in rabbis.

Midrash, however, was the task of every preacher, the humble provincial *sôphēr* of the community in the Diaspora no less than the *ḥākhām*, the learned rabbi in the School of Midrash in Jerusalem. The word midrash derives from *dārash*, to probe or examine.[1] Revelation is a bottomless mine of wealth: no pious man can be content to take what merely lies on the surface—he must *dārash*, dig and bring up treasure. There are seventy faces to scripture: we must *dārash*, examine it, and find it revealed from glory to glory. Revelation is, to take a more familiar image, a treasure-chest, out of which the wise householder can bring things new and old—old things, the tradition handed down by others, new things, whatever may be revealed by the Spirit to him now.

Midrash comes to mean, by the second century of our era, commentary on scripture, the probings, the results of the examination. Four books of homiletic midrash on the legal parts of the Law come from this period, and are a foretaste of the Midrash Rabbah codified from the fifth century on. But midrash was already a technical word centuries before. We read in 2 Chronicles of the midrash of the prophet Iddo (13.22)[2] and the midrash of the Book of Kings (24.27),

[1] The classic, all too brief, statement of the meaning and scope of midrash is Mlle R. Bloch's article of that name in *Dictionnaire de la Bible*, Supplément v, cols. 1263–81.

[2] W. Rudolph comments (*Chronikbücher* (Tubingen 1955), p. 238): 'ein Midrasch ist in späteren Judentum die lehrhafte oder erbauliche Bearbeitung und Weiterbildung älterer Erzählungsstoffe. Diesen Sinn nimmt man meist auch hier an, zumal da (2 Chron.) Kap. 13 eben diesen Character des Midrasch aufweist. Aber besonders die Rede Abias zeigt so viele den Chronisten eigentümliche Gedanken und Wendungen, dass man sie als seine eigene Komposition ansehen muss. Man wird deshalb gut tun, *midrash* hier mit Ewald in seinem gewöhnlichen Wortsinn als Erforschung, Ausarbeitung, Studie, Werk (βίβλιον) zu fassen.' But it is not only Abijah's speech which is full of the Chronicler's style of writing. The whole

works of the Chronicler's own predecessors commenting on Kings, and on which he was free himself to comment or to leave by. But midrash is in fact the way in which our whole Old Testament grew up. Deuteronomy is a midrash on the ancient Israelite laws, the Priestly Code is another; our book of Isaiah is the monument to centuries of midrash.

The purpose of midrash is broadly twofold. First, there is the duty to edify, to proclaim God's word in the community, to interpret. This may lead to moral exhortation, or frequently to moral exhortation concealed in the form of a story. We have referred before to von Rad's essay showing that the speeches in Chronicles are Levitical sermons,[3] but the glorification of the account of the building of the Temple is no less edifying in intention. The Testaments are largely quaint moral discourses; 'Now, my children', says the dying Judah, 'I remember how when I was young I got very drunk . . .'[4] Or the need to edify may take the form of laying down Halakah, as is the case with much of the Mekilta.

Second, there is the duty to reconcile. With time come developments in theology, and midrash is necessary in order to square the old with the new. The theology of Samuel/Kings is Deuteronomic—the insights of the seventh century dictate the attitude of the historian of the sixth. But theology moves on. Two more centuries and the priestly theologians have tightened up many details of daily practice which had seemed unimportant before. The Law, which was in written form in the Book of Deuteronomy could be brought up to date step by step as the Priestly Code was glossed into the tradition. *Pari passu* the history of the nation revealed impossible situations which needed to be rewritten with a careful gloss in order to reconcile the traditional story with the newly accepted view of God. Hence the work of generations of chroniclers, culminating in our Chronicler. 1 Samuel had said that God had moved David to the census, in his anger against Israel. But with time it seemed less proper for God to concern himself so directly—and perhaps so immorally—with the affairs of men. A

---

story is a fabric of interwoven strands: from 2 Sam. 24 (the census number); Judg. 9 (Abimelech made king at Shechem, and the young Jotham reproving him in a mountain speech for taking vain fellows to usurp the kingdom; and an ambush); Judg. 17 (Micah and his false Levite and his sacrilegious image at Dan); Judg. 20 (the battle at Gibeah, with a second ambush); Josh. 8 (a further ambush, ending with the capture of Bethel: the priests sounding with the trumpets); and above all the contrast of the true Levites (Lev. 24) with Jeroboam's false priesthood. The chapter is one of the clearest cases of 'Bearbeitung und Weiterbildung' in Chronicles. And 2 Chron. 24 is another.

[3] ch. I, n. 1.　　　　　　　　[4] Test. Jud. 11.2; 12.3.

Satan, an angelic *agent provocateur*, exists in the Book of Job for such
purposes, and the Chronicler turns the task, and the odium, over to
him.[5] 2 Samuel says loosely that David went and brought up the ark
from the house of Obed-Edom, and when they had gone six paces
he sacrificed an ox and a fatling. The Chronicler, taught by P, supplies
Levites to carry the ark—no doubt 2 Samuel had intended them: and
also has the Levites perform the sacrifice—a rough reading of 2
Samuel would leave one with the impression that King David killed
the animals himself, which would of course have been unthinkable.[6]
Similarly in the Testament of Levi, and elsewhere in apocryphal
writings,[7] Levi is praised for destroying Shechem. Admittedly
Genesis would allow the view that Jacob was upset, temporarily, with
Levi for this action: but how could the father of God's priesthood be
thought to do wrong, especially in so virtuous an act as the avenging
of his sister's honour? The same motive is common in the Midrash
Rabbah.

So much for the purpose of midrash. Some of its methods we will
consider shortly. But first three general considerations should be
mentioned, with respect to the attitude of mind of the midrashist, or,
as we may call him less barbarously, the *darshān:* his creativity, his
view of inspiration, and the limits on his licence. We recognize
plainly that midrash is a creative activity. The rabbis did not have a
long secret tradition that Isaac gave himself willingly to be sacrificed
by Abraham. They made it up. Our Chronicler, and his predecessors,
possessed no direct line back to Davidic times by-passing 2 Samuel,
so as to know that it was Levites who carried the ark and performed
the sacrifices 700 years before. They made it up. Many midrashic
stories, and the non-traditional speeches put into the mouths of
scriptural characters, have been made up. Now nothing would be
more shocking to a *darshān* than the suggestion that he had made
anything up. The very derivation of the word midrash would seem to
him the guarantee that he was digging for what was there before: to
invent would be blasphemy. One place in scripture will show him
what is missing in another. His activity is nothing but to examine one
passage in the light of other relevant passages. Furthermore, he would
point confidently to others who had trodden the path before him.
The Chronicler looks back to the Midrash of Iddo, the rabbis saw
their own teachings as nothing but the teachings of their masters with
a shine on. One rabbi would tell a parable in the name of another, the
Amoraim would ascribe their words to their Tannaite forebears.
Nevertheless, in fact, midrash is a creative activity. The presupposition

[5] 2 Sam. 24.1; 1 Chron. 21.1.   [6] 2 Sam. 6.12ff; 1 Chron. 15.26.
[7] Test. Lev. 6.4; 5.3; Jub. 30.18ff.

that the Priestly theology was known to David, or the glory of the
Levitical priesthood to Jacob, is not historically valid. The historical
conclusions drawn from these theological presuppositions are false,
and the stories based on them are legends. Further, however much
we may emphasize that midrash is the creation of a school, and that
the Books of Chronicles, the Testaments, the Midrash, etc., as we now
have them, are the accumulated work of generations, the fact is that
some one person has been the first to invent each detail. We cannot
solve the matter by an infinite regression. Each *darshān* has had a
share in the creative activity of the community of expositors and
apologists.

Now this activity would be impossible without some belief in
inspiration. The basis is granted in the belief that one passage of
scripture will illustrate another. But how is one to know that the right
passage is being taken for enlightenment? In the cases we have
mentioned it might be felt to be obvious. Clearly the Levitical laws are
relevant when it is a question of carrying the ark and sacrificing, or of
our attitude to Levi at Shechem. But midrash does not limit itself to
such vital questions. In the same verse from 2 Samuel we noted that
David sacrificed an ox and a fatling; but in the Chronicles version the
Levites sacrifice seven bullocks and seven rams. Now no doubt this
change is inspired by the feeling that the Samuel offering was inadequate, and that David would hardly have had the Levites offer less
than Balaam had. But if we ask, how does the Chronicler know to go
to Num. 23 for his details, there is no answer. The modern secular
may say, He was already there with the sword-bearing angel, it seemed
appropriate; the Chronicler must have felt that this appropriateness
was a kind of inspiration. The leaps of logic that he makes are nothing
to the extravagances of the rabbis; and since the labours of the
preacher were felt to be charged with divine responsibility, the method
used must presuppose a doctrine of divine guidance. This guidance
gives an *a priori* certainty to the finished account. Things must have
been so (in view of the light cast by passage x): therefore they were so.

Third, it is important to note that the midrashic expansion may be
of considerable length, even in Chronicles, so long as the importance
of the occasion makes it desirable, and suitable material lies to hand.
In the Midrash Rabbah there is no limit: proem after proem can be
inserted to the first verse of Lamentations. But this is because the
Midrash Rabbah is a compendium of midrash, and not a new version
as Chronicles or Jubilees are. In these latter works the authors may
be content to copy out whole chapters verbatim. Or they may make
brief changes, and expansions of a few verses. But when the Chronicler
feels his subject, as in the preparations for the Temple, or the battles

and sermons in 2 Chronicles, or when calendrical enthusiasm falls on the Jubileeist, it is not too much to compose four chapters on end —much of them a cento of texts from elsewhere in scripture, or a list of names supplied from tradition or contemporary life.

Now if Matthew is a provincial scribe, nothing is more probable than that he should wish to write a midrashic expansion of Mark. Both internal and external evidence show that Mark was to him an authoritative book. The internal evidence is his care to present the book whole to his readers. Even on Streeter's conservative count, 606 of the 661 verses in Mark are represented in Matthew.[8] When allowance is made for verses which have been expanded rather than omitted, such as the Seed Growing Secretly or the Doorkeeper parables, some of this leeway is accounted for, and the remainder are mostly omitted for the sake of brevity, by compression, with one or two doctrinal motivations. Matthew shows a reverence for Mark which surpasses the respect of Luke for either of his documents, or of John for any of his. Our external evidence can be nothing else but the well-worn words of Papias on Mark.[9] Whether Papias was right or not, his belief that Mark's Gospel embodied Peter's tradition is quite likely to have been known to Matthew: and indeed the frequent occurrence of the names of Peter, James, and John in Mark make it highly likely that Mark's tradition did ultimately, if not directly, stem from that root.[10]

Matthew had, therefore, an authoritative account of the Lord's ministry: but, as a scribe, he had the midrashist's double motive for expanding it. The people need teaching, and Mark is short of teaching; his record of enigmatic sayings and epigrams will have occupied the Christian preacher in exposition week by week. If the End was near, at the very gates, when Mark was exhorting the reader to understand, how much more urgent is it to be ready now that Jerusalem has fallen, and year succeeds to year! Who can be content with a little parable such as the Doorkeeper? Better give some scriptural parallels—Noah, Lot, the Exodus—and the longer parables which have been developed out of the Doorkeeper in homiletic use, and close with a peroration based on a Marcan saying from elsewhere. Or how can the modern missionary go out fortified merely with the five verses of the Marcan Missionary Charge? Preaching was dangerous and unrewarding in the 70s. The earlier promise of support from the converted requires expansion, and the fact of persecution necessitates the transfer of the whole Warning of Persecutions from Mark 13. And what about a basic Christian style of living? When, in Mark 10, Peter asked what

[8] B. H. Streeter, *FG*, pp. 152, 159.   [9] In Euseb. *H.E.* III. 39.
[10] See pp. 140–2 below.

they should have who had left all and followed Jesus, the Lord had promised blessings with persecutions. This arose out of the Rich Man who had kept the Commandments, but would not sell all and have treasure in heaven. So, when Matthew has described Peter's leaving all in 4, the time is ripe to put into words the Lord's blessings, to expound the Christian way with the Commandments, and the need for all to lay up treasure in heaven.

But Matthew was not only a homiletic *darshān:* he was also a man under acute theological tension. The task of the *darshān* in reconciliation is his no less than in edification. We have seen him at work already in the last chapter struggling with the traditional and the radical attitudes to the Law. Later we shall see him striving to reconcile his doctrine of Israel with the Gentile Mission, in both of which he passionately believed. Truthfulness to the Marcan picture of the apostles' faithlessness wrestles with the desire to honour the princes of the Church; and in many other ways he has to do what the Chronicler had done before him, gloss one theology with another.

In all this we see exemplified the three general traits of midrash to which we have referred: creativity, inspiration, and willingness to expand by a few words, a few verses, or a few chapters. Matthew makes stories up: the Infancy stories, the Temptations, the details of Judas. While it might be very generally conceded that the anonymous community had worked over the tradition creatively, thus pushing the odium back to where it can be dissipated, this is not only improbable for reasons we can see at once, but impossible for reasons which must be set out later. The improbability of many hands having taken part rests on the Church's poverty of Jewish professionals. Midrash is skilled work. A man must know his scriptures well to have the confidence to pick one parallel passage out of the whole and say, 'It is to this that the Spirit is pointing me.' There has been some midrashic working in Mark, the use of the Elisha feeding story, say, to gloss the 5000, but it is not a lot, and the scriptures used are the most familiar ones, Moses, David, Elijah–Elisha, Isaiah. Matthew's Gospel draws on a much bigger area of the OT. The number of scribes in the Church was, on all our evidence, pretty small. The *impossibility* of many hands rests on the structure of the Gospel, which must be the work of one mind; but the evidence for this must wait.

Midrash may be of four different *genres*: Versions, like the LXX and Targums, whose expansions are limited in the nature of the case; Re-writings, like Chronicles or Jubilees, where the author has considerably more freedom; Juristic Commentaries, like the Mekilta and Sifre, where the biblical text is above the line, so to speak; and homiletic matter, such as we find in the Testaments, or compressed in the Midrash Rabbah. Clearly Matthew has most in common with the second of these *genres*: it is neither a free paraphrase of Mark, nor a mere commentary, but a re-writing, a second edition. We shall find ourselves most often therefore looking to the Chronicler for parallels, though some points are well illustrated from the versions, and for parables and poetry we shall need to turn to the rabbis.

Transcription

First, then, Matthew on occasion *transcribes*. The Chronicler transcribed with negligible changes the whole of 1 Sam. 31, the death of Saul, and other whole chapters. We should be at a loss to find so long a section of Mark unaltered in Matthew, but the greater part of Mark 13, and of the Passion story, go in almost word for word, with occasional insertions.

Omission

The Chronicler omits large units from both Samuel and Kings, for dogmatic and apologetic reasons. Almost all the history of the northern kingdom is left out because the northern kingdom was an apostasy; the whole Bathsheba–Absalom cycle is omitted because it brings discredit on David. The things which Matthew felt called upon to omit were naturally much fewer: the Young Man in the Sheet (Mark 14.51f) as being of dubious relevance; the Widow's Mite (Mark 12.41–4) probably as breaking the thread of the Woes discourse in 23; the Strange Exorcist (Mark 9.38f) as bringing discredit on John—but the logia at the end of the unit find a place elsewhere in Matthew; and a general statement at Mark 3.20, which disappears in Matthew's reformation of the Beezebul incident. This gives a total of nine verses which have disappeared without trace, $1\frac{1}{2}$ per cent of Mark. This figure is noticeably less than those customarily suggested, because we are accounting for such passages as the Seed Growing Secretly, or the coming of Jesus' relatives to lay hold of him, as being altered, and not omitted.

Abbreviations

The Chronicler does not normally abbreviate. If he tells a story, he tells it whole, even when, as in Ahab's battle at Ramoth-Gilead, it is largely irrelevant to his purpose. He will expand, but he will not abbreviate. This may be due to personal method: to some it is easier to copy than to worry over what may be being missed. More probably it is doctrinally motivated. Samuel–Kings was scripture: some irrelevant scripture, omittable; but if judged relevant not to be shortened. If so, there is a difference of attitude in Matthew's view of Mark. Mark is authoritative to him, but is clearly not yet scriptural. Almost every pericope is shortened. 20 per cent abbreviation is normal, 65 per cent is reached on occasion, as with the martyrdom of the Baptist, or the Gadarene Demoniacs. Matthew abbreviates for the reasons Form-Critics give. He cuts out the colourful details, reducing some of the Marcan healings to shades of their full-bodied reality, but leaving their theological tendencies in all the stronger relief.

Inconsistencies

Abbreviating is a skilled business, and Matthew leaves frequent traces of his activity in minor contradictions. Large crowds attend Jesus down from the mountain, and apparently witness the healing of the leper; who is told, however, following Mark, to tell no one (8.1,4). The sick are brought to Jesus at sunset in Mark 1.32, it being the end of Sabbath: Matthew gives us the evening scene also, but lacks the Sabbath to give it point. Matthew saves the credit of the sons of Zebedee at 20.20 by having their mother claim the seats of glory for them; but Jesus is soon discovered addressing James and John themselves—'Jesus said, *Ye* know not what *ye* ask' (RV). There are perhaps thirty minor muddles of this kind.

Fatigue

Closely related is the phenomenon of fatigue. When an editor begins a story, he may amend freely to suit his interest; later the magnet of the text he is following pulls him into more docile reproduction. At 6.14 Mark has 'King Herod', which Matthew amends, for accuracy, to 'Herod the tetrarch' (14.1): but at 14.9, in line with Mark, he has become 'the king'. At 9.16f he leaves out the first of Mark's εἰ δὲ μή's, a phrase he is not fond of, but leaves in the second. Having spared the scribes, as we have seen, in a number of cases, he includes them among the mockers at the cross, following Mark. The whole Gospel is an illustration of the same tendency. In 1—12, he rearranges Mark freely, and adds large units of new material. After 13, he follows Mark's order with hardly a variation, and with only minor insertions, mainly exegetical parables. The Chronicler is similarly much freer earlier in his work than he is with Manasseh, Josiah, and the end of the Monarchy.

Doublets

The process of midrashic exposition often involves the glossing of one context with another later in the story, so that the author is involved in borrowing forward from his own material. The Chronicler, for example, wishes to set out Hezekiah as a great reformer, and for the purpose borrows forward much of the matter relative to Josiah, much of the Deuteronomic reform and especially the Passover celebration. Then when he comes to Josiah we have a doublet: the same details now recur in their own right. Or it may happen the other way round. The Chronicler glorifies Jehoshaphat, and sets him out as a kind of Solomon redivivus. Jehoshaphat walks in the first ways of his father David (2 Chron. 17.3), he has riches and honour in abundance (17.5; 18.1), the Arabians bring him presents (17.11), his heart is lifted up (17.6), there is no war (17.10): and then in time of invasion he leads the people in prayer in the Temple in a seven-verse intercession based closely on Solomon's prayer at the Temple Dedication (20.6–12). This gives us a doublet by process of borrowing back. Both habits are common in Chronicles, and account in large measure for the repetitive impression the book makes.

Now just as it is not normal to think that the Chronicler had an independent tradition of Hezekiah's Passover or Jehoshaphat's Temple prayer, so it is unnecessary to posit independent traditions behind the twenty-one Matthaean doublets.[11] They may be readily understood as similar instances of borrowing from his material, with or without minor amendments. Half of the 21 cases are borrowing forward:

(1)   the topic of purity of the eyes (5.29f) suggests the Marcan logion, 'It is better to enter life with one eye' (Mark 9.43ff);

(2)   adultery leads on naturally to divorce (5.32) and the Marcan ruling on the subject (Mark 10.11);

(3) & (4) Matthew draws on Mark 13 in advance for matter relating to persecution, which he inserts in the Missionary Charge in 10, including, 'You will be hated by all for my name's sake. But he who endures to the end will be saved' (10.22);

(5) & (6) he closes the Charge with two verses closely similar to Mark 8.34f, 'If any man would come after me . . . For whoever would save his life . . .' (10.38f);

[11] The doublets are catalogued in J. C. Hawkins, *Horae Synopticae*, p. 64, and in many more recent works.

(7) & (8) he expands the Beelzebul Controversy by drawing on the Pharisees' demand for a sign, with the Lord's reply on the Sign of Jonah (12.38f/Mark 8.11ff);

(9) he takes the saying on Faith as a Grain of Mustard-Seed to answer the Apostles' 'Why could we not cast it out?' (17.20/Mark 11.22f);

(10) he adds the Pharisees' blasphemy, 'He casts out demons by the prince of demons', at the healing of the dumb demoniac at 9.34, and indeed assimilates other details of the healing at 12.22ff (Mark 3.22);

(11) he puts Jesus' preaching, 'The Kingdom of God is at hand' into John's mouth (3.2/Mark 1.15).

In all these cases he also inserts the saying in its Marcan context later in the book. The changes that he makes will be commented on in later chapters.

Four further cases are of Marcan epigrams given in their Marcan contexts and either then or later filled out and repeated. 'To him who has will more be given . . .' comes at 13.12 (Mark 4.25), and is expounded by the Talents and then repeated (25.29); 'The last shall be first . . .' comes at 19.30 (Mark 10.31), and is repeated after the explanatory Labourers in the Vineyard; 'Watch therefore, for you do not know when the master of the house will come' (Mark 13.35) comes in a similar way both before and after the parable-series in 24.42—25.13. Such double use of a saying is self-explanatory. A case of borrowing back would be, 'He who is greatest among you shall be your servant' (23.11), which sums up the earlier fuller form of the same saying in its Marcan context at 20.26f (Mark 10.43).

The remaining doublets are simply explained as repetitions of favourite Matthaean phrases—repetitiveness is too common a rabbinic trait to need illustration. Twice he cites Hos. 6.6 (9.13; 12.7), a statement of the antithesis between the old legalism and the new love. Twice he develops the contrast between the good and rotten trees and their fruit (7.16–20; 12.33), twice he gives us the fire as the fate of the fruitless tree (3.10; 7.19). He repeats the description of Jesus' progress, teaching and preaching and healing (4.23; 9.35), and the logion 'It shall be more tolerable on the day of judgment . . .' (10.15) in a similar context (11.24). There are many other passages which involve repetitions of language, but which are not so exact as to deserve the name of doublets (e.g. 4.24/14.35; 4.25/12.15; 9.27–31/ 20.29–34). The similarity between, 'Whatsoever thou bindest . . .' (16.19 AT) and 'Whatsoever ye bind . . .' (18.18 AT) is, of course, intended, the keys of the kingdom being first given to Peter, and later to the Twelve.

In this way it can be seen that the doublets constitute no argument for the use by Matthew of two different sources. More than half of the instances are most easily explained as borrowing forward on the analogy of the Chronicler; the others as natural repetitiveness. Matthew borrows forward rather than back, because he is doing his freer work in the first part of the book.

Explanatory Changes

These are common in the Targums, where any phrase likely to cause difficulty or offence is liable to be glossed, paraphrased, or otherwise explained. There are instances in the LXX, for example at Prov. 13.15:

Hebrew: 'Good sense wins favour' LXX: 'Good sense gives favour, And to know the Law is of good understanding.'

Stenning cites more than a hundred major instances in the Targum of Isaiah.[12] We find frequent minor changes of this kind in Matthew, for instance:

Mark 8.15	Matt. 16.6
Beware of the leaven of the Pharisees and the leaven of Herod.	Beware of the leaven of the Pharisees and Sadducees . . . Then they understood that he did not tell them to beware of the leaven of bread, but of the teaching of the Pharisees and Sadducees.

The Herodians have disappeared into the stock Pharisees-and-Sadducees, and an explanatory sentence is added to make sure that leaven is really understood to mean false teaching, just as in the Proverbs citation above good sense is explained as knowledge of the Law.

Modification

While the notion of explanatory changes by Matthew is a commonplace of criticism, the suggestion that he modified Marcan sayings would be more controversial. Yet modification is the universal practice of the rabbis in forming Halakah.

Deut. 23.24
When you go into your neighbour's vineyard, you may eat your fill of grapes, as many as you wish; but you shall not put any in your vessel.

[12] J. F. Stenning, *The Targum of Isaiah* (Oxford 1949).

Sifre
The worker in the vineyard may eat grapes, but not figs . . . R. Elazar b.
Hisma said, He may not eat more than his day's wage; but the Sages say
that the words 'as many as you wish' show that he may.[13]

R. Elazar was modifying the Law, that is, he was aligning it with the
intention of fair play found elsewhere in scripture, so expressing a
limitation which he took to be present in the author's mind; but the
sages prefer an interpretation *au pied de la lettre*. Similar modifications
can be found in the Targums.[14]

Isa. 26.19	Targum
Thy dew is a dew of light, and on the land of shades thou wilt let it fall.	Thy dew is a dew of lights unto them that observe thy law: but the wicked to whom thou gavest might, but who have transgressed thy Memra, shalt thou deliver to Gehinnam.

The Targumist modifies the general statement of scripture, interpreting God's dew as a blessing surely limited to the righteous only,
while a more appropriate reward will await the reprobate.
   In just the same way it seems natural to interpret a number of
modifications of Mark which we find in Matthew as the work of the
evangelist's own hand, especially as the changes are in line with his
theology.

Mark 10.11	Matt. 19.9
Whoever divorces his wife and marries another, commits adultery against her.	Whoever divorces his wife, except for unchastity, and marries another, commits adultery.
	Matt. 5.32
	Everyone who divorces his wife, except on the ground of unchastity, makes her an adulteress.

We have already cited the Divorce passage in Mark as a case where
Matthew found his two theologies in conflict. It is natural therefore
for him to modify the apparently anti-scriptural 'Whosoever divorces
. . . commits adultery' of Mark by glossing it with a guarded interpretation of Deut. 24; and accordingly he adds an except clause to
both presentations of the saying. Similarly:

[13] Sifre Deut., Ki Teze, 266, f. 121b fin.
[14] cf. J. Bowker, *The Targums and Rabbinic Literature* (Cambridge 1969),
pp. 93–300.

Mark 8.12	Matt. 16.4
Truly, I say to you, no sign shall be given to this generation.	No sign shall be given to it except the sign of Jonah.

Matt. 12.39
No sign shall be given to it except the sign of the prophet Jonah.

Surely, any Christian might feel, it is not quite true to say that *no* sign is given to this generation. Has not God by the Resurrection[15] designated Jesus as his Son in power? It might well seem appropriate to Matthew therefore on both occasions when he cites this logion to add an 'except' clause as with the unchastity question. He makes it plain in 12 that to him the sign of Jonah means the Resurrection.

Deliberate Change of Meaning

Not infrequently we find in the Targums, not so much modification as deliberate change of meaning. For example, Hezekiah prays:

Isa. 38.10	Targum
I said, In the noontide of my days I must depart; I am consigned to Sheol for the rest of my years . . .	In the sorrow of my days I shall go into the land of Sheol: but because of my memorial for good my years are increased . . .
But what can I say? For he has spoken to me, and he himself has done it. All my sleep has fled because of the bitterness of my soul.	What praise shall I utter and declare before him? Seeing that he has shown me so much goodness. How shall I serve and repay him all the years which he has added to my life, and delivered my soul from bitterness?

The Targum has changed the prayer of the dying king into a thanksgiving for (presumed) salvation, and altered the meaning of most of the phrases in the original on his way. There are many instances of such deliberate change well-known in Matthew:

Mark 3.20f	Matt. 12.33
And the crowd came together again . . . And when his friends heard it, they went outside to seize him, for they said, He is beside himself.	And all the crowds were beside themselves . . .

[15] Rom. 1.4.

The improper suggestion that the Lord had been out of his mind is excised by transferring the verb ἐξιστάναι to the crowds.

Mark 10.18
Why do you call me good?

Matt. 19.17
Why do you ask me about what is good?

'Why do you ask me about what is good?' A deliberate change here is obvious, whether, as is usually said, to avoid the suggestion that Jesus was other than good, or in line with rabbinic discussion about the good, which is the subject of the coming interview.

Other examples are to be found at 13.32; 13.58; 14.12,15; 21.3; 22.31; 24.3; 28.7,8.

Added Antithesis

Matthew often adorns the plain Marcan prose with antitheses of his own making. This is in line with Matthew's generally poetic character as a writer, and is not something common to Jewish authors.

Mark 6.6
And he went about among the villages teaching.

Matt. 9.35
And Jesus went about all the cities and villages, teaching in their synagogues and preaching the gospel of the kingdom, and healing every sickness and every infirmity.

Mark 11.25
And whenever you stand praying, forgive, if you have anything against anyone; so that your Father also who is in heaven may forgive you your trespasses.

Matt. 6.14f
For if you forgive men their trespasses, your heavenly Father also will forgive you; but if you do not forgive men their trespasses, neither will your Father forgive your trespasses.

Antithesis is similarly often found in the new material:

6.13: And lead us not into temptation, but deliver us from evil.
25.21: You have been faithful over a little, I will set you over much.

There are some cases where the antithesis is added to a Marcan logion, to form an epexegetic antithesis:

Mark 7.23
All these evil things come from within, and they defile a man.

Matt. 15.20
These are what defile a man; but to eat with unwashed hands does not defile a man.

Sometimes the antithesis comes before the Marcan logion, thus forming an anticipatory epexegetic antithesis:

Mark 13.13	Matt. 24.12
But he who endures to the end will be saved.	And because wickedness is multiplied most men's love will grow cold. But he who endures to the end will be saved.

On three occasions there is even a doubled lead-in to emphasise the third, Marcan, line:

Mark 9.41	Matt. 10.40ff
For truly, I say to you, whoever gives you a cup of water to drink because you bear the name of Christ, will by no means lose his reward.	He who receives a prophet because he is a prophet shall receive a prophet's reward, and he who receives a righteous man because he is a righteous man shall receive a righteous man's reward. And whoever gives to one of these little ones even a cup of cold water because he is a disciple, truly I say to you, he shall not lose his reward.

The same figure is found in the preceding verses, Matt. 10.37ff/Mark 8.34, and in Matt. 11.7ff/Mark 1.2. Antitheses, both double and triple, abound in the new matter, and will be analysed in ch. 4, pp. 83–4 below.

Expansion

When the Jewish translator or editor felt that a situation needed clarification, he was content to expand the text until it was clear. This is true even of the Targums on occasion:

Isa. 43.12	Targum
I declared, and saved, and proclaimed.	I declared to Abraham your father what was about to come. I saved you from Egypt as I sware to him between the pieces; I proclaimed the instruction of my law from Sinai.

The three straightforward verbs are each in turn glossed by a reference to the history of salvation. *A fortiori* the same may be true in a work such as Chronicles: nor is the Thucydidean distinction between freedom with the words and strictness with the facts at all in line with

Hebrew thinking. The deeds as much as the words are liable to clarification, midrash. The last verses of 2 Samuel run:

2 Sam. 24.24f	1 Chron. 21.25—22.1
So David bought the threshing-floor and the oxen for fifty shekels of silver. And David built there an altar to the Lord, and offered burnt-offerings and peace-offerings. So the Lord heeded supplications for the land, and the plague was averted from Israel.	So David paid Ornan *six hundred* shekels of *gold* by weight for the site. And David built there an altar to the Lord, and offered burnt-offerings and peace-offerings, and called upon the Lord; *and he answered him by fire from heaven upon the altar of burnt-offering. And the Lord commanded the angel; and he put his sword back into its sheath. At that time, when David saw that the Lord had answered him in the threshing-floor of Ornan the Jebusite, . . . Then David said, Here shall be the house of the Lord God, and here the altar of burnt-offering for Israel.*

The first thing the Chronicler clarifies is the price. Fifty shekels of silver is not much for the site of the Temple, so he interprets this as fifty per tribe, to make six hundred, and *keseph* he interprets as money, precious metal, which he takes to be gold; after all, silver was nothing accounted of in the days of David and Solomon. But the big thing is that in the staying of the plague God had revealed to David the site of the Temple, and had authorized sacrifice away from the Tabernacle altar at Gibeon. If God was revealing so great a matter by 'being intreated for the land' then he will have done so in the classic manner of Lev. 9, by sending celestial fire to consume the sacrifice; and no doubt the angel will have been commanded to sheathe his sword also. We may compare the angel with the sword in the Balaam story again; and Jacob's 'This is none other than the House of God'. There are very considerable expansions of this kind throughout the book, especially in 2 Chronicles, where the six-verse expansion made here seems very moderate.

My thesis is that a great deal of Matthew is to be interpreted in this way. Many of the expansions are minor, and perhaps uncontroversial:

Mark 3.14	Matt. 10.7
To be sent out to preach.	And preach as you go, saying, The Kingdom of heaven is at hand.

Mark 1.14f	
Jesus came . . . preaching, . . . The kingdom of God is at hand.	

Mark 14.21	Matt. 26.24
Woe to that man by whom the Son of Man is betrayed! It would have been better for that man if he had not been born.	Woe to that man by whom the Son of Man is betrayed! It would have been better for that man if he had not been born. *Judas, who betrayed him, said, Is it I, Master? He said to him, You have said so.*

The last verse in Matthew makes it clear that Jesus really did know that the traitor was Judas: from Mark one might think he merely knew it was one of the Twelve.

Mark 1.9	Matt. 3.13ff
In those days Jesus came from Nazareth of Galilee and was baptized by John in the Jordan.	Then Jesus came from Galilee to the Jordan to John, to be baptized by him. *John would have prevented him, saying, I need to be baptized by you, and do you come to me? But Jesus answered him, Let it be so now; for thus it is fitting for us to fulfil all righteousness. Then he consented.*

Matthew is concerned to answer a question that has vexed Sunday school teachers from that day to this, If Jesus was sinless, why should he be baptized? The presence of two words not otherwise found in Matthew is not an adequate objection to the conclusion that this is a Matthaean expansion.[16] The language in general, as well as the manner and the theology, is very typical of him. Similarly Mark tells us that the stone was rolled away from the sepulchre, Matthew describes the angel of the Lord doing so; Mark implies resurrection appearances in Galilee, Matthew supplies one; Mark tells how one of the disciples cut off the man's ear, Matthew expands to show that the Lord's reaction was to reject violence. And many such-like things he does.

Composition Miracles

On occasion the Chronicler fuses two stories from Kings into one, or includes details from a different incident to fill out a story. For instance, he describes the wickedness of King Jehoram in the words of 2 Kings 8. 17–22, including his marriage to Ahab's daughter; then he adds that he made high places, and made the inhabitants of Jerusalem to go a-whoring, and appends a letter from Elijah, pronouncing divine judgement on him.[17] The drawing of Ahab's influence into the story

[16] See p. 244 below.   [17] 2 Chron. 21.

suggests the activity of Elijah pronouncing God's judgement on Ahab, and the two themes are run together by means of an anachronistic letter. Similarly, 2 Kings 16.5–6 described the overwhelming of Ahaz by the armies of Samaria and Damascus; while earlier, in 2 Kings 6, Elisha is described as delivering a Syrian army prisoner to the King of Israel, and then persuading the King to feed them with bread and water, and to let them go from Samaria. The Chronicler combines the two stories. Ahaz's armies are defeated, and 200,000 prisoners taken to Samaria: there Oded, as a latter-day Elisha, persuades the Samaritans to release the captives and feed and clothe them.[18]

In a similar way, Matthew combines elements from different Marcan miracles. For example, the healing of the Two Blind Men in 9.27ff begins by recalling Bartimaeus in Mark 10.46ff.

Mark 10.47	Matt. 9.27
And when he heard that it was Jesus of Nazareth, he began to cry out and say, Jesus, son of David, have mercy on me.	And as Jesus passed on from there, two *blind* men followed him *cry*ing *out and saying, Have mercy on* us, *Son of David.*

The faith of Bartimaeus and the two men are stressed in the two stories also. However, in some respects the Matthaean story is more like the healing of the other Marcan blind man, at Bethsaida. They are healed privately, Jesus touches their eyes, and commands them to silence, all of which are traits of the Bethsaidan, but not of the Jericho, blind man. For the last point, Matthew draws on the words of the command to silence in a third miracle, the Marcan Leper.

Mark 1.43f	Matt. 9.30f
And he sternly charged him, and sent him away at once, and said to him, See that you say nothing to anyone; but go, show yourself to the priest . . . But he went out and began to talk freely about it, and to spread the news.	*And* Jesus *sternly charged* them, *See that no one* knows it. *But* they *went out and spread the news* of him through all that district.

The verbal coincidences of rare words and phrases make the conclusion irresistible.

Matthew does this a number of times. The deaf demoniac of Mark 9, the blind man of Mark 10, and the controversy with the scribes over casting out a demon in Mark 3 are all put together in an omnibus healing controversy at Matt. 12.22ff. The Demoniac in the synagogue (Mark 1) is omitted, only to be run together with the Demoniac by the Lake (Mark 5) at Matt. 8, where two Demoniacs are restored. The two

[18] 2 Chron. 28.1–15.

Blind Men are run together a second time when Matthew reaches Jericho. Last, and most interesting of all, a second version of the paralytic at Capernaum, and of the Gentile woman's daughter, are run together, with other matter, to give the Centurion's Boy, the only healing in the new material.[19]

[19] See pp. 319ff. below.

3

THE MIDRASHIC PARABLE

In the previous chapter we have been able to parallel Matthew's methods of expanding Mark from the literature most akin to it, the Books of Chronicles and the Targums. However, Matthew's most typical method of expounding Mark is by means of parables, of which there is no instance in these works. The new parable matter in Matthew, with its accessories, covers some 120 verses of the Gospel, or 20 per cent of the total new material, and for this we must seek for parallels in the rabbis. In this chapter we shall examine what I take to be a cross-section of one hundred rabbinic parables,[1] selected at random, and will pick out from them a number of features, or characteristics, some of which they have in common with OT parables, and in others of which they differentiate themselves. We shall then proceed to ask how far these characteristics are shared by the parables in Mark, Matthew, and Luke. I have tried to show elsewhere[2] that the parables in the three Synoptic Gospels are of very different types, and my conclusion there as here is that the Matthaean parables were composed by Matthew. What I had not then noticed, and what presses home my conclusion, is that Matthew's parables are in the rabbinic style in every way, while Mark's and Luke's in most respects are not.

The OT uses the word *māshāl* in a wide variety of senses: indeed Professor Jeremias distinguishes sixteen different uses of the word.[3] Nevertheless, it is possible for us to pick out the growth of what we call the parable, that is, a comparison between things divine and human in form of a story, however slight. There are, we may say, five parables in the OT: Jotham's parable of the Trees in Judg. 9; Nathan's parable of the Poor Man and his Ewe-Lamb in 2 Sam. 12; Jehoash's parable of the Cedar and Thistle in 2 Kings 14; Isaiah's parable of the Vineyard in Isa. 5; and Ezekiel's parable of the Vine and Eagle in Ezek. 17. There is clearly some variety here: Jotham's Trees and Jehoash's Cedar and Thistle are fables, for example, which the others are not. Yet they stand together in a number of respects, in which we may compare them with their rabbinic counterparts.

---

[1] See appendix to the chapter, pp. 66–9, for references.
[2] 'Characteristics of the Parables in the Several Gospels', *JTS* xix, Pt i (April 1968), pp. 51–69.
[3] J. Jeremias, *The Parables of Jesus* [*PJ*] (6e., 1962; ET, 2e., London 1963), p. 20.

Indicative Parables

They are all *indicative*, not imperative, parables. They point to the situation as it is. This is what the men of Shechem have done in making Abimelech king, and this will be its consequence. This is what Amaziah has done in his hybristic folly, and this is what he will suffer. This is the sin that David has committed, and he speaks his own fate. God has tended Israel his vineyard, and will lay it waste for its wild-grape harvest. The king has turned from Babylon to Egypt, and the country will not prosper. They are not, even indirectly, appeals to be righteous. What is done is done, and must now be seen to have been done; and God's hostile action can be confidently pronounced.

Rabbinic parables are indicative, too. They differ from OT parables in that they are rarely parables of prophecy, but they are concerned to demonstrate the world's situation in the perspective of the action of God. They are sometimes, indirectly, concerned with edifying the hearer, but they do not set out to exhort him to pray, or to beware of riches. They usually arise out of a text that needs exposition, or a question of doctrine. Their subject is most commonly Israel, but other subjects are the Fathers, the Torah, Nebuchadnezzar, the Talmîdh Hākhām, the soul and the body, the world and its destiny, suffering, death, resurrection, and so on.[4] It will be convenient to cite a few rabbinic parables to illustrate this and subsequent points.

'Israel disappointed the fond hopes which God had placed in them by making a golden calf soon after the Revelation. R. Ḥama, the son of R. Ḥanina [third century] said: "This might be compared to one who had a bed full of vegetables, but rising up early in the morning, he found they had withered." '[5]

'And the heart of Pharaoh was turned' (Exod. 14.5). R. Jose the Galilean said: To what may this be compared? To a man who inherited a farm requiring a *khor* of seed, and he sold it for a small price. The purchaser opened some wells in it, and planted gardens and parks. Thereupon the seller began to feel sore because he had disposed of his inheritance for a trifle. Even so was it with the Egyptians, who sent Israel out of their land and did not realize the treasure they were thereby losing. It is of them that the text speaks (Cant. 4.13): 'Thy shoots are an orchard of pomegranates.'[6]

---

[4] These subjects are all instanced in A. Feldman, *The Parables and Similes of the Rabbis* [*PSR*] (Cambridge 1927), to which I am much indebted. Feldman gives no instance of an imperative parable.
[5] Lev. R. 18.3.   [6] Mekilta, ad loc.

Both of these parables are to biblical texts on the story of Israel's
salvation. A longer parable expounds the doctrine of judgement:

'[The Emperor] Antoninus said to Rabbi [sc. Judah the Prince, second
and third centuries]: The body and the soul can free themselves from
the Judgement. How so? The body will say, "It is the soul that hath
sinned, for from the day that she departed from me, I have been lying
in the grave silent as a stone." And the soul will say, "It is the body
that has sinned, for from the day that I quitted it I have been flitting
like a bird in the air." And Rabbi replied: I will tell thee a parable.
Unto what is this like? Unto a human king possessed of a beautiful
Pardes,[7] which had in it some fine early figs. He placed therein two
watchmen, of whom one was lame and the other blind. Then said the
lame to the blind, "I see some luscious early figs in the garden, come
and carry me on thy back and we shall delight ourselves with them."
The lame mounted the shoulders of the blind, and gathered some of
the fruit, and they ate it together. After a time the owner of the
Pardēs came and said unto them, "Where are those fine early figs?"
The lame said, "Have I then legs to walk with?" The blind said,
"Have I eyes to see?" What did the king? He made the lame to ride
upon the back of the blind and sentenced them together. Even so will
the Holy One, blessed be He, bring the soul, cast it into the body and
judge the two together; as it is said, "He calleth to the heavens from
above and to the earth that he may judge his people." He calleth to the
heaven above for the soul, and to the earth for the body, to judge his
people.'[8]

It is evident that just as much for a doctrinal parable as for a parable
expounding a historical text, the story aims to set forth the actions of
God and men in the indicative. Man cannot hope to escape judgement
by the exercise of imperial sophistry, for God will see through him,
and will judge him, soul and body put together. Of our hundred
parables, only two, Hillel's Royal Statues, and the Passenger Overboard from the Tanḥuma, could be described as being imperative.

Now in the case of the Gospel parables we find a sharp cleavage in
this respect between Mark and Matthew on the one side, and Luke on
the other. Mark's three Seed parables in 4 speak of the growth of God's
kingdom; the Wicked Husbandmen of its rejection by Israel; the
Fig-Tree and the Doorkeeper of its coming consummation. In the
same way all but possibly one of the Matthaean parables are indicative parables, kingdom of heaven parables. In 13 all but the Marcan
Sower begin, 'The kingdom of heaven is like . . .'; they are about

[7] The *Pardes* (Paradise) is a large park which features often in rabbinic parables.
[8] B. Sanh. 91a; Lev. R. 4.5.

God's action in inaugurating his kingdom, and man's response, the devil's opposition, the kingdom's silent growth like mustard-seed and leaven, its transcendent value like buried treasure or pearl, its consummation, like the pulling in of the dragnet. The Unmerciful Servant in 18 also begins, 'The kingdom of heaven may be compared . . .', and concludes, rather to our surprise, 'So also my heavenly Father will do to everyone of you, if you do not forgive your brother from your heart'; the parable is about God's judgement on the unmerciful, and only secondarily suggests an imperative about our own behaviour. The Labourers in the Vineyard describes God's merciful generosity to the unrighteous Last, and the resentment of the righteous First; the Two Sons the ultimate obedience of the sinners, the real disobedience of the Pharisees. The Wicked Husbandmen and the Great Feast speak of the rejection of Christ by Israel, and the substitution of the Gentiles—the latter ending with the judgement of the hypocritical churchman. All five parables in 24—25 testify to the coming of Judgement at the Parousia; they carry no more than the general moral, Watch. The Two Builders in 7 is similarly a Judgement parable: those who hear and do have built their houses on a rock, and vice versa—only a general moral can be drawn. The only parable with an imperative sense is the Lost Sheep, where the moral is plain, and for the apostles, *Pascite agnos meos*: though Matthew himself still sees the parable in indicatives, 'It is not the will of my Father who is in heaven that one of these little ones should perish'.

The contrast with Luke is very striking: his parables are almost all imperative parables, carrying a direct suggestion of what the Christian should do. Even to the Marcan Sower he makes four small changes to emphasize the moral of faithful endurance by the Christian. Those on the rock 'believe for a while'; those among the thorns are throttled 'as they go on their way'; the fruitful do not merely receive the word but 'hold it fast in an honest and good heart'; they bear fruit 'with patience'. Thus even the Sower becomes an exhortation. The same is true of many of the Q and all the L parables. The Lucan parables are told to encourage the Christian to pray,[9] to be faithful,[10] and to count the cost,[11] and to warn him of the perils of money.[12] Luke introduces an almost unbroken element of imperative parables into an almost unbroken tradition of indicative parables. Mark and Matthew are in the Jewish tradition, Luke is not.

A corollary of this is the introductory formulas used in the different

---

[9] The Friend at Midnight, the Unjust Judge.
[10] The Pounds, the Servant of all Work.
[11] The Tower-builder, the Embassy.
[12] The Rich Fool, the Unjust Steward, Dives and Lazarus.

Gospels. Jeremias writes; 'Most of the rabbinical parables begin with the words: *mashal. l^e* . . . This usage is an abbreviation of: *'emshol l^ekha mashal. l^ema haddabhar dome? l^e* . . . (I will relate a parable to you. With what shall the matter be compared? It is the case with it as with . . .) Hence, occasionally, all this may be reduced to the bare dative (*l^e*).'[13] Now two of the Marcan parables open with such formulas (4.26,30): 'With what can we compare the Kingdom of God, or what parable shall we use for it? It is like a grain of mustard-seed . . .'; one has simply, 'It is like'; the others all have the word παραβολή to introduce them. Matthew similarly introduces all his long parables but one with some such formula as, 'The kingdom of heaven may be likened to . . .' and many of his shorter ones too. Such formulas come ten times in Matthew: twice there are shorter intro-ductions: 'It will be as when . . .' (25.14), 'Everyone who . . . does them will be like . . .' (7.24); twice we find, 'What do you think? . . .' (18.12; 21.28); and once 'Who then is the faithful . . .' (24.45). The Marcan Sower and Wicked Husbandmen retain their introduction as 'He told them many things in parables', 'Hear another parable'. Luke on the other hand never uses introductory formulas except when they lie in previous tradition. His parables either begin, 'A certain man . . .' or 'Which of you . . .'. While there are rabbinic instances of such an opening, the Marcan–Matthaean tradition is the Jewish norm; and this is not accidental, because Mark and Matthew are giving analogies for the coming of the Kingdom, but Luke is making an appeal to the Christian.

Nature and Personal Parables

The OT parables are essentially comparisons between the human–divine situation and an analogue in nature. Indeed such an approach is assumed in the description of King Solomon's *m^eshālîm*: 'He also uttered three thousand *māshāl*, and his songs were a thousand and five. He spoke of trees, from the cedar that is in Lebanon to the hyssop that grows out of the wall; he spoke also of beasts, and of birds, and of reptiles, and of fish' (1 Kings 4.32f). Jotham and Jehoash spoke of trees; Isaiah spoke of a vineyard; Ezekiel of an Eagle and a Vine. Nathan is the only parabolist to speak of a human situation, though his story also turns on a ewe-lamb. The Marcan parables follow this tradition. The three Seed parables in Mark 4 are all exclusively nature-parables, as is the Fig-Tree—the farmers in the first two are background figures who are incidental; the interest is in the growth,

[13] Jeremias, *PJ*, p. 100.

and the different lessons to be drawn from it. The Wicked Husbandmen is Isaiah's Vineyard parable with a personal situation woven in,
suggested by Cant. 8.11f. The Doorkeeper is brief, but concerned with
personal situations only. Many of the shorter Marcan images are also
taken from nature and inanimate life—the lamp, the patch, the wine,
bread and dogs, the camel and the needle's eye—while the personal
image, like the Strong Man Bound, is rare.

This tradition of nature-parables is foreign to the rabbis. It is rare
to find a rabbinic parable that is not concerned with human relationships: only ten of our hundred are not personal parables. Of the three
parables already cited, one was concerned with the King and the blind
and the lame Watchmen, one with the disappointment of the man
who sold his inheritance for a trifle—like Pharaoh, who let the treasure
of Israel go. The closest to a nature-parable is the farmer who found
his vegetables withered, but here the farmer is not incidental: the
point is that he stands for God, whose estate of Israel has yielded him
no fruit. Rabbinic parables feature kings and farmers, normally
tenant-farmers (*'aris*), their servants and labourers and watchmen,
robbers, the captain of a ship and his passenger, fathers and sons, the
potter, a man and wife, woodcutters, shepherds, slaughterers, a prince
and his tutor, a priest and his messenger, etc.[14] There are many nature
similes as when the delay in Israel's redemption is likened to spices:
'When the spices are gathered, tender and moist, their odour does
not spread, but when they are gathered dry, the scent does spread.'[15]
But for parables in the fuller sense, personal stories are the norm.

Matthew's parables are in the rabbinic, and not the OT tradition.
He even personalizes two of the Marcan nature-parables: intruding
into the Mustard-Seed a man, taking and sowing in his field; rewriting
the Seed Growing Secretly with a very live farmer with his staff of
servants and his enemy. His own parables take over the world of
rabbinic characters: kings for the rabbinic *melekh*, with their nobles
and their slaves, farmers and their *pō'ᵃlîm*, labourers, the good-man
of the house (*ba'al habbayîth*) and his steward (*bēn bayîth*), house-
builders and fishermen, a father and his sons, wedding-guests and
bridesmaids, a woman in the kitchen and children at play, a merchant
and a burglar. The Lost Sheep, the Dragnet, and the Sheep and Goats
we misname. The Lost Sheep is centred on the Shepherd: he has a
hundred sheep and leaves the ninety and nine and goes and seeks the
lost, and if he finds it rejoices. The Dragnet gathers the fish, but the
evangelist is in imagination with the fishermen: 'they' cast the net
and pull it when full on to the shore and sit down and gather the good

[14] For references, see appendix to chapter, pp. 66–9 below.
[15] Yalqut Ps. § 639.

into buckets and throw out the bad. The Sheep and Goats is not only misnamed for content, it is misnamed as a parable also: it is a description of the Last Judgement given straight as the peroration to the Apocalyptic Discourse, and contains the simile of the shepherd, no more. The only nature-parable that is added by Matthew is the Leaven, in parallel with the Mustard-Seed, and that contains a woman. Many of these characters are taken over by Luke, so that in this respect Luke and Matthew both follow the rabbinic tradition against the Marcan parables, which stand rather in the OT nature-parable line.

Contrast-Parables

In most parables there is some sort of contrast latent. Jotham's bramble is set against his fruitful trees, Jehoash's bramble against his cedar, Nathan's rich man against his poor man, Isaiah's wild grapes against the sweet ones hoped for. The emphasis upon the contrast can, however, become much more marked, and in rabbinic parables commonly does. For example:

'This might be likened unto a king who had some concubines and many sons. He also had one son born to him of a Matrona, and for him the king cherished a special affection. He gave fields and vineyards to all the children of the concubines, but to his son (by the Matrona) he presented a *Pardes*, out of which came all his provisions. Thereupon the son went and enquired of his father: "Thou gavest to the sons of the concubines fields and vineyards, but to me thou hast presented one *Pardes* only." So is it with the Holy One . . .'[16]

'R. Joshua of Sichnin said in the name of R. Levi [fourth century]: The trees that bear edible fruit were asked, "Why are your voices not heard?" "We have no need thereof", they replied, "our fruits are our witnesses." Then they asked of the fruitless trees, "Why are you so noisy?" and they replied, "Would that we could make our voices heard louder still so that we might attract attention." '[17]

'R. Eleazar b. Zadok [first century] said, To what are the righteous like in this world? To a tree which stands in a clean place, while one of its branches projects into an unclean place; when the branch is cut off the whole tree stands in a clean place. Even so does the Holy One, blessed be He, bring chastisements upon the righteous . . . And to what are the wicked like in this world? To a tree which stands in an unclean place while a branch protrudes into a clean place; when the

[16] Tanḥuma Lev., p. 78; Yalqut § 615.
[17] Gen. R. 16.3.

branch is cut off the whole tree stands in an unclean place. Even so
does the Holy One . . .'[18]

51 of our hundred rabbinic parables are contrasts of this kind.

In the Marcan parables the contrasts are not strongly marked, if
indeed they are there at all. The Sower has four different sorts of land
bearing seed, which receive equal treatment, although the intention
is to set the fourth against the other three. The Seed Growing Secretly
and the Fig-Tree are not contrasted with anything, nor are there in
Mark any faithful Husbandmen to contrast with the Wicked. The
Mustard-Seed is only generally contrasted with other larger seeds and
smaller plants. It is different with Matthew. His long parables are
without exception black-and-white caricature contrasts: the two
Builders upon sand and rock, the man and his enemy sowing their
Wheat and Tares, the Dragnet with the good fish in buckets and
the bad thrown out, the ninety-nine safe sheep and the wanderer, the
Merciful King and the Unmerciful Servant, the first Labourers in the
Vineyard and the last, the obedient and disobedient Sons, the invited
and the chosen at the Wedding Feast, the faithful and the faithless
servant in charge of the house, the wise and the foolish Virgins, the
two good and faithful stewards and the wicked and idle steward.
Often the contrasts are laboured by repetitive language so that they
shall not escape us, the Two Builders, the Unmerciful Servant, and the
Talents especially, as with the trees in clean and unclean places above.
Usually the contrast is even: wheat with tares, five wise virgins and
five foolish. It is the art of the author that he achieves just as black and
white a contrast when he intrudes third and fourth parties. The
antithesis is not diminished by the inclusion of a second virtuous
steward in the Talents, nor by the hire of various lots of labourers
between the first and the last—and freshness is preserved. We may
compare the son of the Matrona and the many concubine-sons above.
So much is the contrast part of Matthew's manner that he introduces
contrasts of his own into both the long Marcan parables. Mark ends
the Wicked Husbandmen, '. . . and [he will] give the vineyard to
others': Matthew adds, '. . . to other tenants who will give him the
fruits in their seasons', and 'God's kingdom will be taken away from
you and given to a nation producing the fruits of it' (AT). Similarly
with the Sower. The parable is told very much as it stands in Mark,
but the emphasis is changed in the interpretation by the addition of the
significant word συνίημι to the first and last classes. What matters,
Matthew has told us, is understanding. The disciples are blessed
because they do understand; the Jews are punished because they will
not understand. So now those along the path are those who hear and

[18] B Kidd. 40b.

do not understand; those on the good soil are those who hear and do understand. The subtleties of the two intervening classes cannot be forced into this mould, and should not be omitted; and we are left with a complex four-point Marcan parable on which a simple two-point Matthaean contrast has been grafted.

Thus all thirteen of the long Matthaean parables are contrast-parables. There remain a number of shorter vignette-parables, which are not long enough to bear this type of handling. Nevertheless, the weddings and funerals of the Children in the Market-place are a contrast; the Marcan Mustard-Seed is supplied not only with a farmer to take and sow it in his field, but also with a pair in the woman taking and hiding leaven in the meal; and the Pearl makes a pair with the Treasure in the Field. In both the last two pairs the use of repetitive language points the contrast: the man in his farm with the woman in her kitchen, the treasure from the land and the treasure from the sea. The only parables in Matthew which are not contrasts are the Marcan Fig-Tree and Matthew's own Burglar.

It would take us too far afield to analyse the Lucan parables for contrast here. Suffice it to say that while sometimes, as in the Two Debtors, or the Pharisee and Publican, we have contrasts somewhat of the same kind, many of the Lucan parables—the Good Samaritan, the Rich Fool, the Friend at Midnight, for example—are not of this kind. Matthew takes *à l'outrance* a common feature of rabbinic parable-making, a feature which hardly occurs in Mark, and is not noticeable in Luke.

Stock Figures

We notice quickly that the characters of rabbinic parables are stock figures. The kings are stock kings, powerful, generous, wise; the labourers are industrious or idle, honest or cheats, and so on. What else should we expect? The parables are short. Where a figure is sought for God's power, generosity, or wisdom, a king suggests itself —why have a weak, mean, or foolish king? Even in a longer parable such as the Lame and Blind Watchmen above, the king is portrayed merely as just and powerful, the Watchmen merely as cunning. Colourful detail is eschewed.

Now a strong differentiation appears at this point between Matthew and Luke. Since Mark's parables are mostly nature-parables, there are hardly any characters in them. But while Luke's characters are highly individual people, Matthew's figures are all stock figures, most of them straight out of the rabbinic book. People are either good or bad, wise or foolish, obedient or disobedient, merciful or merciless. His Two Builders is typical: one is wise and builds his house upon the rock, the other is foolish and builds his house upon the sand. There are the same rain and the same rivers and the same winds, and the inevitable end. His Two Sons is even more stark, and reveals the essential Matthaean, rabbinic, technique. The boys are stock figures, not human beings. Nine words apiece suffice to sketch in their characters. We even find the Marcan people stylized into the rabbinic pattern. In Mark the Wicked Husbandmen begins simply with a man; in Matthew he has become an ἄνθρωπος οἰκοδεσπότης, a standard *ba'al habbayîth*.

In Luke on the other hand all is alive. His characters are many-sided: prudent despite being crooked, penitent although a publican, thoughtful for their brothers even in Hades. The whole teeming world elbows its way into his parables, rounding off the sharp contrasts: one invited guest has bought a field, another has got married, the beggar is called Lazarus, the traveller is going from Jerusalem to Jericho. The characters soliloquize, as Mark's and Matthew's hardly do.[19] 'What shall I do?' they ask, and we see into their hearts—the Rich Fool, the Prodigal, the Unjust Steward, the Judge, and the Vineyard-Owner at length. A comparison between his Builders and Matthew's is most instructive. He lacks the plain contrasts, wise and foolish, rock and sand; he lacks the repetitious Noah's Ark picture, "the rain fell and the floods came and the winds blew and beat against that house". He has envisaged the situation. It is not primarily the wind and the rain which bring down a house with weak foundation, but the floods. He therefore concentrates on the river, and makes the contrast the presence or absence of a sound foundation. This involves much more of the builder as a man: he digs and deepens and lays the foundation; he has built well, and his house cannot be shaken. How much better we know him, and see it all, than with the Matthaean Wise Man. A comparison between Luke's Two Sons and Matthew's Two Sons is even more instructive, and need not be laboured.

Allegory

I have argued elsewhere[20] that few distinctions have been more ill-starred for the criticism of the Gospels than that between parable and allegory, which are often seen as two different *genres* of literature. Happily this battle does not have to be fought out again here. I am

[19] Mark 12.6/Matt. 21.37, 'They will respect my son'; Matt. 24.48, 'My master is delayed', are the only instances.
[20] 'Characteristics', *JTS* XIX, pp. 58–62.

concerned merely to show that Matthew allegorizes, and that his parables are consistently allegorical in marked degree; that the Marcan parables are less, and the Lucan parables very much less allegorical; and that the rabbinic—and for that matter OT—parables have about the same order of allegory as Matthew. If we are to claim that the parables of one author are more allegorical than those of another, it is necessary to quantify the evidence; and this we can readily do by a simple exercise. Count the number of 'features' a parable has; count the number of these features to which the evangelist ascribes a 'meaning'; and express the second as a proportion of the first.

We might take as an illustration Matthew's own Dragnet, since he gives us the interpretation himself, so there is a minimum of subjectiveness. The parable has ten points, all of which have meanings to Matthew. The casting of the net is the Church's preaching, the sea is the world, all kinds of fish are the various church members, the net's being full is the fullness of Israel and the Gentiles being gathered in, the fishermen are the angels, the pulling up on to the beach is the judgement, the good fish are the just, the bad the hypocritical churchmen, the buckets stand for heaven, the throwing out for hell. At no point does the allegory spoil the story: so the Dragnet has a count of 10/10 or 1.0.

The OT parables have a high allegory-content apart from Nathan. Every point corresponds in Jehoash's Thistle and Cedar except for the offer of marriage—six points out of seven, 0.86. Ezekiel's elaborate Eagle and Vine, so far as one can interpret his contorted imagination, yields 20 correspondences against 23 points in the story, the same figure, 0.86. Isaiah and Jotham have rather more colourful detail without corresponding meaning. In Isaiah's Vineyard, the stones, the tower, the winevat, the pruning and the hoeing are without meanings; in Jotham's case the threefold invitation and refusal to reign. But in both parables the meaning breaks through—when Isaiah's farmer commands the clouds not to rain, or when fire comes out of Jotham's bramble and burns the cedars. Both end with 0.73. On the other hand Nathan's parable is full of non-significant details. The children, the morsel, the cup, the poor man's bosom, the traveller, the rich man's sparing his own flock, the cooking of the ewe-lamb, seven points of fourteen, are without meaning—a count of 0.5.

Now the rabbinic parables are high in allegory-content, and it is for this reason that they tend to clear contrasts, stock figures, and human situations—these are the best bases for allegorical parables, for the more colourful the situations and various the characters, the more interest the author will have in his story, and so the lower will be

the allegory-content. If we take some of the parables we have already
used as illustrations: in R. Hama's Withered Vegetables, God is the
man, the bed of vegetables is Israel, God's plot in which he hopes,
the next morning is 'soon after the Revelation', the withering is the
making of the Golden Calf—all these details are in the interpretation
provided, 4/4, 1.0. In R. Jose's Cheap Farm, the inheritor is Egypt,
the farm is Israel, the cheap sale is letting Israel go, the buyer is
(perhaps) God, the planting of gardens and parks is Israel's later
greatness, the seller's disappointment is the turning of Pharaoh's
heart: but the requirement of a *khor* of seed, and the sinking of wells
are without significance—six points out of eight, 0.75. In the Blind
and Lame Watchmen, the king is God, the *Pardēs* is the world, the
lame watchman is the body, the blind is the soul, the stealing is sin,
the owner's interrogation is judgement, the watchmen's excuses are
Antoninus' sophistry, the king making the lame ride on the blind for
sentence is the resurrection to damnation; only the luscious, early
figs are corroborative detail, nine points out of ten, 0.9. As rabbinic
parables normally carry an appended interpretation, the exegesis is
fairly objective, and something of this order, between 0.75 and 1.00,
might be taken as normal. It is very rare for a rabbinic parable to be
spoiled for the allegory.

The Gospels are not to be treated as a unity, and the allegory-
content varies markedly from Gospel to Gospel. As the analysis of
allegory-content is wearing to follow, and as we shall have opportunity
to take the Matthaean parables with their synoptic counterparts one
by one later, we may content ourselves with the results of the analysis
here. Mark twice achieves an allegory-content of 1, in the Sower and
the Fig-Tree. He has 0.55 for the Seed Growing Secretly, 0.8 for the
Mustard-Seed, 0.65 for the Wicked Husbandmen, 0.75 for the
Doorkeeper. Adding together all the points and all the correspondences we obtain an overall figure of 0.75. Mark never has a spoiled
story.

Matthew shows his propensity for allegory in the Wicked Husbandmen: he inserts the stoning of one servant (Zechariah), and the paying
of fruits (Obedience) by the other (Christian) farmers; he transposes
the throwing of the son out of the vineyard to before his murder, as
Christ suffered without the gate; he omits the unallegorizable share
of the fruits demanded in Mark. Similarly his rewriting of the Seed
Growing Secretly into the Tares results in a much more marked allegory—11 points out of 14, 0.79 against the Marcan 0.55. In general
we find a higher allegory-content in the Matthaean than in the
Marcan parables, which is the more remarkable in that Matthew's
parables are longer than Mark's, and the correspondence rate tends

naturally to be higher in short parables. The following are the figures: Two Builders 1.0, Sower 1.0, Tares, 0.79, Mustard-Seed 0.87, Leaven 0.83, Treasure 0.86, Pearl 0.8, Dragnet 1.0, Lost Sheep 0.86, Unmerciful Servant 0.69, Labourers in Vineyard 0.65, Two Sons 1.0, Wicked Husbandmen 0.76, Marriage Feast 0.95, Burglar 1.0, Faithful and Unfaithful Servants 0.83, Ten Virgins 0.61, Talents 0.72, Fig-Tree 1.0. All in all Matthew has 185 points corresponding out of 226, an average of 0.82. Matthew's greater interest in the meaning of the story, over against Mark, results in the breakdown of the story in two cases. In the Marriage-Feast, the coming of Titus' army to Jerusalem and the burning of the city are represented in an allegory which breaks the story of the King and his Dinner. In the Faithful and Unfaithful Servants, the latter is first cut in half and then has his portion with the hypocrites, in allegory of Gehenna. Often it is said that the breakdown of such stories shows Matthew's interference with earlier versions of the parables which are happily preserved for us in Luke. The naivety of this approach is very surprising. The evidence above, which is widely accepted, shows Matthew to have been both an allegorist and an allegorizer. What should be more natural than that on occasion his interest in the meaning should have led him into spoiling the story, like Isaiah and Jotham? The intrusion of the allegory in the Marriage-Feast is due to his interest in the guilt and punishment of Israel, and in the concluding verses (the man who had not on a wedding-garment) to his worry over the Church as a *corpus mixtum*. Both belong naturally to a Matthaean parable. We do not lack evidence that Luke altered the Matthaean parable in various characteristic ways.[21] The intrusion of an allegory of hell into the Unfaithful Servant is similarly due to Matthew's interest in that subject.

Luke, on the other hand, shows a marked aversion from allegory. The following figures show that, with one exception, the Lucan version of each parable has less allegory-content than either the Marcan or the Matthaean opposite number, and that where there is no close corresponding parable in his predecessors, the figures are lower still. I give the Lucan figures first: Two Builders 0.66 (Matt. 1.0), Two Debtors 0.8, the Sower 0.87 (Mark 1.0), the Friend at Midnight 0.36, the Burglar 1.0 (Matt. 1.0), the Faithful and Unfaithful Servants 0.61 (Matt. 0.83), the Unfruitful Fig-Tree 0.5, the Mustard-Seed 0.83 (Matt. 0.87), the Leaven 0.83 (Matt. 0.83), the Great Supper 0.64 (Matt. 1.0), the Tower-Builder 0.62, the King's Embassy 0.43, the Lost Sheep 0.6 (Matt. 0.86), Lost Coin 0.63, Prodigal Son 0.28, Unjust Steward 0.35, Unjust Judge 0.42, Servant's Wages 0.45, Pounds 0.59 (Matt. 0.72), Wicked Husbandmen 0.85 (Mark 0.65),

[21] See p. 418 below.

Fig-Tree 1.0 (Mark 1.0). Luke's overall average is 0.6, but many of the L parables are less than 0.5. In addition there are four illustrative stories which we call parables, the Good Samaritan, the Rich Fool, Dives and Lazarus, and the Pharisee and Publican, which are a new type of parable not found elsewhere in the synoptic tradition. It is Luke's love of the colourful detail which cuts down the allegory content—shoes and a ring for the Prodigal, the sheep on the shepherd's shoulders and a party to follow. He is interested in the story where Matthew and the rabbis are interested in the meaning. The simplest explanation of Luke's Wicked Husbandmen and Sower alongside Mark's is that by leaving out points which have meanings, and inserting colourful points of his own that have not, he in effect de-allegorizes.[22]

The conclusion to which the evidence of the allegory-content points us is thus clear. Mark has a fairly high allegory-content, Luke a low one. Matthew differentiates himself not only from Luke in this respect, but also from Mark; for he has both a noticeably higher count, and also instances of spoiling the story. In his high count Matthew is closest to the rabbis, as in so much else. In his spoiling of the two stories he is closest to Isaiah and Jotham.

Appended Interpretations

It was, as we have seen, normal for parables to be interpreted. All five OT parables receive interpretations on the spot, and 97 of our hundred rabbinic parables move on at their conclusion with such a comment as 'Even so will the Holy One, blessed be He . . .'. It should therefore cause less surprise and recourse to ingenious theory than is normal, if Mark and his successors append the interpretation to the Sower, and if Matthew does the same for the Tares, the Dragnet, and the Two Sons.[23] It is not natural for Luke to do this, because he is furthest from the Jewish tradition. The most instances of it are found in Matthew because he is closest to the rabbis.

Scale

The scale of rabbinic parables varies. They are content to tell a tale of the humble if it suits them. However, the favourite of all images is the king, and there are many parables in which are featured the *Pardēs*,

[22] But in the Wicked Husbandmen, Luke also (*a*) omits the non-allegorical hedge and winepress and tower, and (*b*) follows the Matthaean allegorized order, 'they cast him out of the vineyard and killed him'; so that in this single case Luke has the highest net allegory-content of the three.

[23] Matthew also appends brief interpretations (so-called generalized conclusions) to the Lost Sheep, the Unmerciful Servant, the Labourers in the Vineyard, the Burglar, and the Virgins.

the royal palace, rich men with extensive lands with parks and gardens, and whatever may catch the imagination and hold the attention. Since God is the central figure of the rabbinic allegories, it is natural that the tendency should be towards royal imagery and the grand scale; even if an individual farmer and his plot of frost-bitten vegetables meet us from time to time. Of our 90 personal parables, 45 are royal, and a further 10 are on the grand scale in other ways.

The Gospel parables are clearly marked off for scale by their Gospel of occurrence. Mark's world is the village, perhaps the Galilean village. The farmers of his first two parables sow the seed unaccompanied. The tiny mustard-seed, the deciduous, dead-looking, fig-tree[24] are magnets to village eyes—the latter forgotten by towny Luke with his 'and all the trees'. The absentee landlord is a standard feature of *latifundia* prevalent in Galilee and elsewhere.[25] When Mark's householder goes away, it is but for a local journey: he will return in one of the watches of the coming night.

Matthew is a lover of the grand scale. He is the oriental story-teller so beloved by the commentators. He makes Mark's mustard-bush into a δένδρον. Mark's owner sends to the Wicked Husbandmen three servants in turn and then a number; Matthew's a group each time, and more the second than the first. His journeying householders are away for weeks, perhaps years: their servants know not the *day* nor the hour. They need a major-domo to supervise them. When he is in the country his scale is such as will tempt the imagination. His farmer in the Tares has a staff of servants to do his bidding. His housewife puts leaven into the meal enough for 162 people, so German accuracy testifies.[26] His shepherd has a hundred sheep. The treasure in the field and the pearl exceed in value all that their discoverers possess. The very fall of the house on the sand is great. In the town things can be still more splendid. There are kings in the Unmerciful Servant and the Marriage-Feast, and the latter runs to an army and the burning of a city, not to speak of a private hell for offensive wedding-guests. Nothing is spared: droves of servants to comb the city, bulls and fatlings sacrificed, a wedding-garment provided per head. Ten bridesmaids in the other wedding-parable are retinue for a rich man's daughter. When it comes to money, Matthew moves among the millionaires. His householder entrusts nothing less than a talent to his servants, ten, twenty, fifty thousand *denarii*,[27] a man's wage for 30,

[24] Jeremias, *PJ*, p. 120.
[25] C. H. Dodd, *Parables of the Kingdom* (2e., London 1936), pp. 124ff.
[26] G. Dalman, *Arbeit und Sitte in Palästina* (Gütersloh 1935) IV, p. 120.
[27] I have followed Jeremias' (Josephus') equivalence, 10,000 denarii = 1 talent; see *PJ*, p. 210, n.6.

60, 150 years. The Unmerciful Servant's debt is astronomical, the tribute of provinces.

Such ostentation is not to be found in Luke. I have tried to show elsewhere[28] that Luke's parables are down-to-earth affairs, and we have not leisure here to analyse them one by one. Two illustrations may suffice. Where Matthew's householder sets his three men up with a seat on the stock exchange, Luke's nobleman sets up his ten with a barrow-load of oranges, a μνᾶ apiece, 100*d.*, a man's wage for three months—the more stingy since he is on his way to a kingdom. The final touch is added when, returned a king, he tips the successful man —now governor of a decapolis—the μνᾶ that has lain idle. This is a community where brass is brass. Similarly Luke's Great Supper is a smaller affair than Matthew's. It is given by a commoner instead of by royalty, and although the guests are many one servant is enough to summon them, and they are few enough for individual excuses to be recorded. The same slave suffices also to bring in both the poor and lame on a second excursion, and those in the roads and hedgerows without on a third. There is no wedding, no bulls and fatlings are mentioned. Every parable in Luke shows the same trend, to a realistic, credible, country-gentleman type of scale. The largest sum of money owed in Luke[29] is a quarter of Matthew's smallest investment.

Here, as in each of the categories that we have taken, the separation of the parables by Gospel of occurrence tells the same story. Matthew's parables are on the grand scale, and are different from Mark's village scale, and Luke's middle-class, realistic scale; and Matthew is closest once more to the rabbinic norm.

Doctrine

The central doctrines of the Matthaean parables are those of Mark, and of the NT: the secret growth of the kingdom, its value, its imminence, the judgement of Israel, and of mankind, the necessity of forgiveness, and the reverse of this world's priorities. There are, however, certain doctrines which are stressed only in the Matthaean parables, or much more than in those in other Gospels, and these doctrines we find both elsewhere in Matthew and also as rabbinic standard teaching. The three most obvious of these are:

(*a*) The substitution of the Kingdom of Heaven for the Kingdom of God as the normal description of the movement founded by God

---

[28] art. cit., pp. 54f.
[29] Jeremias (*PJ*, p. 181), estimates the debt of wheat at 2,500 denarii.

in Christ. *Malkûth hashshāmayim* is to Matthew as to the rabbis the normal way of speaking of Israel's hope, though he is open, as they are, to the use of the Marcan formula when it is God's kingdom as opposed to Satan's (12.28), or when God is being interpreted under the allegory of the father (21.31) or householder (21.43), or in prayer (6.10,33).

(b) Hell.   There is one passage only in Mark (9.43–9) which refers to Hell, and that perhaps poetical. Luke has markedly less Hell than Matthew in and out of Q passages, and makes the distinction between light and heavy punishments in the hereafter that leads to purgatory. But Matthew never wearies of the rabbinic Gehenna. Outer darkness, eternal punishment, fire unquenchable, wailing and gnashing of teeth are the fate of the damned in and out of his parables. It is Matthew who has introduced this harsh motif into the Gospel, and but for him the doctrine, played down by Jesus and foreign to Paul, would not have cast its heavy shadow across history.

(c) The angels play an increased part in the whole Gospel, as opposed to Mark (20 references as opposed to 6), and especially in the parables. We shall later expound Matthew's angelology, which reflects apocalyptic and rabbinic teaching.

We may now perhaps gather together what we have said, and following Matthew's example, set it forth in a parable. Hitherto the parables have been like three rooms of paintings, each roomful discovered in a different Italian city. All have been held in tradition to be Leonardo's, all the Leonardo's there are, but the sophisticated critics have noted and deplored the way in which inferior pupils have painted over the incomparable colours of the master, and marred the simplicity of his lines. Indeed there have not been lacking offers to take off the offensive over-painting, and to reveal the pristine original. Happily no chemical has yet been discovered to do the job. Now our brief survey has revealed two interesting facts which should be fully weighed before the restorers' zeal is allowed further rein. One, the extent to which the paintings in the three rooms are different is far greater than has hitherto been noticed. Room 1 is mainly landscapes, Rooms 2 and 3 are human occasions; Room 1 is all done in a village, Room 3 is of homely scenes, Room 2 is of lords and doges: and so on. In eight different ways the paintings in the three rooms can be seen to differ from each other. Second, a comparison between the paintings in Room 2 and those of Titian, Tintoretto, and Veronese, reveals that in all these eight ways there is a marked similarity to them, which is mostly not shared by those in Rooms 1 and 3. Which of us then will not cry, Hold!, to the restorers? Surely the conclusion forces itself upon us. The paintings in Room 2 are not Leonardo's at all; they are by a pupil of his who settled in Venice.

My parable is an indicative one, and of as noble a scale as I can make it: shall I not follow my master and append an interpretation? The orthodox position of Jülicher, Dodd, Jeremias, and almost all commentaries is untenable. We do not possess a gallery of parables, all of which are substantially the parables of Jesus, but which the handling of the churches or the tendency of the evangelists has distorted and spoiled. The sooner we stop trying to strip off these imaginary accretions in our search for mare's nest originals, the less harm we shall do. The Matthaean parables are Matthew's own compositions. They are rabbinic: in being indicative, against Luke; in being personal, against Mark; in being contrasts, against both; in featuring stock figures, against both; in being more allegorical than Mark, and much more than Luke; in appending interpretations against Luke, and more often than Mark; in scale, against both; and partially, even in doctrine, against both. Matthew writes so regularly: there is not a parable of his that would be in place in either of the other Gospels: where he takes over from Mark, or Luke from him, the change of even a few words at once reveals the writer. If a parable is Matthaean in purpose, in background, in manner, and in doctrine, in what way is it not Matthaean? And since in so many respects his parables differ in these categories both from the Marcan ones which may claim probably to be dominical, and from the Lucan ones which may be alleged to be; and since they follow the rabbis; it is impossible but that their author is Matthew, the Christian scribe.

We said a pupil of Leonardo's—μαθητής, *talmîdh;* Matthew would not refuse our figure. He taught by parables in the name of the Lord, as R. Joshua of Sichnin taught in the name of R. Levi.[30] Often a rabbi would develop the parable of his own teacher. R. Ḥama b. R. Hanina said, 'Compare this'—Gen. 1.31—'to a king who built a palace. He saw it and it pleased him. "O palace, palace", exclaimed he, "mayest thou find favour in my eyes at all times just as thou hast found favour in my eyes at this moment!" Similarly the Holy One, blessed be He, apostrophized the world. "O my world, mayest thou find favour in my eyes at all times just as thou hast found favour in my eyes at this moment!" ' R. Jonathan said, 'Imagine a king who gave his daughter in marriage, and arranged a bridal chamber and a home for her, which he plastered, panelled and painted. He saw it and it pleased him. "My daughter, my daughter", he cried, "may this bridal chamber find

[30] See p. 53 above.

favour in my eyes at all times just as it has found favour at this moment!" Even so said the Holy One . . .'[31] So does the Christian scribe, the evangelist, develop the parables and sayings of his Lord.

Four of the Marcan parables he transcribes. The Seed Growing Secretly he has rewritten in an expanded, humanized, up-scaled, contrasted, allegorized, stock-figure, interpreted, utterly Matthaean version. And he has done the same with the Doorkeeper. Having transcribed the eschatological discourse from Mark almost word for word, he cannot bear to close with so frail a simile. He therefore expands the Doorkeeper into a chain of four parables, taking care to bring out in each of them a different facet of the original. The surprise at an unknown watch suggests the Burglar (already in Christian teaching at 1 Thess. 5.2); the departing master giving authority to his slave suggests the major-domo; the warning to watch suggests the Ten Virgins (given the bridegroom image from Mark 2.19). The mysterious 'To him who has will more be given . . .' (Mark 4.25; Matt. 25.29) joined to the master's departure abroad and giving authority, combine to give him the plot of the Talents. It is such enigmatic sayings which clamour for exposition. 'Many that are first will be last, and the last first' (Mark 10.30) is just such another. Here it is the sayings on the generous and mean eye from Matt. 6, closely related as they are to Mark 10, which provide the second text, and so the plot of the Labourers in the Vineyard. The Treasure in the Field is similarly a parabolic exposition of 'There is nothing hid, except to be made manifest' (Mark 4.22), and the Unmerciful Servant of Mark 11.25, 'Forgive if you have anything against anyone'. Matthew doubles parables, as he doubles so much else. The Tares is a pair for the Sower, the Leaven for the Mustard-Seed, the Pearl for the Treasure, the Servant for the Burglar, the Talents for the Virgins; the Sons in the Vineyard and the murderous guests at the Marriage make a trio for the Wicked Husbandmen. The Dragnet and the harvesting on the shore are suggested by Jesus preaching from the boat to the crowd on the αἰγιαλός. The two Houses are suggested by the two gates and two ways. One parable, one alone, is drawn from the OT, the Lost Sheep from the sheep-and-shepherd passage in Ezek. 34. The converted scribe has faithfully followed the expository tradition of his trade, glossing text to text and drawing out the meaning with parables and similes as they suggested themselves: on the rabbinic principle, 'Each [idea] finds confirmation in a verse of scripture, in a parable, in a figure of speech'.[32]

[31] Gen. R. 9.4.   [32] Cant. R. i. 1.6.

APPENDIX

A HUNDRED RABBINIC PARABLES

The parables listed below are a random selection in the sense that they are the first hundred parables I have encountered. Many of them are to be found in P. Fiebig, *Ältjudische Gleichnissen und die Gleichnissen Jesu* (Tübingen 1904); A Feldman, *Parables and Similes of the Rabbis* (Cambridge 1927); and G. F. Moore, *Judaism*. I have eschewed slanted selections like I. Ziegler's *Königsgleichnissen* (Breslau 1903).

Mekilta

1b–2a	Priest's Son	—
18b–19a	Son and Daughter	—
	Wolf and Lion	Simeon b. Yohai
25a	King and Lantern	Antoninos
26b	Bad Fish	—
26f	Cheap Sale (p. 48)	Jose
29b	Son Turned Out	Absalom the Old
30a	Traveller and Son	Judah b. Ilai
30b	Inner Garden	—
31a	Awakening the King	Meir
32b	Hawk and Dove	—
37a	King and Retinue	Eliezer
41a	Robber in Palace	—
44a	Robbers in Palace	—
55a	Son in Palace	—
67a	Gold and Straw	Simeon b. Eleazar

Sifra

Lev. 26.9	Long-Service Labourer (pp. 407f)	—
Lev. 26.12	King and Hiding Tenant	—

Sifre

Num. 31.2	Two Dogs and Wolf	—
Deut. 11.10	Nobleman and Labourers	—
Deut. Ekeb 43	Corn and Thief	Joshua b. Korhah

MIDRASH RABBAH

Genesis R.

9.4	Palace (p. 64)	Hama b. Hanina
9.4	Bridal Chamber (p. 64)	Jonathan
12.1	Thicket of Reeds	Nahman
	Ball of Cord	Nahman
16.3	Fruitful and Fruitless Trees (p. 53)	Joshua

22.5	Tenant and Firstfruits	—
22.9	Cabbage and Thief	—
30.9	Sour Wine	—
42.3	King's Three Enemies	—
	Tutor and Prince	—
44.4	Thorns in *Pardes*	Levi
55.2	Two Cows	Eleazar
	Potter and Vessels	—
61.6	Medicinal and Poison Trees	Hama
65.10	Palace and Smoke	Eleazar
65.15	Curly-Headed and Bald	Levi
86.4	Driver and Oxen	Judah

Exodus R.

2.2	*Pardes* and Tower	Jannai
7.4	Fruitless Trees	Levi
15.19	Priest and Figs	Nissim
21.7	Shepherd and Wolf	Hama
30.14	Produce and Storehouses	—
30.17	Vineyard Robbers	—
36.1	Pounding Olives	—
48.1	Two Boats	

Leviticus R.

4.5	Lame and Blind (p. 49)	Rabbi
4.6	Auger in Boat	Simeon b. Yohai
5.8	Two Tenant-Farmers	Hanina
9.4	King and Three Farmers	Phineas
13.2	Ass and Dog	Simeon b. Yohai
18.3	Withered Vegetables (p. 48)	Hama
23.3	Lily and *Pardes*	Azariah
30.2	Two Litigants	Abin
34.3	Royal Statues	Hillel

Numbers R.

7.4	Gone to Seed	Hama
8.2	Stag and Flock	—
8.9	Olives	—
15.25	Watchmen	—
18.17	House of Straw	—
20.19	Tree-Fellers	—

Deuteronomy R.

5.7	Youngest Prince and *Pardes*	Levi
6.2	Wages per Tree	Abba b. Kahina
7.4	Two Tenant-Farmers	Simeon b. Halafta
45	Bandage	—

Psalms R.
37.3   Delayed Reward (p. 408)   —
118.3   Tenants and Retainers   —

Eccles. R.
5.11   Labourers in Vineyard   Zeera
                 (p. 408)
5.11   Early Figs   Hiyya Raba
5.14   Fox and Vineyard   Geniba
7.13   Son in Prison   —

Cant. R.
1.2   Royal Wine-cellar   Eleazar
3.10   Sea and Cave   Levi
5.11   Mound-Clearers   Johanan
7.3   Straw and Wheat   Menahem

Lam. R.
Proem II   King and Two Sons (p. 414)   Simeon b. Lakish

TALMUD

Aboth
2.22   Root and Branch   Eleazar
Aboth de R. Nathan
8.18b   One and Many Fields   Meir
15   Unfruitful Field   Simeon b. Yohai
18   Wheat, Spelt, Barley, Beans   —
Baba Bathra
10a   Prince in Prison   Aqiba
Berakhot
Jer. 5c   Good Worker   Zeera
Jer. 5c   *Pardes* Destroyed   Hiyya
Kiddushin
40b   Tree and Unclean Ground (p. 53) Eleazar b. Zadok
Megillah
14a (top)   Mound and Trench   Abba
Sanhedrin
91ab   Courtier and Villages   Rabbi
Shabbat
31a   Preserving Wheat   Raba
152b   Royal Garments (p. 416)   —
Soṭah
40a   Tinsel and Precious Stones   Abbahu
Ta'anit
5a   Tree and Brook   Naḥman
Jer. 65d   King's Jewel-Box   Simeon b. Lakish

Yebamot
21b   Watchman   Ashe

OTHER WORKS

Pesiqta Rabbati
10.35b   Israel as Wheat   Levi
Pesiqta
55b   Watchman and Thief   Aha
128ab   Vineyard Destroyed   Abin
Tanḥuma
Shelaḥ, ad fin.   Passenger Overboard   —
Lev. p. 78   Matrona's Son (p. 53).   —
Qedoshim, 38a   Two Vineyard Owners   Simeon b. Halafta
Yalqut
§ 766   Palace Foundation (p. 309)   —

4

MATTHEW'S POETRY[1]

Much of the teaching in the Synoptic Gospels is in poetry: that is, it is in rhythmical and semi-rhythmical sentences marked by parallelism and antithesis in the Semitic manner. Hebrew and Aramaic poetry are marked by other features besides (regularity in number of stresses, alliteration, rhyme) which do not appear in Greek translations of the OT, nor in our Gospels. But the parallelism and antithesis are the stuff of Semitic poetry, and survive translation; the stress-regularity, rhyme, and alliteration are not in any case invariable features, and the latter two are contingent.

Brave attempts have been made to retranslate the Gospels into Aramaic, and so recover the original poetic forms.[2] This must be judged a hazardous enterprise. We do not know that the evangelists have left untouched the tradition as it came to them: indeed comparison of the Gospels shows that frequently they have not. We do not know that the tradition that reached the evangelists was that which left Jesus: what has Form-Criticism been discussing all these years? We do not know which Aramaic words should be used to retranslate the Greek: the lexicon of the LXX shows an alternative of two or three Hebrew words for very many entries. To argue that the most poetic form will be the original is to beg the question (and leads inevitably to the conclusion that Matthew, which is the most Semitic Gospel, is the most original). We do not know that whenever the evangelists changed the words of a saying they made the rhythm worse: they had read the LXX and (except Luke) were familiar with the Hebrew, and Semitic rhythms rang in their ears. The occurrence of rhyme in the retroversion of such a passage as 'I was an hungred and ye fed me . . .' is not surprising in a language of terminations and suffixes. The occurrence of (fairly) regular stress is not surprising when there are often three Gospels and sometimes variant readings to choose from. The attempt is not always made to translate all the sayings.

It is unfortunate that a natural zeal to attain the Aramaic original has been a distraction from the simpler and more fruitful analysis of the rhythms as they stand in the Greek. For the Gospel rhythms are

[1] The citations of scripture throughout this chapter are not taken from RSV, but either are from older versions for the sake of the associations, or are the author's adaptation for the sake of the rhythm.
[2] Especially by C. F. Burney, *The Poetry of Our Lord*.

more complex than those of the Psalms or Proverbs: there is an obvious difference between Luke's psalm-rhythms in the canticles, with their traditional parallelism:

'He hath shewed strength with his arm: he hath scattered the proud in the imagination of their heart',

or antithesis:

'He hath put down the mighty from their seat: and hath exalted the humble and meek',

and the more epigrammatic style we find in the logia:

'For all they that take the sword shall perish with the sword',
'Lay not up for yourselves treasures upon earth . . .'

There are in fact a number of rhythms in the Gospels which hardly occur, or do not occur, in the OT, but which are developed out of OT, and especially prophetic, rhythms. Their essence is a certain paradoxical flavour. We may isolate the basic, most common, synoptic rhythm as a four-point paradoxical antithesis, such as we find occasionally in the prophets:

'Can the Ethiopian change his skin, or the leopard his spots?'
Jer. 13.23
'He looked for judgement, but behold oppression, for righteousness, but behold a cry.'
Isa. 5.7

We shall require a name for sayings of this form, and in piety to Jeremiah I shall call them *pardics*. A pardic is defined as any four-point antithesis which has a paradoxical element, and is sufficiently crisp. It commonly has, but does not require, 4 nouns, and a link-word, usually a verb—'change', 'looked for' in the instances I have given. About 12 Greek words is normal.

There are about 50 different pardics in the Synoptic Gospels. 4 of these occur in Mark:

	Mark
The *spirit* is *willing*, but the *flesh* is *weak*.	14.38
For what doth it profit a man to *gain* the *whole world* and *lose* his *soul*?	8.36
It is not good to *take* the *children's bread*, and *cast* it to the *dogs*.	7.27
Is it lawful on the Sabbath to *do good* or to *do evil*, to *save life* or to *kill*?	3.4

44 pardics occur in Matthew:

	Matt.	
Do men gather grapes from thorns, or figs from thistles?	7.16	Q
The harvest is plenteous but the labourers are few.	9.37	Q
Be ye therefore wise as serpents and harmless as doves.	10.16	M
For many are called but few are chosen.	22.14	M
Let not your left hand know what your right hand doeth.	6.3	M
The disciple is not above his master, nor the servant above his lord.	10.24	Q
We piped to you and you did not dance, we wailed and you did not mourn.	11.17	Q
For my yoke is easy and my burden is light.	11.30	M
He that is not with me is against me, he that gathereth not with me scattereth.	12.30	Q

Matthew is so fertile in pardics that we find them in pairs:

Should his son ask him for bread, will he give him a stone?
Or should he ask too for a fish, will he give him a snake?   7.9–10 Q
What I say to you in the dark, speak ye in the light,
And what you hear in the ear, proclaim ye upon the
housetops.   10.27 Q

There is a chain of 6 pardics in the Sermon on the Mount:

Whosoever smiteth thee on thy right cheek, turn to him
also the other.
And if any man would go to law with thee and *take away*
thy *coat*, let him *have* also thy *cloak*.
And whosoever shall impress thee for one mile, go with him two.
To him that asketh thee give, and from him that would
borrow from thee turn not thou away . . .
Thou shalt love thy neighbour, and hate thine enemy . . .
Love your enemies, and pray for them that persecute you.   5.39–44 Q

Almost always Matthew sharpens the antithesis in any saying he draws from Mark:

Mark 4.22	Matt. 10.26
For there is nothing hidden except to be opened,	For there is nothing veiled but it will be revealed,
Nor was it in hiding but to come into the open. (17 words)	And hidden, but it will be known. (12 words)

Mark 8.35	Matt. 10.39
For whosoever wills to save his life shall lose it,	He that finds his life shall lose it,
And whosoever will lose his life for my sake and the gospel's shall save it. (24 words)	And he that loses his life for my sake shall find it. (17 words)

Mark 10.31	Matt. 20.16
And many that are first shall be last, and the last first. (9 words)	So the last shall be first, and the first last. (9 words)

Of the 44 Matthaean pardics, 7 are drawn or developed from Mark, 26 from Q (i.e. material also found in Luke), and 11 from M (i.e. material peculiar to Matthew—I use the symbols without prejudice to, and certainly without adherence to, the source–document hypothesis). The remaining references are in the appendix (p. 93 below).

There are about 20 pardics in Luke, of which 14 are Q pardics already given under Matthew. There are 5 L pardics as well, however:

	Luke
Bless those who curse you, pray for those who abuse you.	6.28
This my son was dead and is alive again, he was lost and is found.	15.24,32
What is exalted among men is abomination before God.	16.15
It is easier for heaven-and-earth to pass away than for one dot of the law to become void.	16.17

Two points occur immediately an examination is made of the poetic nature of Luke. One is that there is very little poetry in the teaching sections of the book, other than what is derived from Mark or Q/Matthew. The Lucan canticles show the evangelist to have been the master of Septuagintal rhythms, but the L matter, whether derived from written or oral sources, or spun from his own mind, is on the whole prose. Its strength is in its parables. The other is that in almost every case where Luke has a differing version of a saying from his predecessors, he has a less rhythmical version:

Mark 8.36	Luke 9.25
For what doth it profit a man to gain the whole world and lose his own soul?	For what is a man profited who gains the whole world but loses or forfeits himself?

Matt. 7.21	Luke 6.46
Not everyone that says to me, Lord, Lord, shall enter the kingdom of heaven, but he who does the will of my Father who is in heaven.	Why call ye me Lord, Lord, and do not the things which I say?

Matt. 20.16	Luke 13.30
So the last shall be first and the first last.	And lo, there are last who shall be first, and there are first who shall be last.

Matt. 6.19f
Lay not up for yourselves treasures upon earth, where moth and rust corrupt, and thieves break through and steal: but lay up for yourselves treasures in heaven . . .

Luke 12.33
Sell your possessions and give alms: make you purses that grow not old, an unfailing treasure in the heavens, where no thief approaches, nor moth destroys.

Mark 9.19
O faithless generation, how long shall I be with you? How long shall I suffer you?

Luke 9.41
O faithless and perverse generation, how long shall I be with you and suffer you?

Mark 13.24
But in those days after that persecution, the sun shall be darkened and the moon shall not give her light, and the stars shall fall from heaven, and the powers in the heavens shall be shaken.

Luke 21.25f
And there shall be signs in sun and moon and stars, and upon earth distress of nations in perplexity at the roar of sea and waves . . . and the powers of the heavens shall be shaken.

There are instances in the opposite sense, for example:

Matt. 5.44
Love your enemies, and pray for them that persecute you.

Luke 6.27
Love your enemies, do good to those who hate you, bless those who curse you, pray for those who abuse you.

but they are rarities, and explicable by other Lucan characteristics, in this case the catena. The weight of the evidence would indicate both that poetry was rare in L, and that in differences from both Mark and Q/Matthew, Luke is less rhythmical. The fact that in the Q material we are able to count 26 pardics to Matthew but only 14 to Luke is eloquent.

The pardic, as we have defined it, is a four-point antithetical paradox. There are two specialized kinds of pardic which may be isolated: the *machaeric* where two of the four terms are the same, and the *caesaric*, where the four terms fall in two pairs. The *machaeric* draws its name from Matt. 26.52:

For all who take the sword will perish with the sword.

and the *caesaric* from Mark 12.17:

Render unto Caesar the things that are Caesar's, and unto God the things that are God's.

There are three rather rough machaerics in Mark:

Heaven and earth shall pass away, but my words shall not pass away.	13.31
For he that is not against us is for us.	9.40
For whosoever is ashamed of me . . . of him will the Son of Man also be ashamed.	8.38

Matthew is rich in machaerics: there seven single, and a considerable number of converse ones in his Gospel. The single ones are:

	Matt.	
Freely ye received, freely give.	10.8	M
He that receives you receives me, and he that receives me receives him that sent me.	10.40	Q
Leave the dead to bury their dead	8.22	Q
For by your words you shall be justified, and by your words you shall be condemned.	12.37	M
If *all* shall be scandalised in thee, I will never be scandalised.	26.33	Mk
The poor you have always with you, but me you have not always.	26.11	Mk

and 26.52 above. But the recurrence of converse machaerics is formidable:

For if you forgive men their trespasses, your heavenly Father will also forgive you; but if you forgive not men, neither will your heavenly Father forgive your trespasses.	6.14f	M
And whatsoever thou bindest upon earth shall be bound in heaven, and whatsoever thou loosest upon earth shall be loosed in heaven.	16.19 18.18	M M
Everyone therefore who confesses me before men, I will confess before my Father who is in heaven; and everyone who denies me before men, I will deny him before my Father who is in heaven.	10.32f	Q
Either make the tree good and its fruit good, or make the tree rotten and its fruit rotten.	12.33	Q

Matthew is particularly given to converses, and others which are not converse machaerics may be mentioned here:

So whosoever shall break one of these least commandments and teach men so, he shall be called least in the kingdom of heaven; but whosoever shall do and teach them, he shall be called great in the kingdom of heaven.	5.19	M
And bring us not into temptation, but deliver from the evil one.	6.13	Q
If then your eye be generous your whole body shall be full of light; But if your eye be mean your whole body shall be dark.	6.23	Q
For either he will hate the one and love the other, or else he will hold to the one and despise the other.	6.24	Q

Other instances are in the appendix (p. 93 below).

Luke has the single machaeric rhythm in the Q verse 9.60 only, and the converse machaeric rhythm in the Marcan passage 9.48, two Q/Matthaean passages 6.43, 12.8–9, and three L passages:

Luke

He who is faithful in a very little is faithful also in much,
And he who is unrighteous in a very little is unrighteous
also in much.   16.10 L
Her sins which are many are forgiven because she loved much,
But he to whom little is forgiven loves little.   7.47 L
From everyone to whom much is given shall much be required,
And from him to whom they entrust much they will ask more.   12.48 L

Similar converse logia are the two Q examples, and 16.11f.

If then you have not been faithful in the unrighteous
mammon, who will entrust to you the true riches? And if you
have not been faithful in that which is another's who will give
you that which is your own?   16.11f

For *caesarics* the three Gospels all have the four Marcan examples:

Render unto Caesar the things that are Caesar's and unto   Mark
God the things that are God's.   12.17 par.
For nation shall rise up against nation and kingdom against
kingdom.   13.8 par.
For whosoever wills to save his life shall lose it,
And whosoever will lose his life for my sake and the gospel's
shall save it.   8.35 par.
But many that are first will be last, and the last first.   10.31 par.

Mark also has:

Mark

For brother shall deliver up brother to death, and the father
the child   13.12

which is reproduced in Matthew, but the rhythm is spoiled by Luke; and:

The sabbath was made for man, and not man for the sabbath,   2.27

which is reproduced by neither.

Matthew adds:

For he who shall exalt himself shall be humbled,   Matt.
And he who humbles himself shall be exalted.   23.12 Q

which Luke has twice, at 14.11 and 18.14. Luke also has another Q saying in this rhythm, where Matthew has a different one:

And judge not and ye shall not be judged,
And condemn not and ye shall not be condemned;
Give and it shall be given to you,   Luke
Release, and you will be released.   6.37 Q

Four further simple rhythms may be noted here. First there are a
number of two-part parallelisms with chorus, which we may name
mylics after the instance in Matt. 24.40f:

Then shall there be two in the field; one is taken and one is left:
Two shall be grinding at the mill; one is taken and
one is left.

Mark gives us one example of this rhythm:

When I broke the five loaves for the 5,000, how many
hampers of crumbs did you take up?
And when the seven for the 4,000, how many basketfuls of   Mark
crumbs did you take up?   8.19f

Matthew reproduces this example in abbreviated form, and has four
other instances beside the name-instance:

For if you love those who love you, what reward have you?
    Do not even publicans do the same?
And if you greet your brethren only, what advantage have you?   Matt.
    Do not even Gentiles do the same?   5.46f Q

Lay not up for yourselves treasures upon earth,
    Where moth and rust corrupt, and thieves break through
        and steal;
But lay up for yourselves treasures in heaven,
    Where neither moth nor rust corrupt, and where thieves   Matt.
        break not through and steal.   6.19f Q

For broad is the gate and wide the way that leads to destruction,
    And many are they that enter through it;
For narrow is the gate and straitened the way that leads to life,
    And few are they that find it.   7.13f Q

The remaining example is an abbreviated instance of Mark's three-
point parallelism to which we shall return:

If thy right eye offends thee, pluck it out and cast it from thee;
    For it profits thee that one of thy members should perish
        And not thy whole body be cast into hell;
And if thy right hand offends thee, cut it off and cast it from thee;
    For it profits thee that one of thy members should perish   Mark
        And not thy whole body depart into hell.   5.29f

Although there are two Marcan and four Q instances in Matthew, Luke has only two examples. One is at Luke 17.34f:

On this night two shall be in one bed, the one shall be taken
and the other left;
Two shall be grinding together, the one shall be taken and the
other left,

where the bed has apparently been inserted for the Q/Matthaean field, as more appropriate to the night. The other is at 6.32ff, where the rhythm is rougher than in the Matthaean version, but where a third unit is added:

And if you love those who love you, what thanks have you?
For sinners love those who love them.
And if you benefit those who benefit you, what thanks have you?
Sinners too do the same.
And if you lend to those from whom you hope to receive again, what
thanks have you?
Sinners too lend to sinners that they may receive back as much.

In view of the third unit, this might better be classed with the scandalics below.

A shorter form of stylized line of which we find a number of instances in the Gospels is of the form 'Wheresoever . . . there will . . .', or 'As it was . . . so will . . .' These we may call *aetics* after the classic instance in Matt. 24.28:

Wheresoever the carcase is, thither will the vultures be gathered together.

There are no sentences of this form in Mark, but there are seven in Matthew:

	Matt.	
As were the days of Noah, so will be the coming of the Son of Man.	24.37	Q
For as in those days before the flood they were eating and drinking . . . so will be the coming of the Son of Man.	24.38f	Q
For where your treasure is, there will your heart be also.	6.21	Q
For as Jonah was three days and three nights in the belly of the whale, so will the Son of Man be three days and three nights in the heart of the earth.	12.40	Q
For as the lightning comes from the east and shines as far as the west, so will be the coming of the Son of Man.	24.27	Q
For where two or three are gathered in my name, there am I in the midst of them.	18.20	M

As will be noticed, this balance of sentence is a favourite with Matthew for closing a paragraph: four of these instances sum up and round off the substance of preceding teaching. Five of the six Q instances come in the Lucan versions also; there is none in the L matter, but an extra Q instance 'As it was in the days of Lot . . .'

Another simple pattern of sentence which we find in Matthew and Luke is the offensive rhetorical question opening with an abusive vocative. These we may call *echidnics* after the Q logion ascribed to John the Baptist:

	Matt.	
You brood of vipers! Who warned you to flee from the wrath to come?	3.7	Q
	Luke	
	3.7	Q

There are four further instances in Matthew:

	Matt.	
You brood of vipers! How can you speak good, when you are evil?	12.34	Q
You blind fools! For which is greater, the gold or the temple . . .?	23.17	M
You blind! For which is greater, the gift or the altar . . .?	23.19	M
You serpents, you brood of vipers, how are you to escape being sentenced to hell?	23.33	Q

It is interesting, and perhaps significant, that the only example of this rhythm in Luke is at 3.7. Two of the remaining instances are in Q contexts, and are omitted by Luke.

A further simple sentence-form is a proverb-type saying closing a paragraph, with the formula: predicate, subject/referent, αὐτοῦ/-ῆς, the copula being suppressed. These we may call *arcetics*, after:

ἀρκετὸν τῇ ἡμέρᾳ ἡ κακία αὐτῆς	6.34	M
ἄξιος γὰρ ὁ ἐργάτης τῆς τροφῆς αὐτοῦ	10.10; cf. Luke 10.7	Q
καὶ ἐχθροὶ τοῦ ἀνθρώπου οἱ οἰκιακοὶ αὐτοῦ	10.36	M
καὶ ἐδικαιώθη ἡ σοφία ἀπὸ τῶν ἔργων αὐτῆς	11.19; cf. Luke 7.35	Q

There are no instances in Mark or L. While the arcetics and echidnics perhaps should not be classed as poetry, and I have excluded them from the count at the end of the chapter, both are evidence of Matthaean creativity, there being no example outside Matthew/Q.

The last simple rhythm which I shall propose is the anticipatory epexegetic prohibition, which is also almost peculiar to Matthew, and which we may call the *thesauric* after the pattern:

| Lay not up for yourselves treasures upon earth . . . | Matt. |
| But lay up for yourselves treasures in heaven . . . | 6.19f Q |

We are not concerned here with the 'not . . . but . . .' assertions, of which there are a number of examples in all the Gospels, such as:

	Mark
I came not to call the righteous, but sinners to repentance.	2.17
The Son of Man came not to be ministered unto, but to minister . . .	Mark 10.45

but with *prohibitions*, the point of which is to emphasize the command or assertion following:

	Matt.
And think not to say within yourselves, We have Abraham to our father,	
For I say unto you that God is able of these stones to raise up children to Abraham.	3.9 Q
Think not that I came to destroy the Law or the Prophets;	
I came not to destroy but to fulfil.	5.17 M
But when you pray jabber not as the Gentiles;	
For they think that they shall be heard for their much speaking.	
Therefore be not ye like them; . . .	
Thus therefore pray ye . . .	6.7ff M
To a road of the Gentiles go not away, and to a city of the Samaritans go not in,	
But journey rather to the lost sheep of the house of Israel.	10.5f M
And bring us not into temptation, but deliver us from the evil one.	6.13 Q
Think not that I came to cast peace on the earth;	
I came not to cast peace but a sword.	10.34 Q
And fear not those who kill the body, but cannot kill the soul;	
But fear rather him who can destroy both soul and body in hell.	10.28 Q

Mark has no thesaurics. Luke has 2 of the 8 Matthaean instances at 3.8 and 12.4f, the latter in a 42 word version.

In addition to the above rhythms, all of which are based upon a straightforward parallelism or antithesis, we may isolate a number of *triple* rhythms. The basis of these is formed by the use of the same root three times in a sentence, which we may call a *poteric:*

	Mark
Can you drink the draught that I am drinking?	10.38;
Or be baptized the baptism that I am baptized?	cf. 39
With the measure you measure shall it be measured to you, and more to you.	4.24

Similarly:

	Mark
He that hath ears to hear let him hear.	4.23

Matthew retains the first half of Mark 10.38, 'Can you drink . . .'
omitting the second for brevity. He improves the rhythm of Mark
4.24, the measuring logion, first by transferring the unrhythmical last
clause to 6.33, and then by prefixing a second poteric (cf. misthics
below):

For with the judgment you judge will you be judged,	Matt.
And with the measure you measure will it be measured to you.	7.2

Matthew has also two doubled poterics not in Mark:

The good man out of his good treasure-chest brings forth good,	
And the bad man out of his bad treasure-chest brings forth bad.	Matt. 12.35 Q
Many prophets and saints desired to see what you behold, and saw not,	Matt.
And to hear what you hear, and heard not.	13.17 Q

But he reduces Mark 10.39 to,

	Matt.
My draught you shall drink,	20.23

and Mark 4.23 to,

	Matt.
He that hath ears let him hear,	13.43

which is evidence of his preference for double over triple rhythm, as
also is his doubling of the other poterics.

Luke omits the Mark 10.38–9 ('Can you drink . . .') pericope, from
embarrassment. He has the measuring logion in a more rhythmical
form like Matthew's, but without the Matthaean prefix; he has the
two Q doubled poterics at 6.45 and 10.24.

More common is a threefold parallelism, which we may call a *scandalic*
from the instance at Mark 9.43ff. There are two examples in Mark,
both of them very long and repetitive.:

And if thy hand offends thee, cut it off;
 It is good for thee to enter into life maimed,
  Than having two hands to depart to hell, to the unquenchable fire:
And if thy foot offends thee, cut it off;
 It is good for thee to enter into life halt,
  Than having two feet to be thrown into hell:

And if thine eye offends thee, pluck it out;
  It is good for thee with one eye to enter into the kingdom of God,
    Than having two eyes to be thrown into hell,
      Where their worm dies not, and the fire is not quenched.   Mark
          9.43

If a kingdom is divided against itself, that kingdom cannot stand;
And if a house is divided against itself, that house will not be
able to stand,
And if Satan rose up against himself and was divided, he cannot
stand, but has an end.   Mark 3.24–6

Matthew is not content with either of these cumbrous locutions. The former he reproduces twice, once in the context of the Seventh Commandment, where eye and hand are to the point, but foot is suitably omitted (5.28–9), and once in the Marcan context (18.8f), where he combines hand and foot in one clause. In both he thus ends with a not very neat double parallelism. The divided kingdom logion he also alters to remove the triple parallelism:

Every kingdom divided against itself is wasted,
And every city or house divided against itself will not stand;
And if Satan casts out Satan, he is divided against himself—
How then shall his kingdom stand?   Matt. 12.25f

Matthew is not however averse from triple parallelism:

For there are eunuchs who were born so from their mother's womb,
And there are eunuchs who were made eunuchs by men,
And there are eunuchs who made themselves eunuchs for the
kingdom of heaven.   Matt. 19.12 M

Lord, Lord, in thy name have we not prophesied,
And in thy name cast out demons,
And in thy name done many miracles?   Matt. 7.22 M

Ask and it shall be given you,
Seek and ye shall find,
Knock and it shall be opened to you;
For everyone who asks receives,
And he who seeks finds,
And to him who knocks it will be opened.   Matt. 7.7–8 Q

Hallowed be thy name,
Come thy kingdom,
Be done thy will.   Matt. 6.9f M

I say to this man, Go, and he goes,
And to another, Come, and he comes,
And to my servant, Do this, and he does it.   Matt. 8.9 Q

But you, be not called Rabbi,
For one is your teacher, and you are all brothers;
And call no one your father on earth,
For one is your heavenly Father;
Neither be called masters;
Because your master is one, the Christ.   Matt. 23.8ff M

So he who swears by the altar, swears by it and all upon it,
And he who swears by the temple, swears by it and him who
indwells it,
And he who swears by heaven, swears by the throne of God,
and him who sits thereon.   Matt. 23.20ff M

Everyone who is angry with his brother shall be liable
to judgement;
Whoever says Raqa to his brother shall be liable to the council;
And whoever says, You fool, shall be liable to the hell of fire.
                                                          Matt. 5.22 M

There is a closely similar fourfold parallelism on swearing at 5.34ff.
Threefold parallelism may also be seen on a larger scale in the section
on the three duties to God at 6.1–18, and in the Genealogy (cf. 1.17).

An especially interesting group of scandalics in Matthew are those
where the first two lines are original to Matthew, while the third line
is found in Mark. The method of composition here seems to have been
similar to the thesaurics above ('Lay not up your treasures on earth
. . . but lay up . . .'), where the function of the first line is to be a
negative contrast with the climactic second line; or to 7.2, 'The
judgment . . . the measure . . .', where Matthew has prefaced a
poteric of the new material to the Marcan one. These we may call
misthics after

He that receives a prophet in the name of a prophet shall receive
a prophet's reward,
And he that receives a saint in the name of a saint shall receive
a saint's reward,
And he that gives one of these little ones only a cup of cold water
in the name of a disciple, verily I say to you, he shall not lose his
reward!   Matt. 10.41f M

Here the last line is drawn from Mark 9.41:

For whoever gives you a cup of water in the name that you are Christ's,
   verily I say to you that he shall not lose his reward.

The three lines follow a natural de-escalation: 'prophet . . . saint . . .
disciple', as at 23.34, 'Behold I send you prophets, *hᵃkhāmîm,
sôpʰᵉrîm*, or in Matthew's reversal of the Marcan seed's growth,

'100, 60, 30'. Indeed they are a natural bridge from the Marcan, 'He that receiveth me receiveth not me but him that sent me', in the previous line. Matthew's two prefatory poterics are noticeably more rhythmical than his Marcan line. Or again:

He who loves father or mother more than me is not worthy
of me,
And he who loves son or daughter more than me is not
worthy of me,
And he who does not take up his cross and follow after   Matt.
me is not worthy of me,   10.37f Q

where the last line is dependent on Mark, 8.34,

Let him lift his cross and follow me

as the context shows. Or,

Hallowed be thy Name,
Come thy kingdom,
Be done thy will,   Matt. 6.9f Q

where the third line recurs in the Matthaean version of Christ's own prayer at Gethsemane. Or,

What went ye out into the desert to behold?
 A reed shaken with the wind?
But what went ye out to see?
 A man clothed in fine clothes?
  Lo, those who wear fine clothes are in palaces!
But why went ye out? To see a prophet?
Yea, I say to you, and more than a prophet: for this is he of whom
it is written,
Behold I send my messenger before thy face, who shall prepare
thy way before thee,   Matt. 11.7ff Q

where the whole piece leads up to the Malachi quotation with which Mark opens the story of John the Baptist, and which Matthew has omitted from the passage in his Gospel at 3.3.

 Of these four Luke has the last misthic in a very slightly more elaborate form; he is lacking a parallel to Matt. 10.41f; and in place of Matthew's carefully balanced 10.37, he has the prosy list:

If anyone comes after me and hates not his father and mother and wife and children and brothers and sisters, yea and his own soul, he cannot be my disciple.   Luke 14.26

Luke has also a triple rhythm at 10.16:

He who hears you hears me,
And he who rejects you rejects me,
And he who rejects me rejects him who sent me.

where something very similar to the first and last lines comes in
Matt. 10.40. Luke is defective in scandalics otherwise. He omits both
the Marcan examples, and lacks the rhythm in the Q passages Matt.
7.22/Luke 13.26 and the Lord's Prayer. He retains it only in 'Ask,
and it shall be given you . . .' (11.9f), and 'I say to this man, Go . . .'
(7.8): and has one rather wordy example of his own:

I entered your house; you gave me no water for my feet:
    But she has wet my feet with her tears, and wiped them with her hair.
You gave me no kiss,
    But from the time I came in she has not ceased kissing my feet.
You did not anoint my head with oil,
    But she has anointed my feet with ointment.   Luke 7.44ff L

There is nothing unpoetic about this. It has all the leisured beauty of
Semitic parallelism and antithesis. But Matthew could not have
written it: it lacks the epigrammatic, sharp, paradoxical brilliance
which is typical of him.

Matthew not only excels in the triple parallelisms of scandalics
and misthics; he also writes triple pardics and multiple parallelisms,
which we will group together under the name *typhlics* after 11.5f:

The blind see and the lame walk,
The lepers are cleansed and the deaf hear,
And the dead are raised and the poor are evangelised.   Matt. 11.5f Q

The sick heal, the dead raise,
The lepers cleanse, the demons expel,
Freely you received, freely give.   Matt. 10.8 Q

I was hungry and you gave me to eat,
I was thirsty and you gave-me-drink,
I was a stranger and you took me in,   Matt.
Naked and you clothed me,   25.35f M
I was sick and you visited me,   37–9 M
I was in prison and you came to me.   42f M

For they broaden their phylacteries and lengthen their hems,
They love the first seat at dinner and the first chair in synagogue,
And the greetings in the market-places and to be called by men,
Rabbi.   Matt. 23.5f M

There are none of these in Mark, and the Q typhlic at Matt. 10.8 appears in a non-rhythmical form at Luke 10.9, if it appears at all:

And heal the sick therein, and say to them, The Kingdom of God has come upon you.

Luke has a parallel to Matt. 11.5f at 7.22, but the rhythm is unclear—probably:

The blind see, the lame walk, the lepers are cleansed,
And the deaf hear, the dead are raised, the poor are evangelised.

We shall see that Luke has a tendency to catalogue, which may account for the different syndesis.

More elaborate still are the complex series of antitheses which we find in Q passages, and which we may call *crinics*. The Matthaean versions are given here with notes on differences in Luke.

Therefore I tell you, do not be anxious for your life, (a)
what you shall eat, (b)
Nor for your body, (a) what you shall wear. (b)
Is not the life more than food, (c)
And the body than raiment? (c)
Look at the birds of the air; (d)
They do not sow nor reap nor gather into barns, (e)
And your heavenly Father feeds them. (f)
Are you not of more value than they? (f)
And which of you can by being anxious add one cubit to
his stature? (g)
And about clothing why are you anxious? (a)
Consider the lilies of the field how they grow; (d)
They neither toil nor spin; (e)
Yet I tell you that even Solomon in all his glory was not arrayed
like one of these. (f)
But if God so clothes the grass of the field, (h)
Which today is (i) and tomorrow is cast into the oven, (i)
Will he not much more clothe you, little-faiths? (h)
Therefore do not be anxious, saying, (a)
What shall we eat? or What shall we drink? (b)
or What shall we wear? (b)   Matt. 6.25ff

Luke's version has three minor rhythmical changes to this poem. In Line (e), for Matthew's 'They do not sow nor reap nor gather into barns', he gives a double antithesis,

They neither sow nor reap,
Who have no store-house or barn.[3]   Luke 12.24

[3] Luke regularly avoids triple series; cf. p. 336 below.

Less successfully at the opening of the antistrophe, where Matthew has, 'And about clothing, why are you anxious?', he has the somewhat prosaic

So if you cannot do even the least,
Why are you anxious for the rest?   Luke 12.26

Matthew's version ends with his favourite *inclusio*, the (a) and (b) lines being repeated: Luke's less satisfyingly: 'And you, do not seek what you may eat and what you may drink, and do not be of anxious mind.'

A second, briefer, instance, is:

The men of Nineveh shall rise up in the judgement (a)
With this generation and condemn it; (b)
For they repented at the preaching of Jonah, (c)
And lo, a greater than Jonah is here. (d)
The Queen of the South shall rise up in the judgement (a)
With this generation and condemn it; (b)
For she came from the ends of the earth to hear the wisdom
of Solomon, (c)
And lo, a greater than Solomon is here. (d)   Matt. 12.41-2 Q

The two stanzas appear almost unchanged, but in reverse order at Luke 11.32,31.

A third instance where the wording is close is:

To what shall I liken this generation? (a)
It is like children sitting in the market-places, (a)
Who call to the others and say, (b)
We piped to you and you did not dance, (c)
We wailed and you did not mourn. (c)
For John came neither eating nor drinking. (d)
And they say, He has a devil. (e)
The Son of Man came eating and drinking, (d)
And they say, Behold a glutton and a toper, (e)
A friend of publicans and sinners. (e)
And (yet) wisdom is justified by her deeds. (f)   Matt. 11.16-19 Q

There are a number of minor verbal differences in the Lucan version: the only rhythmical difference is in beginning with a doubled antithesis:

To what then shall I liken the men of this generation,
And to what are they like?   Luke 7.31

This simple, and even rather meaningless, duplication is best explained as a Lucan addition on the same basis as

What is the kingdom of God like?
And to what shall I liken it?

at Luke 13.18, where Luke has amended his Marcan *Vorlage*.
    There are two instances in Matthew, where Luke is less successful:

Woe to you, Chorazin, (a) woe to to you, Bethsaida; (a)
For if the marvels done in you had been done in Tyre and Sidon, (b)
Long since in sackcloth and ashes had they repented. (c)
But I say to you, it shall be more tolerable for Tyre and Sidon (d)
On Judgement Day than for you. (e)
And you, Capernaum, shall you be exalted to heaven? (a)
You shall go down to Hades. (a)
For if the marvels done in you had been done in Sodom, (b)
It would have remained till today. (c)
But I say to you that it shall be more tolerable for the land of Sodom (d)
On Judgement Day than for you. (e)   Matt. 11.21–4 Q

The Lucan version stops at '. . . Hades', thus omitting the parallel part of the second stanza. The other instance is the Matthaean version of the parable of the Two Builders in which the extended repetitions: 'The rain came down and the rivers came and the winds blew and fell (beat) upon that house, and it fell (not).' and 'So everyone who hears my words and does them (not) shall be likened unto a wise (foolish) man who built his house upon the rock (sand)' are not given in this form in Luke, but the parable is reproduced in what may be called a prose version.   Matt. 7.24–7 Q
    Luke has one Q crinic which is not in Matthew in this form:

As it was in the days of Noah, (a)
So shall it be also in the days of the Son of Man: (a₂)
They ate, they drank, (b)
They married, they gave in marriage, (b)
Till the day when Noah entered the ark, (c)
And the flood came and destroyed them all. (d)
Likewise, as it was in the days of Lot, (a)
They ate, they drank, (b)
They bought, they sold, (b)
They planted, they built (b)
But in the day Lot came out of Sodom, (c)
'Fire and brimstone rained from heaven' and destroyed them all; (d)
So shall it be in the day when the Son of Man is revealed. (a₂)
                                        Luke 17.26–30 Q

Here the first stanza is closely similar to Matt. 24.37-9, which we might be disposed to think of as an abbreviated version, but for the following verse. Here Matthew writes:

Then shall there be two in the field: one is taken and one left.   24.40

The Lucan context, and especially the mention of Lot's wife, raises the strong suspicion that Luke has interpreted this verse as a reference to Lot and his wife in the 'field' especially as (συμ) παραλαμβάνομαι stands in the LXX of the fate of the laggard. Perhaps indeed Matthew meant the words in this sense. The probability will be then that Luke expanded this verse into a second stanza to fit the Noah strophe.

One more instance of Matthaean poetry may be cited, which is not built in two stanzas, so does not qualify as a crinic, but whose similarity is obvious:

Ye have heard that it was said,
Thou shalt love thy neighbour,
And hate thine enemy;
But I say to you,
Love your enemies,
And pray for your persecutors,
That you may be sons of your Father in Heaven:
For he makes his sun rise on bad and good,
And he rains on just and unjust.
For if you love those who love you,
What reward have you? Do not the publicans the same?
And if you salute your brethren only,
What virtue have you? Do not the Gentiles the same?
So shall you be perfect,
As your Father in Heaven is perfect.   Matt. 5.43-8 Q

There is no more perfect multiple structure of antitheses in any Gospel. The Lucan version here is a pale shadow.

What conclusions can be drawn from this mass of evidence and neologism? I propose three.

1.   There is a certain number of poetic sayings in Mark, of which we have isolated 22. A number of these are epigrams which form the climax of an incident, such as,

The Sabbath was made for man, and not man for the Sabbath,
Render therefore to Caesar the things that are Caesar's . . .,

which are clearly dominical. Therefore Jesus gave some of his teaching in the form of poetic sayings which occur in Mark. However, the bulk of the Marcan sayings, while arresting, are not polished when set alongside the Matthaean versions. In many cases the poetry is of rather a rough kind. Further, 15 of the 22 sayings are single sentences.

The only lengthy piece of Marcan poetry, 'If thy hand offend thee . . .' is noticeably wordy. The impression given is of a country poet; who knows, perhaps Jesus himself.

2. There are 26 poetic sayings in Matthew which are formed out of Marcan logia, 16 of which are from the Marcan 22, and 10 from other Marcan sayings. In the large majority of cases Matthew has polished the Marcan version: he has reduced the number of words, changed them to emphasize the antitheses, added further parallel verses, etc. This shows Matthew to have been more of a poet than the author of the Marcan logia; and there are many passages in the prose narrative which would bear out this conclusion:

And he went round the villages in a circle teaching   Mark 6.6

And Jesus went round all the cities and villages, teaching in their synagogues and preaching the gospel of the kingdom, and healing all sickness and all disease.   Matt. 9.35

The presence of 4 misthics, in which the third, climactic, line is Marcan, and the other two lead up to it, and are without significance on their own, suggests, though it does not prove, that Matthew may have composed poetry of his own to frame the Marcan logia. The same suggestion would explain a number of the 8 Matthaean thesaurics. For instance, in Mark the Lord had said to the rich man, 'Go, sell all you have and give to the poor, and you shall have treasure in heaven.' Matthew writes,

Lay not up for yourselves treasures on earth . . .
But lay up for yourselves treasures in heaven . . .   Matt. 6.19

The sheer volume of poetic sayings in Matthew as opposed to Mark and Luke tells in the same sense. We have isolated 22 sayings or short units in Mark, against 132 in Matthew: but the disparity is considerably greater than this, since Mark has only 2 scandalics among the complex rhythms we have picked out, no typhlics, crinics, nor any sustained unit like Matt. 5.43–8, and Matthew has 24 of these complex units. Thus in all, the volume of poetry in Matthew is of the order of ten times the amount in Mark. On the other side, Luke has 63 sayings and units which we have separated, but of these 44 are Q poetry, 7 are taken over from Mark, and only 12 are from L. Thus, to operate with figures alone for the moment, Mark has brought 22 poetic logia into the tradition, Matthew 110, Luke 12. If we were dealing with the use of a particle, the conclusion would be obvious. If Mark used τότε 22 times, Matthew 132 times, and Luke 63 times, of which 44 were taken over in Q passages and 7 in Marcan, we should say, 'This is a Matthaean word: Matthew has introduced this into the book editorially.' The same conclusion holds with the poetic rhythms. The breakdown of Matthaean poetry validates this. 26 of the 132 sayings we have shown to be improved versions of Marcan logia: of the rest 36 are M logia, 70 Q logia. Included in the M group are 3 thesaurics, 5 scandalics, 1 misthic, and 4 typhlics, all complex units. Thus the M group contains almost exactly half as much poetry as the Q group. A simple explanation of this would be that the Q sayings are just the most poetic and most memorable, and so appealed most to Luke. Mark is preserving tradition, mostly in the form of unitary sayings: that is why he almost never has a long sustained unit of poetry, and the thread is hard to follow in his discourses. Matthew is writing midrash, freely embroidering the tradition he had from Mark: that is why the thread is usually easy to follow in his discourses, and the poetry can move into units of eight and nine antitheses, with strophes and antistrophes.

3. Luke could write a pastiche of a LXX psalm, but his creative genius was not poetic when it came to the logia. We have seen how he not uncommonly spoils the rhythm of some of the Marcan poetry, and usually has an inferior version where there is a difference between him and Matthew—Burney assigned Matthew the palm.[4] He does try on a number of occasions to gild the Q/Matthaean lily, and while often we prefer the lilies as they grow, we cannot but think he has sometimes succeeded. The technique which he uses is most often that of the catena or catalogue, often a catalogue of four.

Blessed are you when men hate you and when they exclude you
and revile you and cast out your name as evil . . .   Luke 6.22 Q

Love your enemies, do good to those who hate you, bless those
who curse you, pray for those who abuse you.   Luke 6.27f Q

And judge not, and you shall not be judged,
And condemn not and you shall not be condemned.
Forgive and you will be forgiven,
Give and it shall be given to you;
Good measure, pressed down, shaken together, running over,
Shall they give into your bosom.   Luke 6.37f Q

The Lucan Beatitudes and Woes are similarly reduced to a catalogue of four virtual synonyms. Or,

---

[4] *The Poetry of our Lord*, pp. 87f.

For there shall be henceforth five in one house divided,
Three against two, and two against three shall they be divided;
Father against son and son against father,
Mother against daughter and daughter against her mother,
Mother-in-law against her daughter-in-law, and daughter-in-law
against her mother-in-law.   Luke 12.51–3

We cannot pronounce upon the originality of one form or another of a logion simply on the grounds of more marked antithesis, the criterion which is often used by Burney, and by many scholars of the inter-war period. Luke generally alters his Marcan original, and for the worse. It would be surprising if he did not do the same with Q/Matthew; and it would also be surprising if he failed every time. Therefore the existence of some pardics and other rhythmical sayings in the L tradition, and the excellence on rare occasion of the Lucan version of a Q rhythmical saying is entirely consonant with the theory that Luke wrote third and knew the other two Gospels. A feeling for rhythmical epigram is a rare gift. The pre-eminence of Matthew's Gospel in this area by so great a preponderance demands an explanation.

The explanation normally given is that Matthew had two teaching sources, Q and M, both of which contained a high element of poetry; while Luke had access to Q only, and to L, a source which contained mostly parabolic matter. This ignores two vital factors which I have tried to expound in this chapter: the distinctive quality of the Matthaean poetry, and the poetic abilities of Matthew and Luke as disclosed by their handling of Mark. On the Four-Source Hypothesis, how are we to explain the absence of any complex rhythm of the kind I have isolated (misthic, typhlic, crinic, Matthaean unit) from both Mark and L? Why is it that these complex rhythms, and the large preponderance of simple rhythms, occur in Matthew, who is shown redactorally to have an ear for such things? Why is it that the Q rhythms are usually inferior in Luke, who is shown redactorally to have little ear for such things? The simple solution suggests itself: Matthew was the Church's poet.

APPENDIX

TABLE OF SYNOPTIC RHYTHMS

MARK	MATTHEW			LUKE		
	R	M	Q	Q	R	L

pardic: 'Can the Ethiopian change his skin, or the leopard his spots?'

MARK	R	M	Q	Q	R	L
3.4; 7.27; 8.36; 14.38	10.17, 26; 10.39; 15.26; 16.26; 19.24; 26.41	5.41; 6.3; 7.6; 7.15; 8.17; 10.16, 11.30; 22.8, 14; 23.34; 25.33	5.39, 40, 42, 43f; 6.13, 25(2); 7.9f; 7.16; 8.20; 9.37; 10.24, 25, 27(2); 11.17, 23, 25; 12.30; 13.16; 24.26, 28; 25.21–3	6.27, 30; 9.58; 10.2, 15, 21; 11.11f, 23; 12.2, 3(2), 22f	6.9	6.28; 15.24 = 32; 16.15, 17
(4)	(7)	(11)	(26)	(13)	(1)	(5)

machaeric: 'For all who take the sword will perish with the sword.'

MARK	R	M	Q	Q	R	L
8.38; 9.40, 37; 13.31	26.11, 33; 10.40 = 18.5	10.8; 12.37; 26.52; 6.14C; 16.19C; 18.18C	8.22; 10.40; 10.32C; 12.33C (C = converse)	9.60; 12.8fC	9.48	12.48; 16.10C
(4)	(4)	(9)	(6)	(3)	(1)	(3)

other converse logia

MARK	R	M	Q	Q	R	L
	12.31, 32; 13.11; 15.20	5.19; 7.17f	6.23, 24; 7.13f; 10.13	6.43; 11.34; 16.13		7.47; 16.11f
	(4)	(2)	(4)	(3)		(2)

caesaric: 'Render to Caesar the things that are Caesar's, and to God the things that are God's.'

MARK	R	M	Q	Q	R	L
8.35; 10.31; 12.17; 2.27; 13.8, 12	16.25; 19.30; 20.16; 22.21; 24.7; 10.21		23.12	6.37(2); 14.11 = 18.14	9.24; 13.30; 20.25; 21.10	
(6)	(6)		(1)	(4)	(4)	

mylic: 'Then two men will be in the field; one is taken and one is left: Two women will be grinding at the mill; one is taken and one is left.'

MARK	R	M	Q	Q	R	L
8.19f	5.29f; 16.9f		5.46f; 6.19f; 7.13f; 24.40f	17.34f; 6.32f		
(1)	(2)		(4)	(2)		

thesauric: 'Do not lay up for yourselves treasures on earth . . . But lay up for yourselves treasures in heaven . . .'

MARK	R	M	Q	Q	R	L
		5.17; 6.7ff; 10.5f	3.9; 6.13, 19f; 10.28, 34	3.8; 12.4		
		(3)	(5)	(2)		

aetic: 'Wheresoever the body is, there will the vultures be gathered together.'

MARK	R	M	Q	Q	R	L
	18.20		6.21; 12.40; 24.27, 28, 37, 38f	11.30; 12.34; 17.24, 26, 37		
	(1)		(6)	(5)		

	C1	C2	C3	C4	C5	C6	C7
poteric:	'Can you drink the draught that I am drinking?'						
	10.38(2) = 39,; 4.24; cf. 4.23	20.22; 7.2(2)		12.35(2); 13.17(2)	6.45(2); 10.24(2)	6.40	
	(5)	(3)		(4)	(4)	(1)	
(simple rhythm totals:							
	(20)	(26)	(26)	(56)	(36)	(7)	(10))
scandalic:	'And if thy hand/foot/eye offend thee . . .'						
	9.43ff; 3.24ff		5.22; 7.22; 19.12; 23.8ff; 20ff,	7.7f(2); 8.9	7.8; 11.9; 10.16		7.44ff
	(2)		(5)	(3)	(3)		(1)
misthic:	'He who loves father/son/does not take up his cross . . . is not worthy of me'.						
			10.41f	6.9f; 10.37f; 11.7f	7.24–7		
			(1)	(3)	(1)		
typhlic:	multiple parallelism						
			23.5f; 25.35f	10.8; 11.5	7.22		
			(4)	(2)	(1)		
crinic:	strophe/antistrophe poems						
				6.25ff; 7.24–7; 11.21–4, 16–19; 12.40–2	7.31ff; 12.24–9; 11.31f		17.26–30
				(5)	(3)		(1)
Matthaean unit				5.43-8			
(complex rhythm totals:							
	(2)		(10)	(14)	(8)		(2))

5
MATTHAEAN IMAGERY

Our generation has seen an intensive study of imagery. Professor Caroline Spurgeon[1] provided a detailed analysis of the images used by Shakespeare, showing both his predilection for images from certain areas of life, such as birds and gardening, and his particular way of viewing the matter of his images, as in his seeing nautical events from the safety of the shore. Professor Spurgeon draws frequent and significant contrasts between Shakespeare's imagery and that of his contemporaries, Bacon and Marlowe, Jonson, etc. Shakespeare, for instance, has many more images drawn from sport than Marlowe, or from the firmament than Bacon; Marlowe is far more given to hyperbolic imagery. Her book includes charts, which would be a sufficient refutation, if one were required, that Bacon or Marlowe wrote Shakespeare.

One of the most valuable studies which has stemmed from Professor Spurgeon's work is Professor W. H. Clemen's *Development of Shakespeare's Imagery*.[2] Clemen shows the organic nature of Shakespeare's images. He does not so much count them across the plays as observe their function in particular plays. Images of shipwreck are active in *The Merchant of Venice* from the first scene,[3] or of blood and confusion in *King John*.[4] Furthermore it is possible, especially after the early plays, to see how the images are not ready-made pieces tagged on to the situation, but how one word suggests another:

For the fifth Harry from curb'd licence plucks
The muzzle of restraint, and the wild dog
Shall flesh his tooth in every innocent.

Curb suggests muzzle, and so to dog, flesh, and tooth.[5]

We have not leisure here, nor am I competent, to enter further into the fascination of these studies. It is remarkable that this widely known discussion has made so little impact on biblical research: for if we can get to know an author so intimately through the study of his images, why should we not settle the OT problems of E or Trito–Isaiah? Or, which is more to the purpose, why should we not examine the

[1] *Shakespeare's Imagery* (Cambridge 1935).
[2] London 1951.
[3] I.1.9ff, and 22ff. Clemen, op. cit., p. 82.
[4] ibid., pp. 85f.
[5] *B Henry IV*, IV. v. 129ff; Clemen, op. cit., p. 75.

imagery of the Gospels, and see if we can make the same sorts of
distinction, and see the same pattern of organic development? It
would seem as if we could apply a series of tests to the Synoptics, and
draw conclusions from them, in the same way as Spurgeon and
Clemen.

1.　Religious imagery differs from dramatic imagery in being all-
embracing. In a play the characters pick up handkerchiefs, see daggers
before them, or exit pursued by bears. Handkerchiefs, daggers, and
bears are not images, they are the furniture of the story. But in
religious teaching all the earthly symbols used are brought in to
express some aspect of divine truth: whether analogically, 'Your
heavenly Father', parabolically, 'like a merchant seeking goodly
pearls', or by example of action, 'If any man strike thee on the right
cheek . . .'. The images of the Gospels are thus more thickly sown
than those of an Elizabethan play. They consist of all those nouns and
verbs which come in the teaching sections of the Gospels, apart from
those which are used ostensively. If Jesus says, 'How many loaves
have ye?' he is pointing to real loaves, and that is no image. If the
man in the parable asks to borrow three loaves, we have the imagination of the teacher at work, and 'loaf' therefore is an image.

Our question is, how far the teaching of the Synoptics reveals a
single imagination at work, and how far the several Gospels reveal
preoccupation with individual areas and uses of imagery. We are
concerned therefore with the teaching of Jesus. I have thought it
proper, however, also to include reference to the teaching of John the
Baptist; since in the theory I am proposing the same creative imagination of the evangelist will have been at work embroidering the
Baptist's teaching as the Lord's. I will draw attention to the John
images in the analysis. Of course, in the theory I am proposing the
same imagination will have been at work also in many places in the
narrative: for instance, Matthew's fondness for celestial imagery is
mirrored by his story of the Star. This area, however, I forswear; the
question of the evangelist's freedom with the narrative is too controversial to be considered at the same time.

In view of the all-embracing nature of imagery in religious teaching,
it is difficult to overestimate the importance of our study. Imagery is
the means by which a religious teacher communicates his doctrine.
Doctrine is related to imagery, if I may make the matter crystal-clear,
as οὐσία is to ὑπόστασις: the one can only be substantiated in the other.
The images which a teacher uses are therefore basic to his mind. They
must, moreover, reflect the mental world in which he lives. In so far,
therefore, as the Gospels reveal a volume of images of various kinds

similar in proportion to the volume of teaching, and a similar handling of them, we have evidence of one mind being behind all the Synoptic teaching, and that the mind of the Lord. Such a finding would substantiate the theory of non-Marcan traditions, and would destroy our own hypothesis. *Per contra* in so far as an imbalance is revealed in any area, or a different style of handling imagery, there we have evidence for our hypothesis, and against the non-Marcan traditions.

The number of verses of teaching in the Synoptics is approximately: Mark 240, Matthew 620, Luke 560. The later two Gospels thus contain roughly two and a half times the volume of teaching in Mark. Our first test then can be a numerical one. If Matthew or Luke has more than three times as many uses as Mark of a particular kind of image, we have evidence of imbalance, and so of Matthaean or Lucan creativity. Three times is only an approximation. We are dealing with statistics, and a statistical analysis of the figures is provided in an appendix to the chapter. Beside the total of image-uses in a particular category I have also noted the number of actual distinct images: Matthew, for example, refers to 22 different animals in his teaching material, and has 44 uses of these in all. The number and selection of distinct images is also highly relevant for judging between the two theories, whether the non-Marcan teaching goes back to Jesus, or whether it is the evangelist's (or his church's) addition: but the figures are much smaller than those of the use of images, and are not amenable to statistical conclusions. I have also noted the Q/M/L breakdown of uses, but these figures should be used with caution.[6]

2. We can ask if images of a certain kind are treated in the same way in the different Gospels. Shakespeare and Bacon look at ships from different points of view: do the three evangelists view animals or farms or the OT in the same sort of way?

3. A third test can also be decisive. If the Q and M material are Matthew's own composition, then we should be able to descry in the images some regularity, some organic relationship; and this should be a differentiable relationship from what is seen in Mark and Luke. If on the other hand the logia were ready-made, a smooth development of images of the curb—muzzle—dog—tooth kind will be impossible.

---

[6] The Q material is, in my understanding, that part of Matthew which Luke took over, and the M material that part which he rejected: sometimes, as with religious imagery, Luke found the matter not to his taste, and the Q figures are low and the M figures high. Thus there is no reason for expecting Q and M figures to be comparable. The interesting comparisons are between Mark and L and M + Q on my theory, and between the four 'sources' on the non-Marcan traditions theory.

Leaps of the *stichwort* kind or general imaginative inconsequence
are what we should expect from ready-made logia.

4.   We do not have different plays to consider as artistic unities, but
we have different units of teaching in the five Discourses of Matthew
and occasional teaching appended to them, and it will be worth while
asking whether one particular area is dominated by a single image or
image-group. In so far as this is found to be so it is to be seen as further
evidence of Matthaean activity, since nobody believes that the
Discourses came to him ready-made. If they show signs of being a
unity, it is he who has made them so.

The clue I propose to follow is one which I noted in ch. 2 above, and
examined more fully in ch. 4. Matthew's mind is basically antithetical:
towns and villages, preaching and healing, every sickness and every
disease. He tends at every point to think of a pair to the image he has
inherited from Mark, or which he has written himself; or to provide
a complete pair to round off the phrase. In the Lord's Prayer he rounds
off the Third Petition with 'on earth as it is in heaven', a pair of an
obvious kind which he has 15 times against once in Mark and 6 times
in Luke (3 in L). In the same way, for example, he tends to add a
female to a male image: Mark gives him the Mustard-Seed parable
to which he adds the farmer sowing the seed in his field; and then he
sets alongside, phrase for phrase, a parable of the woman hiding
leaven in the meal. He modifies Mark's blank refusal of a sign for this
generation by the sign of Jonah; and as a pair supplies the Queen of
the South. 'Look at the birds of the air; they neither sow nor reap nor
gather into barns . . . Consider the lilies of the field, how they grow;
they neither toil nor spin.' 'Two men will be in the field; one is taken
and one is left. Two women will be grinding at the mill . . .' The
unwatchful servant is followed by the unwatchful bridesmaids, linked
by the repeated, 'Watch therefore, for you know neither the day nor
the hour.' The girls playing at mourning are paired with the boys
playing at wedding-dances. There are instances of this in Luke, the
Sheep and the Coin for one, but I am not so much pleading an exclusive Matthaean trait as proposing a habit of mind, of which I shall
suggest that there are a large number of exemplifications. Matthew,
I shall maintain, develops his images antithetically: heaven and earth,
male and female, and so on.
     In the matter that follows I have isolated thirteen areas of imagery,
and attempted to draw conclusions from them. It should be noted
that *any* areas of imagery are both licit and dangerous. Shakespeare
and I are both fond of images from sport, but closer inspection may

reveal that I never use images from bowls nor he from cricket. Nevertheless, while similar figures may disguise differences, disparities will always be significant: and it is disparities which are our interest. We have only to be alive to the possibility that other areas might reveal further disparities.

Orchard

Mark has 10 orchard images in 19 uses, all in parables: the vineyard, the vine, fruit, branch, leaf, and fig-tree, the hedge, the tower, the vat, digging. Matthew has 59 uses adding the axe, root, tree, cutting down, fire (all in John), cluster, and fig: 23 of these are in Q, 18 in M, the large majority in both being in logia material. Luke takes over 29 uses from Q and Mark: he adds 17 uses of his own, including digging, dung, and a sycamine tree. Ten of Luke's new uses come in the Unfruitful Fig-Tree.

Mark has the obvious features, and is concerned only with the tree and its growth and fruit. Matthew multiplies the uses by more than 3 if we include the John images; he specifies the fruit, and is interested in the whole life of the tree, including its end. Luke takes over rather more than half of the Marcan and Matthaean uses: he is fond of digging and manure, and imagines more of the total process than Mark.

The antitheses rather than the numbers are the most significant Matthaean side of the orchard imagery: good fruit and bad in 7 and 12, good trees and bad in 7 and 12, clusters and figs; trees and fruit, axe and root in 3 (John). There are no logia of this type in Mark or L.

The development of the images comes smoothly in Matthew. John preached to the repenting crowds in Mark: Matthew adds a foil, the unrepenting Pharisees and Sadducees. They stand beside the penitent, but they do not really repent—where is the earnest, the fruit of their change of heart? From fruit to tree, from tree to axe and root, to felling and the bonfire. It is the same process in 7. The false prophets are the Church's peril: how can they be told beneath their sheep's clothing? Their fruits: no clusters, no figs, they are bad trees not good, with rotten fruit not good—cut them down and throw them in the fire. Pharisaic hypocrisy in 12 evokes the same syndrome, a bad tree to bear such bad fruit. The shadow of Mark's Vineyard parable in Matt. 21 suggests the Vineyard as the background to two more parables in 20—21, the Labourers and the Two Sons.

Farm

Mark has 51 uses of farming images, including 22 different ones; Matthew has 122, of which 37 are Q and 57 M. Luke retains 50 of these uses and adds 24 new ones. Mark has many of the most obvious features of farm-life: a field, earth, rocky ground; three words for seed, sow, germinate; shoot, grow; corn, root, fruit, fruitless, bear fruit, ear; sickle, harvest; thorns, choke; mustard-seed, plant. Matthew introduces a number of more colourful aspects, especially at the latter end of the year, among the farmer's enemies, and in his herbarium: gathering, a barn, harvesting, harvesters, workers, a load, a yoke; a winnowing-fan, a threshing-floor, chaff, harvest bonfires (these in John), uprooting; thistles, tares; scattering, treading down; mint, anise, and cummin. Luke retains three-quarters of these different images, and adds on his own: ploughing, a plough, a store-house, rue, a garden, a bramble, moisture, and sifting.

The interpretation of these figures seems clear. Mark conveys a sturdy interest in the farm as a major locus of Jesus' teaching. His 51 uses are only doubled by Matthew, and his 22 images less than doubled. Luke is not much interested in farms: he adds only 50 per cent to the Marcan uses. The striking difference is in Matthew's much increased emphasis on the harvest, which stems from his theological interest in the End. Mark shares this interest, but to him the farm images convey growth. The only harvest images he has are sickle and harvest at 4.29. By contrast the Matthaean emphasis on the harvest with nine new harvest images is striking: they are introduced into both John's and Jesus' teaching, and are surely Matthew's own. This is borne out by their occurrence in pairs and antitheses, which are not instanced in Mark and L: wheat and chaff, fan and threshing-floor (both John), thorns and thistles, yoke and load, labourers and harvest, gather and scatter, field and meal, mustard-seed and leaven, mustard-seed and mountain.

The smoothness with which they fit in also bears this out. The orchard-bonfire at 3.10 leads on to the Christian baptism with fire, and suggests its pair in the harvest-bonfire; and so to winnowing, threshing, the storing of grain, and the burning of chaff. At 9.36 Matthew follows Mark's, 'He had compassion on them because they were as sheep without a shepherd'. The pastoral suggests a pair with the agricultural: 'The harvest is plentiful but the labourers are few'. The apostles are called to shepherd Christ's flock, and to gather in his grain: he himself is not sent but to the lost sheep of the house of Israel.

Animals

Mark has 4 animal images, the camel, the sheep, the puppies, and the
birds: in all 6 uses. Matthew has 22 different animals, of which there
are 44 uses. He introduces the dog, the pig, the bull, the fatling, and
the goat; the snake and the viper; the wolf and the fox; the dove, the
sparrow, the hen and chickens, and the vulture; the fish and the
whale; the gnat and the moth. 13 of the animals, with 19 uses, come in
Q passages; 12 of them with 21 uses in M passages. Luke retains 19
of these uses and adds as many of his own: he introduces the lamb,
the kid, the ass, the raven, and the scorpion. Most of these, new uses
as well as retained ones, occur in Q contexts.

Mark, then, is not strong in animal imagery. His animals are the
most commonplace, three domestic animals and the birds. Matthew,
on the other hand, delights to draw in the whole zoological panorama.
He fills out the domestic section to 8, adds wild animals, reptiles,
particular birds, fish, and insects. Each animal is to him symbolic of
one aspect of human behaviour: the camel of size, the dog and the pig
of profanity, the sheep of wandering helplessness, the ox and fatling
of wealth, the snake and viper of underhand hostility and cleverness,
the wolf of cunning, the fox of wild life, the dove of harmlessness,
the sparrow of cheapness, the hen of motherliness, the vulture of
ubiquity, the gnat of smallness, the moth of destruction. It is noticeable that in all but one of the L passages where animals are introduced
this is not true. Luke's dog and pigs and oxen and kid and calf are all
introduced incidentally in the course of his parables; his fox is a term
of abuse for Herod. The only exception to prove the rule is Luke
10.19, '. . . to tread upon serpents and scorpions . . .' where OT
images are in part responsible. It is not that Luke is insensitive to the
Matthaean (Q) symbolism, which he takes over, and indeed improves:
his lamb is more helpless than Matthew's sheep, his ox harder to get
out of the pit than Matthew's sheep; his raven more the object of
God's providential feeding in scripture than Matthew's birds; his
scorpion nastier to find on the plate than Matthew's stone. It is just
that he does not play this kind of animal symbolism off his own bat.
A further distinguishing characteristic of the Matthaean animals is
the way in which they come in pairs and in fours: dogs and pigs, sheep
and wolves; sheep and wolves, serpents and doves; foxes and birds;
gnats and camels; sheep and goats; hen and chickens; moth and rust.
Luke misses most of these, and his own attempts to pair animals,
'untie his ox or his ass from the manger', 'having a son or an ox fallen
into a well', by no means convey the same epigrammatic effect.
Matthew's symbolic thought is so rich that he makes some images

stand for two, even contradictory, concepts. His serpents are both contemptible as underhand and admirable as clever, his sheep are both the errant and the blessed, the apostle, the Christian and the Jew; just as he boldly has leaven as symbolic of the gospel as well as of Pharisaic hypocrisy, and the sons of the Kingdom are now the Jews and now the Christians.

Matthew's animal images are black and white like so much else of his thought. The Pharisees are vipers from John on, and in the strongly anti-Pharisaic passages in 12 and 23 this and the snake-image recur: they are a brood of snakes and vipers, straining at gnats, swallowing camels; while the Lord is as a hen with her young. The godless being like dogs and pigs lead on to the false prophet who is a wolf masquerading as a sheep. The traditional sheep is the basic image. The crowds are harassed and helpless like sheep, whom the apostles are sent out to tend, sheep in the midst of wolves themselves, pastors to the lost sheep of the house of Israel. The man whose hand was withered is like a sheep fallen into the pit on the Sabbath. In 18 the Twelve are told how the lost sheep are to be sought and won; in 25 they take their place by the Shepherd-King dividing his sheep from the goats. It is not surprising that the animal images fall in clusters, in 7, in 10, in 23, and 25 especially; they suggest and develop each other.

Country

For the rest of the country, Mark has 9 images in 15 uses: the mountain, the field, the stone, the cave, nesting, the shepherd, summer and winter, and the sea. Matthew retains all of these and has a further 13 images of his own—54 uses in all. He adds: the wilderness, waterless places, the ground, the dry land, the rock, the sand, foxholes; grass, lilies, a reed; a flock; a river and the deep sea. Luke retains half of all these images and adds 10 of his own: shepherding, watering, and feeding the flock, the stall, husks, wood (green and dry), a hill and a dell; a flood and a wave: 41 uses in all. 14 of the Matthaean uses are in Q, 26 in M sections.

The countryside is a natural locus for Marcan imagery, even if it is again only the plainer features of the landscape which catch his eye. Matthew has rather more than three times the uses of country images, and again we notice the detail of observation which has introduced so many of the most colourful countryside images—the wild plants, and the different kinds of ground. Again, too, the Matthaean images fall in pairs: stones and children (John), the rock and the sand, the birds' nests and the foxholes, the birds and the lilies, the river and the rain: compare Luke's the green wood and the dry. But Luke is not a countryman. He drops half the imagery in the tradition, and has the fewest uses in proportion, as he has also in the Farm section.

Cosmic Images

Mark has 7 cosmic images in 9 uses: the sun, moon, stars, powers, the world, the clouds, and the wind. Matthew adds the lightning, the *kauson*, rain and raining, and the rising of the sun, to the Marcan images, all of which he retains: 23 uses in all. Luke retains all these images, often in different uses, and adds the south wind, and a shower, 16 uses in all.

There is a noticeable difference in the Matthaean use from that of Mark and Luke. The Marcan cosmic images are all called forth to describe the portents of the End, and many of the Lucan ones are slanted the same way: fire and brimstone raining on Sodom, the cloud and the shower, the south wind and the kauson all being signs of the times. But the Matthaean images stand for God's providence in the rain and the rising of the sun; or the brilliance of Christ and his angels and saints, who are repeatedly likened to the sun or lightning.

Parts of the Body

Parts of the body are the basis of images in number in all three Gospels. Mark has 14 images in 43 uses: the flesh, the body, the soul, the spirit, the heart, the blood, the eye, the lips, the ear, the neck, the hand, the feet, the belly, and the womb. Matthew has all these, and as many more, in 122 uses: he adds the face, the head, the hair, the right eye, the mouth, the tooth, the right cheek and the other, the limbs, the shoulders, the right hand and the left, the finger, and the bone. Six of these are lacking in Luke, but he adds the finger-tip, the tongue, the loins, the breast, the breasts, and the bosom: 103 uses. 36 of the Matthaean uses are from Q, 47 from M passages: 44 of the Lucan uses are introduced by Luke.

Numerically the images are nearly in proportion to the teaching matter. Again, however, it is noticeable that the Marcan images are all the most obvious ones: it is Matthew and Luke who have recourse to almost every visible part of the body, especially Matthew.

It is interesting to examine the development of parts of the body images in the Sermon on the Mount. 'Blessed are the pure in heart . . . adultery with her already in his heart. If your right eye causes you to sin . . . If your right hand causes you to sin . . . And do not swear by your head, for you cannot make one hair black or white . . . An eye for an eye, and a tooth for a tooth: but I say to you . . . If anyone strikes you on the right cheek, turn to him the other also . . . Do not let your left hand know what your right hand is doing . . . the eye is the lamp of the body. So if your eye is generous (AT), your whole body will be full of light; but if your eye is mean (AT), your whole body will be full of darkness . . . Therefore, I tell you, do not be anxious about your life . . . nor about your body . . . Is not life more than food, and the body more than clothing? . . . And which of you by being anxious can add one cubit to his stature . . . Why do you see the speck that is in your brother's eye, but do not notice the log that is in your own eye? . . . your eye . . . your own eye . . . your own eye . . . your brother's eye.' Such a catena of images is hard to understand unless a single mind is at work. Especially noticeable is the magnetism of the eye image. In a number of places the imagery link explains what otherwise would seem to be a puzzle: swearing by one's head seems a come-down after heaven, earth, and Jerusalem; increasing one's stature seems out of place in the carefully balanced contrasts of food and clothes, birds and lilies. The generous and mean eye appear to interrupt the train of thought between the treasures in heaven of 6.19–21 and the two masters in 24.

Matthaean antitheses include: body and soul (four times), hand and foot (twice), eye and tooth, left hand and right hand, right cheek and left, mouth and heart, heart and treasure. Mark has spirit and flesh; Luke has womb and breasts, shoulder and fingers.

Town

It is time we came to the affairs of men. In the town Mark has 11 images in 28 uses: the market-place, the way, the mud, building, sanhedrin's, a house, the headstone of the corner, the roof, the door, and the drain. Half of these uses are in the house. Matthew has all these except the mud, and he adds 17 of his own images, 91 uses in all: the town, the gates, the key, to lock, the village, the lanes, the corners, the streets, the highway entrances, dust, and stumbling-blocks; the roof-covering, the store-chamber, the beam, the foundation, to live in, and the collapse. Luke lacks 2 of these images, but has the gateway. The breakdown between the four teaching sections is: Mark 28, Q 28, M 41, L 38.

For the first time we find the sort of spread numerically that we should expect across the three Gospels on the non-Marcan traditions hypothesis. The uses in the four sections are fairly level, and the totals in Matthew and Luke are about the same and three times that of Mark. Against this, however, we find our customary ordinariness of image in Mark: Mark's interest is concentrated on the house and its parts, whereas the available features in the streets of the town, as well as in the structure of the house, seem very nearly to be exhausted by Matthew's and Luke's list. Often, as with the parts of the body, we feel the magnetism of the image-group on Matthew's writing. 'You are Peter, and on this rock I will build . . . You are my stumbling-block' (AT). 'The gates of Hades shall not prevail . . . I will give you the keys of the kingdom . . .' Curb—muzzle—dog—tooth. The road is an important image in the Sermon, perhaps with the thought of the Christian *halakah*. 'Make terms with your creditor quickly, while you are on the road with him . . . whoever impresses you for one mile, go with him two . . . They sound the *shofar* in the synagogues and in the lanes . . . they like to stand praying at the corners of the streets . . . you don't see the roof-beam in your own eye . . . knock and it shall be opened to you . . . go in by the narrow gate, for broad is the gate and wide the road, . . . narrow is the gate and straitened the road . . . a wise man who built his house upon the rock . . . its foundation was upon the rock' (AT). There is something of the same kind within a single pericope in Mark in the Beelzebul controversy, where the divided house and the strong man keeping his house bear out the lord-of-the-house imagery: but such continuity of images is exceedingly rare in Marcan discourses.

Matthaean pairs are: gates and ways (twice), synagogues and lanes, synagogues and street-corners, town or village, town or house (all M): Luke has store-house or barn.

Religion

All three Synoptic Gospels have a great deal of religious imagery, but much the most is in Matthew. Mark has 19 images in 57 uses: the house of God, the offering, the sacrifice, the shewbread; mystery, the commandments, the tradition, the sabbath, the synagogue, the chief seats therein; prayer, fasting, sin, blasphemy, repentance, a hypocrite, defiling, a priest and a prophet. Matthew has all these and 35 further images: 204 uses in all. He adds: two more words for the Temple, its gold, the altar and the throne of Moses; law, a tittle, righteousness, a trumpet and blowing it, phylacteries, hems, sack-cloth, ashes, washing, tithing, alms, a vow, swearing and peace in the sense of blessing; wise men, learned men, rabbis, teachers, cathegetes, scribes, saints, pupils, and proselytes; to bind and to loose, sorrow for sin, mourning for sin, another word for defile, oath-breaking. Luke retains 29 of these 54 images, and adds Levite and apostle: in 109 uses. The breakdown by teaching blocks is: Mark 57 uses, Q 38, M 120, L 42.

These figures must be considered a very strong argument for the thesis we are urging. Teaching involving the uses of religious symbols must have been part of the ministry of Jesus, which we should have expected *a priori* to be reflected in nearly equal proportions in the evangelists, if all the Gospel teaching goes back to him. We cannot argue that Matthew's church was more interested in Judaism than Mark's and Luke's, and therefore would remember more of Jesus' teaching on the subject. For the whole point of imagery is that its use is largely unconscious, and arises in the course of teaching on other subjects—Pharisaic hypocrisy, say, or humility, or the hiding of revelation, or apostolic powers. Mark in any cases has 57 uses, and Luke 109, of which 40 are new uses in L material, so neither of the other evangelists can be said to avoid religious imagery. The simplest explanation is a personal one. We have shown that Matthew was a *sôphēr*. In this capacity he was constantly handling holy things, and it is natural that his imagination should run among the *sacra*. Mark has only 6 references to the Temple and its appurtenances: Matthew adds 23. Mark mentions only prayer and fasting among pious acts; Matthew adds 13 others. Mark has only 2 classes of religious person —the most obvious, the prophet and the priest: Matthew adds 9 further classes, all of them, be it noted, classes from the synagogue system. There are 5 different words introduced for the various grades of learned Jew: of Luke's innovations, the Levite comes from classical, not practical Judaism, the apostle from Christianity. With such a background, we should have no difficulty in accounting for Luke's handling of the situation. He is not a scribe: the minutiae of the scribal hierarchy or of Jewish piety are not relevant to his concern. No less set than his predecessors against Pharisaic hypocrisy as the principal enemy of the Lord and the Church, he reinforces their doctrine with new examples drawn from the central stock of religious images: sin, repentance, prayer, prophet, disciple are among his favourite thoughts. The peripheral images he omits; they are Matthaean additions, and so optional extras.

Pairs and antitheses are numerous in Matthew: temple and gold, altar and offering, jot and tittle, Law and prophets, σοφοί and συνετοί, phylacteries and hems, sackcloth and ashes, scribes and Pharisees, disciple and master, binding and loosing, mercy and sacrifice. Mark has the commandments of God and your tradition, Luke has priest and Levite.

The religious images pervade Matthew, and can be traced at length in many parts of the Gospel, especially the first half of the Sermon, and 23, where the diatribe is carried on by means of associated religious symbols, from Moses' throne in v.2 to 'your house' in v.38.

The detailed exposition of this chapter, and its links with the Sermon must await full exposition later. A shorter example of a clear kind comes in 12. The sabbath, David's entry into the Temple and eating of the Shewbread, only permitted to the priests, are given in Mark. The mention of priest leads Matthew on to seek for a case of permitted sabbath-breaking among the priests, and to the conclusion, 'Something greater than the Temple is here', a phrase soon to be paralleled twice. The Temple leads on to Matthew's Hosea text, 'I desire mercy and not sacrifice'. These verses did not come to Matthew as ready-made independent logia. The sequence of images runs so smoothly because they are midrash, embroidered on to the Marcan story.

Crime and Punishment

We pass from man's highest endeavours to his confessed failure. Considerable use is made of images from criminal life in the Synoptics, especially in Matthew. Mark has 12 images in 27 uses: a robber, murdering, hitting on the head, spoiling, killing, tying up, plundering, sexual fault, adultery; witness, judgement; thrashing, the cross. Matthew has all these but κεφαλαιόω and a further 24, 90 uses in all. He adds: men of violence, forcing, snatching, extortion, a thief, digging through, stealing, a murderer, harlots, becoming drunk, beating; a legal adversary, settling, the judge, condemning, the prison officer, the prison, the torturer, punishment, the sword, cutting in half, stoning, crucifying, and flogging. One might wonder how much was left for Luke to initiate. He adds: stripping, blows, wounds, half-dead; the magistrate and a different prison officer, dragging to court and accusing, but lacks 10 of the Matthaean images: in all he has 69 uses of 30 images, nearly three-quarters of the Matthaean figure, which is over three times that of Mark. The four teaching blocks are: Mark 27, Q 25, M 46, L 34.

Although there is less disparity here than in some other areas, there remains a noticeable preponderance in Matthew. This is not due to any noticeable doctrinal angle on the images, since comparatively few of the uses are in connection with hell, for example. Mark has the crimes against the Commandments, but is limited to 2 images apiece of the court and punishment. Both Luke and Matthew introduce a considerably broader area of crime, and more court-images. Matthew adds 8 punishment images to the Marcan 2; half of these are not in Luke, and there are no L punishment images. It is hard not to conclude that it is Matthew's super-ego with which we have to do.

Rites of Passage

Mark has 8 images drawn from the fields of birth, marriage, and death, in 20 uses: being born, a bridegroom, the sons of the bride-chamber, marrying and giving in marriage and divorce; a corpse and inheriting. Matthew has all these, and twice as many besides in 66 uses: the marriage-hall as such, the marriage, the bridesmaids, dancing, flute-playing, the procession, the guests, the wedding-garment; a second word for corpse, wailing, breast-beating, weeping, burying, chalking, and two words for tomb. Luke lacks 7 of these images, and introduces no new ones; he has 46 uses in all. For the teaching-blocks the figures are: Mark 20, Q 13, M 29, L 17.

The preponderance of Matthew is again impressive. If the total of uses in Matthew is not far above three times those in Mark, yet the tripling of the different images used is surely remarkable. Nor is this due to the accident of a single parable. It is the presence of two wedding parables in Matthew and the saying on the Children in the Market-Place and various other logia which combine to emphasize the themes of marriage and death in the Gospel. There is noticeably less marriage, though just about as much death in Luke. Luke has no innovations, and only two-thirds of the uses of Matthew. As a synagogue official, Matthew might be expected to turn his mind to the Rites of Passage.

The theme of Christ as the Bridegroom is Pauline, Marcan, and no doubt dominical. The Church is the bride to Paul, but the sons of the bridechamber in Mark: the former figure does not submit to allegorizing, so Matthew keeps to the latter. Christians are individuals, in need of warning not to presume on their vocation; they can be represented as guests or bridesmaids, not as the corporate bride. Mark has the wedding as the time of the ministry, while the bride-groom is with them; Matthew's mind turns more towards the Lord's return, when the eternal marriage can be celebrated, and so the exploitation of the theme is kept to the end of the book. The Marriage-Feast is set as a pair to the Wicked Husbandmen, the same teaching, the same villains, the same emissaries, the same abuse of them, the same destruction. Only the image is different. Matthew appends his common concern, the warning to the lukewarm Christian, in guise of a wedding-guest who has brought no robe of righteousness. A wedding similarly forms the ideal mode for a parable on watching in 25. We have had the watchful and the unwatchful steward; the brides-maids form a female companion piece.

Matthaean pairs are: marrying and giving in marriage, piping and dancing, mourning and breast-beating, the carcase and the vulture, the bidden and the elect. There are none such in Mark and L.

Economic Life

Mark has 8 images in 9 uses drawn from trade: sell, barter, work, pay, make and lose money, measure, livelihood. Matthew has all these and 21 more, 29 images in 82 uses. He adds: buy, owe, debt, debtor, borrow, loan, wage, hire, make account, possessions, mammon; tax-collector, banker, interest, merchant, pearl, unemployed, grind, oil, furnace, and mill. Luke, for the first time, exceeds Matthew, both in number of images and in uses. He has 44 images in 98 uses. As he lacks 12 of the Matthaean/Marcan images, he has in fact introduced 27 new images into the tradition: creditor, another word for debtor, to do business, remit a debt, purse, wallet, profit, another word for lend, pay, spend, expense, property, bill, bank, inn, innkeeper, completion, steward, stewardship, hireling; test, extort, exact, swindle, beg, corn and portion of corn. The division into teaching-blocks runs: Mark 11, Q 14, M 52, L 81.

Few figures are more revealing than these. Jesus lived in a Galilean village where trade was done at the village store, where credit was not a large feature of life, and nobody made a fortune. The Gospel tradition matured, and the Gospels were written, in large cities, where money was made as well as earned, where dishonesty forced itself on the attention, where there could be institutions for credit, where businessmen bought luxuries worth the earnings of a lifetime, and invested money by the talent. The images in which a man's teaching is conveyed reveal the environment in which he lives, and it speaks volumes for the accuracy of Mark that the images of the city, of Jerusalem, Antioch, and Rome, are absent from his book. In most other areas of natural and human interest we have found Mark to be in the same numerical order as the other three teaching blocks. If his figure has been only a third as many as Matthew or Luke, we have thought that to be significant, and we have found the distinctions to lie rather in particular ways of looking at a given part of life than in lack of interest. But in images of economic life there is a numerical chasm between Mark and the two later evangelists: Matthew has nine times, Luke eleven times the volume of such images. There can be no explanation for this by appealing to *Sitz-im-Leben* differences, for all our evidence is that the Marcan tradition was funnelled through cities, where it would be natural to retain and elaborate trade imagery. Much of the trade imagery is in parables, especially in Luke, but there would still be an embarrassing surplus of logia on pearls and purses, mills and mammon, extortion and exaction without. The most natural explanation is that Mark faithfully reflects the teaching of the Lord in the Galilean hills; that Matthew has sought to edify a city congregation with midrashic parables and midrashic epigrams reflecting the city environment; and that Luke, who knew the ways of businessmen from travelling and personal contact rather than from the safety of the synagogue school, rewrote and rehandled the Matthaean matter. It is significant that Luke takes over only 14 of Q/Matthew's trade images. Here, for the first time, we find a field where Luke's imagination is at home. He has a parable of Two Debtors of his own for Matthew's Unmerciful Servant, and the Pounds for Matthew's Talents. He has 81 uses of trade imagery in L.

It is not my task to urge a theory of the composition of Luke, except in so far as this is involved in my own thesis of the creativity of Matthew. It is useful, however, to note that whereas I have set out ten different areas of imagery where Matthaean imagination seems to predominate in the synoptic tradition, there are also areas where Luke's imagination has been still more influential. Mark has no image relating to credit; Matthew introduces 7 and Luke a further 6. Mark has only κερδαίνω and ζημιόω that might relate to the whole world of business; the language of business is second nature to his successors, and their parables are full of it. In the Marcan community there is little worth stealing: thieves, sharp practice, defaulting, extortion, dishonesty, swindling are introduced by Matthew and abound in Luke. The money in Mark, as we shall see, is the peasant's coins; silver and gold, pearls and talents belong in the strange world of the city-church.

The trade imagery grows naturally out of the Matthaean text. The basic equivalence is the rabbinic commonplace that sin is a kind of debt which we incur, and which we depend upon God's mercy to remit. We have this in the Lord's Prayer, whither it comes from Jesus' words in Mark, 'Whenever you stand praying, forgive . . . so that your Father also who is in heaven may forgive you your trespasses.' Matthew cites this, and its converse, at the close of the Prayer: in the Prayer itself the trespasses have become debts, and the trespassers debtors. Similarly in 18, 'If thy brother sin . . .' (AT), the apostle is to tell him his fault, visit him, accuse him, excommunicate him: which leads on naturally to, 'How often shall my brother sin against me . . .', and the command to forgive him seventy times seven. Sin = Debt. God, Peter, Peter's brother: King, Debtor, Debtor's Debtor. 'So also my heavenly Father will do to . . . you if you do not forgive your brother.' The growth of the Talents from the master leaving home in Mark's Doorkeeper we have expounded before.

Measures

A similar conclusion is to be drawn from the images of length, capacity, and money in the three Gospels. Mark has two measures of capacity, the μέτρον, a general term, and the μόδιον, a corn measure of about a peck, or 2 gallons. He mentions the denarion twice, and has Jesus instruct the apostles to put no brass in their pockets. Matthew has 13 terms for measuring and money, in 22 uses: a mile, a cubit, and stature; a σάτον, about a peck and a half, or 3 gallons; a *kodrantes* ($\frac{1}{64}$ of a denarion), an *assarion* ($\frac{1}{16}$ of a denarion), a silver piece or shekel (4 denaria), a stater (4 denaria, equal to a shekel), a coin, gold, and a talent (10,000 denaria)—as well as the Marcan uses. He has Jesus instruct the apostles to put no gold or silver or brass in their pockets. Luke has a similar number of terms and uses. For measures he has the *bath* which was about 8 gallons, and the *kor*, which was about 11 bushels, or 80 gallons. For money he has the *lepton*, which comes in the Marcan narrative elsewhere ($\frac{1}{128}$ of a denarion), the drachma, which was about 1 denarion, and the *mna*, which was 100 denaria. He has Jesus instruct the apostles to take no silver for the journey.

There is no need to labour the point which has been made in the previous section. While Mark retains the Palestinian simplicity, Matthew indulges in the large figures of one who has only the imagination with which to pay; Luke's measures show a business-like restraint, but are still far from life up-country. The environment of a trading community is stamped on both books.

Domestic Images

Within the house it is different. Here Mark has 22 different images in 36 uses: the doors, goods, a table, a bed, a lamp, a lampstand, a *modion*, a wineskin, a cup, treasure, a millstone, a drain, the chief seat; salt, bread, crumbs, leaven, wine, water, to quench, to leave home, and to sleep. There are in addition a number of clothes images, which we will not consider here. Matthew has 36 images in 78 uses, only a little over double the Marcan number. He has all the Marcan images, except that he makes the water cold. He adds a dish, a torch, a jar, and a splinter; food, fish, a gift, oil, and rust; to burn a light, to spin, to labour, to sweep, to adorn, to strain wine, to shut a door, and to nod. Luke has 36 domestic images in 73 uses. He lacks 8 of the Matthaean images, and replaces them with 8 of his own: the platter, arms, another word for bed, an egg, a portion of food, to light a lamp, a towel, and a ring. The four teaching sections break down: Mark 36, Q 18, M 38, L 35.

It is evident that in this area Mark holds his own. His uses of domestic imagery are as numerous as those found in either M or L, and are double those in Q: or to put the matter in another perspective, he has proportionately more uses than either of the other two Gospels. The house is likely to have been a centre on which Jesus' own imagination fixed, and we can get no help for our thesis numerically from this group of images. There is a way of looking at household images which is Matthaean and not Marcan, and that is in the observation of household activities rather than furniture. 18 of Mark's 21 images are nouns: furniture and food. Putting wine into wineskins, and the light on the stand, giving water to apostles, finding treasure, and sleeping are the only actual home activities mentioned. Matthew has much more of the woman's work: spinning, sweeping, straining the wine, adorning the house, labouring, burning and trimming the lamp; and there is cleaning the dish, giving food to the children, and shutting the door as well. Matthew's love of pairs is instanced as usual: swept and garnished, the dish and the cup, to toil and to spin, to strain and to swallow, the salt of the earth and the light of the universe, a city on a hill and a lamp on a stand, to slumber and sleep, bread and fish, moth and rust, the beam and the splinter. Mark's only pair, the patch and the wineskins, is not much to set against such a galaxy.

Our analysis has revealed four areas out of thirteen in which there is so great a disproportion in the volume of imagery between Mark and Matthew as to require the hypothesis of a different mind. In animal imagery Mark has 6 uses against Matthew's 44; in religious imagery Mark has 57 uses against Matthew's 204; in economic imagery Mark has 9 uses against Matthew's 82; in measures Mark has 6 uses against Matthew's 22. Even if we put economics and measures together, we are left with one-quarter of the imagery analysed in which there is a large, or overwhelming, preponderance in Matthew. There is further a remarkable, but not overwhelming, disproportion in the Orchard, Country, Crime and Punishment, and Rites of Passage areas. We cannot explain this on the grounds of selection of material by either churches or evangelists. A random selection would not give such disproportion; a conscious selection cannot be accounted for. The Non-Marcan Traditions view is thus driven into a Bacon-wrote-Shakespeare position. How do we know Bacon did not write Shakespeare? Read Professor Spurgeon. In five Shakespeare plays selected from all periods there are 48 bird images; in as much Bacon there are 12; 43 tree and plant images to 20; 21 celestial bodies against 4; while Bacon outweighs Shakespeare in science and religion. Shall we argue that different booksellers selected the Bacon writings and the Bacon pseudo-Shakespeare writings? No: the imagination is different between the two men. And so does Matthew's imagination differ from the Lord's: it is only that so venerable a tradition has prevented us from asking the question.

To examine the images in detail is to assure ourselves that this is so. Not only is the Marcan—I should say, the dominical—imagination limited to the house and farm life of the Galilean hills: it is also restricted to the salient features of that world. In area after area we have seen how Mark draws on the most obvious and commonplace images. The *major* features of life are turned over and brought into religious use: the sowing and growth of the field, the domestic animals, the house itself, the principal religious figures and pious practices. Matthew's imagination is different. He can use the salient features— the sheep or the way or the house—as themes to develop through his book. But also his mind goes into every corner. When we have given a list of animals, or crimes and punishments, or parts of the body, or religious characters and practices, or marriage and death images from Matthew, we feel we have covered the whole field: all that is left to Luke is the gleanings. It is not till we come to an area such as Trade, or Social Life, that Luke is able to show an even wider observation.

Finally, Matthew's mind is antithetical in a way in which the Marcan tradition and L are not. In area after area we have found pairs and antitheses leaping to mind, five, six, ten at a time from Matthew. This habit straddles the Q–M division, and indeed is not uncommon in the redaction as well. There are pairs in Mark and L, but they take some thinking of. There is thus a cleft in the handling of images between Matthew on the one side, and Mark and L on the other. This antithetical habit of mind enables us to follow the development of Matthew's paragraphs as well as of his sentences. We have seen, all too briefly, instances of how he moves from one thought to the next: we can observe his mind at leisure in later chapters. But images and their use give us an infallible insight into an author's mind; and what seems to be revealed by this study is that the mind behind the First Gospel is Matthew's.

APPENDIX
TABLE OF SELECTED CATEGORIES OF SYNOPTIC IMAGES

		IMAGES			USES			USES	
	MARK	MATT.	LUKE	MARK	MATT.	LUKE	Q	M	L
1. Orchard	10	17	15	19	59	46	23	18	17
2. Farm	22	39	38	51	122	74	37	57	24
3. Animals	4	22	22	6	44	36	17	21	17
4. Country	9	22	18	15	54	41	14	26	20
5. Cosmic	7	11	13	9	23	16	2	12	7
6. Parts of Body	14	28	28	43	122	103	36	47	44
7. Town	11	27	23	28	91	89	28	41	38
8. Religion	19	54	31	57	204	107	38	120	42
9. Crime and Punishment	12	35	30	27	90	69	25	46	34
10. Rites of Passage	8	24	17	20	66	46	13	29	17
11. Economic	8	29	44	9	82	98	14	59	81
12. Measures	5	13	13	6	22	20	8	12	10
13. Domestic	22	36	36	36	78	73	18	38	35

If we limit the comparison to Mark and Matthew, we may apply a statistical test as follows. Let p be the proportion of Marcan uses we might expect from the volume of Marcan teaching, and q be the proportion of Matthaean uses we might expect from the volume of Matthaean teaching: and let n be the total number of uses (Mark + Matthew) in any category. Then in 95 per cent of the categories, the number of uses found in Mark in that category should lie between $np \pm 2\sqrt{npq}$. There are about 240 verses of teaching in Mark and about 620 in Matthew, so $p = 28$ per cent and $q = 72$ per cent. For example, if there were 100 uses in one category between the two Gospels, we should expect the number in Mark to be about np, that is 100×28 per cent, or 28: and the statistical formula tells us that it is only significant if Mark has $2\sqrt{\frac{28}{100} \times \frac{72}{100}} \times 100$ $(2\sqrt{npq})$ uses, which works out at 9 uses, more or less than this figure. So if Mark had more than 19 $(28 - 9)$ and less than 37 $(28 + 9)$ uses in this category, there would be nothing surprising: and even then this goes for only 95 per cent of the cases—once in 20 we could expect the Marcan uses to fall outside this area without seeking an explanation.

The categories which seemed to us most striking were the Animals, the Religious, and the Economic images. In the case of the Animals, there are 50 uses between the two Gospels, so we should expect to find in Mark 14 uses ± 6.4: but actually there are 6 uses, which is too few. In the case of Religion there are 261 combined uses, so we should expect to find in Mark 73 uses ± 15.5. Mark has in fact 57 uses, which is just outside the area. In the case of Economic images, there are 91 uses between the two Gospels, so we should expect to find in Mark 25.5 uses ± 8.5, i.e. between 17 and 34. Mark has in fact only 9 uses. Thus in three cases out of thirteen the number of uses in Mark show a statistically significant shortfall. As this is much more than the 5 per cent permitted, the theory of a common source in Jesus behind the non-Marcan parts of Matthew is invalid.

6

LANGUAGE AND USE OF SCRIPTURE

The First Gospel was written in Greek, but its thought is Semitic; indeed at a number of points its thought is Aramaic rather than Hebrew. Two hypotheses might account for this. The evangelist might be a Greek-speaking Jew; or he might be retailing Aramaic traditions which had come to him in their original language, or in a literal Greek translation; or, of course, both. It will not cover the data to think of him as an imitator of the LXX, because that would leave the Aramaisms out of account. The prestige of Professor Black's *An Aramaic Approach to the Gospels and Acts* [*AAGA*][1] has done much to promote the second view, which would be fatal to our thesis: for if there are Aramaic traditions to be discerned behind the new material, then plainly Matthew was not a creative scribe.

Black assumes as axiomatic what we are contesting for Matthew. He writes: 'Jesus must have conversed in the Galilean dialect of Aramaic, and his teaching was probably almost entirely in Aramaic. At the basis of the Greek Gospels, therefore, there must lie a Palestinian Aramaic tradition.'[2] Three groups of phenomena lead him to believe that he can see that Aramaic tradition behind the Greek: (*a*) there is a number of common Aramaic constructions which are rare or non-existent in Greek, and which occur with some frequency in the Gospels; (*b*) there are many instances of Semitic rhythms in the poetic passages, especially in Matthew; and sometimes when retroverted into Aramaic these give instances of rhyme and alliteration; (*c*) in a number of cases retroversion into Aramaic provides a plausible explanation of a suspected mistranslation, or a varying form of a saying between two Gospels, or a textual variant. The suggestions under (*c*) we will deal with as they come up, since they are limited in number, and may require extended discussion. The poetic argument we have already considered in ch. 4 above, and found that the Matthaean poetry is adequately explained as the creation of the evangelist himself; and indeed that no other explanation suffices. The first group, the common Aramaisms, we will consider now.

Clearly numerous instances of Aramaic constructions in Matthew could be explained on either of our two hypotheses. *Prima facie* it is just as likely that Matthew was an Aramaic-thinking Greek-speaker,[3]

---

[1] 3e., Oxford 1967. [2] p. 16. Black's 'therefore' is a non sequitur.
[3] cf. S. Brock, reviewing *AAGA* in *JTS* (April 1969), pp. 274–8.

as it is that Aramaic versions of the Lord's words came to him (or that he had them unchanged from their first translator). It is unfortunate that Black uses the ambiguous term 'translation Greek' to cover what is in fact both hypotheses: for he has not considered the possibility of midrashic activity of the kind we are suggesting, and the false syllogism which I have quoted above lulls him into supposing that translation Greek means the translating of an Aramaic tradition into Greek words, when in fact it can equally easily be the original expression of an Aramaic mind. When my Chinese servant says, 'Me go Kowloon side', she is using translation English, i.e. putting her original Chinese thought into English words. Black writes, 'That asyndeton should so preponderate in the Words of Jesus . . . points to the conclusion that a sayings-tradition, cast in translation Greek and reflecting faithfully the Aramaic construction, has been utilised by the evangelists.'[4] But it might equally easily point to the conclusion that they thought in Aramaic, without a lot of 'and's', and so omitted the και's when they came to write in Greek.

We are not at leisure to weigh Black's conclusions for the other evangelists; but for Matthew the choice is certain. He had an Aramaic mind. The trouble is that Black proves so much too much. He gives a list of references for each of his Aramaic locutions, but does not note in which passages Matthew (or Luke) is overwriting Mark. No doubt this is intentional, for the question of Marcan priority is not closed, and the occurrence of Aramaisms in the redactional passages of the other two may be the means of opening it further. But the arguments for Marcan priority remain very weighty, and are assumed to be valid in this book—as indeed they are on occasion by Black. All we have to do therefore is to take the lists of Matthew references instanced by Black, and inquire how many of them occur in passages overwriting Mark.[5] About half of Matthew is redaction of Mark. So if half, or indeed merely a considerable number, of the Aramaisms are introduced by Matthew redactionally, it will be certain that Matthew thinks in Aramaic, and we can dispense with the Aramaic traditions hypothesis. If none of the Aramaisms is written into Matthew's redaction, but thev are found to occur frequently in the new material, then the traditions hypothesis is right, and we can dispense with the

---

[4] pp. 60f. The full sentence is, 'That asyndeton should so preponderate in the Words of Jesus and be virtually absent in the longer narrative portions of the Synoptics, except in Mark's Gospel and in certain Jewish Greek formulae chiefly in Matthew, points to the conclusion . . .'. Mark's Gospel is a large exception: are we to think the whole book faithfully reflects the Aramaic? For the formulas in Matthew see p. 118 below.

[5] cf. H. D. F. Sparks, 'Some Observations on the Semitic Background of the NT', *Bulletin of the SNTS* II (1951), p. 39.

rest of this book. If there are occasional introductions of Aramaisms in the redaction, and many in the new material, the question will be open whether we need both hypotheses.

Casus Pendens,

or resumptive pronoun: 'Yahweh, he is God'. While found in Greek on occasion, this is a natural Semitism. Black cites 15 instances of this in Matthew:[6] but 9 are from redactoral passages. 2 of these are copied in direct from Mark, (24.13; 25.29), but the remainder are introduced by Matthew, for example:

Mark 4.16	Matt. 13.20
And these . . . are the ones sown upon rocky ground.	What was sown on the rocky ground, this is he who . . . So Matt. 10.11; 12.32; 13.22,23; 15.11; 26.23.

Asyndeton

Black refers to 29 instances of asyndeton in Matthew,[7] all with λέγει, λέγουσιν, ἔφη, though he gives only 19 references, of which 10 are introduced by Matthew in redactoral passages (19.18,20,21, 22; 21.27; 22.37D,20D,21; 26.34; 27.23D. The fact that Matthew can introduce asyndeton four times in five verses in the Rich Young Man pericope is sufficient explanation for his writing it on his own three times in two verses in the Tares (13.28f).

Parataxis[8]

It is natural for the Greeks to write sentences with subordinate participles, and for Semites to write main verbs joined by w^e. The latter construction is very common in Mark, and in narrative Matthew frequently improves the Greek by the introduction of nominative aorist participles. In the Q passages of Matthew, however, Black notes that there is only about one participial construction per page of Greek text. This is, however, very natural, for the Q passages are for the most part those poetic passages which have also appealed to Luke, and aorist participles are undeniably prosy. When the parables are included, of which the bulk are usually classed with M, we find no lack of hypotaxis. Black himself notes 11 hypotactic aorist participles in the Unmerciful Servant. There are occasions when

---

[6] *AAGA*, pp. 51–5.　　　　　　　[7] ibid., pp. 55–61.
[8] ibid., pp. 61–9.

Matthew writes paratactically in the Semitic way. Black gives 9 instances drawn from Codex Bezae, but 8 of these are in passages where Matthew is overwriting Mark (11.28,29; 19.3; 20.30; 26.66,74; 27.49,58).

D^e–Clause

The all-purpose Aramaic d^e-clause can be translated seven ways into Greek, and is often suspected of lying at the root of Gospel variants. Black suggests only two possible cases in Matthew:

6.5: 'You must not be like the hypocrites, ὅτι φιλοῦσιν . . .'[9]

The Vulgate reads 'qui amant', supported by Diat. arab. Since d^e can be translated by both a relative and 'because', he proposes to explain the variant by reference to an Aramaic *Vorlage*. However, the parallel, 'When you fast, do not look dismal, like the hypocrites; for they (γὰρ) . . .', has no *varia lectio*. A simpler explanation is that Matthew wrote his favourite causal ὅτι, which was misread as οἵ. The other is at 13.16:

'Blessed are your eyes ὅτι βλέπουσιν
Luke 10.23: 'Blessed are the eyes οἱ βλέποντες what you see.'

The Matthaean ὅτι-clause and the Lucan relative are alleged to go back to the same Aramaic d^e.[10] The proposal does not account for the word 'your' in Matthew, or the phrase 'what you see' in Luke. Black himself suggests that Matthew's ὅτι-clause is in antithesis to the crowds who are addressed in parables *because* they do *not* see. Luke's change would easily be accounted for by his fondness for participial phrases, for example 8.12; 11.4.

Pronouns

Semitic usage of the article, demonstratives like ἐκεῖνος and αὐτός, or the reflexive, may be widely instanced in Matthew;[11] but again many of the instances fall in redactional areas, and merely show that Matthew thought more Aramaically than Mark. The Hebrew construct, not an Aramaic usage, interestingly, lies plainly behind the anarthrous βασίλισσα νότου; but then we find the same in the Passion story:

Mark 14.3	Matt. 26.6
While he was at Bethany ἐν τῇ οἰκίᾳ of Simon the leper.	Now when Jesus was at Bethany ἐν οἰκίᾳ of Simon the leper.

[9] ibid., p. 72.   [10] ibid., p. 70.   [11] ibid., pp. 93–100.

On the other hand, the Semitic ostensive use of the article is retained from Mark at 5.15 'Nor do men light *the* lamp and put it under *the* bushel' (AT), and similarly at 12.24,27; as well as being written into Marcan contexts at 12.12; 15.29; and 19.17. Pleonastic ἐκεῖνος is common in Matthew, especially in parables. Two cases where he writes it into a Marcan context are 9.26,31. Black himself concedes[12] that ἀπὸ τῆς ὥρας ἐκείνης 'at that very moment' is especially rabbinical, and that this may account for its frequency in Matthew. Five uses of αὐτὸς are claimed to be well-known Aramaisms.[13] Two of these are very disputable. At 3.4 Matthew, who has introduced John, but lost sight of him in the long citation of Isa. 40, resumes with αὐτὸς δὲ ὁ Ἰωάννης, which Blass–Debrunner take as 'the aforementioned John'. There seems no need to concede Wellhausen's claim of a proleptic pronoun, as used in Aramaic for emphasis. At 3.12 οὗ τὸ πτύον ἐν τῇ χειρὶ αὐτοῦ is not a case of a resumed relative: we say in English, 'whose fan is in his hand'. Of the remaining three cases one (10.11D) is an over-writing of Mark. The two cases of ethic datives[14] μαρτυρεῖτε ἑαυτοῖς (23.31) and μὴ καλέσητε ὑμῖν (23.9D) are not exampled outside the new material.

Indefinite Pronouns[15]

These are similarly intruded by Matthew in the redaction no less than written naturally in the new material. Of six instances of εἷς used adjectivally three are written into Marcan contexts (9.18; 21.19; 26.69); of two instances of partitive εἷς, as in 'one of the soldiers', one follows Mark, one is redactoral. Of 22 instances of ἄνθρωπος = τις 8 are redactoral: again the expression is common in parables as with ἄνθρωπος οἰκοδεσπότης. εἷς . . . εἷς, one . . . another, comes three times in the new material, partitive ἐκ, one of, some of, comes twice; for these there is no redactoral parallel.

Miscellaneous

Semitic languages lack comparatives and superlatives.[16] Two instances are given in Matthew: 2.16D, and 22.36, which overwrites Mark:

Mark 12.28: Which commandment is the first of all?
Matt.: Which is the great commandment in the law?

Semitic languages tend to weak auxiliary and inchoative verbs,

[12] ibid., p. 110n.   [13] ibid., pp. 96ff.
[14] ibid., pp. 102, 104. μαρτυρέω, however, is very commonly with the dative in Greek; cf. μαρτυρεῖς σαυτῷ (Eur. *Ion* 532).
[15] ibid., pp. 104–8.   [16] ibid., pp. 117f.

ἄρχομαι, λαβών, etc. Eleven instances are cited in Matthew,[17] four of which follow Mark (14.19; 15.36; 16.26,27) and four overwrite Mark (21.35,39; 27.48,59). Aramaic tends to impersonal plurals where the French write 'on'. Five examples are given in Matthew,[18] one of which overwrites a citation (1.23), one follows Mark (24.9), and two overwrite him (5.15, Q context, 9.17). The latter runs:

Mark 2.22	Matt.
No one puts new wine into old wineskins . . . but new wine into new wineskins. (AT)	Nor do they put new wine into old wineskins . . . but they put new wine into new wineskins. (AT)

Two examples are given of τίς (interrogative) used as a kind of condition, which is claimed to be Semitic by Joüon, as 'Who then is the faithful and wise servant . . .?'[19] Four cases of gnomic aorists, which probably stand for Semitic perfects, are also cited.[20] All the last six cases are in the new material.

From the brief survey that we have given, it will be seen that the balance tilts heavily in favour of the view that Matthew is a Greek-speaking Jew, whose own personal Aramaic thinking shines through his Greek. Just about half of all the instances of Aramaisms cited by Black occur in the redactoral material. While it would be possible to complicate the hypothesis by assuming an ever greater alternative version of the Lord's words and deeds which was in Matthew's hands and ran parallel with the Marcan matter, the most likely explanations seem to be the simpler ones, which reduce to two. Either greater numbers of Semitisms betoken an earlier tradition, in which case we should reject Marcan priority; or we may conclude that Matthew's Aramaic thinking is widely evidenced in his alterations of Mark, and may be taken as natural therefore in his writing of the new material.

Having been at pains to establish the Semitic nature of Matthew's thinking, we should not omit to observe that his Greek is at the same time more educated than that of Mark. He has a much wider vocabulary, including such words as σεληνιάζομαι, προβιβάζομαι, καταπον-τίζομαι, βαρύτιμος; he introduces the passive voice; in the narrative he has frequent hypotactic participial phrases, genitive absolutes, etc. This is no place to give a full account of Matthew's style, for which we may refer the reader to Lagrange's Introduction to his great commentary.[21]

---

[17] ibid., pp. 125f. [18] ibid., pp. 126f.
[19] ibid., pp. 118f; see below, p. 437, n. 22.
[20] ibid., pp. 128–30.
[21] M-J. Lagrange, *L'Evangile selon S. Matthieu* (3e., Paris 1927).

Matthew's writing is very regular, and we shall have occasion to appeal to his habits, both those which are instanced in the redaction and those which come frequently in the new material without occurring in the redaction. For this purpose I shall make use of an extension of Sir John Hawkins' principle. In *Horae Synopticae* Hawkins gives 95 words and expressions which he calls characteristic of Matthew; the criterion that he uses is that each word or expression must occur at least four times in Matthew, and either not at all in one of the other two Synoptics, or at least twice the number of uses in the other two combined. Further expressions meeting Hawkins' criterion have been isolated by Jeremias and others, but there are still other locutions which do not, which have seemed to many (including Hawkins himself, who provides a second list) to be Matthaean. Wherever a word or phrase is introduced by Matthew in the Marcan matter even once, that fact shows something of the evangelist's habit of mind. Or the same is true where he has a word noticeably more often than both Mark and Luke, as say μεταμέλεσθαι (3 times in Matthew, never in Mark or Luke), or ἀμὴν λέγω σοι/ὑμῖν (31 times in Matthew, 13 in Mark, 7 in Luke). In any case where the Matthaean uses are over twice the Marcan ones and also more frequent than the Lucan ones, we have some ground for thinking the writing typical of Matthew. However, since Hawkins' use of the word Matthaean is clear, and I do not wish to be suspected of eroding for my advantage the distinction he has set up, I shall refer to such usages as fall in the last two brackets, that is the redactional uses and those I have just described, by the term semi-Matthaean. In asking whether any passage is to be seen as the creative composition of the evangelist, part of the evidence is linguistic. Matthaean and semi-Matthaean uses will tend to establish creative composition; ἅπαξ λεγόμενα and rare uses comparative to the other Synoptics will count against creative composition. It is important not to overstress the linguistic evidence. It is perfectly easy to retell a traditional story inserting characteristic expressions of one's own; *per contra* everyone uses some words in his vocabulary once and once only in a given composition. ἅπαξ λεγόμενα do not prove derivation. Linguistic phenomena of this kind are straws in the wind, and should be evaluated as such.[22]

The possession of a Matthaean vocabulary, a list of characteristic words, enables us to put my theory, and other theories, to a simple statistical test. First we can test the Marcan priority theory. In the passages where Matthew is usually believed to be over-writing Mark, taken together, we can form three percentages: (*a*) the overall percent-

---

[22] There is a list of Matthaean and semi-Matthaean words on pp. 476–85 below.

age of characteristic words; (*b*) the percentage of characteristic words in the actual words which Matthew and Mark have in common; and (*c*) the percentage of characteristic words in the words they do not have in common. If Marcan priority is false, there is nothing singular about the words in common between the two Gospels so far as Matthew is concerned—they are merely the words from Matthew which Mark selected. If Marcan priority is false, therefore, we should expect all three percentages to be about the same. But if Marcan priority is true, the percentages will vary widely: percentage (*b*) will consist of those words which are characteristic of Matthew which Mark happened by chance to use before him, and will be very low; percentage (*c*) will consist of those words which are characteristic of Matthew in Matthew's own editorial changes, and will be high; percentage (*a*) will be the weighted average, and will lie between. In fact (*a*) is about 15 per cent, (*b*) is about 3 per cent, (*c*) is about 28 per cent: therefore the Marcan priority theory is true.

We can now use the same figures to form a base for testing my own theory against the orthodox position. In the orthodox view the Q and M material, together with any introductory framework in which the units stand, are Matthew's over-writing of further alien sources. We now know roughly what to expect when Matthew is over-writing an alien source because we have just seen what he does with Mark. There might be some difference in his handling of teaching matter as opposed to narrative, but this does not appear very obviously in the teaching sections of Mark. If the orthodox view is correct, therefore, we should expect the percentage of Matthaean characteristic words in the Q and M material to be about 15 per cent. On my view, however, Matthew is not over-writing an alien source, or hardly at all: he is composing, somewhat as he is in the editorial changes he makes to Mark. If my hypothesis is right, we should expect the percentage of characteristic words in the M and Q material to be about 28 per cent. As we examine, in Part II, the units of new material, I shall list the characteristic words in each paragraph, and note the totals: there is a statement of the results in Chapter 23. It should be noted that it is immaterial whether Q and M are taken to be written or oral: a story told us orally has as alien a form as one we read, and this will show itself just as much when we retell it in our own words.

A further study which Hawkins reports briefly in the course of his invaluable *Horae Synopticae* is into the LXX background of the three Gospels. He does this by the simple test of making a list of all those words which are peculiar to each of the three, and finding what percentage of them occur in the LXX. Of 71 words peculiar to Mark he finds that 31 are not in the LXX; of 112 words peculiar to Matthew he finds 36 not in the LXX; of 261 words peculiar to Luke he finds 73 not in the LXX—42 per cent Mark, 32 per cent Matthew, 28 per cent Luke. This would suggest *prima facie* that Matthew was more soaked in the LXX than Mark, and Luke than either. This conclusion leads us on to the study of the citations of scripture in Matthew, which have been the subject of considerable writing in recent years. We shall set out briefly the conclusions that seem to be established from a consideration of the 40 formal and 108-odd allusive quotations in the Gospel, and will then consider the theories proposed to explain the phenomena by K. Stendahl, B. Lindars, and R. H. Gundry.[23]

The study of the quotations is highly complex.

(a) There is a considerable degree of assimilation in the NT texts, especially in Mark to Matthew, so that it is often hard to be sure whether Matthew has made an alteration to Mark.

(b) There is a considerable degree of assimilation of the LXX texts, especially Codex A to Matthew, so that it is often hard to be sure when we have a genuine agreement of an uncorrupted LXX text and Matthew.

(c) Even if we were confident that our LXX texts were uncorrupted by NT influence, we often cannot be sure which, if any, of them is likely to have been in use in first-century Syria.

(d) Our knowledge of which Targum Matthew is likely to have been familiar with, if any, is equally sketchy, even if much improved by the researches of the last generation.

(e) In allusive quotations we cannot be sure how close the evangelist intended to keep to any OT reference.

(f) Since Matthew often draws on more than one passage, we cannot always be sure to which secondary passages, if any, he may be referring. Nevertheless, the following results seem to emerge:

1. Matthew was familiar with, and drew on, the LXX. Out of 16 formal quotations which he takes over from Mark, 7 follow the LXX

---

[23] Since the delivery of the Lectures, two considerable further discussions of the question have been published: R. S. McConnell, *Law and Prophecy in Matthew's Gospel* (Basle 1969), and W. Rothfuchs, *Die Erfüllungszitate des Matthäus–Evangeliums* (Stuttgart 1969). There is also a balanced review of these works and of Gundry in 'Les citations d'accomplissement . . .', by F. van Segbroek, in *L'Evangile selon Matthieu* (Bibl. Ephemer. Theol. Lovan. 29, Gembloux 1972), pp. 107–30. Both McConnell and Rothfuchs see the creative hand of Matthew in the selection and partial retranslation of the citations.

exactly, and in two further quotations he follows Mark in minor differences from the LXX. Of the remaining 7, he brings 2 closer to the LXX. Mark, followed by Luke, has the Commandments at 10.19 in the form μὴ φονεύσῃς, μὴ μοιχεύσῃς, etc.: Matthew (19.18) has the form οὐ φονεύσεις, οὐ μοιχεύσεις, etc., which is in all the LXX texts, albeit in varying orders. Similarly Mark opens the Isa. 29 citation at 7.6 οὗτος ὁ λαὸς against LXX ὁ λαὸς οὗτος: Matthew follows the LXX word-order. The context here requires the LXX sense and not the sense of the Hebrew. There are also three of four allusive quotations taken over from Mark which are assimilated to the LXX. For example, Mark refers to Mal. 4.5f 'Behold I send you Elijah . . . ὃς ἀποκαταστήσει the heart of the father . . .' The Hebrew here is *hēshîbh* so the Greek verb is quite a striking translation. Mark's own reference, 9.12, is in the form 'Ηλίας μὲν ἐλθὼν πρῶτον ἀποκαθιστάνει πάντα. Matthew gives the actual LXX form ἀποκαταστήσει with Mark's πάντα.

Of the 24 formal quotations which Matthew introduces independent of Mark, at least 9 follow the LXX without significant variation, and a further 8 can be demonstrated to contain some LXX traits against the Hebrew. The celebrated 'ἡ παρθένος shall conceive . . .' for example, gives the sense of 'virgin' which is not required by the Hebrew '*almāh*; and the LXX version is required in 'Out of the mouth of babes . . .' (21.16) also. It seems therefore that Hawkins' conclusion is valid, that Matthew knows the LXX well, and at times better than Mark.

2. Matthew also on occasion shows such close adherence to the Hebrew, against the LXX, that it is hard to resist the conclusion that he knew and drew on a text very close to our MT. We cannot avoid the possibility that he was following a Targum very close to our Hebrew, but the only wisdom we can have is to follow the evidence we possess, and this leads inevitably to the conclusion that Matthew was master of the Hebrew.[24] There is one clear example in his change of a Marcan citation. The Hebrew text of the Shema‘ gives three 'tones': 'Thou shalt love Yahweh thy God with (b^e) all thy heart (*lēbhābh*) and with (b^e) all thy soul (*nephesh*) and with (b^e) all thy m^e'*ōdh*.' The LXX texts vary in their translation of the nouns, and Lucian gives a fourth tone, but b^e is always rather freely translated ἐξ. Mark in both 12.30 and 12.33 reproduces the LXX ἐξ. Matthew goes back to the Hebrew with ἐν. At 12.30 (that is the actual quotation), Mark gives four tones. Matthew goes back to the original three. The muddle over the fourth tone arises from the ambiguity of the Hebrew m^e'*ōdh*, which

[24] He translates the name Jesus somewhat roughly at 1.21, and Emmanuel at 1.23; and puns on Beelzebul at 10.25.

can mean property, force, or strength. Gerhardsson argues that Matthew is closest to rabbinic interpretation here;[25] but it seems clear that at least in the use of the preposition, if not in the number of nouns and their interpretation, Matthew goes back to the Hebrew.

The plainest instance of dependence on the Hebrew is at 8.17, where there is a citation of Isa. 53.4. Here the Hebrew gives, 'Surely our sicknesses he bore, and our diseases (or pains) he suffered (or carried)'. The LXX and Targum give a spiritualizing rendering. LXX: 'This man bears our sins, and is in grief (ὀδυνᾶται) for us.' Matthew gives the citation as a proof of the foretelling of Jesus' healing of disease, so he requires the Hebrew, and not the LXX sense. His version 'Himself took our infirmities and bore our diseases' is different from the LXX in every word except καὶ and τὰς, and his opening αὐτὸς is as likely to be a translation of *'ākhēn hû'* as a link with the LXX οὗτος. There are many less complete instances where a link with the Hebrew looks virtually certain. For example, in the long Isa. 42 citation at 12.18ff, the Hebrew gives, 'He shall not make himself heard *bᵉhûts*'; the LXX translates 'He shall not be heard outside (ἔξω)'; Matthew takes the *hûts* more literally, 'No one shall hear him in the streets (ἐν ταῖς πλατείαις).'

3.   Gundry[26] claims 16 possible contacts with the Targums, and 10 possible contacts with the OT Peshitta, the official Syriac translation of the OT. In many cases these must remain as no more than possibilities. For instance, at Deut. 13.1–3 the Hebrew has, 'If there shall arise in your midst a prophet or a dreamer of dreams and shall give you a sign or a wonder', and is closely followed by the LXX. Both the Targum of Jonathan and the Old Palestinian Targum give the interpretation 'false prophets', and both Mark and Matthew have 'There shall arise (false Christs and) ψευδοπροφῆται and shall give signs and wonders' (AT). But the evangelists are not translating Deuteronomy: they are giving Jesus' prophecy of the time of troubles in terms of Deuteronomy, and the interpretation 'false' is required to give the sense. This is true of many of the instances given. A more promising case is Matt. 11.19 ἰδοὺ ἄνθρωπος φάγος καὶ οἰνοπότης. The LXX rendering of Deut. 21.20 gives συμβολοκοπῶν οἰνοφλογεῖ—a reveller in drunkenness, for the Hebrew *zôlēl wᵉsōbhē'* a spendthrift and drunkard; where Jonathan and the OPT have 'an eater/glutton in flesh and drinker in wine.' But perhaps no reference to Deuteronomy is intended. The strongest case is to be made for Matt. 26.52: 'For all

[25] B. Gerhardsson, 'The Parable of the Sower and its Interpretation', *NTS* 14.2 (January 1968).
[26] R. H. Gundry, *UOTSM*.

who take the sword will perish by the sword.' H. Kosmala[27] refers to the Targum on Isa. 50.11: 'All you . . . who take a sword, go, fall . . . on the sword which you have taken . . . you will return to your destruction.'

The most widely-claimed link with the Peshitta is 27.3ff, the 'double fulfilment' of Zech. 11.13, 'And the Lord said to me, Cast it to the potter (*yôtsēr*)'. Here the Peshitta reads *'ôtsār*, treasury. Wellhausen suggested[28] that Matthew knew both readings, and saw them as fulfilled first by Judas, who tried to throw the money into the κορβανᾶς, and then by the priests who paid it for Aceldama, the Potter's Field. Gundry correctly says, 'Whether or not Matthew himself knew of another reading, he cannot have intended κορβανᾶς to have fulfilled a reading of *'ôtsār* in Zechariah; for his narrative expressly states that it was not permissible to put the money εἰς τὸν κορβανᾶν, and Judas had merely thrown the money εἰς τὸν ναόν.'[29] In fact the Hebrew text is corrupt, and the probability is that the Peshitta, like the LXX χωνευτήριον, 'I threw them into the foundry', is doing its best to interpret the difficult 'founder', who melted the metal down for the treasury.[30] Matthew tells us that he associated the prophecy with Jeremiah, and we can make sense of his narrative with the Hebrew of Zechariah, and the LXX of Jeremiah 19 and 32, and some other associated references, without recourse to the Syriac.

It appears, therefore, that the evidence for the use by Matthew of other versions of scripture than the Hebrew and the Greek is somewhat debatable: the instance at Matt. 26.52 is the best hope.

4. Matthew, like Mark before him, combines on occasion two or more passages of scripture together. Mark begins his Gospel with a citation said to be from Isaiah, but in fact combining similar words from Exod. 23, Mal. 3, and Isa. 40. Matthew similarly, in the citation we have just discussed, claims to be quoting the major prophet Jeremiah, but in fact the purchase of the field for 17 pieces of silver in Jer. 32, and the potter in Jer. 19 only account for a minority of the matter, more of which comes from Zech. 11. There are many instances of this habit, which derives from the Jewish preaching habit of glossing a Torah text with a prophetic text that opened with, or contained a series of the same words.[31] Many of the Matthaean quotations merely

---

[27] 'Matt. 26.52—a Quotation from the Targum' in *Novum Testamentum* 4 (1960), pp. 3–5.

[28] *Das Evangelium Matthaei* (2e., Berlin 1914), p. 145.

[29] Gundry, *UOTSM*, p. 123.

[30] So C. C. Torrey, 'The Foundry of the Second Temple at Jerusalem', *JBL* 55 (1936), pp. 247–60; cf. Stendahl, *SSM*, p. 124.

[31] cf. Mann, *BRPOS*, pp. 11f.

combine two prophetic texts of similar wording. For example, Isa.
62.11, LXX^B: 'Tell the daughter of Sion, behold thy Saviour has
appeared for thee . . .'; Zech. 9.9: 'Rejoice greatly, O daughter of
Sion! Shout aloud, O daughter of Jerusalem! Behold your king is
coming to you . . .'; Matt. 21.5, 'Tell the daughter of Sion, Behold,
your king is coming to you'. There are apparently about three times
as many references to the prophets as to the Law in Matthew, which
would be strange for an author who accords the Law such esteem, as
any Jew would—'Not an iota, not a dot, will pass from the Law' (5.18).
In fact we shall often find a Torah reference embedded in a prophetic
quotation. Behind the marvellous conception by the παρθένος of
Isa. 7 stands the classic marvellous conception by Sarah, foretold in
almost the same words in Genesis; and Matthew's mind here is
indicated by his tracing the Lord's ancestry to Abraham at the beginning of the chapter.

5. Matthew shows himself to be a Targumist in small ways and
large. He not only chooses the textual form he is going to cite, and
perhaps includes reference to the Targum, he not only combines one
scripture with another, he also writes his own interpretation into
scripture. This is shown most clearly in one or two minor instances in
his altering the Marcan quotations. Mark, following both Hebrew
and Greek texts of Zech. 13.7, writes, 'and the sheep will be scattered'.
Matthew has, 'and the sheep of the flock will be scattered'. Zahn
suggests this is to underscore the antithesis between the shepherd and
sheep, which sounds quite Matthaean; or perhaps the phrase is
inserted from Ezek. 34.31. More interestingly, Hebrew and Greek
give Mic. 5.1: 'And thou Bethlehem (house of) Ephratah, thou art
least (*tsā'îr*, ὀλιγοστός) among the thousands of Judah . . .' This is
clearly, Matthew will have felt, in need of interpretation: least in size,
but greatest in destiny. He therefore inserts οὐδαμῶς, '*by no means
least*': the plea that he read the statement as a rhetorical question—
'Art thou the least? (By no means)'—is only another way of saying
the same thing. There is much free interpretation in 12.18ff, the long
Isa. 42 citation. Hebrew and Greek read, 'Behold (LXX Jacob) my
servant ('*abhdî*, ὁ παῖς μου), I will help him, (LXX Israel) my chosen
(*b^eḥîrî*, ὁ ἐκλεκτός μου)'. Jesus is no mere servant chosen and helped
by God: other scriptural terms will make the matter plainer. παῖς
may stand, it means son as well as servant in Matthew; ὅν ᾑρέτισα
is put for 'I will help him'—'whom I have chosen', a favourite LXX
word for God's choice of David and Solomon to be king;³² ὁ ἀγαπητός

<hr>

³² 1 Chron. 28.4,6,10; 29.1; or of Jerusalem to be his seat, Ps. 132.13,14;
Zech. 1.17; 2.12.

μου, ὃν εὐδόκησεν ἡ ψυχή μου, 'my beloved with whom my soul is well pleased', the words from the Baptism.[33]

Sometimes the course of the Lord's ministry results in an alteration to the course of scripture. Matthew believed that every syllable of the Law had been fulfilled in Christ, and he looked to scripture for prediction of every new turn of fate in his story. Every geographical move, his place of birth, his sojourn in Egypt, his settlement at Capernaum; every change of policy, his healing mission, his speaking in parables, his turning to the Gentiles, all are proven from scripture. If he grew up in Nazareth, that must have been foretold too: hence the puzzling 'Ναζωραῖος κληθήσεται' (2.23). Whether the traditional *nētser* of Isa. 11 lies behind this, or, as we shall argue, 'Ναζιραῖος ἔσται, he shall be a Nazirite' from Judg. 13—or any other passage—it is clear that some violence has been done to scripture. In doing this Matthew is only doing what we have earlier illustrated as the habit of the Targumists, edifying his readers by aligning prophecy with fulfilment. More often, as we shall see, he aligns fulfilment with prophecy.

Such is, in brief outline, the way in which scripture has been treated in Matthew in the citations and open allusions. Three recent theories have been propounded to explain the milieu from which such an operation arose.

1 *The School of St Matthew*

Stendahl[34] was impressed by the fact of Jesus being a rabbi, and suggests that this was likely to have been an enduring influence on church life.[35] Luke mentions ὑπηρέται τοῦ λόγου who had handled the Gospel material before him, and Stendahl suggests that these were *ḥazzānîm*, who taught in the Christian schools, and were something on the way to a rabbinic *bêth-hammidrāsh*.[36] In Matthew he sees the flowering of this movement. The Gospel contains considerable elements of church discipline, as in 18, rulings given to Peter, etc., which make it unsuitable for liturgical use.[37] It has much more in common with the *Didache*, which is only in the earlier part simple instruction for catechumens, but in the later chapters is designed to provide for the

---

[33] 'With whom my soul is well pleased' translates the Heb. against the Greek. Matthew's uninterest in any 'servant'–Christology is shown (*a*) by his suppression of the weak 'I will help him'; (*b*) by the choice of αἱρετίζω for ἐκλέγομαι to translate *bāḥar*; (*c*) by the insertion of the association-laden ὁ ἀγαπητός μου. See further below, pp. 329f.

[34] K.Stendahl, *SSM*.   [35] ibid., p. 34.
[36] ibid., pp. 35, 32.   [37] ibid., pp. 22ff.

regulation of the church.[38] Outside Christianity, the Qumran Community's *Manual of Discipline* gave an even closer parallel, with its ethical provisions, disciplinary rules, and eschatological note.[39]

The main part of Stendahl's book is a learned and balanced study of the citations in Matthew, in which he comes to conclusions similar to those I have briefly set out. He also comes to another conclusion which I have not set out, because it is more debatable. This is that the citations which Matthew introduces into the narrative with a formula, such as 'All this came to pass . . .' fall into a class by themselves and are marked by considerably greater freedom than the quotations shared with Mark and Luke and other non-formula quotations.[40] Now the freedom which Matthew uses in this group seems to Stendahl to have much in common with the method of the Qumran school of commentators on the Book of Habakkuk.[41] They, like Matthew, do not 'take refuge,' in Stendahl's phrase, in a single text, in the way that Luke and Hebrews and most of the NT authors do, in the LXX. They appear to draw freely on several texts, some of them known to us through the Peshitta, the Targum, the LXX, Lucianic Mss. etc., others apparently adapted *ad hoc* to the needs of the Covenanters' theology. All is designed to align the text and exegesis to the experience and teaching of the community, and the interpretation is introduced with the phrase: *pishrô 'al*, its meaning refers to. . . This formula appears to Stendahl to be the Qumran equivalent of the Matthaean formulas, just as the aligning of scripture with the community's experience, and the drawing on and expansion of different texts of scripture, seem to be a common method. The fact that the Covenanters drew on occasion on two readings of the same verse simultaneously seemed to find a ready echo in Matthew's use of the *yôtsēr*/*'ôtsār* readings at 27.9, though, as we have seen, this may be challenged.

These methods in common give Stendahl the *Sitz-im-Leben* of the Matthaean Gospel. It is the production of a *bêth-hammidrāsh*, where a group of learned Jewish Christians have laboured, like the Qumran scholars, to produce a Manual of Discipline for the Church. They have sought out variant readings, and used the best alternatives to accord with the tradition of the Lord's ministry: where readings gave out, they have been willing to targumize, to gloss the text, themselves. They have left their hallmark on the Gospel in the formulas intro-

---

[38] ibid., pp. 23f.   [39] ibid., pp. 23, 27.

[40] The distinction is not original to Stendahl, and is widely held; cf. F. van Segbroeck, 'Les citations d'accomplissement . . .', op. cit., p. 128. It is at least as old as Hawkins.

[41] Stendahl, *SSM*, pp. 183–202.

ducing these scriptural creations; their method was the Qumran method, *midrash pesher*.

It was perhaps unfortunate that Stendahl wrote his thesis in 1954, when the Qumran fever was at its first height. He has established that the handling of the Old Testament in Matthew is different from the more or less straight quoting of the LXX which we find elsewhere in the NT, and that we require the hypothesis of a more scholarly, more Jewish mind, and of a learned tradition familiar with the varieties of a text not yet finally set; and of a scholar's confidence to make bold in interpretation. But from this picture to the scriptorium by the Dead Sea is a long jump.

Jesus was a rabbi, but he was not a rabbi like Hillel with a concern for learning. Nothing looks more remote from a learned school than the Church of the Epistles, whose concern, like Matthew's, is the urgent evangelization of the world. It is Matthew who has given us the saying, 'You are not to be called Rabbi'; in his Gospel as in Paul there is one rabbi, who commands through the spirit. Stendahl does not distinguish the different degrees of learning. The *ḥazzān* whom he sees behind the Lucan prologue is often interchangeable with our *sôphēr*, the provincial teacher-cum-lay-reader, moving in a very different milieu from the *beth-hamidrash* of Jerusalem, aped in Qumran. Quite apart from the strangeness of such an institution in the first-century Church, we do not require it. A *sôphēr* whose profession was to teach the children the Hebrew and to understand it in their native Aramaic or Greek is quite sufficient.

The formula citations are deceptive. Put in a section by themselves, they contain 260 words, of which 146 are from the LXX, on Hawkins' counting, and 114 not. This contrasts with 251 LXX words and 61 non-LXX words in the non-formula citations. But the formula citations actually sub-divide:

	LXX	Non-LXX		LXX	Non-LXX
1.23	13	2	2.6	8	16
2.18	14	6	2.15	2	4
13.14f	47	1	2.23	0	2
13.35	6	4	4.15f	20	13
21.5	10	7	8.17	2	7
			12.18ff	20	31
			27.9f	4	21
	90	20		56	94

The five citations in the first column show an average of LXX words *higher* than the non-formula citations. Further there are quotations peculiar to Matthew without formulas in the Sermon on the Mount which have as heavy a non-LXX proportion as the first group (5.31, 33,43). There seems thus to be no basis for isolating the formula-citations. In the Marcan citations Matthew used the Marcan form, with minor amendments, sometimes towards the familiar already underlying LXX, sometimes with a recollection of the Hebrew or other freedom. In the new writing he is more free. Sometimes he uses the LXX: as the Church's Bible it is the best. Some of the citations, as 1.23, 21.16, require the LXX meaning. Luke, who knew only the LXX,[42] naturally takes only LXX quotations over from Q/Matthew: in fact he becomes wary after the Temptations. For the rest, whether introducing with a formula or not, Matthew uses his Hebrew, the Targum, and his wits, with or without a LXX base. To call this midrash is to use the proper rabbinic term: to call it pesher seems to me to obliterate the distinction between Matthew's restraint with, and the Covenanters' liberties with, Holy Writ.[43]

2 *New Testament Apologetic*

Fr Lindars[44] proposes a different line of explanation. The early Church used OT citation as a means of justifying Christian claims to Jewish opponents: the habit of quotation is thus apologetic, designed to show that the events surrounding Jesus had been foretold in God's providence.[45] This use of scripture developed from proof-texts of the Resurrection, the first doctrine to be proclaimed, rejected, and justified;[46] and spread to Jesus' sufferings, rejection, humble ministry, giving of the Spirit, second coming, incarnation, ascension, pre-existence. The earlier quotations will have been according to the Hebrew, or the Targum:[47] later the Greek church added LXX

---

[42] M. Wilcox, *The Semitisms of Acts* (Oxford 1965), claims the presence of considerable influence of Semitic texts, especially Targumim, on the forms of citation in Acts: but he takes these to be significant of earlier versions of speeches, especially of Stephen's and Paul's speeches in Acts 7 and 13, which came to Luke in Greek.

[43] W. H. Brownlee sets out as the two first principles of pesher interpretation: (1) Everything the ancient prophet wrote has a *veiled, eschatological meaning*. (2) Since the ancient prophet wrote cryptically, his meaning is often to be ascertained through a *forced or abnormal construction of the biblical text*—'Biblical Interpretation among the Sectaries of the Dead Sea Scrolls', *The Bibl. Archaeol.* 14 (1951); cf. Stendahl, *SSM*, p. 191. The differences, as well as the points in common with Matthew, need to be stressed.

[44] B. Lindars, *The New Testament Apologetic* (London 1961).

[45] ibid., pp. 19f.   [46] ibid., pp. 32–74, 252.

[47] ibid., p. 284, and *passim*.

quotations, and assimilated previous quotations to the LXX. Sometimes we can trace this development by observing different uses of the same text. Ps. 2.7,[48] for example, 'You are my son, today I have begotten you', is first used of the Resurrection, as in Acts 13.33; Heb. 1.5; 5.5, and later applied to the Baptism. Sometimes we can trace the development within a single citation, as in the mixed text of Matt. 12.18ff, citing Isa. 42.[49] Here the long citation justifies four different doctrines, which have been disputed at different stages of development:

(a) The Resurrection, proved by 'Behold my servant, my chosen', the earliest Christology, cited from the Hebrew against the Greek;

(b) the Baptism, proved by ὁ ἀγαπητός μου, ὃν εὐδόκησεν . . .', and by the giving of the Spirit;

(c) Jesus' patience in his Passion, proved by 'He will not wrangle or cry . . .'; and

(d) the Mission to the Gentiles, proved by 'In his name will the Gentiles hope', according to the LXX.

Only the last stage in the development can bear any relation to the context in the Gospel; here Matthew has misapplied words first seen as referring to Jesus' silence at his Passion, and taken to be a prophecy of his gentle ministry.

The theory is attractive, but it is a house of cards. We cannot claim that the Church's use of quotation was only, or even mainly, apologetic. Most of the quotations in Matthew, the Lord's birth at Bethlehem, his going to Egypt, settling at Nazareth, preaching at Capernaum, and so on, do not have an apologetic air: they proclaim the Lord who has fulfilled the scriptures, every jot and tittle. We cannot claim that quotation began with the Resurrection. Jesus must often have quoted scripture in his ministry, and at least the interpretation of his death in terms of the Exodus covenant must be historical, and ante-date the Church. The evidence does not permit of the Resurrection-to-Pre-existence, Hebrew-to-Greek construction. There is LXX in the quotations covering the most central doctrines, and non-LXX in the most marginal ones, as in Matthew's version of the end of Judas. The Resurrection use of Ps. 2.7 in Acts and Hebrews comes later in order of writing than the Baptism use in Mark 1. Above all, the neat construction does not fit the facts of the Matthaean picture. The context into which Matthew has inserted the long Isa. 42 quotation is Jesus' gentle ministry. In view of Pharisaic hostility (12.14), Jesus withdrew from there (15), and enjoined silence on those whom he had healed

[48] ibid., pp. 139–44.   [49] ibid., pp. 144–52.

(16), that he might fulfil Isaiah (18–21). But Matthew's context fulfils just those parts of the citation which are *not* in the LXX form; ἐρίσει and κραυγάσει are in neither Greek nor Hebrew, and much of v. 20 is not Septuagintal. The text fits the context perfectly: it is an arbitrary assumption, dignified by the name of 'the principles of Form-criticism', that it was earlier applied to a conjectured different situation, and then misunderstood and misapplied by Matthew. This does not prove Lindars wrong: it is merely that here, as so often, his construc-tion does not go with the evidence. A better solution is bound to be one with fewer presuppositions, and which allows for creative uses of different versions of scripture in the last, rather than the early, stages of composition.

3 *Matthew the Note-taker*

The fullest analysis of the material is given by an American scholar, R. H. Gundry, in *The Use of the Old Testament in St Matthew's Gospel*.[50] Gundry examines the allusive quotations as well as the formal ones, and although he sometimes seems optimistic in hoping to recover the text-form of words which have confessedly been adjusted to the syntax and context of the Gospel, it seems that he has established his conclusion that non-Septuagintal forms and LXX forms alike underlie much of the allusive material as well the formal citations: and that this goes for the allusive quotations in Mark as well. This conclusion is a further nail in the coffins of both Stendahl and Lindars. The LXX-element in the earliest allusive quotations, ante-dating Mark, goes against Lindars, who requires the LXX late; while the working together of Hebrew, Aramaic, and Greek texts before Mark is an embarrassment to Stendahl, whose Christian School is called into existence to explain this phenomenon for a section of Matthew.

Gundry's own theory is that the presence of Aramaic, Hebrew, and Greek elements in the pre-Marcan matter requires first-century Palestine as the origin of the Gospel tradition: 'For where else were these three languages used alongside one another?'[51] There is sufficient archaeological evidence to show that all three languages were in common currency among all classes, even in Judea: how much more in Hellenized Galilee. Matthew the publican would be one especially likely to be able to speak and write all three,[52] and the habit of note-taking is sufficiently attested in Greek and Jewish milieus to make it

---

[50] Leiden 1967, NT Suppl. xviii. Gundry includes a critique of earlier theories, including Stendahl's and Lindars', to which I am indebted.
[51] Gundry, *UOTSM*, p. 178.   [52] ibid., p. 183.

a likely hypothesis that he made a short-hand outline, *à la* Papias, of the Lord's deeds and words.[53] Included in this would be references to scripture in all three forms familiar to him, Hebrew, Targum, and LXX, intermingled from the beginning. Mark took over this material, and assimilated the formal quotations to the LXX, but left many of the allusive ones untouched: his Gospel was thus a conflation of the brief Ur-Matthäus and the oral Petrine tradition. Matthew himself wished to be loyal to the Petrine–Marcan Gospel, which he took as his own outline, and followed faithfully, adding his own matter, and further formal quotations, many of them carrying further his addiction to varying texts and targumic freedom.

The theory lacks the sophistication of the analysis. A mixed text for the earliest quotations of the OT in Greek is just what we should expect without the need for Matthew the publican and his notes. The Marcan Church knew enough Hebrew to know that *ba'al z^ebhûl* meant the lord of the house; the tradition had come from the hands of apostles who would naturally have known the Targum best, and the missionary outreach of the Church was in Greek to Greeks who used the LXX. We certainly cannot assume that Hebrew was unknown outside Palestine: how did the learned manage in Babylonia? But the worst feature of the theory is its requirement of Matthew twice over. It is not enough to have him drawing on all three textual traditions at an early stage: we require his knowledge of the LXX for the passages where he has brought Marcan quotations closer to the LXX, as well as his knowledge of other texts for the mixed citations. The slavish following of Mark in the second half of the Gospel, and especially in the Passion, where the insertions, such as Pilate's wife's dream, or the guards at the tomb, are of such a secondary stamp, is incomprehensible in an independent apostle-eyewitness. The theory is more complex than is needed, and lacks credibility.

The Sopher

I am much indebted to the scholars of whose solutions I have written critically, both for their painstaking analysis and for pointing the way to a solution which accords so well with what we have set out in the earlier chapters. Stendahl is right in seeing a development in use of scripture culminating in Matthew as the most learned of the NT authors; in positing a learning which was master of several traditions and authoritative to targumize on its own. Lindars is right in seeing the development of the use of texts from central to peripheral doctrines. Gundry is right in seeing Semitic and Greek OT texts at the base of

[53] ibid., p. 182.

the pre-Marcan tradition, and exemplified at its fullest in Matthew. Stendahl's and Gundry's evidence leads to a Christian scribe in Syria. Qumran parallels are interesting but distracting: the same use of scripture was habitual in mainstream Judaism, and was practised inevitably wherever Jewish children were taught and Jewish religion expounded with Pharisaic orthodoxy. Hebrew was what the children were taught to read: all we need is a community where Greek and Aramaic were spoken. Such a background is demanded by Matthew's alterations to Mark, as we have seen, and is generally conceded by the hypothesis of a Syrian provenance. The improbable, and contradictory, features of a *bêth-hammidrāsh* or of a note-taking apostle can be ignored. We have thus further, and massive, evidence of our Christian scribe, bringing forth from his chest scriptural treasures: treasures old in the original *miqrā'*, and in the authoritative[54] versions of Greek and perhaps Aramaic; and treasures new in the combinations and glosses which he is inspired to introduce on his own.

[54] Philo regarded the Hebrew and LXX as deserving of equal reverence, as sisters, *De Vit. Mos.* II.40.

7

THE NON-MARCAN TRADITIONS

Professor Bornkamm, in the opening sentence of a book of influential Matthaean essays, writes: 'It belongs to the established conclusions of Synoptic research that the first three evangelists were, in the first place, collectors and editors of traditions handed on to them.'[1] So speaks with measured, and perhaps ominous confidence, the orthodoxy of a hundred years. The manner of collection, the motive of editorship, may be matter for learned dispute. The presence of a line of traditions, hidden from us but extending behind the Gospels of Mark, Matthew, and Luke alike, is common ground, and an established conclusion of Synoptic research. Three great schools of critical archaeologists have turned over the soil of these narrow fields, and sifted it with devoted patience for two centuries. First the subsoil was examined, and the documents revealed from which our Luke and Matthew were formed. Then the strata beneath received attention, and the effect upon the tradition of oral transmission through a living Church was disclosed by the Form-critics. Finally redaction-critical scholars have re-examined the topsoil itself to observe the trend of the evangelists' own mind. But it has not been open to doubt that the archaeological image, and method, were sound. Troy was beneath our feet. Somewhere, at the bottom, was a residuum of true tradition of the life of Jesus; transformed, corrupted, superimposed upon, fossilized, and refashioned, by a hundred unnamed preachers and teachers, and three familiar evangelist-editors.

In the opening chapters of this book we have seen a number of reasons for thinking that Bornkamm's confidence is misplaced, at least as regards Matthew. So far from being an editor in the modern sense, comfortably tied by the reports he receives, selecting, smoothing, adjusting, Matthew has seemed to be an editor in the ancient sense, a *darshān*, rewriting and expounding as appeared necessary for edification. And so the archaeological image looks less persuasive: perhaps there is no Troy beneath the Matthaean field except where it overlaps the Marcan. The matter, it might be thought, could be resolved by digging. As we turn over each unit of the Matthaean material—as we shall do in Part II—we can sift it for evidence of an earlier tradition and see. But unfortunately a sifting of the evidence is not enough, for the confidence of the orthodox rests upon two planks,

[1] G. Bornkamm in *TIM*, p. 11.

the one evidential, the other *a priori*, and it is the combination of the two which has sustained the non-Marcan traditions hypothesis so long. It is to the *a priori* plank that we now turn.

Surely, it is said, the primitive Church was not a simple or highly cohesive society in which one set of traditions could conceivably dominate: the Church was a disorganized, scattered body, its mission proceeding by private initiative. As each man remembered, or had been told, traditions of Jesus, so they would be passed on and treasured in this community or that. Vagueness is inescapable in our picture of the development of the tradition; but whatever else, we should expect a manifold, not a single, tradition. I have called this an *a priori* argument because it is based not on the evidence of the text, or of any tradition about the text, but upon what we should expect, upon what must have been. It is in fact extremely difficult to find the case argued in form-critical works: it seems too obvious to require argument. The classic form-critical work, for example, Professor R. Bultmann's 450 page *The History of the Synoptic Tradition* assumes throughout the circulation of the tradition in the Palestinian and Hellenistic churches, and is content to say 'The history of the tradition is obscure.'[2] Hitherto obscurity has been enough because it has been possible to go on and say, 'And here, in Luke and Matthew, is the evidence before our noses': but now a second possibility is before us, that the non-Marcan material, at least in Matthew, is nothing but the evangelist's own writing. Perhaps the evidence is not evidence at all; but the *a priori* picture remains.

I should like to propose a second, slightly less obscure, *a priori* picture. There were, I would suggest, from the very beginning, three communities in the Church. We cannot accept Luke's account that the Twelve Apostles ruled a united church in Jerusalem, and supervised an ever-extending cloud of daughter-churches. Our earliest evidence is that the Eleven returned to Galilee after the Resurrection,[3] and this is borne out by the state of affairs referred to in Acts 6, where the Jerusalem church is not a unity, but is divided by language into two communities, one under the Apostles, one under the Seven. I have argued elsewhere[4] that the Hellenist church at Jerusalem arose spontaneously while the Eleven were in the north, and that this best

---

[2] (Göttingen 1931; 2e., E.T., 1968), p. 3. No attempt is made, similarly, to give a sketch of a history into which the theory could be fitted in M. Dibelius, *From Tradition to Gospel* (2e., E.T., London 1934); V. Taylor, *The Formation of the Gospel Tradition* (London 1935), pp. 168ff; or F. C. Grant, *The Gospels: Their Origin and Their Growth* (London 1957), pp. 52ff.

[3] Mark 14.28; 16.7; Matt. 28.16.

[4] *Type and History in Acts* (London 1964), pp. 189f.

accounts for its independence and vigour, as well as for the Marcan tradition: but however it arose, there were, in a matter of months, three communities of Christians—one in Galilee, presumably under the minor apostles, whom we may call the Nine, one in Jerusalem under the Three major Apostles and James, and one among the Hellenists, stemming from the community around Stephen and Philip.

It is hard to believe that the Nine went anywhere else but Galilee. They are not referred to in Paul's letters, or in the mission-story in Acts. They were not responsible for missions to Samaria or Antioch, and probably not to Damascus. They were not in Jerusalem when Paul called on Peter in the late-middle 30s,[5] nor when he and Barnabas and Titus returned in the late 40s.[6] Galilee was their home, and Luke testifies to the existence of flourishing churches throughout the tetrarchy, whose natural leader they would have been. The example of the Judean mission warns us not to look for more ambitious missionary zeal. Till persecution compelled them, it did not occur to the leaders of the Jerusalem church to sow the seed of the word beyond the city environs: then it was not the Three, but the more adventurous Hellenist leaders who took the word to such places as Samaria and Caesarea. The Church grew under the hand of humble, zealous, anonymous missionaries in Lydda, Sharon, Joppa, and the rest, and Peter staged his visitations to established churches as occasion required. Energy and imagination, then, which were lacking in the Three, we should not expect from the Nine. Whether as whole-time or occasional pastors, they will have tended the Galilean churches. The word will have increased and multiplied easily among those who had seen and heard the Lord. We have no evidence of missions from Galilee: a barrier of Gentiledom lay about them.[7]

It would be a mistake to regard the Galilean church as in any way cut off from the Judean Christians. Every year at the feasts the Galilean Christians would come to Jerusalem, and there would be happy reunions, with much reminiscing no doubt during the weeks of Unleavened Bread, Pentecost, and Tabernacles. On these occasions there would be a fusion of memories: stories forgotten in the north would be revived, and vice versa; problems of church order which had been settled on the basis of dominical logia in one region would be discussed and applied in the other. No doubt memories of marginal matters would go unmentioned, but in such constant fraternization

---

[5] Gal. 1.19.   [6] Gal. 2.1–10.

[7] The Lucan picture deserves credit in so far as Luke wishes to ground the Church's Mission in the activity of the Apostles, and is very restrained about it; cf. M. Hengel, 'Die Ursprünge der christlichen Mission', *NTS* 15.1, pp. 15–38.

in weeks of fellowship the memories of the two apostolic communities would be continually aligned.

The second Christian community was that of Judea, with its centre at Jerusalem. Peter, James, and John had come in early days to settle, and had gathered round them the mother-Church of Christendom, as it appeared to Luke. Peter was there in the mid-30s when Paul came to ask some questions,[8] and the three pillars—now with another James in place of the martyr—negotiated with Paul and Barnabas in the late 40s.[9] If there were any memories independent of the Three—Simon the leper, members of the Passover crowd, the 'goodman' of the upper room, etc.—they would soon become part of the Peter–James–John tradition. These were the inner circle of the apostles, and the repositories of *the* authentic paradosis. Luke bears witness to the importance of this aspect of apostleship in the Matthias story. He had been to Jerusalem and had seen apostles in action, and knew them as those who had 'companied all the time that the Lord Jesus went in and out among us, beginning from the baptism of John'. As witnesses of certain special incidents, the raising of Jairus' daughter, the Transfiguration, Gethsemane, individual post-Resurrection appearances, they enjoyed a natural pre-eminence over the Nine, and as time advanced they, or the survivors among them, were bound to enjoy increasing prestige as living links with Jesus' ministry. Even Paul, who was not anxious to incur obligation to the 'pillars', could not evade this indebtedness. All knowledge of the historical Jesus in Judea would be likely to stem from the Peter–James–John tradition, or PJJ, as we may abbreviate it.

The major work of mission was not, so far as our evidence goes, undertaken by the 'Hebrew' church, but by the third community, the Hellenists[10]—Stephen in Jerusalem, Philip at Samaria, the Negev, Azotus, Caesarea, Barnabas at Antioch, Cyprus and on, Saul in Nabat, Tarsus, Antioch and on; and so on. It is this community which had the natural contacts with the outside world, and which undertook all the missions for which we are able to give credit outside Palestine. Indeed, how should it be otherwise? They were the Jews who spoke Greek. Since they stemmed from a community in Jerusalem, the traditions they passed on must have been a part of PJJ, but our

---

[8] Gal. 1.18; cf. G. D. Kilpatrick, 'Galatians 1.18', in *New Testament Essays*, Studies in memory of T. W. Manson, ed. A. J. B. Higgins (Manchester 1959).
[9] Gal. 2.1–10.
[10] cf. E. Haenchen, *The Acts of the Apostles* (E.T., Oxford 1971), pp. 264–9, esp. p. 266, 'The whole story becomes transparently clear if Stephen had *led a mission* among his compatriots and erstwhile companions of the synagogue, the more so if that mission had been crowned with great success' (Haenchen's italics).

evidence would suggest that their knowledge of the paradosis was defective. Apollos was a leader of the Alexandrian church, but had a garbled account of the tradition on baptism. The Antiochene church required the supervision of Barnabas. Paul was catechized at Damascus, but required further enlightenment at Jerusalem. The pattern presented to us in Acts and the Epistles is of a series of attempts by the Jerusalem church to amplify and correct the defective Hellenist paradosis. Peter and John follow up Philip at Samaria; Peter goes round Judea confirming the churches; later he visits Antioch, and probably Corinth and Rome.

An *a priori* picture can thus be developed in contrast to the manifold tradition view normally assumed. Like all *a priori* pictures it is speculative: but where we have no facts we must use our imaginations with as much control as we can. The conclusion towards which we find ourselves led is in fact of one dominant tradition, the Peter–James–John tradition at Jerusalem, which was the fountain-head for the paradosis of the missionary, Hellenist, community, and a constant correcting and amplifying force. The Galilean tradition did indeed develop independently, but was liable to alignment with PJJ at the thrice-yearly Festal gatherings. We should expect some differences of memories in Galilee, but we should expect them to be marginal.

There, then, is an alternative view to the standard one. What evidence can we call upon to choose between them?

First, we are compelled to identify Mark's Gospel as the kernel of PJJ. Not only did Papias believe in the 130s that Mark had his material from Peter; and 1 Peter, perhaps thirty years earlier, speak of Mark as 'my son'; but the content of the Gospel shows a constant inside knowledge of the Christian story from Peter, James, and John's angle. The name Peter occurs 19 times in Mark, Simon 8 times, James and John 10 times each. In contrast none of the other eight faithful apostles is ever mentioned independently: their names are catalogued, and Andrew is twice appended to his brother. It is inconceivable that such a tradition should have had its origin in the community where the Eight were leaders; or that if it had, it should not have provoked an authoritative statement of PJJ from Jerusalem. Mark is a theological development of PJJ, perhaps a reaction from it even, no doubt a selection of it: but ultimately it is from the community of the Three that it has come.

There are two ways in which the posited non-Marcan traditions could have come to Matthew and Luke:

(*a*) They could have been part of the Galilean traditions which were *not* assimilated to PJJ. South Syria is the most likely locus for

Matthew's church: perhaps the church was founded from Galilee, and had such traditions from the beginning. Perhaps Luke met Galilean Christians—Mnason, the 'old disciple', could have been such—and questioned them for their memories of Jesus.
(b) They could have been part of PJJ which Mark omitted.

The trouble is that the new material in Matthew (to leave Luke aside for the moment) does not look like either of these. For (a) there is again the name test. One of the features that has led critics to postulate a non-synoptic tradition behind the Fourth Gospel is the mention of non-synoptic characters—Philip, Andrew, Thomas, Jude, Nathanael. Luke may have known a friend of Cleopas, Susanna, and Joanna the wife of Chuza. Where are such names in Matthew? There is one only, the apostle Matthew for the Marcan Levi: and here the apologetic motive, of supplying an apostle's name for one called, seems the obvious solution, rather than supposing that the evangelist knew better than Mark. The Matthaean material might have come early from a part of the Galilean church which had no contact with the Eight, but it would be surprising: much of the new material, for example in 10 and 18, is represented as private teaching to the apostles.

But the conclusive feature, which tells against an early independent development of PJJ just as much as a Galilean tradition, is that the non-Marcan materials in Matthew cover a different ground from Mark.[11] In all the narrative contexts which Matthew takes over from Mark I cannot think of one sentence in which it can be plausibly argued that Matthew was drawing on a parallel source. He improves the Greek, he abbreviates, he adds doctrinal glosses and clarificatory excursions, but there is no point at which we seem to have a rival wording, let alone a correction or factual addition. Why do we not, to take the example we have just used, think Matthew was the tax-gatherer? Well, if he were, surely, we feel, he would include some detail not in the austere Marcan account: or at least he would not be content to copy out the Marcan wording. And the same is true of all the Marcan narratives—the healing stories, the Jerusalem ministry, the Passion. Every commentator descries Matthew's tendencies; none, in modern times, descries a second source. Matthew *adds* one healing, the Centurion's Boy: he covers new ground, but he corrects nothing. When he does insert narrative additions into the Marcan context—Peter walking the water, the Coin in the Fish's Mouth, Pilate's Wife —they are just the points where we are most sceptical of them as history, that is, truly primitive tradition. In the teaching additions the

[11] cf. B. H. Streeter, *FG*, p. 502—'The narratives peculiar to Matthew . . . stand to Mark as the mistletoe to the oak.'

case is more controversial, but in the narrative we have nearly common ground. Either Matthew knew no other narrative source, or he totally disregarded it: the non-Marcan materials do not overlap the narrative sections of Mark, but cover new ground.

Now so far as the Matthaean material is concerned, this situation faces the Form-critics with a chasm not easily crossed. They have studied the evolvement of single pericopes, or groups of pericopes, within an unspecified church. But no church was concerned with one or a few pericopes: each church had, however defectively, a Gospel outline. It is true that the Gospel of Thomas provides us with an instance of a sayings-document without narrative content: but then a sayings-document without narrative content is the interest of a Gnostic community, and the Matthaean material is not tainted with Gnosticism. The church that carried the tradition of Jesus' answer to John Baptist in prison was a church that knew how he had healed the sick and cleansed the lepers. And are we to believe that this tradition was able to supply no independent account of a single healing that Jesus had done, of those described by Mark? Some non-Marcan tradition, according to the standard view, has supplied Matthew with more than 450 verses of material, some from PJJ perhaps, some from Galilee: of which a high proportion is widely believed to go back to logia and parables of Jesus. Is it really credible that so well-informed a source or sources had nothing, no facet of any story, no detail that escaped Mark's memory, no distinctive wording of any kind, that overlapped the Marcan narrative and was considered worthy of mention by Matthew: but that his community's own memories of the Lord's mighty works and Passion, made sacred by constant repetition over two generations, should, on the arrival of Mark, be consigned without a pang to the eternal oubliette? I do not think so. Nor is the situation made easier by the postulation of documents, Q and M. If some community, for reasons not easy to specify, did put together such documents, which in the case of Q include a narrative element, they can still hardly have been the community's total tradition of Jesus. The Church lived by the Gospel, not by collections of teaching, and Matthew's church as much as any. Nothing enables us to escape the dilemma: if Matthew had a good narrative before he had Mark, why did he throw it away and follow Mark, wording and all, like a lamb, never allowing his previous version to obtrude at all? If he did not have a good narrative, but some minimal substitute, how did he come by 300 verses of genuine dominical teaching?

The quickest solution would be to suppose that the new material in Matthew was the teaching side of the PJJ material, which Mark, whether by intention or ignorance, left by. This would be to desert the manifold traditions view, for now the non-Marcan traditions, like the Marcan, would all be developed in Jerusalem. But it is not an attractive solution. We can hardly believe that Mark had committed to memory the entire Jerusalem narrative tradition, and preserved it word for word. The same objection then applies as before. If the post-Marcan authorities were able to pass to Matthew so much genuine teaching, was there no point that was worth mentioning in all the narrative to pass also?

To prove the impossibility of the whole form-critical endeavour so far as it concerns Matthew is not within any man's power: it must suffice to show its implausibility. But what is the alternative? Are we to think that the Matthaean church had no tradition of the words and acts of Jesus before Mark's Gospel reached it other than a sketchier, perhaps a very sketchy, version of PJJ? Are we to suppose that the primitive communities together remembered no more of their Lord's teachings than is contained in Mark, with perhaps some additional matter preserved in Luke; and that, these apart, the pearls of Jesus' doctrine, instead of being gathered, treasured, and re-set on the form-critical pattern, were trampled under Galilean feet and lost forever? Yes, that is exactly what we are to think, for it is exactly the situation presented in the Pauline Epistles.

The attitude of Paul to traditions of Jesus' teaching is plain: where it is known it is authoritative. There are three passages in which Paul certainly cites Jesus, all in 1 Corinthians. There is a disputed reference in 1 Thessalonians. There are many places where there is sufficient wording in common between the Epistles and the Gospels to make a relationship likely or possible: and there are a number of places where we should have expected Paul to cite Jesus if he knew our Gospel tradition. The likeliest hypothesis into which we can fit these facts is that Paul was familiar with something less than our Mark, and that Matthew was familiar with our Pauline corpus.[12]

In 1 Cor. 7.10f Paul writes, 'To the married I give charge, not I but the Lord, that the wife should not separate from her husband . . . and that the husband should not divorce his wife. To the rest I say, not the Lord . . .'. This is a satisfactory passage exegetically, because two points about it are certain. First, the contrast between the Lord's command and Paul's own makes it clear that he is appealing to a tradition of a saying of Jesus. Second, the form of saying which we have preserved in Mark 10.11f exactly covers the points for which Paul claims dominical authority: 'Whoever divorces his wife and marries another, commits adultery against her; and if she divorces

---

[12] See ch. 8 below.

her husband and marries another, she commits adultery.' Only Mark makes reference to the possibility of the woman divorcing: this is mentioned neither by Matthew nor by Luke. Thus we have a strong presumption that Paul is appealing in detail to a saying from PJJ, later transcribed by Mark. The citation of Jesus' teaching settles the remarriage question without appeal to other arguments.

The situation is not so straightforward at 1 Cor. 9.14, 'In the same way the Lord commanded that those who proclaim the gospel should get their living by the gospel.' It is clear that appeal is being made to a tradition of Jesus' words, but the phrasing is so general that *prima facie* there is no reason for choosing between the Marcan charge to the Twelve, 'to take nothing for their journey . . . no bread, no bag, no money . . .' (Mark 6.8ff), and the more detailed *oratio recta* commands in Matt. 10.9ff, and Luke 10.4ff. Paul's method of argument is complex, but the Lord's commands are final. The question is whether as an apostle Paul has the right to be supported by the Church, and Paul answers it by appealing, first to reason ('Have Barnabas and I not the same right as Cephas and the rest', vv. 4–6), second to analogy (soldier, vineyard-worker, shepherd, v. 7), third to scripture (vv. 8–10; Deut. 25.4), fourth to more reason (if we sow spiritual good, we should reap some material good, vv. 11f), fifth to two further illustrations from scripture (Deut. 18.1, those who serve temple and altar get their living thereby), and only then to the words of the Lord. But this does not signify any less reverence for dominical authority. The case is argued at length because Paul feels so strongly about it. The Lord's words come last as the final blow.

But with which form of the tradition is Paul familiar? A reference so slight might incline us to think that he knew only the indirect speech of the Marcan form. What is evident is that Paul is not drawing on the Q epigram, 'The labourer deserves his food/wages', but that Matthew is drawing on something very like 1 Cor. 9, and Luke on something very like Matthew. Matthew has already compared the apostles to ἐργαταί going to work in the harvest at 9.37f: ἐργάτης and ἄξιος are both semi-Matthaean words, and τροφή is Matthaean. The rhythm is Matthew's favourite arcetic—cf. 'Sufficient to the day its evil' (AT)—favourite especially when closing a paragraph.[13] The only thing that is untypical in the saying is that the labourer is paid in truck: whereas Matthew is accustomed to his labourers being paid in cash (20.1ff; cf. the Matthaean ἀποδίδωμι, μισθός). This suggests that he was drawing on an earlier tradition where the payment was in kind: and we have in 1 Cor. 9 a reference to Jesus' command that

---

[13] See p. 79 above.

the apostles be paid alongside a series of illustrations from farm-labourers, all of whom are paid in kind. Paul uses none of the three Matthaean words in a passage that must have recalled the Q-logion to his mind if he knew it. Luke takes over two of the Matthaean words, but, being even more used to a cash economy, puts 'wages' for 'food'.

The third passage in 1 Corinthians is 11.23ff, the tradition of the Eucharistic Words. Our best authority in a highly complex subject is Jeremias,[14] whose conclusion is that the Marcan account is closest to Jesus' historical words, and that the Pauline version represents an expansion of this. It is at any rate certain that Paul's form is unrelated to Matthew's, which follows Mark closely with the addition of the phrase, 'for the forgiveness of sins'. The shorter Lucan text follows Mark's word-order against Paul's: if Luke wrote the longer text, it is certainly influenced by Pauline practice, and not vice versa.[15] There is thus no evidence from the three certain citations of Jesus by Paul of any knowledge of a non-Marcan tradition going back to Jesus. In 1 Cor. 7 Paul is close to Mark and against the other two. In 1 Cor. 9 the issue is more open, but if anything the Marcan tradition is Paul's most likely source.[16] In 1 Cor. 11 the Pauline is an expansion of the pre-Marcan tradition, against Matthew and the shorter text of Luke: there is no evidence, even in this liturgical area, that Paul goes back to anything more reliable than PJJ.

There is a fourth possible citation of Jesus at 1 Thess. 4.15: 'For this we declare to you ἐν λόγῳ Κυρίου, that we who are alive . . . shall not precede those who have fallen asleep. For the Lord himself will descend from heaven . . .' There are three difficulties in understanding these words.

(a) Does ἐν λόγῳ Κυρίου refer to a traditional saying of Jesus, as is maintained by Frame, Dibelius, Jeremias, and others?[17] Or is it merely the standard LXX expression for a word of Yahweh communicated through the Church's prophets, as Professor J. G. Davies has suggested?[18]

(b) It is not plain where the 'word of the Lord' begins or finishes. Was it, 'Those who are alive, who are left at the coming of the Lord, shall not precede those who have fallen asleep', that is, the words

[14] *The Eucharistic Words of Jesus* [*EWJ*] (E.T., London 1966), pp. 173–89.
[15] ibid., p. 156. [16] See pp. 345f below.
[17] J. E. Frame, *The Epistles of St Paul to the Thessalonians* (I.C.C. 1912), pp. 171ff; M. Dibelius, *An die Thessalonicher* (3e., Tübingen 1937), pp. 25f; J. Jeremias, *Unknown Sayings of Jesus* (E.T., London 1957), pp. 64ff; W. Forster and G. Quell, *Lord* (E.T., London, 1958), p. 105 (*TWNT* III, p. 1092).
[18] 'The Genesis of Belief in an Imminent Parousia', *JTS* XIV, Pt. I (1963).

immediately following the formula, with ὅτι at the beginning of
v. 16, amplifying from Paul's more general picture? Or is this just
the substance of the word of the Lord, which is then cited,
following the ὅτι, in 16–17a, finishing '. . . to meet the Lord in
the air'?[19]

(c) If we accept the latter, Jeremias' interpretation, and take λόγος
Κυρίου as a reference to a saying of Jesus, we are still not out of the
wood, because a few verses earlier Paul refers to 'instructions we
gave you through the Lord Jesus' (4.2), which plainly means
teaching based on that of Jesus and interpreted by the OT through
the inspired mind of the apostle.[20] Paul might therefore have in
mind a word of Jesus such as Mark 13.26f, 'Then they will see the
Son of Man coming in clouds . . . and then he will send out the
angels, and gather his elect from the four winds.' That the last
phrase must be interpreted to include the dead is certain from
Dan. 12.1f, the book of the Son of Man prophecies, 'At that time
your people shall be delivered, . . . and many of those who sleep in
the dust of the earth shall awake, some to everlasting life . . .', and
the sharing of the dead saints in the messianic judgement was a
part of Jewish eschatology which Paul presupposes. So even if
Paul is referring to a tradition of Jesus' words here, he still may
mean no more than what we have in Mark glossed with standard
Jewish teaching.

Beyond these citations, there are many passages where the wording
is sufficiently close to suggest a connection with our Gospel tradition:
but there is no passage where there is a plain dependence of Paul on a
non-Marcan tradition. Thus Rom. 13.7, 'taxes to whom taxes are due',
may recall Mark's, 'Render to Caesar the things that are Caesar's';
Rom. 14.14, 'I know and am persuaded in the Lord Jesus that nothing
is unclean in itself', probably goes back to something like Mark 7.19,
'Thus he declared all foods clean';[21] 1 Cor. 13.2, 'If I have all faith

---

[19] J. Jeremias in *New Testament Apocrypha* I, ed. R. McL. Wilson and W.
Schneemelcher (London 1963), p. 88.

[20] cf. W. Neil, in *Peake's Commentary* (1962), p. 999. I. B. Rigaux (*Les Epîtres
aux Thessaloniciens* (Paris 1956)) writes similarly, 'Nos préférences iraient donc,
non à une révélation particulière, mais à ce message apocalyptique de Jésus dans
le genre de celui rapporté par les synoptiques (Marc XIII et par.). Nous verrions
le contenu de cette parole dans IV. 16–17, ou nous trouvons précisément des
expressions parallèles aux révélations du discours eschatologique. Sur cette
parole du Maître Paul s'appuie pour introduire sa révélation.' See also L. Cerfaux,
Christ in the Theology of St Paul (1951; E.T., New York 1958), pp. 36–8.

[21] cf. C. H. Dodd, ῎Εννομος Χριστοῦ, *Studia Paulina* (in hon. J. de Zwaan,
Haarlem 1953), reprinted in *More New Testament Studies* (Manchester 1968),
p.144.

so as to remove mountains', recalls Jesus' words at Mark 11.23, 'Whoever says to this mountain, Be taken up . . . and does not doubt in his heart but believes . . .'. In all these cases the dependence of Paul upon PJJ, no doubt in a less accurate and structured form than our Mark, would seem a likely explanation.[22]

Now it is certainly true that there are similar verbal links between Pauline sayings and passages in Matthew. We have mentioned 'The labourer deserves his food' already as similar to 1 Cor. 9; or 'Be prudent as serpents and guileless as doves' (AT) is close to Rom. 16.19, 'I would have you wise to what is good, and guileless as to what is evil'; or 'Where two or three are gathered in my name, there am I' strongly recalls Paul's instruction in 1 Cor. 5.4, '. . . in the name of our Lord Jesus. When you are gathered, and my spirit is present . . .' (AT), both contexts being concerned with the excommunication of the unrepentant.[23] But we should be most unwise to assume from these links a dependence by Paul on a non-Marcan tradition: for Matthew was writing a generation after Paul, and might with equal ease be dependent upon him. The case will be argued as the passages occur in Part II.

One point, I do not know how weighty, should be made here. The theory of dependence by Paul on non-Marcan traditions in such passages as the ones I have just mentioned, seems to assume a familiarity with the tradition far beyond anything we might reasonably expect. 'I would have you wise to what is good, and guileless as to what is evil', does not recall to the casual reader the logion about serpents and doves. Paul is not slow to cite the OT, and we have shown that he regards a word of Jesus as final in any argument: why does he not say, 'Even as the Lord commanded, Be prudent as serpents . . .'? This failure to appeal to texts which would have been highly effective had he known them becomes critical on occasion. In 1 Cor. 6 he is arguing against the practice of Christians going to law, and gives eight verses to shaming the Corinthians by logic: why does he not ram the point home, 'Even so the Lord said, If anyone would sue you and take your coat, let him have your cloak as well'? Two chapters of 2 Corinthians are devoted to appealing for support for the collection (8–9). One cannot but admire the variety and quality of the arguments Paul uses: emulation, compliment, Christ's generosity in the incarnation,

[22] B. Gerhardsson (*MM*, p. 306) claims that Κυρίου ἐντολή in 1 Cor. 14.37 refers to a word of Jesus. The subject of the ἐντολή is that women should keep silence in church—in the light of form critical research, an ironic subject for Jesus to have legislated on!

[23] cf. C. H. Dodd, art. cit., p. 134, 'An obscure relation'; more fully in 'Matthew and Paul', in *New Testament Studies* (Manchester 1958), p. 60; see p. 154 below.

sweet-reasonableness, the precedent of Exodus, Paul's humiliation if they fail, the rewards of generosity, the citation of Proverbs and Psalms. Why does he not cap it all, 'So I give charge, not I but the Lord, Give, and it shall be given to you, It is more blessed to give than to receive, Lay not up for yourselves treasures on earth', or one of a dozen other Matthaean or Lucan texts? We cannot say, Paul prefers logic to citation, for he proves his point three times elsewhere in Corinthians by citing Jesus. The most obvious answer is that he does not quote the non-Marcan traditions because he does not know them.

Such a state of ignorance by Paul of the greater part of Jesus' teaching is in line with the theory of the diffusion of the tradition which I have developed in this chapter. Paul was converted in Damascus, and catechized by Ananias, himself a sketchily instructed Hellenist. He knew the great facts of the faith, as he says in 1 Cor. 11 and 15, and went off on mission to Nabat: two years later, aware of his limitations, he came to repair his lack of knowledge by a fortnight's visit to Peter. Many of the best-known stories about Jesus, and the logia most important for teaching, all from PJJ, would be passed on to him by Barnabas during their long association in Antioch and elsewhere. But for Paul, the lack of tradition of Jesus' words was no great handicap. He had the great facts of the faith to preach: the incarnation, the crucifixion, the resurrection, the gift of the Spirit, the Second Coming. For the rest there was the whole OT.

Professor Kilpatrick has adduced a number of considerations suggesting that Matthew's church is a city church in Syria: (a) πόλις is used 26 times against 8 times in Mark;[24] (b) the references to silver and gold as against the Marcan brass, especially 10.9, 'Get no gold or silver or brass in your purses', point to a wealthier community;[25] (c) Matthew calls Mark's Syrophoenician woman a Canaanite, and the word Canaan was used in the Semitic world for Phoenicia;[26] (d) the cities of the Levant were in general hellenized, while the country-side retained its Semitic character, so the Greek language and Semitic thought of the Gospel would both be accounted for.[27] It is also true that the stater (Matt. 17.27) was a Syrian coin.[28] We are able to add two further arguments to the same purpose: (a) the imagery of trade and credit is far more widely used in Matthew than in Mark (82 uses to 9) and suggests a mercantile background;[29] (b) the substitution of the small town of Gadara for the better-known Marcan Gerasa, as being nearer the Lake (8.28), and of Magadan for Dalmanutha (15.39),

[24] Kilpatrick, *Origins*, p. 124.   [25] ibid., p. 125.
[26] ibid., p. 132.   [27] ibid., p. 133n.
[28] cf. B Bekh. 49b; S–B I, p. 293. See also Streeter, *FG*, p. 504.
[29] See pp. 109f. above.

both show a familiarity with the geography of the Decapolis which is best explained if the evangelist lived not far away.

The principal cities in southern Syria are Tripolis, Berytus, Sidon, Tyre, and Ptolemais on the coast, and Damascus inland. There were churches in Damascus in the 30s, and at Tyre and Ptolemais, at least, in the 50s. Such communities might be founded as extensions of Philip's evangelism at Caesarea, thirty miles south of Ptolemais, or of the Antiochene mission in the north of the province. In either case they would be Hellenist foundations, and heirs to the same weakened form of PJJ which was all that Paul had. There is nothing in Matthew to suggest one origin rather than the other. The church at Antioch, so far from being steeped in Pauline theology, went over to hard-line Christian Judaism to a man, Barnabas and all, at the first puff of pressure from 'those of James':[30] they were basically as conservative as everyone else, only they had let the god-fearers in without circumcision. The circumcision issue is dead in Matthew: that was what the Jerusalem Council had been about, and the Pauline view had triumphed. Matthew could not commend the Gentile mission as enthusiastically as he does unless he had accepted this as a *fait accompli*. But for a church that had a competent *sôphēr* and a majority of Jews, as would be likely in the Syrian cities with their large Jewish populations,[31] a generally conservative position on the Law is just what we should expect, if the apostles of the church were, shall we say, Manaen and Symeon called Niger.

One straw in the wind that points to Antiochene foundation is the names of the church officers. In the Pauline churches, and no doubt elsewhere, these were called elders, ἐπίσκοποι, and deacons: at Antioch they were prophets and teachers.[32] Teacher (διδάσκαλος) is a general Lucan word for a number of technical Jewish terms that appear in Matthew—σοφός, scribe, rabbi, καθηγητής.[33] Christian prophets come in Matt. 10.41; 23.34, and there are warnings against false prophets at 7.15ff; 24.11,24. At 23.24 prophets and wise men and scribes, or as Luke would say, prophets and teachers, are linked together. At Caesarea there were prophets, but Philip was called ὁ εὐαγγελιστής.

In the 50s and 60s such a church would continue very much as its

[30] Gal. 2.13.
[31] J. Juster (*Les Juifs dans l'Empire Romain* (Paris 1914), pp. 194–7, 210), provides some details of Jewish colonies in Syria, and reckons the total at about a million. Even if (as I should suspect) this is a considerable exaggeration, the most populous Jewish settlements were certainly in Egypt, Syria, Asia Minor, and Rome.
[32] Acts 13.1.   [33] cf. Kilpatrick, *Origins*, p. 126.

members had before their conversion: the same Law, written and oral, was valid on the authority of the Sanhedrin—they were not less Jews because they were Christians, but more; the same pattern of synagogue worship would be maintained round the year.[34] Faith in Christ would show itself only in the Christian exposition of the Law in sermons, and in the Eucharist on Saturday nights: and, we may hope, in a deeper spiritual life. Prayer would be made for the conversion of Israel as a whole: there would be strained relations with synagogues not accepting Jesus as Christ. After 64 if not before, copies of the Pauline letters would be received. In his lifetime Paul was a controversial figure, as Cranmer was in the Church of England. After his martyrdom Cranmer was whitewashed by all Protestants, and we may expect the same for Paul. He was the good apostle who had spread and died for the faith, and his letters were para-scriptural to the apostolic fathers, as far back as they take us.[35] Galatians and parts of Romans would be stiff reading in the Matthaean church: as 2 Peter says, 'There are some things in them hard to understand, which the ignorant and unstable twist to their own destruction, as they do the other scriptures' (3.16). But the religious mind is accommodating: think of the millions of Christians who have read Matt. 23.2f, for 1900 years, 'The scribes sit on Moses' seat: so practise and observe whatever they tell you', without so much as buying a copy of the Mishnah.

In the 70s worship would be revolutionized by the arrival of Mark. The full wealth of PJJ was now at Matthew's disposal. The skilful *sôphēr* found himself able, week after week, to expound OT texts in terms of the new tradition, and vice versa: drawing sometimes on the Pauline letters, and sometimes on the stock of rabbinic wisdom, especially in the matter of parables. The narrative was the Marcan narrative, for it supplanted a thin thing, a Form-critics' PJJ, worn down to its bones: the full body of Mark's story, backed by the authority of Peter, left nothing of the older tradition worth preserving. The additional matter was an amplification of Mark, because it was Matthew's midrash. As year followed year, a more and more perfect amplification could be provided: and when its author felt it could not be bettered, it could be written down and passed out to other churches.

In the 80s the Jewish authorities at Jamnia authorized the insertion in the synagogue sabbath liturgy of a curse on the Nazarenes and other sectaries, the so-called Birkath-ha-Minim. All Christians were thus excommunicated. Jews would no longer beat them in synagogues or chase them from town: they were extirpated. On the other side, it

---

[34] See pp. 172–94 below.
[35] cf. R. M. Grant, 'The New Testament Canon', in *The Cambridge History of the Bible* I, pp. 284–308.

became impracticable to expect Christians to subscribe to the Temple tax, or to conform to the Jamnia regulations: they no longer belonged. Matthew is written before this crisis: he belongs to Jewry and expects to be persecuted for his heterodoxy. So the Gospel was probably written within a couple of years either way of A.D. 80. This gives time for Matthew to embroider Mark, and for Luke to embroider Matthew.[36]

Such a conclusion is a challenge to 'the established conclusions of Synoptic research', for it means that Matthew collected no traditions, and his editing was what other people call composing: but it fits with the best picture that we can form of the diffusion of the memories of Jesus, and with the nature of the Gospel, in a way that the established conclusions do not.

[36] Kilpatrick (*Origins*, pp. 128f) argues for a date in the 90s: (*a*) he sees the Birkath-ha-Minim as the cause of the synagogue–church tension in Matthew; (*b*) there are misunderstandings of earlier Semitic traditions, as in the Death of Judas story; and the Trinitarian formula in 28.19, among other material, is late. On the other hand (*c*) Nerva's abolition of the poll-tax in 96 would make a later date than that impossible in view of 17.24ff. But the Birkath-ha-Minim produced a situation in which the Matthaean position to Judaism would become untenable almost overnight; cf. on Matt. 5.11/Luke 6.22, pp. 279f. The XIIth 'Benediction' ran: 'For persecutors let there be no hope, and the dominion of arrogance do Thou speedily root out in our days; and let Christians and *minim* perish in a moment, let them be blotted out of the book of the living and let them not be written with the righteous' (*Berakot* (*Die Mischna*), ed. O. Holtzmann (Giessen 1912), cited in W. D. Davies, *Setting of the Sermon on the Mount* [*Setting*] (Cambridge 1964), p. 275). The Christians were thus 'delivered to Satan', 'removed from among' the Jews (1 Cor. 5.1–5), and became 'as Gentiles and tax-collectors' to them (Matt. 18.17); cf. D. Hare, *Persecution*, pp. 125ff; R. Hummel, *Die Auseinandersetzung zwischen Kirche und Judentum im Matthäusevangelium* (Munich 1963) pp. 28–33.

I do not accept that Matthew has misunderstood any earlier Semitic traditions, and contest such suggestions in the following chapters. There is no evidence of the lateness of the Trinitarian formula, if lateness is to mean the 90s rather than the 70s. Pauline Christians were baptized into Christ (Jesus), and in the Lucan church it was in, on, into the name of (the Lord) Jesus (Christ). But Paul uses the Trinitarian combination several times, and since the Spirit is an essential part of Pauline doctrine of Baptism, it was inevitable that the threefold name should come to be used. This use must have developed at some stage in parallel with the single name, and there is nothing whatever to show that this development is post-Lucan. It occurs in *Did.* 7.1, alongside the single name at 9.4; cf. D. G. Delling, *Worship in the New Testament* (Göttingen 1952; E.T., 1962), pp. 55–9.

8
MATTHEW AND PAUL

Matthew, we have maintained, was a Christian scribe; and if so we should expect to see in his book the doctrine of the rabbis as well as their characteristic methods of targum and midrash, their free writing of parables and poetic epigram. It is well known that such an expectation is not misplaced; both in phrasing and content we find that Matthaean changes of Mark, and Matthaean new material, often run parallel with rabbinic expressions. But such parallels will not suffice to explain more than a proportion of the doctrinal innovations in Matthew. For Matthew is not merely a scribe, but a Christian scribe; and the rabbi to whom he owes far and away the most is Paul.

This statement is so far a challenge to orthodox opinion that before we can begin to marshal the evidence for it, we must fend off three prior objections which may be lurking in the reader's mind.

1. 'Are not Paul and Matthew the most disparate of the NT authors? Surely Paul, if there is any sense to the old Tübingen view, represents the open, Gentile-church theology, with its abolition of the ritual and oral Law; while Matthew embodies the view of the Jewish church, maintaining the validity of the whole Law, and viewing the Gentile mission with reservation?' No, I do not think so. Dr Dodd puts the matter better when he writes, 'Matthew represents a first approach from the Jewish–Christian side to the Catholicism which was to provide the Hegelian synthesis.'[1] The evidence is that Matthew was a Jewish Christian; but the evidence is also that he is a Jewish Christian under influence of Pauline words and Pauline theology, and we can see the struggle of the two views in his book.

2. 'Granted that there are phrases and ideas in common between the two authors, is not the simplest and most probable explanation that both Matthew and Paul belonged to churches in which were current floating traditions of words of the Lord? Such has been the working basis of Form Criticism these last fifty years. What more natural than that such logia should turn up in slightly different form in Matthew and in the Epistles?'[2] We have seen in the last chapter how uncertain are the foundations of the form-critical view of Matthew in general.

[1] C. H. Dodd, 'Matthew and Paul' (1947) in *New Testament Studies* (Manchester 95 3), p. 53.
[2] Such was Dodd's own conclusion, op. cit., p. 66.

But whenever we come to analyse logia which Paul and Matthew have in common, we shall find reasons for thinking that the Matthaean form is secondary, and presupposes something like the Pauline form. We have already seen an example of this in 'The labourer deserves his food'. Two further instances may suffice:

1 Thess. 5.2	Matt. 24.43
The day of the Lord will come like a thief in the night.	If the householder had known in what part of the night the thief was coming, he would have watched . . . The Son of Man is coming . . .

Paul gives the general simile: the unexpectedness of the Parousia will be like the unexpected coming of a thief. Matthew has made this into an allegory. The thief is now the Lord, the Christian is the householder.

1 Cor. 5.3–4	Matt. 18.17, 20
I have already pronounced judgment on the man who has done such a thing *in the name* of the Lord. When you *are gathered*, and my spirit is present, with the power of our Lord Jesus, you are to deliver this man to Satan . . .	If he refuses to listen even to the Church, let him be to you as a Gentile and a tax-collector . . . For where two or three *are gathered* in *my name*, there am I in the midst of them.

The coincidence of Greek words is quite striking, ἐν τῷ ὀνόματι τοῦ Κυρίου Ἰησοῦ συναχθέντων ὑμῶν in Paul, συνηγμένοι εἰς τὸ ἐμὸν ὄνομα in Matthew, and the context of a church excommunicating is the same. Dodd correctly argues[3] that the Matthaean version has been adapted to the epigram known to us from the Pirqe Aboth, 'When two sit and there are between them words of the Torah, the Shekinah rests between them.'

3. 'What possible grounds are there for thinking that Matthew had ever seen the Pauline epistles?' Dodd himself writes, 'The presumed sources of this Gospel [sc. Matthew] and the process of its composition . . . would seem to belong to a milieu remote from that of Paul . . . in Matthew traces of [Pauline] influence are indeed difficult to find.'[4] Dodd does not really mean that they are difficult to find: the excellent essay in which these sentences occur expounds 35 or 40 of them. It is just assumed as impossible that Matthew could have read Paul and been influenced by him. Nor should we blame Dodd: one of the most widespread, and, if I may say so, one of the most idiosyncratic presuppositions of this century in NT scholarship has been the watertight compartment view of the churches. The picture given us in

[3] ibid., pp. 58–61; M Aboth 3.2.   [4] ibid., pp. 53f.

Acts and the Pauline Epistles is of the Hellenist apostles and their lieutenants in continual movement, linking the churches together in a constantly renewed network of visits and letters. Paul, Barnabas, Mark, Silas, Timothy, Luke, Sosthenes, Aquila, Apollos, Erastus, Sopater, Aristarchus, Gaius, Secundus, Tychicus, Trophimus, Phoebe, Chloe's people, Peter, Stephanas, Fortunatus, Achaicus, Titus and the anonymous brother, certain of James, Epaphroditus, they post o'er land and ocean without rest, from the late 40s to the early 60s. The Pastorals, if we allow their evidence, extend the period and the area.[5] Yet orthodoxy would have us believe that in the 70s and 80s the Church of God was like the battleship *Bismarck*, subdivided by watertight bulkheads, so that those who would pass from one to the next cannot, with the treasures of Pauline theology, or the L, M, and Q logia. How should this be? The letters treasured in Corinth or Thessalonica, sent round Galatia, even ordered by the apostle to be read in other churches such as those in Colossae and Laodicea, these were soon to form the Pauline corpus. If we locate Matthew in Syria, was not Paul fourteen years at Antioch, his theology formative and dominant in the mother-church of the Syrian mission? What milieu was there in the 60s even (unless perhaps Jerusalem) remote from that of Paul? After his martyrdom, what indeed? Nothing is more natural than that Matthew should have read the whole Pauline corpus; as a scribe, trained to reverence the Aboth, and as a Christian evincing a marked reverence for the apostles, we should expect him to treat Pauline doctrine as authority.

Many features of the Matthaean teaching on God are standard rabbinic doctrine, frequently expressed in Greek translations of standard rabbinic terminology. 'Our Father in Heaven' is a common rabbinic phrase,[6] as is the *malkûth hashshāmayim*, the Kingdom of Heaven, only and commonly found in Matthew. The rabbis often compare God to a king, as Matthew does in two parables, Mark never. The God who sees in secret is a rabbinic commonplace;[7] he searches the hearts in prayer in Rom. 8.27 also. His providence is well known: in the Mishnah it is said that his mercy extends even to a sparrow's nest.[8] The two norms of God's character in rabbinic thought are the *middath haddîn* and the *middath hāraḥᵃmîm*, the norm of judgement and the norm of mercy:[9] κρίσις and ἔλεος are two

---

[5] The same picture is valid for the sub-apostolic period too, of constant linking and communication between churches; cf. M. Goguel, *The Primitive Church* (1947; E.T., London 1964), pp. 171–5.

[6] Moore, *Judaism* I, p. 359.   [7] ibid., pp. 368f, 372.

[8] M Meg. 4.9; Moore, *Judaism* I, p. 365; cf. Matt. 10.29,31.

[9] Moore, *Judaism* I, p. 387.

favourite Matthaean concepts—and on the human side also, judgement and mercy and Pauline faith are the weightier matters of the
Law.[10] The rabbis prayed for and looked forward to the hallowing of
God's name: as is well known, almost all the Lord's Prayer can be
paralleled from Jewish prayers.[11] The two main rabbinic periphrases
for God, his wisdom and his spirit,[12] are found in Matthew.

For the expressly Christian doctrines, time and again we find Paul's
teaching reappearing, if not actually echoed, in Matthew.

Christology

Jesus' *dual sonship*, of the seed of David according to the flesh, of God
in power (Rom. 1.4) is testified by Mark, but is emphasized by
Matthew. The first verse of the Gospel and the second fourteen of the
Genealogy make concrete the Davidic sonship, which is a frequent
theme later in the Gospel. The virginal conception gives a physical
basis to the divine sonship, which is stressed in the Temptations—'If
you are the Son of God . . .' and *passim.*

Jesus' *authority*, especially after the Resurrection, is a constant
Pauline theme: at his name every knee should bow (Phil. 2.10); God
has put all things under his feet (Eph. 1.22;[13] 1 Cor. 15.27). Matthew
exalts Jesus' authority beyond what is expressed in Mark: 'All things
have been delivered to me by my Father' (11.27); 'All authority in
heaven and on earth has been given to me' (28.18).

Jesus' *unique relationship* with the Father is expressed at its highest
in Col. 1.19: 'In him all the fulness of God was pleased to dwell'.
Although Matthew does not go as far as this, he makes more explicit
the relationship which is set forth in the dominical 'Abba' when he
writes, 'No one knows the Son except the Father, and no one knows
the Father except the Son' (11.27). 'The Son' absolutely is found in
Paul at 1 Cor. 15.28; 'the Father' absolutely at Eph. 2.18; Col. 1.12.
The exploitation of this usage is left to St John.

Jesus' *glory* is emphasized in Matthew over Mark in the Transfiguration in that Matthew adds, 'and his face shone like the sun'
(17.2). The detail of Moses' face shining (Exod. 34.29ff), which is the
type of this passage, is expounded by Paul in 2 Cor. 3.7ff.

The *relationship of Christ to the Church* is expressed in the doctrine
of the Body, which can find no part in a Gospel: but it is often taught

[10] 23.23.
[11] Moore, *Judaism* I, p. 424.   [12] ibid., p. 416.
[13] I accept Pauline authorship of Ephesians: those who do not will know how to
discount my arguments.

by means of the prepositions ἐν and σύν—'in you', 'crucified with Christ', 'raised with him'. Matthew introduces this doctrine at two significant places: at the beginning of the Gospel Jesus is proclaimed by the angel as Emmanuel, translated 'God with us'; at the end he promises the Eleven, 'Lo, I am with you always.'[14] Matthew also introduces the teaching that where two or three of the apostles meet, he is there ἐν μεσῷ αὐτῶν. While these expressions are hardly adequate to the full force of the Pauline teaching, they are a fuller expression of it than anything in Luke.

The Pauline teaching of *saving* from sin is also introduced as the interpretation of Jesus' name—'he will save his people from their sins' (1.21)—and Matthew glosses the words of the Eucharist, 'This is my blood of the covenant, which is poured out for many *for the forgiveness of sins*'. The last expression is not common in Paul but occurs at Col. 1.14; cf. Eph. 1.7. The word ἀφιέναι is introduced redactionally three times into Marcan passages. A favourite word of Paul for the same thing is justification, which occurs once in Paul's sense at Matt. 12.37, 'By your words you will be justified'. An attempt has been made to maintain that Matthew uses δικαιοσύνη in something of the Pauline sense,[15] of the righteousness of God, but I agree with Schlatter[16] and Strecker[17] that this is vain. Matthew's idea of righteousness is through and through rabbinic, something to be attained by man. It is facile, however, to conclude from this that Matthew was uninfluenced by Paul: after all Peter lived with Jesus the length of the ministry, and emerged a vacillating legalist. Nevertheless the Gospel stories of the faith of sinners in Christ, and his acceptance of them enshrine the justification teaching; the goodness by which Matthew's vineyard-owner pays a full penny to those who have worked but one hour sounds like an echo of Pauline grace; and he comes close to expressing it in words when he writes 'The tax-collectors and harlots believed [John] . . . they go into the kingdom of God before you' (21.32,31). Matthew's 'before' is a meiosis: he did not think the Jewish authorities would go in ever. The Pauline emphasis on faith is also near to Matthew's heart: 'Be it done for you as you have believed', 'Not even in Israel have I found such faith', 'Do you believe that I am able to do this?' 'If you have faith and never doubt.'

---

[14] W. D. Davies (*Setting*, pp. 97f), speaks of 'a real identification' of apostles and Lord, and cites 10.24,40; 18.5,10; 25.37ff.
[15] See G. Schrenk, *TWNT* II, p. 200; E. Lohmeyer, *Das Evangelium des Matthaus* [Lohmeyer], ed. W. Smauch (3e., Göttingen 1962).
[16] A. Schlatter, *Der Evangelist Matthäus* (Stuttgart 1929), p. 140: but I shall argue for a double meaning at 5.6; see p. 262 below.
[17] *WG*, pp. 149–57.

Ethics

Ethical teaching is scanty in Mark, and is greatly expanded in Matthew: the greater part of the new Matthaean doctrine may be paralleled in Paul, often verbally, and often independently of the rest of the NT.

Mark records Jesus as saying that the love of God and of our neighbour constitutes the two great commandments. Paul says that Commandments VII, VI, VIII, X and any other commandment are summed up in this sentence, 'You shall love your neighbour as yourself'. Love is the fulfilling of the Law: he who loves his neighbour has fulfilled the Law. Paul is free to be as one outside the Law when it is expedient—not that he is without law towards God, but he is ἔννομος Χριστοῦ, under Christ's law. The search through the Epistles for a series of provisions of this law of Christ has been ill rewarded:[18] it seems wise to take ἔννομος Χριστοῦ in line with Rom. 13. Christ's law has one provision only, ἀγάπη, and we are to interpret it by being imitators of Christ. Matthew expounds the Pauline view. The two great commandments are a *kelāl*, a summing up: 'On these two commandments depend all the law and the prophets.' The ethical teaching of the Sermon may be summed up in the Golden Rule: 'For this is the law and the prophets.' To the rich young man Jesus sums up the commandments: Commandments VI, VII, VIII, IX, V, and 'You shall love your neighbour as yourself'—against Mark's 'Do not defraud'. 'You shall love your neighbour' in a full Christian interpretation is similarly the sixth and last of a series of Christ's Commandments in the Sermon, also beginning with murder and adultery. The Sermon is Matthew's exposition of the νόμος Χριστοῦ. Christ has come to fulfil the law, and what is laid upon the Christian is no series of casuistical rules, but the exemplification of ἀγάπη: the love of our neighbour (ch. 5), of God (6.1–18), and of the poor (6.19–34). It is true that Matthew assumes the validity of the whole Torah, written and oral, a doctrine which Paul laboured to extirpate, *contra mundum*: but then Paul was *contra mundum*, and we could hardly expect him to have succeeded in expelling nature with his fork. Matthew is expounding Mark first with the aid of Pauline doctrine, and second with that of the rabbis: and we can not reproach him with not normally giving Paul the highest seat.

Scandal and scandalizing are themes that bulk large in Matthew, and Paul, against Luke, and for the noun, Mark (σκανδαλίζω Matthew 14, Mark 8, Luke 2, Paul 4; σκάνδαλον Matthew 5, Mark 0, Luke 1,

---

[18] C. H. Dodd, ''Ἔννομος Χριστοῦ', in *More New Testament Studies* (Manchester 1968), pp. 144ff.

Paul 6). The whole of Rom. 14 is given to the care of the man who is weak in faith, and the peril of scandalizing him. Who is scandalized, and Paul does not burn? 1 Cor. 8 carries the same theme. Similarly Matthew teaches that Christians should pay their Temple half-shekel still lest they scandalize the Jews; that the apostles must beware above all of scandalizing the little ones who believe in Jesus (Paul's men weak in faith, his weak brother); scandals must come, but woe to those responsible. συμφέρει, from the same context, is another Matthaeo–Pauline word (Matthew 4, Mark 0, Luke 0, Paul 7).

Paul and Mark follow the radical dominical tradition on divorce, which Matthew glosses in favour of the Shammaite doctrine. But Paul holds even more radical views on marriage itself. In view of the impending distress he thinks it is better to remain in one's present condition, i.e. for the unmarried to remain single, as he does: but if they cannot exercise self-control, it is better to marry than burn. Matthew adds to the Marcan divorce teaching in the same sense, in a characteristic rhythm: it is not expedient to marry—some are eunuchs born, some made, some have kept themselves as eunuchs for the kingdom's sake. Nevertheless, not all men can receive this precept, but only those to whom it is given.

Matthew introduces the prohibition of Christian swearing: let their ναί be ναί and their οὐ οὐ, for more than this is of the evil one. It is hard to believe that this is not connected with Paul's protests in 2 Cor. 1.17: 'Do I make my plans like a worldly man, so that with me should be the ναί ναί and the οὐ οὐ?' (AT). The meaning is rather different: Paul means he does not vacillate, say ναί and οὐ one after the other; Matthew that ναί ναί and οὐ οὐ are quite enough to guarantee a Christian's statement of intention. But Paul's protest arises naturally in the course of his self-defence; and it would be equally natural for Matthew to take his words of a serious statement of intention as a paradigm for Christians, who should abjure swearing. ὁ πονηρός, the devil, is also Matthaeo–Pauline (Matthew 4, Mark 0, Luke 0, Paul 2).

Matthew has Jesus foreswear the *lex talionis*: Christians are not to oppose the evil one in physical attack, in lawsuit (κριθῆναι), in impressment, in solicitation for money. He is very close to Paul: 'Repay no one evil for evil . . . do not be overcome by evil, but overcome evil with good'; 'To have lawsuits (κρίματα) at all with one another is a defeat for you. Why not rather suffer wrong? Why not rather be defrauded?'; 'You bear it if a man takes advantage of you, . . . or strikes you in the face'. Matthew stresses the Christian's duty to rejoice in persecution, and be glad; and to pray for those who persecute him. So had Paul before him: 'Bless those who persecute you; bless and do not curse them'; 'Rejoice always'; 'We rejoice in our sufferings'; 'The sufferings of this present time are not worth comparing with the glory . . .'. Matthew sums up, 'You must be perfect'—τέλειος, another Matthaeo-Pauline word (3/0/0/8)—'wisdom among the perfect', 'as many as be perfect' (AT).

Matthew's warning against judging lest one be judged is likewise a familiar Pauline theme. 'Therefore you have no excuse, O man, whoever you are, when you judge another; for in passing judgement upon him you condemn yourself . . . We know that the judgement of God rightly falls upon such.' The whole of Rom. 14 is given to this topic, and Paul revolts against human judgement in 1 Cor. 4 and elsewhere. Matthew says that those who mourn are blessed, i.e. those who repent of their sins, and judge themselves: so Paul, 'Ought you not rather to mourn?' Paul would have the Romans wise to what is good and guileless (ἀκεραίους) to what is evil: Matthew, with his characteristic φρόνιμος, animal imagery, and pardic rhythm, has, 'Be ye prudent as serpents and guileless (ἀκέραιοι) as doves' (AT).

Evangelization

Matthew takes over the expressly Pauline doctrine of Mission, and presents it whole. The apparent contradiction in Matthew between a particularist view and a universalist view arises entirely from the failure to perceive that the Pauline teaching is assumed.

Jesus himself had, according to Mark, limited himself virtually to the Jews. He preaches and ministers to Israel, and shows himself reluctant to heal in Phoenicia. Nevertheless heal he does, a crumb of hope for the future. Matthew underscores this emphasis: the lost sheep of the house of Israel, the theologically significant Canaanite woman for Mark's colourless Syrophoenician, silence, embarrassment, and more decent reluctance to breach the dam. But he gives two crumbs of hope for the future, a Gentile centurion's boy as well as a Canaanite woman's girl. The former is as reluctant a miracle as the latter: the healing is again done at a distance, and there is amazed praise for the faith of the centurion as for the woman of Canaan.[19]

Both Paul and Matthew have a low opinion of Gentiles. Non-Jewish Christians are Gentiles no more, but members of God's Israel: but for the rest Paul warns his flock not to live in the passion of lust like the Gentiles who know not God, and he told Peter in a heated moment that he lived like a Gentile (ἐθνικῶς). So Matthew recognizes that Gentiles seek after earthly things, salute each other for what they

---

[19] Many commentators punctuate 8.7 as a question: ἐγὼ ἐλθὼν θεραπεύσω αὐτόν;The emphatic ἐγὼ certainly bears this out, and stresses Jesus' reluctance.

can get out of it, babble their prayers away, lord it over each other, and are to be avoided by the godly.

Paul said the gospel was God's power for salvation to all believers, first the Jew and then the Greek. Since Jesus' healing mission typifies the saving power of the gospel, Matthew establishes the theological order from the start: the first sufferer Jesus heals is an Israelite leper, the second is a Gentile boy. Similarly he sets out the commission to evangelize and the cost in persecution twice. In 10 the Apostles are directed only to the lost sheep of the house of Israel, and are promised betrayal, trial, and martyrdom in their own land. In 24 the disciples' testimony is to be given to all nations, they will be hated by all nations, this gospel will be preached throughout the world, and worse trials will befall them. The nations will come to Judgement in 25. Jesus' last words to the Eleven and to 'his brethren' who doubted, are that they should go and make disciples of all nations. Thus Matthew, like Paul, sees the evangelization of the world as a double mission, first to the Jew and then to the Greek.[20]

Nevertheless, the picture of a double sending, first to Israel, then to the Gentiles, is oversimplified. Historically, the Twelve had felt themselves sent to Israel only. In the famous Council described in Gal. 2, Paul had divided the world with the Jerusalem apostles: they would have the circumcision, he and Barnabas the Gentiles. Christ, then, had given the mission to the lost sheep of the house of Israel to the Twelve, and in their ordering (Matt. 10) they are commanded not to go to Samaritan or Gentile towns; if persecuted in one place to flee to the next; for before the circuit of Israel is complete, the Parousia will have come. In 28 a clear distinction is drawn between the Eleven and the others who did not worship in faith, but doubted: the exalted Christ reassures them, and entrusts the mission to the whole world to the whole Church. The original Twelve must care for Israel, in Matthew as in Paul, but the Church—no doubt through further apostles—must carry this gospel of the Kingdom to every nation.

Mark had set out briefly the apostle's rights to food and shelter from his converts, and Paul, not without some rhetoric, amplifies this (1 Cor. 9.1–14). The apostle is like a labourer planting a vineyard, a shepherd with his flock, a ploughman ploughing, a thresher threshing, in expectation of reward. Matthew too amplifies Mark: the harvest is plenteous, but the labourers are few—and the labourer is worthy of his food. Or, continues Paul, 'Do you not know that those who are employed in the temple service get their food from the temple?' Matthew too justifies the apostles' eating on sabbath—'have you not

---

[20] For a full exposition of the double mission in Matthew, see pp. 338ff. below.

read how the priests in the temple profane the sabbath, and are guiltless?' (12.5). The Lord's provision for his apostles is thus made in Paul and Matthew under the same images.

Mark reports that the Pharisees asked Jesus for a sign, and were refused. Paul gives the *Sitz-im-Leben* of this saying in church life: 'For Jews demand signs and Greeks seek wisdom, but we preach Christ crucified, a stumbling-block to Jews and folly to Greeks' (1 Cor. 1.22f). Signs in the Jewish sense are refused: but God's own mysterious sign in the crucifixion and resurrection of Jesus is provided and proclaimed. Hence Matthew is led to qualify the Marcan refusal: no sign shall be given this generation—but the sign of Jonah. For Jonah was three days beneath the waters of death and returned to life, and the Ninevites repented at his preaching; a greater than Jonah was crucified and returned from three days in the heart of the earth, and is preached but not believed. Paul's doctrine of the hardening of Jewish hearts is Mark's, and Matthew's; but Paul looks beyond the temporary hardening, which in God's providence is the occasion of the Gentile mission, to the ultimate gathering in of all Israel. Here Matthew follows him as Mark does not. Jerusalem, bent on killing and stoning God's messengers, has refused her Lord's motherly care, and must suffer the ruin of her Temple. Christ leaves her now, not to be seen again till the Parousia; when she will greet him: 'Blessed is he who comes in the name of the Lord' (23.37–9). Jerusalem can only say 'Blessed' of one in whom she recognizes her salvation: any other exegesis is a twisting of the plain words. The change of tone of the discourse is sudden because the repentance will be sudden. In another place Matthew says that the sons of the kingdom will be cast into outer darkness (8.12); but then in another place Paul says that the wages of sin is death.

The Church

Matthew is the only synoptist to follow Paul in the image of the Church as a building: 'On this rock I will build my church' (16.18; 1 Cor. 3.9–17; Eph. 2.19–22); as for the gates of Hades, the inability of the powers to suppress the Church is a Pauline theme—God has raised us up with Christ, and made us to sit in heavenly places with him (Eph. 2.6). The Matthaean teaching on the apostles is identical with the Pauline teaching, and despite common opinion may be confidently derived from Eph. 2.[21] Paul says that the Christians are ἐποικοδομηθέντες on the foundation of the apostles and prophets, Christ Jesus himself being the ἀκρογωνιαῖον, in whom the whole

[21] For a full exposition, see pp. 386–90 below.

οἰκοδομή grows into a holy Temple in the Lord. Mark recorded that Jesus had surnamed Simon Cephas, Petros, but had given no occasion for the name. Matthew takes the Confession at Caesarea as the best occasion for the surnaming, and explains the name by reference to the Ephesian text. Jesus is the Christ, and as Christ, son of David, he will build his new Temple, the Church; and Paul had taught that the apostles and prophets were the foundation. Here, then, is the justification for the name: Peter is the first rock on which it is to be built (οἰκοδομήσω). οἰκοδομέω here cannot mean edify, and almost certainly carries the Temple image. To be the rock *means* to hold the keys of the Kingdom, like the Pharisaic scribes who lock men out of it; or to be precise, to have the power of binding and loosing, *'āsar* and *hittîr*, like the Pharisaic scribes on Moses' seat. Two chapters later, the same power of binding and loosing is extended to the full Twelve: 'Whatsoever ye bind on earth . . .' They share in the power of the keys; they are rocks also, part of the foundation of the Temple. That Christ Jesus himself is the κεφαλὴ γωνίας is expressly said, following Mark, at 21.42. John gives the same teaching of the apostles' position as foundation-stones in the twenty-first chapter of the Apocalypse.

The apostle's work, binding and loosing, is exemplified in 1 Cor. 5, a passage with strong verbal echoes in Matt. 18.[22] The Church should gather with the Apostle as chairman, but since Paul is in Ephesus this cannot be done: the judgement is clear in view of the scandal and obduracy of the sinner, so ἐν τῷ ὀνόματι τοῦ Κυρίου ἡμῶν Ἰησοῦ συναχθέντων ὑμῶν with Paul spiritually in the chair, the man can be handed over to Satan; that is, excommunicated. 'Have nothing to do with him', it is said elsewhere, 'that he may be ashamed' (2 Thess. 3.14); or, as Matthew puts it, let him be to you as a Gentile and a tax-collector. 'Truly, I say to you, whatever you bind on earth shall be bound in heaven': your excommunication expels from the kingdom, and so hands over to Satan. They can dare to do this because they are Christ's vice-gerents: where two or three (of them, we must understand from the context) are gathered in my name (συνηγμένοι εἰς τὸ ἐμὸν ὄνομα) there am I in the midst of them. Paul shows himself in 2 Cor. to be the good pastor caring for this straying sheep (Matt. 18.12–14). His zeal to gain (κερδαίνω, Matt. 18.15) his brethren is often exemplified; the word is a technical term.[23] At Gal. 6.1 he bids the spiritual restore any man taken in a trespass, in the spirit of meekness, just as the Matthaean Jesus tells the apostles to speak to the sinner alone. The resource of taking two or three witnesses, as in

[22] See p. 154 above.
[23] In distinct, but closely related senses: Paul is anxious to gain converts, Matthew penitents.

Deuteronomy, is also mentioned by Paul in another connection (2 Cor. 13.1). ἐκκλησία is used both of the Church universal in 16, and of the church local, as here, following Paul: 'my Church', the Church of Christ, is Pauline teaching in Ephesians and Colossians only. ἀδελφός of a Christian is common to Paul and Matthew. The necessity of trouble within the church (σκάνδαλα, Matt. 18.7; αἱρέσεις, 1 Cor. 11.19) is also common ground.

Many things in church life Matthew has taken from his Jewish background, rather than from the radical apostle: such matters as divorce rules, dietary laws, and the keeping of the Oral Torah would not be common ground between them, and the reason for this I have explained in ch. 1 above. I have urged already, following Dr Dodd,[24] that the influence in 18 cannot be from Ur-Matthew to Paul, and it seems reasonable to think that dependence, whether indirect, or as I should think, direct, is from Paul to Matthew. The Matthaean rhythms and imagery in 16 suggest the same conclusion.

Anti-Pharisee Polemic

Matthew much increases the volume and virulence of the anti-Pharisaic matter in Mark, and his new material shows strong links with two passages in Paul, Rom. 2—4 and 1 Thess. 2. Paul had taught in Rom. 4 that the essential was not physical descent from Abraham but the following of the example of faith which our father Abraham had; and Matthew has this thought in the mouth of John the Baptist, 'Do not presume to say to yourselves, We have Abraham as our father' (3.9). Paul goes on to teach that God brings life from the barren womb, from the sepulchre; Matthew that he can raise children from the stones.

The Marcan polemic is reproduced in Matt. 12, and amplified in 23. The new material for the seven Woes is partly drawn from Rom. 2—3. The fault of the Pharisees is that they say and do not (23.3); even so Paul warns his Jewish readers that 'it is not the hearers of the Law who are righteous before God, but the doers' (Rom. 2.13). They bind heavy burdens, hard to bear, and will not lift a finger to ease them (23.4); while Paul taught that Christians should bear one another's burdens, and so fulfil the law of Christ (Gal. 6.2). All their phylacteries and salutations and the rest are done for show (23.5-7), like their alms and prayers and fasting in 6. They perform the outward tithe punctiliously, but neglect the weightier matters of the heart (23.23f); they cleanse the outside of the cup, but within seethes their rapacity (23.25f). So Paul taught that he is not a real Jew who is one outwardly (ἐν τῷ

[24] See p. 154 above.

φανέρῳ), nor is true circumcision something external (ἐν τῷ φανέρῳ), but he is a Jew who is one inwardly (ἐν τῷ κρυπτῷ): whose praise is not from men but from God (Rom. 2.28f). In 23 Matthew draws his contrasts between ἔξω and ἔσω; in 6 between ὅπως φανῶσιν and ἐν τῷ κρυπτῷ/κρυφαίῳ, and between men's approval and God's reward. Matthew twice calls the Pharisees blind guides (ὁδηγοὶ τυφλοί, τυφλοὶ ὁδηγοὶ τυφλῶν), and warns of the fate of the blind led by the blind (15.14); Paul with heaviest irony derides the *soi-disant* Jew, sure that he is a guide to the blind (ὁδηγὸς τυφλῶν, Rom. 2.19). In Rom. 3 Paul continues into diatribe: the Jew is as bad as the Greek—their throat is an open sepulchre (τάφος), the poison of asps is under their lips. Matthew compares the Pharisees to chalked sepulchres (τάφοι); similarly, three times he calls the Pharisees vipers, once snakes, with both expressions in 23. Lohmeyer says that such abuse is unexampled in rabbinic literature.[25]

If these parallels, many of which are noted by Dr Dodd, seem impressive, the link between 1 Thess. 2.15f and the peroration of 23 is unmistakeable. The Jews, says Paul, (*a*) killed both the Lord Jesus and the prophets, and (*b*) persecuted us out, and (*c*) displease God and oppose all men by hindering us from speaking to the Gentiles that they may be saved—so as (*d*) always to fill up the measure of their sins. But (*e*) God's wrath has come upon them at last. (*a*) They killed the prophets: 'You witness against yourselves, that you are sons of those who murdered the prophets.' (*b*) They persecuted us out (ἐξεδίωξαν): 'Therefore I send you prophets and wise men and scribes . . . some you will persecute (διώξετε) from town to town.' (*c*) They hinder us from speaking to the Gentiles that they may be saved: 'You shut the kingdom of heaven against men; for you neither enter yourselves, nor allow those who would to go in.' (*d*) So as always to fill up the measure of their sins (ἀναπληρῶσαι τὰς ἁμαρτίας): 'Fill up, then, the measure of your fathers (πληρώσατε τὸ μέτρον). . . that upon you may come all the righteous blood shed on earth', from Abel to Zechariah. (*e*) But God's wrath has come upon them at last: 'All this will come upon this generation . . . your house is forsaken.' The concentration of the five themes in two verses of Paul and eleven of Matthew is too singular to be coincidence: the prevention of preaching and the filling up of a notional measure of sins are both exceedingly rare ideas, hardly instanced elsewhere in the NT. The brevity of the Pauline version, and the highly Matthaean character of the Matthaean version leave no doubt which is primary and which secondary. Direct dependence is hardly escapable.

[25] Lohmeyer, p. 38, n.2.

Eschatology

Matthew's eschatology is rather more developed than Mark's, and the developments are in many places clearly due to Paul, and in others to the rabbis. παρουσία is a Matthaean word, four times in Matthew, one of them redactoral, never in the other evangelists: it comes seven times in 1 and 2 Thessalonians, and not elsewhere in the technical sense in the Pauline Epistles. The Thessalonian teaching is closely followed in Matthew:

To wait for his Son from heaven, who delivers us from the *wrath* to come.	1 Thess. 1.10
To flee from the *wrath* to come.	Matt. 3.7

ὀργή, a common Pauline term for impending judgement, is only found in the Synoptics in this passage, John's preaching (Q).

Unblameable . . . at the coming of our Lord Jesus *with all his holy ones* (AT).	1 Thess. 3.13
When the Son of Man comes in his glory, and *all the angels with* him.	Matt. 25.31

The Son of Man is unaccompanied by angels, apparently, at Mark 13.26. 1 Thess. 3.13 is closely similar to Zech. 14.5, where the 'holy ones' are angels, which makes this meaning probable, as does the context, rather than 'saints'.

The Lord himself will descend from heaven with a cry of command, with the archangel's call, and with the sound of the *trumpet* (σάλπιγξ) of God.	1 Thess. 4.16

Matthew inserts, of the Lord's despatch of the angels, 'with a loud *trumpet-call* (σάλπιγξ) (24.31). The ἐπισυναγωγή, the gathering of the faithful from the four corners to meet the Lord on clouds (1 Thess. 4.17; 2 Thess. 2.1) is already in the Marcan tradition, and is retained in Matthew (24.31b).

The times and seasons are unknown to the Thessalonians (5.1), as the day and hour are in Mark and Matthew (24.34ff), who stresses the point with the illustrations following: Paul then continues,

For you yourselves know well that the day of the Lord *will come* like *a thief* in the night.	1 Thess. 5.2

Matthew then immediately appends the parable of the Thief (new material). Paul warns of the suddenness of the Day, and that Christians must live as sons of light: 'so let us not *sleep*, as others do, but let us *keep awake*' (5.6). Mark has the sleeping/waking contrast, but

Matthew much more forcibly, and after the Thief, in his Ten Virgins.
Paul continues: 'For those who sleep sleep at night, and those who
get drunk *are drunk* (μεθύουσιν) at night.' Mark lacks any reference to
drunkenness: Matthew introduces the Unfaithful Servant, who drinks
with the *drunkards* (μεθύοντες). Matthew has thus seven features of
the Parousia in 24—25 in common with 1 Thessalonians, of which the
trumpet, the thief, and the drunkards are intruded into the Marcan
framework, and probably the angels and sleeping/waking as well.
Direct dependence of Matthew on Paul is a high probability.

Other features are in common from elsewhere in the Pauline
Epistles. Paul speaks of the unknown blessings which 'God has *prepared* for those that love him' (1 Cor. 2.9, amending Isa. 64.4), and
speaks of their election 'before *the foundation of the world*' (Eph. 1.4):
Matthew combines the two phrases at 25.34, 'Come, O blessed of my
Father, inherit the kingdom *prepared* for you *from the foundation of
the world*'. The last phrase, and the doctrine of election that goes with
it, is found once elsewhere in Matthew, once without the doctrine in
L, not in Mark. Judgement by both God and Christ are commonplaces of Pauline writing. Christ is the judge both in the preaching of
John Baptist and at 16.27, 'The Son of Man . . . will repay every man
for what he has done'; and at 25.34, 'Then the King [that is Christ]
will say to those at his right hand . . .'. The kingdom that follows is
the Messianic kingdom: 'Before they see the Son of Man coming in
his Kingdom' (16.28), 'Then the King will say . . .' (25.34). Paul tells
the Corinthians that the messianic kingdom will last for a period:
'Then comes the end, when he delivers the kingdom to God the Father
after destroying every rule and every authority and power' (1 Cor.
15.24).[26] Matthew pictures the Messianic Kingdom under the standard
rabbinic image of the Feast with Abraham, Isaac, and Jacob and the
Church seated (8.11; 20.21). Every Corinthian Christian knew that
he would judge the world (1 Cor. 6.2); Matthew associates the Church,
'these my brethren', with the King at the Great Assize in 25,[27] and
has Jesus promise the Apostles judgement of the tribes of Israel (19.28).
The passing of heaven and earth, with the implication therefore of
their replacement, comes at 5.18 and 13.43.

[26] Dr Dodd (op. cit., p. 55) points to the contrast in the Tares parable as evidence
of Matthew also making this distinction: 13.27, 'In *your* field', i.e. the Son of
Man's; 13.43, 'Then the righteous will shine like the sun in the kingdom of their
Father.' I fear this is too optimistic: the kingdom of their Father is just another
way of speaking of the Kingdom of Heaven, 'thy kingdom come', which will be
actualized in the reign of Messiah. But the destruction of the devil and his angels,
the Matthaean form of the Pauline authorities and powers, is referred to in
Matt. 25.41.
[27] See pp. 443f below.

One feature of Matthaean eschatology which is not common to Paul is the prominence of Hell. Gehenna is a strong theme of Jewish writing of all kinds from the inter-Testamental period on. It is in the targums, the pseudepigrapha, and the rabbis alike. It is scarcely mentioned in Mark, and its constant presence both in the parables and in other Matthaean matter must be due to the rabbis. It is of interest that Paul, to whom this doctrine must have been just as natural, has so completely purged this old leaven out of his system. Luke diminishes the Matthaean stress considerably. It hardly comes in John.

At Rom. 2.12–16 Paul speaks of the godly heathen, recognizing the possibility that their thoughts may excuse them on the day when God shall judge the hidden things of men; and we find the same recognition in the Matthaean Sheep and Goats. On the other hand, Paul is well aware of the possibility of himself and his converts being 'castaways', and the *corpus mixtum* view of the Church comes in the Dragnet and the Marriage-Feast and elsewhere in Matthew. These two points hardly come elsewhere in the NT.

Citations

There are seven citations, or references to scripture, which are common to Matthew and Paul, which it would be natural to explain as being derived by the evangelist from the apostle:

1. Ps. 61.13, LXX: 'For thou shalt repay to each according to his deeds'.

Virtually the same text occurs at Prov. 24.12. Paul cites word for word but for an introductory 'who' at Rom. 2.6: Matthew cites at 16.27 with τὴν πρᾶξιν for τὰ ἔργα approximating to the singular $k^ema^{'a}ṣēhū$ in the Hebrew. The obvious relevance of the verse made it popular in the next generation, and it is quoted in the Pastorals, twice in the Apocalypse, and in 2 Clement. The quotation is redactoral in Matthew and therefore secondary.

2. Deut. 32.5, LXX: 'A crooked and perverse generation'.

Paul quotes word for word, in the genitive case, at Phil 2.15. Matthew quotes in the form, 'O faithless and perverse generation' at 17.17, where he is expanding the Marcan 'O faithless generation'.

3. Paul combines the two Isaiah stone texts 8.14; 28.16 at Rom. 9.33: 'Behold I am laying in Zion a stone that will make men stumble and a

πέτραν σκανδάλου.' At Matt. 16.18 Jesus says to Peter that upon this πέτρα he will build his Church: and at verse 23 he tells Peter that he is a σκάνδαλον to him. The second reference is again redactional. The combination is taken up again in 1 Pet. 2.

4. Isa. 29.14, LXX: 'I will destroy the wisdom of the wise, and the understanding of the understanding will I hide.'

Paul cites this at 1 Cor. 1.19, amending 'hide' to 'thwart'. Matthew alludes to the passage at 11.25: 'Thou hast hidden these things from the wise and understanding.' This is in the new material.

5. Deut. 19.15b: *'al-pî shᵉnêi 'ēdhîm 'ô 'al-pî shᵉlōshāh 'ēdhîm yāqûm dābhār.*

LXX^B: ἐπὶ στόματος δύο μαρτύρων καὶ ἐπὶ στόματος τριῶν μαρτύρων στήσεται πᾶν ῥῆμα [SA etc. σταθήσεται][28]

2 Cor.: ἐπὶ στόματος δύο μαρτύρων καὶ τριῶν σταθήσεται πᾶν ῥῆμα. Matt. [ἵνα] ἐπὶ στόματος δύο μαρτύρων ἢ τριῶν σταθῇ πᾶν ῥῆμα.

Paul quotes this at 2 Cor. 13.1, in the form, 'At the mouth of two witnesses and three shall every word be made to stand' (AT) Matthew quotes the text at 18.16 as a ἵνα clause, agreeing word for word with the Pauline version,[29] against LXX^B whose repetitiveness and middle voice exactly translate the Hebrew. This is in the new material also.

6. Gen. 2.24, LXX: 'Therefore shall a man leave his father and his mother, and cleave to his wife, and they two shall become one flesh.'

The text is cited in Mark 10.7, probably without the clause, 'and shall cleave to his wife' (om ℵ B syr^sin Nestlé). Both Paul, at Eph. 5.13, and Matthew, at 19.5, cite the text (*a*) including the cleaving clause, and (*b*) dropping the word αὐτοῦ after both father and mother. While there is textual doubt about all four passages, it is simplest to argue that Matthew was familiar with the Ephesians version.

7. Isa. 42.4 LXX: 'And upon his name shall Gentiles hope.'

Paul cites at Rom. 15.12, without the word 'name', which anyhow is not in the Hebrew. Matt. 12.21 cites with the 'name' but without ἐπί. The quotation of this verse is likely to be secondary in Matthew: the context is of Jesus' gentle ministry which is justified by the first

---

[28] The passive is likely to have been introduced into SA by assimilation to Paul and Matthew.
[29] Except for ἢ, which echoes the Hebrew *'ô*, against καὶ (Paul, LXX).

three verses—'He will not wrangle or cry . . . he will not break a bruised reed . . .'—and the mention of the Gentiles is irrelevant.

Four of these seven references occur in passages where Matthew is closely following Mark, so that influence from pre-Matthaean tradition on Paul may be ruled out. Direct influence from a written text seems likely in the Deut. 19 and Gen. 2 citations where Paul and Matthew agree against the LXX and Mark: but for the purpose of the present argument indirect influence from Paul via hypothetical catechisms and testimony-books is quite enough.

I do not wish to appear to be arguing the impossible thesis that Matthew was a Pauline Christian. It is quite evident that his theological sympathies are far apart from the apostle's: as I have tried to show in ch. 1 above, whenever there is a point of decision—on the status of the Law, on the oral tradition, on the authority of the Jewish Council and on many related questions—Paul always opts for a radical, Matthew for the conservative position. The only issue which Matthew concedes to the radicals is the circumcision question; and he concedes this tacitly because it had been decided a generation before. The great Pauline doctrines of the body of Christ, of the Spirit, of justification by faith, are only distantly echoed in Matthew, and the Matthaean *nova lex* is not a project for which the apostle would have felt any enthusiasm. What I am concerned to press is that the ignorance of the Pauline writings which is normally postulated for Matthew is both improbable on general grounds, and also flat against the evidence. The hypothesis that the Pauline letters were discovered in various church safes round the Mediterranean about A.D. 100 is totally implausible. If they were scripture to Basilides, they were being read in church for a good time before that, and the best view is one of continuous use from Paul's martyrdom on. We could only combine this with Matthaean ignorance at the cost of siting the Matthaean church on the Sea of Azov or in Portugal, and hardly then.

The evidence for a direct link from Paul to Matthew may be described as massive. In the development of anti-Pharisee polemic between Rom. 2, 1 Thess. 2, and Matt. 23, of eschatology between 1 Thess. 4—5 and Matt. 24—25; of the redactional OT citations; and of the doctrine of the apostles between Eph. 2 and Matt. 16—18, the evidence even for a documentary link is strong. Such a relationship we have no need to press. If, as we have argued, Matthew was without non-Marcan traditions in any volume, nothing is likelier than that he possessed the substance of the Pauline teaching, and nothing would be more natural than that he should make it a part of the doctrinal basis of his midrash.

9

MATTHEW AND THE JEWISH YEAR

Hitherto our attention has been concentrated on the details of the Matthaean text: why such a word, such a rhythm, such an image is used, and whether they can be traced to Mark, or midrashic use of Mark. But even more significant is the shape of the whole Gospel, for unless we understand the structure of a book we do not understand the book, and no theory can claim to account for Matthew which does not propose an explanation for why the book is as it is.

When chronological theories[1] were abandoned after the 1914 War, a variety of 'theological' theories took their place. These sometimes consisted of theories of arrangement by topic[2]—'The Healings of the Master', 'Master and Disciples', 'The Master and his Opponents', etc.—which were unexciting but unexceptionable; and sometimes of typological theories. The most widely received of the latter was the theory of B. W. Bacon,[3] who drew on the evident fact that there were five teaching Discourses in the Gospel, each sealed off with a formula at its end, to suggest that Matthew had in mind to arrange his book round Five Books of the New Law, in parallel with the Torah. While this seemed attractive, it did not explain very much, for the first teaching block, the Sermon, bore no relation to Genesis, but a strong relation to the law-giving of Exodus, and Bacon's theory was carried a step further by Farrer. Farrer suggested[4] that Matthew had not five but six 'set-pieces' in the Gospel, of which the first was the Genealogy, opening with the words, 'The Book of the Genesis of Jesus Christ . . .' The Sermon was then a natural Exodus law-giving; the commissioning of the Apostles in 10 was a new Leviticus, with the Twelve as the priests of the New Israel; 13 described the gathering of the Numbers into the Church; 18ff contain a number of references to Deuteronomy; and thereafter the new Jesus/Joshua crosses the Jordan, enters Jericho, and establishes the Kingdom in the land. The theory is among Farrer's brilliant suggestions: it is not strong on Leviticus and Joshua, and its

---

[1] W. C. Allen, *A Critical and Exegetical Commentary on the Gospel according to St Matthew* [Allen] (Edinburgh 1912), pp. lxiiiff, and McNeile, pp. xiiff, still assume a chronological outline to be the dominant structural feature.
[2] e.g. Lohmeyer, J. Schniewind, *Das Evangelium nach Matthäus*, NTD (11e., Göttingen 1964), p. 8.
[3] *Studies in Matthew* (London 1931) pp. 80ff and *passim*,
[4] 'On Dispensing with Q', in *Studies in the Gospels*, ed. D. E. Nineham (Oxford 1954); *St Matthew and St Mark* (2e., London, 1966) pp. 179–99.

Numbers is decidedly thin, but it explained too much to be entirely wrong.

All these theories were literary theories; they took it that Matthew was writing a book, and proposed to explain the structure of the book. But there are also lectionary indications in the Gospel, for instance in the natural divisions of the Passion story into three-hour units, which not only were used in Good Friday vigils in the fourth-century Church,[5] but look as if they were designed for such a use. The liturgical use of Matthew was urged by Kilpatrick as the mode of the work's development of Mark,[6] but Kilpatrick did not suggest any consecutive use of the Gospel in liturgy. He viewed it as a book from which preachers selected passages and developed them, just as Matthew (in his view) took passages of Mark and combined them with M and Q material: in other words, his theory gave no account of the structure of Matthew as it stands.

The theory that I wish to propose is a lectionary theory: that is, that the Gospel was developed liturgically, and was intended to be used liturgically; and that its order is liturgically significant, in that it follows the lections of the Jewish Year. Matthew, I believe, wrote his Gospel to be read in church round the year; he took the Jewish Festal Year, and the pattern of lections prescribed therefor, as his base; and it is possible for us to descry from Ms. evidence for which feast, and for which Sabbath/Sunday, and even on occasion for which service, any particular verses were intended. Such claims do not err on the side of modesty, but I hope to show that the nature of the evidence is so exact and so cogent that no other conclusion is possible. Such a theory not merely accounts for the general structure of the Gospel, and makes many of the details within individual pericopae significant within that structure: it also provides a credible *Sitz-im-Leben* for the Gospel as a *genre*, the bourn of a long quest.[7] A Gospel is not a literary *genre* at all, the study of Matthew reveals: it is a liturgical *genre*. A Gospel is a lectionary book, a series of 'Gospels' used in worship week by week in *lectio continua*. Such a conclusion is in every way consonant with the view of the evangelist which we have established as a *sôphēr*, a provincial schoolmaster/synogogue official, presupposing Jewish ways at every step. He officiated, week by week, year after year, at worship that was Jewish in root and mainly Jewish in branch. He expounded Jewish readings with Christian traditions in the Jewish

---

[5] See p. 432 below for an abbreviated table, and references.
[6] Kilpatrick, *Origins*, pp. 72–100.
[7] See C. F. Evans, *The Cambridge History of the Bible* I, pp. 270f, and references there.

manner: and as the Jews read the Law by *lectio continua* round the year,[8] so did he come in time to put together the elements of his now developed *paradosis* into a continuous book. The same conclusion is true for the other Gospels, with some adjustments: I have done no more than tabulate the evidence for Mark in appendix B at the end of this chapter, and set out the outline for Luke in ch. 21 below—each Gospel requires exposition in a full book. But the way in is by Matthew: he is the most Jewish of the evangelists, and the lectionary system that he follows is both simpler and better evidenced than that underlying the other three.

The Jews in the first century followed a dual system of synagogue readings, not unlike that of the Book of Common Prayer. The Church of England begins reading from Genesis at Morning Prayer on Septuagesima, and provides a *lectio continua* day by day till Holy Week: then there are special readings for the Easter season, and similarly for Ascension Day, Whitsunday, etc. In the same way the synagogue had both a sabbath cycle and a Festal cycle of readings: but there is no first-century Prayer Book to tell us what they were. The sabbath cycle is a matter of controversy in at least two major respects. We do not know whether the cycle ran for one year or for three, or for some other span;[9] and we do not know whether it began in Nisan (April) or in Tishri (October).[10] It is even open to doubt whether there was an accepted sabbath cycle before Jamnia, and all these questions will concern us later. But the Festal cycle is older than the sabbath cycle. In many cases the nature of the Feast dictates the scriptures used, as

---

[8] *Lectio Continua* is first attested documentarily in the Mishnah, Meg. 3.4: 'On the fourth (sabbath in Adar, they read) the section, "This month shall be for you . . ." (Exod. 12.1–20). On the fifth they revert to the set order (only)'; cf. Danby, p. 205. Chapter 10 gives evidence for a continuous reading before the Chronicler's time: it goes back probably to Ezekiel and the Deuteronomistic community in the 6th century B.C. See also below, p. 227, n.2.

[9] A three-year cycle was accepted by A. Büchler in two articles, 'The Reading of the Law and the Prophets in a Triennial Cycle', in *JQR* v (1893), pp. 420–68, and vi (1894), pp. 1–73; and by J. Mann, *BRPOS*; and in reliance upon them by most scholars since. Dr A. Guilding's *The Fourth Gospel and Jewish Worship* is largely dependent upon their triennial cycle theories. The triennial view has been widely disputed following the publication of Dr Guilding's book, most notably by J. R. Porter, 'The Pentateuch and the Triennial Lectionary Cycle', *Promise and Fulfilment* (Essays presented to S. H. Hooke, ed. F. F. Bruce (Edinburgh 1963)); L. Morris, *The New Testament and the Jewish Lectionaries* (London 1964); L. Crockett, 'Luke 4.16–30 and the Jewish Lectionary Cycle' *JJS* xvii (1966), pp. 13ff; and J. Heinemann, 'The Triennial Lectionary Cycle', *JJS* xviii (1968), pp. 41ff).

[10] Büchler supported a cycle beginning from Nisan, Mann a cycle beginning from Tishri, Guilding both.

Purim is connected with Esther, or Passover with the Exodus.[11] In some the dates are given in the OT text, as when Israel came to Sinai in the third month[12] (Pentecost), and Solomon dedicated the Temple in the feast of the seventh month[13] (Tabernacles). There are festal lessons prescribed in the Mishnah,[14] and others in the Talmud,[15] both of which traditions are certainly older than the documents in which they occur. It is the festal cycle which is the basis of Matthew.

The Jewish Festal Year has pre-biblical roots, and the three pilgrim-feasts, ordained as occasions for all the sons of the commandments to appear at the Temple, combined Canaanite agricultural traits with Israelite historical ones.[16] Unleavened Bread/Passover was both the feast of the deliverance from Egypt, expressed in the sacrifice of the lamb and other ceremonies, and the barley harvest celebration, expressed in the eating of unleavened bread.[17] Pentecost was both the feast of the giving of the Law on Sinai, and the celebration of the wheat-harvest.[18] Tabernacles was both the feast of the Temple, which Solomon dedicated in an eight-day feast in the seventh month, and the Feast of Ingathering, the thanksgiving for the whole of the year's produce, of the winevat and the threshing-floor.[19] Passover/Unleavened Bread was celebrated for a week from the spring full-moon, that is normally[20] the full moon after the spring solstice (Nisan 14–21). Tabernacles was kept at the point diametrically opposite in the calendar, for eight days following the autumn full-moon, that is normally the full-moon after the autumn solstice (Tishri 15–22). Pentecost was celebrated on slightly different days in different Jewish communities,[21] but the Pharisaic practice, which was normative in the first century, was to take it on the fifty-first day from Passover, as a one-day festival (normally Sivan 6).[22]

[11] There was no synagogue celebration of Passover, since 'all Israel' was at Jerusalem; the Passover scripture passage was in fact Deut. 26.5ff. The Exod. 12 passage was read in the synagogues on the last Sabbath in Adar (March) in preparation for the feast.
[12] Exod. 19.1.　　　　　　　　　[13] 1 Kings 8.2
[14] Meg. 3.4–6　　　　　　　　　[15] B Meg. 31a.
[16] H.-J. Kraus, *Worship in Israel* (E.T., Oxford 1966), pp. 26–69; J. van Goudoever, *Biblical Calendars* (Leiden 1959), ch. 2.
[17] Kraus, op. cit., pp. 45ff.
[18] ibid., pp. 55ff.　　　　　　　[19] ibid., pp. 61ff.
[20] Jewish intercalation appears to have been determined by the state of the crops and was made at the time of the New Moon after Adar, cf. T. Sanh. II. 6: so a relationship to the solstice would not be invariable. According to Josephus (*Ant.* 2.317), an eight-day ἄζυμα was kept in the Dispersion; cf. Jeremias, *EWJ*, p. 24.
[21] For details see van Goudoever, op cit., ch. 2.
[22] The Pharisees' interpretation was already glossed in LXX Lev. 23.11: for its normalcy in the first century cf. Jeremias, *Jerusalem in the time of Jesus* (E.T., London 1969), p. 264.

In the course of time three further feasts and two major fasts came to be incorporated into the liturgical year. New Year came to be celebrated separately from Tabernacles after the Exile, on 1st Tishri: but while the traditional autumn New Year was still observed, albeit a fortnight earlier, the Babylonian custom was also adopted of counting the months from the spring (when the Babylonian New Year was celebrated). We thus have the anomaly of a New Year festival 'in the seventh month, on the first day of the month'.[23] New Year was from ancestral times the season when Yahweh came to judge the world,[24] and it looks forward to the New Age when the Holy One will establish the Kingdom of Heaven, and judge mankind. On New Year's Day, Rosh Hashshanah, says the Mishnah, 'all that come into the world pass before God like flocks of sheep' for judgement.[25] It was said in the name of R. Johanan (third century) that on Rosh Hashshanah three books were opened: the Book of Life for those whose works had been good, the Book of Death for those whose works had been thoroughly evil, and a third book for those whose case was to be decided on the Day of Atonement.[26] Second, there was the feast of Dedication, Ḥanukkah, on 25th Kislev (December). Ḥannukkah coincides in date with the old Canaanite Feast of Midwinter,[27] and was not celebrated in Judaism, at least officially, until Judas Maccabaeus reconsecrated the Temple on 25th Kislev, 165 B.C. Its similarity to Tabernacles, the other Temple feast, is marked by its coming also to be celebrated for eight days, 'with gladness as at Tabernacles'.[28] Whether or not it was in origin a sun festival, the name Ḥanukkah means Dedication, and it is taken to celebrate the descent of the glory of God, the Shekinah, to invest Tabernacle and Temple, and of the divine fire to consume the altar sacrifice.[29] The third additional feast is Purim, celebrating the deliverance of the Jews through Esther. The day of its celebration varies between 11th–15th Adar (March),

[23] Lev. 23.24.
[24] Many of the psalms in the 90s, which celebrate Yahweh's coming in judgement, are probably New Year Psalms of the monarchy period; cf. S. Mowinckel, *The Psalms in Israel's Worship* (E.T., Oxford 1967), I, ch. 5.
[25] M R.H. 1.2.
[26] B R.H. 16b; cf. Moore, *Judaism* I, pp. 495f; II pp. 63–5.
[27] Kraus (op. cit., pp. 88ff) ignores, R. de Vaux (*Ancient Israel* (2e., E.T., London 1965), pp. 513f) disputes, the claim of a pagan origin for the feast; cf. p. 393f below for further discussion.
[28] 2 Macc. 10.6.
[29] 2 Macc. 1.22; 2.8f. Jeremiah hid the Tabernacle and the Ark, 'until God gather the people together, and mercy come; and then the Lord shall disclose these things, and the glory of the Lord shall be seen, and the cloud: as also it was showed unto Moses; as also Solomon besought . . .' The Maccabaean victory marks the coming of mercy.

according to details set out in the Mishnah.[30] The two major fasts are 9th Ab (August), commemorating the destruction of the Temple in 586 B.C., and other disasters;[31] and the Day of Atonement (Yôm Kippûr) on 10th Tishri, falling between New Year and Tabernacles.

There are thus eight major liturgical occasions in the Jewish Year by the beginning of our era:

Nisan (April)[32]	14–21	Passover (Pesaḥ)
Iyyar (May)		
Sivan (June)	6	Pentecost (Shābu'ôth)
Tammuz (July)		
Ab (August)	9	9th Ab (Tish'āh be-Ābh)
Elul (September)		
Tishri (October)	1	New Year (Rō'sh Hashshānāh)
	10	The Day of Atonement (Yôm Kippûr)
	15–22	Tabernacles (Sukkôth)
Cheshvan (November)		
Kislev (December)	25–	Dedication (Ḥanukkāh)
Tebeth (January)	–2/3	
Shebat (February)		
Adar (March)	11ff	Pûrîm

Between these high-days stretched the sabbaths of the twelve Jewish lunar months. These followed the new moon, and consisted of not less than twenty-nine days nor more than thirty. Which was which depended upon the actual observation of the new moon,[33] and in the tables which I have appended to this chapter I have represented them as the months of an ideal year with alternating thirty and twenty-nine days. As the twelve-month year had thus 354 days, or nearly so, there was a constant $11\frac{1}{4}$ days falling behind to the solar year, and roughly seven years in nineteen this was made up by having an extra month, Second Adar.[34] The number of sabbaths between feasts was bound to vary slightly, and I have taken the 4th Nisan as the date for the first sabbath in the year, as the median between the 1st and the 7th. There are minor complications in both these facts, which can be explained in due course, but my aim has been to set out a normal year as far as possible.

We are able to form an idea of the likely pattern of worship in the Matthaean church from the following considerations. Jewish sabbath worship consisted of one major service in the morning, and one lesser

---

[30] M Meg. 1.1–2.   [31] M Taan. 4.6,7.
[32] The English months in parenthesis are approximations.
[33] M R.H. 1.3—3.1.
[34] The institution of a regular intercalation on this basis is believed to go back to R. Hillel II, A.D. 358—*The Jewish Year Book, 1970*, p. 8.

service in the afternoon. There were also week-day services on Mondays and Thursdays.[35] The morning service included readings from the Torah by seven readers, the afternoon one by only three; the afternoon lections, along with those read on Mondays and Thursdays, were all read again the following sabbath morning. At first Jewish Christians continued to worship in the synagogues; and where there was tension they would naturally tend to form their own synagogues.[36] In all churches, whatever was done over the sabbath morning worship, the Christians met together on the Saturday night for a meal and the bread-breaking.[37] In the predominantly Gentile churches, the sabbath worship dropped away, and both of the descriptions that we have in the NT of Christian worship imply one service only on Saturday night. In 1 Cor. 11–14 we have the impression of lively worship including a meal with formal breaking of bread and communion; much of the evening is in fact consumed in ecstatic seizures, but the intention of the apostle was that these should be kept to a minimum, and that prophesying, that is, inspired preaching, should take the centre. In Acts 20.7ff Luke writes, 'On the first day of the week, when we were gathered together to break bread . . .', as if this were the normal procedure for the churches. Since Paul was a Jew, instituting services for Christians who had either been Jews or adherents of the synagogue; and since Luke is telling the story, and he is from the same tradition; it is proper to assume a Jewish counting of the week, in which the first day ran from sundown on Saturday to sundown on Sunday.[38] And if, which is remotely unlikely, Paul decided to follow, and Luke accepted, a Roman week, the Christian worship would still be on Saturday night, because the first day of the Roman week was Saturday.[39] In Acts, as in Corinthians, there is the preaching of the word, and the occasion ends with the breaking of bread and communion. Relations with Judaism are clearly distant in the Pauline churches, and there can be little doubt that what is described in both passages is the one service of the day, consisting of both word and

---

[35] M Meg. 4.1.   [36] cf. Matthew's 'their synagogues'.

[37] H. Riesenfeld, 'Sabbat et Jour du Seigneur', *New Testament Essays* (in memory of T. W. Manson), ed. A. J. B. Higgins (Manchester 1959).

[38] W. Rordorf (*Sunday* (E.T., London 1968), pp. 202ff) maintains a Sunday evening celebration in the first century, by reading back from second-century evidence: but 'the first day of the week' does not mean that in a Jewish context, nor can it be explained why the Church should have celebrated the Resurrection, which happened on Sunday at dawn, on Sunday night. Luke 23.54, 'It was the day of Preparation, and the sabbath was beginning', shows Luke's Jewish thinking: the use of τῇ ἐπαύριον at Acts 4.3; 23.31; 20.7b is not counter-evidence of Roman thinking, as Rordorf himself says on the previous page, 'this expression cannot be pressed to mean that another day of 24 hours will have begun'.

[39] Rordorf, op. cit., pp. 33f, 41.

sacraments: something of a Jewish synagogue service to begin, and culminating in the Eucharist, the whole being set at a meal.[40] The famous picture given by Justin in the *Apology*[41] would be a straightforward development from this, with the principal change the move to Sunday morning, since the Gentiles could not see the sense in a first-day-of-the-week service being held on a Saturday night. The Jewish week is still there, but the Jewish day, sundown to sundown, has been superseded. Justin specifies the readings: the prophets, i.e. the Old Testament, for as long as time allows; the ἀπομνημονεύματα of the Apostles, i.e. the Gospel; the Sermon.

The fact that our evidence is so largely from the Hellenizing church must not lead us into the monolithic fallacy.[42] The first-century churches were developing their common Jewish liturgical heritage at different rates in different places, and the Pauline pattern is hardly likely for the Jewish–Christian churches, of which Matthew's is one. We have already seen that Matthew is at pains to rescind the Marcan abrogation of the sabbath:[43] he will not say that the sabbath was made for man, and he waters the sabbath controversies down to the happy conclusion that 'it is lawful to do good on the sabbath'.[44] It would be natural then to suppose that the Matthaean church observed the sabbath, including sabbath worship. It had parted company with 'their synagogues', but was determined to prove its adherence to true Judaism by keeping all that the Pharisaic scribes taught from Moses' seat:[45] and what more basic than the pattern of Jewish worship? We

---

[40] cf. O. Cullmann (*Early Christian Worship* (E.T., London 1953), p. 31): 'In the early Church there are only these two celebrations or services—the common meal, within which the proclamation of the word had always a place; and Baptism' (italics). D. G. Delling (*Worship in the New Testament* (E.T., London 1962)) says boldly, 'The order of the synagogue service has obviously not influenced the early Christian one' (p. 42), a statement which contrasts sharply with sensible confessions of our ignorance higher on the same page. Delling explains neither the growth of Christian worship from a Jewish matrix, nor the synagogal order of the synaxis in Justin.

[41] I, 67.

[42] Books on New Testament worship are particularly liable to this fallacy, despite experience of variety hard learned in later liturgical study. Cullmann's statement in italics in n. 40 above is an astonishingly unwary generalization. Rordorf's study is partly vitiated by his failure to imagine the likely practice of the Jewish–Christian churches; and Delling writes: '[Jewish] formulae would be retained by the Jewish Christians when they took part in Jewish Worship' (p. 7), without considering what they did when they took part in Christian worship. Scholarship requires imagination as well as evidence. An honourable exception to the rule is C. W. Dugmore, *The Influence of the Synagogue upon the Divine Office* (2e., London 1964).

[43] p. 18 above. [44] 12.7/Mark 2.27; 12.12/Mark 3.4.
[45] 23.2f.

might as soon expect Archbishop Cranmer to have dropped the Lord's Supper. In earlier times no doubt Christians had been to Jewish synagogues in the morning and church at night, much as some Oxford undergraduates might attend College Chapel as a duty at 8.00 a.m., and repair for true spiritual nourishment to St Ebbe's at 11.00 a.m. But now Christians had their own synagogue, and their own *sôphēr*, and we may rely they duplicated the Jewish system rather than settled for the spirit of the matter like the pragmatic Paul.

Later echoes of such practices are not lacking. For the Bithynian church which Pliny persecuted,[46] the church women confessed under torture that they had an evening Eucharist *stato die*, which there is not the least evidence for taking as Sunday; and that in the early morning they sang the Kyrie's, or some suitable psalm (a *carmen* to Christ as a god), and recited the Commandments (bound themselves with an oath (*sacramentum*) not to steal, etc.). The pressures of the working day have driven the synagogue service before dawn, and reduced it to a skeleton, but there are plainly two Saturday services in Bithynia forty years after Matthew.[47] Elsewhere, Saturday Eucharists may have come into vogue very early, and are evidenced in the *Egyptian Church Order* (=Hippolytus' *Apostolic Tradition* in Ethiopic).[48] Saturday worship may have been observed in Irenaeus' time,[49] and has been observed specially in the Greek church from early days.[50] 'To suggest that the holding of services on Saturdays was a fourth-century innovation is to . . . ignore the fact that the Church grew out of the synagogue.'[51]

What is more to our purpose, we may depend that the Matthaean church, struggling to maintain its orthodoxy, will have followed the Jewish Calendar, with its feasts and fasts, and that the lections used will have have been the Jewish lections. If we have tassels and phylacteries, rabbis and *sôphᵉrîm*, we require a good reason for dispensing with Jewish high days and readings. What we *should* expect by way of a change is a series of Christian readings which showed how the Law and the Prophets had been fulfilled.

If the Matthaean church read the Torah in series as did the synagogues, and followed the Jewish Festal Year, what would be more natural than that it should also read the Gospel in series, and that the

[46] Pliny the Younger, *Epist.* x, 96–7.
[47] The theory that the worship was on a Sunday cannot explain either the origin of the dawn synaxis or the desuetude of the evening Eucharist.
[48] 24.1; cf. Dugmore, op. cit., p. 33. [49] *Adv. Haer.* IV. 16.1.
[50] The lections for Saturdays and Sundays are in one cycle, those for the weekdays in another.
[51] Dugmore, op. cit., p. 37.

Gospel should be aligned to the Jewish Year? But to achieve such alignment the Gospel would need to be tailor-made. The Christian material suitable for the feasts would need to occur at the proper intervals, and to have the number of paragraphs in between equal to the number of intervening sabbaths. That Matthew should have rewritten Mark in this way is a promising hypothesis: but how shall we have confidence rightly to divide the text? Happily there survive in some of our early and many of our later Mss. divisions which can be our guide, and which, if followed faithfully, provide an exact fit with the Jewish Year which we are postulating as in use in the Matthaean Church.

Matthew is divided in Mss. ℵ[52] B and 579 into 170 sections, which are sometimes as short as a single verse: von Soden[53] took these to be reference numbers, and with them we are not immediately concerned. Even older, in his opinion, are the 68 numbered divisions with titles, which occur in Codd. Alexandrinus (A) and Ephraemi (C), of the fifth century; the Dublin codex (Z), the Rossano codex (Σ), the Sinope codex (O), and Nitrensis (R), of the sixth century, and many later Mss. Nestle similarly calls these the old Greek divisions,[54] and they are marked in italic numbers in the margin of later editions of his text. Alexandrinus[55] and others have a table of the titles of the paragraphs at the head of the Gospel, and the name of the particular title at the top of each leaf: for a sample folio see the Frontispiece. In every case the divisions begin with 2.1ff περὶ τῶν μάγων, and count the first chapter as a Preface, as is the usual practice with NT Ms. divisions, and indeed with some secular books. Thus including ch. 1 there are 69 paragraphs or κεφαλαῖα in A's Matthew: the titles (which are not in Matthaean Greek) are given in von Soden's *Die Schriften*,[56] and I have translated them in the appendix. It is to be noted that while normally the title covers the substance of the whole unit, in a fair number of cases this is not so, and in these the titles refer to the opening incident of the κεφαλαῖον only, and I have indicated the

---

[52] For ℵ see F. G. Kenyon, *Handbook to the Textual Criticism of the NT* (2e., London 1912), pp. 80ff.
[53] H. von Soden, *Die Schriften des Neuen Testaments* (Berlin 1911) I, p. 402. There is a fairly full description of the details of the divisions in the Mss. in F. H. A. Scrivener, *A Plain Introduction to the Criticism of the New Testament* (4e., Cambridge 1894) I, pp. 58ff, and a briefer modern account in B. M. Metzger, *The Text of the New Testament* (2e., Oxford 1968), pp. 21ff.
[54] Nestle–Aland, *Novum Testamentum Graece* [Nestle-Aland] (e.25, 1963), p. 29.
[55] Alexandrinus itself is lacking the first twenty-four chapters of Matthew, but the numbers and titles are there for the rest of the Gospel, and the tables of titles at the head of the other Gospels show that the same is likely to be true for Matthew.
[56] ibid.

remainder of the matter in a parenthesis. For example, κεφαλαῖον no. 5 is the Sermon on the Mount, but the τίτλος is περὶ τῶν μακαρισμῶν; no. 67 is the Passion story, but is called 'The Remorse of Judas', with which it opens. The antiquity of the divisions is indicated (*a*) by their occurrence in Mss. of Egyptian (Z)[57] and Caesarean (OΣ)[58] as well as Byzantine provenance (ACRω),[59] and (*b*) by their widespread use in later Mss.: there is every reason for treating them as seriously as we would any verbal reading of similar attestation.

Von Soden suggested[60] that the divisions in A were, unlike those in B, intended for synoptic purposes. Eusebius, and Ammonius before him in the third century, had marked the Gospels into sections to facilitate comparison and to form diatessara; and the A divisions might be another attempt of the same kind. But if this were the case, then the A divisions in Mark would correspond with those in Matthew, and they do in the majority of cases. But in a number they do not. The six last units in Matthew are paralleled by four in Mark, for example, and the break at Mark 14.18 would require a corresponding break at Matt. 26.21, not 26 which we have. There are similar difficulties at Mark 2.13; 3.13; 5.25. Unless these points can be explained, the synoptic theory breaks down.

Two points about the divisions suggest a lectionary purpose. If the Gospel were used for readings, then the first reading will begin at the beginning of the book, and there is no need to mark it specially; and we have an explanation for the otherwise curious phenomenon of division 1 coming in ch. 2. The preface, which I have styled 0, would require no title. Similarly, if one is looking for readings, all that matters is where one starts, and the title must therefore give the essence of the *first* part of a complex paragraph. A table at the beginning of the book, and the title at the head of the page, and a number in the margin, are perfectly adapted for the purpose. We are not, however, concerned

[57] Codex Dublinensis (Z) is a palimpsest of the sixth, or possibly of the fifth century, whose text agrees chiefly with the Codex Sinaiticus; cf. Metzger, op. cit., p. 58.
[58] B. H. Streeter regarded O and Σ as weak members of the Caesarean text ('Codices 157, 1071 and the Caesarean Text', *Quantulacumque*, Studies presented to Kirsopp Lake (London 1937), pp. 149f; cited in Metzger, op. cit., p. 55).
[59] After a century of low regard, the Byzantine Mss. have recently been somewhat rehabilitated; see G. D. Kilpatrick 'The Greek New Testament Text of Today and the *Textus Receptus*', *The New Testament in historical and contemporary perspective: essays in honour of G. H. C. MacGregor* (Oxford 1965), pp. 189ff. Kilpatrick writes, 'A should be rehabilitated as a manuscript as worthy of serious consideration throughout as the other uncials of the fourth and fifth centuries A.D.' I am grateful to Dr Kilpatrick for kindness in advising me on several textual points.
[60] op. cit. I, p. 426.

merely with whether the divisions were used for lectionary purposes in later centuries: what we want to know is whether they were part of the original design of the evangelist.

The suggestion that this might be so was made by Dr Carrington in *The Primitive Christian Calendar*.[61] I am not now concerned with Carrington's scheme, which has little in common with my own: but to acknowledge his seminal suggestion, and to consider the criticisms of principle that have been levelled against it. It was dismissed by Casey,[62] partly with the argument that the Marcan church would not have been likely to take over the Jewish Calendar; and partly with vilification. Even if Casey's comments on the reaction from Judaism in the Marco–Pauline church are just, they would not apply to Matthew. W. D. Davies, in a long discussion,[63] remarks, 'I am not sure that we can dismiss the lectionary significance of the divisions in the manuscripts as surely as does Casey.' He notes against the hypothesis: (*a*) that the divisions are missing from the Chester–Beatty papyri (third century); (*b*) that Carrington assumes an annual reading, whereas the Jewish cycle was triennial; and (*c*) that many of the divisions delimit sections which are either too long or too short as lectionary units. None of these objections is final. For (*a*), although the Chester–Beatty papyrus (p[45]) has no divisions, the Bodmer papyrus (p[75]) has divisions for Luke which are close to those in A— unfortunately its text is defective for Matthew.[64] But the absence of the divisions from some papyri cannot be fatal to the lectionary hypothesis. If the Matthaean lections follow the Jewish Year closely, they would rapidly become meaningless to any church which parted company with Jewish ways, as the majority did. The wonder is that they have survived so late and so widespread in their pristine form. For (*b*) Davies is relying on the Büchler–Mann view,[65] which was still

---

[61] P. Carrington, *The Primitive Christian Calendar* (Cambridge 1952). Carrington was primarily concerned with Mark, which he believed (correctly) to begin with matter suitable to be read at New Year; he styled the 48 divisions for twelve four-week months, and was impressed with the coincidence of the Feeding of the 5000 with Passover.

[62] R. P. Casey, reviewing recent writing on 'St Mark's Gospel', in *Theology* (October 1952), pp. 362–70.

[63] 'Reflections on Archbishop Carrington's *The Primitive Christian Calendar*', in *The Background of the N.T. and its Eschatology*, ed. W. D. Davies and D. Daube, in honour of C. H. Dodd (Cambridge 1964), pp. 140n, 144ff.

[64] The A-group divisions of Matthew are rational, except for a number of sections which begin a verse or two late, at the point where the chief character of the pericope is named (see below, pp. 325f, n. 39). In a number of cases the A-group divisions of Luke are irrational; p[75] is closer to a rational division of Luke, but has added sub-divisions. See p. 455, n. 6).

[65] See above, p. 173, n. 9.

orthodox in the 1950s: but it is irrelevant to our thesis which length of cycle was being followed, because the Jewish Festal year was invariable, and it is with this that Matthew shows strict agreement. He does also show a relationship to an annual sabbath-by-sabbath lectionary system, but that is secondary, and will be expounded in a later chapter.[66] For (*c*), the great disparity in length of sections, which at first sight seems incredible as an intentional feature of the Gospel, turns out to be the cornerstone of the structure. Some of the lections are only two or three verses long; one is the Sermon on the Mount: but then neither Carrington nor Davies set out the Matthaean A sections against the Jewish year—they were disputing about Mark, and Matthew was but a makeweight.

If Matthew were written to be the Church's reading round the year, when would the readings begin? It would be natural to suppose that the Passion story was read at Passover/Eastertide. The story is set then, and this is the only direct Festal reference in the Gospel. In the earliest lectionaries that we have, Roman, Greek, Syriac, and Armenian, the Passion according to Matthew was read in Holy Week.[67] Further it is likely that the Matthaean church would have celebrated the octave of Easter.[68] Passover was, with Unleavened Bread, an eight-day festival, ending on the 21st Nisan, and Tabernacles and Hanukkah were eight-day festivals, so Matthew would not have lacked precedent for regarding the Queen of Feasts as an octave. There are already traces of an Easter octave in John, in the story of the confirmatory appearance to the Eleven with Thomas on the eighth day,[69] and all Christian calendars from Etheria on celebrate Low

---

[66] pp. 227ff below.   [67] See p. 433 below.

[68] Matthew is likely to have followed the later Catholic rather than Quartodeciman practice over Easter. Some first-century churches celebrated the death-and-resurrection of Jesus on Passover, 14th Nisan, since it was on Passover that he died; others on the Saturday night following Passover, since it was on the first day of the week that he rose again. In the second century these became Quartodeciman and Catholic parties. Although the Quartodecimans sprang from Jewish–Christian origins, there is nothing Gentile–Christian about the Catholic use, and the issue was not fought on general Jewish *v*. Gentile Christian issues. The Quartodecimans were largely confined to Asia, and the Syrian bishops Cassius and Clarus were used to the Catholic practice and voted for it: since Matthew is likely to be a Syrian document, and the Quartodecimans claimed Johannine authority, it is best to suppose that the Matthaean church celebrated Easter on the Saturday night. Eusebius, *H.E.* v. 23–5; E. Lohse, *Das Passafest der Quartadecimaner* (Gütersloh 1953).

[69] John 20.26.

Sunday as the Easter octave. The likelihood is then that Matthew
began to be read on the second Saturday[70] after Easter.

The first five sections are of reasonable length. The whole of ch. 1
is the Preface, and so would fall to Easter II, but the Genealogy alone
would be dry. Ch. 2 is divided between Easter III and IV, with the
break at the most rational place. The Baptism and Temptations fall
together, and would form a long reading for Easter V, thirty-four
verses; the Call of the first Apostles would be read on Easter VI, nine
verses. The next section is the whole Sermon on the Mount, and would
fall on Easter VII, that is, the Saturday between 5th and 11th Sivan;
the eve of, the day of, or the Saturday after Pentecost. Now, as I have
said, Pentecost is the feast of the Giving of the Law. The reading for
Pentecost in the Toseftah and the Talmud[71] is Exod. 19—20.23:
Exod. 19 tells how Israel came to Mt Sinai, and Moses went up the
mountain, Exod. 20 tells how God gave Israel the Law, beginning
with the Ten Commandments. Matt. 5 describes Jesus going up the
mountain and sitting down to teach the New Israel the New Law. He
prefaces the Sermon with the rider that he has come to fulfil the old
Law, and proceeds to draw a series of antitheses between six of the
old precepts and six of the new dispensation of fulfilment. Of the six,
the first two are from the Ten Commandments, the fourth and sixth
are from the Ten Commandments combined with other texts,[72] and
the fifth ('An eye for an eye . . .') is from the next chapter in Exodus.
In Matt. 6 Jesus contrasts the spirit in which Christians are to perform
the traditional duties to God with that customary in Pharisaism: in
their prayer for God's name to be hallowed we have a further echo of
the Commandments.[73]

Exod. 19.1 records that on the third new moon after the Exodus
Israel reached Sinai, that is 1st Sivan; Exod. 16.1 that on the 15th day
of the second month they left Elim, and that during the following
week (16.22,30) they were fed with manna. Thus before the close of
the redaction of the Bible, the events between the Exodus and Sinai

---

[70] The 'Gospel' began as homiletic comment on the Sabbath morning OT
readings, and may have been used by Matthew at the sabbath a.m. service as
well as at the Eucharist in the evening: 'Saturday' covers both.

[71] J Meg. III.7; T Meg. IV.5; B Meg. 31a. The association of the Law-giving and
Covenant with Pentecost is repeatedly made in Jubilees (6.19 Sinai itself, 6.10
Noah, 14.20 Abraham, 15.1 Circumcision), and was made by the Qumran
community; cf. B. Noack, 'The Day of Pentecost in Jubilees, Qumran and Acts',
in *Annual of the Swedish Theological Institute* I (1962). The Mishnah reading,
typically, is Deut. 16.9–12 (Meg. 3.5). The rabbis at Jamnia were on the defensive,
and in most instances appointed a lection that commanded the observance of a
feast.

[72] See p. 271 below.   [73] See p. 276 below.

were being assigned to dates between Passover and Pentecost, and this interest is further elaborated in the Mekilta[74] and the Seder 'Olam.[75] The stories of Israel's hunger for bread and God's supply of their need, and of Israel's thirst for water, and their tempting God at the Waters of Massah, Temptation, were thus the subject of rabbinic meditation and homily the last two sabbaths in Iyyar. Two weeks before the Sermon on the Mount (20–26th Iyyar) would come Matt. 3.1—4.16: how Jesus was baptized and tempted forty days in the desert. His first Temptation was his hunger, to turn stones into bread; and the reply he gives is the words that comment on the giving of manna in Deuteronomy—'that he might make you know that man does not live by bread alone, but that man lives by every word that proceeds from the mouth of God'.[76] At his second Temptation he replies to the devil in words that recall Israel's second tempting of God, 'You shall not put the Lord your God to the test, as you tested him at Massah' (Deut. 6.16; Exod. 17).[77] In the next chapter of Exodus, before Sinai, Moses appointed Seventy to be judges over Israel: in the next section of Matthew, before Pentecost, Jesus appoints the first four of his Twelve, who will one day sit on thrones judging the twelve tribes of Israel.

The Sermon is Pentecostal in a further way. Pentecost is the fiftieth day from the day after Passover, the Feast of Weeks, *Shābu'ôth*: it is a perfect octave, the final day to the Week of Weeks. From ancient times it has been observed with an all-night vigil, and through the night and day the gift of the Law has been celebrated by the reading of the beginning and end of each of the biblical books.[78] These were reckoned as twenty-two in number according to one tradition,[79] twenty-four according to another.[80] Now a part of the traditional liturgy for Pentecost is Ps. 119,[81] which is ideally suited to it as a praising of the Law. The Psalm is divided into twenty-two stanzas,

---

[74] cf. A. Büchler, art. cit., *JQR* v, pp. 434ff.

[75] ch. v, vi, x; cf. Büchler, as above.   [76] Deut. 8.3 (AT).

[77] The name of the chapter (*seder*) in Hebrew is *wayassa'*, 'And he tempted'.

[78] 'Therefore the pious ones of old used not to sleep on this night [sc. Pentecost], but they used to study the Torah and say, "Let us acquire a holy inheritance for ourselves and our sons in two worlds" ' (Zohar, Emor 98a); cf. *J.E.*, art. 'Pentecost', IX, pp. 592ff.

[79] So Josephus, *c. Ap.* I 39–42, Melito, Origen, Jerome, *Prologus Galeatus*; see G. W. Anderson, 'Canonical and Non-Canonical', *Cambridge History of the Bible* I (Cambridge 1970), pp. 135ff.

[80] 2 Esdras 14.44–6. The official Hebrew canon is of twenty-four books. Both figures involve an amount of double counting, so as to keep the number down to the ideal—an inevitable process when new books were to be added to a canon whose total of books was fixed.

[81] Tractate *Sopherim*, 29.

according to the twenty-two letters of the Hebrew alphabet, which open the eight lines of the respective stanzas in order. It contains a considerable number of references to praise at different times in the day: 'I remember thy name in the night, O Lord' (v. 55), 'At midnight I rise to praise thee' (v. 62), 'It is my meditation all the day' (v. 97), 'I rise before dawn and cry for help' (v. 147), 'My eyes awake before the watches of the night' (v. 148), 'Seven times a day I praise thee' (v. 164). The last reference invites us to suppose that the Psalm was in fact composed for the celebration of Pentecost: that the stanzas were sung three at a time at the three-hourly watches in honour of the triads of biblical books; that the twenty-second stanza completed the series with the eighth watch;[82] the references to the night (v. 55) and 'at midnight' (v. 62) would fall at the third watch, at midnight; the reference to 'seven times a day' would fall at the seventh watch, at midday. Now the Sermon is itself an octave. It opens with an octave of blessings, of which the reward of the first blessed, the poor in spirit, and the last blessed, the persecuted for righteousness, are the same, the Kingdom of Heaven. The Sermon is an exposition of these Beatitudes,[83] and divides accordingly into eight sub-readings, one for each watch. So we have an answer to Davies' hesitation:[84] the Sermon is far longer than a normal lection because it is the Church's Pentecostal lection. As a Jewish–Christian synagogue, the Matthaean church celebrated Pentecost the day through. It required an octave of readings to expound the fulfilment of the Law in Christ's Torah,[85] and that is precisely what the Sermon on the Mount supplied.

After the Sermon the lections become short. There are seven from ch. 8 and six from ch. 9, one of them being as short as two verses. However, the same principle covers all lections in the Gospel: that each division should describe one incident. Most of the sections are about the length of some of the shorter modern Gospels:[86] some are the same. The next holy day of the Jewish Calendar is the Fast of 9th Ab (August). Now Lection 14, Matt. 9.9–17, would fall either on 9th Ab or on one of the six days following, if we pursue the A divisions: the Call of Matthew, the dispute about Jesus' table-fellowship, and the controversy about fasting. Jesus teaches that fasting is out of place

---

[82] As long as the canon was limited to twenty-four books as a maximum, there would be no embarrassment.

[83] See ch. 12 below. [84] See p. 182(c) above.

[85] The Beatitudes are formed as a unit on the model of the opening stanza of Ps. 119: eight verses of which the first two open, 'μακάριοι . . .' ('ashrei).

[86] Short lections are not anomalies. In the Anglican 1928 Book the Gospel for Thanksgiving for the Institution of Holy Baptism is three verses (Matt. 28. 18–20): the Epistle for the Second Sunday after Christmas is one verse (2 Cor. 8.9).

during his ministry, but will be incumbent upon his disciples after his departure. It is the most direct injunction to fast in the Gospel. Further, 9th Ab was no ordinary fast-day, for which fasting alone was prescribed, but the day of mourning for the double destruction of the Temple: and mourning involved more elaborate ascesis than fasting. Matthew at 9.15 substitutes 'mourn' for the Marcan 'fast'.

Matthew has rearranged the Marcan healings in such a way as to yield a crescendo of controversy. At first Jesus is the popular healer in 8, but he comes under increasing criticism in 9, which ends in the accusation that he exorcizes through the arch-demon. In 10 he warns his disciples that they will be rejected like their master; in 11 he upbraids the fickle generation and the cities among whom he has shown his healing powers. With 12 comes the climax. Three bitter controversies are described, the Cornfield, the Withered Hand, Beelzebul, taking up the end of 9. Jesus is rejected, and he proclaims the Pharisees rejected by God in their turn. All this refashioning is in favour of the theme of New Year, which is judgement, and the possibility of repentance before the coming of the Kingdom of the Heavens. In 10 the apostles are chosen and sent to proclaim the coming of the Kingdom. In 11.2—12.8 we have a long lection, which in most years would be for the week including 1st Tishri. Jesus quotes the New Year lection from Isa. 35,[87] 'The blind receive their sight ...' to show that the Age-to-Come has begun. Tyre and Sidon, Sodom, would have repented, but not this generation. The warning of judgement and the call to penitence extend in Judaism from New Year to Atonement. Lection 21, the Withered Hand, introduces the word κρίσις twice in the Matthaean version: 'He shall proclaim judgement to the Gentiles . . . till he brings judgement to victory' (AT). Lection 22, Beelzebul, has Jesus telling the Pharisees that they will not be forgiven, either in this age or in the age to come; that on the day of judgement men will render account for every careless word they utter; and that by their words they will be condemned. The principal *haphtārāh* reading on Atonement Day was the Book of Jonah, which according to the Talmud was read entire.[88] Its theme is apt, for the Ninevites repent in sackcloth and ashes at Jonah's preaching, as Israel is called to do on Yom Kippur. The 23rd Matthaean section compares Christ to Jonah: 'The men of Nineveh will arise at the judgement with this generation and condemn it; for they repented at the preaching of Jonah, and behold, something greater than Jonah is here.'

Five days after Atonement comes Tabernacles, the eight-day Feast

[87] See below, p. 312, n. 5.
[88] B Meg. 31a. The passage is a Baraita, and likely to be old.

of Ingathering, and celebration of the Temple. The lection following
the Jonah passage in Matthew comprises the whole Parables chapter,
13. The parables are ingathering parables: the seed that bears a
hundred, sixty, or thirty-fold, the gathering of the wheat into garners
and the tares for the bonfire, the net that gathers fish of every kind.
The minor parables not so markedly, but the theme is not far away:
the mustard-tree growing to its fulness, the leavened meal that brings
the harvest to table. It was a theme that the Lord had taught, and
Mark had put together: in Matthew it is expanded and emphasized.
The second theme of Tabernacles was the Temple, dedicated by Solomon in the Feast of the seventh month, and celebrated each year with
processions round the altar. It is in ch. 12, in the readings for the first
half of Tishri, that the Temple–Solomon theme comes forward: one
greater than the Temple, than Solomon, one who shows his wisdom
in parables, who speaks of trees and fish.

Tabernacles was an eight-day feast, and the great length of the reading would resolve itself if, like the Sermon, it were subdivided into
eight, and the sub-divisions in this case used over the eight days. It
divides into eight easily enough: vv. 3–9 The Sower; vv. 10–17 The
Reason for Parables; vv. 18–23 The Sower Interpreted; vv. 24–30 The
Tares; vv. 31–5 Mustard-Seed, Leaven, and a second citation on
Parables; vv. 36–43 The Tares Interpreted; vv. 44–52 Treasure, Pearl,
and Dragnet (Interpreted); vv. 53–8 Jesus' wisdom disbelieved. There
were short mid-Festival services in the synagogues, for which the
Mishnah provided lessons from Num. 29 specifying the offering for
each day; and there were holy convocations, days of solemn rest, on
the first and eighth days, on the former of which was read the law of
the set feasts from Lev. 23.[89] The church could have used the eight
Matthaean sections in series as they stood, or perhaps longer pieces
on the first and last days, and the Saturday.

Yom Kippur had by the first century an importance far beyond
such other one-day feasts as Ninth Ab, New Year, or Purim: it was
the Mishnah's Yoma, 'The Day', and it is inconceivable that the
Matthaean church should have done other than celebrate it on 10th
Tishri. The other feasts might well be assumed under the liturgy of the
previous Saturday,[90] and have the Gospel repeated on the day itself.
The vagaries of the calendar must involve some complications around
New Year, and the Matthaean text allows for this. The median year
which we have set out involves no problem. Lection 20, with the Isa.

[89] M Meg. 3.5.
[90] cf. M Meg. 3.4, 'If the first day of the month Adar falls on the Sabbath, they
read the section *Sheqalim*; if it falls in the middle of the week they read it earlier,
on the sabbath that goes before . . .'

35 quotation, contains New Year within its week (on the Friday); there are two Lections, 21 and 22, both on the judgement theme, for the two Saturdays, 2nd and 9th Tishri; Lection 23, with the Jonah reference, can be taken on 10th Tishri; and there is no further Saturday before 15th, when Lection 24, the Harvest Parables, can begin to be read. Should the Saturdays fall two or three days earlier, there would be the complication of a fifth Saturday in Elul. Now Lection 20, unlike the other units we have treated,[91] involves two distinct incidents, for the Upbraiding of the Cities is in no way related to the story of the Cornfield: this could then be divided, and the Cornfield read on the last Saturday in Elul. This would leave only one Saturday between New Year and Atonement, so Beelzebul would have to be combined with the Jonah paragraph, to which it belongs; and the Mother and Brothers, which is a distinct incident within Lection 23, could be divided off for use on a Saturday between Atonement and Tabernacles. These are the only cases in the Gospel where the A divisions provide more than one incident within a κεφαλαῖον, and both are necessary to provide for the fluctuations of the calendar. Should the Saturdays fall later than the median, the second and/or third of these adjustments can be made. The Jonah unit can thus always be read at Atonement and the Harvest Parables at Tabernacles.

The next synagogue feast is Dedication, which falls on 25th Kislev (December) and the seven days following, after an intermission of nine weeks. It celebrates the investing of the Tabernacle and Temple with the divine glory as the sun breaks through the darkness of midwinter; and secondarily, the gathering together of God's Israel when mercy comes. An intermission of nine sections in A brings us to Matt. 17.1–13: the Transfiguration, when the cloud of glory descends upon Jesus, and his face shines like the sun, and his garments grow white as the light. He has declared himself one greater than the Temple in 12. As God took possession of the Tabernacle in Exod. 40/Num. 9, and of the Temple in 1 Kings 8,[92] with the descent of the Shekinah; so it is given to the three apostles to see the Shekinah upon Jesus on the mountain, God's living Temple indwelt by his glory. The *sidrāh*[93] for Dedication was Num. 7ff,[94] when the gifts for the Tabernacle were dedicated: gifts originally commanded in Exod. 30, and given in the free-will

[91] For the cohesiveness of the Baptism and Temptations in one unit see p. 245 below.
[92] 2 Macc. 2.8ff, where the two incidents are referred to in connection with Hanukkah.
[93] The term *sidrah* is used to signify the section of the Torah set for reading on a feast-day or sabbath in the *annual* cycle: the term *seder* for the same in the triennial cycle.
[94] M Meg. 3.6; B Meg. 31a.

offering. Now the Exod. 30 passage was well known to every Israelite. It was called *Sheqalim*, and was the appointed additional reading seven weeks before Passover, so that all could pay their half-shekel in time for the feast.[95] Matt. 17.24–end makes the half-shekel incumbent upon the church; and since the money is to be dedicated for Temple use, he sets the pericope at Dedication.

John 10, or at least John 10.22–39, is dated at Dedication, and the theme of much of the chapter, including vv. 25–31, is Jesus as the Good Shepherd. The gathering theme is evidenced for Dedication in 2 Macc. 1.27; 2.18, and it would be natural to think that Ezek. 34 was a Jewish reading for the feast.[96] Matt. 18 begins from the Marcan injunction to beware of scandalizing the little ones, and expounds this duty under the image of the lost sheep: first Christ's pastor is given the parable, and then it is applied in detailed illustration. For the rest of the eight days the apostles are given the Church's law: Peter, later the Twelve, is made the rock upon which Christ's Church is to be built as a New Temple, and the laws they are to bind and loose are then set out. Later centuries continued to celebrate 'Encaenia of the Church', the Church's Dedication, at Midwinter.[97]

Purim, commemorating the deliverance of the Jews through Esther, falls on a slightly variable date between 11th and 15th Adar (March): that is, about ten weeks after the end of Hanukkah. The tenth lection after the Hanukkah series in Matthew (Lections 34–41) would be Lection 51, Matt. 22.1–14, The Royal Marriage-Feast: new material, introduced into the Marcan sequence by Matthew. In the Esther story, King Ahasuerus marries, and the book is largely taken up with a series of banquets; while Haman is still at home, the king's chamberlains arrive and bring him in haste to the feast that Esther has prepared; and the unworthy wedding-guest is cast out and hanged on his own gallows. The Matthaean parable adapts the preceding Marcan

---

[95] M Meg. 3.4; cf. Shek.

[96] Guilding (op. cit., p. 131) claims that Ezek. 34 was a *haphtārāh* reading for Dedication, but she depends upon the evidence of late Yemeni, south Italian, and Persian use, she presupposes a triennial cycle, and according to her table on p. 234 the passages would fall six weeks after Hanukkah.

[97] Dedication (Encaenia, the Greek approximation to Hanukkah) remained long in the Church's calendar. It was still celebrated around 400 in Jerusalem for eight days, and the OT lection was 2 Chron. 7—8, the Dedication of Solomon's Temple. Monks attended from as far as Mesopotamia and Egypt, and at least 40–50 bishops, amid great pomp and solemnity. The date had been transferred to mid-September, in celebration of the consecration of the two great basilicas, the Martyrium and the Anastasis, in 335 (*Peregrinatio Etheriae*, ch. 48): but a late December date was still in use among the Palestinian Melkites and Nestorians, who celebrated the feast of *Encaenia Ecclesiae*, not *Ecclesiarum*; cf. M. Black, 'The Festival of Encaenia Ecclesiae', *JEH* 5 (1954), pp. 78–85.

Husbandmen to the Purim theme. There is a royal wedding, a feast to which the guests are summoned by the king's servants, and the unworthy guest is cast out into hell.

Sometimes there are fifty-one sabbaths in the 354-day Jewish year, sometimes fifty: and then every third year or so there is a Second Adar intercalated, so that there will then be fifty-four sabbaths or fifty-five. No system of fixed lections can be flexible enough for such variation. The Matthaean text provides one lection beyond what is requisite for a fifty-one Saturday year: in short years combination would be required (as is normal in modern synagogue worship), in long years repetition.

Ch. 23 would fall, then, to the first Saturday in Nisan; 24.3–35 to the Saturday before Passover. There is every probability that the early Church, back to the Matthaean generation and even before, celebrated the weekdays leading up to Passover, and the watches of Passover night. Mark 14.1 and Matt. 26.2 note that the authorities' plot was two days before the Passover; the supper at Simon's house is evidently remembered to be on the Wednesday night; and the watches through Passover night are marked in both Gospels, and underlined in the preceding Apocalyptic discourses. In the earliest Eastern lectionaries we find Matt. 24ff being read serially from Tuesday in Holy Week, in the Greek lectionaries from Monday, and in both Matthew is used at three-hourly watch-services through Maundy Thursday night.[98] The period from 10th Nisan when the lamb was taken, till 14th when it was eaten, is marked out as a time of preparation in Exodus, and in Jewish domestic practice.

Lection 57, Matt. 24.3–35, is well suited to a Paschal context. The Passover celebrated the deliverance of the Exodus, and looked forward to future deliverance, and to the coming of Elijah, Messiah's fore-runner.[99] Matt. 24 looks to the Parousia of the Son of Man. The Noah story was read in synagogues the second sabbath in Nisan.[100] Jesus warns his disciples to flee to the mountains: as it was in the days of Noah, so shall it be in the days of the Son of Man. As at the Exodus the first-born children were killed throughout Egypt from Pharaoh on his throne to the woman grinding at the mill, but the Israelites spared, so now two women shall be grinding at the mill, one will be taken and one left. Matthew's Apocalypse describes the Passion of the Church, fittingly read at the beginning of the week of the Passion

[98] See p. 433 below.
[99] Moore, *Judaism* II, p. 42. The setting of a chair for Elijah is a later practice. cf. Jerome, cited below, p. 438, n. 27.
[100] In an annual cycle; cf. pp. 227f below.

of her Lord.[101] There are five lections (58–62) available for the maximum of five days between Lection 57 and Passover. In the Virgins
(59) the cry goes up at midnight that the bridegroom has come, just as
a great cry went up at midnight at the Exodus; and the door is shut
upon the community of the saved, as upon Noah. The Sheep and
Goats (61) continues on to 26.5, and includes Jesus' words, 'You
know that after two days the Passover is coming': it would be suitably
read two days before Passover, as the Anointing story (62) would be
suitably read the following evening. 26.17–25 (63), the preparation
and eating of the Last Supper, would be read at the Christian Passover,
at sunset; as it says, 'When it was evening . . .' (v. 20). 26.26–46, the
Institution of the Eucharist, the closing psalm, and Gethsemane,
would fall naturally at 9.00 p.m.: the Passover meal was a full-length
occasion. 26.47–68, the Arrest and Trial, is marked off from the
previous section by the threefold, 'Could you not watch with me one
hour?', and would be read at midnight. Luke adds the apt comment,
'This is your hour, and the power of darkness' (22.53). 26.69—27.2,
Peter's Denial and Jesus' delivery to Pilate would follow at cockcrow,
3.00 a.m. (26.74). 27.3–56, the whole story of the Passion from Judas'
remorse to the women's watching of Jesus' death, would be taken at
the one main service in the daytime of Passover. 27.57—28 would be
the reading for Easter Saturday. The opening words, 'When it was
evening . . .' assign it to sabbath; the opening words of 28, 'Now
after the sabbath, toward the dawn of the first day of the week . . .'
assign it to Saturday night. No doubt it was in practice divided between
the two Saturday services. 28.19f supplies the dominical authority for
the Easter baptisms; and the whole of 28 would be repeated on the
octave.

The 69 sections of the A group of Mss. thus correspond to the
lections of a church which celebrated a Christian version of the Jewish
Festal Year from beginning to end. The sections provide exactly the
number of readings to go round; ideal passages occur on the occasion
of all the six major Feasts and both major Fasts. There are Discourses,
formally introduced and closed with rubrics, for the three pilgrim-
feasts of Pentecost (5—7), Tabernacles (13), and Passover (24—25),
and for Hanukkah (18), and a week ahead, in preparation for the two
principal Festal Seasons of Passover (23) and New-Year-Tabernacles
(10). There are less formal blocks of teaching for New Year (11),
Atonement (12.38–end, or 22–end), the remainder of Hanukkah (17,
19) and Purim (22.1–14). Between these Discourses run a series of
stories, in each case providing exactly the right number of lections for
the intervening sabbaths. The chances against this pattern occurring

[101] cf. R. H. Lightfoot, *The Gospel Message of St Mark* (Oxford 1950), ch. IV.

by accident are very large. The liturgical structure is clearly integral
to the writing, and could not have been imposed by the later Church
on material not designed for the purpose. The Gospel was written to
be read round the Jewish–Christian Year, and was formed by repeated
preaching round the Jewish–Christian Year, by Matthew.

What became of Matthew's masterpiece? The widespread and long-
continued use of his divisions, as testified in the Mss. of the A group,
show that the first-century Church, which everywhere was still conscious of its Jewish roots, knew what Matthew was doing and appreciated it. In some places the readings will have been understood and
used by Jewish Christians for centuries as they were intended. In others
the set lections will have been read serially, perhaps for as long, for
motives of conservatism, without any understanding of their significance, other than at Easter. In others, as testified by the Chester–Beatty
papyri, the lections made no sense and ceased to be used. In ℵ and B
we have an example of an attempt to improve on Matthew's irregular
handiwork. Their 170 divisions are mainly of even length, and often
fall in threes—three parts of the Genealogy, three Temptations, three
parts to ch. 18, etc.—enough, perhaps, for three readings a week in a
church like the Didachist's, that celebrated Wednesdays, Fridays, and
Sundays.

Matthew is the Gospel most often quoted by the second-century
Fathers,[102] and it is natural to think therefore that they read him most
often in church. Neither Mark nor John provides lections for a year.
Matthew was before Luke, and his poetry is more memorable, and the
book carries the name of an apostle. It is normally supposed that in
early times the bishop selected the passage to be read at will,[103] but
there is no evidence for this; nor is it likely, as Etheria seems to suggest,
that the same Gospel was read every week.[104] Our first lectionaries
provide only lections for feast days, the first and fourth weeks in Lent,
Holy Week, and Easter Week: the likelihood is that the Gospels
were read serially for the remainder of the year. The Syrian church
read Matt. 4—11 through serially the first week in Lent before 500,[105]
and Matt. 24—28 was read serially everywhere in Holy Week. In the
Greek church the Sermon on the Mount is read serially to this day

---

[102] E. Massaux, *L'Influence de l'Evangile selon S. Matthieu* (Louvain 1950).
[103] G. G. Willis, ed., *St Augustine's Lectionary* (London 1962), pp. 5ff. But
Willis himself shows that Augustine selected the lections at Hippo serially.
[104] *Peregrinatio*, ch. 27, 43, says that the Jerusalem church had the Resurrection
as the Gospel every Sunday: but this does not preclude a changing Gospel
besides, just as many modern churches have used John 1. 1–14 every week as
well as a changing Gospel.
[105] BM Add. 14457, cited in F. C. Burkitt, 'The Early Syriac Lectionary System',
Proc. B.A. xi (1923).

through the week-days after Pentecost, almost as the evangelist intended, and the succeeding healing stories are read, almost in series, on the Saturdays and Sundays thereafter.[106] With the rise of a non-Jewish Christian year in the fourth century the old rational ways were ploughed under in the commemoration of martyrs real and fictitious, and in a meaningless eclecticism. Augustine, who established new lections with a free hand at Hippo, reproved his congregation for tumultuous behaviour because he abolished the reading of the Passion according to St Matthew on Good Friday in favour of lections from all four Gospels.[107] Well might they complain. In the West today only the Passion according to Matthew survives in its intended place in the Church's liturgy: whether removed to Palm Sunday for the Gospel, or sung to majestic German music, often on its own Good Friday. Purim, Dedication, New Year, the two Fasts are forgotten: Pentecost is surrendered to Luke. Perhaps we may smile at the irony which has replaced the Jewish with an English feast of Ingathering: when we sing 'The Sower went forth sowing', Bourne's version of Matthew's Sower, and 'Come, ye thankful people, come', Alford's version of Matthew's Tares.

[106] cf. Scrivener, op. cit., I p. 81.
[107] Aug. *Serm.* ccxxxii. i.l, cited by Willis, op. cit., p. 9. The Matthaean Passion was also established in the Mozarabic and Ambrosian rites at an early date.

APPENDIX A

1. THE A DIVISIONS OF MATTHEW AND A JEWISH–CHRISTIAN YEAR

NISAN

4 Saturday	56	23.1	Reviling of Scribes and Pharisees
11 ,, before *Passover*	57	24.3	The Consummation
Sunday to 14 Nisan	58 59 60 61 62	24.36 25.1 25.14 25.31 26.6	The Day and the Hour The Ten Virgins The Receivers of the Talents The Coming of Christ She who anointed the Lord with Myrrh
15 *Passover* 6 p.m.	63	26.17	The Pasch
9 p.m.	64	26.26	The Mystic Type (Gethsemane)
midnight	65	26.47	The Betrayal of Jesus
3 a.m.	66	26.69	The Denial of Peter
a.m.	67	27.3	Judas' Remorse (Trial and Crucifixion)
18 Saturday	68	27.57	Request for the Lord's Body (Resurrection)
25 ,,	68		(Octave)

IYYAR

2 Sat.	0	1	(Genealogy, Birth)
9 Sat.	1	2.1	The Magi
16 Sat.	2	2.16	The Slaughtered Children
23 Sat.	3	3.1	John first preached the Kingdom of Heaven (Baptism Temptations)

SIVAN

1 Sat.	4	4.17	The Saviour's Teaching (Call of Four)
6 *Pentecost* 8 Sat.	5	5.1	The Beatitudes (Sermon on the Mount)
15 Sat.	6	8.1	The Leper

SIVAN

| 22 Sat. | 7 | 8.5 | The Centurion |
| 29 Sat. | 8 | 8.14 | Peter's Mother-in-Law |

TAMMUZ

6 Sat.	9	8.16	Those Healed of Various Diseases
13 Sat.	10	8.19	The Man Not Commanded to Follow
20 Sat.	11	8.23	The Rebuke of the Waters
27 Sat.	12	8.28	The Possessed of Demons

AB

5 Sat.	13	9.2	The Paralytic
12 Sat. (*9th Ab*)	14	9.9	Matthew the Publican (Eating, Fasting)
19 Sat.	15	9.18	The Daughter of the Synagogue Ruler
26 Sat.	16	9.20	The Woman with Flux

ELUL

3 Sat.	17	9.27	The Blind Men
10 Sat.	18	9.32	The Dumb Demoniac
17 Sat.	19	10.1	The Directing of the Apostles
24 Sat. *New Year* }	20	11.2	Those sent by John (Upbraiding of Cities, Cornfield)

TISHRI

2 Sat.	21	12.9	The Man with Withered Hand
9 Sat.	22	12.22	The Blind and Dumb Demoniac
10 *Day of Atonement*	23	12.38	Those who asked for a Sign (Mother and Brothers)
15–22 *Tabernacles*	24	13.3	The Parables
23 Sat.	25	14.1	John and Herod
30 Sat.	26	14.15	The Five Loaves and Two Fishes

CHESHVAN

7 Sat.	27	14.22	The Walking on the Water
14 Sat.	28	15.1	The Transgression of God's Commandment
21 Sat.	29	15.22	The Canaanite Woman
28 Sat.	30	15.29	The Crowds Healed

KISLEV

6 Sat.	31	15.32	The Seven Loaves
13 Sat.	32	16.5	The Leaven of the Pharisees
20 Sat.	33	16.13	The Question at Caesarea
25 Th. *Ḥanukkah*	34	17.1	The Transfiguration of Jesus
26 F	35	17.14	The Epileptic Boy
27 Sat.	36	17.24	Those who asked for the Didrachma
28 Sun.	37	18.1	Those who said, Who is greatest
29 M	38	18.12	The Parable of the 100 sheep
30 Tu	39	18.23	The Man who owed 10,000 Talents

TEBETH

1 W	40	19.3	Those who asked if one may divorce one's wife
2 Th	41	19.16	The Rich Man who questioned him
4 Sat.	42	20.1	The Hired Labourers
11 Sat.	43	20.20	The Sons of Zebedee
18 Sat.	44	20.29	The Two Blind Men
25 Sat.	45	21.1	The Ass and the Colt

SHEBAT

3 Sat.	46	21.14	The Blind and Lame
10 Sat.	47	21.18	The Withered Fig-Tree
17 Sat.	48	21.23	The Chief-Priests and Elders who questioned the Lord
24 Sat.	49	21.28	The Two Sons

ADAR

1 Sat.		50	21.33	The Vineyard
8 Sat.		51	22.1	Those Invited to the
(11–15 *Purim*)				Marriage
15 Sat.		52	22.15	Those who asked about
				the Tax
22 Sat.		53	22.23	The Sadducees
29 Sat.		54	22.34	The Questioning Lawyer
2ND ADAR		55	22.41	The Lord's Questioning

The dates are for an 'average' year, i.e. midway between having the first sabbath on 1st and 7th Nisan. The titles are those in the Mss. with suitable additions in brackets.

2. THE MATTHAEAN LECTIONARY

	TORAH	OTHER OT	LECTION (A)	MATT.
IInd–VIth Saturdays after Easter (5)	(Exod. 16—18)		0–4(5)	1—4
Pentecost (Eight Watches)	Exod. 19—20	Ps. 119	5	5—7
(and Saturday)				
IInd–IXth Saturdays after Pentecost (8)			6–13(8)	8—9.8
9th Ab (and Saturday)		Lamentations	14	9.9–17
XIth–XIVth Saturdays after Pentecost (4)			15–18(4)	9.18–34*
Saturday next before New Year Season			19	9.35*—10
New Year (and Saturday)		Isa. 35	20	11*—12.8
Ist (and IInd) Saturdays after New Year			21(–22)	12.9–37(21)
Yom Kippur	Lev. 16	Jonah	23	12.38(22)—end
Tabernacles (Eight Days)	Lev. 23	1 Kings 8	24	13*
Ist–IXth Saturdays after Tabernacles (9)			25–33(9)	14—16
Hanukkah (Eight Days)	Num. 7ff	Zech. 3—4	34–41(8)	17—19
Ist–IXth Saturdays after Hanukkah (9)			42–50(9)	20—21
Purim (and Saturday)		Esther	51	22.1–14
Saturdays after Purim (2–7)			52–5(4)	22.15–end
Saturday next before Passover Season			56	23
Saturday before Passover			57	24.1–35
Sunday—14th Nisan (1–5)			58–62(5)	24.36—26.16
Passover (Four Watches and Day) (5)	(Exod. 12)		63–7(5)	26.17—27.56
Easter (and Octave)			68	27.57—28

*Minor adjustment of connecting verses (see 14.11)

APPENDIX B

THE A DIVISIONS OF MARK AS LECTIONS FROM NEW YEAR TO EASTER

If Matthew is a lectionary book, what about Mark?

The Codex Alexandrinus and its allies divide Mark into forty-eight κεφαλαῖα and a Preface, twenty units less than Matthew. Since there cannot be less than fifty Saturdays in a Jewish year, and several of the κεφαλαῖα belong to the Passion, Mark cannot be a book of Gospels for a year. But it could be a book of Gospels for half a year, that is, from Jewish New Year on 1st Tishri to Easter. Two facts suggest this: (*a*) Matthew took twenty lections (0–19) to reach the week before New Year, and New Year would be a natural place to begin a lectionary series; (*b*) in the Preface (Mark 1.1–20 (A–22)[1]) John comes preaching repentance and the advent of the Kingdom of God—the themes of New Year, and the very passage expounded in Matt. 11,[2] the Matthaean New Year lection. In addition, at Jesus' baptism God addresses him in the words of the traditional New Year psalm, Ps. 2,[3] 'You are my Son'.

We are so ignorant about the Marcan church that any *a priori* assumptions of Jewish–Christian or other practice are rash: Mark is much more radical than Matthew about the Law and the Sabbath, but what does this tell us about his church's observance of Tabernacles or Hanukkah? We should not expect him to have observed Ninth Ab or Purim (especially as Matt. 22.1–14 is new material), but beyond that it is hard to be sure. We might expect three tests to show whether the hypothesis of a half-year lectionary book is valid or not: (*a*) Would Mark 4.1–34, the Marcan Harvest Parables, fall in Tabernacles? (*b*) Would Mark 9.2–9, the Marcan Transfiguration, fall in Hanukkah? (*c*) Would the intervening number of Saturdays correspond with the intervening number of lections?

The κεφαλαῖα can be set out in the following arrangement, and provide an exact correspondence:

---

[1] The divisions in Mark, as in Matthew, often begin with the name of the principal character, where a rational division would come a little earlier.
[2] See pp. 355ff below.
[3] cf.S. Mowinckel, *The Psalms in Israel's Worship* I, pp. 62ff.

	LECTION (A)	MARK
New Year (and Saturday)	0	1.1–20 (A–22)
Atonement	1	1.21 (A23)–28
Saturday after Atonement	2	1.29–31
Tabernacles (Eight Days)	3–10 (8)	1.32—4
Ist–IXth Saturdays after Tabernacles (9)	11–19 (9)	5—7.30 (A–33)
Hanukkah (Eight Days)	20–7 (8)	7.31 (A 34)—9
Ist–XIVth Saturdays after Hanukkah (14)	28–41 (14)	10—12
Saturday before Passover	42	13.1 (A3)–31
13th–14th Nisan	43–4	13.32—14.11
Passover (Two evening, one day services)	45–7	14.12—15.41
Easter	48	15.42—16.8

The Atonement lection draws on the *sidrah*, Lev. 16, where Matthew drew on the *haphtārāh*, Jonah. The high priest was to go in full robes into the Holy of Holies and make atonement for the uncleannesses (ἀκαθαρσίας) of the whole congregation (συναγώγης) of Israel, sending them out in the scapegoat to the desert: on his brow was the gold plate inscribed, Holiness of the Lord. Jesus goes into the synagogue and casts out the unclean spirit from a man who hails him as the Holy One of God.[4] The Harvest Parables fall on the seventh day of Tabernacles, 'the great day of the Feast'.[5] The Transfiguration falls on the sixth day of Hanukkah: 'And after six days Jesus took with him . . .' (Mark 9.2). The number of lections after Hanukkah to the first Saturday in Nisan fit the normal year exactly, without provision for intercalation. From the Saturday before Passover the arrangement is as in Matthew, but there is provision for only two days immediately before Passover, and the Paschal liturgy is less demanding than in Matthew. The later Gospel, as one might expect, provides a more elaborate liturgical structure.

[4] There is no known instance of 'the Holy One of God' as a title of Messiah: the High Priest's title is the closest parallel; cf. Ps. 106.16.
[5] The seventh day of the Feast was marked with a sevenfold procession round the altar, and was known as *Hôshʻānāh Rabbāh* ('The great "Deliver" ') from the recitation of Ps. 118. The ceremonies of Tabernacles, including those of Water-drawing and Light, were limited to the first seven days of the Feast. It seems likely therefore that 'the great day of the feast' of John 7.37 means the last day of the week, and not the eighth day appended in Leviticus. So R. E. Brown, *The Gospel according to John* (New York 1966) I, p. 320; S–B ad loc.; cf. Mishnah Suk. 4,5; Moore, *Judaism* II, pp. 47ff. The eighth day is preferred by other commentators who do not think the symbolic reference of the day to be important.

Mark had regard not only for the Festal cycle, but also for the sabbath cycle. Dr Farrer wrote: 'The greatest weight of Levitical topics falls in the first line of (Marcan) healings; "Numbers" themes are mostly strongly felt in the second and third, while Deuteronomy prevails in the fourth and after.'[6] The interested reader may work out the lectionary correspondences for himself with the aid of the appendix to ch. 21, pp. 472f below.

Why should anyone compose a lectionary book for half a year? Such books are not desk-compositions: they grow. It was natural to start a series of stories about Jesus with the ministry of the Baptist, and it was natural to describe his preaching of the coming kingdom and repentance at New Year's tide. Christians told of the demoniac in the synagogue as a fulfilment of Atonement before Mark, no doubt, and of the Passion at Passover. Mark has linked them up into a continuum. Six and a half months' readings are not satisfactory: well, Mark only promised to give us 'the beginning of the Gospel',[7] and very likely (he may have felt) someone else might like to write a second volume about Pentecost, and the continuance of the Gospel in the Church. Mark's unsatisfactoriness is Matthew's invitation. What he has done is to add a first half to Mark: Matt. 12—28 follows Mark 3—16 with occasional insertions, Matt. 1—11 borrows forward and elaborates.

[6] *Materials on St Mark* (unpublished), p. 46.
[7] So C. P. M. Jones, in the Bampton Lectures of 1970.

10
THE CHRONICLER AND
THE JEWISH YEAR

No new theory, however compelling its evidence, can hope to persuade if it covers only a narrow front. The structure of Matthew, and its Ms. divisions, may urge us to the conclusion that the evangelist wrote with a liturgical purpose, and to a liturgical pattern; and perhaps, it may be felt, there is a *prima facie* case for Mark also to have written in the same way. But who will believe that these two authors, alone of Jewish antiquity, will have composed their books like this? If the theory is true, it must be true of more writers than Matthew and Mark: if it is not true of others, it will hardly be credible for them.

I am thus in a dilemma. I am writing a book about Matthew, and to establish in detail the lectionary theory which I have just proposed in outline must involve 200 more pages of argument; and many points which I have briefly touched upon require urgent amplification if I am to carry my reader with me. Yet to continue will be self-defeating for the reason I have given. But if I turn aside and argue a similar conclusion for a part of the OT, I only redouble the dilemma: for an outline such as I have drawn in the last chapter for one book of the OT would require similar amplification, and would raise an identical question about further books. Since I cannot write a series of books simultaneously I must propose a compromise. I will set out a case for thinking that one major work of the OT is lectionary in character, and leave it at that: a detailed justification and an examination of further works must await another occasion.

The work of the Chronicler is again our best hope. As the last considerable stratum of OT scripture, it lies closest in date to Matthew, and we have argued that its midrashic method of composition is close to Matthew's also. It was written before the close of the OT canon, and it tells a continuous but episodic story, like the Gospel: so it could conceivably have been built up as a series of 'second lessons' by recitals in the synagogue/Temple in the same way that I have posited for Matthew. Indeed, a *Sitz-im-Leben* for the book that envisaged its regular reading out in public, before and after its fixation in its final form, would in any case seem more probable than that of a history-book designed for the better instruction of the priesthood.

The Chronicler's aim is to write a cultic history of Israel; exalting the Temple, the Ark, Jerusalem, the Levites, the Southern Kingdom, all summed up in the character of David; denigrating the North with its independent tradition. He begins the continuous narrative with the death of Saul leading into the deliverance under David, and the tendency of the story thereafter becomes obvious. He begins to transcribe the work of his Deuteronomic predecessor at 1 Sam. 31. What is not immediately obvious is why a work of this scope should begin with Adam, and occupy at least eight chapters with Genealogies.

The genealogical chapters may be described as a midrash on Genesis. 1 Chronicles sets out a formal parallel. 'Adam, Seth, Enosh . . .', ten patriarchs named without relationship down to Noah; Shem, Ham, Japheth, Noah's sons; seventy descendants, the seventy nations of Gen. 10; 'Shem, Arpachsad, Shelah . . .', ten more patriarchs set out without relationship down to Abram; Isaac and Ishmael, the sons of Abraham; seventy descendants of Abraham, as described in Gen. 25 and 36. One or two names are omitted to keep the numbers square. The kings and dukes of Edom of old are then somewhat curiously recited from Gen. 36, and the sons of Israel in the order of Gen. 35; and there follows, in the next seven chapters, an extension, a bringing up to date, a midrash on the patriarchal families as enumerated in Genesis. Judah is promoted to first place for doctrinal reasons which are given, and is awarded three genealogies. In the first he absorbs, surprisingly, a number of the Esau clans of Gen. 36;[1] in the second we have the line of David; in the third various side-lines: all of which goes back to the *affaire* with Tamar in Gen. 38, as we are told. After Judah comes Simeon, without apology. Then the remaining tribes, briefly, much as given in Gen. 46.8–27, except for Levi, who is given at length, as befits the priestly tribe: only that Reuben, Gad, and half-Manasseh are said to have been sent into exile to this day, while Zebulun and Dan are suppressed completely, and Benjamin is given twice. Judah now has three parts in Israel, and Benjamin two, and the remote northern and eastern tribes, one the centre of idolatry, are better forgotten. We find the same pattern when the hosts are numbered under Jehoshaphat—three brigades of Judah and two of Benjamin.

It is noticeable that the names of many of the heads of families are those of towns in the tribal area. The names of the descendants of Noah in Gen. 10 would read to the Chronicler as what they are, the names of the surrounding peoples: how simple therefore to supply

[1] Hori (Gen. 36.22) = Hur (1 Chron. 2.19,50); Shobal (Gen. 36.20,23) = Shobal (1 Chron. 2.50,52); Ithran (Gen. 36.26) = Jether (1 Chron. 2.53), Ithrites; Manahath (Gen. 36.23) = Menuhoth (1 Chron. 2.52); Onam and Aran (Gen. 36.23, 28) = Onam and Oren (2 Chron. 2.25ff); Akan (Gen. 36.27) = Jaakan (1 Chron. 1.42); Korah (Gen. 36.5) = Korah (1 Chron. 2.43).

for the names of descendants of Judah on a like principle Etam, Ephratah, Bethlehem, Tekoa, Ziph, Socoh, Zanoah, Keilah, Mareshah, etc. In this way he not only begins from the Genesis beginning, and expands Genesis tribal families, but he actually does so by the same method as P in the Genesis genealogies.

The remainder of 1 Chronicles is given over to the exploits of David, and his preparations for the building of the Temple. Now the Kings story of the building of the Temple already lay in natural parallel with the story of the building of the Tabernacle, because the Jews were ignorant of the structure of the Tabernacle, and retrojected on to it, from earlier times, the image of the Temple.[2] The principal difference which the Chronicler makes to the Temple story is to approximate it more closely to the second half of the Book of Exodus. Down to ch. 26 the story is mainly in the words of Samuel–Kings. He begins at the moment of Israel's nadir of oppression under the Philistines, with the death of Saul. He moves rapidly over David's establishment as king, and his victories. By 11 Jerusalem, the future cultic centre, is taken; by 13 the ark is recovered, and is brought with impressive Levitical escort (15) and massive psalmody (16) to its temporary tent-home; in 17 the Temple is adumbrated; in 21 its site is bought, and thereafter it absorbs the narrative. The whole Absalom story is suppressed, partly for brevity, partly because David's share in it is not too creditable: and in everything David is exalted, as befits the *alter Moses* in whose type he is cast.

The Tabernacle story in Exodus is in two halves, divided by an interlude. In Exod. 25—31 God gives Moses the 'pattern' (*tabhnîth*)[3] of the Tabernacle: first the ark, then the cherubim, the shewbread table, the lampstand; the hangings and structure of the Tabernacle itself, with its veil and porch; the altar and the court; the vestments and so on. The manner of consecrating priests and altar are given, provision is made for incense, and craftsmen in chief are nominated, Bezalel b. Uri b. Hur, and Oholiab of Dan. There is then the interlude of the Golden Calf, when the sons of Levi establish their position on the side of Moses and the Lord, and Moses returns to the mountain-top. In 35 he gathers the people and commands an offering, which the people bring with a willing heart till there is too much. In 36—39 Bezalel and Oholiab and other wise-hearted and cunning men make all the things that were commanded in 25ff, and bring them. In 40

---

[2] Modern studies have justified the existence of a Tent from early times, but Wellhausen's conclusion (*Prolegomena zur Geschichte Israels* (3e., Berlin 1886), pp. 351ff) on the structure is said to be 'only too obvious', by R. de Vaux, *Ancient Israel* (2e., E.T., London 1965).
[3] Exod. 25.9,40.

the Tabernacle is erected; the ark and other furniture are introduced; the cloud of Shekinah covers the tent of meeting and the glory of the Lord fills the Tabernacle.

The 2 Samuel story already contains the suggestion of a division into two, David wishing to build a Temple but forbidden, establishing the ark at Jerusalem, buying the Temple site; Solomon executing the work. But while Solomon's building in Kings, as I have said, covers much of the same material as Bezalel's in Exodus—altar, cherubim, shewbread table, lampstand, laver, etc.—and while the conclusion of the story is the same, as the glory-cloud fills the house of the Lord with the introduction of the ark, there is nothing corresponding to God's giving Moses the pattern, and there is no free-will offering by the people. Far from it, the people's share in the work is by means of a forced levy. As we should see it, the D historian glorifies the Temple all he can, but the Priestly writer in Exodus succeeds in telling the story twice, once in the pattern and once in the execution, and adds the edifying scene of the free-will offering in between.

The Chronicler assimilates the D Temple story to the P Tabernacle story.

1. He provides a preview of the construction by assigning to David the whole planning of the edifice. From 1 Chron. 22 to the end of the book we have the first considerable block of his own writing of narrative. David counsels Solomon to build, he provides precious metals, and materials, and workmen, Levites and priests and singers and gatekeepers and officials, a chapter of each.[4] In 28 he assembles them all and commissions Solomon to begin: and (it is said) 'David gave Solomon his son the pattern (*tabhnîth*) of the vestibule of the Temple, and of its houses, its treasuries, its upper rooms, its inner chambers, and of the room for the mercy seat; and the pattern of all that he had by the spirit for the courts of the Lord's house . . .' (11f AT). He tells Solomon the weight of gold for each article of the furniture: the lampstand, the altar of incense, the cherubim, etc.[5]

[4] Rudolph, *Chronikbücher* (Tübingen 1955), regards the whole mustering of 23—27 as a later insertion, breaking the continuity between 23.2 and 28.1ff; the interpolator(s) having covered their tracks by further insertions at 28.1, 12b, 13a, 21a; 29.6, 8. The objection that a numbering of the Levites is in contrast to Joab's exclusion of them at 21.6 is not fatal, since here they are numbered for liturgical purposes, not at Satan's behest (for David's self-glorying). See Rudolph, op. cit., pp. 152ff, 185.

[5] Rudolph excises vv. 14–18, the detail of the Temple vessels, as destroying the balance of the presentation, and as being irrelevant: he thinks the Chronicler was concerned with David's giving Solomon the gold and silver, not the details of its use. He sees the Exodus parallel (p. 188), but he misses its force: David, like Yahweh, provides for every detail of the Temple furniture.

The *tabhnîth* is not his own, but God's. He has it 'in the spirit', as the spirit was in Bezalel in Exod. 31.3. He makes all clear 'by writing from the hand of the Lord' (v. 19), as Moses and Ezekiel had written. He concludes by handing over on paper 'all the work to be done according to the *tabhnîth*', as God bade Moses, 'See that you make them after the *tabhnîth* for them, which is being shown to you on the mountain.' 'Every willing man that hath any skill for any kind of service' will help (28.21; Exod. 35.25ff). In this way we are given an account of the Temple in the giving of its pattern as well as in the execution, as in Exod. 25—31.

2.   Despite the overwhelming mass of material which the King has provided, there is then a free-will offering by the people of precious metals and precious stones. A counterpart is thus provided to the offering in Exod. 35—36.

3.   The building covers the first five chapters of 2 Chronicles, and is told very much in the D words. It culminates, like both 1 Kings and Exodus, in the introduction of the ark and the descent of the glory-cloud. But where there are variations we can see the influence of the Tabernacle. The veil of purple and blue and scarlet with its cherubim (3.14) is after Exod. 26.31: the use of the lavers and sea for washing, in place of their earlier numinous function, reflects Exod. 30.17ff: there are references (4.7,20) to practices *kᵉmishpātām*, according to their ordinance, which must mean Exod. 25.31ff, 37. Moses has a brazen altar made for the Tabernacle: Solomon's altar is fifty times as big in volume, but he makes a platform of brass of the identical dimensions of Moses' altar, $5 \times 5 \times 3$ cubits, on which he makes the prayer of dedication (6.13; Exod. 38.1) before the altar. Solomon's helpers in Kings in the building of the Temple had been King Hiram of Tyre and a craftsman of his,[6] a worker in bronze, described as being the son of a widow of the tribe of Naphtali, married to a Tyrian. The Chronicler describes the same man as a man skilled to work in metals, stone, wood, and fabrics, a master of all trades, exactly like Bezalel and Oholiab (Exod. 35.35); and furthermore as the son of a woman of Dan, which is surely an assimilation to the tribe of Oholiab. And what about Hiram? The Chronicler always in these chapters, but nowhere else,[7] writes his name Huram, which can hardly be accidental; and it is mere speculation that Huram was Hiram's throne-name. Elsewhere he shows himself willing to change and adjust names, and

---

[6] 1 Kings 7.13; 2 Chron. 2.13. The Kings account appears to give the craftsman's name as Hiram; the Chronicler glosses this to Huramabi, Huram-is-my-father, a neat solution.

[7] 1 Chron. 14.1.

to invent them on purpose: Achan becomes Achar, since Achar ('*ākhar*) means to trouble, and he was the troubler of Israel (1 Chron. 2.7); Zabdi, his ancestor, becomes Zimri, like Zimri who troubled Israel by sleeping with the Midianite woman (1 Chron. 2.6); Rehoboam is set out as another David, with a favourite junior wife, and a daughter by her, Shelomith, like Solomon (2 Chron. 11.18ff). So here Hiram lengthens the yodh to Huram, to assimilate him to Bezalel of the line of Hur. Bezalel is expressly referred to as the maker of the old altar in 2 Chron. 1.5.

What, we feel, could be more natural than this assimilation of Kings to Exodus? Or, for that matter, of Kings to Leviticus? For when the Tabernacle was complete, Moses gave Aaron the law of the sacrifices (Lev. 1—7), and sanctified Aaron and his sons (8); the first sacrifices were offered (9), and 'fire came forth from before the Lord and consumed the burnt offering and the fat upon the altar' (9.24). Similarly, when in Kings the Temple was complete, Solomon offered massive peace offerings, and the burnt offering (8.62f). The Chronicler again assimilates: in 2 Chron. 7.1, as *not* in Kings, fire comes down from heaven and consumes the burnt offering and the sacrifices; in 8.14, he appoints the divisions of the priests not in Kings, for their service, as in Lev. 8, and the Levites and gatekeepers. Or again, Kings has Solomon celebrate the feast of Tabernacles seven days, and then send the people away on the eighth day; the Chronicler makes the eighth day a solemn assembly, in accordance with later practice, and the Levitical law (23.36), and he gives the correct dates according to Lev. 23.34,39. The same chapter is referred to at 2 Chron. 8.12f, when Solomon institutes the daily, monthly and festal sacrifices 'according to the commandment of Moses'.

What is more interesting is that the influence of Leviticus remains on the Chronicler's writing through the reigns of Solomon, Rehoboam, Abijah, and Asa, in ways that do not seem natural. The issue between Rehoboam and Jeroboam is made to turn upon the possession of the true priesthood in Judah, and the false priesthood and worship instituted by the latter. The priests and Levites that were in all Israel resort to Rehoboam out of all their borders (11.13). The Levites leave their suburbs and their possessions and come to Jerusalem because Jeroboam cast them off; the latter appoints priests of his own for the he-goats (*śeʿîrîm*) and calves which he has made (11.15). Now there is no lack of texts in the Torah to insist that sacrifice must be in the Temple, under the official priesthood: Lev. 17.1–9 is but one of many. But what is singular is the use of the word *śeʿîrîm* for false gods: this occurs only once elsewhere in scripture, and that is at Lev. 17.7. As the Chronicler has inserted the word into a Kings context, direct

reference is virtually certain. The Levitical passage forbids sacrifices
in the open field, 'that they may bring them to the Lord, to the priest
at the door of the tent of meeting . . . so they shall no more slay their
sacrifices for *šeʿîrîm*.'

There is another striking reference to Leviticus in ch. 13, which is
devoted to Abijah, Jeroboam's successor. Abijah makes a long speech
to Jeroboam emphasizing the difference between the true and the false
priesthood. They have the golden calves with them; they have driven
out the priests of the Lord, and anyone can consecrate himself; but
as for us, we have priests, sons of Aaron; they burn the morning and
evening sacrifice, and incense, set out the shewbread, and light the
lamps (13.11). Given the Chronicler's theology, an emphasis on the
true and false priesthood is natural, and Levitical: what is out of place
in an eve-of-battle speech is a description of the true priests setting
out the shewbread and lighting the lamps, and this shows that the
Chronicler's eye is on the opening verses of Lev. 24, where these duties
are laid on the priesthood. The whole Abijah chapter is a tangle of
midrash from Judges and Joshua. The ambush, and the references to
Gibeah, recall the battle at the end of Judges over the Levite's con-
cubine: the reference to Micaiah and the consecration of false priests
recall the Levite and the silver idol of Judg. 17ff: all come into the
story because this was the foundation legend of the original false
worship at Dan, which Jeroboam has now made permanent. And this
too has its roots in the Torah, because there it is the son of a Danite
woman who first blasphemes the name: in the same chapter, Lev. 24.

The theme is continued into the reign of Asa, which is cast as an
enactment of Lev. 26, and a re-enactment of the Gideon story, and,
at the end, of chapters in the life of Jeremiah. Lev. 26 opens with a
veto of idols and pillars, and these are later specified (v. 30) as high
places and sun-pillars (*bāmôth, ḥammānîm*). Asa opens his reign with
a purge of foreign altars and pillars, and he takes out of Judah the
high places and sun-pillars ('*eth-habbāmôth weʿeth-haḥammānîm*). The
word *ḥammān* occurs eight times in the OT, and the combination of
the two is limited to these two passages and Ezek. 6.6. Leviticus
promises that if this is done, 'I will give peace in the land' (26.6), and
for ten years of Asa's reign 'the land had rest' (14.6). And in the next
verse of Leviticus it is said, 'You shall chase your enemies . . . five
of you shall chase a hundred, and a hundred of you shall chase ten
thousand.' The scene in Chronicles moves at once to the Ethiopian
invasion, when a million enemies are defeated by Asa's much smaller
army, and flee before them, and are chased as far as Gerar (14.9ff).
It is difficult to think that this series of parallels is accident.

Once our attention is drawn to the Levitical background of this section of 2 Chronicles, other more general correspondences suggest themselves. The great Consecration Prayer of Solomon in 6 is made before the altar, and has as its recurrent theme, 'If [trouble comes] then hear thou in heaven, and forgive the sin of thy servants . . .' Israel's confidence was that peace with God and forgiveness of sin was to be had through the sacrifices of the altar, and especially the sin offerings which are the central theme of Lev. 1—7. Direct reference is made to true and false oaths before the altar (6.22f), which are the topic of Lev. 5.1ff; 6.1ff. The Chronicler adds to the King's Prayer an ending from the Psalms, 'Let thy priests, O Lord, be clothed with salvation', which would fit well with the vesting of Aaron and his sons in Lev. 8. Or again, Kings related that Solomon provided a personal house for Pharaoh's daughter: the Chronicler glosses, 'For he said, My wife shall not live in the house of David, for the places to which the ark of the Lord has come are holy.' Rudolph comments that she is kept from the palace not because she is a heathen but because she is a woman, and refers to Lev. 12.4, 'A woman [after childbirth] shall not touch any hallowed thing'. Or again, Rehoboam's marriages to two of his first cousins (11.18ff) respect the laws of consanguinity in marriage of Lev. 18, and are abundantly blessed.

Now I must draw attention to a very striking fact. With the exception of the references to the Lev. 23 feast, all the above correspondences between 2 Chronicles and Leviticus *fall in order*. We may write down a brief table:

(i) Induction of Ark, Descent of Glory-Cloud	Exod. 40	1 Kings 8.1–11;	2 Chron. 5
(ii) Forgiveness from Altar Sacrifices	Lev. 1—7	8.12–61	6
(iii) Clothing of Priests	8		6.41
(iv) First sacrifice, Fire from Heaven	9	(8.62ff)	7.1–7
(v) Woman away from the holy	12		8.11
(vi) Worship God at Jerusalem, not he-goats	17.1–9		11.13ff
(vii) Consanguinity in marriage	18		11.18ff
(viii) Shewbread, lamps; Danite blasphemy	24		13.8ff
(ix) Sun-pillars: peace: 5 chase 100	26.1–13		14

This is the more significant because in one or two places it is a little contrived. Commentators note that the section (vii) on Rehoboam's marriages interrupts the flow of the story; or that the peace consequent on Asa's reform (ix) is broken abruptly by the Ethiopian invasion.

If, as it appears, the Chronicler begins with Genesis, assimilates the later part of the David story to the later chapters of Exodus, and provides a serial midrashic expansion of Solomon and his three successors from Leviticus, we can hardly avoid asking whether the following chapters of 2 Chronicles bear relation to the Book of Numbers. Perhaps, we might even feel, it is natural that they should do so.

The later period of the Kings was a time of national apostasy, punished by national humiliation: the same themes that distinguish Israel's weary passage through the desert, b^emidhbār, in Numbers. But the correspondences are far too detailed and too numerous to permit of explanation on the ground of accident.

The Book of Numbers draws its English, and Greek, name from the two numberings (p^equdhāh, 1.44; 26.51) of the tribes which Moses institutes: one in Num. 1—4 when they leave Sinai; one in Num. 26 when all the old generation are dead and they are approaching Canaan. The people are numbered from twenty years old and up in both cases, by father's houses, according to tribes, there being twelve tribes and a leader for each. Jehoshaphat begins his reign by sending out his princes to teach the people, one of the five being Nethanel (17.7; Num. 1.8; with Judah, Num. 2.5), while others are called Obadiah and Micaiah, from the faithful leaders under the contemporary Ahab in Kings. He then numbers his men of war according to fathers' houses—only two tribes now, but in five divisions, amounting to twice Moses' host. The names of the captains are taken from David's mighty men in 1 Chron. 12—14. They go out to war with Ahab to Ramoth–Gilead. It is a puzzle why this long incident of primarily Samaritan history should have been included verbatim by the Chronicler. It may well be that the two reminiscences of Numbers in the story were a factor in his mind:

Num. 24.12	2 Chron. 18.12f
(Balaam): Did I not tell your messengers, What the Lord speaks, that will I speak?	The messenger said, Let your word be like the word of one of them and speak favourably. But Micaiah said, As the Lord lives, what my God says, that will I speak.

Num. 27.16	2 Chron. 18.16
Moses prayed that the congregation of the Lord may not be as sheep which have no shepherd.	I saw all Israel scattered upon the mountains, as sheep which have no shepherd.

There is a second numbering of the host by fathers' houses under commanders of thousands and hundreds, twenty years old and up, under Amaziah in 25.5. These are the only two formal musterings of the host in Chronicles. We are told the size of Asa's army, and there is the Satanically inspired numbering under David, but in neither case is the procedure of the two musters in Numbers followed: minimum age, family grouping, tribal total, individual commanders. These are found only for Jehoshaphat and Amaziah: neither is in Kings.

Jehoshaphat's later career continues to be reminiscent of Numbers. At 19.5ff he appoints judges over the people as Moses did at Num. 11.16, and a later description makes plain the reference:

Deut. 1.17	2 Chron. 19.6
I charged your judges at that time [Num. 11], Judge righteously . . . You shall not be partial in judgement . . . For the judgement is God's.	You judge not for man but for the Lord . . . Let the fear of the Lord be upon you . . . There is no perversion of justice with the Lord our God, or partiality, or taking bribes.

As an appointer of judges Jehoshaphat fulfils his name, Yahweh–judges: this also is an innovation of the Chronicler. His reign closes with an expansion of the war against Moab and Edom from 2 Kings 3, turning on the statement therein, 'The kings have surely fought together, and slain one another' (3.23), a feature which is made much of. But a war with Edom suggests Num. 20–21, and Jehoshaphat says in his prayer, 'And now behold, the men of Ammon and Moab and Mt Seir, whom thou wouldest not let Israel invade when they came out of Egypt, and whom they avoided and did not destroy—behold how they reward us!' (20.10f). The reference is thus explicit, and again the Chronicler's own.

The same is true with the prophecy of Zechariah in 24, which is modelled on the scene at the return of the spies in Num. 14. Joash in Kings had been a good king, but the Chronicler turns him over to idolatry after Jehoiada's death, and introduces Zechariah, Jehoiada's son, to rebuke him: and this he does with a sermon almost word for word that of Moses on the day of national apostasy:

Num. 14.41	2 Chron. 24.20
Why now are you transgressing the commandment of the Lord, seeing it shall not prosper? (RV)	Why do you transgress the commandments of the Lord, so that you cannot prosper?

Then all the congregation bade stone Joshua and Caleb with stones, but the glory of the Lord interposed (Num. 14.10): now the people conspire against Zechariah and stone him with stones to the death (21).

Uzziah's reign has similarly been expanded with midrashic matter taken over from Numbers. The Kings account recorded that the people were still burning incense in the high places, and that the Lord smote the king so that he was a leper to the day of his death (2 Kings 15.4f). This invites exposition, and the lead is provided by the mention of incense-burning, and perhaps also by the later sacrificing by King Ahaz in Kings. The burning of incense was a priestly prerogative (Num. 4,16,18) which had been usurped by Korah and his company in Num. 16; and for this they had been smitten by God, censer in hand. Indeed Miriam herself had challenged Moses to be his equal, and had been smitten with leprosy in Num. 12. The Chronicler fits these types to the story in hand: Uzziah enters the temple of the Lord to burn incense on the altar of incense; he is rebuked by the high priest who cites the Numbers law; he turns in anger censer in hand, and the leprosy breaks out on his forehead, because the Lord had smitten him (26.16ff).[8]

Hezekiah's reign also shows a marked use of Numbers by the Chronicler. As a hero of the faith he is suited to be the institutor of cultic splendour, and some of the details of Josiah's reformation are drawn on in advance, especially the celebration of the Passover, which fills 30: but the important difference is that Hezekiah's Passover is celebrated in the second month, because insufficient priests were sanctified in time for the normal date (v. 3), and because celebrants were to attend from Dan to Beersheba (v. 5). Now the law providing for a second month Passover is found only in Num. 9.10f, where it is said that 'if any man of you is unclean through touching a dead body, or is afar off on a journey, he shall still keep the passover to the Lord in the second month on the fourteenth day.' The priests and Levites arise and bless the people at the end of the feast (v. 27; Num. 6.23ff). At the beginning of 31, Hezekiah provides for all the offerings in turn which are laid down in Num. 28—29: the daily burnt-offerings (Num. 28.3), the sabbath burnt offerings (Num. 28.9), the new-moon offerings (Num. 28.11ff) and the set-feast offerings (Num. 28.16—29.19); and commands the people to provide firstfruits and tithes for the priests (31.4–end; Num. 18.8–24). The celebrated deliverance from Sennacherib is the reward of his piety.

With so rich a background of influence from Numbers of a kind which is fairly obvious, we may feel encouraged to look for further references which may also have been in the Chronicler's mind. Num. 4—5 prescribe the duties of the sons of Kohath, and of the priests in judgement by ordeal; Jehoshaphat appoints priests to judge in Jerusalem, and the Kohathites take the lead, here alone, in the Edomite campaign (19—20). Later, in Num. 31 a victory is won over Midian, and a portion of the spoil is given to the Levites, while in Num. 35 the Levites are given their cities and suburbs: in 2 Chron. 31 Hezekiah directs the people to give the Levites their portion, and makes a reckoning of them in their cities and suburbs.

Some of the parallels which we have mentioned are taken over from Kings, and in all cases the order of the kings and their characters

[8] The two passages are linked in Sifre Num. ad loc., and in Shoḥer Tobh on Ps. 118.3.

and histories are to a large extent beyond adjustment: so to expect that all of them will fall in series as the Leviticus ones did is to ask the impossible. Nevertheless, if we tabulate them, we cannot refuse the suggestion that so far as possible the Chronicler has again made a series of correspondences in order:

	NUM.		2 CHRON.	
(i)	1—4	First Numbering of Host	17	Jehoshaphat's Host
(ii)	3—4	Levites	20.14–18	Spirit on Jahaziel the Levite
(iii)	9	2nd month Passover	29—30	Hezekiah's 2nd month Passover
(iv)	14	Spies nearly stoned	24	Zechariah stoned
(v)	16	Korahites offer incense, smitten	26	Uzziah offers incense, and is struck with leprosy
	12	Miriam struck with leprosy		
	18	Priests' prerogatives		
(vi)	20ff	Moab refuses passage	20	Moabite War
(vii)	24, 27	Balaam, sheep	18	Micaiah and Ahab
viii)	26	Second Numbering of Host	25	Amaziah's Host
(ix)	28f	Law of Offerings for Feasts	31	Hezekiah provides Offerings and Tithes for priests and Levites, in their cities and suburbs
(x)	31	Portion of spoil for Levites		
(xi)	35	Levites' cities and suburbs		

Hezekiah's Passover, the Moabite War, Micaiah and Ahab, Amaziah's victory: these are the points that fall out of order, and they are all fixed by the account in Kings. The remainder are broadly in the Chronicler's hands, and they fall in order.

The Numbers assimilations are not natural; but a parallel between the last chapters of 2 Kings and the Book of Deuteronomy is self-evident. The end of 2 Kings describes the Deuteronomic reform, and the parallel rests ultimately on history. Manasseh had been an idolatrous king whose ways were overturned under his grandson Josiah. The reforming party had treasured traditional laws of a Yahwist, centralizing, Levitical-priesthood, anti-*bāmôth* emphasis in a document: and this document played a decisive part in the reformation, and afterwards became the nucleus of the canonical Deuteronomy. It is not surprising, then, that we find Manasseh in Kings breaking all the Deuteronomic laws, which are then reinstated as authoritative by Josiah. Further, the sixth-century Deuteronomic editor, living under the shadow of the exile, makes it his business constantly to expound the threat of Yahweh's judgement upon the people should they disobey; a threat which had come to fulfilment under the last kings. It is therefore no labour to the Chronicler to introduce Deuteronomic motifs into the last chapters of 2 Chronicles: they were the stuff of the story from the beginning.

It is, however, demonstrable that he has allied art to nature. The tithes and cities of the Levites, which formed the theme of the last chapters of Numbers, occupied Hezekiah in 2 Chron. 31. 2 Chron. 32, the Sennacherib story, reads like a synopsis of the opening third of Deuteronomy. Hezekiah exhorts the people, 'Be strong and of a good courage. Do not be afraid or dismayed before the King of Assyria . . . with us is the Lord our God, to help us and to fight our battles' (vv. 7f), as Moses had said before, 'Be strong and of a good courage' (Deut. 31.6), 'You shall not fear them; for it is the Lord your God who fights for you' (Deut. 3.22). Sennacherib demands, 'Who among all the gods of those nations . . . was able to deliver his people out of my hand, that your God should be able . . .?' (v. 14). Sennacherib asks ironically, but Moses rhetorically, 'What god is there in heaven or on earth who can do such works and mighty acts as thine?' (Deut. 3.24; cf. 4.7). Sennacherib's great host withdraws discomfited. It is a persistent theme of the first chapters of Deuteronomy that 'the Lord will drive out before you nations greater and mightier than yourselves' (4.38; 7.1). After the war Hezekiah is crowned with wealth: precious metals, grain, wine, oil, cattle—all the riches promised on condition of obedience in Deut. 8. 'And in the matter of the envoys of the princes of Babylon', we read, 'God left him to himself, in order to try him, and to know all that was in his heart' (v. 31). So, Moses said, God had tried Israel, to know what was in their heart (Deut. 8.2).

With Manasseh and Josiah we come to the central Deuteronomic law-section. Manasseh rebuilds the high places (Deut. 12) which Josiah destroys (33.3; 34.3); and the Baalim, which Josiah has ground to powder (Deut. 9.21); and the Asherahs (Deut. 16.21); and the worship of the host of heaven (Deut. 17.3; 4.19). He practises augury and sorcery, has recourse to wizards, and makes his children pass through the fire, all of which are forbidden in Deut. 18.9ff. He sets in the Temple the image of the idol which he has made—the Chronicler virtually quotes Deut. 12.5—'in this house, and in Jerusalem, which I have chosen out of all the tribes of Israel, I will put my name for ever' (33.7). In the next verse he cites the promise of Israel's perman-ence in the land 'if only they will be careful to do all that I have com-manded them, all the law, the statutes and the ordinances given through Moses' (v.8). In these last two details he has gilded the Kings lily. In the next chapter Josiah undoes his predecessor's misdeeds; he is obedient to 'the Law which is in charge of the Levitical priests' (Deut. 17.18; 2 Chron. 34.19ff); and then goes on to celebrate a massive, and much enhanced Passover (Deut. 16.1–8).

The closing Deuteronomic exhortation is likewise made to match. In Deut. 28.36 the exile is foretold: 'The Lord shall bring you, and your king whom you set over you, to a nation that . . . you have not known'—so Jehoiakim, Jehoiachin, Zedekiah. Moses had continued,

'The Lord shall bring against you from afar . . . a nation of stern countenance, who shall not regard the person of the old, or show favour to the young' (v. 49); and so the Chronicler describes the end, 'Therefore [the Lord] brought up against them the king of the Chaldeans, who slew their young men with the sword . . . and had no compassion on young man or virgin, old man or aged' (36.17). But beyond judgement there is mercy. In Deut. 30 it is said, 'When all these things come upon you, the blessing and the curse . . . and you call them to mind among the nations where the Lord your God has driven you, and return to the Lord your God . . . and obey his voice . . . then the Lord your God will restore your fortunes, and have compassion upon you, and he will gather you again from all the peoples. . .' The story has a happy ending. And so does the Chronicler add a happy ending to Kings: he finishes the book with the accession of Cyrus, and the first steps towards the Return.

A table of virtually consecutive correspondences between the last five chapters of 2 Chronicles and Deuteronomy may thus be added to the tables we have already set out:

	DEUT.		2 CHRON.	
(i)	1ff	Moses exhorts people	32	Hezekiah exhorts people
(ii)	4,7	God will drive nations out		God drives Sennacherib out
(iii)	8	Tries Israel; beware of wealth		Hezekiah's wealth, tried by embassy
(iv)	12ff	High places. etc. forbidden	33 34	Manasseh builds high places, which Josiah destroys
(v)	16	Law of Passover	35	Josiah celebrates Passover
(vi)	17	King to be obedient to Book	34	Josiah obedient to Book
(vii)	28	Exile for disobedience No mercy on the weak	36	King and people into exile Chaldaeans merciless
(viii)	30	Repentance in exile, then return		Cyrus authorizes Return.

The Chronicler's work did not finish at 2 Chronicles. He also wrote the Book of Ezra, and ch. 7–9 of Nehemiah, of which Neh. 7, the list of the returning families, is virtually a duplicate of Ezra 2. He saw himself as living in a time of Restoration. The laws laid down by Moses, enforced by David, were now being observed in faithful Temple-worship; the apostasy of the past was repented of. A natural consequence of this view is a parallel between the first coming into the promised land under Joshua, and the return under Zerubbabel and Ezra. For what it was worth tradition gave the same suggestion, for the high-priest of the return had been another Joshua, ben-Josadak. Joshua had brought the people of God into the land, with all the trouble and disobedience of that first coming: the second coming, with another Joshua, although not without similar troubles and disobedience, had been the beginning of better things.

Ezra 1 tells the story of the release of Israel by the Great King, and

Sheshbazzar/Shealtiel's preparation for the Return. In 3—6 Jeshua
and Zerubbabel build the Temple and the wall, and the returned
exiles take the Passover in celebration. Joshua's great exploit at
Jericho is recalled at 3.9ff. Then the walls of the city had fallen to
Israel at the sound of the priests' trumpets, when the people shouted
with a great shout: now Jeshua and his company set the priests in their
apparel with trumpets, and the Levites to sing; the people shout with
a great shout (3.11,13) and the foundations are laid. At Josh. 5.10
was celebrated the first Passover in Canaan.

In Ezra 7—8 Ezra's own coming is described, and in 9—10 he leads
the people in confession for the sins of the past, and especially for the
taking of forbidden wives from the people of the land, who are then
put away. The local peoples are represented as being substantially
those of Joshua's time (Josh. 9.1; Ezra 9.1)—the Canaanites, the
Hittites, the Perizzites, the Jebusites, the Ammonites, the Moabites,
the Egyptians, and the Amorites. Ezra rends his garments (9.3,5),
puts earth on his head, sits astonied until the evening oblation, and
makes confession among the princes (9.6–end): the guilt of the people
has brought upon them their defeat by the kings of the lands, and
confusion of face as it is this day. So had Joshua rent his garments and
put dust upon his head among the elders of Israel (Josh. 7.6), and
fallen on his face before the ark until evening; and confessed the
guilt that had brought defeat at Ai (7.7–15). The guilty who had taken
foreign wives come before Ezra; on pain of their goods being devoted
(*yoh°ram*) they are commanded by him to confess to the Lord, to
give him glory (*t°nû tôdhāh l° Yahweh*, Ezra 10.11), and put away their
wives from them; as Achan had been commanded by Joshua to confess to the Lord, to give him glory (*ten-lô tôdhāh*, Josh. 7.19), and
Israel had put away the devoted thing from them. Josh. 9 is concerned with the prohibition of assimilation to the peoples of the land—
the story of the Hivites and their mouldy bread: the actual prohibition of marriage with them comes in Josh. 23.12. The hewers of
wood and drawers of water of Josh. 9 are the Nethinim of Ezra
8.17,20.

The Chronicler will not have written out his list of returning
families twice. The more difficult placing should be preferred: if he
wrote it after Ezra 10, a scribe might well feel that its better place
would be when the return began, and insert it after Ezra 1. A placing
after Ezra 10 would, however, coincide with the chapters of settlement
under Joshua, Josh. 13—21. Joshua settles all the tribes: the returning
exiles are named partly by families, partly as the men of Bethlehem,
Etam, Jericho, etc., the villages of Benjamin and Judah. Both lists
close with the priests and Levites.

The concluding two chapters give a happier hope for the future. In Neh. 8 Ezra holds a formal reading of the Law with full panoply of ceremonial; and Jeshua and the priests cause the people to understand what is read. So had the earlier Joshua read all the words of the Law, the blessing and the curse, according to all that is written in the book of the Law, to the whole people between Mt Ebal and Mt Gerizim, before all the elders, officers, judges, and priests (Josh. 8.30–5). Ezra closes the reading with a celebration of Tabernacles in booths, of which it is said that since the days of Joshua the son of Nun the children of Israel had not kept the feast so (8.17). Jeshua and the priests then stand upon the stairs of the Levites, and Ezra rehearses the mighty acts of God who has brought them to where they stand (9.4–end). They begin with Abraham, and the covenant to give him the land of the Canaanite, the Hittite, and the rest, and bring the story through Moses and the first occupation to the exile and the return. So had Joshua (24) rehearsed the mighty acts of God, beginning from Abraham, through Moses to his own day. Joshua ended by joining with the people in a covenant with God (24.25); and the Chronicler closes his work, 'Because of all this we make a firm covenant, and write it; and our princes, our Levites and our priests set their seal to it' (Neh. 9.38).

We may sum the matter up with a further table of correspondences, which again are close to a series in order:

	JOSH.		EZRA	
(i)	1—3	Israel enters the Land	1	Israel returns to the Land
(ii)	5	First Passover in Land	6	Returned exiles celebrate Passover
(iii)	6	Walls of Jericho fall to trumpet and shout	3	Walls of temple laid to trumpets and shout
(iv)	7	Joshua confesses Israel's sin: Achan confesses taking devoted thing	9—10	Ezra confesses Israel's sin: sinners confess on pain of devoting property
(v)	9, 23	Israel mingles with peoples Intermarriage forbidden Hivites become Nethinim	8	Israel has intermarried with peoples Nethinim return with Ezra
			NEH.	
(vi)	13ff	Land allotted by towns	7	Returning families by towns
(vii)	8	Joshua reads Law in public	8	Ezra reads, Jeshua interprets Law
(viii)	24	Joshua recites tradition from Abraham to date	9	Ezra recites tradition from Abraham to date
(ix)		and renews the covenant		and renews covenant.

The question now arises: what explanation are we to give for the formidable series of correspondences which we have adduced? Three possibilities suggest themselves: a form-critical theory, a folk-art theory, and a liturgical theory.

A form-critic might argue as follows. The parallels are in part just

what one would expect, and in part they are fantasy. What more
natural process than that the Kings Temple story should be assimilated
in the telling by later generations to the current P theology expressed
in the second half of Exodus? Of course the Leviticus fire from heaven
would tend to creep in; and the occasional detail of a Numbers story
of national disobedience would find its way in the telling into the tales
of the later kings. Did the generations which told and retold the
story of Manasseh and Josiah and the Exile not steep themselves in
Deuteronomy? How else should we expect the story to be adapted
but by the glossing of a phrase here and there from the end of the Law?
So far the parallelism is just what might be expected, and indeed is
commonplace in the commentaries. Beyond this we have to remember
that the Chronicler is highly allusive: there are many hundreds of
texts to which he refers from the prophets and the Law. Only a small
selection has been made here: but there are Leviticus texts in the
Deuteronomy section, and Deuteronomy texts in the Leviticus section.
The pattern being discerned of a serial midrash on Genesis to Joshua
is but pictures in the fire; reminiscent only of Monsignor Knox's
proof that *In Memoriam* was written by Queen Victoria.

I would submit that such a reading refuses to take seriously the
evidence. The further on one reads into the Chronicler's work,
roughly speaking, the more impossible it is to interpret it this way.
In 1 Chronicles the writer sticks fairly closely to Samuel; in 2 Chronicles he goes increasingly his own way; in Ezra–Nehemiah he is
writing freely. Some of the Leviticus parallels, like the $s^{e\epsilon}\hat{i}r\hat{i}m$ or the
lamps and shewbread are not in the least natural, and can only be
drawn from Leviticus: most of the Numbers parallels, such as the two
numberings, Zechariah's sermon and stoning, or Uzziah's leprosy,
are clearly artificial and belong to Numbers alone: ch. 31 and parts
of ch. 32 refer openly to six passages in the end of Numbers and the
beginning of Deuteronomy in such a way that it is hard to think the
writer is doing much else but provide antitypes—the odds against
these occurring in series at the place in order must be thousands to
one: the Joshua parallels are so close as to be unanswerable. It is
recorded of the Duke of Wellington that on one occasion he walked
down the steps of Apsley House in full dress uniform to be greeted
by a stranger, 'Mr Smith, I believe': to which the Duke replied, 'Sir,
if you will believe that you will believe anything.' A form-critical
approach seems equally credulous.

A second, if remote, possibility might be that the Chronicler was
an artist: seeing the natural parallel between the Kings story and the
Pentateuch, he has elaborated it with the touches we have seen. Such
a theory does not impress. Who wrote, who read, works of art in the

Jerusalem of 350 B.C.? The suggestion seems foreign to the Jewish mind, unpractical and pointless.

The third possibility, which I would commend, is a liturgical one. Chronicles was not written to preserve for future ages the traditions of the camp-fire: it was written to be used, to be read aloud; and if to be read aloud, to be read in liturgical practice. Its sermons are intended to edify the Israelite, and as a ministry of the word presuppose a reading of the word. Ezra's reading of the Law in Nehemiah, and Joshua's reading from the D tradition show the contemporary enthusiasm for the word of God in the Torah: why should we not suppose that sabbath practice in the Chronicler's day already included a serial reading of the Law round the year, as is first directly testified for the synagogue by the Mishnah?[9] But from very early times the prophets formed a second and inferior canon to the Law, and the reading of a second, *haphtārāh*, lesson which must coincide in theme with the Torah reading is certainly much older than its first testimony in our Luke 4. It seems a highly circumstantial hypothesis that the Chronicler saw himself as writing a continuous series of *haphtārāh* readings to run parallel with the Law. Nor need we suppose that the Chronicler invented such a practice. David and Moses, the Temple and the Tabernacle, Jeroboam's gods and the Golden Calf, Josiah and Deuteronomy—the parallels were already woven into the fabric of scripture by the Deuteronomic historian who provided the readings for sabbath worship two centuries earlier; and their roots lie buried further back still. The Chronicler was perfecting a system of liturgical correspondences which already stretched back to immemorial antiquity.

But how would such a cycle run? The Torah runs from Genesis to Deuteronomy, and Joshua is not part of it: if the Chronicler is writing a parallel to the Torah, why has he included a Book of Joshua in his work? Well, he has not merely included a Book of Joshua: if we may trust the Hebrew order—as we surely must, it being the harder—*he has begun with it*.[10] This is the solution to our problem, and the guarantee that we are on the right line. No sense can be made of a version of Israelite history that runs first from Sheshbazzar to Ezra and then from Adam to Jeconiah, unless it is a cyclical sense. Jeshua is parallel to Joshua, and Joshua is already, in the D form, a second lesson to the first part of Genesis. Joshua inherited the promises made to Abraham. He circumcised the people and renewed Abraham's covenant of circumcision. He overcame the Canaanites, the Hittites,

[9] M Meg. 3.4.
[10] The Hebrew order is Ezra, Nehemiah, Chronicles: with which the Canon closes. I am grateful to Dr H. D. F. Sparks for this point.

the Girgashites, and the rest as was promised to Abraham. He fought his first campaign against Ai and Bethel where Abraham pitched his tent. His conquest of Adonisedek and the four kings recalls Abraham's victory over the kings, and Melchisedek. Abraham's exploits begin the rehearsal of the mercies of God with which he ends his life, and he dies having sworn Israel to the covenant first made with Abraham. And before all this God held back the waters of Jordan at Adam, as he had subdued the waters at Creation and we may speculate that behind the legend of Rachab the harlot lies the myth of Rahab the dragon. The Chronicler inherited a system in which Joshua was the *haphtarah* readings to Gen. 1—17, and his Jeshua comes first because it is a third reading in parallel, and with it therefore his cycle begins. The Genealogies form a midrash of the rest of Genesis; the fathers from Adam to Jacob are taken at a gulp in 1 Chron. 1, the remainder at somewhat more leisure. For the detailed parallels, and for those in the first half of Exodus, I refer the reader to the appendix to this chapter.

In the appendix I have divided the Torah as it has been divided since Talmudic times, into 54 units; of which the last units are short, and may be compressed for the 50/51 sabbaths in the normal year. Other divisions would be possible, but the traditional is our best guide. An annual system is to be preferred to the triennial and other systems because (*a*) an annual system must have come first as the simplest development of the old festal year, with its three feasts and a recital of tradition at each; (*b*) units 42–46 of the Chronicler's work are too short to be subdivided into three apiece; (*c*) an annual system beginning in the first month (Nisan) would have Joshua's (and Jeshua's) Passover read at Passover, Lev. 16 read at Yom Kippur, and Lev. 23, the law of the Feasts, read at Tabernacles. All three are the traditional readings for the occasions.[11] Unfortunately no divisions of Ezra–Chronicles survive.

The thing that is decisive in favour of such a liturgical system is that the parallels with the Law–Joshua do not merely run in order, but are spaced out in a way that liturgical use requires, and accident could never ensure. Of the 51 lections into which I have divided the work, 35 contain one or more striking parallels with the words and theme of the given Torah reading, and a further 10 show a more general, but often obvious parallel. A further 3 are expositions of a Torah theme one or two sabbaths apart: for only 3 lections has the Chronicler's ingenuity, or my own, given out—and even though I might blush to suggest a forced parallel, I should not put it past him

---

[11] B Meg. 31a; M Meg. 3.5.

to see a sermon in the law of leprosy and Jeroboam's rebellion, or the Holiness Code and Rehoboam's fall from grace.

So the writing of a continuous liturgical book was not first done by Matthew. The Chronicler did it with Chronicles–Ezra, and the Deuteronomic historian did it with Joshua–Kings, and the Priestly editor did it with the Law. That Matthew knew about it, and that Matthew himself used an annual lectionary, become open hypotheses which we must test in due course. But that such writing was congenial to the spirit of the times seems past question.

APPENDIX

THE CHRONICLER'S LECTIONARY SYSTEM

(The numbers follow the modern annual cycle. * signifies the Chronicler's additions to Kings, (*) a change of Kings order. *Italics* signify striking coincidences, and/or more general parallels.)

		GENESIS	JOSHUA	EZRA
NISAN	1.	1—6.8 *Creation.* Fall. Cain. Genealogy.	1—3 Be strong. Rahab. *Waters part for Israel to enter promised Land.*	1*Sheshbazzar. *Israel returns to land.*
	2.	6.9—11 Noah. *Babel.* Genealogy.	*4—6 Circumcision. Passover. Walls of* Jericho fall to *trumpets and shout.*	3—6* *Jeshua and* Zerubbabel raise temple and *walls to trumpets and shout. Passover.*
PASSOVER				
	3.	12—17 Abraham (a): In Canaan by *Bethel and Ai.* Promise to *inherit land from peoples. Circumcision. 5 Kings; Melchisedek*	7—12 *Achan. Ai/Bethel. Reading Law. Mixing with peoples. 5 Kings; Adonisedek*	7—10* *Confession of* Ezra. *Intermarriage with peoples.*
				NEHEMIAH
	4.	18—22 Abraham (b): Birth and binding of Isaac. *Promise renewed.* Genealogy.	13—16 Joshua conquers Canaanites and *allots land* to first five tribes.	7* *Returning Families.*
	5.	23—25.18 Abraham (c): Sarah Rebecca Keturah. Genealogy.	17—22 Joshua continues to *allot land* to remaining seven tribes.	8* Ezra *reads,* Jeshua interprets *Law.*
	6.	25.19—29.8 Jacob and Esau.	23—24 *Rehearsal from Abraham. Covenant.*	9* *Rehearsal from Abraham. Covenant. (Jeshua)*
	7.	28.10—32.3 *Jacob* and Laban. Leah Rachel. Birth of Patriarchs.	1 CHRONICLES 1.1—42* Adam—Noah (10). Descendants of sons of Noah (70) Shem—Abram (10). Descendants of sons of Abraham (70).	
	8.	32.4—36 Jacob and Esau. *Sons of Israel. Esau's descendants. Kings and chiefs of Edom.*	1.43—2* *Kings and Chiefs of Edom. Sons of Israel* (=Gen. 35.22ff). Judah *clans.*	
	9.	37—40 *Judah tries to save Joseph. Judah and Tamar.* Joseph in prison.	3* *Sons of David.*	
PENTECOST	10.	41—44.17 Joseph in power. *Judah* and brothers. *Simeon* hostage.	4* Villages of *Judah. Simeon.*	
	11.	44.18—47.27 Joseph recognized. Israel to Egypt. *Sons of Patriarchs.*	5—7.13* *Families of Reuben. Gad, half-Manasseh, Levi, Issachar, Benjamin, Naphtali.*	
	12.	47.28—50 Jacob blesses *Manasseh* and *Ephraim,* the Patriarchs (. . .*Joseph, Benjamin*): dies.	7.14—8* *Manasseh, Ephraim Benjamin.*	

EXODUS

13. 1—6.1 *Oppression in Egypt.* Moses *kills Egyptian, draws water* from *well. Moses raised to deliver Israel,* enter land of *Jebusites,* etc.

    10, 11(*) Death of Saul (*Oppression under* Philistines). David made king, takes *Jebus.* Mighty Men *draw water* from *well.* Benaiah *kills Egyptian.**

14. 6.2—9 Egypt smitten with seven plagues. Moses' *Thirty* (6.14ff).

    12* David's army. Amasai chief of *Thirty.* Ark from Kiriath–Jearim: God 'breaks forth'.

15. 10—13.16 *Last three plagues.* Passover. *Exodus.*

    13—14 *David smites Philistines.*

16. 13.17—17 Red Sea. *Moses' Song.* Timbrels and *Dancing* (15.17). Manna. Meribah. Amalek.

    15—16* Ark processed into Jerusalem. Cymbals and *Dancing. David's Song* by Asaph.

17. 18—20 Jethro. Sinai. X Commandments.

    17—18 Temple adumbrated. (17.21) David's victories over Philistines.

18. 21—24 Laws of Covenant: so '*enemies driven out, bounds from Red Sea to sea of Philistines desert to Euphrates'.*

    19—20 *Syrians, Edomites, Ammonites . . . to the River.*

19. 25—27.19 *Tabernacle* (a): Pattern of Ark, structure Altar, Court, etc.

    21—22 Census. Site of *Temple. Temple planned.*

20. 27.20—30.10 *Tabernacle* (b): *Pattern* of *Priests' cothes,* consecration, Incense, Altar.

    23—28* Levites, *priests,* acolytes officers for *Temple.* David gives Solomon the *pattern.*

21. 30.11—34 *Tabernacle* (c): *Half-shekel. Fezalel and Oholiab.* Golden Calf. Moses' *Visions.*

    2 CHRONICLES
29*; 1—2 *Freewill Offering.* Solomon's *vision.* Huram.

22. 35—38.20 Tabernacle (d): *Freewill Offering. Bezalel and Oholiab. Construction.*

    3—4 *Construction.*

23. 38.24—40 Tabernacle (e): Gold. Priests' clothes. *Induction. Glory-cloud.*

    5 *Induction. Glory-cloud.*

LEVITICUS

24. 1—5 *Burnt Offering. Cereal Offering. Peace Offering. Sin Offering. Swearing.*

    6.1–23 Solomon *before Altar.* 'Hear and forgive'. *Swearing.*

25. 6—8 *Burnt Offering, Cereal Offering. Sin-Offering. Guilt Offering. Ordination of Aaron and sons.*

    6.24—end '*If they confess . . . hear and forgive.' 'Let thy priests be clothed with salvation'.**

26. 9—11 *Sacrifice: fire from heaven.* Priests replaced. Clean and Unclean.

    7—8.10 *Sacrifice: fire from heaven heaven.** Solomon's building.

NEW YEAR

27. 12—13 Uncleanness: *Women,* Leprosy.

    8,11—9 *Solomon's wife away from ark.** Queen of Sheba.

28. 14—15 Lepers. Discharge.

    10 Division of Kingdom.

YOM KIPPUR

29. 16—18 Atonement. *Worship only for God at Tabernacle, not he-goats. Marriage and consanguinity.*

    11 *Priests secede to Rehoboam at Temple.* Jeroboam's he-goats.* Rehoboam marries cousins.**

30. 19—20 Holiness code.

    12 Rehoboam forsakes Law. Shishak.

TABERNACLES

31. 21—24 Priests' cleanness. Feasts. *Shewbread, lamps, blasphemy.*

    13 Abijah and Jeroboam. *Shewbread and lamps.**

32.	25—26.2 Jubilee. Redemption. (*If faithful, peace, 5 chase 100*).	14—15 Asa *destroys idols.** *Peace. Chases million Cushites.**
33.	26.3—27 *But if not* . . . Vows.	16 *Asa unfaithful: War, disease,** *Death.*
	NUMBERS	
34.	1—4.20 *First Numbering of Host.*	17*, 18 *Jehoshaphat's host.** With Ahab to Ramoth–Gilead.
35.	4.21—7 Levites (*Kohathites*). *Judgement* by Ordeal. Nazirites. Offerings.	19—20* *Judges. Levites and priests to judge.* Moabite War (*Kohathites*).
36.	8—12 *Lamps.* Passover, (*2nd month*). Quails and 70 elders. Miriam's *leprosy.*	21—22 Jehoram, Ahaziah. *Lamp* for David.
37.	13—15 *Spies.* Sacrifices.	23—24 Joash. Jehoiada. Zechariah.*
38.	16—18 *Priestly prerogatives. Korah* and incense. Priests' incomes.	25—26 Amaziah and Edom. *Host numbered.** *Uzziah's incense and leprosy.**
39.	19—22.1 Red heifer. *Edom refuses passage.* (2 Chron. 20) Brazen Serpent. Sihon, Og.	27—28 Jotham. Ahaz.
40.	22.2—25.9 *Moab* obstructive (2 Chron. 20). Balaam (2 Chron. 18).	29 Hezekiah: (a) *2nd month Passover* preparations (Num. 9).*
41.	25.10—30.1 *Second Numbering. Feasts and Offerings.*	30—31.3 Hezekiah: (b) *Passover* kept. *Provision of offerings.**
42.	30.2—32 Vows. Midianites. *Portion of spoil to Eleazar and Levites.* Gad, Reuben.	31.4—13 Hezekiah: (c) *Portions and Tithes to priests and Levites.**
43.	33—36 Stages of Journey. Borders. *Levites' cities and suburbs.* Zelophedad.	31.14—end Hezekiah: (d) Reckoning of *Levites* by cities and suburbs.
	DEUTERONOMY	
44.	1—3.22 *Moses encourages People* (3.22).	32.1-8 *Hezekiah* (e) *encourages* people (32.7).*
45.	3.23—7.11 Commandments. *Driving out nations greater and mightier.*	32.9—23 *Hezekiah:* (*f*) *Sennacherib.*
46.	7.12—11.25 *Trying Israel to know all his heart.* Wealth.	32.24—end Hezekiah: (g) *Wealth.** Babylon Embassy.
47.	11.26—16.17 *High places* forbidden. Jerusalem worship. Passover.	33 *Manasseh builds high places. Augury, sorcery, wizards, fire.* (Deut. 18) Amon.
48.	16.18—21.9 *Destroy Asherah.* Host of Heaven not to be worshipped. *King to study book of law under priests.*	34 *Josiah destroys Asherahs, etc. Follows book of law produced by Hilkiah.*
49.	21.10—25 Various laws.	35 Josiah's *Passover and death.*
50.	26—29.8 Blessing and Curse. *Exile foretold: no mercy on weak.*	36.1-21 Last Kings. *Exile. No mercy on weak.**
51.	29.9—34 (As many readings as are necessary) Repentance and *Return.* Moses' Song, Blessing Death.	36.22—end *Cyrus authorizes Return.**

PART II

The Matthaean
Year

11

THE NEW ISRAEL 1—4

The Chronicler, we have surmised, used an annual cycle for the Torah, and composed an annual cycle of *haphtārāh* readings. Matthew, we have suggested, wrote his Gospel to follow an annual Festal cycle: but if he followed the Jewish Festal system, what did he do, we have yet to ask, about the cyclic readings, sabbath by sabbath? Did he follow an annual cycle for them too, or a triennial cycle as was in use in Palestine in A.D. 500?[1] The evidence is all centuries away. We may reasonably conjecture that the triennial system arose when reading and Targum together became unbearably and unprofitably long: but then they were never felt to be unbearable in Babylon, where the annual system was used continuously. Perhaps the triennial system came in with Jamnia:[2] we do not know. The second-century evidence shows only that the period between Passover and Pentecost was the subject of calendrical meditation: the events between Exod. 12 and 19 were dated in the Mekilta for the period between 14th Nisan and 6th Sivan, and this period was the centrepiece of the three-year cycle. All we can do with Matthew is ask the question whether there is any relationship to either cycle. The conclusion I shall suggest is that Matthew is familiar with the annual cycle *and* with the Mekilta pattern: I find no evidence of his knowing the triennial cycle as a whole.

The Gospel reading for the first sabbath in Nisan was, we concluded, Matt. 23; this includes one open reference to Genesis in its peroration, 'that upon you may come all the innocent blood shed on earth, from the blood of innocent Abel . . .' (v. 35). Abel's murder, in Gen. 4, comes in the first *sidrāh* of an annual cycle, the third of a triennial cycle. It is also said of the Pharisees that they are serpents (ὄφεις) and that they close the kingdom of heaven before men: if these are references to Gen. 3, they would also fit an annual cycle only. The Gospel

---

[1] B Meg. 29b.
[2] It is evident that lectionary arrangements were in flux in the second century. R. Meir laid down an arrangement under which it would take rather over two years to read the Pentateuch, while his contemporary, R. Judah b. Ilai's scheme would have taken 5½ years (T Meg. IV.10; B Meg. 31b; I. Elbogen, *Der jüdische Gottesdienst* (3e., Frankfurt 1931), p. 160). Under an annual cycle the reading of an average *sidrāh* might take twenty minutes for the Hebrew and thirty minutes for the targum; and there was the *haphtārāh* besides. As targums became universal in the last century B.C. and the first A.D. there was bound to be pressure either to drop the Hebrew or to abbreviate the lections, and we do not need to speculate which would be the rabbis' preference.

readings for the second week in Nisan were Matthew 24—25, in which the first considerable Matthaean insertion begins, 'For as were the days of Noah, so will be the *parousia* of the Son of Man . . .' (24. 37). Now Noah was the name, and the subject, of the second *sidrāh* of the annual cycle, and the 4th–6th of the triennial. God shut the door on those saved with Noah, also, as the bridegroom shuts the door on the wedding-guests in Matt. 25. We have thus a strong suggestion that Matthew was working with an annual, and not a triennial cycle. Now the third *sidrāh* is Gen. 12—17, Abraham, Melchisedek, and the promise of the birth of Isaac. These are not referred to in Matt. 28, the Easter Gospel, though we cannot but notice that Melchisedek provides the text for the Passion-orientated sermon of Hebrews, and that Abraham and Adam and Noah and the Exodus are the themes of almost all the baptismal Easter sermons from St Paul for five hundred years.[3]

Proem. Jesus' Genealogy and Birth 1.1—25

Matthew begins, if the Festal cycle theory is right, on the fifth sabbath of the year. The annual cycle *sidrāh* was Gen. 23—25.18: the burial of Sarah 23; the marrying of Isaac, 24; and the generations, *tôledhôth*, of Abraham, 25. Paul had taught the Church that Christ was the seed of Abraham: here then let us begin, with the *tôledhôth* of Abraham ending with Christ, a βίβλος γενέσεως as the Greek Bible puts it.[4] Indeed, to begin with a genealogy is to follow the lead of scripture, for does not the Chronicler begin in just such a way? First the Chronicler gave the line from Genesis to David, then the line of David through to the Return under Shealtiel and Zerubbabel;[5] the Christian fulfilment is to complete the third section. The Chronicler saw David as an *alter Moses*, the Kingdom establishing the Law; and Joshua ben-Jozadak as an *alter Joshua*, with Abraham in turn behind him, the Return fulfilling the Entry, and the sojourn of the Patriarchs. To Matthew is given the secret of the matter—the Kingdom itself came to fulfilment under Christ the Son of David, Jeshua of Nazareth, seed of Abraham and divine High-priest. He begins, 'βίβλος γενέσεως of Jesus Christ, the son of David, the son of Abraham'. Or again, the Chronicler was given to artificial stylizing of schemes of generations—10, 70, 10, artificial 70;[6] or he makes the high-priesthood up

[3] See J. Daniélou, *The Bible and the Liturgy* (1951; E.T., London 1960).
[4] Gen. 2.4; 5.1.
[5] 1 Chron. 1—2.17, 3. Matthew suppresses Zerubbabel's descendants in Chronicles in favour of his own symbolic names.
[6] 1 Chron. 1.1–42; cf. p. 203 above.

to an artificial 24, twelve from Aaron to Ahimaaz, high-priest under David, eleven to Jozadak, and Jeshua the twelfth.[7] So Matthew follows this lead too: fourteen names from Abraham to David, as the Chronicler gave them; the kings assimilated to a second fourteen. Ὀχοζίας, bad king Ahaziah, asks to be assimilated to Ὀζ(ε)ίας, good king Uzziah,[8] and with the intervening two bad kings Joash and Amaziah that eliminates three names; bad king Jehoiakim makes a fourth, and that is fourteen. The third section is no problem as only the first three names are scriptural. It is unfortunate that Matthew has miscounted and given us only thirteen new names,[9] but he tells us his intention in v. 17.

The names in the third section have been filled up in the same way as the Chronicler filled up the list of the high-priests: he neglects high-priests such as Jehoiada who feature in his own story, and makes up the second dozen with a second Zadok and Ahitub and Azariah.[10] Judith 8.1ff is another example of a fictitious genealogy with such names as Simeon, Gideon, and Hananiah, whose stories are referred to in the text as foreshadowing the work of the heroine of their line.[11] So have the spare places in Matthew's table been filled up with symbolic names, some of them the same as the Chronicler's fill-ins. Eliakim is the name of Hezekiah's vizier, to whom it was prophesied that the government would be committed to his hand, and that the

---

[7] Zadok, David's famous high-priest, comes 11th, with Ahimaaz his son 12th, in just the same way as Josadak is the 23rd and last of the line in 1 Chron. 6.3–15, looking forward to Jeshua, the hero of Ezra–Neh. to complete the figure. Ahimaaz is clearly a second high-priest to David despite 1 Chron. 29.22, since Azariah is the 14th name in the list and is said to have served Solomon. The great kings span two high-priests apiece. cf. Rudolph ad loc., J. R. Bartlett, 'Zadok and His Successors at Jerusalem', *JTS* (April 1968), pp. 1–18.

[8] Ὀζ(ε)ία(ς) actually occurs by error for Ὀχοζία(ς) in Matthew's text, 1 Chron. 3.11, though followed, naturally, by Joash, Amaziah, Azariah (= Uzziah).

[9] The mistake is characteristic; cf. the minor muddles instanced on p. 35 above.

[10] 1 Chron. 6.10–13.

[11] Judith is given a genealogy of eleven, or in some texts fifteen names, and the relevance of these comes out in the story. She is ultimately the daughter of Salamiel ben Salasadai, the phylarch of Simeon in Num. 1: she prays, 'O Lord God of my father Simeon', and recalls how Simeon avenged Dinah's profanation with the sword—so is she to take the sword and save the Temple from profanation. cf. also the play *tsûrîshaddāī* Num. 1.6, *sela'shaddāī* Judith 8.1—*tsûr* = rock = *sela'*. She is of the line of Elihu who sat silent before Job's three comforters— so does she sit silent before the three elders of her city, and at length bursts forth (8.12). She is of the line of Gideon, and her enemies approach like locusts (2.20). She is of the line of Ananias, and shows herself to be as the Holy Children, who opposed Nebuchadnezzar by refusing food (12.2). For the same habit among the Bedouin today, cf. D. M. Emmet, *Function, Purpose, Powers* (London 1958), p. 20.

key of the house of David would be laid on his shoulder.[12] But while Jesus is descended from the line of Zerubbabel, the prince of Judah, he also fulfils the high-priestly office of his namesake, Jeshua, Zerubbabel's companion. Zadok and Eleazar are the most high-priestly of all names. Azor and Achim bear a strong resemblance to Azariah and Achimaaz, high-priests in 1 Chron. 6 to Solomon[13] and David. Matthew has already shown himself wise to the practice of amending names. As the Chronicler turned Hiram to Huram and Zabdi to Zimri, so Matthew reads Jobed as a more Jahwist Obed, Amos as a more prophetic Amon, and Asaph as a more musical, a more Chronicular, Asa.[14] Mattan may similarly be an abbreviated Mattathias, founder of the Maccabaean high-priesthood. But Jesus had been no Messiah of Levi;[15] he had been of the tribe of Judah. Hence, perhaps, Abiud, Judah is my father, at the head of the first five symbolic names; Eliud, God of Judah, at the head of the second. Jacob at the end of the list is the ideal name to be father of Joseph, whose name I take to be historical, and to be part of the oral tradition which Matthew received.

The suggestion of fictitious, symbolic names is not modern. Julius Africanus,[16] the third-century father, wrote a letter in which he aspires to reconcile the Lucan and Matthaean genealogies. He begins by remarking: 'Some incorrectly allege that a discrepant enumeration and mixing of names was made, both of priestly men, as they think, and royal: properly (δικαίως) in order that Christ might be shown rightfully to be both priest and king'. Africanus regards this as impious, and fudges an improbable solution to save the historicity of both Gospels. The presence of such as belief as that which Africanus feels called to disprove shows that a symbolic explanation of the names was in circulation 150 years after Matthew was written. In view of the similarity of method which we find in the Chronicler's genealogies, it is hard to resist the conclusion that Africanus' opponents were right.

Such would suffice as an account of the Genealogy: but it is the exordium of the Gospel, and there are a number of points about it which may be highly significant for the whole book, just as the Chronicles genealogies foreshadow the greatness of Judah and Benjamin.

---

[12] Isa. 22.20ff.   [13] 1 Chron. 6.10.

[14] In all three places the Mss. vary, some giving the LXX spelling: this is most easily explained as assimilation to the LXX. The non–LXX spelling is given by both Nestle–Aland and BFBS.

[15] The contemporary doctrine of a Messiah of Levi as well as/instead of a Messiah of Judah is testified in the Testaments of the XII Patriarchs, the Dead Sea Scrolls, and some rabbis; see M. D. Johnson, *The Purpose of the Biblical Genealogies* (Cambridge 1969), pp. 120ff.

[16] Epistle of Africanus to Aristides 1, *ANCL* IX, p. 164.

1. It certainly suggests a simple recurrent pattern. Abraham sojourned in Babylon and removed to Canaan, and after fourteen generations came David's Kingdom, the full occupation of the land: another fourteen and Israel is again removing from Babylon to Canaan, and a further fourteen sees the Kingdom of the Son of David, the Kingdom of Heaven. Luke actually uses the verb μετοικίζω of both Abraham's move from the Euphrates and Jeconiah's deportation.[17]

2. A remarkable parallel occurs in the Exodus Rabbah on 12.2: 'This month shall be unto you the beginning of months; just as the moon has thirty days, so shall your kingdom last until thirty generations. The moon begins to shine on 1st Nisan, and goes on shining till the 15th day, when her disc becomes full: from the 15th to the 30th day her light wanes, till on the 30th it is not seen at all. With Israel too there were fifteen generations from Abraham to Solomon. Abraham began to shine . . . When Solomon appeared, the moon's disc was full . . . Henceforth the kings began to diminish in power . . . With Zedekiah the light of the moon failed entirely . . .'[18] Matthew's way of counting means that David comes both at the end of the first section and the beginning of the second, which would give him a 29-day month, and with Christ a second full moon. The association of the moon-phases with Exod. 12 raises the suggestion that even here Matthew has the Paschal season in mind as well as the Genesis Sidrah.

3. The three fourteens are to a Jew who had read Daniel six weeks of generations; and if six, then looking forward to a seventh, to make a week of weeks. We may compare the rabbinic 2000 years of chaos, 2000 years of Torah, 2000 years of messianic age—then the age to come, all sabbath.[19] This, then, is to be the last week, initiated by the coming of Jesus in humility, to be crowned by his coming in power: but it is not a week that will run its course. If those days had not been shortened, no human being would be saved: this will be the half-week foretold by Daniel, a time and times and half a time.[20] As the evangelist writes, the third generation is already passing since the days of Herod the king: he is near, at the very gates.[21]

[17] Acts 7.4, 43.
[18] Exod. R. on 12.2, Soncino edn, p. 196, cited by W. D. Davies, *Setting*, p. 76.
[19] B Sanh. 97a; J Meg. 70d; Pes. R. 4a–c; Moore, *Judaism* II, pp, 323f; S–B IV.2, 799ff.
[20] Matt. 24.22.
[21] 24.33. The emphasis on the approaching end is exemplified by the additional parables which Matthew piles up in 24—25.

4.   It is possible that we should take the weeks even more seriously. Aminadab is the eighth name, the phylarch of Numbers: the Exodus therefore takes place after the first week of names. Among the kings the break between the two weeks falls after Ozias, Uzziah, by Matthew's device: now it was in the year that king Uzziah died that Isaiah saw his vision. As part of the substance of the vision was the fall of Samaria and birth of Emmanuel (Isa. 7), this gives us an attractively neat pattern:

Exodus from Babylon	King David	Exodus from Babylon
Exodus from Egypt	Fall of Samaria (Emmanuel)	
King David	Fall of Jerusalem	Christ, Fall of Jerusalem Messianic Kingdom.

5.   Four women are mentioned as mothers in Israel, but not Sarah, nor Leah. They are the four whose marriages are irregular: Tamar who acted the harlot to Judah, Rahab the harlot, Ruth the Moabitess, and the unnamed adulteress, the wife of Uriah. They foreshadow Mary's being the mother of Jesus, also through an irregular marriage. Matthew's Genealogy is a poem, and comment upon it should perhaps be likewise.

> Exceedingly odd is the means by which God
> 　　Has provided our path to the heavenly shore—
> Of the girls from whose line the true light was to shine
> 　　There was one an adulteress, one was a whore:
> There was Tamar who bore—what we all should deplore—
> 　　A fine pair of twins to her father-in-law,
> And Rahab the harlot, her sins were as scarlet,
> 　　As red as the thread that she hung from the door;
> Yet alone of her nation she came to salvation
> 　　And lived to be mother of Boaz of yore—
> And he married Ruth, a Gentile uncouth,
> 　　In a manner quite counter to biblical lore:
> And of her there did spring blessed David the King,
> 　　Who walked on his palace one evening and saw
> The wife of Uriah, from whom he did sire
> 　　A baby that died—oh, and princes a score:
> And a mother unmarried it was too that carried
> 　　God's Son, and him laid in a manger of straw,
> That the moral might wait at the heavenly gate
> 　　While the sinners and publicans go in before,
> Who have not earned their place, but received it by grace,
> 　　And have found them a righteousness not of the law.[22]

[22] There is an extended treatment of a more prosaic kind in Johnson, pp. 152ff.

6. Each of the three fourteens foreshadows Jesus' mission. The first column is primary because it consists of the heroes of the Torah, together with the names from the Book of Ruth which lead up to David's birth. Jesus is to be displayed throughout the Gospel as the fulfilment of the Torah, and the fulfilment begins with Abraham. A secondary theme, but a very important one, is the Son-of-David, greater-than-Solomon conception, which is found in many places, and becomes dominant after 12. And a third theme is the fulfilling of the μετοικεσία Βαβυλῶνος, which dominates the end of the Gospel. The prophet of the Fall of Jerusalem was Jeremiah, the prophet in Babylon was Daniel, the prophet of the Return was Zechariah. Daniel was already important in Mark, but Matthew doubles the Daniel citations, and introduces freely from the other two. The disaster of 586 B.C. had been duplicated in A.D. 70, when God sent his armies and destroyed those murderers and burned their city; and another Jesus than the son of Jozadak will be crowned as the royal priest of the ultimate Return.

How many of these schemes were in the mind of the author is a matter of opinion: myself, I should think that all except 4. are probable. The more that are thought to be valid, the more closely is the Genealogy tied in to the fabric of the Gospel, and the more rabbinic is the mind of the author. The acceptance of 3. and 6. especially would tend to make the evangelist the author of the Genealogy on grounds of unity, while 2., 4., and 5. would show him to have considerable familiarity with rabbinic thought. But in any case the beginning from Gen. 25, and the detailed use of Chronicles, and of the Chronicler's methods, would indicate that Matthew the *sôphēr* has composed it. Only the name Joseph would seem to be traditional.

The Lucan Genealogy is an artificial composition, like its Matthaean counterpart. For Matthew's six weeks Luke has eleven, looking for a twelfth: he goes back to Adam, and derives the later names through Nathan, the next elder brother to Solomon, and homonym of the prophet. The details of Luke's composition I have discussed else-where,[23] and many of them are not germane to our argument: but it is significant that Luke includes the Matthaean Eliakim and four versions of Mattathias;[24] that his final week includes the priestly names of Jannai, Melchi, Levi, Matthat, and Eli; and that both Melchi and Matthat look as if they are abbreviated forms of names, Melchisedek being a pagan form—the god Sedek is my king. We would thus have parallels for three features we have suggested in Matthew:

[23] *Type and History in Acts*, Appendix (London 1964).
[24] Matthat (2), Mattathias (2)—also Mattatha. Luke's creativity is most obvious in the series Levi, Simeon, Judah, Joseph (3.29f).

the series of weeks leading up to the Incarnation and the final half-week of generations before the Parousia, the formation of symbolic names by abbreviation, and the use of priestly symbolism.

1.18–25   It was to Abraham's seed that the promise had been made. The raising by God of seed from the dead womb had seemed to Paul to be a type of the Resurrection. 'He did not weaken in faith . . . when he considered *the barrenness of Sarah's womb* . . . [faith] will be reckoned to us who believe in him that *raised from the dead* Jesus'.[25] Matthew takes the step of seeing the birth of Isaac as a foreshadowing of Jesus' marvellous birth, rather than his rising from death. He forms the story of Jesus' genesis first, following the *sidrāh*, from Abraham: in Gen. 17 the wonderful birth of Isaac is foretold to his father by an angel, and not only do these features recur in Matt. 1, but the words of that annunciation are seminal also, 'Behold, Sarah thy wife shall bear thee a son, and thou shalt call his name Isaac'.[26] The Torah thus foreshadowed the coming of Christ, and the Prophets prophesied it; the thread that draws Matthew's mind to Isa. 7. is the verbal similarity that was basic to rabbinic exposition. Isaiah wrote, in the Greek version, 'Behold, ἡ παρθένος, the virgin, shall conceive and bear a son, and thou shalt call his name Emmanuel.'

The most interesting of all the questions of tradition in Matthew falls on the first page. We should like to know: Did Matthew have it in the tradition before him that Mary was a virgin at the conception of Christ, or is this a part of his midrash? The answer to this must depend upon the general picture that is formed of Matthew's method of writing, and in particular upon the possibility of accounting fully for the details of this narrative. If, on other grounds, Matthew appears regularly to have been a *darshān*, freely writing apologetic and edifying stories for the church, putting flesh on the Marcan skeleton, then this particular story will seem to fall into the pattern without recourse to non-Marcan tradition. Paul, and the liturgy, drew Matthew's mind to Abraham, Abraham drew it to Isaiah. The presence of the key-name Emmanuel in the Isaiah text must seem to be confirmation of divine guidance: what was Jesus but God with us? And if, as Christians never wearied of maintaining, he was the son of God, what could be more in keeping than that his birth should have taken place without the seed of a human father, that his mother should have been a virgin at his conception? The Hebrew, *'almāh*, is indeterminate, as Matthew well knew—it corresponds to the English 'girl'. But the Greek, a translation not less inspired, has the suggestive παρθένος. There are few clearer cases of the steps by which an evangelist has found history in scripture. This process does not, of course, disprove the

[25] Rom. 4.19,24.   [26] Gen. 17.19.

historicity of the story as traditionally believed, but it takes away the evidence for it. Matthew believed in the virginal conception of Jesus, but he believed on *a priori* grounds, that it was foretold in a 'given' piece of scripture. We may also continue to believe in the virginal conception of Jesus; but if so, this will be not on grounds of evidence but on *a priori* grounds also, that the Church is not likely to have been wrong on so central an issue.[27]

A third thread from scripture, which goes to make up the story, is drawn from the name of Joseph.[28] Abraham's angel(s) of annunciation came to him openly at noon: the dreamer of Genesis is Joseph, and God reveals the future to him in a series of dreams, as is done also to the Matthaean Joseph. The rest of the story of Matt. 1 is entailed by these three elements. If Mary was virgin and yet the announcement was to be made to Joseph, then they were not yet married, but must be engaged. If they were engaged and she pregnant, then the proper attitude (cf. 5.32, no divorce except on the ground of unchastity) was dissolution. Nevertheless mercy is still proper even in such cases— not like Judah, who was minded to make a public example of Tamar, but she was more just than he. The angel calls Joseph the son of David, which also underlines the ironical contrast between Joseph's restraint with Mary and David's laxity with Bathsheba.

The language of the paragraph is characteristic of the evangelist: οὕτως εἶναι, ἐνθυμεῖσθαι, ἰδού after gen. abs., κατ' ὄναρ, φαίνομαι, (γεννάω), ἐκ of parenthood, πληρόω, τὸ ῥηθέν, διὰ τοῦ προφητοῦ, ἐγερθείς are Matthaean; μὴ with the aor. subj., δίκαιος, θέλω, ἀπολύω = divorce, ἄγγελος Κυρίου (2), παραλαμβάνω (2), τοῦτο δὲ (ὅλον) γέγονεν ἵνα, λέγων, –οντος, γινώσκω of people are semi-Matthaean. Mary as subject of both a gen. abs. and the main sentence in 1.18, and the introductory nom. aor. part. in 1.24, are also typical.

So Matthew's introductory lection is complete. The second half grows from the first, and the midrashic method and the language alike dispose us to take the evangelist for the author.

---

[27] It is often maintained (e.g. by McNeile, pp. 10–13) that the thought of divine conception is uninstanced in Jewish writing, and would be abhorrent to the Jewish mind. Compare, however, D. Daube, *NTRJ*, pp. 5–9, and comments in W. D. Davies, *Setting*, pp. 63f. The argument is in any case invalid. Messianic speculation is post–biblical, and all rabbinic writing comes from a time when anti-Christian reaction was strong: should we expect the rabbis to play into Christian hands by suggesting a virgin birth for Messiah? Aquila was quick enough to revise the translation of Isa. 7.14.

[28] Although it would be possible to argue that Matthew had invented the name from Genesis, this seems to me altogether improbable, and I concede the name as coming to Matthew in non-Marcan, non-Pauline tradition: too much is built on it for it not to be traditional.

1. The Magi 2.1–15

(a) 2.1–12   The *sidrāh* for the sixth sabbath of the annual cycle was
Gen. 25.19—28.8, the birth, struggles, and blessings of Jacob and Esau,
or Edom as he is also called. When Isaac blesses Jacob he says, 'May
nations (ἔθνη) serve thee, and princes bow down to thee (προσκυνησ-
άτωσάν σοι); and be thou lord of thy brother.' Esau is minded to kill
Jacob, and he flees. Matthew's περὶ τῶν μάγων describes how Gentiles
came and bowed down to Christ (προσεκύνησαν αὐτῷ). Herod the
Edomite has made himself king by usurpation, but the true king of
the Jews is born after him and will supplant him. Herod is minded to
kill Jesus, and he flees.

The worship of the Gentiles draws in other texts: Isa. 60.3, 6: 'Kings
shall come to thy light, and nations (ἔθνη) to thy brightness . . . all
from Saba shall come bearing gold (χρύσιον) and shall bring frankincense (λίβανον)'; and Ps. 72.10, 15, 'The kings of Arabia and Saba
shall bring gifts. And all kings shall bow down to him (προσκυνήσουσιν
αὐτῷ) . . . To him shall be given of the gold of Arabia . . .' The myrrh
is drawn from the Song of Solomon, 'Who is this that comes up from
the wilderness, censed with myrrh and frankincense (σμύρναν καὶ
λίβανον)? Behold Solomon's bed.' (Cant. 3.6; cf. 4.6).

But Jesus is not only the new Jacob/Israel: he is also the son of
Joseph. Now the greatest of old Joseph's dreams had been of the star
that was his before which all else should bow;[29] Pharaoh's wise men
(σοφοί, ἐξηγηταί)[30] had given place before his power to interpret
dreams, and so his brothers came to bow down to him (προσεκύνησαν
αὐτῷ). The brothers came with gifts of money and incense and nuts,
and at the last saw his face: and so Joseph brought the family of the
people of God down to Egypt. The new Joseph, son of another Jacob,
continues to dream dreams. At Jesus' birth wise men (μάγοι) follow
his star and do him obeisance: they bring gifts of gold and frankincense and myrrh, and see the child. Then with more dreams Joseph
brings the Holy Family down to Egypt. The theme of Jesus' birth-star
is developed with manifest reference to Joseph by Ignatius.[31]

Other scriptures have played a secondary part. The star of Num.
24.17 became a key text for rabbinic Christology,[32] and will certainly
have reinforced Matthew's inclination to use the star image. And,
what is significant for our general thesis of the influence of cyclic and
paschal readings, the star went before the Magi and guided them till

[29] Gen. 37.8.
[30] Gen. 41.6. Symmachus translates μάγοι.
[31] Ign. *Eph.* 19.
[32] See S–B I, 76f: Bar-Kokhba took his name from the text. cf. also Test. Lev.
18.3; Test. Jud. 24.1; Lohmeyer, p. 20.

it came to rest over Jesus: as did the pillar of cloud and fire go before
Israel at the Exodus, and guide them each day and night, till it had
brought them to the divinely chosen resting-place. Daniel interprets
Nebuchadnezzar's dream in a story that is already a midrash on
Joseph and Pharaoh: and Nebuchadnezzar's wise men were μάγοι
and φαρμακοί.[33] μάγοι, astrologers, are more to Matthew's purpose
with the star. But Jesus is not just, like Joseph, of the family of Abraham: he is also the son of David. David's birthplace must be Jesus'
birthplace, then, and Micah had prophesied as much: 'But you, O
Bethlehem Ephrathah, who are little to be among the clans of Judah,
from you shall come forth for me one who is to be ruler in Israel . . .
he shall feed his flock. . . .' This Matthew improves for the occasion:
a repointing of '*alphê*, clans, gives '*alluphê*, rulers:[34] the gloss οὐδαμῶς,
by no means least, shows Bethlehem's greatness of destiny, more
relevant than her numerical littleness: and the mention of shepherding
leads him to take the citation straight on to God's word to David in
2 Sam. 5.2, 'You shall be shepherd of my people Israel'. Gifts of gold
are foreshadowed in David's own psalm for his son, Ps. 72, and of
myrrh and frankincense in Solomon's Song as son of David.

Midrashic reference is to be intuited rather than proven. Schniewind
maintains that we have to do here with remembered history,[35] and
who can prove him wrong? The strength of the construction that we
have given rests on the following points:

(*i*) Both the annual cycle *sidrāh* and the Paschal story are seen to
furnish the central theme of the pericope. The coming of the
Gentiles to worship Christ, led by the divine light, and the
murderous intent of rejected Edom, are given, so to speak, by the
liturgy, and must seem to be inspired. These are passages of
scripture which neither Matthew nor his interpreter are in a
position to select.

[33] Dan. 2.2. It is because of the star that they have to be μάγοι, not just σοφοί.
The notion that in them the powers were doing obeisance to Christ is a later
construction of Ignatius, Tertullian, and Origen: had Matthew intended this he
could have written the ambiguous ἄρχοντες. cf. Lohmeyer, p. 21, n. 2, and
literature there cited.
[34] Stendahl, *SSM*, pp. 99f. The citation is a fine illustration of the *sôphēr* getting
the most out of his text—repointing, glossing, combining quotations through the
keyword ποιμανεῖ. He also substitutes γῆ 'Ιούδα for 'Ephratha': Ephratha is
not theologically significant, but it cannot be made too clear that Christ comes
from Judah. He puts ἡγούμενος for *moshēl* to smooth the transition from
ἡγεμόσιν.
[35] *Das Evangelium nach Matthaüs, NTD*, pp. 16ff. So also Allen, p. 14.

(*ii*) The gold, myrrh, and frankincense are gifts from the Gentiles to the son of David in prophecy, and Bethlehem is cited as his prophesied birthplace.

(*iii*) The midrash on the name Joseph is probabilified by six points of correspondence: Joseph son of Jacob in 1.16, the dreams, the star, the going down to Egypt, the obeisance, and the wise men. Although the star and the obeisance are well explained in other ways, the remaining points are especially connected with Joseph, and the story moves on to a midrash on Exod. 1—4. The importance of the name in Israel, and the expectation that a man would be the true son of his 'father' or eponym, are commonplaces: we have seen the styling of the Jeshua stories to match the Joshua tradition, and Judith's ancestors, and there are several examples in so 'straight' a history as 1 Maccabees.

(*iv*) The whole content of the story is covered by these passages, with which there are not only verbal but thematic bonds, and a clear imaginative connection is easily traceable. Lohmeyer has suggested a more complex use of the Balaam story,[36] and a connection with the Philonic legends of Moses' birth is often asserted:[37] such would be optional extras.

The section contains much characteristic Matthaean diction. προσκυνέω (3), συνάγω, a favourable view of γραμματεῖς, φαίνεσθαι, σφόδρα, τότε, κατ' ὄναρ, ἕως + ind., δῶρα, προσφέρειν, ὅπως, διὰ τοῦ προφήτου, ἀναχωρέω are Matthaeanisms, and there are no less than thirteen nominative aorist introductory participles. ἀνατολή (3), γεννᾶν (2), ἰδού, πᾶσα Ἱεροσόλυμα, πάντας, λέγοντες, ἐλθών (2), οὕτως, γῆ, ἐλάχιστος, ἡγέμων, πορεύομαι, ἀνοίγω, κἀγώ, ἐπάνω, officers τοῦ λαοῦ, χρῦσος are semi-Matthaean; as is the use of celestial imagery. There are words which are rare in Matthew: πυνθάνομαι, ἐπάν, ἀκριβοῦν, ἐξετάζω, λίβανος, σμύρνα, χρηματίζομαι, ἀνακάμπτω, θησαυρός = chest: so that Lohmeyer can claim evidence of an independent source.[38] But some of these are from passages in the LXX consciously

---

[36] p. 25.

[37] e.g. by W. D. Davies, *Setting*, pp. 78ff, citing Josephus, *Ant.* 2.9.2; cf. 7. I agree with Davies that Herod and the slaughter of the children are a midrash on Exod. 1, but the rest of the argument has come in uncriticized under this impressive umbrella. The sorcerers of Exodus are hostile figures who are Moses' enemies, and are hardly to be seen as types of the pious Magi. The central place occupied by the star in the story is not explained, nor the provenance of the Magi from the East, nor the dream motif. So we need a midrashic hypothesis as well as the borrowing of contemporary Moses legends: and the latter procedure might seem to Matthew, as it seems to me, rather a paltry notion.

[38] p. 20, n. 1.

referred to; others are instanced elsewhere in Matthew—ἐξετάζω at 10.11 (redactoral), θησαυρός as a treasure-chest at 13.52; ἐπάν is here alone, but ὅς ἄν, ὅσος ἄν, ἐάν are common and even Matthaean. Dr Kilpatrick's verdict is, 'Some of these expressions are required by the subject-matter, and the few that remain are quite outweighed by the general similarity with the style of the [*sic*] editor'.[39]

(*b*) 2.13–15.   Joseph, we have said, like Joseph of old, brings the new Israel down to Egypt. To call Jesus the new Israel is no tendentious whim, for Matthew states as much: this fulfilled Hosea, 'Out of Egypt I called *my son*'. Israel was God's son in the prefiguring language of the OT: and it is in connection with the Exodus that he is so called. In Exod. 4.22 Moses is to say to Pharaoh, 'Thus says the Lord, Israel is my πρωτότοκος υἱός.' Otherwise the God/Israel relationship is spoken of directly as father/son only in Deut. 4.37, and in five prophetic texts, of which Hosea is one. The LXX translated Hosea's 'my son' by the more respectful, 'Out of Egypt did I call their children', but Matthew has recourse to the Hebrew which alone can fit his purpose. The literal Son of God, the true Israel, follows the path of his foreshadowing forebear. The language is very strongly Matthaean: ἀναχωρέω (2), φαίνομαι, κατ' ὄναρ, ἐγερθείς (2), πληροῦν, τὸ ῥηθέν, διὰ τοῦ προφήτου λέγοντος, ἰδού + gen. abs. Other words are semi-Matthaean: ἐκεῖ (2), ἴσθι, νυκτός, ἄγγελος Κυρίου, παραλαμβάνω (2), λέγων, ἕως (2), μέλλω. τελευτή is found here only, but τελευτᾶν (2.19) is semi-Matthaean.

2. *The Innocents 2.16–end*

On the seventh sabbath the *sidrāh* was Gen. 28.9—31, the birth of Jacob's sons, and Rachel's grieving for her childlessness: the Gospel was the death of the Innocents, in fulfilment of Jer. 31.15. Now of all the citations in the Gospel, this is the most clearly artificial. According to Matthew, the voice was not heard in Ramah but in Bethlehem; the babies were Judahite babies, and their mother therefore is Leah, not Rachel. There are many prophecies of lamentation in scripture: why choose this one? Because the sidrah was the story of Rachel, Rachel cheated of her husband while her sister bore him six sons, Rachel's childlessness and envy, Rachel's offer of her handmaid in her place, and the ultimate birth of Joseph: as Jeremiah puts it, Rachel weeping

[39] Kilpatrick, *Origins*, p. 54.

for her children because they are not.[40] In Gen. 35 Rachel gives birth at Bethlehem to the son of her sorrow, Benjamin.

The use of Exodus to gloss the Rachel story is obvious. Pharaoh ordered all the Hebrew boys to be killed in his fear of Israel; and the new tyrant follows in his steps in slaughtering the boys of Bethlehem. Murderous Pharaoh is thus superimposed on murderous Esau. More especially Pharaoh sought to destroy Moses (ἐζήτει ἀνελεῖν Μωύσην) and Moses fled (ἀνεχώρησεν, Exod. 2.15); Herod destroyed the boys —Matthew uses ἀναιρέω here alone in the Gospel—and the family ἀνεχώρησαν and avoided destruction. In Exod. 4.19 Moses is told to return, 'for all the men who were seeking your life are dead': in Matthew Joseph is told, 'For those who sought the child's life are dead'. Only Herod has died in his story: the Exodus plural οἱ ζητοῦντες betrays his dependence on the Exodus type.

The section ends with the famous conundrum, 'And he went and dwelt in a city called Nazareth: that what was spoken by the prophets might be fulfilled, ὅτι Ναζωραῖος κληθήσεται'. The most popular solution remains Isa. 11.1,[41] 'There shall come forth a shoot (*nētser*) from the stump (of Jesse)', where the Targum interprets the *nētser* as Messiah; although the wording is certainly much closer to Judg. 13.5, 7, 'Νάζιρ (αιος) ἔσται'.[42] The latter seems to me the more convincing. κληθήσεται is a favourite word of Matthew. He is looking for a prophecy to justify Jesus' sojourn in Nazareth, just as he justifies every other move of geography and policy, and this is the closest. The alteration of the *i* of Nazir to the *o* of Ναζωραῖος is easily understood in the light of similar adjustments in the rabbis,[43] and in the Dead Sea Habakkuk commentary.[44] We may compare Hiram/Huram in the Chronicler, and Azariah/Azor in the Matthaean genealogy. Matthew was led to the text by the parallel situation and wording of the birth of Samson to that of Isaac and Emmanuel. Manoah's wife is barren, and the angel of the Lord (so in Judges and Matthew, not in Genesis or Isaiah) says to her, 'ἰδοὺ σὺ ἐν γαστρὶ ἔχεις καὶ τέξῃ υἱόν . . . He shall be a Nazir of God and shall begin to save Israel.'[45] It is objected by

---

[40] Matthew veers between the LXX and his own version of the Hebrew. πολύς is his own, in place of the third noun in Greek and Hebrew: the scale of the disaster bespeaks it. παρακληθῆναι is similarly more graphic than παύσασθαι, and follows the Heb. *l*ᵉ*hinnāhēm*. But τέκνα is required by the Rachel parallel in Genesis: she was not sonless but childless; cf. Matt. 22.24, 'If a man dies, having no children (τέκνα)'. This is against Greek and Hebrew, and shows the evangelist's interest.

[41] Stendahl, *SSM*, pp. 103f, 198f; Gundry, *UOTSM*, pp. 97f.

[42] So H. H. Schneider, *TWNT* IV, pp. 879ff.

[43] e.g. *tsûr*/*tstr*, Gen. R.I. 9; Shoher Tobh 18.26; A. Feldman, *PSR*, p. 12.

[44] cf. Stendahl, *SSM*, pp. 183ff, esp. p. 192, point 10.

[45] Judg. 13.3,7 (LXX).

Gundry[46] that Jesus was no Nazirite, and was known as a winebibber: but to Matthew it is the marvellous birth of a saviour that is relevant, and not his subsequent view of asceticism. Luke saw Gundry's difficulty, and transferred the text to the annunciation of the Baptist's birth.[47] Thus the wording, the midrashic method, and the Lucan change all support a primary reference to Judg. 13. But, at the same time, it would hardly be possible for a community that was known as the Ναζωραῖοι,[48] and which regarded their leader as the scion of Jesse, and Isa. 11 as a Messianic prophecy,[49] to miss the *double entendre*: so Matthew says τὸ ῥηθὲν διὰ τῶν προφητῶν—the plural, 'prophets', in such a formula, is not instanced elsewhere in the Gospel.

The language is very strongly Matthaean;[50] ἀναχωρέω, φαίνομαι κατ' ὄναρ (2), γῆ + name (2), ἐγερθείς (2), τότε (2), ὅπως, πληρόω (2), τὸ ῥηθέν (2), διὰ τοῦ (τῶν) προφήτου (–ων) λέγοντος (2), ἰδού, λεγόμενος. Other words are semi-Matthaean: πάντας (2), ἐκεῖ, λέγων, πορεύομαι, ἄγγελος Κυρίου, κατοικέω, παραλαμβάνω (2), τελευτάω, εἰς τὰ μέρη, κληθήσεται. Septuagintal phrases are θυμέομαι, ἀναιρέω, ζητεῖν τὴν ψυχήν, ἀπὸ διετοῦς καὶ κατωτέρω. Only ἀκριβόω and χρηματίζομαι are not found outside the Infancy narratives.

But what of Luke? Since we are abjuring Q, and supposing Luke to have copied and adapted parts of Matthew, we cannot escape the corollary that he will have read Matt. 1—2 also. What then has he done with Matthew's *haggādāh*?[51] Well, basically he has done what Matthew has done: but what Matthew has done with brilliance, he has done with genius. The same texts that have served Matthew serve him. Isa. 7 establishes the virgin conception, Mic. 5 Bethlehem. Abraham becomes the type of the father of the Lord's predecessor, Zechariah: well advanced in years, childless, to whom the angel announces the birth of his son, incredulous. Manoah and his wife lend their Nazirite overtones to the ascetic John; and the parallel, and greater, marvellous birth of Samuel to Hannah is then suggested as the type for the birth of Jesus, worked out in the Magnificat. The freedom of association which is the basis of haggadic midrash enables Luke to lay in fee the archangel Gabriel and the dumbfounding of Daniel;[52] the witness of Zechariah in Isa. 8 and the writing of the name of the prophet's son on the tablet; Zechariah and Malachi at

[46] op. cit., p. 98.
[47] Luke 1.11, 'The angel of the Lord appeared to him' (cf. Judg. 13.3,13,15); Luke 1.15, 'He shall drink no wine or strong drink' (cf. Judg. 13.4,7,14).
[48] Acts 24.5. The Talmud speaks of Jesus as *nôtsᵉrî*; see Lohmeyer, p. 32.
[49] Rom. 15.12; 2 Thess. 2.8.
[50] See Kilpatrick, *Origins*, p. 54, cited above.
[51] For a fuller exposition see my 'St Luke's Genesis' in *JTS* VIII.1 (April 1957).
[52] Dan. 9—10.

the end of the prophets; and much other matter which would take us too far afield. But Luke's reading of the Matthaean infancy story, and his understanding of it, are not an embarrassment to interpreting the third evangelist, but a prerequisite.

3. John's Preaching, the Baptism and Temptations 3—4.16

(a) 3.1–12 Matthew now reaches the opening of Mark, and at this point the relationship with the sabbath *sidrāh* fades away, to be replaced by the type of Israel in the desert. The *sidrāh* for the eighth sabbath in the annual cycle was Gen. 32.4—36; in the opening chapter of which Jacob comes to the ford of Jabbok, he wrestles with the man until he sees the Face of God (εἶδος θεοῦ), and he is named Israel instead of Jacob. In the same week the Gospel was Jesus' Baptism and Temptations: he comes to the Jordan, he persuades John to baptize him, he sees the spirit of God (Mark πνεῦμα, Matt. πνεῦμα θεοῦ) coming upon him. It is conceivable that Matthew is still thinking in terms of the sidrah, but if so he has left no verbal traces. At the most we can find an indirect link in Isa. 42.1 (LXX): '*Jacob* my son whom I have adopted, *Israel* my beloved, in whom my soul is well-pleased. I will set my spirit upon him.' The text is scarcely visible in the Marcan account: with Matthew's third person, and relative ᾧ and ἐπί (coming *upon*), it is almost word for word the form that he actually cites at 12.18. The new Jacob, God's son—υἱός not παῖς—has seen the πνεῦμα θεοῦ, the spirit coming upon him, and is named the new Israel, the beloved in whom God is well-pleased. Perhaps: but then Matthew suppresses the names.

Matthew transfers to his beginning Mark's 1.4a to give a less clumsy opening, and the vague 'in those days' is similarly brought in from Mark 1.9. John had preached a baptism of repentance;[53] Matthew characteristically gives the *oratio recta*, 'saying, "Repent . . ." ', and adds the message of Jesus from Mark 1.15, 'The kingdom of God is at hand'.[54] Jesus' preaching and John's preaching are, as often in Matthew, the same. The citation of v. 3 is taken over from Mark: only that Mark said it was from Isaiah, so his opening sentence, which is from Exod. 23/Mal. 3, is omitted, and saved for later. If, as is probable, Mark had John clothed only in camel-skin, then Matthew has glossed this with, 'and a leather girdle around his waist'. John

---

[53] Perhaps the forgiveness of sins has been deliberately suppressed, as the prerogative of Jesus (9.9; 26.28, a Matthaean addition).

[54] cf. 28.7/10 for a similar transfer of words to a speaker different from that given in Mark: from Mark's angel to the risen Lord.

is Elijah returned, as Mark hints and Matthew states ' "Elijah has already come . . . ." Then the disciples understood that he was speaking to them of John the Baptist':[55] so Matthew assimilates John to Elijah as he is described in 1 Kings 1.8. Mark's Jerusalemites become 'Jerusalem',[56] and 'all the region about the Jordan' is added for magnification.

So far, by general consent, so good: but 3.7–10, 12 lack a Marcan parallel—only v. 11 in the paragraph derives from Mark 1.7f. Well, Matthew adds to the eschatological preaching of Jesus in 24—25, so it is not surprising that he should wish to stress the Baptist's eschatological preaching, which is hardly mentioned in Mark. He does this by introducing a stock audience of Pharisees and Sadducees—so coupled five times in Matthew, never in Mark or Luke. He opens the onslaught with an abusive vocative and rhetorical question (an echidnic),[57] a form found five times in Matthew, never in Mark, only here in Luke. Matthew has Jewish officialdom berated three times[58] as a brood of vipers, twice by Jesus, once by John: never in Mark, only here in Luke. The wrath to come, and the contrast of the children of Abraham in flesh and in spirit are both Pauline doctrines.[59] The Abraham antithesis grows out of the genealogy. Repentance is the keyword of the paragraph (v. 8); John preached repentance in Mark, and Matthew's exposition is in terms of a tree bearing fruit or facing the axe[60]—again a motif which comes twice later in Matthew in the mouth of Jesus:[61] never in Mark, in Luke only in Q passages and the Fig-Tree parable.

The imagery develops in the entirely natural way of free writing. The Pharisees and Sadducees are *snakes* escaping from the wrath to come—like snakes escaping from the *fire*,[62] since God's wrath is fire; they are like the barren *trees* that go for the fire at the *axe* of judgement; the fire in the orchard leads on to the fire by the *threshing-floor*, when the *fan* succeeds the axe and the *chaff* the deadwood. Harvest-imagery abounds in Matthew above the other evangelists,[63] and the contrast of wheat/chaff, barn/fire is typical of his black and white approach.[64] The imagery of fire and stubble, of the destruction of root and branch, is not Matthew's invention: it is given already in Mal. 3.2; 4.1, 'Behold a day comes burning as an oven . . . and all that do wickedly shall be as stubble: and the day that is coming shall set them on fire

[55] Matt. 17.12f. [56] cf. 2.3, the town = the people.
[57] See p. 79; cf. 12.34; 23.17,19,33. [58] 3.7; 12.34; 23.33.
[59] 1 Thess. 1.10; Gal. 3; Rom. 4.
[60] A common simile in the rabbis; cf. Feldman, *PSR*, p. 103.
[61] 7.17–19; 12.33 (more briefly); Luke 3.8f Q; 6.43f Q.
[62] cf. Acts 28.3. [63] See p. 100 above.
[64] See p. 54.

. . . and there shall not be left of them root or branch' (LXX): the day before which, four verses later, Elijah is to come and turn the hearts of men. The rhythm of verse 9, 'Do not think to say . . . for I say unto you . . .' (AT) is the thesauric rhythm,[65] 'Do not think that I have come to bring peace on earth: I have not come to . . .', 'Do not think that I have come to destroy the law and the prophets: I have come . . .' (AT)—found eight times in Matthew, never in Mark, twice in Matthaean parallels in Luke. The language is characteristic. συνάγω is Matthaean; μὴ + aor. subj., ποιεῖν κάρπον (2), ἄξιος, δένδρον(2), πῦρ(2), γεννήματα, ἔχιδναι, μέλλω, ἐκκόπτω, καλός, βάλλομαι, λέγω ὑμῖν ὅτι, κατακαίω are semi-Matthaean. ὑποδεικνύω alone is non-Matthaean. The harvest words are only found here, but the theme is typical. The passage is thus Matthaean in doctrine, in language, in imagery, and (in two verses at least) in rhythm; and is naturally to be seen as Matthew's own composition. Luke copies it almost word for word, with a characteristic, 'Begin not . . .' for Matthew's 'Think not . . .'[66] All the points we have shown to be Matthaean are less characteristic, or uncharacteristic of Luke.

(b) 3.13–17 Since baptism is said to be of repentance, and even (by Mark) for remission of sins, the question suggests itself why Jesus should have offered himself as candidate;[67] and Matthew's insertion resolves this question, just as his insertion of, 'You are a stumbling block to me' resolves the reason for Jesus' indignation with Peter at Caesarea Philippi, or his insertion of a rebuke to Peter at the arrest resolves the question of Jesus' attitude to violence in his defence. The Baptist, Matthew glosses, tried to prevent him with words of humility: but Jesus replied, in a general remark,[68] that this was the will of God. Seven of the 36 words in 3.14f are on the list: τότε, ἄρτι, δικαιοσύνη (Matthaean), λέγων, ἀποκριθεὶς εἶπεν, οὕτως (semi-Matthaean): and the concept of total fulfilment of the will of heaven (πᾶσαν δικαιοσύνην) is crucial to Matthew—we are not to break one of the least of these commandments; all that the scribes lay down we are to do. δικαιοσύνη is naturally taken in its normal Matthaean sense of man's obedience to God,[69] as when our righteousness must exceed that of the scribes

[65] See p. 79ff. above.
[66] Pleonastic ἄρχομαι comes twice as often in Luke as in Matthew. Other Lucan changes are: κάρπους (pl.), added καὶ (v. 9, typical of Luke), a return to the Marcan wording (v. 16b), infinitives of purpose (v. 17).
[67] Jerome, *Adv. Pelag.* III.2, cites the Gospel to the Hebrews to the same problem.
[68] cf. 4 Macc. 13.12: 'Isaac, for righteousness' sake, offered himself to be a sacrifice.'
[69] cf. A. Schlatter, *Die Kirche des Matthäus* (Gütersloh 1929), p. 32; G. Barth, *TIM*, pp. 137ff; A. M. Farrer, *The Triple Victory* (London 1965), p. 24: *contra* Lohmeyer, McNeile, ad loc.

and Pharisees, and we must be careful not to do it before men. Strecker's argument[70] that the passage is a Matthaean version of a pre-Matthaean apologetic seems over-subtle. It rests on the presence of two ἅπαξ λεγόμενα, διεκώλυεν and πρέπον. As Matthew introduces eight other δια–compounds into the Gospel, the presence of the former is not very striking, and some untypical vocabulary is to be expected in any passage. πρέπειν comes three times in the Greek Psalter, eight times in all in the LXX.[71]

The account of the opening of the heavens is assimilated to Ezek. 1.1, καὶ ἠνοίχθησαν οἱ οὐρανοὶ καὶ εἶδον . . .[72] Otherwise the Baptism follows Mark closely.[73] Abraham and David are already present in the Marcan tradition: Isaac was Abraham's ἀγαπητὸς υἱός, and 'You are my son' was spoken to David. In his Genealogy and Infancy stories Matthew might feel that he has brought old things out of his treasure-chest in a new form.

(c) 4.1–11 Mark affixes to the Baptism a brief statement of Jesus' temptation. The close link between Baptism and Temptation may be gauged from the fact that both Paul in 1 Cor. 10 and the author of Hebrews in ch. 5 draw baptism/sonship into their sermons on temptation:[74] so it is the less surprising that the fifth-century manuscripts of Matthew, and the evangelist himself, should see the two as an integrated whole, even at the cost of a long lesson. Mark's brief account cries out for expansion: what were the trials to which Satan put the Lord through those seminal forty days? What but the temptations that Israel of old underwent and failed for forty years in the desert? Was it not written that Israel had tempted God, and that Moses had fasted forty days and forty nights? Where Israel of old stumbled and fell, Christ the new Israel stood firm: this is what Matthew meant by fulfilling every jot and tittle of the Torah.

The midrash virtually writes itself. Mark wrote that Jesus was forty days in the desert tempted by Satan and fed by angels. If he had no human food, then what would his first temptation be but hunger— just as Israel, having crossed the water in Exod. 14, hungered in Exod. 16 and was fed with angels' food? Matthew adds to the forty days 'and forty nights' following Moses' fast: 'I remained on the mountain

---

[70] *WG*, p. 15.
[71] G. Barth (*TIM*, p. 137) takes the passage to be editorial; so also apparently Kilpatrick, *Origins*, p. 5.
[72] Gundry, *UOTSM*, p. 28.
[73] The words from heaven are closer to Isa. 42.1 than is the Marcan version, cf. p. 242.
[74] cf. Farrer, *The Triple Victory*, pp. 20ff.

forty days and forty nights: I neither ate bread nor drank water.'[75] Christ is the fulfilment of Moses, the intercessor, the leader of God's people; and the fulfilment of Israel itself, now no longer succumbing to the first pang of hunger. Christ, as God's Son, has power to speak and to create: God has power to raise up children to Abraham from the stones—could not God's Son speak and turn the loaf-shaped stones to bread? But no: for what had been the divine word to Israel after the hunger-temptation of Exod. 16? 'Man shall not live by bread alone, but by every word that proceeds from the mouth of God.'[76]

From Exod. 16 the story proceeds to a second fall, the thirst of Exod. 17: when Israel tempted God, and his need was supplied by the Waters of Temptation (Massah). But the midrashic method can plumb deeper than to tell us that Jesus resisted the temptation of thirst as he had that of hunger. Hunger was resisted also for ten days by Daniel and the Three Children in Dan. 1. Now Daniel is a book of the temptations of the saints, and it is furthermore the book in which alone the coming of Messiah is foretold: 'Know therefore and understand that from the going forth of the word to restore and build Jerusalem to the coming of an anointed one, a prince, there shall be seven weeks . . . and after the sixty–two weeks, an anointed one shall be cut off . . . and upon the pinnacle of abominations ('al kᵉnaph shiqqûtsîm, LXX ἐπὶ τὸ ἱερόν, upon the temple, Theod. ἕως πτερυγίου τοῦ ἀφανισμοῦ, up to the pinnacle of desecration) shall come one who makes desolate.' (Dan. 9.25–7). So, now that Jesus has been anointed with the Holy Ghost, the desolating devil takes Messiah to the πτερύγιον τοῦ ἱεροῦ, with intent to cut him off, and takes into his mouth the words of God to David, the Lord's anointed of old, 'Under his wings (kᵉnāphāiw, πτέρυγας) you will find refuge . . . He will give his angels charge of you',[77] and the rest. The situation of the second trial is thus drawn from Daniel, the substance from David: and the last word from Moses, 'You shall not tempt the Lord your God', God's word on the incident at Massah.[78]

Moses fasted not once but twice: the first time because 'you provoked the Lord your God to wrath in the wilderness',[79] the second time because 'in Horeb you provoked the Lord to wrath', in the matter of the Golden Calf.[80] Israel's third and greatest temptation was at the mountain, where they fell and worshipped the idol of gold: and Daniel also speaks of an idol of gold before which God's saints refused to bow down, and of the kingdoms (βασιλείαι)[81] and the glory (δόξα)[82]

---

[75] Deut. 9.9,18.
[76] Deut. 8.3.
[77] Ps. 91.4,11f.
[78] Deut. 6.16.
[79] Deut. 9.7.
[80] Deut. 9.8–17.
[81] Dan. 6.1 and *passim*.
[82] Dan. 2.37; 4 *passim*.

of them which they might have if they recanted. Daniel and Deuteronomy combine to form the third of Christ's temptations, when he refuses to bow down to the devil for the βασιλείαι of the world and their δόξα: and the last word is again with Moses, 'You shall worship the Lord your God, and him only shall you serve.'[83]

The texts in Matt. 4 are from Deuteronomy, but the puzzle is the order. Moses' fasts are in Deut. 9; 'Man shall not live by bread . . .' from Deut. 8; 'You shall not tempt . . .' from Deut. 6.16; 'Thou shalt worship . . .' from Deut. 6.13. Farrer suggested that Matthew works backwards from the fasting texts towards the Shema', and gives us a chiastic order:[84] but such a procedure does not seem *a priori* likely, and I know of no other instance of Matthew reversing the order of scripture by intent. It seems simpler and more probable that he follows the order of Exodus: the hungering theme already puts him in Exod. 16, and this suggests the Tempting of Exod. 17, and so to the mountain at Exod. 19, and the climactic Golden Calf. For Luke's change of the order I refer the reader to p. 460 below.

If we exclude the words quoted from the LXX, there are 101 words of new material in 4.3–10, and of these 19 are characteristic—προσελθών, τότε (2), ἔφη, πεσὼν προσκυνέω (Matthaean); ἀποκριθεὶς εἶπεν, παραλαμβάνω (2), ὁ διάβολος (2), ἵστημι, γέγραπται γάρ, ὁ κόσμος (semi-Matthaean). We should add ἡ ἀγία πόλις which Matthew intrudes redactorally at 27.53. ὁ πειράζων is found here only in Matthew, but occurs also in Thessalonians; εἰπεῖν ἵνα is also here only, but such expressions as θέλειν ἵνα occur. With 'the kingdoms of the world and their glory', compare 'the kingdom of God and his righteousness'.

(*d*) 4.12–16; cf. Mark 1.14f, 21a. The move, like all changes of policy in Matthew, has its scriptural justification. Matthew, with rabbinical skill, blends together the LXX and Hebrew, with καθημένος/οις from Ps. 107.10, and ἀνέτειλεν as his own rendering.[85]

---

[83] Deut. 6.13.   [84] Farrer, *The Triple Victory*, pp. 16ff.
[85] See Stendahl, *SSM*, pp. 104ff; Gundry, *UOTSM*, pp. 105ff. The sense of neither Greek nor Hebrew is entirely satisfactory for Matthew's purpose, and he omits the irrelevant introductions of both. He remains close to the Hebrew at first, with repeated γῆ (γῆ + a name is Matthaean) and καὶ: ὁδὸν θαλάσσης is a literal translation of *derek hayyām*, and is included in virtue of 4.13, Κ. τὴν παραθαλασσίαν. τοῖς καθημένοις is the Hebrew (Greek κατοικοῦντες), emphasizing their haplessness; cf. Ps. 107.10, LXX; and καθήμενος (16a) follows suit. ἀνέτειλεν is more graphic than the Greek or Hebrew.

4. The Ministry Begins: The Call of the Four Disciples
4.17–25

Cf. Mark 1.15–20, 39; 3.10, 7f. The Call of the Four, which is part
of a much longer first lection in Mark, stands on its own in Matthew
in virtue of its echo of Exod. 18—19. Matthew shows the Four as not
merely called, but witnessing the Lord's ministry of preaching and
healing which they will later share (10). The crowds, which are an
essential part of the Exodus background, have to be borrowed
forward from Mark 3.

What we have seen is the process of midrash, the crossing of one
scripture with another. The *darshān* is weaving a fabric of which the
warp is visibly provided by the liturgy, the annual cycle readings from
Gen. 25 in the fifth week to Gen. 32 in the eighth: the woof is the
paschal season stories from Exod. 12—19, which become increasingly
important as the stage is set for Pentecost. The midrash is done with a
keen sense of the rabbinic method, exemplified most clearly in the
Chronicler, many of whose traits we have seen paralleled. Other
passages are adduced by association. When the association is provided
by the story of the desert-temptations of Exod. 16, suggestive of
Christ's desert-temptations, Mark is introduced, the scripture that is
to form the main fabric of the Gospel: by Lection 4 we have Mark and
Exod. 18 and Genesis drops out—we have had Joseph already. We
have accounted for virtually the whole of the story on this basis:
it is necessary to posit only the name of Joseph from oral tradition.

But could not the midrash be the work not of Matthew, but of the
anonymous Church? I should not myself think that the book was
written quickly. I should see the midrash as growing year by year for
the five to ten years since Matthew's church acquired a copy of Mark:
first the cyclic and Festal readings providing inspiration, then the
subsidiary Exodus themes, and so on, till suitable passages were
reached in Mark. But the dominant hand has been one man's. The
language is one man's language. The familiarity with rabbinic ways
is considerable—there is knowledge and use of Hebrew not available
to Mark or Luke, and many a Chronicular twist: and there cannot
have been many *sôpherîm* in the church.[86] Certain themes, such as the
dreams, or Solomon, come again in the book. The fairy-tale Magi
are as Matthaean as the everyday shepherds are Lucan.[87] The theology
of the fulfilment of the whole of scripture is everywhere. The more one
tests them out, the more the two possibilities converge. It is not the
church which preaches but her *darshān*, St Matthew.

[86] 'Not many of you were wise', 1 Cor. 1.26.
[87] cf. p. 459 below.

APPENDIX
TABLE OF LECTIONARY CORRESPONDENCIES WITH MATTHEW, WEEKS 1–9

		Annual Cycle	*Festal Cycle*			*Matthew, ΑϹΟΣΖ, etc.*
4	Nisan	Gen. 1—6.8		56	23(.35 Abel)	
11		6.9—11		57ff	24–5 (24.37; 25.10, Noah)	
15			Exod. 12.21	62ff	26–7 (Passover)	
18		12—17	13.1	68	27.57—28 (Easter)	
25		18—22	14.15		(Octave)	
2	Iyyar	23—25.18	15.1	0	1 (Toledoth of Abraham)	
9		25.19—28.9	15.22	1	2.1 (Jacob-Esau, Joseph's Star	
					Pillar of Cloud)	
16		28.10—32.3	16.4	2	2.16 (Rachel's childlessness,	
					Out of Egypt)	
23		32.4—36	16.28	3	3.1 (Baptism, Temptations)	
1	Sivan	37—40	18.1	4	4.17 (Judges for Israel)	

Sources:

Annual Cycle: Jewish Yearbook
Festal Cycle: A. Büchler, art. cit.
Matthew: appendix to ch. 9.

12

PENTECOST:
THE UNITY OF THE SERMON (5—7)

For the thesis which I am arguing, the crux is the Sermon on the Mount. Much of the early chapters of the Gospel is commonly regarded as *haggadah:* a critic of good will may allow on the linguistic evidence, aside from the suggestions of serial midrash which I have adduced, that the whole may be the composition of the evangelist himself. But the Sermon is the stronghold of traditional criticism: how, you may ask, am I to scale this citadel, fortified generation after generation with conflations of M and Q, with bastions of apophthegms and catechetical outworks? You will not come in here, the critic will be thinking, but the blind and the lame will keep you out.

My strategy for taking the stronghold of Zion is twofold. The conduit by which I propose to insinuate my men in this chapter is the suggestion that the Sermon has a unity of its own, that it coheres in a well thought out and carefully worked out whole: Jerusalem is a city that is at unity with itself. If it can be shown that this is so, then one mind formed the plan of composition. Neither Streeter's scissors and paste, nor Dibelius' pebbles, gathered, smoothed, and mossed by the brook, could produce a work of art. Jesus, perhaps, or Matthew's teacher, or Matthew: but not the chance of church life. It would still remain possible, at this stage, for Matthew to have obtained much of his material by selection from previous tradition, but it will be seen that some considerable place must be found for the evangelist's free activity: thus I hope at least to smite the blind and the lame who call Matthew the editor. Secondly, in the following two chapters, I shall try to show the extent to which Marcan matrices, and especially the passage of the Rich Man, dominate the Sermon, and that these, and their development through OT references and regular Matthaean ways of writing, taken in conjunction with the scheme I am outlining now, account for the whole of the Sermon without remainder. In this way I hope finally to smite the Jebusites, and to lay out a city of David worthy of the name, wherein all true daughters of Zion may rejoice and defy their enemies.

It was an ancient Jewish practice, if a series of matters were to be expounded, to set them out in order and then give the exposition in reverse. We are taught to say in our sermons, 'I have three points this morning, a, b, c: now a . . ., now b . . ., now c . . .'. The Jew might say, 'My three points are a, b, c: now c . . ., now b . . ., now a . . .'. 'These are the generations of the sons of Noah, Shem, Ham, Japheth . . . The sons of Japheth . . . The sons of Ham . . . To Shem, also, the elder brother of Japheth, children were born' (Gen. 10). This habit was especially natural to our friend the Chronicler—his most recent commentator calls it 'a regular pattern':[1] 'The sons of Abraham: Isaac and Ishmael. These are their genealogies: the first-born of Ishmael, Nebaioth . . . Abraham was the father of Isaac.'[2] 'When David was old and full of days, he made Solomon his son king over Israel. David assembled all the leaders of Israel and the priests and the Levites' (1 Chron. 23.1f). The Levites are then catalogued in 23, the priests in 24, with the choir in 25 and the gatekeepers in 26; then the leaders of Israel in 27, and the making of Solomon king in 28. Mattathias' dying speech follows the same pattern in 1 Macc. 2: '(49) Now have pride and rebuke gotten strength and a season of overthrow . . . (50) And now, my children, be ye zealous for the law . . . (51) And call to remembrance the deeds of our fathers . . . (52–61) Abraham, Joseph, Phinehas, Joshua, David, Elijah, the Three Children, Daniel; (62–64) And ye, my children, be strong, and show yourselves men in behalf of the law . . . (65–68) Behold Simon . . . and Judas . . . render a recompense to the Gentiles.'[3] We find the same method of exposition carried *à l'outrance* by R. Isaac in a Proem to Lamentations: 'Had you been worthy you would have read in the Torah . . .'—he then gives 22 texts of blessing—' . . . but now that you are unworthy you read . . .' and there follow 22 texts of misery and degradation, Lam. 1.22, 21, 20, . . . 1, 'Ekah'. The proem sets out in reverse order what the book is to expound.[4]

Now I would suggest to you, following but amending A. M.

---

[1] J. M. Myers, Anchor Bible (New York 1965) ad 1 Chron. 23.1.

[2] 1 Chron. 1.28,29,34.

[3] cf. Jerusalem Targum, Gen. 3.24: 'He created the Law, and prepared Gehinnom and the Garden of Eden. He prepared the Garden of Eden . . . He prepared Gehinnom . . . For the Law is the tree of life. . . .': P. Borgen, 'Observations on the Targumic Character of the Prologue of John', *NTS* 16, p. 293. Compare also the famous description of Wisdom in Wisd. 7 in three sevens of adjectives, which is similarly structured. It is the last heptad, 'philanthropic, stedfast, sure, unworried, all-powerful, all-surveying, *penetrating all spirits*' which is expounded first, 'For wisdom is more mobile than any motion, yea, she pervadeth and penetrateth all things . . .': then the middle heptad, '*unpolluted*, distinct, unharmed, right-minded, keen, unhindered, beneficent'—'Nothing defiled can find entrance into her . . . an unspotted mirror of the working of God': while the first heptad, '*intelligent, holy, only-born*, manifold, subtle, mobile, lucid' is worked out last, 'She, being only one, hath power to do all things . . . passing into holy souls' (Wisd. 7.22–7). The method is only an elaboration of the familiar *inclusio*.

[4] Midr. Lam. R. Proem XI.

Farrer,[5] that the Sermon on the Mount is of the same construction: that the texts of blessing which head the Sermon are expounded in reverse order in its body. We are given a clear lead that this is the case by 5.11, for after eight Beatitudes of the form, 'Blessed the . . .', of which the last is 'Blessed the persecuted . . .', the following verse opens 'Blessed *are* you, when men revile you and persecute you . . .' The eighth beatitude is plainly expounded in the first verses of the main body of the Sermon.

Of the Beatitudes themselves I shall say little now, since I am maintaining that their meaning is explained by the relevant passages of the Sermon. They are the summing up, the *kelāl*,[6] of the teaching of the Sermon, and, as I should think, were thought out last. Their most striking feature as a group is their eight-foldness,[7] stressed by the identity of the reward of the first and last blessed: for of both the poor in spirit and the persecuted is it said, 'for theirs is the kingdom of heaven'. The reason for this is the place of the Sermon in the Year: this is a Pentecostal Sermon, to be read at the eight watches of the Feast of Weeks,[8] a series of eight lections proclaiming the fulfilment of the Law and the Prophets. A new Christian Law, to be enunciated at Pentecost, requires a Pentecostal exordium, and an octave of blessings gives the authentic Whitsun note. As the Pentecostal Psalm, 119, with its eight-line stanzas, opens with a double *'ashrê*, μακάριοι (οἱ), so can the evangelist reveal in Eight Beatitudes who are the truly blessed. It is to be observed also that of the five blocks of teaching in Matthew the first opens with a catalogue of blessings, and the last with a catalogue of woes. This leads us to suspect the influence of Deuteronomy where 27—28 are a list of blessings and curses. Deuteronomy is to a Greek-speaking Christian already a second law,[9] and its influence on all the NT documents is clearly profound. It would be naturally seen by Matthew as a precursor of the law of Christ. The opening blessing in Deut. 28 is a kind of double fourfold blessing:[10]

---

[5] *St Matthew and St Mark* (2e., London 1964) ch. X. Farrer's analysis, both of the Beatitudes and the second half of the Sermon, is more subtle than mine, and considerably more elaborate. Matthew again makes use of the reverse order exposition for the Beelzebul Controversy in 12.22–45; see pp. 331ff below.
[6] cf. p. 20, 25 above.
[7] Suggestions of an original Seven Beatitudes are, of course, a groundless speculation.
[8] cf. p. 311 below.
[9] cf. Farrer, *St Matthew and St Mark*, p. 163. In the Qumran community Pentecost was the Feast of the Renewal of the Covenant, and its celebration included rituals based upon the liturgy of Deut. 27—28; see Community Rule I–II, G. Vermes, *The Dead Sea Scrolls in English* (London 1962), p. 44.
[10] Deut. 28.3.

'Blessed shall you be in the city, and blessed shall you be in the field. Blessed shall be the fruit of your body and the fruit of your ground, and the fruit of your beasts, the increase of your cattle, and the young of your flock. Blessed shall be your basket and your kneading-trough. Blessed shall you be when you come in, and blessed shall you be when you go out.'

The language of the Beatitudes is largely characteristic—19 words out of 71. Matthaean are διώκειν, δικαιοσύνη (2), ἡ βασιλεία τῶν οὐρανῶν (2). Semi-Matthaean are: κληθήσονται, κληρονομεῖν, γῆ, πεινᾶν–καὶ–διψᾶν, ἐλεεῖν, καθαρός, πραΰς. For an adjective with τῇ καρδίᾳ/τῷ πνεύματι cf. 11.29. πενθέω is inserted redactorally at 9.15, παρακαλέω into the citation of Jer. 31.15 at 2.18, against Heb. and LXX. The only word untypical of Matthew is εἰρηνοποιός, which does not occur elsewhere in the Greek Bible, though the verb εἰρηνοποιεῖν comes in Proverbs and Colossians.

The common view that the Lucan Beatitudes are original, and the Matthaean version a secondary, ecclesiasticized form,[11] adapted for catechism,[12] has little basis. Matthew, it is true, is enthusiastic about the spiritual life—purity of heart, hunger and thirst for righteousness, etc.—but this is equally, indeed better, explained by our view that Matthew was the author of the Beatitudes. Equally it is to be observed that Luke shows himself elsewhere concerned about poverty,[13] and it would be natural for him to abbreviate the Matthaean version, as he so often abbreviates Mark,[14] omitting the pleonastic 'spiritual' phrases. Poor in spirit? What God cares about is the πτωχοί, the poor-and-faithful. When Matthew thought of the blessedness of hunger, he thought of fasting on Mondays and Thursdays; when Luke thought of the blessedness of hunger, he thought of the Macedonian Christians of 2 Cor. 8, penniless but contributing. Luke does here then exactly what he does with the Q/Matthaean Woes: he divides the eight Matthaean Beatitudes in two, replacing them with four Beatitudes and four Woes, just as he divides the seven Matthaean Woes on the scribes and Pharisees in two, replacing them with three woes on the Pharisees and three on the lawyers.[15] Four is the favourite Lucan series.[16] His Beatitudes are slightly awkward, retaining the Matthaean μακάριοι οἱ form, but moving over to the second person

[11] e.g. T. W. Manson, *The Sayings of Jesus* [*SJ*] (London 1937), p. 47.
[12] H. T. Wrege, *Die Überlieferungsgeschichte der Bergpredikt* (Tübingen 1968), pp. 5–26.
[13] cf. Magnificat, Luke 14, Lazarus, etc.
[14] See, e.g., Mark 4.1–25/Luke 8.1–18; Mark 8.34—9.1/Luke 9.23–7.
[15] Luke also divides the crucified thieves into two, one blaspheming, the other repentant.
[16] See p. 91.

in the reward. Luke again moves over to the second person against Matthew in 7.31f (Matt. 11.18f): 'To what shall I compare . . . *this generation*. . .? *They* are like children . . . For John has come eating no bread . . . and *you* say . . . and *you* say . . .': Matthew retains the 'they' throughout.[17] The linguistic changes strongly suggest Lucan editorial activity. He inserts his favourite νῦν and his favourite κλαίειν for the Matthaean πενθοῦντες, but the tell-tale πενθήσετε slips back in the Woes.[18] ἐμπεπλησμένοι and κατὰ τὰ αὐτά which he introduces are semi-Lucan. He inserts the non-Lucan ἀπέχετε from Matt. 6 and παρακλῆσιν from παρακληθήσονται in Matt. 5.4. γελᾶν, which only occurs in this passage in Luke and is sometimes urged as evidence that it must stem from a tradition earlier than Luke,[19] is merely the obvious antithesis to the very Lucan κλαίειν: compare Eccles. 3.4, 'a time to weep, and a time to laugh'. The evidence for the standard view is not simply reversible in the sense that we might regard Matthew as an ecclesiasticised Q/Luke, or we might regard Luke as a socialized Q/Matthew: it leaves unexplained the reminiscences of specifically Matthaean style in Luke. The Lucan version contains four typically Lucan expressions which are not in the Matthaean version, and three Matthaean expressions which are rare in Luke: while there are no expressions strange to Luke in the Lucan version, other than those also in Matthew, that might point to an independent original. It is plain that Luke has adapted something very close to the Matthaean version, and that the whole of the latter, words and theology, are extremely Matthaean. The simplest explanation[20] must be that Matthew wrote the Beatitudes, and that Luke rewrote them.

First, then, Matthew expounds the Eighth Beatitude: and here, as throughout the Sermon, he follows the practice, rabbinic[21] as modern, of triple illustration: μακάριοί ἐστε. . . ὑμεῖς ἐστε. . . ὑμεῖς ἐστε. . .; your reward in heaven, the salt of the earth, the light of the universe. The repeated ἐστε[22] and the triple balance of the images suggest that the paragraph runs from vv. 11–16 or even 11–20, and not 13–16 as

---

[17] Luke changes Mark similarly to the second person at 5.30,34; 6.2.

[18] πενθησετε και is omitted by 1424, Ir., Hil. The doubled verb is clumsy, and this is the only reward of the eight to have it: hence the tendency to assimilate and drop it; cf. X 213 vg (1 MS) Marcion and Jerome, who read πενθησετε alone. There is no justification for Dr Kilpatrick's suggestion (*Origins*, p. 15) that πενθησετε και is a manuscript gloss from Matthew. *Origins* was written at a time when the Q hypothesis was unquestioned, but it is in fact this type of argument which has prevented its discard and held up the advance of scholarship: Q can only be defended from behind a barricade of *variae lectiones*.

[19] Wrege, op. cit., p. 17.

[20] For a more complex solution see Wrege, op. cit., ch. 1.

[21] cf. Mann, *BRPOS*, p. 25n.   [22] So Lohmeyer, ad loc.

is normally printed.[23] The first unit simply expands the Beatitude: the blessedness *is* the reward in heaven. Heaven/earth is then a standard Matthaean antithesis, and the salt image, already in Mark in a context of purification and salvation through loss, suggests itself for the occasion. Better, the Lord had taught, to suffer the loss of a limb and so attain life: for we must all be salted with fire,[24] we must all attain life with loss. Simeon b. Lakish was to teach (*c.* A.D. 250): 'Just as salt removes the impurities from the meat and seasons it, even so do sufferings penetrate and purify the human body.'[25] To Luke also salt was a symbol of salvation through suffering: he appends the salt logion to his teaching on the cost of discipleship. 'Whoso carries not his cross and follows me, cannot be my disciple.' Like a tower-builder, like a king, we must count the cost, perhaps all we have. 'Salt is good; but if the salt is blunted what will it be seasoned with?'[26] So to Matthew: the Christian is the earth's salt, the means of the world's salvation, through his sufferings. If the salt is blunted, if he refuses the sting of persecution, his use is over and cannot be restored; he is fit only for the dustbin—or, since culture had not yet risen to dustmen, for the garden path.

The heaven, the earth, the cosmos. The Christian is to be as the sun to the cosmos, giving it light—a common rabbinic conceit;[27] as a city on a hill; as a burning lamp. The primary sense of the light images is the Christian's witness. In Mark 4 the light is the preaching of the Church.[28] But the introduction of καίουσι suggests that the persecution theme is still in Matthew's mind. Mark: 'Does the lamp come?' Matthew: 'Nor do they burn a lamp' (AT). A lamp on the stand gives light to all in the house, but it burns as it does so. John uses the same figure of the Baptist:[29] he was ὁ λύχνος ὁ καιόμενος καὶ φαίνων, whose witness to the truth was ultimately martyrdom. In Rev. 11 the two witnesses to the death are called λυχνίαι. The same two themes are worked out side by side, often in the same words, in 1 Peter: 'If you are reproached (ὀνειδίζεσθε) for the name of Christ, blessed are you (μακάριοι), for glory (τό τῆς δόξης)... rests upon you. Let none of you suffer as' an evildoer but for doing good.[30] 'Having

[23] The unity of the paragraph is urged by W. D. Davies, *Setting*, p. 290, and by G. Barth, *TIM*, p. 102, n. 1.
[24] Mark 9.49.
[25] T Ber. 5a; cf. S–B I, p. 235. 'The model here is the salt which seems to "die" in the sacrificial meat, but which, when it vanishes, in fact makes the whole sacrifice like itself and pleasing to God', B. Gerhardsson, 'The Seven Parables in Matthew XIII', *NTS* XIX (1972), p. 23.
[26] Luke 14.27–35 (AT).　　　　　[27] S–B I, pp. 237f.
[28] Mark 4.21.　　　　　[29] John 5.35.
[30] 1 Pet. 4.14f (AT).

your behaviour seemly among the Gentiles that wherein they speak against you as evil-doers they may by your good works (ἐκ τῶν καλῶν ἔργων) which they behold, glorify God (δοξάσωσι τὸν θεόν) in the day of visitation.'[31] The wording is so close that it is very probable that 1 Peter is writing in reminiscence of Matthew.[32] The Christian's witness, in word or life, cannot be hid, and he must expect to suffer for it.

Thus all three sub-paragraphs, the prophet's reward, the salt, and the light, read naturally as comments on the blessedness of persecution, expounding the Eighth Beatitude. 5.17–20 form the introduction to the second theme of the Sermon, the Fulfilment of the Law, with which we shall be concerned in the next chapter: but they follow naturally as from the Persecuted for Righteousness. The Christian's good works (5.16) must include every iota and tittle of the Law; not one must be relaxed in teaching or practice. Unless his *righteousness* exceeds that of the Pharisaic scribes he will never enter *the kingdom of heaven*. Matthew thus closes the new paragraph with a reminiscence of the old: 'Blessed are those who are persecuted for *righteousness*' sake, for theirs is *the kingdom of heaven.*'

5.21–6 expound the Seventh Beatitude, 'Blessed are the εἰρηνοποιοί'. We are accustomed to understand the blessing as upon those in the exacting role of mediator, the U Thant's and Gunnar Jarring's of this world, following the meaning of εἰρηνοποιεῖν as 'reconcile' in Col. 1.20. Blessed they no doubt are, but the words have a simpler and more workaday reference—those who do or make peace between themselves and others. A work with close relation to the Sermon, almost our first commentary on it, is the Epistle of James: advising meekness and the avoidance of jealousy James says, 'The harvest of righteousness is sown in peace by those who make peace (τοῖς ποιοῦσιν εἰρήνην).'[33] Similarly Prov. 10.10: 'He who boldly reproves makes peace (εἰρηνοποιεῖ)', that is, a few straight words make for better relations between two men than does dissembling. In neither case is there question of third parties. How then are we to make peace? First by not being angry with our fellows. The old commandment said, 'No murder', but the root of murder to which the new Moses goes, is commonly anger: so, too, the Didachist.[34] He who is angry with his fellows shall now be liable to serious penalties.

---

[31] 1 Pet. 2.12.
[32] E. G. Selwyn comments, 'Based on the *verbum Christi* in Matt. 5.16', *The First Epistle of Peter* (London 1947), p. 171.
[33] Jas. 3.18.
[34] *Didache* 3.2, 'Be not angry, for anger leads to murder'; cf. B Derek Erets 10; S–B I, pp. 282f.

Triple climaxes are a feature of the Gospel. I have called them scandalics,[35] and there are two in Mark, eight in Matthew, and four in Luke (3Q). It would not be surprising if there were one such here, but the puzzle is to sort out the nature of the progression. For the three penalties we have (a) 'judgement', (b) 'the sanhedrin', and (c) 'the gehenna of fire'. The phrase, 'liable to judgement' for the murderer in 5.21, is used of a normal Jewish court, and the same phrase in 5.22 must mean the same thing. Murder in biblical times was tried locally, and in the Mishnah any city that could muster 120 men (230 men on another opinion) could try a capital charge.[36] 'Judgement' in 22a must therefore mean judgement in a local Beth Din, and the twenty-three traditional judges in serious cases were called a lesser Sanhedrin.[37] This gives us a convincing climax for the three courts of judgement— the local sanhedrin, *the* Sanhedrin, the divine judgement. Neither Jesus nor Matthew could have thought literally of trying cases of angry speech before at least the first two of these tribunals: but then hyperbole is a stock feature of Matthew, and of him almost exclusively.[38] Since by Matthew's time the local church was not on speaking terms with the neighbouring orthodox synagogue, he clearly has a local Christian court in mind, as in 18.15ff and 1 Cor. 5. The Sanhedrin is probably still the central Jewish council at Jamnia, since Matthew subscribes to the authority of Moses' seat: but there was also a central Apostolic Council which Paul had attended, and which Matthew knew of, with powers to bind and to loose, and he may have had his eye on that.

The three offences therefore should also form a climax. Being angry is an inner disposition: it is almost always associated in the NT with a verb of action making the anger effective,[39] and should be understood in its literal sense of internal anger. *Reîqā* is a common address of contempt in rabbinic writing,[40] and despite the puzzle of the alteration of the first vowel must be the word intended by ῥακά. We have the phrase instanced on a papyrus from near Lachish, ''Αντίοχον τὸν ῥαχᾶν', Antiochus the ass,[41] so there is no substantial difficulty about the form or the meaning. μῶρος is the word used twenty-eight times by ben Sirach for the fool who is morally and religiously as well as mentally depraved: no doubt some of its overtones come from the Heb. *mōreh* (part. *mārāh*), a godless rebel. Triple climaxes of this kind are instanced by Strack-Billerbeck:[42] for example, 'He who says to

[35] See p. 81ff above.
[36] Sanh. 1.6.
[37] M Sanh. 1.1,2,6, etc.
[38] See p. 397 below.
[39] Matt. 18.34; 22.7; Luke 14.21; 15.28; Rev. 12.17; cf. Eph. 4.26.
[40] S–B I, pp. 278f.
[41] C. C. Edgar, *A new group of Zenon papyri* (Manchester 1934), no. 2 (257 B.C.); cf. Lohmeyer ad loc.
[42] S–B I, pp. 280ff.

his neighbour, You slave, shall be put under the ban; he who says to
him, You bastard, receives the forty [lashes]; he who says to him,
You evildoer (*Rāšaʿ*) is liable for his life.'[43] This Baraita is similarly
hyperbolic. We have thus a satisfactory triple climax. Anger in the
heart will be punished in the local court, rudeness at the central
assize, insult at the bar of heaven.

First then we are to make peace by not being angry; but Matthew
is a realist preacher—what if we have been angry? Then we are to
make peace by humility. If we are offering sacrifice in the Temple and
remember some offence we have caused, we are to go and make it up.
Matthew ignores the destruction of the Temple. It may well be that
sacrifices continued to be offered at the altar in Jerusalem between
A.D. 70 and 135;[44] or he may, like the rabbis, have taken the optimistic
line that they soon will be. This at all events is a second way of peacemaking; and a third illustration follows. If the quarrel has reached the
stage of litigation,[45] make terms quickly—10 per cent now, and the
rest over two years—with your creditor as he drags you to court, or
the creditor will hand you to the magistrate and the magistrate to the
debtor's prison, and you will not come out of there till you have paid
the last sou. It is ironical that the form-critics should force hortatory
secondariness on Matthew:[46] for the meaning is plain in the context,
and exactly fits as a third illustration of peacemaking. The whole
hangs together as comment on the Beatitude. Blessed are those who
make peace: first by not being angry, second by humbly making it
up if they have caused offence, third by paying up their debts as
promptly as they can. Debts are closely associated with sins in Matthew's mind.

[43] B Kidd. 28a.
[44] K. W. Clark, 'Worship in the Jerusalem Temple after A.D. 70', *NTS* VI (1960),
pp. 269ff.
[45] Jeremias, *PJ*, p. 43. Note the second triple climax: angry words (v. 22),
scenes requiring a formal reconciliation (vv. 23f), lawsuits (vv. 25f).
[46] ibid., pp. 43ff; Dodd, *Parables of the Kingdom*, pp. 136ff. Jeremias and Dodd
assume that the piece goes back to Jesus. They admit that the Matthaean words
fit the Matthaean context but their theory makes a virtue of ignoring the context.
They do not like Matthew's prudential morality, so they regard it as a hortatory
or paraenetic debasement of the original. They admit that the uttermost farthing
does not fit the Lucan parabolic form, but their theory makes a virtue of parables
not fitting too well. It is inconvenient for them that Matthew has the Jewish and
Luke the Hellenistic court background, but then, they say, both of the evangelists
have 'developed' the original in different ways. Would it not be easier to think
that Matthew developed the illustration out of a logion in Mark (7.21, p. 286
below), and that Luke, just as Dodd and Jeremias, preferred eschatological
parables to prudential morality? He has done something similar with the Marcan
Cursing of the Fig-tree. For the secondariness of the Lucan version see p. 288f
below.

The Sixth Beatitude was 'Blessed are the pure in heart: for they shall see God', and this is now filled out with a further triple illustration. The pure in *heart* shall *see* God; but anyone who *looks* at a woman in lust is an adulterer in *heart*. Purity of heart means firstly sexual purity: the eye that wanders lustfully deprives itself of the divine vision, for the adulterous heart has no place with the pure. Mark had written of the need to excise the source of temptation, be it hand or foot or eye.[47] Matthew applies the saying to a new context. He promotes the eye to first place because he is speaking of the sin of the eye: then the hand, because adultery is first a sin of the eye and secondly a sin of the hand. The foot he omits because the feet are not much used in adultery.[48]

A second form of impurity, following naturally on from the first, is remarriage. Mark had again given the material: both the Torah text and the Lord's transcendence of it.[49] Matthew fits it to his 'It was said . . . but I say to you . . .' formula, and glosses it with the stricter of the rabbinic exceptions. Our concentration, legalists that we are, is given to the meaning of the excepting clause, but to Matthew as to Mark most remarriage was just legalized adultery, and a cause of the loss of the vision of God. Matthew does not say here that the divorcing husband remarries but that his wife will be driven to remarry, and so both she and her second husband will be committing adultery for which he is responsible: this he would not be if πορνεία had already taken place—hence the excepting clause. But 19.9 shows that he expected the husband to remarry too, with the same consequence.

For the third instance, he has recourse to a new line. Matthew is never obvious. He will not give thirst as Jesus' second temptation after hunger, and he will not give a third instance of sexual impurity. Indeed there is no obvious one: lust is a sin of heart and eye, a bill of divorce is written and delivered by hand. He moves from impurity of eye and hand to impurity of the lips. A constant feature of the Sermon is the dominance of parts-of-the-body images: in these verses he moves to head and hair, in the next to eye again, and to tooth and either cheek. The superfluous oaths are in two pairs: heaven and earth, Jerusalem as the joy of the earth, the head because Matthew's mind is following the parts-of-the-body groove. The visible skipping from one member

[47] Mark 9.43ff.

[48] cf. Mekilta de–R. Simeon b. Yohai on Exod. 20.14 (ed. Hoffman, p. 111), 'Thou shalt not commit adultery. Neither with hand nor foot nor eye nor mind . . .'; R. Simeon b. Lakish in Lev. R. 23.12, 'One who commits adultery with his eyes is called adulterer'; Sifre Num. 15.39, 'Do not roam, following your own heart and your eyes, which you go a-whoring–after'. See Moore, *Judaism* I, p. 486; II, p. 268.

[49] Mark 10.2ff.

to the next shows the movement as natural: purity of the heart, of the eye, of the hand, of the lips. The third illustration of purity is linked to the previous two by Matthew's weak πάλιν, which similarly introduces the third Temptation and joins the Pearl to the Treasure, and the Net to the Pearl.[50] In the old law impure lips came from false oaths. 'Who shall ascend the hill of the Lord? . . . He who has clean hands, and a pure heart: who . . . does not swear deceitfully.'[51] So does the psalmist link the pure heart and the clean hands to the fulfilment of oaths: but in the new law all swearing is *de trop*, purity consists in the simple truth. It is highly probable that Ps. 24 lies behind Matthew's thinking here: it is the only place in the Greek Bible where the phrase καθαρὸς τῇ καρδίᾳ occurs. It links purity with swearing, and refers to God several times as the king of glory entering his city Jerusalem. It salutes the pure who go up to τὸ ὄρος τοῦ Κυρίου.

The fifth Beatitude, 'Blessed are the pitiful, for they shall be pitied' (AT), is taken up in a further three paragraphs. 'An eye for an eye' was ruthless justice: there is no sign that either Moses or Matthew thought it was mercy compared to the feuds that went before. A Christian is to claim no such right, he is to have pity: not to withstand the emissaries of Satan, as his Lord did not, but to turn the other cheek; to have pity for the litigant who would have his shirt and give him his coat as well,[52] to have pity for the Roman and his load; to have pity for the beggar and the borrower. The chain of illustrations moves from the pity of not claiming an eye for an eye to the pity that lets our money go to those in need, through instances of not withstanding evil, where pity is not the first word we should have thought of: but the aptness of the general bracket of ἐλεημοσύνη is plain. Similarly, in a second paragraph, we are to care for our enemies and pray for them, just as God cares for saint and sinner alike. We are to love those who do not return our love, and bid them a respectful good day; and be perfect as our Father is perfect. Luke, who understood the point, writes, 'Be merciful (οἰκτήρμονες), even as your Father is merciful'. It is God's pity that leads him to bless all alike with rain and sun, and we can allow our hearts to be moved with ἐλεημοσύνη for the difficult if we try. The third paragraph links on in a surprising but clear way. The three pious duties of prayer, fasting, and almsgiving are a rabbinic commonplace: but although we find them frequently, they are never in the order in which Matthew gives them. Almsgiving is never first, a position normally taken by prayer. The reason for the transposition will, I hope, be clear. Matthew is already expounding ἐλεημοσύνη. Blessed are the ἐλεήμονες, ὅτι αὐτοὶ ἐλεηθήσονται. No

---

[50] cf. J. D. Kingsbury, *The Parables of Jesus in Matthew 13* (London 1969), p. 14.
[51] Ps. 24.3f.　　　　　　　　　[52] NEB.

talio: have ἐλεημοσύνη on the beggar. No hatred: have ἐλεημοσύνη like God. No parade: when you do your ἐλεημοσύνη do not sound a *shôphar* in front of you . . . but when you do ἐλεημοσύνη let not your left hand know what your right hand does, that your ἐλεημοσύνη may be in secret . . .' (AT). The same method of triple illustration holds good for the exposition of each of the Beatitudes: we do not expect the theme to bridge over from the six Antitheses to the three pious duties, but when we look the verbal evidence assures us that it is so.

It is often urged against unity of authorship of the Antitheses that the attitude to the old Law vacillates in marked fashion.[53] In the first two Antitheses, and the fourth, Jesus is portrayed as *deepening* the meaning of the Torah: no murder, no adultery, no false oath then; now not merely these outward sins but the attitudes that lie behind them are forbidden to the Church. But in some at least of the other three, Jesus is seen as *abrogating* the Torah: Moses permitted a bill of divorce, but Jesus forbids it, with rare exception; Moses commanded the injured to take an eye for an eye, and is countermanded by Jesus; Moses prescribed hatred for our enemies, Jesus love. Now not only are these two attitudes widely disparate in themselves, but also the second is in flat contradiction with Matthew's general attitude to the Torah, which is of complete adherence, and is set forth in detail in 5.17–20. Therefore, it is concluded, matter from a different church, with an altogether different theology, is being incorporated, and according as the Gospel is seen to come from a Gentile or a Jewish–Christian church, so the foreign body can be identified.

It must be said that this is a scholar's dilemma: analysis reveals that πληροῦν, 'I have come not to abolish . . . but to fulfil', is being used to cover the two different senses of Jesus' deepening and transcending the Law. None of us noticed the discrepancy, I dare say, until scholars pointed it out; and it is clear that Matthew himself was as innocent as we, for had he noticed it, he would certainly not have included material in flat contradiction to his own beliefs. Well, if he could change the meaning of πληροῦν from deepen to abrogate and back again twice, in incorporating traditional material, on the usual hypothesis, so could he in developing the theme himself, on mine. Words are deceptive, they slip; in the first two Antitheses Jesus is standing by the Law, and 'fulfil' means 'deepen', just as Matthew

---

[53] Wrege, op. cit., pp. 35–94; Strecker, *WG*, pp. 143ff; Barth, *TIM*, pp. 62–75. Daube (*NTRJ*, pp. 55–62) attempts to palliate the difficulty by reference to the rabbinic formula, 'You have heard . . . you will say . . .': but the formula is not the same, and the argument seems over-subtle. Daube, and W. D. Davies (*Setting*, pp. 101–8), are right in seeing Matthew's intention as being mild and not radical in his attitude to the Law: cf. p. 15ff.

intended. But historically Jesus had a radical attitude to the Law; he knew himself to be abrogating it, and one of the three test occasions which prove this is Mark 10,[54] from which Matthew takes the third Antithesis, on Divorce. Small wonder then that πληροῦν slips, to mean transcend, and that it slips back and forth for the rest of the chapter. Jesus' attitude was at variance to Matthew's on this important issue, and we have analysed, in the first chapter, Matthew's embarrassed but skilful reaction to this dilemma. It is, of course, impossible that Matthew should have been aware of any discrepancy between his Lord and himself: that is why he not merely transcribes the Marcan stories with slight gloss, but freely incorporates their material into his main exposition of Jesus' teaching, in the Sermon: and the ambiguous πληροῦν provides the required smokescreen.

The Fourth Beatitude is, 'Blessed are those who hunger and thirst for righteousness.' Hungering and thirsting are to us a forceful metaphor for desire; to Matthew they are the sacramental expression of it. Those who hunger and thirst for righteousness are, as the next passage in the Sermon, 6.5–18, explains, those who pray and fast for it. R. Tanhum b. Hanilai (*c.* A.D. 280) said similarly, 'He who imposes hunger on himself in this world for the sake of the Torah, him will God satisfy in the world to come.'[55] Strack-Billerbeck comment, 'It is not spiritual hunger for the Law which is in question here, but physical hunger undertaken willingly to devote oneself to the study of the Torah.'[56] The Matthaean Christian is devoted to the higher δικαιοσύνη, of the new Law, and he willingly imposes hunger on himself that he may attain it. What is this righteousness? Matthew follows the double meaning of *ts^edhāqāh:* it is not a matter of either a Protestant–Pauline righteousness of God being done, or a Catholic–Jewish–Christian good works, but of both. Righteousness is normally in Matthew good works:[57] in 6.33 it is the kingdom of God and his righteousness. The righteousness for which we are to hunger and thirst is expounded in the Prayer which we are given as the expression of our prayer and fasting: whose first half is concerned with God's righteousness being done in this world—'thy kingdom come, thy will be done, on earth as it is in heaven'—and whose second half is concerned with our righteousness, that we forgive, and that we be not brought into temptation.

A widely held theory[58] is that the repetitive comments on Almsgiving, Prayer, and Fasting, formed an original 'poem', and that the

[54] cf. H. Merkel, 'Jesus und die Pharisäer', *NTS* 14.2 (January 1968), pp. 194–208.
[55] B Sanh. 100a. [56] S–B I, p. 201.
[57] 3.15; 5.20; 6.1; 21.32; and probably 5.10.
[58] Since Manson, *SJ*, pp. 163f.

non-repetitive matter, including the Lord's Prayer, has been inserted by the evangelist from other sources. There are passages in the rabbis as tedious as this hypothetical poem; but while in our study of Matthaean poetry we found triple parallelism of a repetitive kind (scandalic, misthic),[59] we never found an instance as unrelieved as this—indeed Matthew twice abhors the tedium of Mark's, 'If your hand causes you to sin . . .'. The theory thus postulates a repetitiousness which is not merely unevidenced in the Gospel but rebutted: and seems therefore unjust. We shall have later to examine the Matthaean nature of the language, images, and rhythms, which count heavily against such a view: but in the meantime I am concerned to show how neatly this section of the Sermon fits together. While expounding mercy, the evangelist is drawn to contrast Pharisaic and Christian giving of 'mercy': this suggests the other two Pious Works, which he then commends in closely similar paragraphs. The other two Pious Works expound the previous Beatitude, on hungering and thirsting; the righteousness for which we are to pray and fast comes out in the Lord's Prayer, and the satisfaction which is promised in the Beatitude is given more fully in the text, 'Your Father who sees in secret will reward you'. Although there are not three illustrations of the Beatitude in a strict sense, the teaching on Prayer is subdivided into the formal contrast with the Pharisees and the Our Father, and the fasting paragraph makes a third unit.

I am assuming, with all the principal editions, that B א are right in placing the Mourners as the second Beatitude and the Meek as the third; it seems easiest to explain the reversal in D syr° Cl, etc., as an assimilation to Luke, where the mourners are third, and the filling of the hungry comes second. The Third Beatitude then, 'Blessed are the πραεῖς, for they shall inherit τὴν γῆν' is virtually a citation from Ps. 37,[60] οἱ δὲ πραεῖς κληρονομήσουσι τὴν γῆν. We are accustomed to translate πραεῖς as 'meek' and to think of them as doormats, but this is not quite the picture of the πραΰς in the psalm. The πραΰς frets himself not because of the ungodly (1, 7, 8), but hopes in the Lord (3, 5), waits on the Lord (9, 24) and does good (3), and the Lord will deal with the sinner and his tricks (*passim*). The Lord supports the πραεῖς and in the days of famine they shall have enough (17–19), he will not forsake his saints (28). They have compassion and give (21), they are merciful and lend (26), they will be fed (3f) and they will inherit the γῆ (9, 11, 29). In a word the πραΰς trusts God and is liberal with what he has: and God looks after him.

We could hardly ask for a more exact description of the theme of the second half of 6. We are to be liberal: not treasuring treasure for

[59] See p. 81ff above.   [60] Ps. 37.11.

ourselves on earth, but in heaven. The separate paragraph in which
the verses on the 'single eye' are usually enclosed is an error: the sense
follows straight on. 'The light of the body is the eye. So if your eye be
generous, your whole body is light . . .' (AT). ἁπλοῦς means generous
in Jas. 1.5, 'If any of you lacks wisdom, let him ask God, who gives to
all men generously (ἁπλῶς) and without reproaching'; as in Rom. 12,
'He who contributes, in liberality (ἐν ἁπλότητι)'.[61] '. . . But if your
eye be mean, your whole body is dark' (AT)—Matthew himself speaks
of the mean eye in 20, 'Is your eye mean because I am good?', RSV
'Do you begrudge my generosity?' The Semitic idiom speaks of the
generous eye and the mean eye where we say generous-hearted and
mean-spirited, but the continuance *from* laying up treasure and *to*
the Two Masters is transparent: do not pile up wealth, be generous-
eyed, you cannot serve God and money.

The πραΰς of the psalm was liberal, he gave and lent; and he hoped
in the Lord to feed him in time of trouble. διὰ τοῦτο, continues
Matthew, having determined to love and hold to one master, God, and
to hate and despise Mammon, do not be worried. God looks after the
birds and the flowers; verily you shall be fed, you will have enough,
you will not be forsaken. Do not worry, that is the way of the heathen:
your Father in heaven knows your needs. Be doing good, be righteous;
seek first his kingdom and righteousness, and all these things will be
added unto you, you will inherit the land. Do not be worried about
tomorrow: the Lord supports the meek. The whole paragraph forms
a perfect Matthaean version of the character and faith of the πραΰς
expounded in Ps. 37. The πραεῖς come seven times, generally in the
same sense, in the Greek Psalter. A second text which lies behind the
Matthaean passage, and which drew the eye of Luke is Ps. 147.6:
'The Lord lifts up the πραεῖς . . . he clothes (περιβάλλοντι) the heaven
with clouds . . . he brings forth grass (χόρτος) on the mountains . . .
he gives the beasts their food (τροφή) and the young of the ravens
(τῶν κοράκων) that call upon him. The Lord takes pleasure in all that
hope in his mercy' (LXX).

The Second Beatitude is 'Blessed are those who mourn, for they
shall be comforted'—a text all too familiar from many funerals: and
yet the pastor wonders eventually, in view of the manifest difference
in response among the bereaved, whether such a blanket blessing can
be thought of as anything else but pious nonsense. There is no com-
pulsion to render the saying meaningless in this way. πενθεῖν means
often to mourn for one's sins, to go humbly, to repent. 'It is actually

[61] Verse 8; cf. 2 Cor. 8.2; 9.11,13. See H. J. Cadbury, 'The Single Eye', *HTR* 47
(1954), pp. 69–74; J. Amstutz, ΑΠΛΟΤΗΣ (Bonn 1968).

reported that there is immorality among you', cries Paul,[62] 'And you are arrogant! Ought you not rather to mourn (ἐπενθήσατε)?' Matthew himself tells us that the Pharisees and John did ascetic practices, but that the Lord had said, 'Can the wedding-guests mourn (πενθεῖν)?', where Mark has 'fast'.[63] It is the humble penitent, mourning for his sins in ashes and sackcloth, who is promised the comfort of God, not the merely unhappy or deprived: and it is humility and the regarding of our own sins and not those of our brother which are commanded in 7.1–6. Do not be critical: for the criticism you deal out to your neighbour is the criticism you will receive from God, the measure you give is the measure you will get. Why criticize your fellow-Christian's peccadilloes when your own sins are as scarlet? Go humbly, mourn, pluck the beam out of your own eye, and then you will be more fit to give spiritual advice around. The exposition, like the others in the Sermon, falls in three parts: (*a*) don't criticize (in your heart); (*b*) don't criticize your brother to his face; (*c*) don't criticize your brother behind his back. Don't give the sacrifice to the dogs, don't throw your pearls to the pigs, don't expose what is precious, your brother's character, to the malice of the godless: otherwise they will trample them under foot, they will join happily enough in your back-biting, and then turn and rend you, and serve you right. In this third precept, Matthew follows a popular rabbinic theme going back to the talebearer of Proverbs.[64] The Tannaite R. Eliezer said, 'Let the honour of thy brother be as dear to thee as thy own':[65] backbiting was called the evil tongue (*lāshôn hārā'*) or in Aramaic the third tongue (*lisan telita'e*). Matthew is close to the thought of ben Sirach, 'Blame not before thou hast examined . . . and where sinners judge, sit not thou with them.'[66]—first don't be quick to criticize, second don't criticize in company with the malicious. This is the most difficult text in the Gospel on any account, and this solution seems to me by far the most satisfactory:

(*a*) It gives the proper significance to dogs and pigs, of the godless, the malicious. The words are clearly meant to be offensive, and it is quite unsuitable to interpret them of the Gentiles, who are never so thought of in Matthew: κυνάρια of the Canaanitess is a different word as well as in a different tone, and the animal names of wolves, vipers, etc., elsewhere in the Gospel signify the enemies of God. This rules out all interpretations forbidding the preaching of the Gospel, or the giving of the sacrament, to the Gentiles.[67]

---

[62] 1 Cor. 5.2. [63] Matt. 9.15; Mark 2.19.
[64] G. F. Moore devotes half a chapter to it—*Judaism*, Pt v, ch. v.
[65] M Aboth 2.10. [66] Ecclus. 11.7–9.
[67] Sacrament: *Didache* 9; Tert., *De Praescr.* 41. Word: Allen, ad loc.

(b) The NT regards the brother for whom Christ died as precious above all else, and although he is nowhere compared to a pearl—μαργαρίτης occurs only in Matthew in the Greek Bible—he is said to have been bought with a price,[68] and Paul does expressly call his converts an offering (προσφορά).[69] The preciousness of the 'brother' is a theme of Matthew's own, set out in the Lost Sheep whom the apostles are to seek out.[70] The matter of the brother's honour is not found elsewhere perhaps in the NT, but there is no dearth of rabbinic references to this point, as R. Eliezer just cited. No interpretation of the sacrifice and the pearl as the preaching of the word forbidden to the hard-hearted[71] is likely to be right, because it is precisely this which is enjoined and expounded in Jesus' most celebrated parable of all, the Sower.

(c) This interpretation gives point, as hardly any other does, to the second half of the verse: the experience of trampling our acquaintance under foot with third parties, and then having them turn and rend us, is distressingly familiar. More particularly these phrases do not suit the 'Discriminate in your preaching' interpretation: most of chapters 10 and 24 are given to the theme 'Preach freely and expect persecution'.

(d) While it may seem to a hardened Form-critic even a virtue to have interpreted a verse in defiance of its context, it must seem likely at least that Matthew thought the words had a reference to the passage in which he set them. It is the chief glory of my interpretation to have made sense of them in their context, I think alone of all proposals.[72] Those interpretations which set v. 6 against the previous verses—'Don't judge in general, but be discriminatory in extreme cases'[73]—cannot be right. Matthew frequently adds sentences without connecting particles as here: sometimes building up an argument, sometimes crowning it, sometimes starting a new paragraph. But nowhere in the Gospel does he omit a 'but'. The sense I am suggesting fits the symbolism of both the animals and the precious things, gives full meaning to the whole verse, and fits the context. Those who go humbly, who mourn, neither judge nor try to improve their brother, but endeavour to get rid of their own sins: least of all do they join in backbiting.

---

[68] 1 Cor. 7.23.　　　　　　　　　[69] Rom. 15.16.

[70] Matt. 18.12ff.

[71] So J. Schniewind, *Das Evangelium nach Matthäus*, NTD (11e., Göttingen 1964), Allen.

[72] Farrer took v. 6 as going with vv. 7–11, but the sense is strained, *St Matthew and St Mark*, p. 172.

[73] So McNeile, and apparently J. C. Fenton, *The Gospel of St Matthew* (London 1963), but the writing is obscure.

And so to the First Beatitude, 'Blessed are the πτωχοὶ τῷ πνεύματι: for theirs is the Kingdom of Heaven'. The normal interpretation of the classic phrase[74] is to take it of the '*ᵃnāwîm*, the πτωχοί of the Psalms, in line with the Lucan, 'Blessed are you πτωχοί': as those trying to lead holy lives in obedience to God and so condemned to poverty through the oppression of the proud; as those for whom God is the only hope; not some self-conscious group of Ebionites, but the faithful of God's people to whom the evangel was promised in Isa. 61: 'The Lord has anointed me to bring good tidings to the πτωχοί.' Part of the attraction of this view has been the easy reconciliation of Matthew and Luke: Luke says plain οἱ πτωχοί, meaning the poor-and-faithful; Matthew makes the meaning clear—not the beggars, but the poor spiritually speaking. Nothing is wrong with this interpretation but the emphasis: the Lucan parallel, and the association with οἱ πενθοῦντες in Matthew as in Isaiah, make it certain that it is on the right lines, and we now have, in the Scrolls, a parallel to the phrase, 'poor in spirit'. What is latent in the word πτωχός, however, and what Matthew desires to stress by the addition of τῷ πνεύματι, is the God-ward aspect. Isaiah sets the poor in parallel with the contrite in heart (61.1), and soon to the mourners (61.3). Mourning and contrition are *religious* activities: Israelites mourned not merely because they felt miserable, but as an appeal to God to make them less so. Isaiah soon continues, 'Upon your walls, O Jerusalem, I have set watchmen; all the day and all the night they shall never be silent. You who put the Lord in remembrance, take no rest, and give him no rest . . .' (62.6). Poverty and contrition and mourning are silent appeals to God, as the watchmen's prayers are vocal appeals to God. So did David fast and weep for his dying child. The reason why '*ᵃnāw*, πτωχός, carry the overtone poor-and-faithful is that *by nature* poverty is an appeal to God. That the poor commits himself to the Lord goes without saying; the Lord is his only hope. That the Lord cares for the poor and needy is a cardinal point of Israel's faith; he is moved by the appeal. Matthew emphasizes the appeal, glossing τῷ πνεύματι on Isaiah's πτωχός. The spirit is the God-ward aspect of man: blessed, then, are the beggars with respect to God, the destitute before heaven, the men of prayer. Such a stress suits the Scrolls context well: 'By the poor in spirit (He has scattered) the hard of heart, And by the perfect of way all nations have come to an end'.[75] In the preceding verses the Covenanters have been described as 'them that staggered', 'the fearful

---

[74] So Zahn, Allen, McNeile, Schniewind, Bonnard, Fenton, Lagrange, Wrege, pp. 6ff.
[75] War, xiv.7, tr. G. Vermes, 'The Dead Sea Scrolls in English'. The Hebrew is '*ᵃnāwê rûaḥ*.

of heart', 'the dumb', 'the feeble': to continue, 'By the men of prayer
. . .', is extremely apt. Such an interpretation would fit admirably
with the exposition in Matt. 7.7–11, 'Ask and it will be given you, seek
and you will find, knock and it will be opened to you'. The beggars in
spirit pray of God and are answered, they scavenge (as Eastern
beggars must) and are rewarded, they hammer on the gates of heaven
and are not refused. If we, sinners that we are, grant our children's
requests, how much more our heavenly Father. The main body of
the Sermon once more expounds the best meaning of the Beatitude.

Our theme is at an end. 7.12, the Golden Rule, sums up the theme
of the fulfilment of the Law and the Prophets, which I have left till the
next two chapters. The remainder is peroration.[76] It was normal for
rabbinic sermons to end with a peroration: the Judgement-scene in
25 is Matthew's peroration to Mark's Apocalyptic Discourse, and
'O Jerusalem, Jerusalem . . .' is a peroration to 23. There are two
gates and two ways[77] we can go, and two places we can end up. There
are two kinds of teacher we can follow, like two kinds of animal, like
two kinds of tree bearing two kinds of fruit. We must beware: we
must be doers and not mere sayers. There are two kinds of builder
and two kinds of foundation and two kinds of house, and two kinds
of end to the storm.

[76] See p. 26 above.
[77] Ps.1, as well as Ps.119, is traditional for Pentecost (B Sopherim 29): '*Blessed
is the man who* walks not . . . nor stands in *the way* of sinners . . . but his
delight is in *the law* of the Lord, and on his law he meditates *day and night*. He
is like *a tree* . . . that *yields its fruit* . . . The wicked are not so but are like *the
chaff* . . . the Lord knows *the way* of the righteous, but *the way* of the wicked
will perish.'

APPENDIX
THE UNITY OF THE SERMON

Beatitudes cf. Pentecost.

(8) Persecuted	(*a*) Reward in heaven	5.11–12
	(*b*) Salt of earth	5.13
	(*c*) Light of cosmos	5.14–16
	Law and Prophets fulfilled	
(7) Peacemakers	(*a*) No anger, rudeness, insult	5.21–2
	(*b*) Reconciliation	5.23–4
	(*c*) Come to terms	5.25–6
(6) Pure in heart	(*a*) No lust (heart/eyes/hands)	5.37–30
	(*b*) No remarriage	5.31–2
	(*c*) No false oaths (Ps. 24.6)	5.33–7
(5) Merciful	(*a*) No *talio*	5.38–42
	(*b*) No hatred	5.43–8
	(*c*) No parade in 'mercy'	6.1–4
(4) Hunger and Thirst for Righteousness	(*a*) No parade in prayer	6.5–8
	(*b*) Lord's Prayer	6.9–15
	(*c*) No parade in fasting	6.16–18
(3) Meek (Ps. 37.11)	(*a*) Treasure in heaven	6.19–21
	(*b*) Generous eye	6.22–4
	(*c*) No anxiety	6.25–34
(2) Mourners	(*a*) No judging	7.1–2
	(*b*) No reproving	7.3–5
	(*c*) No backbiting	7.6
(1) Poor in spirit	Ask, seek, knock	7.7–11
	Law and Prophets in a Kelal	7.12
Peroration	(*a*) Two Gates, Two Ways	7.13–14
	(*b*) False prophets. Two Trees and Fruits	7.15–23
	(*c*) Two Builders	7.24–7

13
PENTECOST:
THE LAW FULFILLED 1

I set myself in the last chapter to expound the Sermon as a unity stemming from the Beatitudes, and claimed to be laying out its foundations as that of a city. My readers can hardly but have felt that the structure proposed was defective, in that it overran and ignored the celebrated Antitheses in ch. 5 and 6: my wall was full of breaches, and a fox, if he went up on it, should break it down. It is my task now to repair these breaches, and in face of the Sanballats and Tobiahs: for we must go about our building sword in hand. Not only have we to show that the Sermon makes good sense if seen as the construction of the evangelist, and that each individual section makes good sense if seen as the construction of the evangelist: we must also stand by at all points to examine the claims of Lucan priority for any saying, or of non-Matthaean strands witnessing to an alien oral tradition, or of traces of mistranslation from an Aramaic original. A task for a Nehemiah: but be of good heart, I shall not lightly do sabbath-trading with the Form-Critics, or permit a mixed marriage with Proto-Luke.

The Six Antitheses of 5 ('It was said . . . but I say unto you'), and the Three Antitheses of 6.1–18 ('not like the hypocrites before men . . . but to your Father who is in secret'), are clearly formal arrangements of which we must take account. They have often been taken to be the basis of the Sermon's structure, most famously by Windisch and Jeremias. Windisch[1] takes the Sermon to be a counterblast to Pauline antinomianism: the saying ascribed to Simeon the Just, one of the Great Synagogue of Ezra, gives the structure to his polemic. 'By three things is the world sustained: by the Law, by the (Temple-) service, and by deeds of lovingkindness.'[2] The Christian version of the Law is set out in 5, the Christian service in 6.1–18, the Christian loving-kindness in the remainder of the Sermon. Jeremias[3] takes his text, even more convincingly, from within the Sermon itself: 'For I tell you, unless your righteousness exceeds that of the scribes and Pharisees, you will never enter the kingdom of heaven.' The Antitheses of 5 are then a contrast with scribal interpretation of the Law, in its harsh legalism; those of 6.1–18 are expressly a contrast with Pharisaic

[1] H. Windisch, *Der Sinn der Bergpredikt* (2e., Leipzig 1937).
[2] M Aboth 1.2.
[3] J. Jeremias, *The Sermon on the Mount* (E.T., London 1961), pp. 22ff.

hypocrisy; while the rest of the Sermon sets out the Christian righteousness which lays up its treasure in heaven, and judges not.

I do not think either of these proposals is correct. Matthew is, as
Windisch says, soaked in rabbinic lore, but we can hardly believe
that he formed the pattern Christian sermon on so obscure, and non-
biblical a text. Further, although the two groups of antitheses fit
Windisch's categories, it is by no means obvious that the rest should
be classed as 'acts of lovingkindness', especially, 'Ask, and it will be
given you . . .', which is plainly about prayer. Jeremias has a better
text, but his exegesis is worse: the Antitheses of 5 are between Christ's
Law and Moses', not between Jesus' interpretation and that of the
scribes, who are never mentioned. 'An eye for an eye', for example,
was Moses' commandment, and was not enforced by the scribes.[4]
Furthermore, scribes and Pharisees occur ten times in Matthew as a
pair undifferentiated, and in 23 the phrase plainly means 'Pharisaic
scribes': it seems unlikely that Matthew meant two distinct groups
at 5.20 only. Nor is the Christian righteousness in any sense limited
to 6.19—7.12: it is described throughout the Sermon.

The Antitheses of 5 bear a strong family likeness to the second
table of the Ten Commandments, the Duties to Man. The first is with
the Sixth Commandment, 'Thou shall not kill'; the second with the
Seventh, 'Thou shall not commit adultery'. The third carries on from
the second with the divorce theme, and is unrelated to the Eighth
Commandment; but the fourth, 'You shall not swear falsely (οὐκ
ἐπιορκήσεις)', is closely similar to, and in fact a more generalized form
of, the Ninth Commandment, 'Thou shall not bear false witness'
(οὐ ψευδομαρτυρήσεις)'. The fifth is different, 'An eye for an eye', but
this in turn is drawn from Exod. 21.24, where the Book of the Covenant
expands the Ten Commandments. There is reason for thinking that
the last Antithesis is a positive version of the Tenth Commandment:
'You shall not covet *your neighbour's* house . . .'/'You shall love
your neighbour . . .'. For in the Matthaean account of the Rich Man,
Jesus urges the young man to keep 'the commandments',[5] and then
specifies them as nos. VI, VII, VIII, IX, V, and 'You shall love your
neighbour as yourself'. In the Antitheses Jesus expressly refers to
what was said to them of old time, i.e. at Sinai, and contrasts his New
Law with Commandments VI, VII, the Divorce Law, IX, an eye for
an eye, and 'You shall love your neighbour as yourself'. The two lists
are close. Jesus had given Love of Neighbour as summing up the law
of our duty to man in Mark 12: Matthew inserts it, in both 19 and 5,
as a positive form of the Tenth Commandment, crowning and summing up all the rest. Paul had similarly written, 'The commandments

[4] Daube, *NTRJ*, pp. 254ff.   [5] 19.18.

(VII, VI, VIII, X), and any other commandment, are summed up in this sentence, You shall love your neighbour as yourself'.[6] But where he cites both the Tenth Commandment and the summary, Matthew has glossed the latter for the former in both places. There is no fulfilment of 'You shall not steal', for which I shall shortly suggest a reason. Honouring parents is sufficiently catered for in the Korban passage in Matt. 15, which does not fit in here: Jesus did not in this matter lay down a more stringent Christian version, but simply pointed to Pharisaic evasion and double-face.

The links of the Sermon with the Rich Man pericope are powerful, and should now be enumerated:

(a) Christian righteousness is seen in both cases as founded on, but transcending, the Six Commandments of the Second Table, and in both passages the Tenth Commandment is given in the same positive form.

(b) The aim, both in the last verse of 5, and in Jesus' challenge to the Rich Man, is perfection: 'You therefore must be perfect', 'If you would be perfect'. τέλειος is used in these passages only in the Gospels.

(c) The one thing that the Rich Man lacks is to be gained by giving his wealth to the poor, and so gaining treasure in heaven, θησαυρὸν ἐν οὐρανῷ in Mark, ἐν οὐρανοῖς in Matthew—Matthew prefers the plural, *shāmayîm*. All disciples are bidden at 6.19 not to lay up treasure on earth, but treasures in heaven, θησαυροὺς ἐν οὐρανῷ.

(d) Jesus speaks in Mark 10 of the perils of wealth, and Peter comments, 'Lo, we have left everything and followed you. What then shall we have?' The Sermon follows immediately on the story of how Peter had left his calling and followed Jesus (4.20).

(e) Jesus had answered Peter in Mark with the promise that everyone who has left home or family for his sake will receive the same a hundredfold now in this time, with persecutions, and eternal life beyond. As so often Matthew divides the theme. In Mark 10.30, the blessings and persecutions are now in this time, and in the age to come eternal life. The present blessings and persecutions are proclaimed in Matt. 5.3–10: the blessings of 19.29 are when the Son of Man shall sit on his glorious throne. The Sermon opens with the blessings of the disciples, of which the last is, 'Blessed are those who are persecuted for righteousness' sake'.

So much coincidence, I would suggest, can hardly be accident. Three forces have been at work upon Matthew in the construction of the Sermon:

[6] Rom. 13.9.

1.   The Jewish Pentecost lection was Exod. 19—20.23.[7] Matthew has had Jesus gather his first disciples, like Moses in Exod. 18, and now, to fulfil Moses, he must go up the mountain and deliver the new Christian commandments. This dictates the setting, and in some measure the pattern, of 5, with its predominant background of material from Exod. 20ff; it dictates the octave form of the Beatitudes, and some later details of the Sermon.

2.   Peter's willingness to leave all and follow Christ had been in Mark the occasion of Jesus' promise to the Twelve of blessings with persecutions; and this incident had followed from the Rich Man to whom Jesus had spoken of the Commandments, and of going beyond them. The double reference is an assured invitation to midrash. Matthew does not therefore begin the Commandments from the First and work through them, but takes the Second Table, since that was where the Lord had begun from in Mark 10. He makes the sixfold transcendence of the Duty to Man the substance of 5: but he makes Mark, throughout, his primary inspired text, opening with the blessings-and-persecutions, and completing the persecution theme before he introduces the Commandments with the proem, 'Think not that I have come to abolish the law and the prophets . . .'. The Rich Man's influence continues in the command to be perfect, and to the end.

3.   The Beatitudes cannot therefore have existed as an independent unit of fixed form. Matthew himself has put the Persecuted last, and has awarded them the Kingdom of Heaven, as a pair to the reward of the first blessed, the Poor in Spirit. The Seventh and Sixth Beatitudes, the Peacemakers and the Pure in Heart, are determined by the Sixth and Seventh Commandments, no murder or adultery; since these must be transcended first, following Mark 10. But once the Beatitudes are down, even on the back of an envelope, they exert their independent force. To keep one's eyes from women is the first step to purity of heart: but how can the evangelist refrain from adding that refusal to divorce or remarry was a second? Here was a natural pair to the lustful eye, and a *cause célèbre* that had been fully described by Mark, and known even to Paul. So the fulfilment of Deut. 24 takes the place of the Eighth Commandment—call it stealing another man's wife if you will, but Matthew need not have thought so. Purity of the lips makes a happy third illustration, and enables the Ninth Commandment to be included under the umbrella of purity of heart. 'Who shall ascend into the hill of the Lord? . . . He that is clean in hands and καθαρὸς τῇ καρδίᾳ, who has not lifted his soul to vanity, nor sworn

[7] See above, p. 184, n. 71.

(ὤμοσεν) deceitfully to his neighbour.' The same constriction imposed by the Fifth Beatitude shapes the following paragraph.

To retain an identifiable Six Duties to Man, the last Antithesis is fixed, or nearly so: the glossing of the positive 'Love your neighbour. for not coveting your neighbour's goods is as far as Matthew dare go' The Christian is to love his neighbour in the deepest sense, including his enemy: to put it in a word, he is to be merciful. Indeed, this is scripture's word, for does not God say in the Decalogue that he is a God ποιῶν ἔλεος to thousands? Moses indeed says that God limits his mercy to those who love him (τοῖς ἀγαπῶσίν με) and repays their sins to those who hate him (τοῖς μισοῦσίν με): but later on Sinai (Exod. 23.5ff) the Israelite is bidden to care for his enemy's (τοῦ ἐχθροῦ σου) lost animals, and God says ἐλεήμων γάρ εἰμι (22.26): that God has mercy on good and bad alike is the lesson of the sun and the rain. Mercy then must be the topic of the Fifth Beatitude, and this means that the Fifth Antithesis comes under the same bracket. The honouring of parents is out of place for reasons we have given, but the harshness of the ancient 'An eye for an eye', from Exod. 21, clamours for inclusion in its place. The old rule was dead, but no matter: what Matthew is concerned with is the rhetoric of contrast, and the edification of the Church. For the Christian to spare his adversary is mercy, a lesson never taught enough, and it is Moses, not the scribes, who is being 'fulfilled'.

We began by thinking that the guiding force from the Torah was the Decalogue: but we have now seen that we have to do not with the Ten Commandments only, but also with their amplification in the three chapters following. Indeed Mark also glosses the Decalogue in the Rich Man passage, for he gives the Tenth Commandment as μὴ ἀποστερήσῃς, and the phrase οὐκ ἀποστερήσεις comes in Exodus 21.10. Now the Book of the Covenant is to a large extent a formless jumble of ancient legislation, but if one approaches it with the eye of a first-century Christian scribe, looking for an *ābh weathôleathdhôth* arrangement, the heads being set out first and the detailed application second, a rough and ready arrangement is not far to seek. For what we plainly have is: (*a*) the Decalogue, set out in 20 in starkest formulas; (*b*) 21—22.19, the detailed application in the laws of slavery, concubinage, manslaughter, dishonour of parents, wounding, stealing, swearing, seduction, and like matters, all of which belong with the Second Table; (*c*) 22.20—23.19, the detail of the feasts and sacrifices due to Yahweh, the keeping of the Passover and forbidding of idolatry, interspersed with repeated commands not to oppress the alien, the widow, and the poor; (*d*) 23.20–end, a peroration, promising that if Israel hears and does the commandments (ἐὰν ἀκοῇ ἀκούσητε . . .

καὶ ποιήσῃς), they will drive out their enemies and inherit the land. The only break in this arrangement is the law of the altar, which comes first, at the end of 20. Furthermore the opening part of (*b*), 21.1–16, gives every evidence of being constructed on Matthew's own chiastic pattern: 1–6, the laws of slavery, classed presumably under VIII with other property; 7–11, the laws of concubinage, under VII with *nāshîm;* 12–14 manslaughter under VI; 15f, striking and cursing parents under V.

This being the case, we now see more clearly what Matthew is doing.

(*a*) He has set out the proem of his Sinai as a series of formulas of blessing, for the message of Jesus is εὐαγγέλιον, not ἐντολαί.

(*b*) He has developed these in reverse order, with or without regard to Exod. 21.1–16, now making open the contrast between the old Law and the new, and taking, like Moses, the Second Table first. Matthew could hardly have begun with the Second Table on account of the Rich Man alone, but Jesus is now seen to have been following Moses there, in beginning with the Duty to Man.

(*c*) He then goes on to the First Table, like Moses, in which he expounds the Christian duty to God (6.1–18) and to the poor (6.19ff). The *gēr* is mentioned in the Decalogue under the Fourth Commandment, and the stranger, the widow, and the poor come frequently alongside the worship of God in Exod. 22.20—23.19, so it is natural for him to continue the two themes together.

(*d*) He finishes with a peroration, like Moses, urging his congregation to hear and to do. The parallels and contrasts, both general and particular, are striking.

It would be meaningless, as well as inartistic, to open 6, 'It was said to them of old, You shall have none other gods but me, but I say. . .' The prohibitions of polytheism and idolatry are in themselves ultimates, unless we are to expect Matthew to contrast them with the doctrine of the Trinity. What can and must be surpassed, however, is the spirit of worship exemplified by the Pharisees: duty to God in the Church shall be directed to God and not to man. The theme is near to Matthew's heart, and the means of expressing it is already latent in his last paragraph. He has been speaking of ἐλεημοσύνη— but is ἐλεημοσύνη not one of the three basic duties to God, almsgiving, prayer, and fasting? Rabbinic practice in coupling the three together merely echoed Moses' joining of the service of God and the poor in the second half of the Book of the Covenant. The first of the new Antitheses follows in under the wing of the old Beatitude: the other two write themselves in parallel, and require a joint Fourth Beatitude, those who hunger and thirst after righteousness.

The Church is thus taught its distinctive way of doing its duty to God: but although the first two Commandments are intractable to Matthew's rhetoric, the Third is more pliable. For, although all Jews believe in one God and idols are by the first century unknown, the honouring of God's name is another matter. There are many, even in the seats of authority, who take his name in vain; nor will it be properly honoured till the age to come. Matthew therefore sets it as the first petition of the prayer that sums up the Lord's prayers and the Lord's teaching on prayer: 'Hallowed be thy name.' The sense of the petition is that of the Third Commandment, 'You shall not take the name of the Lord your God in vain': the positive form used and the verb ἁγιασθήτω are assimilated from the Fourth Commandment, 'Remember the sabbath day, to keep it holy (ἁγιάζειν)'. There is nothing else about Sabbath here: the Fourth Commandment had been a battlefield throughout Jesus' ministry, and is sufficiently expounded elsewhere. What we have in 6.1–18 is the Christian mode of keeping Commandments I–III: we are to pray with fasting and almsgiving for God's name to be hallowed. We have a triple contrast with the Pharisees, and a triple petition for true worship on earth, for a triple Commandment.

There are thus nine Antitheses in 5.21—6.18, the Law of Christ fulfilling the Law of Moses as a spiritual keeping of what had become a dead letter. But nine Antitheses leave us wondering: Moses gave ten Commandments, where is Christ's Tenth Word? It is the story of the Rich Man which supplies it. There, when Jesus had been assured that the man had kept the commandments from his youth, he had said, 'You lack one thing.' Here, then, is the final Christian commandment, the one thing that the Lord had added to Moses: that we should let our earthly wealth go, provide for the poor, and have treasure in heaven. Moses had prohibited the oppression of the poor as part of Israel's duty to God: Christ said to sell and give all. Matthew caps his nine Antitheses with a Tenth, 'Do not lay up for yourselves treasures on earth . . . but lay up for yourselves treasures in heaven'. The first part of the contrast is not merely to give rhetorical emphasis to the second, as in the common Matthaean thesauric phrases: it is necessary to provide the formal Tenth Antithesis of the series. In view of the close links we have traced between the Rich Man and the Sermon, this conclusion seems inevitable. The Sermon is set up as a new Pentecost, a delivering of the New Commandments from the Mountain. Matthew had in mind from the beginning that the climax was to be the Lord's one thing lacking, the Last Commandment. The new first six *dᵉbhārîm* are adapted, as we have seen, from the Second Table as found cited in Mark 10. The First Table has to be reduced to three in order to leave space for the new Last Commandment, the Treasure in Heaven. The first three Commandments belong together, and can suitably be bracketed as the honouring of God's name. Sabbath may be left by for another time. Similarly, not stealing, the Eighth Commandment, is transcended in fact by the Lord's attitude to property. We could have had at 5.31, 'It was said, You shall not steal, but I say to you, Go, sell all that you have . . .': but Jesus had not presented this teaching as a gloss on the old commandment, but as the additional new one needful for perfection. Matthew therefore, with theology as sound as his artistic sense, suppresses the Eighth Commandment: its substance belongs as the climax of the whole. The interplay of the triangle of forces constituted by Exodus, Mark 10, and the Beatitudes, reveals the architecture of the Sermon as the work of a mind supremely logical and artistic: we knew it was a poetic masterpiece, but it is a masterpiece of design no less.

The 'treasures in heaven' theme in the second half of 6 dictates therefore the Third Beatitude. Matthew finds the description of the man who gives to the poor and trusts God for his own future in Ps. 37: there he is characterized as πραΰς and it is said that he will possess the land—what more suitable as the reward of the third μακάριοι than that they should possess the fullness of what they had given away? And did not God promise Moses besides (Exod. 23.30) that if Israel kept the old covenant, this should be their reward, to inherit the land? There is no one, the Lord had said in sorrow for the Rich Man's failure, who has left lands for my sake, who will not receive a hundredfold.

It is not, therefore, until the beginning of 7 that Matthew is, so far as Exodus and Mark are concerned, his own master. It would be enough to close the Sermon with a peroration now, and have six Beatitudes starting from the third. However, this would do scant justice to Jesus' historic preaching, and furthermore the Pentecostal sermon requires liturgically an octave of blessing to set it on its way. Jesus had come (Mark 1.15) saying, 'The time is fulfilled, and the Kingdom of God is being inaugurated: repent and believe the εὐαγγέλιον' (AT). Now the text in scripture which Mark and Matthew and Luke, and indeed the whole early Church,[8] associated with these words, was the opening verses of Isa. 61. 'The Spirit of the Lord is upon me, because he has anointed me (ἔχρισέ με): he has sent me to evangelize (εὐαγγελίσασθαι) the poor (πτωχοῖς), to declare the acceptable year of the Lord . . . to comfort all that mourn (παρακάλεσαι πάντας τοὺς πενθοῦντας), to give to those that mourn (τοῖς πενθοῦσιν) in Sion glory for ashes, the oil of joy to the mourners (τοῖς πενθοῦσιν)

---

[8] Mark 1.9–15, πνεῦμα . . . εὐαγγέλιον; Matt. 3–5 (see below); Luke 4.18f: Acts 10.38; 1 Thess. 1.5.

. . .'. In verse 7 of the same chapter it is said, κληρονομήσουσι τὴν γῆν. Matthew expressly refers to the evangelizing of the poor at 11.5. Now the presence in Christian tradition of such a prophetic commentary on the Lord's baptism and first preaching cannot but have impressed Matthew. For a full statement of his teaching, this should stand first: and Luke thought the same. Luke makes the reading of the passage the context of Jesus' first sermon, and the exposition of it the occasion of his first rejection. For Matthew the εὐαγγέλιον, the good news of God's action, is that the time is fulfilled: and those who hear it are blessed. The first to whom it comes in Isaiah are the πτωχοί; the ones emphasized by threefold repetition are the πενθοῦντες. Thus the first two Beatitudes grow out of Isaiah's prophecy of the Lord's inspired preaching of the gospel. He glosses πτωχοί with the spiritualizing τῷ πνεύματι. The πενθοῦντες he inserts as they stand: but their meaning is also spiritualized when he expounds the blessing as on those who go humbly in 7.1-6. Jesus began to preach and say, Repent (4.17): the πενθοῦντες are those who mourn for their sins, who pluck the beam from their eye and judge not. For the third illustration, the backbiting, Matthew glosses once more with Exod. 23.1: 'You shall not utter a false report. You shall not join hands with a wicked man to be a malicious witness.' The image he takes from the previous verse, 'You shall be men holy to me (ἅγιοι); therefore you shall not eat any flesh that is torn by beasts in the field; you shall cast it to the dogs (τῷ κύνι).' To a Christian his fellows are ἅγιοι; to utter a false report of them, or join hands with the wicked against them, would be like casting them to the dogs (τοῖς κύσιν); and he will only end by being torn by the beasts himself. So whereas the last six Beatitudes are governed by the Ten Commandments structure of the Sermon, the first two are derived from Isaiah, and the exposition in 7.1-11 is governed by them.

The rewards in the Beatitudes are mostly straightforward. The poor in spirit are awarded the kingdom of heaven because Isaiah's anointed one preached the gospel to the poor, and Jesus had come preaching that the kingdom of heaven was inaugurated, and that men should believe the gospel (Mark 1.15). The mourners are comforted because Isaiah's Christ had come παρακάλεσαι πάντας τοὺς πενθοῦντας. The meek inherit the earth because that is what they do in Ps. 37.11, and as it happens in Isa. 61.7 and Exod. 23.30 as well. The naturalness of the mourners being comforted suggests much that follows. These who hunger and thirst for righteousness are satisfied: the pitiful are pitied. The pure in heart see God because in Ps. 24 it is the pure in heart who ascend into the hill of the Lord, and seek the face of the God of Jacob.[9] The makers of peace are to be called the sons of God because as a

[9] Ps. 24.5f; cf. also λήμψεται ἐλεημοσύνην παρὰ θεοῦ.

Christian blesses his enemies he will become, so the Sermon teaches us, the son of his Father who is in heaven. This is the least pointed of the rewards. The persecuted receive the kingdom of heaven so as to make an octave with the poor in spirit: in Mark 10 Jesus had promised his persecuted apostles eternal life, and the kingdom of heaven is a fair approximation.

For the thesis which I am arguing, the creativity of Matthew, the Beatitudes may be seen as a kind of turning-point. They are commonly regarded as one of the strongholds of the Q hypothesis, being, to this view, an ecclesiasticized version of the more primitive Lucan form. In fact, as I suggested earlier, the Lucan form is linguistically and structurally secondary, being a socialized version of the Matthaean. All the modern literature attempts to trace the formation of the Beatitude tradition into its present forms by form-critical and redactional techniques, and commonly urges an original Aramaic form. What we now see is that the Matthaean form is Matthew's own creation. It is not merely that the *order* of the Beatitudes is forced on him, but the *content* is as well. Had he fifty beatitude-form logia to choose from, he could not have hoped to find eight so much to his purpose. We can watch him at work, developing Isa. 61, moving back and forth between the Commandments and the Rich Man as the architecture of the Sermon requires of him. The Sermon was not written at a run: its accurate dovetailing bespeaks careful forethought and painstaking revision Pentecost after Pentecost—and not all the bricks were ready-made. It is, if I may use a domestic parable, as if you are being shown round an ancient, but marvellously modernized, kitchen. The walls of the kitchen are full of curves and crannies, yet all are covered with beautifully fitting cupboards. As one with experience of kitchen fitments you say at first glance; these are top-quality cupboards, they will be from Harridge's department store. But the more closely they are seen to fit the ancient stonework, the more you doubt your judgement. Remembering that your host is an able carpenter you suddenly jump to it: 'You did it yourself!', you say. A modest smile is your reply. Then you are taken into the dining-room, and observe some remarkable modern panelling . . . The Beatitudes are the psychological barrier: if these are Matthew's creation, his midrash on Mark 10 from Exodus and Isaiah and the Psalms, then comes the wild surmise, why not the whole Sermon? Why not the whole Gospel? Why, indeed.

5.11–12

Luke and Matthew alike lead on from the Beatitudes with 'Blessed are you . . .' The Lucan version is characteristic in the following ways.

(a) Rhythmically, it has Luke's favourite fourfold exposition: '. . . when men hate you, and when they exclude you and revile you and cast out your name . . .' Compare, 'Love your enemies, do good to those who hate you, bless those who curse you, pray for those who abuse you', 'Good measure, pressed down, shaken together, running over'.

(b) Linguistically, it introduces the characteristic singular οὐρανῷ, the general subjects οἱ ἄνθρωποι, οἱ πάτερες ὑμῶν, for Matthew's impersonal 'they',[10] σκιρτήσατε, κατα τὰ αὐτά, ἐν ἐκείνῃ τῇ ἡμέρᾳ of a non-eschatological day. There are several Matthaean expressions in the Matthew version which Luke has rarely and only in parallel passages: ὀνειδίζω and μισθός he retains, but διώκω he twice changes, and substitutes 'for the sake of the Son of Man' for 'for my sake'.[11]

(c) Historically, Luke is written after the formal break with Judaism. So ἀφορίσωσι, 'they exclude you' is suitable for him as it is not for Matthew, which was written, we are arguing, towards A.D. 80. Matthew, similarly, has 'say all manner of evil against you falsely', which may mean either malicious talk, or delation to the synagogue authorities for discipline: if the latter, it is too late by Luke's day—now the Jews no longer abuse nor delate, they formally curse the Christians in the Twelfth Blessing of the Birkath-ha-Minim. Luke's expression, 'They cast out your name as evil', is a forceful and successful adaptation of Matthew's 'They utter all kinds of evil against you falsely'.[12]

Justin says that the Christians were cursed in the Jewish synagogues,[13] and the formal break must have made a profound impression on them. The double change of wording exactly reflects the change in relations with the Synagogue which has taken place in the decade between the two Gospels.

The Matthaean version is a Matthaean extension of the last Beatitude. It turns to the second person to break the Beatitude sequence; δεδιωγμένοι is expanded into three synonyms; 'for the sake of righteousness' is equated with 'for my sake'; 'yours is the king-dom of heaven' becomes 'rejoice and be glad, for great is your

---

[10] Luke supplies a subject at 8.49/Mark 5.35; 9.7/Mark 6.14; 11.33/Matt.5.15; and here: but he leaves impersonal subjects from his *Vorlagen* at 6.44; 17.23; 18.15,33; 21.27; and he introduces them on his own account at 12.20,48; 14.35; 23.29–31.

[11] cf. 18.29; 21.12.

[12] So Lohmeyer, *Matt.*, p. 95. See W. D. Davies, *Setting*, pp. 274ff. The institu-tion of the anti-Christian curse is usually dated about A.D. 85.

[13] *Dial.* 16.4.

reward in heaven'. 9 words out of 35 are characteristic: διώκω (2) (Matthaean), πονηρός, ἕνεκεν ἐμοῦ,[14] μισθός, οἱ οὐρανοί, οὕτως (semi-Matthaean). πόλυς = is great recurs at 9.37, 'The harvest is great' (AT). The persecution of the prophets before you recurs at 22.3 and 23.29ff. ἀγαλλιάομαι is used here only in Matthew, but for its use in the phrase 'rejoice and be glad' compare Ps. 31.11; 32.1; 50.10.

These verses have been the cause of considerable speculation on mistranslations of the Aramaic.

(a) Wellhausen suggested that Matthew's 'before you' in 5.12 might come from *qadhmêikôn*, which is only one letter different from *qadhmêihôn*, a possible original for the Lucan 'their fathers'.[15] While this is possible, it is unsupported by the Syriac, which reads *d*ᵉ*men q*ᵉ*dhāmaikôn* in Matthew, and *'abhāhāth*ᵉ*hôn* in Luke.

(b) The Matthaean 'be glad' (Syr. *r*ᵉ*wazû*, Aram. conjecture *rûzû*) is similar to the Lucan 'leap' (Syr. *dûtsû*, Aram. conjecture *dûtsû*) (Burkitt).[16]

(c) The Lucan expression ἐκβάλωσιν τὸ ὄνομα ὑμῶν ὡς πονηρόν is similar, but not identical, to the LXX κατενέγκη (ἐξήνεγκεν) αὐτῆς ὄνομα πονηρόν (Deut. 22.14, 19). Here the meaning is 'to publish' her name as evil, which is close to Matthew's 'say all manner of evil against you'. Black suggests an Aramaic *'appeq*, 'make to go forth', corresponding to the Hebrew *hôtsî'* which lies behind the Deuteronomy passage: this was then rendered accurately but roughly by Matthew, and over-literally by Luke.[17] If so, it is a unique error: ἐκβάλλω is never used in Koine Greek or the LXX to mean 'publish'. But we get a much better sense if we follow Lohmeyer and take Luke's phrase to mean what it says and apply to the Birkath-ha-Minim: and the change to ἀφορίσωσιν bears this out. The Aramaic original hypothesis always has to contend with the burden of being conjecture, and in these cases seems merely to be explaining by conjecture what is readily explicable by characteristic habits of Lucan writing.

---

[14] cf. 10.18,39; 16.25. Mark prefers to add 'and the gospel's', Matthew 'for my sake' absolutely.
[15] *Einleitung*, p. 36. Wellhausen omitted the suggestion in the 2nd edition; see Black, *AAGA*, pp. 191f.
[16] Cited by Black, without reference, p. 193. Burkitt's conjecture would seem to require a simultaneous oral and visual error: z is like ts to hear, r is like d to read.
[17] See Black, *AAGA*, pp. 135f.

5.13

The reward of the persecuted is great in heaven: and to Matthew the pair for heaven is earth. How is the theme of persecution to be worked out on earth? The image in Jewish tradition for preservation through suffering was salt, and the Marcan saying on salt can be adapted here. In place of 'Salt is good', Matthew writes, following 5.11, '*You are* the salt of the earth: but if the salt has become blunted'—substituting his favoured μωρ– root for the Marcan 'become saltless'[18]—'with what will it be salted?' (AT). He inserts the epigrammatic ἁλισθήσεται from the previous verse of Mark, 'everyone shall be salted with fire'. He rubs in the moral with typical stress on the fate of the faithless: 'It is no longer good for anything except to be thrown out'—cf. 8.12, 'the sons of the kingdom will be thrown out', or the rude wedding guest, or the unprofitable servant—'and trodden under foot by men' —compare the sacrifice and pearls trodden under foot at 7.6. Characteristic expressions are γῆ, οὐ . . . εἰ μή, βάλλομαι, οἱ ἄνθρωποι = men. Luke has the saying in another context, but also of the cost of discipleship: 'Salt is good' (Mark) 'but if the salt has been blunted, with what will it' (Matthew) 'be seasoned?' (Mark). 'It is fit neither for the land nor for the dunghill' (Luke's interest in manure) 'They throw it out' (Matthew) (14.34, AT). It is, like all else in the Travel narrative, adapted Matthew with reminiscence of Mark. Luke, as often, has his agriculture slightly wrong: the use of salt in this way in Palestine is unevidenced—Luke is introducing Greek farming practice. καὶ = also is characteristic of Luke: μωρός and its compounds are non-Lucan, and witness Luke's secondariness. Thus our evidence points both to Matthaean priority, and to free Matthaean adaptation of Mark.

5.14–16

Matthew customarily gives three illustrations to his themes: and indeed the Decalogue speaks not merely of heaven and earth, but of

---

[18] Black (*AAGA*, p. 166) follows Lightfoot's suggestion that 'μωρανθῇ suits very well with the Hebrew *tāphēl* which signifies both *unsavoury* and a *fool*': there is at least one passage in the Pal. Talmud where *tphl* occurs in Aramaic—'it was probably the only Semitic word for the thing signified and in common use among Aramaic-speaking Jews'. *tphl* means primarily tasteless, unsalted, as in Job 6.6, and is used in a transferred sense for worthless, foolish, e.g. Job 1.22; Jer. 23.13. Exactly the same transference takes place in Syriac where the root *pkh* means first unsalted, tasteless (and is used to translate ἄναλος, Mark 9.50), and so silly (1 Tim. 4.7), foolish (2 Cor. 11.1,17), and translates μωρανθῇ in Matt. 5.13. The transference may have taken place quite easily within the Semitic mind of Matthew without reference to hypothetical originals. cf. Jeremias *PJ*, p. 168.

the heaven above and the earth beneath and the waters under the earth. The κόσμος accordingly makes his third: the persecuted preserve the world, like salt, and they also witness to the universe, like the sun. The opening sentence of the unit then forms itself on the pattern of its predecessor, 'You are the salt of the earth . . . you are the light of the κόσμος.' Perhaps we have an echo of Paul's 'children of God without blemish in the midst of a crooked and perverse generation among whom you shine ὡς φωστῆρες ἐν κόσμῳ'.[19] But for the expansion of the light theme Matthew goes again to the Marcan tradition, 'Does the lamp come to be put under the *modion* or under the bed? Is it not to be put on the λυχνία?' (4.21, AT). The two witnesses in Rev.11 will be called λυχνίαι. Matthew retains all the significant words except 'bed', and rewrites the sentence as an affirmation (AT): 'Nor do they' —Semitic indefinite plural—'burn a lamp'—a hint of suffering witness—'and put it under the *modion* but on the λυχνία': and he adds a characteristic explanation, 'and it shines to all in the house'. The Lord had spoken ironically of putting the lamp under the bed, and had gone on to speak of things being hidden (κρυπτόν, ἀπόκρυφον) and made visible: Matthew leads up to the lampstand saying with the logion, 'A city set on a hill cannot be hid (κρυβῆναι)'. He elsewhere introduces the πόλις as a pair to the οἰκία at 10.14, 'going outside that house or city' (AT), and at 12.25, 'No city or house divided against itself': both in Marcan contexts, and clear evidence of the evangelist's activity. ὁ κόσμος, ἐπάνω are introduced elsewhere into Mark. The paragraph closes with a Matthaean *inclusio*, 'Let your light so shine . . .', which is redolent of typical language, 14 words out of 23: the generalizing οὕτως, λάμπω (2), ἔμπροσθεν τῶν ἀνθρώπων, καλός, ὅπως, and τὸν πάτερα ὑμῶν τὸν ἐν τοῖς οὐρανοῖς—the last two being Matthaeanisms. Luke has a form of only the lamp saying. He introduces the κρυπτή, the cellar of the Hellenistic house,[20] in place of the bed, and has the light put in the window to guide those *coming into* the house, a fitting symbol for his missionary bent:[21] the use of gnomic οὐδεὶς and ἅπτω is semi-Lucan, and also witnesses to Luke's editorial activity.

5.17–20

The persecution theme is done, and Matthew turns to introduce the main outline of the Sermon: this is a new Sinai, and what is being done is to transcend the Sinai commandments. Despite many attempts to drive wedges into the paragraph, separating the 'redactor' from his material, it is hard to believe that so utterly typical a piece of writing

---

[19] Phil. 2.15. [20] Jeremias, *PJ*, p. 27.
[21] 11.33. He adapts Mark with the same words at 8.16.

does not come whole from Matthew's pen. Christ came to fulfil the Law (17), that is, to show the roots from which the old Commandments stem, and so make them more comprehensive. This is exactly in line with the handling of murder and adultery, and, as suggested above,[22] it is no cause for astonishment if the equivocal nature of the Greek πληροῦν and the brilliance of his own rhetoric lead him to miss a lapse of meaning in the second half of the chapter. There is in fact a lapse of meaning in the next verse. 'Till heaven and earth pass away, not an iota, not a dot will pass from the law, till all is accomplished': that is, Matthew begins by meaning, till doomsday the law is valid to the last comma—its legal *provisions* are binding upon the Church. But it is also true, and a truth as dear to Matthew as to any other NT writer, that the *histories* of the Law are fulfilled in the Lord's life, in such matters as the Sermon fulfilling Sinai: so he ends, '. . . not a dot shall perish from the law, till all is accomplished'. The verse has two 'until' clauses, one at the beginning for one meaning of 'not perishing' or being fulfilled, one at the end for the other. Let him who has never changed the drift of a sentence in the writing throw the first stone. But it is the main theme which continues. Every commandment in the Law, even the very least, must be kept and taught in the Church on pain of eternal disgrace (19). We have only to compare 23.2f, 'The scribes and Pharisees sit on Moses' seat: *all* that they tell you, do', (AT), to see how fundamentally Matthaean this attitude is, and that the Oral Torah is included too. Many details of the Gospel, especially in the handling of Mark 2—3 on Sabbath, of Mark 7 on diet and the oral Law, and of Mark 10 on divorce, reveal the same attitude. The Christian must keep it all in its true meaning, in spirit as well as in letter; he must do better than the Pharisaic scribe, or he will never make the grade at all (20). Righteousness is a key Matthaean concept, and Matthew is leading the Church in the quest for perfection. Everything about the paragraph is theologically in character: the fear of antinomianism, the contempt for Pharisaic hypocrisy, the threat of exclusion for the half-hearted, no less than the main theses I have cited. It is required where it stands and admirably performs the function of introducing the Lord's attitude (as Matthew sees it) to the Law. The war on two fronts, against the Antinomians and against the Pharisees, is fought throughout the book, and is here in a nutshell.

Because what we have in fact is Matthew's attitude to the Law, there was little Marcan tradition on which he could draw. Jesus had said, 'Heaven and earth will pass away (παρελεύσονται), but my words will not pass away (παρέλθωσι)', and this governs the form of 5.18, although the meaning is developed, to put it mildly. In Mark Jesus

[22] pp. 261f.

said his words would outlast creation: Matthew has him say that
before creation passes away (παρέλθῃ) the Law of Moses will be fulfilled in him, and that it is valid till then. It was a rabbinic opinion that
the Law was valid until the age to come: 'In this age Israelites contract
uncleanness, and get themselves purified according to the directions
of the priest; but in the future it will not be so, but God himself will
purify them . . .'[23] A similar form of the saying is at Luke 16.17, 'It
is easier for heaven and earth to pass away than for one dot of the
Law to become void'. Luke did not believe in the validity of the Law
to the end of this age, and he clarifies Matthew's statement by omitting
the first of his 'until' clauses. 16.16, 'The Law and the prophets
were until John . . .' is good Lucan theology—sc. 'but circumcision,
etc., is now abolished, and the world can crowd into the kingdom'.
16.17 then means, 'But (δὲ) the life of Jesus (/the Church) fulfils the
Law completely', which agrees with both Luke's thinking and the
context. He retains the Matthaean tittle, and heaven-and-earth; both
signs of his secondariness.

This sentence then has a Marcan *Vorlage:* but the form of the
remainder is conveyed in rhythms which we have shown to be characteristic of Matthew alone. 'Think not that I came to destroy the Law and
the Prophets: I came not to destroy but to fulfil' (AT) is the thesauric
rhythm: cf. 10.34, 'Think not that I came to cast peace on the earth:
I came not to bring peace but a sword' (AT), where the sentence-form
is identical. There are eight such rhythms in Matthew, none in Mark,
and two in Luke (both in Q passages). 5.19 is a repetitive converse
logion: 'Whoever then relaxes one of the least of these commandments
and teaches men so, shall be called least in the kingdom of heaven;
but he who does them and teaches them shall be called great in the
kingdom of heaven'—compare, 'For if you forgive men their trespasses your heavenly Father will also forgive you; but if you do not
forgive men their trespasses, neither will your Father forgive your
trespasses.' There are 13 cases of this in Matthew, none in Mark, 9 in
Luke, of which 4 are in Q-passages. With the structure of 5.20, 'For
I say to you, unless your righteousness exceeds that of the scribes and
Pharisees, you will never enter the kingdom of heaven', compare 18.3,
'Truly I say to you, unless you turn and become as little children, you
will never enter the kingdom of heaven.' 18.3 is redactional, Matthew's
own: the rhythm is not found elsewhere in the Synoptics.

[23] Pesiqta 41b; Tanḥuma, Huqqat 60b; Moore, *Judaism* i, p. 272. Some Jewish
speculation expected the Torah to continue as valid under Messiah: if Matthew
knew of this, he could mean 'until the end of the Messianic kingdom', or perhaps
rhetorically, 'for ever'. See W. D. Davies, 'Matthew 5.18', in *Mélanges Bibliques
redigés en l'honneur de André Robert* (Paris 1957), and comments on a reply by
A. D. Macho in *Setting*, pp. 446f.

When we pass to language, the evidence is so plentiful that I blush to record it: 44 words out of 101. Matthaeanisms are: the kingdom of heaven (3), heaven-and-earth, the scribes and Pharisees, δικαιοσύνη, πληρόω, οὐ μή . . . ἕως ἄν (2), and the familiarity with holy things such as tittles on the law-scroll. Semi-Matthaean are νομίζω, λύω of relaxing laws, νόμος (2), ἐλάχιστος (2), οἱ ἄνθρωποι = men, οὕτως, οὖν, ἀμήν, κληθήσεται (2), resumptive οὗτος, λέγω ὑμῖν ὅτι, περισσεύω, theological ἦλθον (2). There is no non-Matthaean vocabulary. When a paragraph fits its context so well, and when it is so thoroughly Matthaean in theology, in rhythm, and in language, the presumption must be that it is the evangelist's own.

5.21–2

So the antithesis between Sinai and the Lord's teaching can be opened, and I have shown why it begins from the Sixth Commandment. Anger is the obvious root from which murder springs: indeed the Lord had virtually said as much following his comments on the Fifth Commandment in Mark 7.21: 'For from within, out of the heart of man, come evil thoughts: fornication, theft, murder, adultery . . .'. Jesus had spoken of what is again an extension of the Second Table of the Law as coming from within. The πορνεῖαι, κλοπαί, φόνοι, μοιχεῖαι, πλεονεξίαι, and so on are to be the theme of the Sermon; and in each case the Lord is portrayed as putting his finger on the relevant διαλογισμὸς ὁ κακός which proceeds from the heart and leads on to the act. Matthew did not make the theme of anger up: it is implicit in Mark. But around the Marcan grit he lacquers his pearl, a three-tier climax leading to the threat of the gehenna of fire (5.22). Since there is at Mark 9.43ff a threefold threat of gehenna, the unquenchable fire, which is quoted eight verses down Matthew's page, it is likely that his mind is already at work on this passage. But in any case the concepts and language betray the evangelist at work. The threat of hell comes easily to him. The idea of a church organized as a Beth Din is peculiar to him, being instanced at 18.15–20: as a hierarchy of houses of judgement, it is unique within the Gospel, but is entirely in line with the general acceptance of Jewish institutions. If, as is likely, the Sanhedrin means the Jewish Sanhedrin, only Matthew in the NT gives it authority (23.2). If it means an Apostolic Council, it is Matthew who gives instructions for the apostles to make Church Law at 16.19 and 18.18, and not to change biblical law at 5.19; to apply discipline and ultimately sanctions is commanded at 18.12ff. All these passages are without synoptic parallels, though they mirror closely the Pauline picture of church courts in 1 Cor. 5, and a supreme apostolic Beth

Din in Gal. 2. Linguistically Matthaean are (apart from the opening formula) φονεύω, ἔνοχός (3), κρίσις (2), μωρός: semi-Matthaean are ἀδελφός = fellow-Christian (2), λέγω ὑμῖν ὅτι, ἔσται (4), γέεννα, πῦρ— 19 words out of 54. The repetitive triple climax is a form of what we have called the scandalic rhythm. There are close instances at 19.12, eunuchs born so, eunuchs made of men, eunuchs for the kingdom; and at 23.20ff, swears by the altar, swears by the temple, swears by heaven. The only parallel outside Matthew is Mark's a kingdom divided, a house divided, Satan divided. Matthew's fondness for *oratio recta*, and for standard rabbinic expressions, comes through in Raka: a similar instance is at 23.7, 'being called Rabbi' by men. The paragraph is thus typical of the evangelist in concept, rhythm and language, and a Marcan matrix is readily visible.

5.23-4

So much then for not being angry: but if we have quarrelled, then our duty as peacemakers is reconciliation. The first law in Exod. 20 after the Decalogue concerns the building of the altar (θυσιαστήριον) and the offering of sacrifices on it: Matthew grafts the altar naturally on to his first Antithesis, as worship without charity had been forbidden by Jesus, 'Whenever you stand praying' (Mark 11.25) 'forgive if you have anything against anyone (εἴ τι ἔχετε κατά τινος)'. Matthew adapts this to the case in point, 'you there remember that your brother has something against you (ἔχει τι κατά σοῦ)'. The phrase is only in these two passages in the NT. In Mark the peril was resentment, here it is the simpler unrepented injury: in both cases reconciliation must precede prayer. The presence of the altar in Exodus is probably all we need to explain its mysterious occurrence in a post-70 document. I incline to K. W. Clark's thesis that offerings were still made at the altar after the Temple was destroyed,[24] and until A.D. 135; but Matthew may well be living in the rabbis' dream-world where the Temple-service will soon be restored—why should this have seemed absurd in the late 70s? The unit is famous for its Matthaean words, 16 out of 41: προσφέρω (2), δῶρον (3), θυσιαστήριον (2), τότε—the whole background of Temple worship in teaching illustration is peculiar to him: οὖν, ἐκεῖ (2), κατά + gen., ἀδελφός (2), ἐλθών, ἔμπροσθεν are semi-Matthaean. διαλλαγῆναι, on the other hand, is ἅπαξ λεγόμενον.

5.25-6

For the third illustration, we are given a case of injury through an unpaid debt. Where Mark has, 'Forgive if you have anything against

[24] See p. 258 above.

anyone', he continues, 'so that your Father also who is in heaven may forgive you your trespasses (παραπτώματα)': Matthew has the same at 6.14f, but in the Lord's Prayer he writes, 'Forgive us our debts (ὀφειλήματα)'. Similarly at 18.21 Jesus is asked, 'How often shall my brother sin against me and I forgive him?', and answers with a parable on debts. Matthew associates sin and debt: indeed the Aramaic word for the two is *ḥūbhāh*, the Syriac *haubā*', and Matthew thinks in Semitic. It is natural for him to move from seeking reconciliation to paying money owed. Punishment and prisons are congenial to his imagination too, and we may compare 18.34 for the payment of the last farthing in gaol. For the 'chain-reaction' sentence-form—'the creditor hand you over to the judge, and the judge to the warder . . .' we may compare the Matthaean 'Abraham begat Isaac, and Isaac begat Jacob . . .'. Verse 26 is one of Matthew's ἀμὴν λέγω σοι (ὑμῖν) . . . οὐ μὴ . . . ἕως ἄν forms—compare above *'Truly I say to you . . . not* a dot will pass from the Law *until* all is accomplished'. The following are also semi-Matthaean words: ἴσθι, ἀποδίδωμι, βάλλομαι, ἔσχατος, φυλακή = prison, ἐκεῖθεν, and ταχύ—14 words out of 43. εὐνοῶ, ἀντίδικος (2), ἕως ὅτου are only found here, the former two not too surprisingly.

Luke has the unit (12.58f) in an eschatological context. It forms a challenge to the Pharisees: God is the judge, and life is a brief road to the judgement-seat; getting quittance means repenting. Such a message is often believed to be the substance of Jesus' original preaching,[25] and the tendency has been to draw the conclusion that Luke has preserved the Lord's meaning. However, the Lucan *form* is manifestly secondary. He introduces the paragraph, 'As you are going with your accuser before the ἄρχων', the Greek magistrate before whom Paul and Silas were brought in Acts 16.19. The ἄρχων is then equated with the Matthaean κριτής, and hands the debtor on to the Greek πράκτωρ, the constable in charge of the collection of debts.[26] The situation is thus translated into a Greek context, while, as Jeremias concedes, Matthew retains the Jewish background.[27] ἐργασία occurs four times in Acts, and not elsewhere in the NT, and the dragging of opponents to court comes in Acts 16 also. ἐκεῖθεν is rare in Luke (18/6/3) but is retained here from Matthew. Matthew's Latin

---

[25] So Jeremias, *PJ*, pp. 37ff, 43, and *passim*.
[26] See W. Bauer, *A Greek–English Lexicon of the New Testament and other earlier Christian Literature*, tr. and ed. W. F. Arndt and F. W. Gingrich [Bauer] (4e., Cambridge 1952) ad voc., citing U. Wilcken, *Urkunden der Ptolemäerzeit* (1927), p. 118, 15; 24.
[27] *PJ*, p. 43, n. 73.

loan-word κοδράντης is replaced with the genuine Greek λεπτόν[28], in line with Luke's dislike of loan-words. But the significant thing is the change from ἄρχοντα in 58a: it is not natural to write, 'While you are on your way to the *magistrate*, come to terms with your accuser lest he drag you to the *judge*.' The influence of the Matthew *Vorlage* is evident at this point: it is not the only place where Luke reverts to exact copying through fatigue as a pericope progresses.[29] Luke has material about Jesus' challenge to repent over the slaughtered Galileans and the eighteen at Siloam; and what he has done here, as often, is to turn Matthew's illustration of peacemaking into grist for his mill.

The three paragraphs on peacemaking are good examples of the thesis I am arguing. *Prima facie* they are non-Marcan material, M, no doubt, and Q. Once it is seen that they are carefully sited stones in a great edifice, we examine the marks of the mason's hammer more closely: but why should they not be M and Q still, adapted to their place? Then we see that in fact they show evidence of being quarried from Mark and Exod. 20: we see that the rhythmical form is Matthaean, and the thought-sequence is Matthaean, and the images are Matthaean and the language is Matthaean. So the simplest hypothesis becomes, does it not, to dispense with Q and M, and the oral tradition and the Aramaic original? Matthew panelled the dining-room too.

[28] Luke retains Mark's λεπτά at 21.2.
[29] cf. Luke 19.11–27, esp. v.20, ὁ ἕτερος.

14

PENTECOST:
THE LAW FULFILLED 2

In the last two chapters I have tried to set out the main architecture of the Sermon as deriving from the Marcan record of the teaching of Jesus, especially in Mark 10, and from Exod. 20—23, the ancient law-giving on the mountain: these two matrices being amplified by a pattern of Matthew's own, the Beatitudes, as expounded in reverse order. In this chapter we will consider briefly the paragraphs from 5.27 to the end of the Sermon, asking whether there is evidence for pre-Matthaean tradition, or for Matthew's own creativity.

5.27–30

The paragraph on Adultery is straightforward. The Antithesis formula is a shortened version of 5.21, 'You have heard that it was said to the men of old'. The Seventh Commandment follows the Sixth. The lust–adultery link is a Jewish commonplace. 'One who commits adultery with his eyes is called adulterer.'[1] 'Do not roam, following your own heart and your eyes, which you go a-whoring after.'[2] 'Thou shalt not commit adultery. Neither with hand nor foot nor eye nor mind . . .'[3] Matthew limits his expansion to eye and hand, as the limbs most adapted for the purpose: indeed D and syr^{sin} leave out the hand verse inasmuch as it is the sin of the eye which is primarily in question. The scandal of the eye draws his thought to Mark 9.42ff, of which he writes an abbreviated and Matthaeanized form. συμφέρει is Matthaean (Mark καλόν ἐστιν), and Matthew has a much stronger liking for ἀπό and σῶμα than Mark: ἐκκόπτω is semi-Matthaean, as are the specification of the *right* hand, *right* eye, anarthrous γέεννα (2), εἰ for ἐάν. In the earlier part of the paragraph ἐρρέθη, πρὸς τὸ with the infinitive are Matthaean: λέγω ὑμῖν ὅτι is semi-Matthaean. μέλος (2) is found only here in the Gospels, but is in line with Matthew's concern with parts of the body, of which there are 122 mentions in one form or another in his Gospel.[4] There is no other non-Matthaean language.

5.31–2

Jesus gives his ruling on divorce and remarriage in Mark 10, radically doing away with the Deuteronomic permission. Matthew glosses the

---

[1] Lev. R. 23.12.　　　　　　　　　　[2] Sifre Num. 15.39.
[3] Mek. de R. Simeon b. Yohai, Exod. 20.14.
[4] See pp. 103f. above.

Marcan radicalism in that context by the insertion of μὴ ἐπὶ πορνείᾳ;
thus saving the authority of Deuteronomy and aligning Jesus with
the Shammaite school. He produces the same teaching with a similar
gloss here: it is natural therefore to take it for his own. The phrasing
ὃς ἂν ἀπολύσῃ τὴν γυναῖκα αὐτοῦ follows Mark 10.11: 'let him give her
a certificate of divorce' follows Deut. 24.1 (LXX) 'he shall write her
a certificate of divorce, and give it into her hands'. 'It was said' and
'But I say to you' are characteristic, as is Matthew's Jewish concentration of interest on the man. Mark and Paul both refer to the possibility
of the woman's initiative: Matthew, closer to scripture and to the
ancient patriarchy, limits the woman's sin to being forced (by economics) to remarry; the fault is with her first husband for forcing her
out, and her second husband for taking her on. Matthew has thus,
like Mark, a double fault to find, and ends the second clause, as does
Mark, with a firm μοιχᾶται; but he only blames the husbands, because
in traditional Semitic thought the woman is but a vessel: she can be
'adulterated' (transitive, 5.28,32), but she cannot adulterate her
husband. What does πορνεία mean? It has nothing to do with Levitical
laws of affinity.[5] At the least it could refer to cases such as Matthew
himself describes in 1, where Joseph, who was a just man, meant to
divorce his betrothed on finding her pregnant. But the introduction
which Matthew glosses to 19 makes it virtually certain that it means
adultery: Mark 10.2: 'Is it lawful for a man to divorce his wife?',
Matt. 19.3: 'Is it lawful to divorce one's wife for any cause?' When
μὴ ἐπὶ πορνείᾳ is also inserted in the Matthaean text at 19.9, it is clear
that this is the Hillel–Shammai debate. πορνεία is nothing but an
equivalent for μοιχεία on the feminine side: only the wife can behave
like a πόρνη. παρεκτός is non-Matthaean. λόγος is the Hebrew *dābhār*
meaning a matter,[6] which is used in Deut. 24.1 of the unseemly matter.
The passage is a clear instance of the tendency to save scripture which
we have evidenced in Matthew not only in general, but in the very
example in 19.

5.33–7

The second three Antitheses make a fresh start. There is a characteristic resumptive πάλιν, and the longer form of the formula, 'You have
heard that it was said to the men of old . . .', both of which carry us

---

[5] cf. F. W. Green, *St Matthew* (Oxford 1963), ad loc.; H. J. Richards, 'Christ on
Divorce', *Scripture* 11 (1959), pp. 22–32.
[6] So Bauer ad voc. *'erwath dābhār*, translated ἀσχημον πρᾶγμα in LXX,
becomes λόγος πορνείας with the Shammaite view of *'erwath*. cf. Allen,
McNeile, Schlatter.

back to 5.21.[7] The pure in heart not only refrain from lust and re-marriage: they do not swear deceitfully to their neighbour, the psalmist had said (Ps. 24.4). Matthew needs therefore a more general word than the ψευδομαρτυρήσεις of the Ninth Commandment: it is not just perjury in court which was to be avoided under the old dispensation, but false promises greased with the name of God in general. Matthew's citation is therefore somewhat compendious. It starts with the Ninth Commandment, with a more general verb ἐπιορκήσεις to cover the psalm: the second half occurs verbally nowhere in the OT, though the sense comes fifty times. Matthew does exactly the same thing at the end of the chapter: he first modifies the Tenth Commandment as he has the Ninth, to 'You shall love your neighbour', and then he adds the Antithesis 'and hate your enemy', which is not scriptural in word but in substance. The meaning is plain. 'You shall perform to the Lord what you have sworn': *God* requires the payment of promises made to our neighbour under his name. ὅρκος in the LXX means both oaths and vows, i.e. promises made to God under oath, and the second meaning would be possible in the context of 33–7; but all the rest of the chapter is concerned with our duties to our neighbour, so Matthew is likely to have intended this unit in the same sense. Jas. 5.12 takes up the words, and clearly means 'Swear not' rather than 'Vow not'.[8] The contrast between the old faithful performance of oaths and the new plain speaking is probably due to 2 Cor. 1.17 (AT): 'Do I make my plans according to the flesh, that with me should be the ναί ναί and the οὐ οὐ ?'.[9] Paul's meaning is a little different from Matthew's. He does not go saying ναί ναί one moment and οὐ οὐ the next, but he plans in the Lord: Matthew means that every statement is made in the Lord, ναί ναί or οὐ οὐ, and oaths are therefore an irreligious irrelevance. But the basis is common: a Christian does not speak lightly his ναί ναί and his οὐ οὐ —more than that is of the flesh (Paul), or the devil (Matthew). Yea, yea, nay, nay is of a piece with the obviousness of much Matthaean antithesis. The first pair of forbidden weakened oaths is from Isa. 66.1 (LXX): 'Thus says the Lord, The heaven is my throne, and the earth the footstool of my feet.'—Matthew's favourite heaven-and-earth. Isaiah goes on (66.10) to speak of Jerusalem, which is described in Ps. 48.3 as 'the city of the great king'. Heaven and earth, Jerusalem and . . .: the second pair is not so obvious. Matthew has just spoken of the heart, the right eye, the right hand, the whole body:

---

[7] There are to be six Antitheses, so the longer form here, at the Fourth, divides them into two threes: with three further antitheses in 6.1–18. Matthew makes the counting of his Ten New Commandments easy.

[8] cf. T. W. Manson, *SJ*, p. 158.   [9] cf. p. 159 above.

he is about to speak of eye for eye and tooth for tooth, the right cheek and the other. It would not be surprising if it were he who had completed the forbidden oaths with our head whose hair we cannot make black or—obvious antithesis—white. Thus the material of the pericope is readily explicable from scripture, Paul, and Matthew's own imaginative mind. It is he, and he alone, who is concerned with oaths —here and at 23.16–22, a markedly similar passage. It is part of his whole scribal mentality to be concerned with holy things.[10] The language is less strongly Matthaean—8 words out of 61. ἀποδίδωμι, ἐρρέθη, ὅρκος, ὀμνύω (2), ὁ πονηρός, ἔστω are Matthaean, and there is no uncharacteristic vocabulary.

5.38–42

The Antithesis is based on Exod. 21.24 on the one side, and a development of Isa. 50.6f LXX on the other: 'I gave my back to the whips, my cheeks to the blows (τοὺς σιαγόνας μου εἰς ῥαπίσματα): I turned not (ἀπέστρεψα) my face from the shame of spitting (ἐμπτυσμάτων) . . . For he is near who justifies me: who is he that goes to law with me (ὁ κρινόμενός μοι)? Let him oppose me together (ἀντιστήτω μοι ἅμα).' The verbal links are too strong to be accidental: the 'but I say to you' section is a midrashic expansion of Isaiah. Above all the Christian's thought is recalled by these words to the Passion of the Lord: he had been spat upon (ἐνέπτυσαν, 26.67; 27.30), and struck on the face (ἐρράπισαν, 26.68, ἔτυπτον εἰς την κεφαλὴν αὐτοῦ, 27.30)—and, what does not come in Isaiah, they had taken his clothes (ἱμάτια 27.31, 35), and forced (ἠγγάρευσαν, 27.32) Simon to carry his cross. The crossing of the three texts, Exodus, Isaiah, the Passion, give the Christian his pattern of a life of mercy. Retaliation will be his last thought. He will not ἀντιστῆναι the evil one, in form of his oppressor, for God is near to justify him. If hit on the right cheek (ῥαπίζει εἰς τὴν δεξίαν σιαγόνα), he will turn (στρέψον) the other. If sued at law (κριθῆναί σοι) to take away his undergarment, his χιτών,[11] he will let his wraparound, his ἱμάτιον, go too. If put to forced labour (ἀγγαρεύσει) he will go double the distance. He will give to every beggar (ἐλεημοσύνη, 6.2ff) nor will he turn away (ἀποστράφῃς) from the borrower. The links are with the Greek text of Isaiah, so it is in the Greek church that the midrash has been done. The vocabulary of law and credit is congenial to Matthew, as are measures such as

[10] See p. 106 above.

[11] The χιτών was worn next to the skin, and the possibility of wearing two χιτῶνες is seen in Jos. *Ant.* 17.136; Diog. Laert. 6.13, as well as Mark 6.9, Matt. 10.10; cf. Bauer ad voc.

miles and cubits. ὁ πονηρός is Matthaean, as is the *right* cheek—
suggestions about the redoubled insult of a back-handed blow to the
right cheek are over-ingenious,[12] for Matthew customarily names the
right limb. Semi-Matthaean are θέλω (2), and λαβεῖν. The ἱμάτιον
comes in the Book of the Covenant, Exod. 22.26f, 'And if you take
your neighbour's ἱμάτιον for a pledge, you shall restore it to him
before sunset'. Matthew's Exodus text thus represents the 'cloak' as a
man's fundamental possession. Characteristic too are the balanced
clauses, the right cheek and the other, the χιτών and the ἱμάτιον, one
mile and two, the beggar and the borrower. The strongly antithetical
rhythm is a series of pardics: 'Can the Ethiopian change his skin, or
the leopard his spots?', 'Whoever will force you for one mile, go with
him two' (AT).

Luke (6.27–30) has a version of 39b–40,42 combined with the
following paragraph. Matthew has the *talio* section in the second
person singular, and the Love of Enemies in the second person plural.
Luke opens the combined paragraph with the love of enemies in the
plural, then has the *talio* piece in the singular, then reverts to the love
of enemies in the plural: an uncomfortable procedure. He has no
mention of a law situation, and reverses the order of ἱμάτιον and
χιτών. His context appears to be that of a footpad[13] who takes
(αἴροντος) the outer garment first, and is to be resigned the χιτών as
well: to a Greek church that lacked the Israelite's feeling for the
inalienability of the ἱμάτιον, this was a sensible adaptation. Characteristically Lucan vocabulary are τύπτω, παρέχω, καί = also, κωλύω and
singular πᾶς with the anarthrous participle.

5.43–8

The last of the six Antitheses displays the Matthaean antithetical
rhythm at its purest:

(*a*) You have heard that it was said, (*b*) You shall love your neighbour,
        and (*b*) You shall hate your enemy;
But (*a*) I say to you, (*c*) Love your enemies,
    and (*c*) pray for your persecutors,
so that (*d*) you may be sons of your Father who is in heaven:
For (*e*) He makes his sun rise on the evil and the good,
and (*e*) He sends rain on the just and the unjust.
For (*f*) if you love your lovers, (*g*) what reward have you? (*h*) Do not
   even publicans do the same?

---

[12] e.g. J. Jeremias, *The Sermon on the Mount*, p. 27.
[13] T. W. Manson, *SJ*, p. 51.

and (*f*) if you salute only your brethren, (*g*) what more are you doing than others? (*h*) Do not even Gentiles do the same?

(*d*) You therefore must be perfect, as your heavenly Father is perfect.

Such sustained poetry is unparalleled in any Gospel, though we have shown in ch. 4 above how typical of Matthew it is:[14] antithesis piled on antithesis, the contrasts black and white and obvious, the strong last line making an *inclusio* with (*d*) at the end of the first clause. There are no units resembling this in Mark, and all the strophe/antistrophe poems in Luke are Q poems. Other Matthaean features are: persecution (διώκω), your Father in heaven (2), the use of the elements such as the sun and the rain,[15] and contrasts such as the good-and-the-bad,[16] publicans-and-Gentiles;[17] the ideas of perfection (τέλειος) and reward (μισθός)—indeed, virtually the whole substance of the section. The Marcan 'salutations in the market-places' which feature in v. 47 are also handsomely expanded by Matthew with illustrations in 23.9–10. Smaller linguistic points are the Matthaean ἐρρέθη, μόνον, and ὅπως, and the semi-Matthaean δίκαιος, οὖν, οὐχί; ἀδελφός. In all there are 25 characteristic words out of 96. There is no more Matthaean piece of teaching in the Gospel.

Luke has (6.27–36), as we said, rewritten the paragraph, sandwiching the singular *talio* section in the middle of Matthew's plurals. He adapts Matthew's opening antitheses to a four-item Lucan catalogue: 'Love your enemies, do good to your haters, bless your cursers, pray for your abusers' (AT), a continual feature in Luke,[18] never found in his predecessors. He gives for Matthew's loving and saluting a three-bar unit: loving, benefiting, and lending, at the cost of making the poetry somewhat heavy. He drops the Jewish business of salutations from his version of the reviling of the Pharisees in Luke 11 also, whereas the lending of money is most commonly found as a Lucan image. It is also characteristic of Luke that his antitheses are between synonyms,[19] while Matthew's carry a substantial parallel. Matthew's enemies are not identical with his persecutors, nor his publicans with his Gentiles, nor his loving with his saluting. Luke's enemies and haters are the same, so are his cursers and abusers; and his benefiting is very close to either loving if it is abstract, or lending if it is concrete. Characteristically Lucan too are the emphasis on thanks (χάρις (3), and ἀχάριστος), ἁμαρτωλός (4), πλήν, καθώς, ἐλπίζω, ὁμοίως, ἀπο-compounds, καὶ γάρ (2), ὁ ὕψιστος for God. Luke has πονηρός, μισθός,

---

[14] p. 89 above.
[15] cf. p. 103 above.
[16] cf. 22.10; 12.34f (4); 25.21ff.
[17] cf. 18.17.
[18] See p. 91 above.
[19] cf. 12.24, 'storehouse or barn'; 6.37, 'judge not, condemn not'.

and 'your Father' for God, only in Q contexts. οἰκτίρμων alone is not found elsewhere in Luke.

6.1–8,16–18

The theme of mercy, and of reward from God, continues. We have already observed how baseless is the suggestion that Matthew took over a so-styled poem consisting of three repetitive sections on the three pious duties: a modified repetitiveness is his style, and it is made tolerable here by the variations in the centre section. In fact the section is Matthaean in thought, image, rhythm, and language. The ideas are thoroughly congenial to the evangelist: three Jewish duties, the abhorrence of Pharisaic love of the external, rewards from God and man, the jabbering Gentile. Religious imagery such as the σάλπιγξ (shôfār) and synagogue, disfiguring and anointing, is Matthaean; so are the parts of the body, the left hand and right, the face and head, which form the *leitmotif* of the Sermon; and also the lanes and streets and corners. It is typical of Matthew to expound prayer from scripture: 'Go into your room and shut the door' follows closely the Greek version of Isa. 26.20, εἴσελθε εἰς τὰ ταμίειά σου, ἀπόκλεῖσον τὴν θύραν σου, ἀποκρύβηθι; or Elisha went to pray for the Shunamite woman's son (2 Kings 4.23) εἰσῆλθε εἰς τὸν οἶκον καὶ ἀπέκλεισεν τὴν θύραν . . . καὶ προσηύξατο. 'Let not your left hand know what your right hand is doing' has a four-point balanced rhythm, like the pardic. The sentence form, 'Don't do A, but do B', the anticipatory epexegetic prohibition, is a favourite with Matthew. 'Be not as the hypocrites . . . do not be therefore like the Gentiles . . . Thus therefore pray ye . . .' (AT) The language is highly Matthaean: δικαιοσύνη, πρὸς τὸ + inf., μισθός (4), ὅπως (3), your Father in heaven, ἀποδίδωμι (3), φαίνομαι (3), ὑποκριτής (3), ὥσπερ, your Father (6) are on Hawkins' list. Semi-Matthaean are προσέχω, ἔμπροσθεν (2), οἱ ἄνθρωποι = men (5), ἑστώς, οὖν, ὡς (2), κρυπτός (4), θεάομαι, ἀμὴν λέγω ὑμῖν (2), φιλῶ, ὁμοιόω, κλείω, ἐθνικοί, δοκέω: 84 characteristic words in all out of 253. Only found here are ἐλεημοσύνη, though the stem is elsewhere in the Gospel, εἰσακούω, and ἀλείφω.

6.9–15

A widely accepted history of the Lord's Prayer[20] may be set out in

[20] See, for example, E. Lohmeyer, *The Lord's Prayer* (E.T., London 1965); T. W. Manson, 'The Lord's Prayer', *BJRL* 38 (1955–6), pp. 99–113, 436–448; H. Schürmann, *Das Gebet des Herrn* (Leipzig 1957); J. Jeremias, *The Prayers of Jesus* (London 1967, SBT ii.6); J. Carmignac, *Recherches sur le 'Notre Père'* (Paris 1969). What follows is an amended version of my article, 'The Composition of the Lord's Prayer', *JTS*, xi.1 (April 1963).

five propositions: (*a*) Jesus composed the Prayer himself, and taught it to his disciples, drawing on the synagogue liturgies but transforming them; (*b*) The Prayer was modified into two versions, one in Galilee, one in Jerusalem, and this process continued with its transmission in the Greek churches; (*c*) Mark does not record it, but then Mark has only a little of Jesus' teaching; (*d*) Luke's version is shorter, and therefore closer to the original, since liturgical texts tend to grow with time; (*e*) Matthew's version includes considerable elaborations in Matthaean style, which point to a later version modified by Matthew's own hand.

This picture is riddled with difficulties. If Jesus taught the Prayer by heart, why did the Galilee apostles and the Jerusalem apostles not insist on the *bona fide* version in both churches? Which version was used when the pilgrims came to Jerusalem? Since Paul and Barnabas were in contact with the Peter–James–John tradition, why did they not establish the true version in the Greek church and teach it to Luke? In which churches did the apostolic writ not run? What was Matthew doing producing a Matthaeanized version of Jesus' own Prayer fifty years after it had been taught by the Lord and known by heart by two generations of Christians? Is it credible that Mark should have omitted from 200 verses of teaching the only prayer which Jesus taught by heart—and indeed deliberately omitted it? Are we being told that the passage, 'Whenever you stand praying, forgive if you have anything against anyone', would not recall it to his mind? How did the unique ἐπιούσιος get into both versions? If they were assimilated, why were they assimilated at this point only?

Since the picture is so unclear it is not surprising if there is some disagreement between experts on the detail. Streeter[21] and Manson[22] credited our two versions to M and L, Creed gave both versions to Q.[23] Creed correctly observes that the variations in the Lucan version can all be attributed to the style of Luke; Kilpatrick that the variations in the Matthaean version can all be attributed to the style of Matthew. Since we have three unknowns, Jesus' own version, the pre-Lucan Jerusalem recension, and the pre-Matthaean Galilee recension, it is unreasonable to expect anything like agreement on the reconstruction: it is the possession of multiple unknowns which keeps us scholars in business.

The famous canon of liturgical criticism that the shorter text is likely to be the earlier, has been erected by ceaseless repetition from a rule of thumb to an excuse for not looking at the evidence. If we take it to be a sacrosanct principle that the shorter text is always the earlier, then we are happily in possession of a proof that the 1662

[21] *FG*, p. 277.   [22] *SJ*, pp. 165–71 (M), 265f (L).
[23] J. M. Creed, *The Gospel according to St Luke* (London 1930), pp. 155ff.

Anglican Consecration Prayer is earlier than the longer 1549 version: and, for that matter, both Anglican versions will clearly also be earlier than the canon of the Roman Mass. Nothing, Housman might have taught us by now, excuses us from thinking. Luke often shortens the Marcan teaching he takes over, and he is regularly shorter than Matthew in Q-passages. It is entirely an open question whether he might not have shortened the Matthaean Prayer.

For what we have in Matthew is a prayer composed by the evangelist from the traditions of the prayers of Jesus in Mark and the teaching on prayer by Jesus in Mark, amplified from the Exodus context of the Sermon, and couched in Matthaean language. What we have in Luke is a version pruned of the rounded Matthaean periods and slightly obvious antitheses, and couched in Lucan language. This solution has the great merit of simplicity, it avoids all the problems latent in the accepted theory, and accounts satisfactorily for all the evidence.

The only teaching on prayer in Mark is at 11.25, 'Whenever you stand praying (προσευχόμενοι), forgive (ἀφίετε), if you have anything against anyone, in order that your Father in heaven (ὁ πατὴρ ὑμῶν ὁ ἐν τοῖς οὐρανοῖς) may forgive (ἀφῇ) you your trespasses (παραπτώματα)'. Since Matthew includes virtually all of Mark, but omits this verse in the context, it is natural to suppose that he has included it here. Matthew commonly puts Mark's indirect speech into *oratio recta*. He begins the Prayer, πάτερ ἡμῶν ὁ ἐν τοῖς οὐρανοῖς; he includes as the longest petition, 'Forgive us (ἄφες) our debts as we also have forgiven our debtors'; and when the Prayer is complete, fearing that the dominical stress on forgiveness has been underemphasized, he underlines it doubly with the repetitive converse logion, 'For if you forgive men their trespasses (παραπτώματα), your heavenly Father will also forgive you; but if you do not forgive men their trespasses, neither will your Father forgive your trespasses'. The repetitive converse pardic is a typical Matthaean rhythm—cf. 'Whoever then relaxes one of the least of these commandments . . .', 'Whatever you bind on earth . . .', 'Do not lay up for yourselves treasures on earth . . .'. The Marcan teaching thus gives the basic structure of the Prayer, and the appendix. Matthew, thinking in Aramaic, equates trespasses with debts (Ar. *ḥubhāh*, Syr. *ḥaubā'*) as he does in the parable of the Unmerciful Servant: and this gives him the neat play upon words, 'Forgive our ὀφειλήματα as we forgive our ὀφειλέταις', which would be impossible if he had used Mark's παραπτώματα. However in the appendix it is the παραπτώματα which are twice mentioned, a good instance of editor's fatigue.

That is all that the Marcan teaching on prayer can supply: but Jesus had taught his disciples to pray not only by precept but by

example. Above all the Church remembered his praying in Gethsemane. There too he had prayed, 'Abba', a prayer taken over in the
Pauline churches and used ecstatically, 'Abba, ὁ πατήρ',[24] the glossed
form in which Mark also gives the words at Gethsemane.[25] Matthew
renders this, πάτερ μου, Luke πάτερ, and indeed Luke's regular address
to God by Jesus is πάτερ: 'πάτερ, forgive them; for they know not what
they do',[26] 'πάτερ, into thy hands I commit my spirit'.[27] Since he
regularly avoids Matthew's cumbrous 'your Father who is in heaven',
it is natural for him to head his version of the Prayer with a stark
πάτερ, straight from Gethsemane.

At Gethsemane Jesus had prayed (Mark 14.36), 'Yet not what I
will, but what thou wilt.' Matthew gives his words twice, since Jesus
had gone away 'and prayed, saying the same words': the first time
close to Mark's wording, the second time, 'γενηθήτω τὸ θέλημά σου'.[28]
Here was the kernel of Christ's prayer, crystallized in his hour of
agony: and here too is his ideal prayer for all his disciples: γενηθήτω
τὸ θέλημά σου, ὡς ἐν οὐρανῷ καὶ ἐπὶ γῆς. γενηθήτω and θέλημα of God's
will are both Matthaeanisms, and so is the heaven-and-earth antithesis.

Jesus not only prayed in Gethsemane himself, he told his disciples
to pray ἵνα μὴ εἰσέλθητε εἰς πειρασμόν. Matthew puts the words into
oratio recta, μὴ εἰσενέγκῃς ἡμᾶς εἰς πειρασμόν, and supplies the
converse, 'but deliver us from the evil one.' His εἰσενέγκῃς is merely
a Greek Aphel: the Syriac has *teʿalûn* from *'al*, to enter, in the Gethsemane passage, and *taʿalan* from the Aphel, to cause to enter, in the
Prayer, and the same forms are available in Aramaic. The problem
James raises of the devil, not God, tempting men, occurs to Matthew
also. The evil one *is* the tempter, God is the ultimate power who may
permit or restrain him: 'Let us not enter temptation, but deliver us
from the Tempter.' Alas for so many attempts to make the words
mean tempting God, or the ultimate test: the apostles were to pray
against cowardice, haste, sloth, and apostasy, and so are we.
ὁ πονηρός is characteristic. Luke drops the obvious contrast: the
Lord's words to the Twelve in his dark hour were good enough for
him.

The Lord's Prayer was designed, as we have often been told, to
stand in two halves, three petitions for God's honouring, three for
our needs: and Matthew has set the Prayer in the context of a new
Sinai. Each half, therefore, opens with a petition recalling Exodus.
We have already seen that the first petition is a Christian restatement
of the Third Commandment: so far from taking God's name in vain,

[24] Gal. 4.6; Rom. 8.15. [25] Mark 14.36; Matt. 26.39ff; Luke 22.42.
[26] Luke 23.34. [27] Luke 23 46; cf. 15.12; 18, 21.
[28] Matt. 26.42.

we pray for its hallowing. The fourth petition likewise recalls the coming to Sinai. Then God had given manna enough for the coming day, and each day Israel's needs were supplied: now too the Christian prays, 'Give us today our bread for the coming day (τὸν ἐπιούσιον)' (AT). The word is unexampled, but ἡ ἐπιουσία means 'tomorrow', 'the coming day'. Maybe the Messianic banquet and the Eucharist are in view too: but the prime concern is for plain bread, one day at a time. Luke, more boldly, gives a present imperative and τὸ καθ' ἡμέραν: he remembered that the manna had come regularly and knew God to be dependable. καθ' ἡμέραν is Lucan.

All that is now unaccounted for is the second petition, 'ἐλθάτω ἡ βασιλεία σου'. This is no problem: the Sermon is Matthew's full version of Jesus' message, the εὐαγγέλιον of Mark 1.14 for the πτωχοί and πενθοῦντες of Isaiah; the good news that God's kingdom has drawn near. It has indeed, and is at work: the Church's yearning must be for its fullness, its coming in power—'Be come thy kingdom'. In the same sense the Pauline and pre-Pauline churches prayed, 'Maranatha', 'Come, Lord'.[29]

Matthew has thus composed a prayer that may properly be called the Lord's Prayer, since the greater part of it is his own prayers, and teaching on prayer. After the address God's name stands first, as is proper; and the first three petitions stand in elegant Matthaean symmetry, 'Be hallowed thy name, be come thy kingdom, be done thy will' (AT)—cf. 'Ask, and it shall be given you; seek and you will find . . .' The threefold rhythm with the climax a Marcan logion, 'Thy will be done', we have called a misthic rhythm, found only in Matthew (and once in Luke (Q)). In the second half the physical needs precede the spiritual, and each clause has its own balance: 'Give us today bread for the morrow, forgive us our debts as we forgive our debtors, bring us not to temptation but deliver us from the tempter' (AT). Everything Matthew touches he turns to gold; and this time he has been appreciated.

Luke concentrates on pithiness, a virtue less prized in Christendom. Matthew's address he reduces to a word. There is, we must own, no real distinction between God's kingdom coming and his will being done: let the first suffice, and let heaven-and-earth be forgotten for once. More clear than debts are sins, a favourite Lucan word: unfortunately he leaves ὀφείλω in the second half of the verse, to spoil the balance of the sentence, and to betray his Matthaean *Vorlage*. καὶ γάρ, αὐτοί, and πᾶς with anarthrous participle are semi-Lucan. His version is a marked improvement on Matthew's for brevity: but alas

[29] 1 Cor. 16.23.

for Matthew's rhythms and balances. A bulldozer has been through the garden.

6.19–21

So to the Last Commandment, formed like the others into an antithesis, but with its positive point the Marcan word to the Rich Man to give all and have treasure in heaven. The repetitive antithesis is of the thesauric pattern; cf. 10.28, '*Do not* fear those who kill the body but cannot kill the soul: *rather* fear him who can destroy both body and soul in hell'. There are eight such logia in Matthew, none in Mark, two in Luke (Q). The contrast between the perishable and the imperishable treasure is underlined. σής, the moth, is a common figure of destruction in the OT, including Isa. 50.9, the passage already used in the *Talio* section. It is one of the forty-four Matthaean animal images. βρῶσις may be a further animal image, as the word is used to translate '*ôkhēl*, the devourer, i.e. the grasshopper, in Mal. 3.11(A):[30] or, more traditionally, it may mean rust. The balancing of the mineral with the animal wasting agent would be more pointful, and more Matthaean. ἀφανίζει is a carry-over word. The word μισθός at the end of 5 suggested the theme of earthly and heavenly rewards in 6.1–18: the ruining of the face in fasting suggests the ruining of treasured silks and irons.[31] The human thief forms a further pair with the natural thieves—cf. the human enemy of the Tares alongside the natural enemies of the Sower. The thief digs through in Matt. 24.43 also, and κλέπτω is a Matthaean word, and image. 6.21 is one of Matthew's paragraph-closers, of the form, 'For where . . . there shall be . . .', which we have called aetics, cf. 'Wherever the body is, there the eagles will be gathered together.' There are seven instances in the Gospel, four of which close paragraphs. θησαυρός (3), οὐρανός/γῆ are semi-Matthaean, and ἐκεῖ ἔσται is Matthaean—9 typical words in all out of 49. Luke again throws away the wordy Matthaean contrast, and clarifies the meaning (12.33f). The Rich Man had been told to sell (πώλησον) all he had (τὰ ὑπάρχοντα—Matt. 19.21) and give (δός) to the poor, and he would have treasure in heaven. How then is a Christian to lay up treasure in heaven? He is to sell (πωλήσατε) his possessions (τὰ ὑπάρχοντα) and give (δότε) alms (semi-Lucan ἐλεημοσύνη); he is to make himself a lasting purse (Lucan βαλλάντια), treasure (θησαυρόν) that does not fail, cf. Luke 16.9, 'When the unrighteous Mammon fails (ἐκλίπῃ)'. ἐγγίζω is also on Hawkins' Lucan list. It is significant that the plural οὐρανοῖς occurs with certainty in Luke only here and

[30] Syr. has '*akhᵉlā*', both here and at Mal. 3.11.
[31] cf. σῶμα below, 6.22,25, linking two paragraphs.

at 18.22, the Rich Man pericope: it has become a familiar phrase from Matt. 19.21. Luke retains the plural ὑμεῖς throughout: Matthew switches to the singular for the final sentence as he does in the Fasting section preceding, and the judging section, and *passim*.

6.22–4

The theme of generosity recalls the Lord's warning in Mark 7.22 of the ὀφθαλμὸς πονηρός which defiles a man. Prov. 22.9 already speaks of the generous man as 'the good of eye' (*tôbh-'ayin*), but Matthew makes the meaning plain by writing ἁπλοῦς, the generous eye.[32] The light/lamp images run on from 5.14f, the eye/whole body images from the eye-for-eye and gehenna passages in 5; and the mean eye recurs in contrast with generosity in the Labourers in the Vineyard. 6.23 and 6.24 are both repetitive converse logia:[33] if A then B, if non-A then non-B; either hurt A and help B, or help A and hurt B—11 instances in Matthew, none in Mark, 9 in Luke (4Q). The Marcan 'mean eye' as usual forms the climax. Semi-Matthaean are ὀφθαλμός (3), οὖν (2), εἰ, ἔσται, πονηρός, σκότος (2), δύο, ἤ (2), κύριος of an earthly master: 14 characteristic words out of 72. Luke retains the Mammon epigram word for word, with the addition of οἰκέτης to link it to the context of the Steward, and other servants (16.1–9, 10–12, 13). As with the Beatitudes, he somewhat clumsily addresses the lamp logion to his reader: 'The lamp of the body is *your* eye' (AT). He shortens the light-and-darkness converse, realistically substituting 'when' for 'if': 'When thy eye is generous . . .'. Matthew deals in blacks and whites, Luke knows that Christians are sometimes generous, sometimes mean. Luke 11.36 is an adaptation of the unit to the missionary context in which Luke has set it: Jonah went and preached to the Ninevites, the lamp goes on the lampstand to light οἱ εἰσπορευόμενοι, your generosity will light all about you (ἔσται φωτεινὸν ὅλον) just as the lamp lightens you. ὡς = when is Lucan; καί = also (2), μὴ + part. and ἀστραπή are semi-Lucan; σκοπέω is only here in the Gospels.

6.25–34

If we have the generous eye then our whole σῶμα will be light: so we have no need to worry about the σῶμα being clothed, or its companion the ψυχή—here the inner man—being fed. God feeds the πραεῖς in Ps. 37: in the days of dearth they shall have enough. In Ps. 147 he takes up the πραεῖς and clothes (περιβάλλοντι) the heavens, he brings forth grass (χόρτος) on the mountains, and gives τροφή to the cattle and the young of the ravens that call upon him. How should a Christian then

[32] See p. 264 above.   [33] See p. 75 above.

worry? God has undertaken, as of old, to provide bread for the σήμερον as we pray: let the αὔριον look after itself. Harking back to 6.8, our heavenly Father knows that we have need of all these things. Here we are told we are of more value than the birds; at 10.31 than many sparrows; at 12.12 than a sheep. Harvest-imagery is Matthaean, especially the word συνάγω. So is the pairing of a male and female illustration—the birds and the lilies; two men in the field, two women grinding; the sleeping householder and the sleeping bridesmaids, the farmer with the mustard-seed, the woman with the meal. So is the pairing of animal and non-animal—the birds and the lilies, the moth and the rust, the sacrifice and the pearls, sheep and wolves with figs and thistles, sheep without a shepherd and a harvest without workers. Such pairing is rare in both Mark and L, though the sheep and coin in Luke 15 is an instance of both. The cubit-to-your-stature logion which divides the birds and the lilies is paralleled in thought and image by 10.30, 'The hairs of your head are all numbered', which divides the two sparrows logia: for the sentiment cf. 5.36. Cubits and miles, the only linear measures in the Gospels, are in Matthew. The poem, with its texture of antitheses woven into a clearly discernible strophe and antistrophe, is one of five in Matthew, with the Builders, the Children in the Market-place, Bethsaida and Capernaum, Jonah and Solomon: there is nothing of the kind in Mark, and all the Lucan forms are from Q. Solomon is a favourite OT figure to Matthew, foreshadowing Jesus in his glory and wisdom, in his Temple and his being the son of David: he does not occur in Mark, and is a figure of suspicion to Luke. The grass of the field is a standard rabbinic image of worthlessness: 'To King Jeroboam and Ahijah the Shilonite, all scholars were as the grass of the field.'[34] The final sentence, 'Sufficient to the day . . .' is an arcetic.[35]

Luke makes three minor changes to the rhythm of the poem (Luke 12.22–31): (*a*) of Matthew's triple, 'They neither sow nor reap nor gather into barns', he makes a double antithesis: 'They neither sow nor reap, they have neither store-house nor barn'.[36] Luke has perhaps the better rhythm here, but it is a little simple to argue priority therefrom: when a lesser poet edits a greater one, we should not expect him *always* to make the rhythm worse. As usual, Luke's store-house and barn are virtual synonyms.[37] τάμεια comes earlier in the same chapter

---

[34] B Sanh. 102a (R. Judah in the name of Rab).
[35] See p. 79 above.
[36] Luke elsewhere avoids a Matthaean row of three: see p. 336 below. Of the three triple rhythms isolated in ch. 4 above, poterics, scandalics, misthics, there was only one instance in L(7.44ff).
[37] See p. 295 above.

(12.3), also in editorial difference from Matthew; (*b*) at the opening of the antistrophe, Matthew has, 'And about clothing, why are you anxious?': Luke gives the somewhat prosaic, 'So if you cannot do even the least, why are you anxious for the rest?' (AT). λοιπός is semi-Lucan; (*c*) Matthew ends with his favourite *inclusio*, 'Therefore do not be anxious saying . . .', for which Luke gives, 'And do not seek what you are to eat or what you are to drink, nor be of anxious mind'. Luke tends to avoid μεριμνάω and reduces Matthew's six uses of it here to three: μετεωρίζεσθε is a synonym. Other signs of Lucan editorship are the insertion of the Lucan κατανοήσατε twice, and the avoidance of rhetorical questions three times (23, 24, 28), a Lucan habit. The ravens are specified instead of the general birds,[38] since it is they who are the object of divine providence in Ps. 147 which we have quoted, and in Job 38.41, and they are associated with it in the feeding of Elijah: fatigue leads him to reintroduce πετεινά at the end of the verse.

For the vocabulary of Matthew's version, the following are Matthaean; διὰ τοῦτο, τροφή, ἔνδυμα (2), your heavenly Father (2), συνάγω, ὀλιγοπιστός, δικαιοσύνη. Semi-Matthaean are μεριμνάω (6), οὐρανός, διαφέρω, λέγω ὑμῖν ὅτι, Σολομών, ὡς = like, εἰ, οὕτως, μὴ + aor. subj. (2), ἤ (2), ἔθνη, body-and-soul (2), οὐχί, ἄγρος (2), εἰς τούτων, βάλλομαι, περιβάλλω (2), οὖν, λέγοντες, ἀρκέω. Non-Matthaean are: καταμανθάνω, κρίνον, νήθω, κλίβανος, χρήζω, κακία. The linguistic evidence is strongly in favour of Matthaean authorship—54 characteristic words out of 183; and the rhythmical, doctrinal, and imaginative indications are all in the same direction.

7.1–6

The second Beatitude spoke of the πενθοῦντες, and I have shown that 7.1–6 gives three illustrations of going humbly. There is perhaps no obvious Marcan matrix to hand for the subject, but one can be adapted. Mark 4.21–3, the lamp and the bushel, has already been included in the Sermon: 4.24 runs (AT), 'With what measure you measure it shall be measured to you, and it shall be added to you (καὶ προστεθήσεται ὑμῖν)'. Now at 6.33 Matthew has had Jesus promise, καὶ ταῦτα πάντα προστεθήσεται ὑμῖν. It is natural therefore for his mind to run on to the earlier half of the logion, which can well be interpreted to mean, 'The way you treat others is the way you will be treated by God'. This understanding is then made clear by prefixing an epigram in the identical sentence-form: 'With what judgement you judge you shall be judged, and with what measure you measure it shall be

[38] For Luke's heightening of colour in animal imagery, see p. 101 above.

measured to you' (AT). Compare, 'Hallowed be thy name, Thy kingdom come, (Marcan climax) Thy will be done', 'Do not lay up for yourselves treasures on earth . . . but (Marcan climax) lay up for yourselves treasures in heaven'; or the whole class of three-line examples we have called misthics, as 'He who loves father or mother more than me . . ., He who loves son or daughter more than me . . ., (Marcan climax) He who does not take up his cross and follow me is not worthy of me' (10.37f). μὴ κρίνετε . . . then provides the lead-in to the double epigram, cf. μὴ θησαυρίζετε . . . μὴ δῶτε . . . The beam-and-mote figure is found in contemporary Judaism. R. Tarphon (c. A.D. 100) says, 'I should be surprised if anyone in this generation would accept correction. If one says to a man, "Remove the splinter from your eye", he will reply, "Remove the beam from yours." '[39] The image of the eye runs like a thread through the Sermon. For the hyperbolically great and small, cf. the Matthaean Solomon and the lily, 100d. and 10,000 talents—Matthew never spares contrasts of scale. For the impossible beam in the eye, compare the Matthaean swallowing of camels, and dead burying dead: Matthew never spares the hyperbole. We have said enough about the third illustration in 7.6. For the language, ὑποκριτής, τότε are Matthaean; semi-Matthaean are ὀφθαλμός (6), ἐρῶ, ἤ, ἀδελφός (3), ἐκβάλλω = bring out (3), ἔμπροσθεν, μὴ + aor. subj.: 18 typical words in all out of 107. Only here are δόκος, κάρφος, κατανοέω. The Lucan version contains two of Luke's four-item catalogues: judge not, condemn not, forgive, give; good measure, piled up, pressed down, running over. He has four such catalogues in thirty verses of the Sermon on the Plain, and they are not found in Mark or Matthew. Judging and condemning in this context are the same, and good measure *is* piled up: we contrast Matthew, whose judging and measuring are not the same. The generosity commended in Luke 6.38 interrupts the theme of not criticizing which is begun at 6.37, and resumed after further excursions at 6.41. For Luke's, 'How can you say to your brother, Brother . . .', cf. Luke 15.12, 'The younger of them said to his father, Father.' Semi-Lucan are σαλεύω, ἀπολύω = release (2), κόλπος, ἀντι-compounds, αὐτός.

7.7–12

So to the πτωχοὶ τῷ πνεύματι, and to prayer. Matthew has already written that God knows our needs before we ask (αἰτῆσαι), and that we should seek (ζητεῖτε) first his kingdom. Ask then, and it shall be given you; seek, and you will find. The poverty-stricken beg and scavenge, and they ask at the door too: knock, and it will be opened to you. For

[39] B Arak. 16b; S–B I, p. 446.

the triple rhythm, cf. 'I say to one, Go, and he goes . . .', 'There are eunuchs who were born so, made so, made themselves so', 'He that is angry, says Raka, says Fool,' There are 8 such triple rhythms in Matthew, 2 in Mark, 4 in Luke (3Q). More particularly we have been taught to pray for the coming day's bread: and surely our Father in heaven is more anxious to give us good gifts such as bread, than we poor parents to our children. The standard pair to bread is fish. Christ needed bread, and saw only loaf-shaped stones at his Temptation, so λίθος makes the antithesis to ἄρτος: what more suitable to go against the long, slippery, and nutritive fish than the long, slippery, and lethal snake? The antithesis is Matthew's perfect pardic form, 'Can the Ethiopian change his skin, or the leopard his spots?' 'If he asks him for bread, will he give him a stone, or if he asks for a fish, will he give him a snake?' The *a fortiori* argument of v. 11, 'If then you . . . how much more God . . .' is the rabbinic *qal waḥōmēr*, only found in Matthew and Q-Luke in the Gospels. The nutshell statement of v. 12 is the rabbinic *kᵉlāl*, also especially Matthaean. Linguistically Matthaean are: your Father-in-heaven, ὅσα ἐάν. Semi-Matthaean are: ἀνοίγω (2), λαμβάνω, ἤ (2), εἰ, πονηρός, οὖν (2), θέλω, νόμος, οἱ ἄνθρωποι = men, οὕτως—23 typical words out of 97. *Per contra* δόμα is only found here. In the Lucan version, κάθως and ὁμοίως are Lucan at 6.31, the Golden Rule: Luke always gives himself away. In the 11.9ff section he inserts the Lucan ὑπάρχοντες and the singular οὐρανοῦ. He makes the food in the *qal waḥōmēr* more interesting, in the Lucan tradition of colourfulness—egg and scorpion for bread and stone: at 10.19 also he pairs serpents and scorpions. But his improvements are, as always, at a price. It is bread which gives the thematic continuity with the Lord's Prayer; and the point of the paragraph, God's provision of the daily needs of the prayerful, is blurred by the intrusion of 'He will give the Holy Spirit' in 13. No doubt, to the author of Acts, the Holy Spirit is the highest of God's gifts, and that work is full of instances of God's gift of it to the prayerful Church: but that was not the point of Matthew's paragraph. The smoothness of the pardic goes too, with the introduction of ἀντὶ ἰχθύος: 'Which of you as a father will his son ask for a fish, and he for a fish will give him a snake?' (AT).

7.13–14

The Beatitudes are expounded: the fulfilment of the Law and the Prophets is sealed with the Golden Rule: Matthew turns to his peroration. The Rich Man had asked how to inherit eternal life (ζωή), and Jesus had grieved how hard it was for a rich man to enter (εἰσελθεῖν) God's kingdom, so that the apostles had wondered who then could be saved. εἰσέλθατε, begins Matthew, applying the obvious figures of the gate and the road: ἀπώλεια makes the antithesis with ζωή, and the πολλοί with the ὀλίγοι. The text including ἡ πύλη follows on more smoothly from 'Enter by the narrow gate', and is printed by Aland–Nestle, and BFBS: this would give the normal strong Matthaean antithesis, a broad gate and a wide road, a narrow gate and a cramped road: a further instance of the Matthaean converse repetitive logion, with every word including the two ὅτι's having its counterpart. διὰ (2), πύλη (2), and the πολύς/ὀλίγος antithesis are semi-Matthaean—6 words out of 42: the doctrine of the two ways is standard Jewish catechesis. Luke (13.23f) omits the two ways, and replaces the gate with a door: for he is putting together a series of Matthaean judgement-sayings, including a shortened version of the Bridesmaids, who stand outside and knock when the door (θύρα) has been shut (ἐκλείσθη), and say κύριε κύριε ἄνοιξον ἡμῖν, and are told οὐκ οἶδα ὑμᾶς. Push in now at the στένη θύρα, Luke reinterprets, before this happens: everyone forces his way into the kingdom at Luke 16.16 also. ἰσχύω and ζητέω are semi-Lucan.

7.15-20

The broad road is not merely there: Christians are being actually ushered down it by the antinomian false prophets who relax the Law; they come in the editorial passage 24.11 too, as well as at 5.19. Note the absence of δὲ at 7.15: there is no paragraph and the sense runs on.[40] Mark warned of ψευδοπροφῆται (13.22) and said they would lead many astray (ἀποπλανᾶν, Matt. πλανᾶν). This suggests the image of the straying sheep (cf. πρόβατον πλανώμενον 18.12f). The Christian is led through the broad wicket by what looks like a fellow-believer, but in fact one who is after his soul. The animal image is Matthaean, especially the sheep, and the sheep/wolves antithesis comes again at 10.16. ἔνδυμα is Matthaean too, as is the emphasis on works. The tree/fruit, ἀγαθός/πονηρός, καλός/σαπρός contrasts, and the tree being known (γινώσκεται) by its fruit, are all reproduced at 12.33ff, and are closely similar to the cutting down of the fruitless tree that stands in the mouth of John Baptist at 3.10. 'Do they gather grapes from thorns, or figs from thistles?' (AT) is a pardic. Linguistically συλλέγω is Matthaean: semi-Matthaean are ἤ, οὕτως, πῦρ, καρπὸν ποιεῖν, βάλλομαι, ἄραγε beside the contrast-words just mentioned—31 typical words out of 61. Luke (6.43ff) runs the good and bad treasure from the Matt. 12 context in

---

[40] Nestle–Aland and BFBS follow the sense of the Greek and print no new paragraph. The RSV and NEB translators, influenced by form–critical theory, make a new paragraph here, and often.

with the good and bad fruit: somewhat uncomfortably, for he is then left with the Matthew 12 moral, 'Bad will out'—'Out of the abundance of the heart the mouth speaks'—instead of the Matthew 7 moral which forms an *inclusio* at Matt. 7.20, 'Thus you will know them by their fruits'. Luke turns Matthew's rhetorical question, 'Do men gather . . .?' into a negative statement, as usual, replaces Matthew's ἀπό with his preferred ἐκ, and somewhat mars the epigram by adding a second verb τρυγῶσιν. τρυγάω is only here in the Gospels. The false prophets belong in the Matthaean Sermon, because Matthew has made it clear from the beginning that he is fighting a war on two fronts: the Pharisaic scribes on one side and the antinomian Christians on the other. Luke, who is not much concerned with antinomianism, has adapted this, not without some difficulty, to the theme of Christian hypocrisy in the preceding verses.

7.21–3

Mark not only warned of false-prophets; he said they would do signs and wonders (13.22). But, says his successor, it is neither words nor works but doing God's will that counts. Note the three-line climax in 22, 'Did we not prophesy in your name, and cast out demons in your name, and do many mighty works in your name?' It is the third line whose substance comes from Mark, cf. 'Be hallowed thy name, be come thy kingdom, be done thy will', and the other misthics. Their prophesyings can be inferred from their name, their exorcisms are a fill-in, the simplest of σημεῖα καὶ τέρατα. As for 21, 'Not everyone who says to me . . .', the question, 'What shall I *do* to inherit eternal life?', and the difficulty of *entering the kingdom* of God, have been the text of the Sermon from the beginning. Matthaean language includes: the kingdom of heaven, my Father in heaven, τότε, ἀνομία, δύναμις = miracle. Semi-Matthaean are ἐρῶ, σός (3), προφητεύω, θέλημα of God's will, κύριε (4), ὁμολογέω, ἐργάζομαι, γινώσκω of people—27 characteristic words out of 67. Luke (6.46) abbreviates the Lord, Lord logion: he cuts out most of the Matthaean phrases, but retains 'Lord, Lord' here, though he omits it at 12.35. There is a passage similar to 22f at Luke 13.26f, but without the false prophecy context. Eating-and-drinking are semi-Lucan. Luke drops the Semitic οὐδέποτε ἔγνων ὑμᾶς for οὐκ οἶδα πόθεν ἐστέ;[41] he approximates Matthew's quotation to the LXX Ps. 6.9 with ἀπόστητε and πάντες; but Matthew's emphasis on ἀνομία is uncongenial to him, and he replaces ἀδικία, a Lucan word.

[41] cf. Luke 10.22/Matt. 11.27 (*bis*). Matthew speaks of knowing people, Luke of knowing who they are (10.22) and where they come from (13.27).

7.24–7

We have said enough perhaps about the Two Builders in an earlier chapter. It is an indicative parable, not an imperative one, to show that it is doers and not sayers who will enter the kingdom of heaven, which is its subject (7.21). It is a human, not a nature parable. Its characters are colourless stock characters, wise and foolish, black and white contrasts. Luke (6.47ff) tries to make his men people, dropping the μωρός/φρόνιμος labels, having his first man digging and deepening and laying the foundation. Judgement comes on Matthew's builders like Noah's Flood—how suitable—rain from above, rivers from below, and the winds: Luke has, as ever, the more imaginable kind of disaster, a river bursting its banks. So Matthew has the grand scale and a great fall, while Luke keeps to the reasonable: and, by the same token, Matthew's straightforward sand and rock give a plain allegory for doing and not doing, while Luke's digging and the rest have no allegorical meaning. In all these ways Matthew is typical, and Luke is typical in so far as he amends Matthew. For language ὁμοιωθήσεται (2), φρόνιμος/μωρός are Matthaean: semi-Matthaean are οἱ-λόγοι-οὗτοι (2), ὅστις (3) πέτρα (2)—16 characteristic words out of 95. For imagery, the elements are Matthaean. For rhythm the strongly paralleled phrases of the Matthaean form are similar to Matthew's strophe–antistrophe poems, or crinics. Parables about building on rock are rabbinic, too: 'This is like a king who planned to build a palace. He dug in several places seeking proper ground for a foundation; at last he struck rock beneath, and said, Here will I build . . . Even so the Holy One, when he sought to create the world, examined the generation of Enosh and the generation of the Flood, and said, How can I create the world, when these wicked people will rise up and provoke me to anger? When he saw Abraham who was to arise, he said, Now have I found a rock on which to build and establish the world. For this reason he calls Abraham a rock (Isa. 51.1f).'[42] This parable may be very old: perhaps the two themes of Abraham and the Flood in it suggested to Matthew the rock and sand. Such would be speculation: but the Two Builders is so strongly characteristic of Matthew, and so distinct from the parable-types that we find in Mark and Luke, that it must be Matthew's own composition.

There, then, I will rest my case for the Sermon. Its structure is Matthew's structure, built on the twin foundations of the Pentecostal scriptures, Exod. 19ff, and the Marcan teaching on and about the Rich Man. Each of the eight Beatitudes which form the skeleton of the structure has three illustrations or subdivisions, and to each of

[42] Yalqut I. 766 (Num. 23.9); Moore, *Judaism* I, p. 538.

these, and to the paragraphs of the peroration, we can see an iron core of Marcan or Exodus teaching. The building between the structure is characteristic of the evangelist: in doctrine, in language, in rhythm, in imagery, in manner. The natural conclusion is that it is his own work. The house has been built on twin layers of rock, and the wise builder is Matthew.

APPENDIX TO
CHAPTERS 13 and 14
THE LAW FULFILLED

			Exod. 18	Mark 10.28	Isa. 61.1
Call of Four, Jesus' Preaching					

PENTECOST LECTION: EXOD. 19–20.23

			EXODUS	MARK	
Beatitudes	5.3–10		cf. Commandments I–X	10.29f	Isa. 61.1f
(8) Persecuted	5.11f	(a) Reward in heaven		10.30	
	5.13	(b) Salt of earth		9.50	
	5.14–16	(c) Light of Cosmos		4.21f	
	5.17–20	Law and Prophets fulfilled		13.31	
(7) Peacemakers	5.21f	(a) No anger, etc. (A1)	VI	10.19; 7.20ff	
	5.23f	(b) Reconciliation	20.24ff	11.25	
	5.25f	(c) Come to terms		11.25	
(6) Pure in Heart	5.27ff	(a) No lust (A2)	VII	9.43–7	
	5.31f	(b) No remarriage (A3)	Deut. 24	10.2ff	
	5.33f	(c) No false oaths (A4)	(IX)		Ps. 24.6 Isa. 66.1
(5) Merciful	5.38ff	(a) No *talio* (A5)	21.24 22.25ff	14.65; 15.21ff	Isa. 50.6f
	5.43ff	(b) No hatred (A6)	(X) 22.26; 23.5ff	12.31	
	6.1ff	(c) Mercy in secret (B1)			Isa. 26.20 2 Kgs. 4.23
(4) Hunger and Thirst for Righteousness	6.5ff	(a) Pray in secret (B2)	(III) 16.4ff	12.40	
	6.9ff	(b) Lord's Prayer		11.25; 14.36–8	
	6.16ff	(c) Fast in secret (B3)			
(3) Meek	6.19ff	(a) Treasure in heaven (C)		10.21	Ps. 37
	6.22ff	(b) Generous Eye		7.22	
	6.25ff	(c) No anxiety	23.30	4.24	Ps. 147
(2) Mourners	7.1f	(a) No judging		4.24	
	7.3ff	(b) No reproving			
	7.6	(c) No backbiting	22.31f		
(1) Poor in Spirit	7.7ff	Ask, seek, knock			
	7.12	Law and Prophets in a Kelal			
Peroration			cf. 23.20ff		
	7.13f	(a) Two ways		10.17, 24ff	Ps. 1
	7.15ff	(b) False Prophets		13.22; 10.17	
	7.24ff	(c) Two Builders	23.22		Isa. 51.1f

15

THE WORKS OF MESSIAH REJECTED
(8—9, 12)

Pentecost is over, and the next celebration in the Jewish–Christian Year is the Tishri Festal Season, New Year–Atonement–Tabernacles. The Festal Season is as ambivalent to the Jew as Advent is to the Christian, at once a season of joyful expectation and of penitence. New Year looks forward to the establishment of the New Age, when the kingdom of the heavens will be inaugurated, and God will reign in fact. Pss. 93, 97, 99, opening 'Yahweh is king' had been among the New Year psalms in earlier centuries,[1] and the *Malkûyôt*, ten verses from scripture on God as king, were part of the New Year liturgy by the time of the Mishnah.[2] The *shôfār* was blown as a signal for the beginning of God's reign,[3] and formed the distinctive part of the New Year ritual. Gen. 21—22, the New Year *sidrôt*, look back on God's first 'remembering' of his people, and forward to the day when he will remember them at last.[4] Isa. 35, one of the New Year *haphtārôt*,[5]

---

[1] The place of these psalms in the New Year festival in the monarchical period was emphasized by S. Mowinckel in *Psalmenstudien* II (Kristiania 1922), and is accepted by H–J. Kraus, A. Weiser, J. H. Eaton, and others. I am not here concerned with Mowinckel's controversial translation, and reconstruction of the ritual.

[2] M R.H. 4.5.

[3] The Son of Man similarly ushers in the New Age by sending out his angels with a blast on the *shôfār* of heaven (Matt. 24.31; 1 Thess. 4.16; 1 Cor. 15.52). In the Apocalypse, when the seventh trumpet is blown there are voices in heaven saying, 'The kingdom of the world has become the kingdom of our Lord, and of his Christ' (11.15).

[4] T Meg. III.6; B Meg. 31a; J Meg. III.7; Büchler, art. cit., p. 430.

[5] It is likely that in the formative period of the Hebrew canon (sixth to fourth centuries) five alternative books of 'Prophets' were in use as *haphtārāh* lessons (Histories, Isaiah, Jeremiah, Ezekiel, the XII), and that the arrangement of the oracles in the latter four was in part for liturgical convenience, in the same way as I have argued above for the Chronicler. This would account for the breaks at Isa. 34—39 and Jer. 30—31. Isaiah was read from the beginning of the year in Nisan: 34—35 celebrated the expected New Age at New Year; 36—39 describe the mighty acts of Yahweh in Isaiah's time, as a part of the rehearsal of the mighty acts of Yahweh at Tabernacles; there is a penitential section for Atonement in 38; and the position of the section in the book, with 33 chapters before and 27 after, corresponds with the position in the year of the Festal Tishri Season — 1—33, half the book in half the year. When the *haphtārôt* were finally fixed (in the Amoraic period), verbal and thematic links with the sidrah were prized, and God's remembering of Hannah (1 Sam. 1—2.10) took the parallel

describes the New Age: the blossoming of the desert, the coming of God to save, the healing of the blind and deaf and lame, the joy of the Holy Way. Jer. 31.2–20, another,[6] tells similarly of the joy coming when Yahweh saves Israel and brings his sons home to Sion. At the same time the New Age means judgement for all, and the more sombre themes of penitence in face of judgement were to the fore in the practice of mishnaic Judaism.[7]

Matthew believed that the New Age had begun with Jesus, and that Rosh-hashshanah was the season for proclaiming, and for pointing to the signs of, the inbreaking of the Kingdom of Heaven. Jesus had indeed wrought the signs of the kingdom: he had healed the blind and deaf and lame, and the Gospel of Mark had been largely filled with such wonders. It is therefore open to him to fill the sabbaths between Pentecost and New Year with the Marcan healing stories, and then to provide Discourses (10—11) to teach their significance. As in 1—7, a story can be supplied for each bye-sabbath, and a teaching discourse can crown the feast. But as the years went by, an improvement upon the Marcan order of healings would suggest itself. In some of the healing incidents Jesus had spoken harsh words in judgement of the scribes and others who had rejected his message and attacked his healing work, especially in connection with the sabbath-laws—notably in the incidents of the Cornfield, of the Man with the Withered Hand, and the Beelzebul controversy (Mark 2.23—3.6; 3.22–30). These belong best at the New Year–Atonement period when judgement and penitence are the prescribed liturgical themes, and it was in fact in these opening weeks of Tishri that they were read in the Marcan church.[8] What Matthew has done, therefore, is to borrow the remaining healing stories forward, and to leave the controversial incidents in their traditional Tishri setting. He will then be able to proclaim the healing of the blind, deaf/dumb, and lame at New Year,[9]

---

place to Gen. 21, God's remembering of Sarah. Jer. 31 took preference over the other prophetic readings for the second day.

Isa. 35.5f not only underlies Matt. 11.5, and so would seem a *possible* New Year *haphtārāh* in the first century A.D.: it also underlies Luke 7.22, which falls on New Year in the Lucan cycle (see below, appendix to ch. 21); and at John 5 'there lay a multitude of invalids, blind, lame, paralyzed' at 'the feast of the Jews', i.e. the Tishri festal season. So Luke and John also associate Isa. 35 with New Year, and its use as *haphtārāh* then may be considered established.

[6] B Meg. 31a.   [7] See p. 175 above.

[8] See above, ch. 9, appendix B.

[9] The dependence of the healing series upon the logion in 11.5/Isa. 35.5f has been a common speculation since B. Weiss, *Das Matthäusevangelium und seine Lukas-Parallelen* (Halle 1876), and Wellhausen, *Das Evangelium Matthaei* (Berlin 1904): what has not been available is a convincing reason why these two texts should be determinative.

since such healings had taken place without marked controversy, and go on to emphasize the judgement theme in the context of the battles of Mark 2—3.

In the meantime the only liturgical occasion is the Ninth Ab, the Fast for the fall of Jerusalem. The ideal lesson for that occasion will be the Lord's teaching on the Church's coming need to fast in Mark 2.18–22: and this must therefore be separated from the Cornfield incident which follows it in Mark 2, for Ninth Ab is seven weeks before New Year. For New Year itself Matthew provides two discourses, one in 10, one in 11. New Year is both the joyful proclamation that the kingdom of heaven is coming, and the call to penitence at judgement. Jesus' own preaching of the inauguration of the kingdom belongs at the beginning of his ministry, and has already been told at 4.17. This message had been a part of the opening section of Mark, and had been read at New Year in the Marcan church:[10] and it is indeed the Christian fulfilment of New Year. Matthew falls back therefore on an excellent second best: in Mark 6 Jesus had sent out the Twelve to preach that men should repent, and Matthew develops this commissioning into a major discourse, at the head of which is written, 'Preach as you go, saying, The kingdom of heaven is at hand.' For the themes of penitence and judgement, 11 reveals Jesus' healings as the works of Messiah, and grieves at the perversity of this generation, and the impenitence of the cities that had witnessed the works. At both the main festal seasons, in Nisan and in Tishri, Matthew has two discourses: here 10 and 11, there 23 and 24—25.

Matthew is faced, then, with the following liturgical framework:

(Easter V	John, Baptism, Temptations	Mark 1.1–14)
(Easter VI	Preaching, Call of Four	1.15–20)
Pentecost	Sermon on the Mount	(7.28f = Mark 1.22)
Eight Saturdays		
Ninth Ab, and Saturday	Call of Matthew, Fasting	2.13ff
Four Saturdays		
N.Y. Saturday, and Saturday Next		
Before N.Y.	Discourses	Mark 6.7ff
Two first Saturdays in Tishri and		
Atonement	Controversy stories	2.23—3

He has thus two series of 'blanks' to fill, eight before and four after Ninth Ab, and the wealth of the Marcan healing tradition on which to draw for the purpose.

Jesus' healing ministry had been set forth in Mark as the 'saving', among others generally referred to, of twelve representative Israelites,

---

[10] See above, ch. 9, appendix B.

and one additional Gentile.[11] So is symbolized the Lord's ministry of bringing total salvation to the Twelve Tribes of Israel, while not excluding the peoples of the world besides. But a symbolism strung out over ten chapters is easily missed; and Matthew concentrates the whole twelve into a healing 'tractate',[12] so that the hearer may grasp it the more easily. No churchman can count the healings of twelve Israelites in successive weeks, and indeed the recounting of so many wonders on end would be tedious. The series requires subdivision. The natural subdivisions in a series of twelve will be two fives and a two, and this arrangement can square satisfactorily with the liturgical 'blanks'. There can be five Israelites healed before Ninth Ab, five more before New Year, and the two controversial healings, the Withered Hand and the 'Beelzebul' demoniac, between New Year and Atonement. This will involve a number of minor adjustments to the Marcan stories:

1. The Beelzebul incident took place in Mark as a reaction to Jesus' exorcisms in general, and not in face of any specific sufferer. It is necessary, therefore, to form a composite story[13] by transferring the details of another healing, and Matthew makes the possessed and deaf and dumb boy of Mark 9.14–29 the background of the controversy.

2. There are only four Saturdays after Ninth Ab if we are to have New Year expounded in a double discourse. But since some of the healings Jesus did are, in a sense, duplicates, this can be solved by putting the two blind men similarly into a composite story, and Matthew simply makes the blind man of Mark 8.22ff a pair with the

---

[11] A. M. Farrer, *St Matthew and St Mark*, ch. III. I am much indebted to the thesis of this chapter, which I have adapted and amplified. Farrer first proposed the thesis in 1951 in *A Study in St Mark*. It was objected, (*a*) that there is no check on symbolic imaginings, which may so easily be pictures in the fire, and (*b*) that if Farrer were right it is singular that there is no reference to the symbolism in subsequent literature. Farrer countered in 1954 with *St Matthew and St Mark*, in which he showed that the same pattern could be seen, with slight adjustments, in Matthew, the first commentator on Mark; and also in Luke, the second. It was objected that the imagination which could descry numerical symbolism in Mark might see the same picture in any fire. Farrer argues the case most convincingly in his posthumous (unpublished) *St Mark's Material*. He never changed the central outline of the healing-and-calling symbolical interpretation. For contrasting comments on Farrer's thesis see F. N. Davey's review in *JTS* III.2 (October 1952); R. P. Casey's in *Theology* (October 1952); and Professor Helen Gardner's *The Limits of Literary Criticism* (London 1956).
[12] cf. Matthew's 'tractates' of harvest parables, Pharisaic hypocrisy, etc. He has the Mishnaic mind; cf. p. 27 above.
[13] See pp. 44ff above.

blind man of Mark 10.46ff, glossing the details of the two stories together.

3. Since Isaiah foretold that in the New Age the eyes of the blind would be opened and the ears of the deaf unstopped, Matthew brings his tale of healings to a climax before New Year with the blind men (9.27–31) and the deaf μογιλάλος of Mark 7.31ff (9.32–4). These can be preceded by the linked stories of the Woman with Haemorrhage (9.18–22) and the Ruler's Daughter (9.23–6); the latter is the most dramatic of all the Marcan healings, and therefore a claimant to a place among the second five.

4. The essence of any 5 + 5 + 2 scheme is that the two fives should run in parallel, for otherwise they will pass unnoticed. Now the Leper of Mark 1 is a pair to the Woman with Haemorrhage of Mark 5 by virtue of the Levitical taboos upon the two illnesses. The law of the leper is to be found in Lev. 13—14, the law of sexual haemorrhage in Lev. 15.25: the two are bracketed together by Moses, and read on the same sabbath under the heading *M^etsōrā'* (Leper). Matthew therefore alters the Marcan order and promotes the Leper to first place in the first five, parallel to the Woman who is first in the second five. Similarly Simon's mother-in-law, raised from her bed of fever, may seem to be a lesser version of the synagogue ruler's daughter, raised from her bed of death. The leper was the third, Simon's mother-in-law the second healing in the Marcan order. Mark's first sufferer was the Demoniac in the Synagogue, and Matthew deals neatly with him by combining him with the Demoniac in the Tombs, thus forming a composite pair of possessed men to balance the composite pair of blind men. The only remaining healing from Mark is the Paralytic, who is suitably the climax of the first five, since the leaping of the lame was also a part of Isaiah's prophecy. This gives a satisfactory pattern which he who runs may read:

(a)	*Levitical uncleanness* 8.1–4　　The Leper	9.18–22　Woman with Haemorrhage
(b)	*Woman Raised* 8.14–15　Simon's Mother-in-Law	9.23–6　Synagogue Ruler's Daughter
(c)	*A Pair of Shouting Men Healed* 8.28–34　Two Demoniacs	9.27–31　Two Blind Men
(d)	*The Lame and the* κωφός 9.1–8　　The Paralytic	9.32–4　The Possessed κωφός

The leper follows on directly from Pentecost, the Ninth Ab reading (9.9–17) directly divides the two fives, the New Year discourses follow on directly from the possessed κωφός. That such a categorization was in Matthew's mind is evident not only from the general arrangement, and numerous small details to be commented on shortly, but from the actual words of 11.5 with which Matthew adapts the Isaiah text: 'The blind receive their sight (*c*), and the lame walk (*d*1), the lepers are cleansed (*a*) and the deaf hear (*d*2), and the dead are raised up (*b*)—the greatest healing of all—and the poor are evangelized (the Sermon on the Mount).' All four categories are expressly mentioned, and the two members of (*d*), which are not a proper pair, are both mentioned specifically.

5. It was an important part of Mark's message that the healing work of Christ included the giving of crumbs to a Gentile: which very thing Matthew was also eager to do. The Syrophoenician woman's daughter cannot be transferred to Matthew's tractate as she stands, for she belongs in Syrophoenicia: but he requires a Gentile healing to make plain the symbolism of twelve Israelites healed and a Gentile. The gospel of salvation had come first to the Jew and then to the Greek: so he opens his tale of healings with first a Jew and then a Gentile, the faithful Centurion's Boy making a double with the faithful Canaanite Woman's girl later on in the Gospel. He has thus three healings in a row to begin the period Pentecost—Ninth Ab, the Leper, the Centurion's Boy, and Simon's Mother-in-Law: and three to end, the Two Demoniacs and the Paralytic. The interval is partly filled with the Marcan crossing of the Lake, which preceded the Demoniac in the Tombs, and partly with other material.

6. Matthew has thus twelve Israelites and a Gentile in his healing section, and they are, as I hope shortly to show, the thirteen Marcan healings: abbreviated, compounded, and elaborated, but the same stories.

1.	Mark	1.23	Demoniac in Synagogue (3)	1.	Matt. 8.1	Leper (3)
2.		1.29	Simon's Mother-in-Law (2)	(G.	8.5	Centurion's Boy (G, 4))
3.		1.40	Leper (1)	2.	8.14	Simon's Mother-in-Law (2)
4.		2.1	Paralytic (5)	3,4	8.28	Two Demoniacs (1,6)
5.		3.1	Withered Hand (11)	5.	9.1	Paralytic (4)
6.		5.1	Demoniac in Tombs (4)	6.	9.18	Woman with Haemorrhage (7)
7.		5.21	Woman with Haemorrhage (6)	7.	9.23	Ruler's Daughter (8)
8.		5.35	Jairus' Daughter (7)	8,9	9.27	Two blind Men (10,12)
(G.		7.24	Syrophoenician's Girl (G))	10.	9.32	Possessed κωφός (9)
9.		7.31	μογιλάλος (10)	11.	12.9	Withered Hand (5)
10.		8.22	Blind Bethsaidan (8)	12.	12.22	Blind, Dumb, and Possessed Man (11)
11.		9.14	Deaf and Dumb Possessed Boy (12)			
12.		10.46	Blind Bartimaeus (9)			

The numbers in parenthesis refer to the position in order in the other Gospel.

7. The 12 + 1 symbolism is thus conveyed with considerable skill. Arrived at the Day of Atonement no Matthaean Christian can have missed the teaching that Messiah had come to heal all Israel, but that

Israel had been scandalized at his works: however he had foreshadowed the salvation of the Gentiles also. But what becomes of this neat symbolism as we progress through the Gospel and reach first the Canaanite Woman, then the possessed boy and finally two more blind men? For these sufferers were intractably set in later stages of the mission, the Canaanite in Phoenicia, the boy at the foot of the Mount of Transfiguration, Bartimaeus at Jericho: no evangelist could tell the story of the Lord's coming to these places and leave them out. Well, such is Matthew's skill that in fact he has the symbolism twice over. In 8—12 he gives us twelve Israelites healed and a Gentile, but, since two of the sufferers are in pairs, there are only ten Israelite healing miracles. The possessed boy is an eleventh, and the blind men at Jericho a twelfth. We have thus *twelve Israelites* (and a Gentile) *healed* in the tractate, and *twelve Israelite healings* (and two Gentile healings) in the Gospel.

It is not to be supposed that all this was planned by the evangelist in his study. It was the result of years of trial and error, arrangement and rearrangement, in actual liturgical practice. Some such theory as I have just suggested seems to be required by changes from Mark which Matthew has made, and it does not demand a sophistication in advance of the age of the Gospel. We cannot suppose it to be accidental that the fasting lection and the two discourses 10—11 so exactly fit the calendar, and these must be primary considerations: for the rest we have either to account for the Matthaean healing order, or suppose that he changed Mark at random, an unlikely and unprofitable hypothesis.

With so much preamble, we turn to observe Matthew's working in detail.

7.28–9

Matthew closes the Sermon with a rubric, and the crowds are carried over from 5.1: but their amazement at his teaching, and his un-scribal authoritativeness, are drawn from Mark 1.22. It is important to note how closely Matthew is following Mark. The Sermon has been a full statement of the εὐαγγέλιον of Mark 1.14f, the blessedness of those who leave all for discipleship (1.16–20): it is fitly sealed off with the people's wonder of the next verses. We note, '. . . not as *their* scribes': there are good scribes and bad, and the Church has good scribes.[14]

---

[14] See p. 13 above.

(6)[15]*The Leper 8.1–4*

The leper's healing, brought forward for the reasons we have given, is told nearly in Mark's words, but abbreviated by about a third. The Marcan injunction to silence is retained, providing a somewhat comical contrast with the ὄχλοι πολλοί whom Matthew has brought down the mountain in 8.1—such minor muddles are not untypical.[16] Matthew introduces his characteristic 'worshipped' and κύριε, and omits both ὀργισθείς and ἐμβριμησάμενος, all from motives of reverence: δῶρον, λέγων, and προσελθών are also Matthaean.

(7) *The Centurion's Boy 8.5–13*

The leper is succeeded in Mark by the paralytic. Matthew is opening his line of healings with a bold contrast: Jew, Gentile. But Mark's Gentile healing is the Greek woman's daughter, which belongs later in the story, so what Matthew does here is to make her the basis of a new compendium healing, combined with Mark's paralytic: as I have suggested in ch. 2 above[17] and shall shortly instance again. The site of the miracle, Capernaum, and the nature of the complaint, paralysis, he therefore takes over from the next following healing in Mark: the new patient is, as in Mark 2.1ff, a paralytic in a house in Capernaum, and the detail of the Marcan sufferer being let down through the roof (στέγην) is made the subject of midrash, 'I am not worthy that you should come under my roof (στέγην)'. Matthew gives Mark's opening phrase in full (AT): Mark 2.1, 'And as he entered again into Capernaum . . .': Matt. 8.5, 'And as he entered into Capernaum . . .'. Later he will give a shortened account of the Mark 2.1ff healing: only that, since he has already recorded Jesus' entry into Capernaum here, he will write, 'He came to his own city' (9.1), and he will omit the detail of the roof. It is standard Matthaean usage to give a Marcan incident virtually whole in its place, and to borrow forward details for another story.[18]

The centurion as protagonist is suggested by the fact of a centurion having confessed Jesus to be the Son of God at the cross. If a Gentile centurion could believe then, when the sons of the kingdom were responsible for the crucifixion, surely such might be the man whose faith could draw a mighty work from the hands of the Lord, and deserve his praise. It is also true that the leper and the paralytic are tied together

---

[15] The numbers in parenthesis are those given in Alexandrinus and other Mss.; see above, ch. 9, and the table in appendix A.
[16] See p. 35 above.
[17] See pp. 44f above.   [18] See pp. 36f above.

by the type of Naaman, the Gentile soldier–leper of the Old Testament.[19]

For the rest, the main outline of the story is determined by the Gentile woman's daughter, for which the Gentile man's son is the natural pair. παῖς in Matthew normally means a son, not a slave.[20] δοῦλος is used in this story for the centurion's servant (v. 9), and the latter has been adopted as the title for the story thanks to Luke, who was the first to make the mistake. Thus we have a father interceding for his son ill at home, grievously tormented, in place of a mother interceding for her daughter ill at home, badly possessed. The emphatic ἐγώ at the beginning of 8.7 shows that the sentence is a question, and not a statement, as traditionally translated: 'Am I (a Jew, the fulfiller of the Law) to go and heal him?'[21] Thus Jesus baulks at the Gentile father's intercession, as at the Gentile mother's, 'I was sent only to the lost sheep of the house of Israel'. But humility and faith overmaster the Lord's proper reluctance. The centurion holds himself unfit to have Jesus come to his house; the woman compares herself to the dogs beneath the table. Both have trust that the Lord's word can answer their child's need. And so it is: both children are healed by the Lord's word at a distance, the only two miracles of remote healing in the Gospel, and especially fit for Gentiles, to whom Jesus had no direct ministry. In both stories Jesus gives an extraordinary commendation of the parent's faith: 'O woman, great is your faith', 'Not even in Israel have I found such faith.' Jesus' words of healing, and the evangelist's note of their efficacy, are virtually identical in the two stories (AT): 'As you have believed, so be it for you; and the boy was healed in that hour',' So be it for you as you desire: and her daughter was healed from that hour.'

The remaining details of the story do not come from Mark, and might be taken as evidence of independent tradition if they were not so typical of Matthew. The threefold, slightly obvious, illustration of the centurion's authority is Matthew's scandalic:[22]

---

[19] Naaman is mentioned as the type of Christ's healings in Luke 4.27, and seems also to be in mind in John 9.7. Luke often makes explicit what is implicit in Matthew, e.g. Matt. 24.40 'Then shall be two in the field . . .' becomes a stanza on Lot based on the preceding Matthaean stanza on Noah; cf. Farrer, *St Matthew and St Mark*, p. 45.

[20] This is clearly the meaning at 2.16; 17.18 ('The boy was healed'); 21.15. At 12.18, the citation of Isa. 42.1, παῖς means 'servant' in the LXX and Matthew knew that was what the Hebrew meant, but he deliberately exploits the ambiguity, replacing 'I will help him' with 'whom I adopted', and paralleling 'my beloved one'. In 14.2 Herod addresses his παῖδες, which presumably means his servants rather than his sons.

[21] So NEB mg, McNeile, Lohmeyer, Zahn, H. J. Held, *TIM*, p. 194.

[22] See p. 81 above.

I say to one, Go, and he goes, and
to another, Come, and he comes,
and to my slave, Do this, and he
does it.

cf. Ask, and it shall be given you,
Seek, and you will find, Knock,
and it shall be opened to you.

The coming of the Gentiles into the kingdom from east and west
occurs several times in scripture, notably Isa. 59.19, 'They of the west
shall fear the name of the Lord, and they of the rising of the sun his
glorious name' (LXX). The healing is thus openly made a symbol of
the Gentile mission foretold in the OT. The antithesis between the
saved Gentiles and the rejected Jews is drawn with customary sharp-
ness.[23] Verses 12 and 13 consist almost entirely of Matthaean phrases:
'the sons of the kingdom', 'will be thrown into outer darkness: there
men will weep and gnash their teeth', γενηθήτω, ἐκείνη ἡ ὥρα. Other
Matthaean language is: προσῆλθεν, μόνον, the kingdom of heaven.
Semi-Matthaean are: ἑκατόνταρχος (3), λέγων, κύριε (2), παῖς = child
(3), anarthrous λέγει, ἐλθών, θεραπεύω, φημί, πορεύομαι (2), δοῦλος,
ἀμὴν λέγω ὑμῖν, Ἰσραήλ, λέγω ὑμῖν ὅτι, ἀνατολή, βάλλομαι: in all 46
words characteristic of Matthew out of 165. The only non-Matthaean
word is δεινῶς. Once it is accepted that composing compendium
miracle stories is a Matthaean trait, there seems negligible evidence to
suggest an independent tradition for the story.

Luke (7.1ff) retells Matthew's tale, taking the παῖς of 8.6 to be the
δοῦλος of 8.9: and assimilating it to the episode of Cornelius, the
centurion of Acts. Luke knew what Matthew was doing, and carries
the process a stage further. As Cornelius sent (ἀπέστειλεν) messengers
to Peter,[24] so does the centurion of Luke's Gospel send (ἀπέστειλεν) to
the Lord. Cornelius is a righteous and godfearing man, well-spoken
of by all the ἔθνος of the Jews: so is his Gospel counterpart reported
by the Jewish elders as worthy for Jesus to do this service, 'for he loves
our ἔθνος, and he built us our synagogue'. Cornelius was the turning-
point of Acts, the first Gentile in the Church: how proper that his
conversion should be foreshadowed by Christ's grace to a similar
centurion in his lifetime.

Once the Lucan centurion is seen as a synagogue-builder with
sickness at home, the pattern of the Jairus healing asserts itself, as
Jairus was a synagogue elder in a similar predicament. A second party
comes accordingly, to say, κύριε, μὴ σκύλλου, as Jairus was followed
by a second party saying, τί ἔτι σκύλλεις τὸν διδάσκαλον;[25] the centurion's faith echoes Jairus'. Thereafter fatigue develops, and he
copies Matthew faithfully. The replacement of the Jews by those
from the east and west he saves for a better context in 13.

[23] cf. 21.43; 22.1–10. [24] Acts 10.8,22.
[25] Mark 5.35.

(8) Peter's Mother-in-Law 8.14–15

(9) The Sick at Evening 8.16–18

Two short lections follow: Simon's wife's mother, as the second healing in Mark, and the Sick at Evening, as following Simon's wife's mother in Mark. The scriptural justification, from Isaiah, is standard in Matthew for any new departure. Jesus casts out the demons 'with a word', and he healed the Centurion's son λόγῳ: a further instance of a carry-over word.[26] Mark has 'they brought to him all who were sick . . . and he healed many': Matthew reverses the adjectives for reverence.

(10) Two Claimants to Discipleship 8.19–22

After healing the sick at evening in Mark, Jesus left Capernaum. Matthew is going to insert the whole second series of Jesus' wonders from Mark 4.35—5 beginning from now, so he has Jesus leave the evening throng as at Mark 1.35, and command to go εἰς τὸ πέραν as at Mark 4.35. However, he should not reach the end of the first series of five Israelites healed till Lection 13, before Ninth Ab, so he has one lection in hand, which he proceeds to fill by a midrash on Mark's Storm.[27] Mark says (4.36) that other boats were with him, so clearly other people wished to follow Christ, and Matthew provides details of two of them. Mark says also that Jesus was asleep on a pillow (4.38 προσκεφάλαιον), but that the disciples awoke him. Matthew draws out the hardness of Jesus' lot by his words, 'The Son of Man has nowhere to lay his head (κεφαλή)'. Both of these details are omitted when Matthew gives the Stilling of the Storm in Lection 11. The first of the intending followers is a scribe, a calling, as we have seen, favoured by Matthew. He is offering to follow Christ to the other side[28] (ὅπου ἐὰν ἀπέρχῃ) like Mark's 'other boats'. Jesus' reply involves a pair of Matthaean animal images[29]—foxes and birds; and its form is the Matthaean pardic—'The foxes have holes, and the birds of heaven nests'; 'Can the Ethiopian change his skin, or the leopard his spots?' The birds of heaven and their nests are suggested by the preceding passage in Mark, 4.32. The beasts, the birds, Jesus, suggests Adam, in authority in paradise, and so the Son of Man, now in weakness. The Marcan suggestion of 'nowhere to lay his head'

---

[26] cf. p. 301 above.
[27] cf. pp. 32f above. Matthew similarly composes the Two Sons in the Vineyard out of the immediately following vineyard parable (21.28ff, 33ff).
[28] ἀπέρχομαι most naturally means to 'leave (for)': so McNeile, and perhaps Fenton. It is used in this sense in the preceding verse.
[29] See pp. 101f above.

forms the proper climax. The inspiration of the Storm is now exhausted, but the 'other boats' presuppose at least one more would-be disciple. Matthew has recourse to scripture: was not Elijah also driven from pillar to post, and did he not call Elisha from the plough?[30] Elisha requested, 'Let me kiss my father and my mother, and then I will follow you', and received a dusty answer. So Matthew's second disciple requests that he may first go and *bury* his father, kiss him a permanent farewell. Elijah might seem a hard master not to permit a filial good-bye, but to await one's father's demise must seem half-heartedness, and Jesus' stern reply the more reasonable. 'Leave the dead to bury their own dead' is the machaeric rhythm;[31] cf. 'For all who take the sword will perish by the sword', 'Freely you have received, freely give' (AT). Matthaean language includes προσελθών, εἷς = τις, a good γραμμάτευς; semi-Matthaean are κύριε, θάπτω (2). κλίνω is non-Matthaean. There are 6 characteristic words out of 69.

Luke moves the incident to a more suitable general context: after Jesus' rejection by the Samaritans, and before the Sending of the Seventy: he adds a third aspirant, drawing also on the Elisha story with 'No one who puts his hand to the plough and looks back . . .'.[32] Two small touches show Luke's handiwork besides: the second man in Matthew presupposes an invitation by his, 'Lord, let me *first* go . . .'. Luke smoothes this by supplying the 'Follow me' before his request instead of after, as it is in Matthew. Secondly, both Matthaean and Lucan contexts are concerned with discipleship, and not apostleship, but Luke's mind is turning to the sending out of the Seventy in Luke 10: he therefore adds, 'but as for you, go and proclaim the kingdom of God', which is in direct contradiction to the 'Follow me' of 9.59.[33]

There is no question of the *bona fides* of the postulants in Matthew. Just as in Mark the other boats were with Jesus, intending to accompany him, but presumably separated in the storm, so Matthew's scribe is wholehearted, and his 'other disciple' only seems to be less so owing to the shadow of Elisha. But in 8.23 we are told, 'And when he got into the boat, his disciples followed him'. μαθηταί follows on from 21, ἠκολούθησαν from 22.

(11) The Stilling of the Storm 8.23–7

The story is abbreviated from Mark by about a quarter, partly in view of the details used in Lection 10. κύριε σῶσον introduces a liturgical note suggesting the Lord's divinity: Mark's πῶς οὐκ ἔχετε πίστιν

[30] 1 Kings 19.20. [31] See pp. 74ff above.
[32] 1 Kings 19.19.
[33] So J. M. Creed, *The Gospel according to St Luke* (London 1930).

becomes ὀλιγόπιστοί to lessen the reproach to the apostles. The choral speaking at the end is also a Matthaean habit; cf. Mark's 'they said one to another'.[34]

(12) The Demoniacs 8.28—9.1

Mark had two stories in 1—5 of demoniacs, one in the synagogue, one in the tombs. Matthew joins the two together in a single story, again in chorus. The outline of the combination is Mark's Gerasene: but Matthew includes words of the synagogue demoniac also:

Mark 1.24: 'What have you to do with us, Jesus of Nazareth? Have you come to destroy us?' Matt. 8.29: 'What have you to do with us, O Son of God? Have you come here to torment us?'

The plural ἡμῖν in the first phrase in Matthew is a necessary adaptation for the *two* men possessed, but the second phrase, ἦλθες with an infinitive . . .?, occurs in Mark 1 and not Mark 5. Gadara is preferred to the more famous Gerasa, one of the Decapolis, as being six miles from the Lake instead of thirty: perhaps an indication that Matthew's is a Syrian and Mark's a distant Gospel.[35] The Lection ends, properly, at 9.1: Jesus accepts the Gadarenes' rejection, and returns to 'his own city', that is, Capernaum. Jesus came to Capernaum at 8.5 to heal a paralytic, the Centurion's boy, and he returns to heal an Israelite paralytic now.

(13) The Paralytic 9.2–8

The paralytic completes the first series of five Israelites healed in Matthew: they are the first four Marcan healings and the Gerasene demoniac. The story is abbreviated by a third.

(14) The Call of Matthew 9.9–17

The lection for Ninth Ab now divides the two healing series, following on from the Paralytic in the Marcan order. The wording is very close

---

[34] G. Bornkamm's essay, 'The Stilling of the Storm in Matthew' (*TIM*, pp. 52–7) appears to be a piece of serious over-interpretation. Bornkamm sees Matthew as reinterpreting Mark so as to allegorize the Storm as the penultimate persecutions of the Church, which is to be saved by the ultimate coming of Christ. But the introduction of paraliturgical language (προσκυνέω, etc.) is frequent in Matthew; σείω is a Matthaean word; οἱ ἄνθρωποι may refer naturally either to the disciples as a whole, or more probably to the two new followers, without involving mankind at the Parousia.

[35] So Allen, Lohmeyer.

to Mark. The presence of Levi the publican in Mark 2, called just like the first Four Apostles in Mark 1, is an embarrassment when his name does not occur in the list of Twelve in Mark 3. One of the Twelve then must have been the tax-collector, and only Matthew, Mattathias, carries a Levite name. The publican, then, will have been Matthew, son of Alphaeus, a Levite: such logic was congenial to the Chronicler, and many after him.

πενθεῖν at 9.15 is a token of Matthew's familiarity with Jewish piety. The Talmud distinguishes carefully between fasting, the going without food for minor acts of humiliation, and mourning, i.e. refraining from work, washing, anointing, wearing sandals, and marital intercourse, which is suitable for more serious matters.[36] Ninth Ab was no ordinary fast-day, but the day of mourning for the Temple twice destroyed: its liturgy was the Book of Lamentations.[37] An alternative translation of an Aramaic *'ith'anne'*[38] is not likely in a passage where Matthew retains the Marcan νηστεύειν three times. The insertion of the stronger word is intentional.

Matthew replaces Mark's Pharisaic scribes at 9.11 with Pharisees, typically: the Hosea quotation is given in the Hebrew form ('and not'; cf. LXX ἤ), despite Matthew's belief in sacrifice (5.23; 7.6). He is similarly devastating about Pharisaic obedience to the Law in 23 while holding it to be binding. Both the repetition of the citation in 12, and the Hebrew form of the words, point to Matthew the *sôphēr* as its originator here.

(15) The Woman with Haemorrhage 9.18–22 (A–19)
(16) The Synagogue-Ruler's Daughter 9.23–6 (A 20–)

The second series of healings opens with the Levitically unclean woman and Jairus' daughter, together as in Mark 5. There is a tendency in all division in *lectiones continuae* for the division to be adjusted to the place where the new character is named for the first time, cutting across the logic of the story: this is true for OT divisions, such as the Noah story, which begins logically at 6.1, and not at 6.9

---

[36] B Taan. 30a, 'All the laws that are observed in mourning are observed also in keeping Ninth Ab'; cf. M Taan. 1.4–6; 2.8.
[37] cf. the liturgy for Ninth Ab: 'Comfort, O Lord our God, the mourners ('*ōbhᵉlîm*) of Sion, and the mourners of Jerusalem, and the city that is in mourning . . .' (*Daily Prayer Book*, ed. S. Singer (Cambridge 1914)).
[38] Jeremias, *PJ* (e.1), p. 42n; E. P. Sanders, *The Tendencies of the Synoptic Tradition* (Cambridge 1969), p. 287. Jeremias withdrew the suggestion in later editions.

where the *sidrāh* starts with Noah's name,[39] and there are other examples in Matthew, such as the Parables chapter, which begins logically at 13.1, not 13.3, where the Sower starts. As 9.18–19 is an unsatisfactory unit, it seems likely that Matthew intended the story to go on to 9.22 with the healing of the haemorrhage, giving one healing to each sabbath, and the Lev. 15 reference first, as a pair to the Lev. 14 leper: and for what it is worth, this is borne out by the insertion of ὁ 'Ιησοῦς at 9.23 where the new lection would begin.[40] The very great abbreviation, by two thirds, emphasizes the healing ministry seen as a whole, at the expense of individual details: Matthew was not concerned with the history as such.

(17) The Blind Men 9.27–31

The two Blind Men follow, balancing the two demoniacs of the first five. They are the classic case of a compendium miracle.

(a) The main structure is taken from Mark's Bartimaeus. Like him they shout after Jesus, and the words are the same, 'Have mercy on me/us, son of David': they, like him, owe their cure to their faith—'According to your faith be it to you', 'Your faith has made you well.'

(b) Some details recall the Marcan blind man at Bethsaida. Like him, Jesus touches their eyes, as he does not Bartimaeus'. Like him, they are healed in private, and commanded not to tell.

(c) The command to secrecy is given, unmistakeably, from the Marcan story of the Leper, where ἐμβριμάομαι,[41] ὅρα μηδεὶς, διαφημίζειν,[42] ἐξελθών all occur. The likelihood is that this is not careless reminiscence but deliberate selection, as Matthew omits all this from his version of the Leper. 'Their eyes were opened' is a quotation from Isa. 35.5, which is soon to be quoted in more

---

[39] Philo begins the second book of *Questions on Genesis* (and therefore the second *sidrāh*, presumably) at 6.14, where God speaks to Noah about the Ark—even less logically. The following nine Matthaean lections seem wrongly divided in A by the same process, all by a margin of one or two verses (my proposed verse of starting in parenthesis): 6 (7.28), 10 (8.18), 16 (9.23), 24 (13.1), 26 (14.13), 29 (15.22), 40 (19.1), 46 (21.12), 57 (24.1).

[40] Jesus' name occurs in the first verse of Lections 1, 4, 8, 13, 14, 17, 28, 30, 31, 32, 33, 34, 37, 45, 51, 55, 56, 62, 63, 64, 68—21 times, or 30 times including the amended first verses of n. 1. More instances could be obtained by reference to *variae lectiones*: but then lectionary use of the Gospels would be likely to increase the use. Matthew sat down and wrote a book, not a series of detached units, so we should not expect him to insert Jesus' name afresh on purpose at the beginning of each new lection.

[41] Only here in Matthew.

[42] Only here and at Matt. 28.15.

detail (11.5). The insertion of the brief conversation is also typical of Matthew.[43]

(18) *The Dumb Demoniac 9.32–4*

The story is basically the deaf (κωφός) and stammering man of Mark 7, who was brought to Jesus and enabled to speak (ἐλάλει): the crowd in Mark marvelled, saying (λέγοντες) 'He has done all things well'; in Matthew, in more Matthaean manner, 'Never was anything like this seen in Israel'—φαίνομαι, οἱ ὄχλοι, προσφέρω are in Hawkins' list, ἰδού, δαιμονίζομαι, λέγοντες, οὕτως, ἐν τῷ Ἰσραήλ are semi-Matthaean. The evangelist has taken all the colour out of the story, and in place has added the possession of the dumb man and the Pharisees' criticism of black magic[44] from Mark 3—a further instance of his tendency to compound miracles. The criticism of the Pharisees makes the healing a pair with the Paralytic, where the scribes criticize Jesus; the possession and 'prince of demons' theme are later taken up in the final healing in 12.

(19) *9.35–8*

These verses, which lead up to 10, are a development of two Marcan texts. Mark 6.6, 'And he went about among the villages teaching', which introduces the Marcan Sending of the Twelve, is put into perfect Matthaean balances—'all the cities and villages', 'teaching and preaching', 'every disease and every infirmity'.[45] This is the Matthaean *healing* tractate, and the healing mission is included. Introductory ὁ Ἰησοῦς, πάντες, *their* synagogues, 'the kingdom' absolutely, θεραπεύω, νόσος and μαλακία, and οἱ ὄχλοι are all characteristic. 9.36 is a development of Mark 6.34, itself a reference to Num. 27.17: as Moses commissioned Joshua of old to shepherd Israel, so Jesus commissions his apostles. 'Harassed and helpless' are the evangelist's explanatory adjectives,[46] paired as ever. The pastoral image suggests a pair with the agricultural,[47] like the birds and lilies in 6, or the sheep and wolves followed by figs and grapes in 7—animals and growing things in each case—or the vipers and rotten trees of 12. Harvest is a favourite

---

[43] There is an exhaustive analysis of the pericope in A. Fuchs, *Sprachliche Untersuchungen zu Matthäus und Lukas* (Rome 1971), pp. 18–170, establishing Matthaean authorship.

[44] Dak syr⁵ Hil omit 9.34, perhaps as occurring also at 12.24. The verse is presupposed at 10.25. Nestle–Aland, BFBS, and NEB mg read the whole verse: NEB text curiously omits 'But the Pharisees said'.

[45] See p. 90 above.   [46] cf. p. 38 above.

[47] cf. p. 303 above.

Matthaean image—τότε, θερισμός (3), ἐργαταί (2), πολύς/ὀλίγος, οὖν, ὅπως, κύριος + gen., ἐκβάλλω = take out, are characteristic words—12 out of 20. Only δέομαι is non-Matthaean.

It will be convenient, now that we are so far through the healing tractate, to complete it by carrying the discussion over to 12. This means postponing to the next chapter the consideration of the two New Year discourses; and in fact breaking into Lection 20, which, for reasons given on p. 189 above, consists of both the discourse in 11 and the Cornfield episode in 12.1–6. But the healings belong together, and need to be considered together.

(20b) 12.1–8

We have already expounded the paragraph in ch. 1 above[48] as an illustration of Matthaean embarrassment with Jesus' radicalism on the sabbath. All we are now concerned to note is that Matthew omits Mark 2.27, 'The sabbath was made for man', which is apparently an invitation to sabbath-breaking, and *in its place* inserts the editorial verses on the priests in the Temple—Matthew's religious interest[49]— and the second citation of Hos. 6.6. The point of the secondariness of sabbath is thus made effectively, without suggesting its abrogation. The priests at Nob suggest the priests in the Temple: their work in offering sacrifice on the sabbath is lawful according to Num. 28.9f. The substitution has the additional merit of justifying Jesus by a prescription from Torah (ἐν τῷ νόμῳ), rather than by the mere example of the prophet David.[50] The Temple is one of the New Year–Tabernacles themes,[51] which recurs constantly in the next lections. The Temple in turn suggests Hosea on sacrifice: ἔλεος, ἀγάπη, καλῶς ποιεῖν take precedence over the ceremonial law. ἢ οὐκ ἀνέγνωτε; is Matthaean: semi-Matthaean are νόμος, λέγω δὲ ὑμῖν ὅτι, μεῖζον, ὧδε, —11 words characteristic of Matthew out of 41. βεβηλόω and ἀναίτιος do not occur elsewhere in the Gospel.

(21) The Man with the Withered Hand 12.9–14

The New Year season continues with the proclamation of judgement. The rejection of Christ in his early ministry reaches its climax in Mark with this pericope, and Matthew exacerbates it. For Mark's 'the synagogue' he writes 'their synagogue'. He makes the Pharisees' challenge open, 'is it lawful . . .?', where in Mark they watched him

[48] See pp. 17f above; cf. G. Barth, *TIM*, pp. 81f.
[49] pp. 105f above.
[50] Daube, *NTRJ*, pp. 67ff.   [51] cf. p. 174 above.

in silence. Jesus' counter-attack is similarly made more effective by the inclusion of a new appeal to the principle that the Son of Man is lord of the sabbath. The mention of David in the previous story suggests the illustration of the sheep, which is drawn from Nathan's parable in 2 Sam. 12; since the man has but one sheep, just as Nathan's poor man, and Nathan's conclusion, as Jesus', is that Bathsheba was more important than a ewe-lamb. Sheep are a favourite image, and οὐχί, οὖν, and διαφέρω, typical words of Matthew's. Rabbinic *hᵃlākāh* in fact permitted the feeding of a beast fallen into a pit on a sabbath, but not the work of pulling it out—an illustration of the limits of Matthew's knowledge.[52] Matthew's ecclesiastical interest is noteworthy in his transformation of the Marcan challenge, 'Is it lawful on the sabbath to do good . . .?' into a piece of church law, 'So it is lawful . . .'. The legal position is thus regularized. Sabbath is valid, as prescribed in Torah, but charity takes priority, just as the saving of life does in the rabbis. Matthew is thus able to present both a radical Jesus and the Law inviolate. Jesus' anger (Mark 3.5) is suppressed as at Matt. 8.3, from reverence: did not the Matthaean Jesus say, 'Everyone who is angry with his brother . . .'? The Marcan Herodians are omitted, irrelevant history dropping away with time.

12.15–21

Matthew continues the story with a highly abbreviated version of the next Marcan paragraph, Mark 3.7–12, Jesus' withdrawal and healing of the crowds, and his silencing of the demons from revealing him. Three things suggest the extensive citation of Isa. 42 here, the longest quotation in the Gospel.

(a) The Marcan New Year lection[53] had included the voice at the Baptism, 'Thou art my beloved Son, with thee I am well-pleased': a glossing of Ps. 2.7, 'Thou art my Son . . .' with Isa. 42.1, 'In whom my soul is well-pleased'.[54]

(b) The crowds in Mark 3.8 had included people from Edom, Transjordan, and Tyre and Sidon. This makes the last clause of

---

[52] See pp. 21f above; S–B ad loc.; Strecker, *WG*, p. 19.

[53] See above, ch. 9, appendix B.

[54] Matthew freely glosses the LXX from the Hebrew, and from other scriptures. ἰδού is from the Hebrew; ὁ παῖς μου means 'my son' to Matthew rather than 'my servant' (cf. p. 320 above, on 8.5ff) ᾑρέτισα is from the Hebrew, but is introduced out of order to emphasize Jesus' adoption, as in 1 Chron. 28, where David and Solomon are so described; ὁ ἀγαπητός is glossed from Mark 1.9, and ηὐδόκησεν, which is a fair rendition of *rātsᵉthāh*, also recalls the Baptism. 'I will put my spirit upon him' is no less baptismal, θήσω being a more apt translation of the prophetic perfect *nāthattí* than the LXX ἔδωκα.

Isa. 42.1 doubly suitable: 'He will proclaim[55] judgment to the Gentiles.' Mark gives the Gentiles: New Year is the season of judgement. The half-year hitherto has seen Christ's ministry to Israel almost exclusively, and the authorities of Israel will now finally reject Christ, and be rejected: the half-year ahead will gradually open the gospel to the Gentiles, first the Canaanitess, ultimately the world-mission of 24 and 28.[56]

(c) Jesus' withdrawal (12.15) in face of the threat of murder (12.14) fits well with the next two verses. The prophet had spoken of God's beloved son as not wrangling in public, and of his gentle care for the bruised, which are just to the point. He had then made a second reference to the Gentile mission, 'In his name will the Gentiles hope.'[57] Matthew thus has a weighty citation with which to support the New Year themes of divine adoption and judgement: turning to the Gentiles, and Jesus' irenic response to hostility are alike evidenced in Mark and proved in the same passage of scripture.

(22) *The Possessed, Blind, and Dumb Man 12.22–37*

Matthew has now given a version of all the Marcan healings except the epileptic boy. The Withered Hand has completed the original

---

[55] Matthew glosses the requisite ἀπαγγελεῖ 'proclaim', for the colourless *yotsī*, 'bring forth'. The verb is used of Solomon's deliverances to the Queen of Sheba in 1 Kings 10.3.

[56] The LXX gloss of ὀνόματι for *lᵉthôrāthô*, 'his law', is retained at 12.21: for all Matthew's new Torah, he knew that the Gentiles' hope was in the person of Christ before his teaching. cf. W. D. Davies, *Setting*, pp. 133ff.

[57] Matthew makes the reference explicit with οὐκ ἐρίσει for οὐ κεκράξεται: the shouting which Jesus withdrew to avoid was the shouting of quarrel—κραυγάζω is similarly the shout of altercation in Acts 23.9; Eph. 4.31. 'In the streets' is a more pointed literal version of the Hebrew *bahûts*, which normally means 'outside' and is so rendered by LXX. For οὐδέ τις cf. 11.27; 22.46. For Isa. 42.3 Matthew treats the LXX freely. The Heb. has 'A crushed (*rātsûts*) reed will he not break (*yishbôr*)': for the second verb LXX gives συντρίψει which Matthew uses for the first—indeed it is closer to 'crush'—and imports the unequivocal κατεάξει for the second. τυφόμενον,' smouldering', is similarly written in for *kēhah* 'dimly burning' in place of LXX καπνιζόμενον 'smoking': the flax still has the *spark* in it, is the point, not yet *quenched*. ἕως ἄν is brought in from Isa. 42.4 LXX. Gk. and Heb. have 'He will bring forth judgment to truth': Matthew substitutes 'to victory', as a short statement of 42.4a, 'He will not fail or be discouraged till he has established κρίσις in the earth'. ἐκβάλλω = bring out is semi-Matthaean: νῖκος may be influenced by Paul's translation of Isa. 25.8 at 1 Cor. 15.54f. For a full discussion cf. Gundry, *UOTSM*, pp. 110–16; Stendahl, *SSM*, pp. 107ff.

Marcan five of Mark 1—3; the wonders of Mark 5 were redescribed in 8—9, along with the dumb man of Mark 7 and the two blind men of Mark 8 and 10; the Centurion's Boy was a male form of the Syrophoenician woman's Girl. For his final healing of the tractate Matthew combines the epileptic of Mark 9 (τὸ ἄλαλον καὶ κωφὸν πνεῦμα, 9.25) with the Mark 3 incident of the Beelzebul controversy over the casting out of demons (Mark 3.22ff); and for symbolic purposes he draws in the blindness of Mark 10 besides[58]—this is the climax of the Lord's healings, and may be suitably seen as a terrible instance of multiple suffering. Following Mark's epileptic Matthew writes, 'the dumb man spoke' (τὸν κωφὸν λαλεῖν): Matthew omits the epileptic's being dumb from his account in Matt. 17—the subject is already treated here. The wondering crowds are also from Mark 9.15; though the verb ἐξίσταμαι is found only here in Matthew, and may be drawn in from the ἐξέστη of Mark 3.21.[59] Their comment, 'Can this be the Son of David?' recalls the cry of the blind man in Mark 10, and is apt for a series of readings which emphasize Christ as the new Solomon. Matthew replaces the scribes of Mark 3 with Pharisees, as usual, and transcribes the Beelzebul incident.

Matthew's rewriting of Mark is designed to do three things: (*a*) to emphasize the judgement which the Pharisees have brought down on their own heads—the repeated οὗτος in 23f, 'Can *this man* be the Son of David?', 'By Beelzebul *this man* casts out demons', points the contrast between the faith of the simple and the blasphemy of the wise, and Mark is continually expanded in this sense; (*b*) to provide a Christian Atonement Day lesson, taking up the Jewish lesson of Jonah in sadness over Pharisaic impenitence; and (*c*) to develop the threefold symbolic[60] antithesis between the newly healed sufferer and the Pharisees, the spokesmen of 'this generation'. The man was δαιμονιζόμενος τυφλὸς καὶ κωφός: in reverse expository order then,[61] first κωφός, dumb, but now speaking, λαλῶν—whereas the Pharisees abuse their gift of speech with blasphemy: 'Whoever *says* a *word* against the Son of Man will be forgiven; but whoever *speaks* against

[58] cf. also Isa. 42.19, 'Who is blind but my παῖδες, and deaf but οἱ κυριεύοντες αὐτῶν?'

[59] See p. 40 above.

[60] The symbolism of disease is a common feature of all the Gospels. The best-known Marcan instance is Jesus' words to the apostles, 'Having eyes do you not see, and having ears do you not hear?' (8.18) after the healing of the deaf Decapolitan and immediately before the healing of the blind Bethsaidan. Sickness is expressly said to be a symbol of sin at Mark 2.17; Matt. 9.12. The theme is expounded tirelessly by St John.

[61] As in the Beatitudes and the Sermon on the Mount, ch. 11 above.

the Holy Spirit will not be forgiven . . . Out of the abundance of the heart the mouth *speaks* (λαλεῖ) . . . men will render account for every careless *word* they *speak* (λαλήσουσιν): for by your *words* you will be justified, and by your *words* you will be condemned.' The 'speaking' theme is drawn out of the Marcan blasphemy, and continues till 12.37. The blindness theme is taken in 12.38–42, the possession theme in 43–5.

At first Mark is treated editorially: ἐρημοῦται[62] makes a balance with οὐ σταθήσεται, more elegant than Mark's repetitions. Matthew's customary city makes a pair with the Marcan house,[63] and he turns Mark's negative into his favourite rhetorical question, 'How then will his kingdom stand?' He then adds a second rhetorical question of his own, 'By whom do your sons cast them out?' The judgement of the Pharisees by their fellow men is a constant theme of Matthew's— the Ninevites and the Queen of the South in this chapter, all the martyrs in history in 23. Matthew convicts the Pharisees of double-talk by reference to their sons here, to their fathers in 23.29f, 'You witness against yourselves, that you are sons of those who murdered the prophets.' διὰ τοῦτο, ἔσονται, εἰ (2) are characteristic language. Verse 28 is the converse of 27a, a repetitive converse in the Matthaean manner (AT): 'But if I cast out demons by the spirit *of God*'—emphatic, cf. 'by Beelzebul' in 27—'then *God's* kingdom[64]—emphatic, cf. Satan's riven kingdom in 25f—has come upon you. ἄρα is semi-Matthaean. φθάνω is non-Matthaean, but there is a similar use in 1 Thess. 2.16, a passage familiar to Matthew.[65] The contrast of Jesus and the sons of the Pharisees casting out demons draws Luke's mind (11.17ff) to Moses and Pharaoh's magicians both working wonders in Exod. 8, where the latter confess, 'This is the finger of God' (8.19): he writes

---

[62] Not found elsewhere in Matt., but a common LXX word (Lagrange, *L'Evangile selon S. Matthieu.*)

[63] cf. 5.14f; 10.11–14.

[64] Matthew always uses the standard rabbinic 'kingdom of heaven' unless he has a reason. At 21.43 he inserts the phrase ἡ βασιλεία τοῦ θεοῦ *editorially* into Mark's vineyard parable: just as the owner will kill those wretches and let out his vineyard to other tenants, so *God's* kingdom will be taken from the Jews and given to the Church. In exactly the same way, just before (21.31), just as the initially recalcitrant son did the will of his father, so do the publicans do God's will and go into *God's* kingdom before the Pharisees. If it occurs at 6.33 it is from the context of the provident God in 6.32. In each case the word 'God' is used with emphasis to represent the owner or the father of the parables, or to contrast with Satan and his kingdom, as here: the phrase should be translated 'God's kingdom', and not 'the kingdom of God'. cf. also 6.10; 13.43; 19.24 (Mark).

[65] cf. p. 165 above.

'by the finger' for Matthew's 'by the spirit' of God.[66] Verse 29a becomes
a Matthaean rhetorical question. Verse 30: the whole incident is
somewhat reminiscent of Mark's Strange Exorcist, where demons
were being cast out in the name of Christ, and the disciples forbade it.
Then Jesus had said to let them be: 'For he that is not against us is for
us.' Matthew omits the Strange Exorcist from the Mark 9 context,
and gives a reversed form of the logion here. When strangers take
Christ's name for exorcism in a good heart, they are not against him
but for him: when they attack his exorcisms from envy, they are not
for him but against him. Matthew completes the pardic with his
characteristic συνάγω/σκορπίζω antithesis.[67] 'He who is not *with me* is
against me: and he who does not *gather* with me *scatters*'. Matthew
rewrites vv. 31f into two pairs of repetitive converse logia, and spells
out Mark's αἰωνίου into an explicit 'neither in this age, or in the age
to come', the rabbinic '*ôlām hazzeh w^ehabbā*'[68]. For vv. 33–7 the theme
is the λαλεῖν given by the dumb man healed: the imagery is Matthaean,
the two trees and two fruits, good and rotten, the offspring of vipers,
the heart and the mouth, the two treasure-chests, the day of judgement.
Verbally ἀγαθός/πονηρός, ἀποδίδωμι, ἤ, λέγω ὑμῖν ὅτι, ἄργος, ἐκβάλλω
= take out are characteristic besides. In the new material, verses
22f, 27f, 30, 33–7, there are 52 characteristic words in all out of a total
of 174 words. The rhythms are Matthaean too: the echidnic,[69] 'You
brood of vipers, how can you . . .?'; the caesaric,[70] 'Either make the
tree good, and its fruit good, or make the tree bad and its fruit bad',
cf. 'Either he will hate the one and love the other . . .'; and the repetitive converse, 'The good man out of his good treasure-chest brings
forth good things . . .' (AT), cf. 'They longed to see what you see,
and did not see it; and to hear what you hear, and did not hear
it'.

---

[66] cf. T. W. Manson, *The Teaching of Jesus* (Cambridge 1931), pp. 82f. Manson
argues for the priority of the Lucan 'finger': (*a*) πνεῦμα is a favourite word of
Luke; (*b*) Luke would wish to remove, not insert, an anthropomorphism; (*c*)
the Exod. 8 passage goes back to 'our Lord's acquaintance with the Hebrew
Bible'. But (*a*) πνεῦμα (of the Holy Spirit) is actually rare in the teaching of
Jesus in Luke—it comes only at 4.18, and 11.13: the motive for Luke to change
to 'finger' is supplied by Manson himself in (*c*); (*b*) So far from abhorring
anthropomorphisms, Luke introduces the arm of the Lord in 1.51, and the hand
of the Lord at 1.66; Acts 11.21; 13.11; (*c*) is, I fear, only Manson's piety. It is
δάκτυλος θεοῦ in the Greek Bible, and the change would be typical of Luke
not only in a close knowledge of the LXX, but in the practice of gilding the
Matthaean lily; cf. p. 101 above.

[67] cf. 25.24,26; cf. Luke 19.21f.

[68] Moore, *Judaism* II, p. 378.   [69] p. 79 above.

[70] pp. 74ff above.

(23) Those Who Asked for a Sign 12.38–42

The man healed in the last lection was possessed, blind, and dumb: but just as his dumbness was symbolic of Pharisaism's failure to speak the good, so his blindness is symbolic of Pharisaism's failure to see spiritually. Mark had told how the Pharisees had been in controversy with Jesus on another occasion, seeking a sign (Mark 8.11f). Matthew puts their wish into *oratio recta*, and adds 'to see' a sign. He makes them Pharisaic scribes, introducing the scribes who were in altercation[71] with Jesus at the healing of the epileptic boy (Mark 9.14), and who address Jesus as διδάσκαλε (9.17) as here: the phrase πονηρὰ καὶ μοιχαλὶς ἐπιζητεῖ is inserted here as it is editorially at Matt. 16.4. But this incident does not merely instance Pharisaic desire to see what God has not given: it recalls also their refusal to see the sign God has given, the Resurrection—and so gives the opportunity to introduce the Atonement theme of Jonah. The whole Book of Jonah was read on Yom Kippur;[72] the first half, to a Christian, foreshadowing Christ's rising from the dead, as the second half foreshadowed his preaching mission till Judgement Day. Yom Kippur celebrated God's offer of forgiveness to all who repent, as the Ninevites repented at the words of Jonah: a greater than Jonah preaches now, but Judaism, as Paul told the Corinthians,[73] only wants to see a sign, and will not believe the Resurrection. Matthew therefore modifies Mark's, 'no sign shall be given . . .' with an excepting clause.[74] For a second stanza to his poem, Matthew's mind moves back to the Solomon–Temple theme which is all through 12—13, and belongs in the seventh month, when Solomon consecrated the Temple. The Queen of the South makes a fitting feminine pair to the Ninevites, besides.[75] The poem is one of Matthew's five crinics:[76] each word in the Matthaean version balances from strophe to antistrophe. Verse 40 is one of Matthew's aetics[77]— cf. 'As were the days of Noah, so will be the coming of the Son of Man.' ὥσπερ, οὕτως ἔσται are Matthaean. The early Church had been used to say, 'after three days he rose again';[78] Matthew stretches the fact to 'three days and three nights' for the sake of the parallel.[79] For

---

[71] Mark 9.14, with the same verb συζητέω as at Mark 8.11.

[72] B Meg. 31a.   [73] 1 Cor. 1.22.

[74] cf. 5.32; 19.9; 16.4—see Modification, p. 38 above.

[75] For other instances cf. p. 98 above.   [76] pp. 86f above.

[77] p. 78 above.   [78] Mark 8.31; 9.31; 10.34.

[79] Matthew similarly adjusts fact to prophecy by assigning Capernaum to *Zebulon* and Naphtali at 4.13 (Manson *SJ* p. 90), or by adding the ass's colt or the thirty silver pieces from Zechariah. For a similar loose use of three days/the third day, cf. Esth. 4.16/5.1: 'Hold a fast on my behalf, and neither eat nor drink for three days, night or day. I and my maids will also fast . . . On the third day . . .'.

'three days and three nights', cf. Matthew's editorial 'forty days and forty nights' (4.2). For 'something greater than Jonah/Solomon is here', cf. Matthew's editorial, 'Something greater than the Temple is here'. For 'Jonah the prophet', cf. 'Isaiah the prophet' (4/1/2), 'Jeremiah the prophet' (2/0/0). Other characteristic words are: τότε, scribes-and-Pharisees, λέγοντες, ἀποκριθεὶς εἶπεν, πονηρός, οὐ . . . εἰ μή, γῆ (2), man with a following qualifying noun, κρίσις (2), ἰδού (2), ὧδε (2), ἐγείρομαι, Solomon (2)—27 in all out of 121.

Luke (11.29–32) lacks the Atonement context, so he concentrates on the main point, the rejection by 'this generation' of Christ's preaching—perhaps also the fact that Jesus was really only one day and two nights in the tomb leads him to suppress the resurrection reference. He introduces the semi-Lucan κάθως, ἐγένετο, and οἱ Νινευῖται,[80] and moves on direct to the Queen of the South, into which he inserts the Lucan τῶν ἄνδρων which spoils the symmetry.[81] He then goes back to Jonah, now copying Matthew exactly, as he so often does in the later part of a paragraph. The widespread view that Luke preserves the 'authentic' or 'clear' form of the logion,[82] which Matthew has allegorized, rests on the circular argument which selects the sayings of eschatological challenge as the original message of Jesus, and then finds those sayings to be original. Matthew allegorizes, true, but then Luke deallegorizes.[83] The only evidence worth considering is the words of the two versions against the established habits of writing of the two evangelists, and all the differences in Luke correspond to characteristic Lucan vocabulary and editorial traits, and show Luke to be secondary: the Matthaean evidence points strongly to Matthaean authorship.

12.43–5

Just as the healed man's dumbness and blindness had been symbolic of this generation's inability to speak or see truly, so is this generation like the man in his possession by an unclean spirit. The unclean spirit (τῷ πνεύματι τῷ ἀκαθάρτῳ) possessing the boy in the Mark 9 parallel was commanded by Jesus, 'Come out of him (ἔξελθε), and never enter (εἰσέλθῃς) him again' (9.25).[84] Here is the peril of the once possessed,

---

[80] cf. οἱ Κορίνθιοι, οἱ Ῥωμαῖοι, etc., in Acts; cp. Matt's Semitic ἄνδρες N., to which Luke relapses at 11.32.

[81] For Luke's tendency to spoil the rhythm in Mark and his frequently less poetic rhythm in Q passages see ch. 4 above.

[82] Manson, *SJ*, pp. 89ff; Jeremias *PJ*, pp. 84, 130; and most commentaries.

[83] See pp. 59f above.

[84] Omitted at Matt. 17.18, having been already expounded here.

which Matthew proceeds to expound. The unclean spirit (τὸ ἀκάθ-αρτον πνεῦμα) comes out (ἐξέλθῃ) of the man, as in Mark, only to enter (εἰσελθόντα) again with his companions. Waterless places are the proverbial home of the demons.[85] The image of the house is carried on from Beelzebul, the Lord of the House, the divided house, and the strong man's house of 25–9. Matthew writes the triple 'empty and swept and put in order', as elsewhere 'they neither sow nor reap nor gather', 'The rains fell and the floods came and the winds blew', 'prophets and wise men and scribes', 'justice and mercy and faith': in each case Luke avoids the triple in his version, usually cutting down to two, as he does here by omitting σχολάζοντα καὶ. 'Swept and put in order' are an obvious pair: verse 45 describes the return of the spirit. τότε, οὕτως ἔσται are Matthaean: semi-Matthaean are διά + gen., ὅθεν, ἐλθόν, πορεύομαι, πονηρός (2), ἐκεῖ, ἔσχατος, pleonastic ἐκεῖνος, παραλαμβάνω, κατοικῶ—15 characteristic words out of 68. With 'the last state of that man becomes worse than the first' cf. 27.64(M), 'The last fraud will be worse than the first', or 20.16 (R), 'The last will be first and the first last'. The non-Matthaean words ἄνυδρος, σχολάζω, σαρόω are all part of the simile. Matthaean authorship seems the simplest solution.

Luke puts the Return of the Spirit directly after the Beelzebul incident, bringing out the perils of the once possessed with reference to the man himself: he is not concerned with the symbolic aspect of the healing, and omits Matthew's οὕτως ἔσται conclusion. The words are very close to Matthew, almost the only changes being the suppression of 'empty and', to make a simple pair, and the introduction of μὴ εὑρίσκον, a semi-Lucan use of μὴ with participle (Luke 11.24–6).

12.46–50

The die is cast: this generation has rejected Jesus, in face of the evident works of Messiah, and Jesus has pronounced God's judgement on them. Matthew closes the scene with the symbolic pericope from Mark 3: Jesus' mother and brothers stand outside, wanting to parley with him. Who are Jesus' true family? They are his disciples, whoever does God's will. Israel after the flesh is henceforward those without: the divine family is the Church.

Once it is seen that the healings in Matt. 8—12 are the same as the healings in Mark, the case for Matthaean creativity becomes overwhelming. The two blind men, the dumb demoniac of 9.32ff, and the final multiple healing, are plainly compound healings, details of

[85] cf. Joel 2.20; S–B, Exkurs über Dämonologie ɪᴠ, pp. 501–35.

different stories being put together to form a composition, the rationale of which is not hard to seek. Once the method of compound healings is accepted, it is natural to look at the Centurion's Boy, and the later parts of the last healing, and the two would-be disciples, and to ask whether they have not a matrix in Mark also. Once the Marcan matrices are seen, and the OT texts laid bare to which Matthew is referring, we find ourselves inquiring as before, 'How Matthaean are the language, imagery, rhythm, manner, and doctrine?' It is hard to see any paragraph or verse in the three healing chapters which does not look like a case of midrashic expansion. Mark's healings and the Calendar, with the Matthaean manner, account for them all.

16

NEW YEAR:
THE FAILURE OF TWO MISSIONS
(10—11)

We have already seen how the season of New Year evoked in the first-century Jew the twin thoughts of the joyful establishment of God's reign, and the direful concomitant of his judgement: and that to a Christian of Matthew's background this would issue in the thought of the inauguration of the kingdom of heaven in Jesus on the one side, which the apostles had been commissioned to proclaim, and the bewailing of the impenitence of Israel on the other, which must lead to their condemnation. The two themes are implicit in the healing stories which Matthew has been leading to their climax. Jesus is the popular healer in 8. The Gadarenes request him to leave (8.34); he is accused of blasphemy (9.3), of eating with the unclean (9.11), of not fasting (9.14), of black magic (9.34). In all but the last case Jesus replies warmly. Matt. 10 broadens the theme. Jesus' ministry of preaching and healing is now to be extended to his apostles. They are to preach the inauguration of the kingdom, and heal the sick and the leper: and they will be rejected as their master. Matt. 11 carries the war into the enemy's territory. A message from John enables the healings to be seen as the works of Messiah: and Jesus then upbraids 'this generation' for its faithlessness, and contrasts the faith of the simple. The crisis of rejection is reserved for the controversial healings of 12, and the Day of Atonement.

The Matthaean authorship of the three healing chapters, out of a Marcan base, was suggested in the last pages: we have now to examine the same claim for 10—11, *prima facie* a stronghold of M and Q material to rival the Sermon. But we shall find that the same technique of expounding Marcan and related OT texts has been followed here as there, and the same typical Matthaean rhythms, images, vocabulary, and doctrines are everywhere.

In Mark the Twelve are called and named in Mark 3, sent on mission in Mark 6: Matthew's rehandling of the Marcan healings has taken him to Mark 5 and beyond, but Mark 3 is still ahead, so it is convenient to him to take the calling and sending together. New Year sees both the forming of a new Israel under its new patriarchs, and their commissioning to proclaim the presence of the kingdom. 10.1 rephrases Mark 6.7, though the Twelve, who are familiar in Mark, come rather surprisingly for the first time unheralded: the whole epexegetic ὥστε clause is Matthaean in language. The names of the Twelve are (not as in Mark) given in pairs, Peter and Andrew, James and John, etc.: partly from a Matthaean love of pairs, partly because they were sent out two and two (Mark 6.7). The names are as in Mark, but Matthew the publican is moved to the emphatic position at the end of the second four: the four first-called, inner-ring apostles, a second four culminating in the now familiar Matthew, and a third four culminating in the traitor Judas.

With v.5f we reach a famous conundrum, a citadel of contradiction. Matthew is unquestionably a Gospel sympathetic to the Gentile mission. Not only is such activity *prophesied*, following Mark, at 24.14, 'This gospel of the kingdom will be preached throughout the whole world, as a testimony to all nations', and at 26.13, 'Wherever this gospel is preached in the whole world':[1] but it is *commanded* in the final lines of the Gospel with every possible emphasis, 'All authority in heaven and on earth has been given to me. Go therefore and make disciples of all nations . . .'. Nor is this a matter of three isolated texts: it has been shown, most carefully and convincingly by Dr Trilling,[2] that one dominant doctrine of the Gospel is the fault of the Jews and their loss of privilege, with a corresponding turning to the Gentiles.[3] Yet side by side with this general attitude we find the increased stress on Jesus' mission as to 'the lost sheep of the house of Israel'; and here a veto on any approach to Gentile or Samaritan, 'but go rather to the lost sheep of the house of Israel'. The former text is visibly introduced by Matthew into the Marcan Syrophoenician pericope:[4] the latter text is confirmed and expounded at 10.23, 'Truly I say to you, you will not have gone through all the towns of Israel, before the Son of Man comes.' All three occur only in Matthew. We

---

[1] Jeremias (*Jesus' Promise to the Nations* [*JPN*] (E.T., London 1958), pp. 22f) interprets these two texts, with the help of several parentheses inserted into the text, to mean the triumphal proclamation of the Gospel by the Angel of Judgement, but he does not deny the general Matthaean emphasis on the Gentile mission.

[2] W. Trilling, *Das Wahre Israel* [*WI*] (3e., Munich 1964), see esp. p. 99.

[3] 27.15–26; 21.33–45, among Marcan passages overwritten: new material with a positive attitude to the Gentiles includes 2.1–12; 4.15f; 4.24; 5.13f; 8.5–13; 10.18; 12.18,21; 12.41f; 13.37f; 22.10; 25.31ff.

[4] In 15.23 the disciples say, 'Send her away for she is crying after us.' Jesus' reply in 24, 'I was sent only to the lost sheep of the house of Israel' is not an answer to this, but a Matthaean variant of Mark 7.27b, 'It is not good to take the children's bread . . .'. πρόβατον is Matthaean: οὐ . . . εἰ μή and Ἰσραήλ are semi-Matthaean. Jeremias, *JPN*, pp. 26f, argues that the verse goes back to an early Aramaic tradition. See p. 379f below. Cf. J. Schmid, 'Markus und der aramäische Matthäus', in *Synoptische Studien* (Munich 1953), pp. 171–4; Trilling, *WI*, p. 101.

have thus the contradiction of the same evangelist apparently introducing both a universalist and a particularist view of mission into the
tradition.

What can be done to palliate this paradox? Four possibilities seem
open: (*a*) both views might be included, since both were known to
have been held in the Church, despite their contradiction; (*b*) the
particularist view might be included, but transcended by the open
view; (*c*) both views might be included without noticing the opposition;
(*d*) the contradiction might be in some way only apparent.

The first view is maintained by Dr Nepper–Christensen: indeed it
is in some measure this contradiction, with its preponderant emphasis
on the open view, which led him to the improbable theory that Matthew
wrote for a non-Jewish church. He writes: 'Possibly the reason [sc.
for including the particularist texts] is a kind of conservatism. Possibly
there was a desire to make a bow to the past; or the reason can be the
realization that it was of value to stand by the oldest view of mission,
since *inter alia* there was doubt, and even friction, whether this old
view in its radicality might be right.'[5] Matthew then either deliberately
included the contradiction for sentimental reasons, or was prepared
to give support to both sides in a continuing debate. Trilling rejects
this view, which has much in common with the older line of compromise proposed by Holtzmann,[6] 'It is unthinkable that the evangelist
is proposing to his church two quite different mission-policies with
equal binding force.'[7] It may indeed be doubted whether any man
who was devoting himself to the Greek church, as Nepper-Christensen
pictures Matthew, would have been prepared so to hedge his bets as to
allow that his life's work might have been misplaced: nor is there any
document showing doubt or friction about the Gentile mission in the
70s.

Trilling himself takes the second, transcendence view. The particu-
larist view is included for apologetic reasons:[8] Jesus' mission to the
Jews only was evidence of his being Messiah, since Messiah in current
thought was a Jewish leader, without responsibility for world mission.
'The Twelve share this limitation of scope for the same reason . . .
Matthew sees this restriction transcended through the exaltation of
Jesus',[9] and this transcendence is made plain by contrasting the
phrasing of 10.5f with that of the world-mission laid on the Church

[5] P. Nepper–Christensen, *Das Matthäusevangelium—Ein judenchristliches Evangelium?*, pp. 204f; cf. pp. 180–201.
[6] H. J. Holtzmann, *Theologie des N.T.* I (Tübingen 1911), pp. 509ff; cf. pp. 504f.
[7] Trilling, *WI*, p. 102.
[8] Following L. Goppelt, *Christentum und Judentum im ersten und zweiten Jahr-hundert* (Gütersloh 1954), p. 181, 40n.
[9] Trilling, *WI*, p. 102.

at 28.18f.[10] It must be owned that Trilling's view is far from clear. He expressly denies a temporal transcendence: a particularist mission before, a universalist one after, the Resurrection. But in any case it is hard to see what he makes of 10.23. In what sense is the restricted mission 'transcended' by Jesus' exaltation in 28, if the Twelve are told that they will not have gone through all the towns of Israel before the Son of Man comes? The Son of Man's coming in Matthew always means the Second Coming. If the command in 28 transcends, in the sense of abolishes, the limitation of 10.5f, why does Matthew include at 10.23 an ἀμὴν λέγω ὑμῖν saying specifically extending the limitation till Doomsday? 10.23 is the rock on which Trilling's transcendence theory founders, just as it was the stumbling-block of the old historical view that the limitation was valid till the Resurrection.[11]

We could fall back on the older view (c), that Matthew was just the editor, who asked no questions, and, like the Chinese examinee, wrote down all he knew.[12] It could be alleged, by way of parallel, that two contradictory theologies of fulfilment are included side by side in Matt. 5. But whereas the slide from fulfil in the sense of 'carry to the uttermost' to fulfil in the sense of transcend is subtle and elusive, the contradiction between the two theologies of mission is striking and scandalous. We have to ask, Does Matthew in general treat Mark like this, writing down Marcan logia in open contradiction to his new material? We have seen[13] that on the contrary, with the sabbath issue, with the divorce issue, with the food-laws and Oral Torah, he twists and turns every way to avoid contradiction, and labours to provide a compromise. It seems only fair to suppose that he would do the same here.

If all these views fail, contradiction accepted, contradiction transcended, and contradiction ignored, is it possible to maintain the fourth option, contradiction apparent? Kilpatrick suggests a way out of 10.23 by supposing that 'the towns of Israel' means all the towns where Israelites were living, including the Diaspora. 'Verse 23 . . .

---

[10] πορευθέντες/πορευόμενοι, πάντα τὰ ἔθνη/μὴ ἀπέλθητε . . ., μαθητεύ-σατε/κηρύσσετε: following A. Vögtle, 'Das christologische und ecclesiologische Anliegen von Mt. 28.18–20', in *Studia Evangelica* (Berlin 1964), pp. 287f.

[11] See, for example, McNeile, Allen, Manson, and many others, who were content to take 10.5f as historical, and write 10.23 off as 'out of context'. A. Schweitzer, *The Quest of the Historical Jesus* (2e., E.T., London 1911), pp. 357f, alone took 10.23 seriously: but he wrote too early to wonder what Matthew made of it.

[12] See previous note. Even Jeremias, *JPN*, whose theory exculpates Jesus, leaves Matthew in the pit of contradiction. But Jeremias held a low view of Matthew: the allegorizer, embellisher, generalizer, distorter, and muddler *par excellence*!

[13] p. 17ff above.

cannot mean merely the cities of Palestine. It must be read in the light
of such passages as Acts 8.1–4; 9.1f; 11.19–21. It was Paul's custom
also in each city that he visited to go first to the Jewish synogogue. If
we can interpret the phrase τὰς πόλεις τοῦ Ἰσραήλ as meaning cities in
which Jewish communities were to be found, the restrictive implication of the verse disappears.'[14] But can we? Two considerations make
it highly unlikely that we can. The linguistic evidence for such a view
is *nil:* none of the passages Kilpatrick cites uses the word in the
required sense. 'Israel', true, means the community as well as the land,
but 'the cities of Israel' can only make sense in contrast to 'the cities
of the Gentiles' (cf. 10.5). Second, Matt. 10 divides into two halves:
in 5–25 explicit instructions are given for the Mission of the Twelve:
26–end is a more general exhortation to fearless confession. It is hard
to escape the conclusion that 10.23 is a typical Matthaean *inclusio*
with 10.5f: 'Go not into any way of the Gentiles, and enter no town
of the Samaritans, but go rather to the lost sheep of the house of
Israel . . . you will not have gone through all the towns of Israel
before the Son of Man comes.'

Kilpatrick's solution fails therefore: but another possibility is
open.[15] Matt. 10 is Jesus' charge to the Twelve: the Twelve are named
at the beginning, and at the end Matthew writes, 'And when Jesus had
finished instructing his twelve disciples . . .'. Now we know that in
the primitive Church the Twelve did conceive of their mission as being
limited to Palestine, and that this restriction was embodied in the terms
of the Council of Jerusalem as described in Gal. 2. Paul writes, 'They
saw that I had been entrusted with the gospel to the uncircumcised
just as Peter had been entrusted with the gospel to the circumcised—
for he who worked through Peter for the mission to the circumcised,
worked through me also for the Gentiles.'[16] Such was the historical
fact at the end of the 40s: Peter (and the Twelve; but principally John,
and James the Lord's brother) were the pillars of the mission to Israel;
Paul and Barnabas were accepted as having a divine commission to
Gentiledom. Certainly at that time neither Peter nor Paul drew the
line by communities, but by geography. Paul preached to Israelite
and Gentile alike outside Palestine, and his 'Gentile' churches were
all mixed churches: Peter's mission had been entirely a Palestine
mission, but including Gentiles such as Cornelius. Although later

[14] *Origins*, p. 119. Kilpatrick prefers the text of DLΘ abdk, etc., which have,
'. . . flee to the next; and if they persecute you from there, flee to the next; for
verily . . .'. It is not easy to see how this helps his interpretation. See also J.
Munck, *Paul and the Salvation of Mankind* (E.T., London 1959), p. 256.
[15] Partly hinted at in Manson, *SJ*, p. 180.
[16] Gal. 2.7f.

Peter's visits to mixed churches in Antioch, and perhaps Corinth and Rome, raised doubt on this division, such an interpretation of the area of the mission of the Twelve was (*a*) unquestioned for nearly twenty years after the Crucifixion, (*b*) enshrined in the Galatian Epistle, and (*c*) with the sole and doubtful[17] exception of Peter's later tours, was maintained, so far as we know, to the end.

The Matthaean tension may then be resolved on this basis. Whether Matthew had read Galatians, as I should think likely,[18] or not, he would be aware that the mission of the Twelve had been a Palestinian mission. He therefore introduced into Jesus' Mission-charge to them the restriction that they were to evangelize Palestine, and that this would be as much as they could undertake before the Parousia.[19] Gentile governors and others would see their witness (10.18), but their preaching and their martyrdom was to be for the Jews of Palestine. In 24 Jesus is still speaking to the Twelve ('his disciples') and he now adumbrates openly (as he had often hinted before) the world-wide mission which Matthew had seen and believed to be the Lord's will for the Church: 'This gospel of the kingdom will be preached throughout the whole world, as a testimony to all nations.' Note that this is a prophecy, and not a command. The Twelve have their mission in Palestine, but the mission of the Church will outsoar their narrow field, till the wedding-hall is filled with guests. After the Resurrection the world-commission is given, and this time *to the whole Church, not just the Twelve.* Jesus sends for the whole community to come to Galilee: 'Go and tell *my brethren* to go to Galilee, and there they will see me.' (28.10). 'My brethren' must mean the whole Christian group, as at 12.50, 'Whoever does the will of my Father in heaven is my brother . . .'. It is a quite unnatural expression for the Apostles. The Eleven then went to Galilee to the appointed mountain, and when they saw him they worshipped him. Now worship in Matthew always implies faith: it is an extremely common word, and is never associated with doubt, which is its opposite. This is made abundantly clear by 14.31ff; Peter was afraid at the wind, and began to sink, but Jesus 'caught him, saying "O man of little faith, why did you doubt?"

[17] Peter no doubt understood his journeys as 'confirming the churches'; Paul understood them as 'building upon another man's foundation'. It is nowhere suggested that Peter undertook a mission to the Gentiles abroad, although it seemed like this to Irenaeus a century later (*Adv. Haer.* III. 3.1).

[18] cf. p. 153ff above.

[19] The same point is to be seen at Matt. 15.26. Mark 7.27 has, 'Let the children first be fed . . .', which Matthew omits. If the Gentiles must wait till the Jews are converted, they will never hear the word, for the Jews will not obey till the end. The two Missions were to go on simultaneously, and the less πρῶτον the better. cf. also the promotion of a Gentile healing to the second place, 8.5ff.

. . . And those in the boat worshipped him, saying, "Truly you are the son of God." ' While on the water Peter was of little faith and doubted: when in the boat the disciples had faith, and worshipped. It is plain therefore that the phrase οἱ δὲ ἐδίστασαν at 28.17 should be translated 'but others doubted'.[20] οἱ δὲ has precisely this meaning at 26.27, 'Then they spat on his face and struck him: οἱ δὲ ἐρράπισαν αὐτόν',[21] and others slapped him: there is no passage in Matthew where οἱ δὲ means a part of the preceding group, so as to justify the normal translation, 'But some (of them) doubted.' The Twelve, then, Matthew's heroes, now had faith in full, they worshipped: others of the brethren, who had followed at the Lord's behest, were weaker. Jesus confirms their hearts with the proclamation of his now universal authority. The community is to go forth and make disciples, the Twelve in Palestine, the Church at large among all nations.

It is possible thus to reconcile Matthew's particularist and universalist tendencies. He inserts a generally positive view of the Gentile mission, for that had been the Lord's will, as history showed: he inserts also a more limited view of the apostolic mission, since the apostles' work had been the evangelizing of Palestine only. So far as the *doctrine* is concerned, both themes could have been written in by Matthew himself: and the linguistic, rhythmical, and imaginative evidence would suggest this conclusion. Verses 5–8 bear evidence of being an exposition of the indirect commands of Jesus in Mark, in Matthew's *oratio recta*. ἀπέστειλεν and παραγγείλας are from Mark 6.7–8. Jesus had called the Twelve κηρύσσειν (Mark 3.14): and the phrase, 'the kingdom of heaven is at hand' is the standard content of preaching (Mark 1.15; Matt. 4.17). The phrase 'the lost sheep of the house of Israel' comes again in Matt. 15.24, editorially, and is undoubtedly Matthew's own. It may owe something to Jer. 50.6 (LXX, 27.6), πρόβατα ἀπολωλότα ἐγενήθη ὁ λαός μου; the sheep image is in any case typical, and carries on the theme of the sheep without a shepherd in 9.36. If the command is Matthaean, the anticipatory prohibition is Matthaean too, for 5b makes no sense without 6. Anticipatory epexegetic prohibitions are a standard Matthaean feature: there are 8 in Matthew, none in Mark, 2 in Luke (Q). It is no argument against Matthaean authorship that Samaritans come here only in the Gospel, for Matthew is always writing in pairs, and the Gentiles as a disbelieving community go with the Samaritans as a disbelieving com-

---

[20] So Allen, McNeile; cf. I. P. Ellis, 'But Some Doubted', *NTS* 14.4 (July 1968). Ellis distinguishes doubt (διστάζω) from disbelief (διακρίνομαι): but he exactly misses the point at Matt. 14.31ff, where doubt is succeeded by, and contrasted with, worship and confession of faith.
[21] D significantly interprets ἄλλοι δέ.

munity as inevitably as the individual disobedient Gentile goes with the individual disobedient tax-gatherer. ὁδόν is similarly a pair to πόλιν both here and at 10.10f (AT), 'no wallet for the *road* . . . whatever *town* or village you enter.'[22] 10.8 takes up θεραπεύω and ἐκβάλλω from 9.35; 10.1.[23] In 8—9 Jesus had healed the sick, like Simon's mother-in-law, and crowned that by raising the dead girl: he cleansed the leper first at 8.1, and cast out the demon last in 9.32ff. The verse is an example of the multiple antithesis or typhlic, of which there are 6 in Matthew, none in Mark, one in Luke:[24] cf. Matthew's, 'I was hungry and you gave me food . . .', a six-unit antithesis as against the three units here. Linguistically, πρόβατον and the kingdom of heaven are Matthaean: semi-Matthaean are, introductory ὁ Ἰησοῦς, μὴ + aor. subj. (2), ἔθνη, Ἰσραήλ, πορεύομαι (2), λέγων, -οντες, θεραπεύω, λαμβάνω—17 typical words in all out of 52. δωρεάν is found here only, but δῶρον is Matthaean. The conclusion seems probable that the whole section 10.5–8 is Matthew's own amplification of Mark 6.7f.

The same conclusion is likely for the following section, 10.9–15. Where Mark bids the Twelve to take no brass for the journey, Matthew, the evangelist of a wealthier church,[25] has, 'Take no gold or silver or brass'—large units of money are standard in Matthew.[26] He also thinks of the money first, whereas the earlier tradition thinks first of bread and pack. Jesus had permitted a stick to his apostles: they were to depend on their converts for food and shelter, but asceticism in itself was not the point. Matthew, who had not perhaps walked from town to town himself, excludes this also. The neat epigram, 'For worthy the labourer of his food' seals the command: Matthew has already compared the apostles to ἐργαταί going to work in the harvest at 9.37; τροφή is Matthaean, and ἄξιος is semi-Matthaean. For the shape of the sentence as a paragraph-closer, an arcetic, cf. (AT) 'Sufficient to the day its evil', 'And the enemies of a man his house-holders', both Matthaean.[27] It is often noted how close is the thought between this passage and 1 Cor. 9, where Paul cites the Lord's command that those who proclaim the gospel should live of the gospel, and compares the apostle to a ploughman and thresher, working in hope of a share in the crop. The link is unquestionable, but it is to be observed that Paul keeps separate the arguments from analogy—

---

[22] The absence of articles does not denote a Semitic original (cp. Jeremias, *JPN*, pp. 19f), but a Semitic mind: cf. 26.6/Mark 14.3, and p. 119 above. With ὁδὸν ἐθνῶν cf. M. Ab. Zar. 1.4, 'If the road leads to (a Gentile town on feast-day)', it is forbidden.

[23] But the suggestion is already in Mark 6.13, 'And they cast out many demons, and anointed with oil many that were sick and healed them'.

[24] See p. 85f above.

[25] Kilpatrick, *Origins*, p. 125.

[26] See p. 61 above.

[27] cf. p. 79 above.

the soldier, vineyard-tender, shepherd, ploughman, thresher—from the
dominical command which he introduces finally as a last word in the
matter. There is nothing whatever to indicate that Paul knew anything
more elaborate than some such tradition as Mark provides. *Per contra*,
he uses none of the three Matthaean words, ἐργατής, τροφή, ἄξιος. It
would be natural, however, to think that Matthew was familiar with
1 Corinthians[28] which had had twenty years in which to circulate in
the Church, and that he expanded Mark in the light of its agricultural
analogies. Matthaean workers are elsewhere paid in cash, but with
an eye on the Pauline payment in kind he writes, 'The labourer deserves
his *food*': Luke, who also lived in a cash economy ('How many
μίσθιοι of my father . . . Make me as one of your μίσθιοι'), amends,
'. . . is worth his μισθός'. Had not the Macedonian churches sent
Paul aid in cash?

10.11–15

Matthew retains the Marcan sentence-structure, but expands the
substance, giving detailed instructions from what had become the
norm of missionary life.[29] Mark had, 'Where you enter a house . . .'
but he knows the peril of rejection—'And if any place will not receive
you . . .'. Matthew formalizes the situation: 'Whatever town or
village [cf. Matt. 9.35] you enter, find out who is worthy in it [ἄξιος,
link-word with 10.10] . . . As you enter the house salute it [Matthew's
fondness for salutations, cf. 5.47; 23.7ff]; and if the house is
worthy let your peace come upon it [Matthew's religious imagery];
but if it is not worthy let your peace return to you [Matthew's repetitive antithesis].' The house, as well as the town, is to have its dust
shaken off the apostles' feet on leaving (cf. Mark's ambiguous
τόπος).[30] Mark ended, '. . . for a testimony against them', which
Matthew suppresses: the scribal mind turns instead to an illustration from scripture: the classic example of unworthy towns under
divine retribution was Sodom and Gomorrah, which ignored

---

[28] cf. p. 153ff above. There are strong links not only with 1 Cor. 9 here, but with
1 Cor. 1—3 at 11.25f, (p. 361 below) and with 1 Cor. 5 at 18.15–20 (p. 163 above).
In both the other cases it is demonstrable that Paul is not familiar with the
Matthaean logia as they stand.

[29] cf. 18.5–20, where the Marcan tradition of the care of the laity is similarly
expanded with detailed instructions from the norm of Christian synagogue
practice.

[30] Luke in 9.1–6 is following Mark, and uses the Marcan sentence-structures: the
Matthaean version is, however, influential on him: (*a*) in forbidding the staff;
(*b*) in ἀργύριον for χαλκός; (*c*) in εἰς ἣν ἂν, ἐξερχόμενοι, τῆς πόλεως
ἐκείνης, and τὸν κονίορτον.

righteous Lot.[31] Matthew adds now that it will be worse for that town than for them, and returns to the theme in 11. ἡμέρα κρίσεως are Matthaean; ἀμὴν λέγω ὑμῖν, ἔσται, γῆ, Σόδομα and pleonastic ἐκεῖνος are semi-Matthaean.

10.16–25

Matthew has now given, in *oratio recta*, the substance of the Marcan mission-charge. Mark's charge had been limited to four verses, whose attention was mainly upon the tradition, no doubt with an eye also to present practice. Matthew, from the situation of a beleaguered Jewish–Christian community on the point of excommunication, is concerned to treat the mission on a more permanent basis: and the outcome of the Palestinian mission in the decades following had been rejection, persecution, and martyrdom. He therefore transfers into this context the warnings of persecution, first from Mark 13, where they are specific and detailed, later from Mark 8, where they are more general and personal. Mark 13.9–13 goes in almost word for word: μαστιγώσουσιν replaces δαρήσεσθε as a more technical translation of *makkôt*[32] and there are various verbal improvements. The only phrase requiring serious change is Mark's, 'And the gospel must first be preached to all nations', which is precisely not the point of Matthew's mission to the house of Israel: he neatly adjusts the preceding sentence, 'And you will be dragged before governors and kings for my sake, to bear testimony before them', and adds '*and the Gentiles*'. The Marcan sentence ran down to 'them': by adding 'and the Gentiles', Matthew makes αὐτοῖς mean Jews in synagogues, Jewish princes such as Herod, etc;[33] and includes Christian testimony to such as Felix and Festus and their retinues, without implying a Gentile mission.

This Marcan prophecy of the cost of the apostolic mission is framed in Matthaean epigrams. 10.16 has four of Matthew's favourite animal images:[34] sheep and wolves, serpents and doves. The sheep/wolves antithesis comes also at 7.15 and not elsewhere in the Gospels: it is suggested by the *pastoral* theme of the discourse, sheep not having a

---

[31] cf. 2 Pet. 2.6f.
[32] So Hare, *The Theme of Jewish Persecution of the Christians in the Gospel according to St Matthew*, pp. 91n, 104; H. H. Schneider, *TWNT* IV, pp. 521ff.
[33] Hare, op. cit., pp. 106f, argues that αὐτοῖς refers to Gentile governors and kings (the nearest nouns), and claims this to be the meaning here and at Mark 13.9. But (*a*) βασιλεῖς are naturally Jewish kings, since no other try Christians in early tradition: cf. Acts 12.1–12, 25–6; (*b*) for the final phrase in Matthew an ἄλλοις would be required; (*c*) the whole Matthaean context shows *Jewish* persecutors to be in mind.
[34] See p. 101f. above.

shepherd, lost sheep. 'Be φρόνιμοι as serpents and ἀκέραιοι as doves' is likely to be related to the Pauline, 'I would have you wise (σοφούς) as to what is good and guileless (ἀκεραίους) as to what is evil':[35] the Matthaean φρόνιμος and the Matthaean animals show, if so, that Matthew is adapting a Pauline or standard ethical platitude, and not the other way round. The use of ὄφις is of characteristic versatility: Matthew sees the snake as the exemplar of subtlety as well as deceit (cf. Gen. 3), just as he sees the leaven as a symbol of the kingdom as well as of festering evil. The rhythm is a pure Matthaean pardic:[36] 'Can the Ethiopian change his skin, or the leopard his spots?', 'So be wise as serpents and innocent as doves.' ἰδού and οὖν are semi-Matthaean: the doubled ὡς reappears at 10.25, disciple as teacher, slave as master, a feature not found in Mark or Luke. 10.23 marks the beginning of the *inclusio* on the Palestine mission, and takes up 10.5f. The doctrine is the Pauline view of the continuance of the mission to the Jews in failure until the Second Coming, when repentance will come, and Jerusalem will say, 'Blessed is he who comes in the name of the Lord' (23.39):[37] the task of the Twelve in the meantime, as envisaged by both Matthew and Paul, is the holding out of God's hands all day long to a disobedient and gainsaying people. The language of the verse is highly characteristic. διώκω, and ὁ υἱὸς τοῦ ἀνθρώπου ἔρχεται are Matthaean; ἀμὴν λέγω ὑμῖν, τελέω, Ἰσραήλ, οὐ μὴ . . . ἕως ἄν are semi-Matthaean. Two further epigrammatic verses complete the paragraph. 'A *disciple* is not above his *teacher*, nor a *slave* above his *lord*' is a pardic, and so is the following half-verse.[38] δοῦλος (2), κύριος with a genitive (2), ὑπέρ with the accusative (2), the doubled ὡς (cf. 10.16), ἀρκέω, and οἰκοδεσπότης are all characteristic language: the image of the *talmîdh* and rabbi is from the religious area which is Matthew's specialty, and the slave–lord relationship is also typical of him.[39] The final logion, 'If they have called the master of the house Beelzebul . . .', derives from the controversy of Mark 3, to which allusion has been made at Matt. 9.34, 'He casts out demons by the prince of demons'. The form is the rabbinic *qal-waḥômēr*, also a thought-pattern peculiar to Matthew/Q in the Gospel tradition.[40] Matthew makes explicit the Hebrew pun:

[35] Rom. 16.19.
[36] See p. 71ff above.   [37] p. 162 above.
[38] Luke 6.40 omits the second half of the pardic: he is using the logion to show the Christian's future maturity, not his liability to his teacher's sufferings.
[39] It occurs also in the Tares and the Unmerciful Servant, the Faithful and Wise Steward, and the Talents, all new Matthaean material: in Luke only in the last two, and at 14.23; never in Mark. The sentiment of this logion is common in the rabbis, e.g. 'It is enough for the slave that he should be as his master' (B Ber. 58b).
[40] See p. 24 above.

οἶκος = z^e*bhûl*, δεσποτής = *ba'al*. Of the 87 words in 10.16, 23–5, 31 are characteristic.

10.26–33

The Mission-charge and the warning of persecution are now complete: next, logically, is an exhortation to courage in witness. One passage in Mark is plainly to the point: the stern words on saving and losing life in Mark 8.34–8, which are to form the main thread of the rest of Matthew's discourse. But before that, Jesus had also taught his disciples the Sower parable, how he and they must preach the word, and often it would be fruitless: and had added (4.22, AT), 'For there is nothing hidden except that it may be opened; nor was in secret but that it should come into the open.' This somewhat cryptic saying Matthew interprets by the context: 'So have no fear of them: for nothing is covered that will not be revealed, or hidden that will not be known.' He sharpens up Mark's somewhat clumsy pardic (12 words for 17, different verbs for Mark's φανερόω/φανερόν, κρυπτόν/ἀπόκρυφον). Then, like a good scribe, he gives the same teaching in a second form, but retaining the pardic rhythm—'What I *tell* you in the *dark*, *utter* in the *light*; and what you *hear* in the *ear*, *proclaim* upon the *housetops*.' The whispering of arcane teaching was a rabbinic custom:[41] κηρύξατε picks up the preaching commands of 10.7: the visual images of the preceding verse (cover, reveal) are naturally succeeded by auditory images in this (hear, ear). 'Fear not', Matthew writes in 26, to carry over the thought from the warning of martyrdom to courageous witness: and he takes up the word in 28, 'Do not live in fear [present imperative] of your persecutors, but live in fear of God.'[42] The verse has Matthew's thesauric rhythm,[43] cf. 'Do not lay up for yourselves treasures upon earth . . .'. Gehenna, οὖν, κρυπτός are characteristic: for ψυχή/σῶμα antithesis,[44] cf. 6.25ff (in a slightly different sense). For an illustration of God's providence Matthew again turns to the animal kingdom—to the birds, as at 6.26. The sparrows are one of his 22 animals.[45] In the Mishnah it is said similarly, 'Thy mercy extends even to a sparrow's nest',[46] and almost the same phrasing comes in

---

[41] B. Hag. 14a; Gen. R. 3.4. The matter is expounded in full in J. Jeremias, *The Eucharistic Words of Jesus* (3e., E.T., London 1966), pp. 125–32.

[42] God, not Satan, has this authority, cf. Jas. 4.12.

[43] See p. 79f above.

[44] For the judgement of body and soul in Jewish thought, cf. the parable of the Blind and the Lame, cited on p. 49 above.

[45] See p. 101f above.

[46] M. Meg. 4.9; cf. 'If a bird is not captured without Heaven, how much less the life of a man!'; Gen. R. 79.

Amos 3.5, LXX, εἰ πεσεῖται ὄρνεον ἐπὶ τὴν γῆν ἄνευ ἰξευτοῦ; In the Sermon Matthew moved from God's providing for the birds to our inability to add to our stature: here from the sparrows to the numbering of our hairs. Linguistically 'your father' is Matthaean: οὐχί; δύο, γῆ, οὖν, διαφέρω are semi-Matthaean. The *inclusio* at 10.31, 'So fear not . . .' is typical: θρίξ/κεφαλή recur together at 5.36. 10.32f are a Matthaean rewriting of Mark 8.38, 'For whoever is ashamed of me and my words . . . of him will the Son of Man be ashamed . . .'. He makes it a typical repetitive converse logion:[47] 'Everyone who confesses me I will confess, but him who denies me I will deny.'[48] 'My father in heaven' (2) is Matthaean: ὁμολογῶ (2), ἔμπροσθεν (2), οἱ ἄνθρωποι = men (2), κἀγώ are semi-Matthaean—that is, almost every word but ἀρνέομαι is characteristic. Of 137 words in the paragraph, 47 are typical of Matthew.

Luke copies the paragraph at 12.2–9, but with significant changes. The saying, 'Nothing is covered that will not be revealed . . .', he takes to mean 'Hypocrisy will out', and attaches it to his warning to beware of hypocrisy. He then needs to alter the following verse to 'Whatever *you* have said in the dark shall be heard in the light . . .' to give the same sense. His addition, 'What you have whispered in private rooms', draws on the example of Elisha[49] who was able to proclaim what the king of Syria had so spoken. This means that a break in the sense is postponed, but inevitable, and it comes in the next verse, being bridged by the apologetic, 'But I say to you my friends . . .' (AT). Hypocrisy, which had been the Pharisaic vice at the end of Luke 11, now becomes the fear of persecution. The poetic balance of Matthew's killing the body/killing body and soul is, as so often, destroyed in a welter of prosaic additions. As at 6.22, Luke has the more portentous 'The Son of Man' for Matthew's 'I', probably in reminiscence of Mark 8.38.[50] Of the changed words in the Lucan

---

[47] See p. 75 above.

[48] cf. Rom. 10.9. 'If you confess (ὁμολογήσῃς) with your lips that Jesus is Lord . . . you will be saved.' In view of the influence of other texts from Romans, we have to reckon with the possibility of the same here.

[49] 2 Kings 6.12.

[50] It is often argued that in the preaching of Jesus the Son of Man was a figure distinct from Jesus himself, and that in our passage Luke retains the original distinction, while Matthew represents the post–Easter assimilation of the two. So R. Bultmann, *Theology of the NT* (E.T., London 1952) I, pp. 28ff; H. E. Tödt, *The Son of Man in the Synoptic Tradition* (E.T., London 1965), pp. 89ff; G. Bornkamm, *Jesus of Nazareth* (E.T., London 1960), p. 228. The view assumes the Q hypothesis. However, the phrase 'Son of Man' is inserted into Marcan contexts by both Matthew and Luke at Mark 3.28f, by Luke at Luke 22.48, and by Matthew at Matt. 16.13,28; 17.12: so there is unquestionably a tendency in the later tradition to *write the title into Mark*—Matt. 16.13 is a clear case of its insertion

version φίλος, ἐνώπιον (2), μετὰ ταῦτα are Lucan: semi-Lucan are οἱ ἄγγελοι τοῦ θεοῦ = God, μή + part., ναὶ λέγω ὑμῖν, περισσότερον, ὑποδεικνύω, οὐκ ἔχω + inf. Two non-Lucan words which are taken over from Matthew are ὁμολογῶ and γέεννα. Only ἐπιλελησμένον does not occur elsewhere in Luke, and might lead us to suspect another source.

10.34–end

The Marcan warning of persecution (Matt. 10.17–22) contained the threat of treachery from within the family, 'Brother will deliver up brother to death . . . and children will rise (ἐπαναστήσονται) against parents.' This prophecy is already related in Mark to the text in Micah,[51] 'The son dishonours the father, and the daughter will rise up (ἐπαναστήσεται) against her mother, the daughter-in-law against her mother-in-law: those in his house shall be a man's enemies' (Mic. 7.6, LXX). Matthew quotes virtually the whole verse, with the introduction ἦλθον διχάσαι for Micah's weaker ἀτιμάζει. It is prefaced with the peace-and-sword logion. For the structure of the saying cf. Matthew's, '*Think not that I came to* destroy the law and the prophets: *I came not to* destroy *but to* fulfil' (5.17, AT): it is one of the Matthaean thesauric rhythms,[52] unparalleled in Mark or Luke. μή + aor. subj., νομίζω, theological ἦλθον (2), μάχαιρα, κατά + gen. (3), βαλεῖν (2), and γῆ are characteristic, but διχάζω is only here. οἰκιακοί follows on from 10.25. The division of loyalty is now taken further in a three-bar climax which we have called a *misthic*,[53] of which the third bar is Marcan: verses 38–9 here are a sharpened form of Mark 8.34f:[54] λαμβάνω, φιλέω (2), ἤ (2), ὑπέρ + acc. (2), and ἄξιος (3) are semi-Matthaean. There are 4 misthics in Matthew, none in Mark, one in Luke (Q). The climax—he who loves parents more than me, he who loves children more than me, he who does not take his cross after me—bridges beautifully from the Micah text to Mark 8.34f. Two further texts from Mark complete the discourse. In Mark 9.37 Jesus had said of anyone receiving a child in his name, 'he

---

for the sake of its mysterious overtones. This would lead us to suppose that the overall frequency ratio Matt. 30/Mark 13/Luke 24 is to be explained in the same way. Luke has the title where Matthew has ἐμοῦ at Luke 6.22, and he has, 'The Son of Man came . . .' at 19.10 whereas Matthew and Mark invariably write ἦλθον. There are therefore three cases (6.22; 12.8; 19.10) where it is natural to see Luke as writing the title into non-Marcan contexts, as well as two (12.10; 22.48) into Mark. In the case of 12.8 he had the phrase to hand in Mark 8.38.
[51] Hare, op. cit., p. 42.   [52] See p. 79f above.
[53] See p. 83f above.
[54] For the sharpening of the rhythm of Mark 8.35 see p. 72 above.

receives me: and whoever receives me, receives not me but him that sent me.' Four verses later he promises that anyone giving a cup of water 'in the name that you are Christ's' will not lose his reward. Matthew makes this his peroration. Mark's 'one of these little ones' (9.42) he interprets of the lay believer, now assumed in the background, who will also participate in the mission. Mark's child (9.37) becomes Matthew's Christian: so is the open dominical doctrine of the receiving of the Lord assimilated to the Pauline teaching that the Church is the body of Christ—to receive an apostle/Christian is to receive him. We have the same doctrine of the presence of Christ where the Church, and especially the apostles, are, at Matt. 18.20 and 28.20. Between the two Marcan logia, now taken of the apostle and the lay Christian, Matthew builds another bridge as in the previous paragraph. Prophets and saints are an OT pair at Matt. 13.17: here they are a shorter form of the Church's 'prophets and wise men and scribes' of Matt. 23.34. The bridge is again in the form of a misthic: 'He who receives a prophet in the name of a prophet, a saint in the name of a saint, (Marcan) gives a cup of (cold)[55] water in the name of a disciple'—only this time the misthic is in the form of an anticlimax: apostle, prophet, saint, lay Christian.[56] The images are from Matthew's religious group. μισθός, μόνον, and εἰς ὄνομα are Matthaean, λαμβάνω and δίκαιος are semi-Matthaean.[57] There are 73 words in the new material, verses 34–7, 41f, if we omit those from Micah LXX: 31 are typical.

Chapter 10 seems therefore, on examination, to give every sign of being a typical piece of Matthaean midrash. Matthew develops the Marcan Mission-charge in the light of the apostolic mission to Israel,

---

[55] A characteristically sharp image, cf. 'the uttermost farthing'; Mark, 'the mustard-seed . . . becomes the greatest of all shrubs', Matt., '. . . and becomes a tree'; Mark, 'His garments became glistening, intensely white', Matt. '. . . white as light,'.

[56] cf. the Sower: Mark, '30, 60, 100', Matt., '100, 60, 30', 13.23.

[57] Luke has the Micah reference at 12.51ff. He destroys the poetic balance of both Matthaean verses, and gives instead a Lucan catalogue of the six relationships in the typhlic form. Instead of the Matthaean Christian at odds with his unconverted relatives who will hand him over to authority, Luke substitutes a family divided 2 : 3 on the faith—death by the sword is no longer in question. παραγίνομαι, διαμερίζω, οἶκος, ἀπὸ τοῦ νῦν are all Lucan expressions. δοκεῖτε ὅτι; comes three times in Luke, too, never in his predecessors. Luke 14.26f is a version of Matt. 10.38f, with another catalogue of relations: most of them from Mark 10.29f. βαστάζω, ἔτι, ἑαυτοῦ are Lucan, as is approval for leaving one's wife for Christ (cf. Luke 18.29). For ἔρχεσθαι πρός με of discipleship, cf. Luke 6.47 only. For μισέω = put in second place, cf. Deut. 21.15ff, LXX (of a wife): I shall suggest in ch. 21 below (see appendix), that Luke 14 was read alongside Deut. 21.

with all its tragedy of rejection and persecution: he adds the persecution passage from Mark 13, and then expounds what he has written —partly with further Marcan texts, 4.22; 8.34–8; 9.37–42, partly with Mark's Micah passage, partly in his own words. Wherever we have the last we find Matthaean language, Matthaean rhythms, Matthaean images, Matthaean doctrine: and in every case traces of secondariness in the Lucan parallels. It is hard to see what evidence there is of any other pre-Matthaean source than Mark.

(20) Those Sent by John
11.2–end (+ 12.1–8)

Matthew now comes to the actual week of New Year, and expounds the significance of the healing wonders recited over the past months. They are the works of Messiah, foretold by Isaiah in the New Year lesson,[58] the earnest of the inbreaking of the Kingdom; and the evangelist can think of other Isaianic prophecies besides. But they are also the sad occasion of judgement upon Israel which has stumbled at them, and whose failure to repent calls for a New Year sermon.

But with New Year Matthew is no longer quite his own master as he has been hitherto. For New Year marked the opening of the Marcan cycle,[59] and the opening paragraphs of Mark's Gospel had been for a decade the Gospel for Rosh-hashshanah: and a very suitable Gospel too. John Baptist's call to repentance and his announcement of the advent of the kingdom were the Christian fulfilment of New Year, which Matthew had no desire to change: only that he is not in a position to go back to a time before Christ's ministry began. His own arrangement illuminates the fulfilment of the old themes even better than Mark's, perhaps: but liturgical traditions die hard.

In this situation Matthew, with typical resource, draws on a hint in the Marcan pericope following the one he has just been using. When Mark had recounted the Mission-charge of Jesus to the Twelve, he went on to describe the speculations of Herod and others on Jesus' healings, who he might be: and took occasion to tell of the Baptist's death in prison (6.14ff). John Baptist's martyrdom Matthew postpones to a more convenient place, but he makes use of the other suggestions of the Marcan paragraph. The healing wonders of Jesus, as in Mark, cause the stir: Matthew can now proclaim 'the deeds of the Christ'.[60] Again they give rise to speculation, but Matthew allows John to come

[58] See p. 312f above.   [59] See above, ch. 9, appendix B.
[60] Matthew speaks of Jesus as ὁ Χριστός only here and at 1.17. The earlier use is also significant: there were three double weeks of generations from Abraham to the coming of Messiah.

closer to the truth than the idle guesses of the Marcan crowd:[61] 'Are you he who is to come, or shall we look for another?' Again the questioning arises from John's prison. This development of the Mark 6 story brings John back on to the New Year stage, and Matthew keeps him there with what modern dramatic technique would call a flashback. Jesus recalls the ministry of John in the wilderness in a series of rhetorical questions, and cites the Malachi verse with which Mark had opened his book. He had suppressed it in 3, citing only Isa. 40: now is the time to proclaim John's destiny, his greatness and tragedy. The two themes, the signs of the kingdom and John's preaching of it, can now be worked into a sermon. This generation has rejected both, and will be condemned like Tyre and Babylon and Sodom before it. Only the simple can inherit the blessings of the Kingdom. How far Marcan material was able to provide the thread for Matthew's embroidery, how far the embroidery can be seen to be characteristically Matthaean, or how much prior tradition we have to posit, we must now explore.

11.2–6

The forming of John's question enables Matthew to suggest Jesus' Messiahship forcibly without putting it into words: that must await the Petrine Confession. The suggestion comes from putting together a catena of messianic prophecies from Isaiah. Isa. 35.3–6 tell of God's judgement and his coming to save Israel, an apt New Year reading; and the blind, the deaf, the halt, and the stammerer are healed in token. Matthew replaces the stammerer[62] with his first-healed leper. Isa. 26.19f tells of the eschatological wrath of God, when the dead shall rise from the tombs. Isa. 60—61 tell of the coming of God's salvation and the evangelizing of the poor.[63] Isa. 8.14f tell of the stumbling of Israel at Immanuel. The key-phrases are put together in a further triple parallelism, or typhlic,[64] cf. Matthew's, 'Heal the sick, raise the dead, cleanse the lepers, cast out demons, Freely you received, freely give' (AT). Such forms never occur in Mark, only once in Luke. The language again is partly characteristic: σκανδαλίζομαι ἐν is Matthaean; semi-Matthaean are ἀποκριθεὶς εἶπεν, πορεύομαι,

---

[61] These are omitted by Matthew at 14.1ff.
[62] The healing of a μογιλάλος in Mark 7 shows that the Church was already using the prophecy before Matthew's day: as with his use of Mic. 7.6 at 10.35f, Matthew is making more explicit the use of a scripture referred to in Mark.
[63] There is a further 'fulfilment' of Isa. 26 when the saints rise from their tombs, 27.52: for Matthew's use of Isa. 61.1, cf. p. 277f above.
[64] See p. 85 above.

ἀπαγγέλλω, τυφλός, χωλός, κωφός, ἐγείρομαι, χριστός, ἤ, διά—13 characteristic words out of 63. There seems no reason to posit a pre-Matthaean source. Luke gives the paragraph in almost the same words (7.18–23), but with an awkward interpolation[65] at 7.21 to enable John's disciples to witness Jesus' healing of the blind, which has not so far occurred in his Gospel.

11.7–19

The significance of the Baptist, as set forth by Mark, was that he was the Christ's forerunner, and this was shown in the second verse of Mark's Gospel with a citation from Malachi.[66] While Matthew gave the associated Isa. 40 citation in the context (3.3), he omitted the Malachi reference then, so as to give it full play in due course. He cites it now: the Baptist was the preparer of 'thy way'—that is, Christ's way—'before thee', added by Matthew for emphasis. But far greater relief is given to the quotation by making it the climax of a three-bar logion: 'What did you go out to see in the desert? The reed-grass? No. A courtier? No. A prophet? No: my messenger.' This is the Matthaean misthic[67] device, of which we have already seen two examples at the end of 10.

The development of the paragraph is based upon the two Marcan passages on John, 1.2ff and 6.14f. 'John appeared *in the wilderness . . .* and there went out to him all the country of Judea and all the people of Jerusalem; and they were baptized by him in the Jordan' (Mark 1.4f). Hence the question, 'What did you go out *into the wilderness* to behold?' The twice repeated question is shorter each time—'But what did you go out to see?' (AT), 'Why then did you go out?'—like the three denials of Peter,[68] only two of which are given *viva voce* in

[65] 'Very awkwardly interpolated by Luke', Creed, op. cit., p. 106.
[66] The citation combines Exod. 23.20 and Mal. 3.1. The final words are as follows:

Exod. 23.20	. . . *mal'ākh lᵉphāneikhā*	LXX . . . τὸν ἄγγελόν μου πρὸ προσώπου σου . . . τῇ ὁδῷ
Mal. 3.1	. . . *derekh lᵉphānāi*	LXX(B) . . . ὁδὸν πρὸ προσώπου μου
Mark 1.2	. . . τὴν ὁδόν σου	Matt. 11.10 . . . τὴν ὁδόν σου ἔμπροσθέν σου

Matthew is using his Hebrew to take advantage of the Exod. Hebrew. See Stendahl, pp. 49f.
[67] See p. 83f above.
[68] 'I do not know what you mean', 'I do not know the man', 'I do not know the man'.

Mark, or the three prayers in Gethsemane,[69] or the three decreasing formulas, 'You have heard that it was said . . .' twice over in 5.[70] The first ironic suggestion arises from the Jordan. The κάλαμός is used collectively for the reed-grass in Ps. 68.30, 'the wild beasts τοῦ καλαμοῦ'; and reed-grass *is* the wild vegetation of the wilderness of Jordan,[71] and is all there is to see. It is often the subject of rabbinic similes.[72] R. Simeon b. Eleazar said, 'A man should always be pliant as a reed . . . How is it with a reed? All the winds come and blow against it, and it sways to and fro with them. When the winds have been lulled, the reed resumes its normal position.'[73] It is likely that such similes would have been available to Matthew from the rabbinic stock. The second ironic suggestion arises from John's clothing in Mark 1, and his prison in Mark 6. John wore camel-hair, and met his death at the hands of those who wore soft clothing in Herod's palace: the king and his wife and his wife's daughter and his princes. The third suggestion comes from the speculations of Mark 6. The crowd had thought Jesus to be 'a prophet, like one of the prophets', Herod that he was John *redivivus*. Putting the two together, Had John been a prophet? Yes, and more than a prophet, Christ's forerunner. Others in Mark 6.15 had said, 'It was Elijah', and Matthew duly ascribes this identity to John at 11.14, as he later does at 17.13, making the Marcan doctrine explicit: it is he, not Jesus, who was the coming Elijah. So had Malachi prophesied (3.1; 4.5), and so had Mark, and the Church, seen John's destiny.

There is one more probable reference to the little Mark 6 passage. There Herod says, 'John the Baptiser has been raised (ἐγήγερται) from the dead': Matthew says, 'There has arisen (ἐγήγερται) no one greater than John the Baptist'—the word ἐγείρομαι is never used in the NT in this sense except here and in the similar Luke 7.16. John's ministry is thus exalted: but Matthew's ecclesiology requires a qualifying clause too—'He who is least in the kingdom of heaven is greater than he'. The Church, to Matthew, = the Kingdom of Heaven—the good seed sprung from the word = the sons of the kingdom, the kingdom is the Church's net pulling in the fish. But John died *before* the kingdom

---

[69] 'My father, if it be possible, let this cup pass from me; nevertheless not as I will, but as thou wilt', 'My father, if this cannot pass unless I drink it, thy will be done', 'saying the same words'.

[70] 'You have heard that it was said to the men of old', 'You have heard that it was said', 'It was also said': 'Again you have heard that it was said to the men of old', 'You have heard that it was said', 'You have heard that it was said'.

[71] cf. 3 Macc. 2.22; Job 40.16; Isa. 19.6; 35.7. It is conceivable that the κάλαμός of the last verse caught Matthew's eye when referring to Isa. 35.5–6 in the previous paragraph. cf. McNeile, p. 152.

[72] cf. Feldman, *PSR*, pp. 111, 247.   [73] Aboth de R. Nathan, ch. 41.

was established, and has been shown groping after, but not achieving, faith—therefore he is sub-Christian. From John's day on the kingdom is violated[74]—Mark 6.17 tells of the first blood drawn, Mark 9.13 says, 'They did to him whatever they pleased'—and violent men like Herod and the Church's persecutors take it by force. βιάζεται must be passive, like εὐαγγελίζονται in 11.5, since the two halves of v. 12 are Semitic parallelism. The Marcan context shows this to be the meaning, rather than Luke's interpretation of the non-religious forcing their way in. As the coming of Elijah is prophesied on the last page of the (Hebrew) Law and the Prophets, so has John's coming marked the end of the Old Covenant.

The doctrine, and much of the words, of the paragraph, are thus a restatement of the Marcan passages on John: and the old Christian scribe follows his trade[75] and adds a similitude—'L^{e}mā haddābhār dōmē'? To what shall I compare this generation?'[76] ὁμοία ἐστίν occurs eight times with parables in Matthew. The similitude is Matthaean in doctrine: the criticism of the Jews for failing to respond to either John or Jesus comes here and at 21.28–end—it never occurs in Mark, and in Luke only in the Q parallel 7.31ff. It is Matthaean in structure with a male-and-female theme:[77] it was the task of men to pipe and dance at weddings, and of women to mourn and beat their breasts at funerals.[78] It is Matthaean in rhythm as containing the pardic, 'We piped to you and you did not dance; we wailed and you did not mourn'. It is Matthew who has children as a group in their own right three times

---

[74] It is objected by McNeile, and others, that 'in no other passage does "the K. of Heaven" stand, like ἐκκλησία, for the persons who share in it' (p. 155). This is a highly dubious generalization. While the Kingdom is still primarily, as in Mark, seen as the initiative of God, it is also an earthly community: growing from the divine seed to be a great institution, with Gentile ramifications (Matt. 13.31f); to which a scribe can be made disciple (13.52); in which teachers can be counted great or small (5.19), and one can be great (20.26) and least (11.11) here and now. In 18 the thought slips insensibly from the Kingdom (as a *present* reality—ἔστιν 1,5) to the Church.

[75] Cf. ch. 3 above.

[76] Cf. Mark's 'This generation seeks for a sign' (8.12), 'O faithless generation' (9.19): and Deut. 32.5, 'A perverse and crooked generation'.

[77] See p. 98 above.

[78] Jeremias, *PJ*, p. 160ff. Jeremias argues that the piece goes back to Jesus as (a) rhyme is obtained on retranslation into Aramaic, and is present in the Syriac versions; (b) the passage places John and Jesus on a par, whereas the Church always exalted Jesus. But then (a) suffixes always yield rhyme when antitheses are as neat as Matthew's; (b) Jeremias discounts 21.32 as 'not original', 'a surprising application', 'allegorising' (*PJ*, pp. 80, 85); but there it is, a parable in Matthew reproaching the Pharisees for rejecting John, just as the following vineyard parable does the same for Jesus. Neither passage puts John and Jesus on a par.

in the Gospel: here, at Bethlehem in 2, and in the Temple in 21: never in Mark, only in the Q parallel in Luke 7. A concern for the rites of passage, especially marriage, is Matthaean.[79] And so is it Matthaean (and rabbinic) to interpret a parable;[80] and so is the interpretation a carefully balanced antithesis in the Matthaean manner, 'For John came . . . the Son of Man came . . .'. John's *ascesis* repeats what is said in Matt. 3; Jesus' eating with publicans and sinners repeats what occurs in Matt. 9.14–17, where occur also the criticisms and the wine-image. As the section began with the *works* of Christ, so does it end with the comment that God's wisdom is justified by its *works*[81]— both in John and Jesus. *Inclusio*[82] and the gnomic paragraph-closer[83] (arcetic) are alike *spécialités de la maison*.

Linguistically Matthaean are: the kingdom of heaven (2), γεννάω, and ἄρτι. Semi-Matthaean are: πορεύομαι, ὁ Ἰησοῦς, οἱ ὄχλοι, θεάομαι, ἰδού (2), ἔμπροσθεν, ἀμὴν λέγω ὑμῖν, μείζων (2), ἕως, ἐγείρομαι, βαπτιστής (2), ἀπό . . . ἕως, ἁρπάζω, πάντες, εἰ, θέλω, μέλλω, προφητεύω, ὁμοιόω, ὁμοία ἐστίν, κάθημαι, theological ἦλθον (2), ὁ υἱὸς τοῦ ἀνθρώπου ἔρχεται. There are in all 49 characteristic words out of 190 (omitting the LXX words in 11.10). οἰνοπότης is a word of abuse from Prov. 23.20. Only found here in Matthew are μαλακά, φορεῖν, βιάζομαι, προσφωνέω, θρηνέω, and φάγος: also βιαστής, though nouns of this form, like βασανιστής are characteristic. Most of these non-Matthaean words are in part demanded by the context: for example, Christ's 'eating' requires a word for glutton, and funerals involve wailing.

Much of the paragraph Luke reproduces (7.24–35), but character-istic changes betray his editorial touch. ἱματισμός, ὑπάρχω are typical of Luke, and he retains the Matthaean, non-Marcan, non–LXX ἔμπροσθέν σου at the end of the Malachi citation.[84] Verses 29f are a clumsy parenthesis in Luke's own words:[85] all the λαός (Lucan) justified God (to anticipate 'Wisdom is justified by all her children' five verses later—the phrase is unique in the NT); νομικοί, the βουλή of God, ἑαυτόν are all characteristic. For the similitude, the five words τίνι ἐστιν ὅμοιος; ὅμοιός ἐστιν recur at Luke 6.47f; 13.18f; and are

---

[79] See p. 108f above.　　　　[80] See p. 60 above.

[81] The preposition would naturally be ἐκ for 'by' as at 12.37; Rom. 3.20; Jas. 2.21,24; but Matthew has a strong predilection for ἀπό.

[82] So Lagrange, *L'Evangile selon S. Matthieu*, ad loc.: 'Inclusio sémitique élégante'.

[83] See p. 79.

[84] Elsewhere Luke appears reluctant to see John *as* the new Elijah. He goes before in the spirit and power of Elijah, but the real new Elijah seems to be Jesus. If so, then he has imported some Matthaean theology with the citation.

[85] cf. Creed, op. cit., ad loc.

peculiar to Luke. ἀλλήλους, κλαίω, ἐλήλυθα (2),[86] and the turn to the 2nd person (λέγετε)[87] are also all characteristic. The closing sentence, somewhat obscure in Matthew, he amends in the light of what follows. You rejected John, now you reject Jesus, said Matthew: but thank God while the σοφοί have been blind the νήπιοι have seen the light (11.25–7). So, says Luke, it is the children[88] of wisdom who justify God's wisdom —all of them, both under John's and Jesus' preaching: the sinners who went for baptism in Jordan and the sinners who ate with the Lord. The only non-Lucan words are τρυφή and βασίλεια = palace, which cannot suffice to outweigh so strongly editorial an impression. Luke's insertion of 29f results in the omission of Matt. 11.12–15, 'From the days of John the Baptist . . .'. A compressed version of this is added at Luke 16.16 in the context of the abolition of Pharisaic obedience to the Law as a basis for justification: Luke's sense requires the violence to be understood as the pressing of sinners into the kingdom—he substitutes εὐαγγελίζεται therefore for βιάζεται, and uses the latter word in the normal middle sense of 'force one's way'— now anyone can push his way in. εὐαγγελίζομαι with the message as its object, and πᾶς = everyone, are typical of Luke. In almost every respect the Lucan version is seen as secondary.

11.20–4

When Matthew wrote of the towns which rejected the apostolic mission in 10, he compared their coming fate to that of Sodom and Gomorrah: so now he turns to the towns which rejected Christ's own mission. The features of the apostolic mission are but the continuance of their master's rejection, only that his preaching was sealed by δυνάμεις in plenty. Tyre and Sidon were the cities constantly inveighed against in the prophets,[89] Sodom and Gomorrah in the Law. The only lakeside towns mentioned as the sites of healings in Mark were Capernaum and Bethsaida, but he also refers to 'the next towns' (1.38, next, that is, to Capernaum), and the healing of the leper

---

[86] cf. especially the exactly similar substitution of ἐλήλυθα at 5.32 for Mark's ἦλθον.

[87] cf. 6.20f.

[88] It was suggested by Lagarde, and since maintained by T. Zahn, *Das Evangelium des Matthäus* (3e., Leipsic 1910) (p. 434), and J. Schniewind, *Das Evangelium nach Matthäus*, NTD (11e., Göttingen 1964), (pp. 146f), that both ἔργων and τεκνῶν are versions of an original ᵃbhādheihā. But τεκνόν never translates ᵃebhedh in the LXX, so both the original and an error have to be postulated. Lucan editorship is a simpler hypothesis.

[89] Isa. 23; Jer. 25.22; Ezek. 26—28; Amos 1.9–10 (Tyre); Joel 3.4–8; Zech. 9.2–4.

follows. Now Chorazin is $2\frac{1}{4}$ miles north of Capernaum,[90] the nearest place known to us.[91] It may well be that, as with Gadara for Gerasa,[92] Matthew is showing his familiarity with the geography of Galilee: though an oral tradition here cannot be ruled out. A pair of towns is required by the rhythm of the paragraph to balance Tyre and Sidon: but if the lesser places are comparable to Tyre and Sidon, then Isaiah[93] would suggest that the greater, Capernaum, is to be set against Babylon. The phrases, 'Will you be exalted to heaven? You shall be brought down to Hades', are adapted from the dirge for the king of Babylon in Isa. 14.13,15. Nevertheless Sodom, which actually was brought down to Hades in the Torah, has the last word: indeed Isaiah suggests the same a few verses earlier (13.19), 'And Babylon, the glory of kingdoms, will be like Sodom and Gomorrah when God overthrew them.' The passage is doctrinally Matthaean in its emphasis on the day of judgement. It is rhythmically Matthaean in being a balanced strophe/antistrophe poem, or *crinic*:[94] of which all the examples are in either Q or M sections, and Luke normally (as here) has a markedly inferior form of parallelism. It is Matthaean in the religious imagery[95] of repentance in sackcloth and ashes. The following words are Matthaean: τότε, δύναμις = miracle (3), ἡμέρα κρίσεως (2). Semi-Matthaean words are εἰ . . . ἄν (2), Σόδομα (2), πλὴν λέγω ὑμῖν (2), ἔσται (2), prepositional ἕως (2), γῆ. There is no non-Matthaean language. 25 words out of 90 are characteristic.

Luke inserts 11.21–22a almost verbatim in the Mission-charge in Luke 10: the mention of Sodom which he takes from Matt. 10.15 provides the contact, but the context is unsuitable. He drops the second half of the antistrophe in favour of a further midrash on Isa. 14. 'How has Lucifer that rose in the morning fallen from heaven', Isa. 14.12 (LXX), becomes 'I saw Satan fall like lightning from heaven'. Luke avoids ἡμέρα κρίσεως as usual, and writes the article before ᾅδης as at 16.12.

11.25–30

It is a long biblical tradition to end a threat of judgement on a note of blessing, and Matthew closes the lection with a happy antithesis

[90] W. Sanday, *Sacred Sites of the Gospels* (Oxford 1903), p. 24.
[91] *The Westminster Historical Atlas to the Bible*, ed. G. E. Wright and F. V. Filson (London 1945), Plate XIV.
[92] See p. 324 above.
[93] Many prophets inveighed against Tyre and Sidon (n. 89 above), but Isaiah is much the most often-quoted prophet in Matthew, and the two prophecies are from the same block of oracles against the nations (Isa. 13—14).
[94] See p. 86f above.
[95] See p. 105ff above; cf. also Jonah 3 where Nineveh repented in sackcloth and ashes.

here, just as he ends the judgement passage in 12 by pointing to Jesus' true mother and brothers. He develops the matter from two texts: one still Isaiah (29.14), 'I will destroy the wisdom of the wise, and will hide the understanding of the understanding' (LXX); the other the 51st chapter of ben Sirach. Matthew has just shown that the σοφία of God is justified despite the rejection of men, and this is a theme well rooted in church doctrine. Paul had taught (1 Corinthians 1.17—2) that Christ was the wisdom of God (1.24, 30), and the preaching of the gospel was wisdom to the mature (2.6ff), but that the wise of the world had counted it folly and were perishing (1.18): and he cited Isaiah, 'I will destroy the wisdom of the wise, and will thwart the understanding of the understanding' (1.19 AT).[96] However, it had pleased God (εὐδόκησεν, 1.21) to reveal (ἀπεκάλυψεν, 2.10) the secrets of eternity to us, babes in Christ as we were (νήπιοι, 3.1). There is very strong evidence for supposing that Matthew was familiar with this passage.[97] He uses three words from the same verse in Isaiah (ἔκρυψας, σοφῶν, συνετῶν), and contrasts ἀπεκάλυψας and νηπίοις, adding, 'for so it was εὐδοκία' before God. It is likely also that his phrase, 'Lord of heaven and earth', recalls God's making foolish both the (earthly) wise of the world and the (heavenly) rulers of this age (1.20; 2.6). The dependence cannot be by Paul on Jesus because (*a*) both Matthew and Paul use the LXX version of Isaiah,[98] (*b*) virtually all the words not in common with 1 Corinthians are characteristic of Matthew—heaven and earth, ναί, οὕτως, κύριε + gen., ἔμπροσθεν.[99] Luke copies (10.21f) but prefaces significantly, 'He rejoiced in the Holy Spirit': it was, to Paul, in the Spirit that the revelation was given us (2.10), it is the Spirit which searches everything, and comprehends the thoughts of God (2.11). Luke knew the relevance of the 1 Corinthians passage too.

None of the rulers, wrote Paul, understood this: indeed, in the Gospel story, not even Peter has yet come to know Jesus as the Son of God. ἐπιγινώσκω is Paul's word to the Corinthians: after death I shall know, even as I am known. 'All things have been delivered to me' (11.27) is very similar to Matthew's 'All authority has been given to me' (28.18). 'And no one knows the Father . . .' is a repetitive converse logion. τοῦ πατρός μου is Matthaean. οὐ . . . εἰ μή (2) is semi-Matthaean. The following absolute use of ὁ υἱός and ὁ πατήρ is natural; the preceding verses have made the relationship plain without further

[96] cf. p. 169 above.
[97] For the general question of the availability of the Pauline letters and the freedom of movement in the early Church, see p. 153ff above.
[98] Against Heb., '. . . *their* wise . . . *their* understanding . . . *shall be* hidden'.
[99] With ὁ πατήρ, vocative, cf. 7.23 and perhaps 27.29 (ℵ): the use is probably influenced by Mark 14.36. Matthew regularly writes υἱὸς Δαυίδ, vocative, against Mark: 9.27; 15.22; 20.30,31; 1.20.

μου's and αὐτοῦ's: cf. 21.37f, 'He sent his son to them . . . They will respect my son . . . when the tenants saw *the* son', or 24.36, the Marcan, 'No one knows, not even the angels of heaven, nor the Son, but the Father only'. There is nothing un-Matthaean about the diction: indeed the reverse. Talk of a Johannine thunderbolt from the synoptic sky confuses the picture. John adopts the absolute use of 'the Son' and 'the Father' without contextual reference throughout his Gospel. In view of the evidential and *a priori* case for supposing that John had read Matthew, it is possible that Matt. 11.27 was seminal for his theology.[100] Luke copies, but with his Greek sense of knowledge, introduces two τίς ἐστιν clauses: he does the same at 13.27. Including ἐκεῖνος, ἀποκριθεὶς ἔιπεν, and introductory ὁ Ἰησοῦς, Matthew has 21 characteristic words in the paragraph out of 69.

God's Wisdom had been revealed in Christ, but it had not been without foreshadowing under the Old Covenant: much writing of wisdom was there, and indeed the whole Book of the Wisdom of Jesus, the son of Sirach. Perhaps the name drew Matthew's attention, just as Jesus, the son of Nave, and Jesus, the son of Jozadach,[101] in a special way foreshadowed the Lord. At any event the dependence here is indisputable, and it is on the Greek version. Ben Sirach opens his peroration: ἐξομολογήσομαί σοι, κύριε . . . ἐξομολογοῦμαι τῷ ὀνόματί σου: the unrighteous have surrounded him but he gives thanks in confession of God's power to save (51.1–12). He has sought wisdom humbly from his youth and has found it (13–22). 'Approach to me (ἐγγίσατε πρός με), you uninstructed', he cries, 'put your neck under the yoke (ζύγον) and let your soul (ψυχή) receive instruction. I laboured (ἐκοπίασα) a little, and found (εὗρον) for myself much rest (ἀνάπαυσιν)' (23, 26f). Matthew provides the pairs to Ben-Sirach's images. ἐξομολογοῦμαί σοι, πάτερ, κύριε . . . Hither (Matthaean δεῦτε) πρός με all the κοπιῶντες and heavy-laden, and I will rest you (ἀναπαύσω). Take my ζύγον[102] on you and learn of me . . . and you will find (εὑρήσετε) rest (ἀνάπαυσιν) for your souls (ψυχαῖς).'[103] πάντες,

---

[100] See John 3.35; 17.1; 7.29; 10.14,15. 3.35 is in a John Baptist context.

[101] In the NT Joshua features in Heb. 4, and the line of heroes of faith is taken through continuously to him and Rahab in 11: there are many less certain references, such as Jesus coming to Jericho, and the prophet like Moses. The parallel is made explicit in Justin, *Dial.* CXIII, and *passim*, and in Origen, *Homilies on Joshua, passim*. For Jeshua see p. 228f above, and the references to the Jesus–visions in Rev. 1—4 (A. M. Farrer, *The Revelation of St John the Divine*, pp. 67, 76, 95, 226).

[102] The yoke of Torah and its preferability to other yokes are a common rabbinic teaching, MAb. 3.8; S–B I, pp. 608ff.

[103] The wording has been adjusted in reminiscence of Jer. 6.16, καὶ εὑρήσετε ἁγνισμὸν (Heb. 'rest') ταῖς ψυχαῖς ὑμῶν.

κἀγώ, μάθετε, πραΰς, an adjective with τῇ καρδίᾳ are all semi-Matthaean. 'My yoke is easy and my burden light' is a pardic. χρηστός and ἐλαφρός are not elsewhere in Matthew, but hardly outweigh the preponderance of Matthaean characteristics, suggesting that the midrash on ben Sirach is by Matthew.

Our conclusion then, once more, is that 11 is the midrashic work of the evangelist. The basic text on which he works is Mark 6.14ff, which follows the Mission-charge. He amplifies this with further matter on John Baptist from Mark, especially from Mark 1. But for the first time since the Sermon he expands the material freely, on the basis of OT texts: Isa. 35; 26; 61; 29; Mal. 3; Ecclus. 51. The Isa. 29 verse he sees, in addition, through the eyes of Paul. Where these passages do not supply the words, we can pick out at every point the familiar rhythms and images and language and doctrine of our own evangelist. What need have we to posit other sources?

17

THE SEASON OF TABERNACLES (13—16.12)

Matthew's tenth, eleventh, and twelfth chapters had celebrated the Christian New Year and Atonement: with his thirteenth he turns to material for the Christian Feast of Tabernacles. Tabernacles was the ancient Harvest Festival, the Feast of Ingathering. Lev. 23.39, from the *sidrāh* for the first day of the Feast,[1] reads, 'On the fifteenth day of the seventh month, when you have gathered in the produce of the land, you shall keep the feast of the Lord seven days: on the first day shall be a solemn rest, and on the eighth day shall be a solemn rest.' The *lûlāb* and *'etrôg* were to be waved in rejoicing for the harvest[2]— 'when you make your ingathering from your threshing-floor and your winepress'.[3] Both time of year and traditional liturgical observance —and indeed the old name *ḥāg hā'āsîph*, Ingathering—kept the harvest theme central.

It is natural, therefore, for a Christian evangelist to go to Jesus' parables of the harvest for 'fulfilment' of the theme; and Mark had already made a preliminary gathering of such teaching in Mark 4— the Sower, the Seed Growing Secretly, the Mustard-Seed.[4] But there is a second Tabernacles theme which would suggest such a move to be not so much natural as inspired. 'All the men of Israel assembled to King Solomon at the Feast in the month Ethanim, which is the seventh month',[5] for the consecration of the Temple. Passages from 1 Kings 8 have been from ancient times the prophetic readings at Tabernacles—today on the second and eighth days—and the Feast is celebrated in the Mishnah with processions round the altar.[6] The salvation-history theme which the Feast was held to celebrate was thus the foundation of the Temple by Solomon.[7] Now Matthew has already

---

[1] B Meg. 31a. See Jewish Encyclopaedia, vi, art. Haftarah, p. 136. The same passage is specified in the Mishnah, Meg. 3.5.

[2] Lev. 23.40.

[3] Deut. 16.13. The Deuteronomic law of the feast was read, at least from Talmudic times, on the eighth day of the festival, *Shemini 'Asereth*, cf. Jewish Encyclopaedia, art. cit.

[4] Mark 4 is the ninth unit in the series of sections in Mss. A, etc., and would be a suitable reading for the seventh day of Tabernacles in a series of lections starting at New Year, cf. ch. 9, appendix B. In this way Matthew would be expanding a harvest parable liturgy already operating in earlier tradition.

[5] 1 Kings 8.2.   [6] M. Suk. 4.5.

[7] J. van Goudoever, *Biblical Calendars*, p. 35. The traditional reading from the 'Scrolls' for Tabernacles was Ecclesiastes, a further link with Solomon.

been leading up to this in 12: 'Something greater than the Temple is here' (v. 6), 'Can this be the Son of David?' (v. 23), 'The Queen of the South will arise at the judgement . . . for she came from the ends of the earth to hear the wisdom of Solomon; and behold, a greater than Solomon is here' (v. 42). When the biblical historian wrote of Solomon's wisdom, he said, 'He was wiser than all other men . . . and his fame was in all the nations round about. He also uttered three thousand proverbs (Gk. παραβολάς, Heb. *māshāl*) and his songs were 1,005. He spoke of trees, from the cedar that is in Lebanon to the hyssop that grows out of the wall; he spoke also of beasts, and of birds, and of reptiles, and of fish. And men came from all peoples to hear the wisdom of Solomon . . .' (1 Kings 4.31–4). Now Jesus, the greater than Solomon, reveals his wisdom in parables: he speaks of the mustard-seed that grows into a tree, and of the birds that nest in it; and in due course he will speak of fish.

Matthew's lection (24) continues down to the end of 13, a massive fifty-eight verses,[8] a lesson fit for a feast. As we found that the previous major Festal Lesson, the Sermon, subdivided naturally into eight, as if to provide lessons for an eight-watch Pentecost,[9] the same possibility may be open here for an eight-day Tabernacles. Since the synagogue provided a daily liturgy through the eight days, the Church cannot but have desired to crown it with a daily measure of the Lord's teaching. Now Mark provides a simple subdivision of the harvest material, on which Matthew is able to build, with the three-unit opening of his ch. 4: (1) the Parable of the Sower; (2) the Reason for Parables, citing Isa. 6; (3) the Interpretation of the Sower. These three units Matthew inserts, with minor modifications, as they stand. We shall argue that Matthew rewrites Mark's following parable, the Seed Growing Secretly: but what concerns us immediately is that he then repeats the pattern of the three Marcan units—(4) the Parable of the Tares; (5) the Reason for Parables, citing Ps. 78; (6) the Interpretation of the Tares. The only difference from the first three units is that, following Mark, the Mustard-Seed follows (4), now with its companion, the Leaven: and this has the additional advantage of giving more body to unit (5). A seventh unit follows, with a pair of vignette-parables, the Treasure and the Pearl, like the Mustard-Seed and Leaven; and the Net and its Interpretation, like the Tares and its Interpretation. The week of harvest is thus neatly balanced: seven parables in seven days—two threes and a parallel seventh. But whereas

[8] The section in A begins at 13.3, where the parables begin. For the tendency for lections to cut off introductory verses, see p. 326 above. A thus gives 56 verses, but the logical place to begin is certainly 13.1.

[9] p. 186 above.

men came from all nations to hear the wisdom of Solomon and repented at it, this generation stands condemned by its own words.
In Jesus' own country he teaches them, and they say, 'Where did this
man get this *wisdom?*' An eighth unit is thus transferred from Mark 6,
making manifest the prophesied rejection of the greater than Solomon.
Each of the eight units thus grows out of the Marcan stock, the second
three patterned on the first three, the seventh on the second three, the
eighth from Mark 6: each is a self-contained unit like the miracle-
stories—none is less than five or more than nine verses.[10]

13.1–23

It is generally conceded that the Sower is Mark's Sower, transcribed
nearly verbatim; that the Reason for Parables is from Mark, with
some significant editorial changes;[11] and that the Interpretation of
the Sower is also closely modelled on Mark. There is some doubt
whether the Isaiah quotation may be a post-Matthaean intrusion,[12]
though we are wiser to trust the Mss. in my view than the canons of
stylistic criticism. The new material that is of controversial provenance is The Blessedness of the Disciples (13.16f). Here it should be
noted: (*a*) that whereas Mark has Jesus reproach the disciples, 'Do
you not understand this parable? How then will you understand all
the parables?', Matthew omits all such suggestion with his aseptic
'Hear then the parable of the Sower'; (*b*) Matthew introduces both
into the Reason for Parables and into the Interpretation, the concept
of understanding as a moral category. God gave Solomon wisdom and
understanding (συνίειν).[13] Christ has wisdom and those who are his

[1] J. D. Kingsbury, *The Parables of Jesus in Matthew 13*, proposes a significant
division of the chapter after 13.35. Up to then the parables are addressed to the
Jewish crowds, afterwards to the disciples; before from the boat, afterwards in
the house; with four parables before and four (including the Things New and
Old) after. For a criticism of this thesis see my review in *JTS* xxi.1 (April 1970),
pp. 164ff.

[11] All of Mark 4.10–12 is here in Matthaean form (see below), and also 4.25. Of
the other cryptic sayings in 4.21–4 we have already had versions at Matt. 5.15,
10.26, and 7.2: but 4.22 is further expounded in Matt. 13.35, 44ff (see below),
and 4.25 in Matt. 25.14–30.

[12] So C. C. Torrey, 'The Biblical Quotations in Matthew', in *Documents of the
Primitive Church* (New York, London 1941) pp. 66–8; Stendahl, *SSM*, pp.
129–32. The introductory formula is unusual, προφητεία and ἀναπληρόω
being found here only in Matthew: but perhaps ἀναπληροῦται = is completely
fulfilled, cf. 1 Esdras 1.54; and προφητεία is common in Paul. See Gundry,
UOTSM, p. 117. The long text follows LXX almost verbatim, but Matthew does
not have recourse to Hebrew or his own targum unless there is reason; see, e.g.,
citations at 1.23; 12.40.

[13] 1 Kings 3.9,11.

have understanding. 'They', ἐκεῖνοι, the non-disciples, are given only parables *because* they do not understand, they have hardened their hearts; when anyone hears the word and does not understand, that is the seed by the wayside; the seed on good ground is he who hears the word and understands. It is, in other words, essential to the Matthaean theology that the disciples understand[14]—they are not just white-washed by having the reproach dropped: to be a disciple *means* to be an understander, not to understand is not to be a disciple. Now both here and at 16.17 understanding is a gift of God: 'To you it has been given . . . Blessed are your eyes . . .'; 'Blessed are you, Simon: for flesh and blood has not revealed this, but my Father . . .'. The blessedness of the disciples is in fact required by the Matthaean view, and is a substitute for the Marcan reproach. The form of the saying follows on from Isaiah in an antithesis typical of the evangelist: 'This is why I speak to them in parables, because seeing they do not see, and hearing they do not hear, nor do they understand . . . But blessed are your eyes, for they see, and your ears, for they hear.' Verse 16 is a pardic, 17 is a double poteric[15]—'They longed to see what you look at and did not see it, and to hear what you hear and did not hear it' (AT), cf. Matthew's 'The good man out of his good treasure brings forth good, and the evil man out of his evil treasure brings forth evil.' Prophets and saints come together also at Matt. 10.41, alone in the NT.[16] The evidence for Matthaean authorship is thus strong, although only 5 words out of 35 are typical—ὀφθαλμός, δίκαιος, ἀμὴν λέγω ὑμῖν.

13.24–30

There are nine reasons for thinking that the Tares is a Matthaean version of the Marcan Seed Growing Secretly.[17]
(a) The *order* of Mark 4 is Sower, Reason of Parables, Interpretation of Sower, Appended Sayings, Seed Growing Secretly, Mustard-Seed. Matthew has the first three and the last, with the Appended

---

[14] cf. G. Barth, 'Matthew's Understanding of the Law', in *TIM*, pp. 105–11.
[15] See p. 80f above.
[16] Isaiah the prophet here, and David the saint at 13.35 (Ps. 78), were able to see the shadows of the present reality: if this is in Matthew's mind, there is a further reason for thinking that he wrote 16f himself, since the pair subserves the pattern of the chapter. For the suggestion that Luke's change of ὅτι to οἵ is evidence of a common Aramaic *Vorlage*, see p. 119 above. Luke writes 'kings' for 'saints', a more exact and less Jewish term for David: he has given in the preceding paragraph fulfilments of Ps. 91.13 and 69.28. Luke's context requires the phrasing of 10.23, but he drops the 'and your ears . . .' antithesis with his usual tendency.
[17] Such a view has been envisaged at least since H. J. Holtzmann, *Handkommentar zum NT* (3e., Tübingen 1901), p. 248.

Sayings elsewhere, and the Tares in place of the Seed Growing Secretly.

(*b*) There is *no* other considerable unit of Mark *omitted* in Matthew. In all cases of apparent omission of a paragraph we find a Matthaeanized version somewhere in the Gospel.

(*c*) The *teaching* of the parable as it stands in Mark is that God's kingdom is like the imperceptible growth of the corn till autumn, when the sickle is put into the world, and the harvest of men is reaped. Matthew's parable conveys the same basic doctrine, with an elaboration: the kingdom is like a corn-field maturing till autumn, when the angelic harvesters will bring in the harvest of the righteous; and (Matthew adds) there are weeds maturing too, to be harvested into hell.

(*d*) *Words in common* between the two parables are ἄνθρωπος, καθεύδω, σῖτος, βλαστάνω, χόρτος, καρπός, θερισμός: of which καθεύδω, βλαστάνω, and χόρτος are neither common words nor inevitable in a harvest parable.

(*e*) Matthew's elaboration is by a *contrast*:[18] the wheat and the tares. But all the new long Matthaean parables are contrasts: sand and rock, the merciful king and the unmerciful servant, the wise and foolish bridesmaids—even the understanding and the not understanding in the Sower. Contrasted parables are Matthaean.

(*f*) Matthew introduces the burning of the tares at harvest, an evident figure for *hell*, and the harvesters, an evident figure for the angels of judgement: both duly so interpreted at vv. 41f. But hell is a Matthaean doctrine,[19] hardly found in the Marcan–Pauline tradition, constantly inculcated by the rabbinically trained Matthew; and the angels of judgement are Matthaean likewise.

(*g*) The Interpretation suggests that the parable is *allegorically* slanted: that is, it contains many features such as the enemy, the reapers, and the burning, which naturally answer to an allegorical interpretation. But it is the Matthaean parables which always answer to this treatment: when Augustine tries it with a Lucan parable[20] we know at once that the exegesis is false. Matthew visibly increases the allegory-content in Marcan parables, and is thus a proven allegorizer.[21]

(*h*) The *scale* is grander in Matthew's parable than in Mark's.[22] Mark has a single man casting his seed, sleeping and rising, putting in the sickle: Matthew has an owner of the estate with a

---

[18] See p. 53f above.   [19] cf. p. 63 above.

[20] *Quaestiones Evangeliorum* II.19; cf. C. H. Dodd, *The Parables of the Kingdom* (London 1935), pp. 11ff.

[21] cf. p. 56ff above.   [22] cf. p. 60ff above.

staff of δοῦλοι who do the work for him. But Matthew regularly increases the scale of the Marcan parables, in the Husbandmen, in the Nightwatchman, in the Mustard-Seed: and Matthew, of the evangelists, is the lover of the grand scale.

(*i*) The following *vocabulary* is Matthaean: ἄλλην παραβολήν, the kingdom of heaven, φαίνομαι, τότε, προσέρχομαι, φημί(2), συλλέγω (3), συνάγω, πρὸς τὸ with inf., two nominative aorist participles. Semi-Matthaean are λέγων, ὁμοιόω, καλός(2), ἀγρός(2), κατακαίω, σός, οἱ ἄνθρωποι = men, καρπὸν ποιεῖν, οἰκοδεσπότης, οὐχί, οὖν (2), δοῦλος (2), κύριε, θέλω, θερισμός (2), οὗ, ἐρῶ, ἕως (prep.), nouns in –της as θεριστής. The only words not found elsewhere are ζιζάνια and δέσμη, not surprisingly. Thus 43 out of the 137 words are characteristic.

When all the straws blow in the same direction, who can doubt the wind?[23]

13.31-3

Matthew's Mustard-Seed is Mark's Mustard-Seed with the insertion of the man sowing—just as all the Matthaean parables, about people[24] —and the seed becoming a tree—just as all Matthew's large-scale parables.[25] There are some typical linguistic changes: ὁμοία ἐστίν, the kingdom of heaven, λαμβάνω, a nominative aorist participle, ἀγρός, . . . μὲν . . . δὲ. There is no justification for claims of an alternative Q version of the parable.[26] Luke is following Matthew throughout the Journey, and so when he gives the parable at 13.18f he includes the phrases from Matthew, ὁμοία ἐστίν, ὃν λαβὼν ἄνθρωπος, αὐξάνω, καί γένεσθαι [ ] δένδρον, and closely follows the Matthaean wording of the Dan. 4 reference to the birds in the branches of the

---

[23] Jeremias (*PJ* (e.1), pp. 64ff) divides the parable from the interpretation on four grounds: (*a*) 'it passes over in silence the obvious motive of the parable, namely the exhortation to patience, thus missing the point of the parable'; (*b*) it contains such expressions, as 'the world' and 'the evil one', which Jesus cannot have used, since they do not occur in Hebrew or Aramaic; (*c*) the interpretation contains ideas, and (*d*) words, which are Matthaean. The last three points fit extremely well with a thesis that Matthew wrote parable *and* interpretation: as for (*a*) the 'obvious' motive of the parable is only obvious if one assumes with Jeremias that the Matthaean form of the parable is dominical.

[24] cf. p. 51ff above.   [25] cf. p. 60ff above.

[26] So B. H. Streeter, *FG*, pp. 246ff. Both Streeter and B. C. Butler account for certain coincidences of wording between Luke and Mark as reminiscences of Mark by Luke. While this would be conceivable, it is not a necessary hypothesis. Luke always writes 'the kingdom of God' for Matthew's 'kingdom of heaven'; ἔλεγεν is common in Luke; and the doubled opening has its precedent at 7.31.

tree. The doubled, 'To what is the kingdom of God like, and to what shall I liken it?' (AT) is also the Lucan form at 7.31 against Matthew: it is mere verbal doubling without extension of meaning such as Luke does often, Matthew never.[27] Sowing mustard in a garden (κῆπος) is against Jewish law,[28] and is one of a series of Lucan errors in such matters.[29] The passage is, as Butler noted,[30] classic for showing the dispensability of the Q theory: in almost every word Matthew's version is accountable as secondary to Mark, and Luke's to Matthew.

A standard feature of Matthew's antithetical mind is the pairing of female to male:[31] the birds and the lilies, the Ninevites and the Queen of the South, two men in the field and two women grinding, the unwatchful servant and the unwatchful bridesmaids, the boys dancing and the girls mourning—and so here, the man in the field and the woman in the kitchen. Such a feature never comes in Mark, and only in the Sheep and Coin in L. Matthaean authorship rather than selection is likely to be the explanation here, for the wording of the brief parable is based formally upon the immediately preceding Mustard-Seed. 'The kingdom of heaven is like . . .' is identical; ἣν λαβοῦσα γυνή answers to ὃν λαβὼν ἄνθρωπος, ἐνέκρυψεν εἰς τὸ ἔσπειρεν ἐν. The three σάτα would suffice for more than 150 people,[32] and are worthy of a Matthaean household: but the figure may be influenced by the three *seah*'s of fine flour of which Sarah made cakes for the angels in Gen. 18.[33] κρύπτω, ἕως + ind., and ζυμή are all characteristic of Matthew, as are ἄλλην παραβολήν, ὁμοία ἐστίν, and the kingdom of heaven—11 words out of 23. Luke follows almost verbatim: significantly, Luke has ἕως + ind. here alone. The comparison of the kingdom to leaven is extremely bold, as leaven is elsewhere invariably a sinister image (cf. 16.6, 11f). But the rabbis similarly are free with images—wheat may stand for the Torah or for sin,[34] thorns are both entanglements and protection.[35] So cf. Matthew's ambivalence with snakes and pearls.

---

[27] cf. p. 295 above.   [28] M Kil. 3.2; T Kil. 2.8(75).

[29] cf. 11.42, where rue was not subject to tithe (M Sheb. 9.1), and certainly not every herb; 14.35 where salt was not used (to our knowledge) in Palestinian agriculture; 21.29, where the Marcan fig-tree is the point, and Luke's 'and all the trees' would include a lot of evergreens in Palestine.

[30] B. C. Butler, *The Originality of St Matthew* (Cambridge 1951), pp. 2ff. Dr Butler's title is somewhat ironic: the very last thing which he believes in is the *originality* of St Matthew.

[31] cf. p. 98 above.

[32] G. Dalman, *Arbeite und Sitte in Palästina* IV (Gütersloh 1935), p. 120; Jeremias, *PJ* (e.1), p. 90n.

[33] Heb. *sᵉ'āh*; Aram. *sā'tā*'; cf. Bauer ad voc.

[34] Yalqut Gen. §37; B Ber. 61a; Feldman, *PSR*, p. 74.

[35] Gen. R. 45.4; cf. B Erub. 101a; Feldman, *PSR*, pp. 184, 190.

The meaning of the two little parables is so straightforward that no interpretation seemed necessary to the evangelist: nor is any unless we reject evangelical simplicity. The Mustard-Seed, the Leaven are the Word of God (cf. 13.19); the man, the woman, are the Son of Man (cf. 13.37); the field, the three measures are the world (cf. 13.38). From the sowing of the gospel, tiny as it is, comes the great Tree of the Church: like the World-Tree of Ezek. 31 and Dan. 4. The birds are the Gentiles (Ezek. 31.6; Dan. 4.21f) who will come from east and west and sit down in the kingdom. From the leavening power of the yeast the whole of the meal is leavened: the second parable has no counterpart to the Church, but is able better to express the gospel's power to fill the whole world. We have thus two fine allegories, typical of Matthew: only the number 3 is without significance.

13.34–5

Mark followed the Mustard-Seed with two sentences summing up Jesus' use of parables, and Matthew abbreviates these now, adding a second justification from scripture: thus continuing his formal parallel between the first three and the second three units of the Ingathering lection. The formula to the citation is Matthaean. The first clause follows the LXX of Ps. 78.2, the second is Matthew's own adaptation. He writes κεκρύμμενα for προβλήματα (*hîdhôth*) following the Lord's words in Mark 4.22, 'There is nothing κρυπτόν except to be made manifest'—and indeed his own 'she hid' (ἐνέκρυψεν) in the previous verse. Christ, like David, comes to declare what God had hidden. καταβολῆς is clearer than ἀρχῆς (*qedhem*), and is used for creation by Matthew at 25.34.[36] ἐρεύξομαι is stronger than the LXX φθέγξομαι (*'abbî'āh*), and is used to translate the same Hebrew verb at Ps. 19.3: Matthew's acquaintance with the Hebrew, and his ability both to draw on the Hebrew and to write his own targum, are again testified.[37]

13.36–43

The Interpretation of the Tares follows, in parallel with the Interpretation of the Sower. The Matthaean authorship of the passage has been so conclusively demonstrated by Jeremias[38] that there is no need to repeat the evidence.

[36] cf. also 24.21 ἀπ' ἀρχῆς κόσμου; cf. Mark 13.19.
[37] cf. Stendahl, *SSM*, p. 117, 'It is an *ad hoc* Christian interpretation, which, moreover, is closely bound up with its context.' See p. 128f above.
[38] *PJ* (e.1), pp. 81ff.

13.44–6

For the first three units Matthew had followed Mark, for the second three he embroidered Mark; for the seventh he writes freely, but it is still the Marcan texts which he expounds. The kingdom, Jesus had taught in Mark, was like seed put into the ground; and had added, 'For there is nothing hidden except to be brought to light, or in hiding but to come to light' (AT). Mark's two ἵνα's, and his κρυπτόν/ἀπόκρυφον suggest another simile than the grain in the ground: rather wealth which is hidden deliberately now, so as to be brought up later. Matthew repeats κεκρυμμένῳ (cf. 13.35) and ἔκρυψεν and ἐν τῷ ἀγρῷ (cf. 13.31), and forms a new but related parable, just as so many rabbis did with the parables of their masters.[39] Even now he will not desert the dominical teachings which are his sole authority. Christ had taught the Rich Man that the kingdom was a treasure (θησαυρός), for which one should go (ὕπαγε) and sell (πώλησον) all that one has (ὅσα ἔχεις) (Mark 10.21). This text, so influential on Matthew,[40] glossed with Mark 4.22, gives the substance of the one-verse parable. With ὃν εὑρὼν ἄνθρωπος cf. ὃν λαβὼν ἄνθρωπος (13.31), and ἣν λαβοῦσα γυνή (13.33). ὁμοία ἐστίν, the kingdom of Heaven, θησαυρός, κρύπτω (2), ἀγρός, pleonastic ἐκεῖνος, are all characteristic language.

Just as the brief Mustard-Seed is paired by the brief Leaven as male by female, so is the Treasure from the land paired by the Treasure from the sea.[41] We find the same line of thought in 7.9f, 'If he asks for bread . . . or if he asks for fish', and in the following parable, the Dragnet, where the sons of the kingdom, hitherto the harvest of the land, now appear as the harvest of the water. Again there is a close formal parallel in the words, which stresses the pairing: 'He sells all that he has and buys that field'; 'He sold all that he had and bought it.' Again the language is characteristic: ὁμοία ἐστίν, the kingdom of

---

[39] For example: 'R. Ḥama b. R. Hanina said, Compare this (*sc.* Gen. 1.31) to a king who built a palace. He saw it and it pleased him. "O palace, palace", exclaimed he, "mayest thou find favour in my eyes at all times just as thou hast found favour in my eyes at this moment!" Similarly the Holy One, blessed be he, apostrophized the world, "O my world, mayest thou find favour in my eyes at all times just as thou hast found favour in my eyes at this moment." R. Jonathan said, Imagine a king who gave his daughter in marriage, and arranged a bridal-chamber and a home for her, which he plastered, panelled and painted. He saw it and it pleased him. "My daughter, my daughter", he cried, "may this bridal-chamber find favour in my eyes at all times just as it has found favour in my eyes at this moment." Even so said the Holy One, blessed be he, to his world, "O my world . . . this moment." ' Gen. R. 9.4; cf. 9.7–10; Lev. R. 2.4, etc.

[40] cf. pp. 276f above.

[41] cf. also agricultural and pastoral, animals and plants, organic and inorganic images.

Heaven, καλός, πάντα ὅσα, πιπράσκω. With πολύτιμος cf. Matthew's βαρύτιμος at 26.7. The immensely valuable pearl is in line with Matthew's love of the immense.[42] There are 22 characteristic words out of 54 in the two parables.

A parable of R. Simeon b. Judah (fl. A.D. 150) is quoted in the Mekilta: 'To what is the matter like? To one who inherited a large field in a Sea-Province, and he sold it for a trifle. And the buyer went and dug it over, and found in it treasures of silver and treasures of gold and costly stones and pearls. Then the seller began to be vexed.'[43] It may be therefore that such parables were already in the rabbinic stock, and that Matthew is adapting them to a Christian tradition. We should not, however, exclude the possibility, suggested by the pearls, that Jewish tradition has exploited a sympathetic Christian source. In either case the affinity of Matthew to the rabbis is demonstrated.

13.47–50

The seventh day's reading can now close with a seventh parable: and parable and interpretation can carry on the parable-and-interpretation pattern which we have seen established in the Sower and Tares. Mark had limited Jesus' verbal comparison of the preaching of the word to the harvesting of the land: but his actual situation had recalled rather the harvesting of the sea. For he had taught the people out of a fishing-boat: and had he not, in almost his first recorded words, told Simon and his fellows that their fishing trade was to foreshadow a fishing of men? Matthew indeed seems to underscore such a view at the beginning of 13, for he writes, 'Jesus, ἐξελθών from the house, sat down by the sea . . . saying, 'Behold the Sower ἐξῆλθεν' (AT).[44] Christ himself goes forth to sow, he sits in the boat and fishes the multitude: they stand on the αἰγιαλός as he speaks from the sea, of the seine that is thrown into the sea, and the catch that is counted on the αἰγιαλός. Once the movement of imagination is made from land to sea (as it is in the Pearl), the parable tells itself. The net, like the field of wheat and tares, brings up both good and bad. The good fish are saved in buckets as the good corn was saved in the garner; the bad are both cast out. The angelic reapers are succeeded by angelic fishermen. If we may say that the parable tells itself, how much more the interpretation. 'So it will be at the close of the age', is repeated from v. 40, the angels and

---

[42] cf. p. 60f above.
[43] Mek. 26b–27a; P. Fiebig, *Altjüdische Gleichnisse und die Gleichnisse Jesu* (Tübingen 1904), p. 25.
[44] X. Léon-Dufour, *Etudes d'Evangile* 1965), pp. 298f.

the separation of the righteous from the wicked from v. 41, 'they shall throw them into the furnace of fire: there men will weep and gnash their teeth' from v. 42. The doctrine of hell is Matthaean; the participation of angels is Matthaean; the contrast element is Matthaean;[45] the Church as a *corpus mixtum* is Matthaean. Whereas in the Tares the field is the world, and the whole of mankind are wheat and tares, in the Dragnet only some of the fish in the sea (ἐκ παντὸς γένους) are in the net. The net that fishes men is the net of the gospel, and some in the Church are good and some bad, as in 22.1–14. The language of the Interpretation is, as we have seen, a catena of Matthaeanisms: but the parable is not much different. The kingdom of Heaven, συνάγω, συλλέγω, σαπρός are Matthaean: semi-Matthaean are ὁμοία ἐστίν, βάλλομαι, καλός. With ἀναβιβάζω cf. προβιβασθεῖσα in the redactoral 14.8; with ἄγγη cf. ἀγγεῖα at 25.4. σαγήνη is found here only, and is used in preference to ἀμφιβλῆστρον or δίκτυον for the sake of its size.[46] 30 of the 71 words in 13.47–50 are typical.

This conclusion will perhaps come as a relief to some readers whom a form-critical approach has bewildered. The Interpretation, it is argued correctly,[47] is Matthaean, not dominical: therefore, it is inferred falsely, we are at liberty to fix for the parable a suitable meaning from the general message of Jesus—for example, 'Throw out the net, you fishers of men!'[48] But, confesses the honest Manson,[49] 'It is a very curious missionary work which wins people only in order to reject them immediately they are won. As it stands the parable does not make sense.' He resolves the matter by following Otto[50] in the speculation that the original parable is v. 47. Thus not only the Interpretation but half the parable is thrown out, like the bad fish. The Otto–Manson–Jeremias hypothesis is not scientific because it selects as primary only that part of the text which concurs with a general picture of the message of Jesus *also gained by selection:* it is not exegesis because it dispenses with three-quarters of the text. It is that philosopher's delight, a reversible hypothesis: perhaps the Net and its Interpretation were Jesus' original eschatological message, and 'I will make you fishers of men' was a creation of the Church to justify its missionary work. Very likely some other form-critic has already reached this conclusion. The midrashic theory may abstract the dominical authority in part from the parables, but it does leave them

[45] cf. p. 53f above.

[46] It could be used from a boat as well as from the land, cf. references in Lohmeyer, p. 228.

[47] e.g. by Jeremias, *PJ* (e.1), p. 85.   [48] ibid., p. 224.

[49] *SJ*, p. 155.

[50] R. Otto, *The Kingdom of God and the Son of Man* (E.T., London 1938), pp. 99–102.

intact, and meaning what they say: it is also scientific, because it is based on unselected evidence, by which it can be tested.

13.51–2

At Mark 4.34 it was said, 'Privately to his own disciples he explained everything'. At Matt. 13.36ff Jesus interpreted the Tares to them in the house. Now their understanding is ratified, and the seventh day sealed with a characteristic *inclusio*. The disciples were declared blessed at v. 16 because they understood, they were the good ground of those who understood (v. 23). Now the Lord sums up, 'Have you understood all this?' 'Yes', they reply. Matthew appends his own signature. He, a parabolizing scribe made *talmîdh* to the Kingdom, follows a Lord who was himself a master of parable. Here is the scribes' art, as ben Sirach told, 'to seek out the hidden meanings of proverbs, and be conversant in the dark sayings of parables':[51] to take over the parables of his rabbi, and to embroider them into his own, to take out of his treasure-chest things new and old. Matthew has given us two old parables, the Sower and the Mustard-Seed nearly as they stood in Mark; and five new parables, but new only in the addition of one angle or another—all were already implicit in the Marcan text. And so had Jesus before him made his parables—his Wicked Husbandmen begins with Isaiah's Vineyard and continues with Solomon's keepers,[52] his Sower with Isaac's hundredfold harvest,[53] his Mustard-Seed with Daniel's Tree. Here is the midrashic method stretching back up the centuries. The image Matthew uses is his familiar θησαυρός—suggested no doubt by v. 44. The good scribe, the making of disciples, the kingdom of heaven, the householder-man are all Matthaean, rabbinic conceptions, alien to Mark and Luke: λέγουσιν αὐτῷ Ναί, διὰ τοῦτο, ὅστις, ἐκβάλλω = bring out, θησαυρός = treasure-chest, are all characteristic vocabulary—16 words out of 32.

Thus the whole chapter of parables hangs together as a Matthaean expansion of Mark 4. The Sower, the use of parables proved from Isaiah, the Sower Interpreted, came direct. The Tares was an expansion of the Seed Growing Secretly: the Marcan Mustard-Seed suggested its female counterpart the Leaven: the use of parables proved from the Psalter came as a continuation from Isaiah—prophets and saints, Isaiah and David: the Interpretation of the Tares from that of the Sower. The Treasure was developed from the logion on hiding so as to come to light (Mark 4.22) and the command to sell all and gain the great treasure (Mark 10.21). Its pair was its marine counterpart

[51] Ecclus. 39.3.　　　[52] Cant. 8.11f.
[53] Gen. 26.12.

the Pearl, as the pair to the Tares was the Dragnet, drawn also from the situation of Jesus in the fishing-boat (Mark 4.1). The final word was elaborated from the private explanation of Mark 4.34. The elaboration is made, as always, in the Matthaean mode, with characteristic doctrinal emphasis and language: only that with parables we are in a prose medium, and there are no Matthaean rhythms. Instead we are able to apply those parable-categories which we developed in ch. 3 above—the parables of Matt. 13 are indicative parables, personal parables, contrast-parables, stock-figure parables, allegorical parables, grand scale parables, and in three cases with interpretations appended. Seven harvest-parables have been supplied for the seven days of Ingathering: and for the eighth day Matthew selects the rejection of Christ's teaching in his *patris*, 13.53–8. The greater than Solomon has spoken his parables, and they say, 'Where did this man get this wisdom?' Founder of a greater Temple, they say, 'Is not this the carpenter's son?' Let not the Church fret: she is founded on a better rock than their faithlessness.[54]

14—16

The autumn Festal Season over, Matthew takes up the Marcan tale. The wonder-tales that were told in Mark after the parables and before the Rejection at Nazareth have been recounted already in Matt. 8—9. The creative work is complete of writing a first half to Mark for the five months up to New Year. All that is required now is to follow the Marcan stories week by week in order, adding whatever gloss may be required.

(25) *John and Herod 14.1–12 (–14A)*

Mark 6.15 has already been expounded in Matt. 11, and the remainder is drastically abbreviated. Drastic abbreviations tend to contradiction, and Matthew first says (v. 5) that Herod wished to kill John, adding

---

[54] Lohmeyer (pp. 230ff) maintains dependence by Matthew and Mark on a common source. However, the opening clause is standard for Matthew and μετῆρεν is editorial also at 19.1. ἐλθών is a Matthaean nominative aorist part., and the addition of αὐτῶν is characteristic, distinguishing Christian from Jewish synagogues. The colourless and unrelated αὐτούς is an instance of Matthew's fallibility when beginning to copy Mark. 'Is not this the carpenter's *son*?' gives a smooth transition—we know his father, his mother, his siblings, cf. 10.37; perhaps it also saves the suggestion of bastardy. Simon moves before Judas as the senior patriarchal name, cf. the reversal of Thomas and Matthew at 10.3. οὐχί and πᾶσαι in v. 56 are semi-Matthaean, and the repeated πόθεν clause gives a Matthaean *inclusio*. The apologetic motif in 'he did not' (v. 58) for Mark's 'he could not' is obvious.

'he feared the people, because they held him to be a prophet' from the Question about Authority pericope (Mark 11.32); later (v. 9) he was grieved, following Mark, and reluctant. Similarly Matthew first corrects Herod's title to tetrarch, but later relapses into the Marcan 'king'.

(26) *The Five Loaves and Two Fishes 14.13–21 (15–A)*

The first two Marcan verses give the Return of the Twelve from their mission of Mark 6.7ff: this was taken in Matt. 10, and is omitted here, the ἀπήγγειλαν being cleverly transferred to the Baptist's disciples who bury their master and tell Jesus, thus providing a motive, the fear of Herod, for his move into the desert. Unfortunately this involves a further contradiction, as Jesus returns to the west shore, following Mark, on the very next day!

(27) *The Walking on the Water 14.22–36*

The Marcan story is, for the greater part, transcribed. There are, however, two unsatisfying sentences, which Matthew might feel to require exposition. In the middle of the story Mark says, 'He meant (ἤθελεν) to pass by them' (6.48). At the end he says, 'They were utterly astounded, for they did not understand about the loaves, but their hearts were hardened' (vv. 51f). Why should Jesus have wished to pass them by? Vincent Taylor suggests, to test their faith;[55] and the same solution might well have occurred to Matthew. The comments about hard-heartedness and lack of understanding suggest that they did not come too well out of the test either: though of course (Matthew believed) neither hard-heartedness nor lack of understanding could properly be predicated of apostles, the exemplars by definition of open-heartedness and understanding. Hence the midrashic story of Peter's Walking on the Water. 'Take heart', says Jesus, '*It is I*'. 'Lord, if *it is you*', replies the Matthaean Peter, traditional spokesman of the Twelve,[56] and with traditional over-confidence:[57] and he takes heart to join his master on the waters. Peter's fear (v. 30) and his cry continue the 'They cried out for fear' of v. 26. The Marcan 'They were utterly astounded' can now receive a happier interpretation—not so much in consequence of their failure to see the significance of the Feeding (Mark 6.52), as because they have caught a glimpse of Jesus' divinity: they worship and hail him as truly God's son—not yet the

[55] *The Gospel According to St Mark* (London 1952); and many other commentaries.
[56] Mark 1.36; 8.29,32; 9.2ff; 11.21; 10.28.
[57] Mark 8.32; 9.5; 14.29,37,54ff.

concept of the Christ, but the same words with which the Gentile centurion was to grope towards faith at the Crucifixion.[58]

The addition is thus firmly rooted in the Marcan story: and although Matthew's predecessors might have bequeathed it to him, the evidence is for Matthew's own authorship.

(a) Peter is introduced in Matthew again at 15.15, a passage generally conceded to be redactoral, at 16.17–19, and at 17.24ff.

(b) The theme of apostolic 'little-faith' is Matthaean. The word comes five times in Matthew, never in Mark, once in Luke (Q): it is usually substituted for the Marcan ἄπιστος, ἀπιστία. It is noteworthy how much it occurs in this section of the Gospel: 'this generation' is faithless at 17.17 and 13.58, the apostles are 'of little faith' here, at 16.8 and 17.20.

(c) Of the language, κελεύω (2), ὀλιγόπιστος are Matthaean; semi-Matthaean are ἀποκριθεὶς εἶπεν, εἰ . . . εἶ, τὰ ὕδατα (2), κύριε (2), λέγων, εὐθέως, ἐκτείνω τὴν χεῖρα—17 characteristic words out of 66. *Per contra* ἐπιλαμβάνομαι and καταποντίζομαι[59] are found here only.

(d) The addition forms a pair with the 'doubting' in Matt. 28. The Feeding at 14.13ff with its fourfold action foreshadows the Last Supper; Christ's Walking on the Sea foreshadows his triumph over death. After the Resurrection his disciples will have faith and worship him, but others of the brethren will doubt: so now those disciples, typified in Peter, yearn to share in the Lord's power over the waters, but fail in their doubting. διστάζω is found only in these two passages in the NT.

(28) The Transgression of God's Commandment 15.1–20

We have already examined the passage at p. 19 above as an illustration of Matthew's recension of the radical Marcan approach to the Torah, written and oral: Matthew saves an uncomfortable situation by exaggerating the Pharisees' position to a defiance of the Fifth Commandment, and by reading the cleanness of food sayings in a comparative sense. The oral Law then remains unimpugned, the *massôrath hazzᵉqēnîm* of the rabbis, and there is nothing said against laws of Levitical defilement, only that evil thoughts defile worse.

The insertion of vv. 12–14 is plainly a redactoral insertion of Matthew's own. 'Do you know', ask the disciples, 'that the Pharisees

---

[58] Mark 15.39.
[59] But note Matthew's liking for such verbs as δαιμονίζομαι, σεληνιάζομαι.

were offended?' 'Yes', replies Jesus, 'They are blind'. It is not Pharisaism which is wrong, it is the Pharisees.[60] They are among the tares in the field of 13, to be rooted out; they are the guides of the blind of Rom. 2.[61] The insertion is the more easily understood if we read Mark 7.16, 'If any man has ears to hear, let him hear.' This is the reading of the Western, Caesarean, Syriac, and Byzantine witnesses, and of some Egyptian Mss.: it could well have dropped out of a precursor of B ℵ by assimilation to Matthew, where it is apparently missing.[62] But the opening Matthaean phrase would provide a typical instance of Matthew's midrashic development of a Marcan text: 'Do you know that the Pharisees were offended ἀκούσαντες τὸν λόγον?' Ears to hear? Not the Pharisees: they heard and were offended, they are blind and will fall into the ditch. The language is a string of Matthaeanisms: τότε, προσελθόντες, my heavenly Father, metaphorical τυφλός are all on Hawkins' list; ἀποκριθεὶς εἶπεν, ὁδηγός are semi-Matthaean—14 characteristic words out of 44. φυτεία, φυτεύω occur here only. Being scandalized is a spiritual peril especially stressed by Matthew (8/4/0); the likening of Jesus' opponents to unsatisfactory trees and bushes is especially favoured by Matthew; the blind guides theme comes twice again in Matthew (23.16, 24), never in Mark, once in Luke (Q). With the epigrammatic form, 'If a blind man leads a blind man . . .', cf. the Matthaean 'If Satan casts out Satan . . .' (12.26), 'If you love those who love you . . .' (5.46).

(29) *The Canaanite Woman 15.21–8 (22–A)*

The rewriting of the next Marcan pericope, the Syrophoenician Woman, is much more free, and has given rise to the speculation that Matthew is drawing upon an independent source. Thus Jeremias argues[63] that 15.24 goes back to an early Aramaic tradition, and cites four Aramaisms: οὐ . . . εἰ μή, ἀπεστάλην, a passive of respect for God, εἰς = *b^e* and the anarthrous οἴκου Ἰσραήλ for the Semitic construct. But we have seen that Aramaisms are a double-edged argument. Matthew tends to overwrite Mark in a more Semitic, and specifically more Aramaic, direction; so we should expect a Matthaean

---

[60] It is not surprising that Jewish apologists from C. G. Montefiore and I. Abrahams on so often cite Matthew to show that Jesus was nothing but a good Pharisee: for Matthew was a Jewish apologist before them. cf. H. Merkel, 'Jesus und die Pharisäer', in *NTS* 14.2 (January 1968).

[61] cf. p. 165 above.

[62] The verse is consigned to the margin by the RSV and NEB texts, and is not read by Aland-Nestle, or BFBS. If the Matthew passage is not seen as an expansion of it, it would seem to a scribe that Matthew did not contain it. A. M. Farrer reads it in *A Study in St Mark* (London 1951) p. 97n.

[63] *JPN*, p. 26.

rewriting here to be in Aramaic Greek. οὐ . . . εἰ μὴ is a semi-Matthaean phrase; sheep are a Matthaean image; εἰς is found after (ἐξ)αποστέλλω often in the LXX; and the whole last phrase occurs also in 10.6. Such a view can hardly be maintained in face of the characteristic nature of the Matthaean version. Sidon is a pair to Tyre as in Matt. 10 and 11, and comes in Mark 7.31. The woman is a Canaanite: partly, no doubt, as Kilpatrick suggests,[64] because in intertestamental times Phoenicia was called Canaan, partly also to stress her being outside 'the house of Israel' (v. 24), like the Canaanites of old. Mark says first that Jesus could not be hidden but the woman heard about him, then that she came and fell at his feet: this seems to imply what Matthew proceeds to give, two distinct scenes. In the new introductory one she cries, like Matthew's blind men (9.27), 'Have mercy on me, son of David': κύριε and δαιμονίζομαι are both typical language. Jesus showed reluctance in Mark, and no words are at first ascribed to him. Matthew shows Jesus' reluctance[65] by a studied silence. The portrait of the Lord strikes us as harsh, but this was not the evangelist's intention. He ascribes harshness to the disciples, who urge the Lord, ἀπολῦσον αὐτήν, just as they had urged him, 'ἀπολῦσον the crowds' before the feeding miracle. Jesus' reply does not match with their words: Matthew's eye is on his text. Mark opened Jesus' reply to the woman, 'Let the children first be filled'. Matthew cannot use the children/dogs metaphor till the conversation with the woman, so he supplies his own familiar sheep, as at 10.6. The identical sentiment, 'My task is the Jews', thus appears in Matthaean garb, 'I was sent only to the lost sheep of the house of Israel'. The suppression of Mark's πρῶτον is Matthaean too. Paul and Mark might speak as if the gospel was first to the Jew, then the Greek: for Matthew both missions are simultaneous, the Twelve in Palestine, the Church in all nations, till the Son of Man comes.[66] The new phrases in v. 28 are highly characteristic, and recur almost *en bloc* at 8.13.

(30) The Crowds Healed 15.29–31
(31) The Seven Loaves 15.32—16.1,4

After the Syrophoenician Woman, Mark recounted the healing of the Deaf Stammerer. Now the healing of the stammerer (μογιλάλος) and the κωφός was prophesied in Isa. 35.5f, 'Then shall the eyes of the

---

[64] *Origins*, p. 132.
[65] Jesus' reluctance has an apologetic importance for Matthew, who must maintain his orthodoxy in the face of synagogue slanders: Jesus was Messiah, the king of the *Jews*, a figure without a calling to the Gentiles other than conquering them—and he only concerned himself with Gentiles when forced. cf. p. 340, n. 8 above,; Hummel, p. 136.
[66] 10.23; see pp. 161, 343 above.

blind be opened, and the ears of the deaf shall hear. The lame man (χωλός) shall leap as a hart, and the tongue of the μογιλάλων shall speak clearly' (LXX). Mark shows his awareness of the prophecy by writing, Ephphatha[67], 'Be opened'. 'And his ears were opened, his tongue was released, and he spoke plainly . . . He even makes the deaf hear and the dumb speak' (7.31–7). Matthew has already recorded this story as the Deaf/Dumb Demoniac at 9.32ff, and accordingly provides a general scene of healing, with four particular categories of patients, which are told over twice: the lame, the maimed, the blind, and the deaf. All except the second are in Isaiah's list of four: Matthew has paired off as usual, the κωφός with the blind, the armless with the legless—so that the stammerer is subsumed under the κωφός. (N.B. κωφούς λαλοῦντας (v. 31): κωφός means both deaf and dumb, the latter idea being stressed here.) There was previous reference to the Isaiah passage in its eschatological context at 11.5f. Much of the language is characteristic: μεταβὰς ἐκεῖθεν, 'the mountain,' προσέρχομαι, many crowds, are Matthaean. Semi-Matthaean are ἐκεῖ, κάθημαι, θεραπεύω, Ἰσραήλ.

The Four Thousand is told virtually in the Marcan words, the only notable change being the substitution of Magadan for Dalmanutha: a vexing riddle, since we do not know for sure where either place was. The best solution seems as follows. Mark brings Jesus from Tyre via Sidon, 'to the sea of Galilee into (ἀνὰ μέσον) the district of Decapolis' (AT), i.e. in a circuit north and east, avoiding Galilee, to the southeast quarter of the lake-coast. Matthew brings him, not via Sidon, 'along the sea of Galilee . . . to the mountain' (AT). 'The mountain' comes three times in Matthew. First it is the new Sinai, the mountain of Torah, at 5.1; second it is here, the mountain of marvellous healings and the feeding of the multitudes; third it is the mountain of resurrection where Jesus gives his last words to the Church (28.16). As the last τὸ ὄρος is said several times to be in Galilee,[68] and the first is strongly implied to be,[69] it is natural to understand 'along the sea of Galilee' here as at 4.18 as along the west shore, and the mountain as being a mountain in Galilee here also: very likely the ancient holy mountain of Tabor, eleven miles south-west of the Lake, venerated in later tradition. The 'high mountain' of Transfiguration is also in Galilee,[70] and may well be thought of as the same. The phrase 'they glorified the God of Israel' (15.31) implies a mixed crowd of sufferers: but that is exactly what Matthew says of those who came to be healed and taught at the mountain at 4.23–5—'His fame spread throughout

---

[67] cf. the Heb. of Isa. 35.5, 'the ears of the deaf *tippāthahnā*'.
[68] Matt. 26.32; 28.7,10,16.   [69] Matt. 4.23; 8.5.
[70] 17.22: but McNeile and others place it near Caesarea.

all Syria'. Matthew thus (most probably) has the 4,000 fed south-west of the Lake, in Galilee, Mark south-east of the Lake, in Decapolis. There follows a boat journey in both Gospels, Mark to Dalmanutha, which is usually taken to be on the south-west shore therefore, and where an altercation with the Pharisees would be natural, as being in Galilee. Matthew already has Jesus in this district, and a boat journey implies to the east shore, and would give an opportunity to include Decapolis, as testified in Mark. Eusebius says 'Μαγαιδανή is now near Gerasa',[71] i.e. in Decapolis. The following boat journey in both Gospels is northwards, to Bethsaida (Mark), towards Caesarea Philippi (Matthew).

(32) The Leaven of the Pharisees 16.5–12

The Marcan pericope is followed closely, with characteristic suppression, however, of the apostles' lack of understanding. At the close we are told, 'Then they understood . . .'. 'Pharisees and Sadducees' expand Mark's caveat on the Pharisees and Herod: Sadducaic and Pharisaic hypocrisy were evidenced side by side at Mark 12.13ff, 18ff, and the Herodians are mentioned with the latter in the Matthaean parallel. Strecker[72] notes a formal contradiction between the view of Pharisaic teaching as leaven here, but as authoritative at 23.2f: but in view of the attitude to the Pharisees inherited from Mark and expounded in 12, 15.1–20, and 16.1, 4, leaven is a mild and apt expression for a corrupting and anti-spiritual influence. διδαχή is used loosely here under the shadow of a Marcan context that rejects Pharisaism *tout court:* in 23 Matthew is able to draw at leisure his distinction between Pharisaism and the Pharisees, the former good, the latter bad.

In the pericopae following Tabernacles, from Matt. 14—16.12, the midrashic theory has a comparatively easy passage. For most of the new material which we have been discussing a considerable body of scholarly opinion has already taken Matthew's redactoral activity to be the creative force. But the more willingly Peter's Walking on the Water or the Matthaean Canaanite Woman are accepted as instances of the evangelist's own free writing, the harder it becomes to draw a line between such pieces and the parables in the second half of 13, say. The midrashic theory suggests itself out of a careful reading of those passages where Matthew is agreed to be overwriting Mark. It is here that we see his linguistic and doctrinal propensities, the rhythms of his sentences, his imagery and scribal turn of mind: and where the Marcan text would provide a matrix in other passages, filled out by the same traits, there seems no basis for positing another source but a determined conservatism.

[71] *Onomasticon.*   [72] *WG*, p. 16.

18
ḤANUKKAH (16.13—19)

(33) The Question at Caesarea 16.13–28

For the greater part the pericope follows Mark. The major exception is the Petrine logion, vv. 17–19; and there are a number of small glosses.

Professor Cullmann has argued that the words to Peter go back to Jesus, and we are fortunate to have in his *Peter*[1] a statement which has achieved considerable acceptance, and may serve as a basis for re-examining the text. Cullmann proposes a theory that the words are dominical, but were not spoken in the context given. He thinks they were originally spoken at the Last Supper along with the Lucan words, 'Simon, Simon, behold, Satan demanded to have you . . . and when you have turned again, strengthen your brethren.' However, they circulated as an independent unit, and were connected by Matthew to the Caesarea pericope 'because in its context it seemed to fit'.[2] The basis for this is a somewhat complex triangular argument into which we need not enter, associating the Luke 22 logion, taken to be historical, with John 6.66–71, Peter's words after the 5,000, taken to be symbolic of the Last Supper conversation, and our text, taken to be foot-loose.

Cullmann defends the dominical genuineness of the logion by five arguments: (*a*) it is 'of quite Semitic linguistic character'; (*b*) it turns upon a word-play which works in Aramaic, 'You are *Kepha*', and upon this *kepha*' . . .' but does not work in Greek, 'You are πέτρος, and upon this πέτρα . . .'; (*c*) the rhythm is Semitic, and is composed of three strophes of three lines each, like Matt. 11.7–9 and 11.25–30; (*d*) there is no object to ἀπεκάλυψε; which shows the first sentence to have been taken from its context, and therefore to have had a different original context; and (*e*) ἐκκλησία, probably translating *kᵉnishta*, means the people of God, as often in the LXX, and not the church-organization of the apostles. It is not merely a possible concept for Jesus, but an essential one, for implicit in the idea of the Son of Man is the Danielic 'saints of the Most High': there cannot be an eschatology without an eschatological community. The idea of building a community occurs in Amos 9.11, LXX, 'I will build up the tabernacle of David', and Israel is often called a 'house'. As for the rock, that is

[1] O. Cullmann, *Peter, Disciple, Apostle, Martyr* (2e., E.T., London 1962).
[2] p. 191.

a symbol of the people of God in Dan. 2, where the stone cut out by no human hand overthrows the idolatrous metallic empires, and grows into a great mountain, and fills the earth. Cullmann certainly bids fair to rebut the earlier critical position from Holtzmann[3] on, which settled the question on the basis that Jesus never intended to found a Church.

When we consider Cullmann's arguments in the light of patterns of writing which we have established as Matthaean, they seem somewhat double-edged.

1. The Semitic linguistic character might be due to its Aramaic genuineness, but it might also be due to Matthew's proven Semitic Greek. ἀποκριθεὶς εἶπεν, my Father in heaven, κἀγώ, the kingdom of heaven, (binding and) loosing (2), earth and heaven (2), ἔσται (2), πύλη, are all characteristic of Matthew—23 words out of 80. ἐκκλησία as a word is also peculiar to Matthew. Flesh-and-blood is a semitism which does not occur in Matthew, but would be as natural to him as body-and-soul, see-and-hear, or hand-and-foot, which do. On the other hand there is no patronymic other than Bar-Jonah introduced by Matthew, and κατισχύω and κλεῖς occur here only in the Gospel: though κλείω is not uncharacteristic.[4]

2. The word-play argument is irrelevant. The name Kepha' is dominical, as we know from Paul and Mark: what we want to know is if Matthew's interpretation is dominical, and the Aramaic word-play cannot tell us that.

3. It is ironical that Cullmann, and Oepke,[5] on whom he depends for his rhythm argument, should cite two Matthew texts in parallel as evidence for *non*-Matthaean authorship. Rhythmical analysis has to be carried much further than distinguishing three strophes (i.e. sentences) of three lines (i.e. clauses); and we have attempted this in ch. 4 above. The strongest rhythm is in v. 19, 'Whatever you bind on earth shall be bound in heaven . . .', and the converse. But such converse machaeric[6] sayings (bind, bound, loose, loosed) are a regular feature of Matthaean writing: five times in Matthew, never in Mark, twice in Luke (one Q). We have virtually the same saying in the plural form at Matt. 18.18 only, and a closely similar rhythm at 10.32f, 'So everyone who acknowledges me before men, I also will acknowledge

---

[3] pp. 170ff. H. J. Holtzmann, *Handkommentar zum NT* I, ad loc.
[4] 3/0/2.
[5] A. Oepke, 'Der Herrenspruch über die Kirche: Mt. 16,17–19 in der neuesten Forschung', *Studia Theologica* (Lund 1948–50), pp. 150f.
[6] See p. 75 above.

before my Father who is in heaven,' with its converse, and at 6.14f. But the less rhythmical earlier sentences are also rather Matthaean. Logia of the form μακάριος . . . ὅτι . . . occur ten times in Matthew, never in Mark, five times in Luke (3Q). The contrast 'men/my Father who is in heaven' comes repeatedly in Matthew, in the Alms–Prayer–Fasting section, at 6.14f (M), at 10.32, 33, etc. Peter's 'You are the Christ' is taken up by Christ's, 'You are Peter'. Now this is a Matthaean habit. In a moment Matthew will in turn take up 'You are Peter (Rock)' with 'You are my *scandalon* (stumbling-stone)'. Or later Peter will say, 'Lo, we have *left* everything and *followed* you: what then shall we have?': Mark and Matthew both have, 'Everyone who has *left* houses . . .', but Matthew goes on to insert, 'You who have *followed* me, will also sit on twelve thrones . . .' taking up the second verb. Or compare 18.1ff, 'Who is the *greatest* in *the kingdom of heaven*? . . . Unless you turn . . . you will never enter *the kingdom of heaven*. So he who humbles himself . . . he is the *greatest*', in contrast with Mark 9.33ff. The rhythms and sentence-balances are thus typical of Matthew, and constitute an argument for Matthaean and against dominical authorship.

4. The missing object to ἀπεκάλυψεν is not a sign of a rent in context, and therefore of a pre-Matthaean origin, but is a common feature of NT Greek, cf. Matt. 11.14, 'If you are willing to accept (it)', 12.13 (= Mark), 'And he stretched (it) out'; 12.44, 'And going he finds (it) empty'; or, best of all, 11.27, 'To whom the Son will reveal (ἀποκάλυψαι) (him)'.

5. Cullmann shows effectively the necessity for the *concept* of the eschatological community in Jesus' thought: but what he has not done, and cannot do, is to explain why the *term* ἐκκλησία does not occur in Mark or Luke. They also have the eschatological community round the Son of Man, but they call it by some such name as 'the disciples': to belong to the eschatological community is to 'follow after me', or 'come to me' (Luke). It is not enough to prove that the thing was in Jesus' mind: we need to know why, according to Mark and Luke, the word was not in Jesus' mouth. Argument from silence is never final, but there is a lot of silence.[7]

---

[7] Cullmann's argument is weak in other ways. It is not really possible to divide 'the people of God' from 'the church-organization of the apostles'. Matthew speaks of building the Church on a rock, and the Temple metaphor bespeaks an organic Church. Israel is often spoken of as a house, but in the sense of a household: building metaphors are not used of it. Amos 9.11 is not to the point: it is a prophecy of the rebuilding of the Temple. Nor is the Dan. 2 passage very satisfactory as a basis for the rock image: in Dan. 2 Israel is a stone, not a rock, and is not a foundation for building at all.

6. Cullmann's proposal to site the logion at the Last Supper seems somewhat comical. Luke, whom Cullmann is taking to be historical, tells us that it was at the Last Supper that the Twelve quarrelled who was to be the greatest, and that Jesus rebuked them for their unspiritual ambition, and pointed to his own example of humility as the mark of greatness. Are we to believe that he then turned and told Simon that he was the foundation-rock apostle, the leader, the 'greatest', despite all? Luke would not thank him for such an anticlimax! Cullmann insists[8] that his exegesis of the logion is independent of his theory of siting: but, as he himself says, they are strong words and require a site in the incarnate ministry. If we agree in rejecting a post-Resurrection pronouncement theory, we seem obliged to suggest some other convincing context.

If we do not accept Cullmann's theory, can we do better ourselves? It is difficult to see any substantial objection to a midrashic view: that the logion is Matthew's own embroidery. He elaborates the Marcan question, 'Who do men say that I am?', to 'Who do men say that the Son of Man is?': Jesus' later word is to explain his Messiahship in terms of the suffering and rising of the Son of Man (16.21), and the two titles are held together from the beginning. He introduces Jeremiah into the disciples' reply, and glosses Peter's answer, 'You are the Christ', with 'the son of the living God'. Whatever may be said for or against Cullmann's view that 'Messiah' and 'Son of God' are distinct concepts in first-century Judaism, it is certain that Matthew thought they meant the same. He regarded Jesus' baptism as his anointing, and quotes Isaiah to prove it:[9] the voice of God says, 'This is my beloved Son', and is repeatedly echoed by the Tempter, 'If you are the son of God . . . .'. The Petrine Confession is to Matthew the highlight of the ministry: he underlines it by explaining 'Christ' here in v. 16, by adding it to Mark at v. 20, '. . . to tell no one that he was the Christ', and by inserting it in the narrative in v. 21, 'From that time Jesus Christ began to show . . . .'.[10] If Matthew makes three small glosses to emphasize the gravity of the moment, may he not have written a longer gloss? Mark had recorded that Jesus surnamed Simon as Peter, but he gave no occasion. Matthew omitted the fact in the Marcan context (Matt. 10.2), merely writing, 'First Simon, who is called Peter.' So great a name deserves a great occasion, and none greater than Simon's confession that Jesus was the Christ.

[8] p. 191.
[9] Isa. 61.1; Matt. 4.17; 5.3,4, cf. p. 277 above; Isa. 42.1; Matt. 12.18, cf. p. 329 ad loc.
[10] $\aleph$ B bo: other Mss. omit χριστός, or both words, from the unusual nature of the subject phrase.

The new material grows organically from the Matthaean text. 'Christ the son of God' is answered by 'Simon the son of Jonah', 'You are the Christ' by 'You are Peter', 'the living God' by 'the gates of Hades': just as Matthew takes up the phrases of his Mustard-Seed parable with the Leaven, or his Treasure-parable with the Pearl. In the parables chapter Matthew presented the Twelve as understanding his teaching and commented, '*Blessed are* your eyes for they see . . .' —not because of their own openness, but because 'To you it has been given to know the secrets . . .'. In 11.25 Jesus thanks *the Father* that he has hidden his Messiahship[11] from the wise, but *revealed* it to the infant Church. Nothing could therefore be more like Matthew in doctrine or language than to continue, '*Blessed are* you, Simon . . ., for flesh and blood has not *revealed* this to you, but *my Father who is in heaven*': the sentence-structure and the antithesis we have already shown to be characteristic besides.

Simon is saluted as the son of Jonah. Now Matthew has already twice introduced Jonah into the Marcan story, once in the opening verses of the present chapter: and Jonah is said to be a symbol of the Resurrection. Jonah was three days and three nights in the ocean of death, and there he prayed, 'Water was poured around me to the soul: the lowest deep compassed me . . . I went down into the earth whose bars are everlasting barriers.'[12] The bars of Sheol closed over his head, and yet he came out alive. It is the familiar image of the Psalms where the speaker is going under in the trials of life, when the waters come up to his neck,[13] and the waves and storms cover him,[14] and he prays that God will set his feet upon the rock.[15] Jonah also prayed to see God's holy temple.[16] How apt that the son of Jonah should himself be the Rock on which the new Temple, Christ's Church, is to be built; whose members may go down to Hades in death for a space, but its gates[17] will not hold them down (κατισχύσουσιν) eternally, for they share in their master's power of resurrection, prefigured in Jonah of old.

Here again an insight into Matthew's calendar enables us to see into the mind of the evangelist. Lection 33 is read on the sabbath before Ḥanukkah: Lection 34 will bring us to the Transfiguration, and Ḥanukkah itself. Now Ḥanukkah is the second feast of the Temple:

[11] i.e. that his miracles are in fact the works of Christ (11.2–6).
[12] Jon. 2.6,7, LXX.   [13] Ps. 69.2.
[14] Ps. 88.3–7.   [15] Ps. 40.2.
[16] Jon. 2.5.
[17] The gates of Hades occur in the Greek Bible at Isa. 38.10; 3 Macc. 5.51; Wisd. 16.13; cf. Job 38.17. Needless to say, they are always for keeping people down in the underworld.

Tabernacles was its Dedication, Hanukkah its Rededication. The legend of the preservation of the fire, the tabernacle, the ark, and the altar of incense from the Fall of the city in 586 B.C., is given in 2 Maccabees[18] as a part of the Hanukkah tradition, and is ascribed there to the careful hiding of Jeremiah. It occurs therefore to Matthew, writing of 'one of the prophets' whom the people see revived in Jesus, to mention Jeremiah: for that prophet had not merely provided the materials for the future Temple, but had appeared to Judas Maccabaeus in a dream,[19] and was said to be alive and praying for Israel. Solomon and his Temple were never far from the story of Matt. 12—13, the Festal season of Tishri: now that we come to Rededication we return to the Temple, the fulfilled Temple, the Church. Then Jesus was the greater than Jonah, the greater than Solomon, the greater than the Temple: now it is on the son of Jonah that the Church, the greater Temple, is to be built. οἰκοδομέω is used metaphorically of the Church in Rom. 15.20; 1 Cor. 3.9–17; 1 Pet. 2.5; and Eph. 2.22: in every case expressly drawing the analogy with the old Temple. Here undoubtedly the same image is being employed. On the eve of Hanukkah the Matthaean Christ turns his mind to his new Temple; the Feast will see him transfigured with the glory-cloud that filled Tabernacle and Temple of old, and setting out the laws that are to govern his ἐκκλησία henceforth.

The images of the Temple and its foundation-stone were in Christian thinking a generation before Matthew wrote. In both Romans and Corinthians Christ is the sole foundation-stone; in Ephesians the image is reapplied, and the apostles and prophets are the θεμέλιον, and Christ the corner-stone round which the rest are aligned.[20] It is upon the latter doctrine that Matthew draws. Christ was, according to Mark, the headstone of the corner, another expression for ἀκρογωνιαῖος, and Matthew repeats this: but also Peter, and later the Twelve, are to him the foundations of the Church, following the teaching of Ephesians. It is a matter of controversy whether Paul wrote Ephesians: if it is not Pauline, it is still likely to be pre-Matthaean. 'If not Pauline [Dr H. Chadwick writes[21]] it is the work of an . . . admirer of the apostle . . . for the generation after Paul's

---

[18] 2 Macc. 2.1–8.   [19] 2 Macc. 15.13–16.

[20] cf. R. J. McKelvey, *The New Temple and the Church in the New Testament* (Oxford 1969), Appendix C, pp. 195ff, argues for the traditional interpretation of ἀκρογωνιαῖος as a corner foundation-stone, and not a coping-stone, still less an arch-stone. His most convincing arguments are from ancient architecture, and from the sole use of ἀκρογωνιαῖος as a foundation-stone in the LXX (Isa. 28.16).

[21] *Peake's Commentary on the Bible*, ed. M. Black and H. H. Rowley (London 1962), p. 982.

death.' On general grounds I should argue that within a few years of Paul's martyrdom all documents believed to be Pauline would be likely to be in wide currency: in particular we have shown strong grounds for thinking that Matthew knew at least 1 Thessalonians, Romans, and 1 Corinthians.[22] If Matthew knew Ephesians, Eph. 2.20 must seem the inspired comment on the Lord's surnaming of Peter. 'You were', says Paul (or his disciple), 'built (ἐποικοδομηθέντες) upon the foundation of the apostles and prophets, Christ Jesus himself being the corner-stone, in whom the whole building (οἰκοδομή) is joined together and grows into a holy temple in the Lord.' Ephesians is the classic Pauline treatment of the ἐκκλησία: and while the coincidence of the words 'church' and 'build', and the images of Temple and foundation, are not enough to *prove* dependence, they form a strong suggestion,[23] especially in view of the commoner image in Paul and 1 Peter of Jesus as the sole foundation-stone. Peter, then, as Matthew interprets the matter, was named the Rock in view of his inspired insight that Jesus was Messiah; and the name signified what Paul taught, that Peter was an apostolic foundation-stone[24] on which the Church, the new Temple, should be built. Simon alone was surnamed Peter, and he was in many ways the leader of the Twelve: but Paul had taught that all the apostles (indeed and some prophets) were foundation-stones of the Church. Matthew cannot tell us that all the Twelve were surnamed Peter, but he can tell us that all the powers which Jesus gave individually to Peter he later gave in common to the Twelve: and this he does word for word at 18.18: 'Whatever you bind on earth shall be bound in heaven, and whatever you loose on earth shall be loosed in heaven.' Whether this teaching is closer to the Vatican II doctrine of collegiality of bishops, or the Anglican position on the matter,[25] it is clear that Matthew did not think of Peter (let alone his successor) as having any exclusive position of fundamentality. He has no position, no authority, which he does not share with his colleagues: but he was the first to see the great truth, and Matthew takes that to be the reason for the name which only he can bear. The Twelve apostles as the Twelve foundation-stones of the

[22] cf. ch. 8 above.

[23] I hope to show in a later work that the Matthaean church read the Pauline corpus in series round the year for the Epistle: and that Ephesians was read at Ḥanukkah. This would make the suggestion very strong indeed.

[24] The image is of a single foundation-rock, not a whole rocky area (cf. Luke 8.6): cf. McKelvey, op. cit., Appendix B, pp. 193f; J. Jeremias, *Jesus als Weltvollender* (Gütersloh 1930), pp. 62f.

[25] It is inconceivable that Matthew, bred in the rabbinic system of a succession of authority, could have imagined the Church without successors to the apostles; and the care with which apostolic authority is delineated is evidence of the same.

heavenly city are taken on from Paul and Matthew by John in the Apocalypse.

It is Matthew's way first to tell us with an epigram the truth he wishes to convey, then to fill it out with a concrete illustration: an object lesson for preachers. 'Blessed are the peacemakers . . .': so do not be angry; and if angry, be reconciled. 'The lamp of the body is the eye': have a generous eye and be full of light, not a mean eye. 'If a man has a hundred sheep . . . does he not leave the ninety–nine?': if your brother sins, go and tell him his fault; if obdurate, take witnesses. So here: 'On this rock I will build my church, and the gates of Hades will not force it down' (AT). The *māshāl* is memorable but not plain. What does Paul mean by calling the apostles the foundation of the Church? He means that they are its governors. Gates suggest keys, and keys are the symbols of power: elsewhere Matthew writes of the Pharisaic scribes who sit on Moses' seat of governance and lock (κλείετε) the kingdom of heaven in men's faces.[26] Again the image of Eliakim, the vizier of Hezekiah, with the key of the house of David on his shoulder,[27] might suggest Peter's sole vicegerency: but the misuse of the power of the keys by a whole community of scribes is cited by the evangelist, and gives a better idea of Matthew's concept of authority in the Church. So Peter's being the foundation means that Peter holds the keys: and what does that mean? It means, to the scribe turned Christian, the rabbinic power to '*āsar* and to *hittîr*: to make rules in God's name, and to make exceptions to them, to excommunicate and to reinstate. This was, historically, the reality of apostolic power. In every page of the Epistles Paul tells us of what he has ordained in all the churches; and from time to time we hear how he disciplines the defaulters, pronouncing judgement in the name of the Lord Jesus that the Church should not associate with immoral Christians,[28] welcoming back the penitent with joy.[29] It requires Matthew to give such practice the correct rabbinic *termini technici*.[30]

In every point, therefore, a midrashic view would seem to be justified. The language is Matthaean, and rabbinic; the rhythm, especially in the last two clauses is typical of Matthew; the imagery of Jonah and Sheol, and of locking the kingdom, come elsewhere in Matthew, and in him alone; the doctrines of divine revelation of the Messiah, and of apostolic power to bind and loose, are Matthaean. The passage grows out of the Matthaean text, and fits with the

---

[26] 23.13. [27] Isa. 22.22.
[28] 1 Cor. 5.3–5,9ff; cf. 2 Thess. 3.6. [29] 2 Cor. 2.5–11.
[30] Matthew introduces the power to reinstate at 9.8; cp. Mark 2.12: 'They glorified God, who had given such authority [viz. to forgive sins] *to men*.' There is no question of the redaction here.

Matthaean calendar. Nothing is required to be invented: the text of Peter's surnaming comes to hand from Mark, unused; the text of the building of the Church on an apostolic foundation comes to hand, in all probability from Ephesians. There is no remainder. As if to seal his devotion to Paul, Matthew makes a further gloss on the Marcan text. Isaiah had warned that God would be a stone of stumbling (λίθου προσκόμματι) and a rock of offence (πέτρας πτώματι) to both houses of Israel (8.14): a verse which Paul combines with another to produce the phrase πέτραν σκανδάλου (Rom. 9.33). Simon has shown himself worthy to be the πέτρα of the Church by his moment of vision: by his daring to rebuke his Lord he becomes a stumbling-block. At 16.18 Jesus said, σὺ εἶ πέτρος: at 16.23 he says σκάνδαλον εἶ ἐμοῦ. It is the same midrashic mind. The images are from Isaiah, but the words are associated not by Isaiah, but in Romans.

What did the Church make of Matthew's midrash? Luke is following Mark for the Caesarea Philippi incident, and just as he introduces no considerable piece of Matthew in the rest of 8.4—9.50, so nor does he here. The themes of the frailty and greatness of the apostles he holds over till the Last Supper, where Peter's frailty was fixed for ever. First he tells of the Apostles' quarrel who should be greatest, which he takes from Mark 9.34f and 10.42ff: then of their future greatness judging the tribes of Israel, from Matt. 19.28. Jesus assures Peter of having prayed that his faith fail not, and gives him the commission to support (στήρισον) his brethren: going on immediately to prophesy his denial. Cullmann is surely well-grounded in seeing a connection between this and the Matthaean logion.

(a) It has the name-antithesis: 'Simon, Simon . . . Πέτρε . . .'; and what looks like a piece of intended irony, 'I tell you, Πέτρε, the cock will not crow . . .'—not much of a rock yet!

(b) It is a personal singling out of Peter over against the other eleven, a thing which Luke rarely introduces elsewhere in his Gospel.

(c) It is a commission to act like a rock. Luke elsewhere (9.51) uses the verb στηρίζω of Jesus 'firming his face': and there are expressions similar to this in the LXX, of which the closest is Isa. 50.7, 'I made my face ὡς στερεὰν πέτραν.'[31] The root idea of στηρίζω and στέρεος is √ΣΤΡ, firmness, and the association of the rock image in the LXX here shows that the same association is open at Luke 22.31.

Luke will then be giving a midrashic paraphrase and reinterpretation of Matt. 16.17ff. Peter had been historically the rock of the Twelve

[31] cf. also Ezek. 3.8, LXX, 'I have made thy face strong . . . more mighty than a rock (πέτρας).'

because he had been the first to see the Lord, and so had 'supported' the others on Easter Day, and had been the rock of the Church in Acts 1—12: this then had been the Lord's calling for him, and the true meaning of his name, and should be recounted as near as possible to the time of Jesus' death. As for keys and binding and loosing, that was a bit legalistic for Luke: had not Paul spent his life protesting that Peter had no authority over him? Better omit Matthew's passion for the new law.

The status of St John's Gospel remains a battlefield, but it may be well to indicate briefly the approach of the present work to John 1.42; 20.23; and 21.15ff. I suppose, in line with the theory of general communication between the churches argued in this book, that John had read all the Synoptic Gospels, and was writing a concentrated midrashic version of his own. The first 'week' of the book[32] gives a foreshadowing of the whole ministry: one of whose turning-points was the realization that Jesus was the Christ (1.41), with the subsequent surnaming of Peter (1.42). The collocation of these two events is due to Matt. 16.16f, though not their relatedness, for John ascribes the realization that Jesus was the Christ to Andrew, his apostle to the Greeks. For the Easter evening scene (20.19–23), John draws on the similar episode in Luke 24.36–49, which includes the command that 'forgiveness of sins in his name should be preached to all nations': John glosses from Matthew the converse logion, 'If you forgive the sins of any, they are forgiven; if you retain the sins of any, they are retained.' He is using the plural as in Matt. 18.18. John 21.15 also follows Luke in associating the commissioning of Peter with his denial: the threefold 'Simon, son of John', the antithesis of Simon Peter (21.1, 3, 7, 11, 15) with Peter (21.17, 20, 21), the setting by the coal-fire, all recall the denial. The shepherding imagery is drawn from Matt. 9.36; 10.5f; 18.12ff; and of course from John 10. The Lost Sheep parable in Matthew is especially related to apostolic binding and loosing.

What does all this leave us with as an historical basis for the great theological systems that have been built on the Matthaean logion? We know that Jesus called Simon Kepha', Rock, and Cullmann is surely right in saying that the name, like other scriptural surnames, will be of theological significance:[33] it is not a nickname, like Stonewall Jackson, or Rocky Marciano. We do not know on what occasion

---

[32] John 1.19—2.12. John's witness is on the first of a series of four days, of which the last three are specified, 'On the next day . . .'. Then, 'on the third day', i.e. on the sixth of the series, comes the Cana marriage. 'After that' Jesus goes down to Capernaum.

[33] op.cit., p. 21.

Jesus gave the name. Mark does not tell us; Matthew has sited it at Peter's Confession as the best context available in his view; Luke at the Last Supper as the best context available in his: modern theories of post-Resurrection words have little to commend them. For the significance of the name scripture gives us two alternative views. Matthew and the Apocalypse interpret in line with St Paul: the Church is the new Temple, and the apostles are its foundation-stones, and Peter, as his name implies, is the foundation-stone *par excellence*. Foundation-stone is an image for authority: Peter and the Twelve are called to govern the Church. Luke and John interpret in line with history. Peter never had any legislative primacy. James and John thought they might share the primacy between them, and even squabbled about such unspiritual questions to the end: Peter was the foundation-stone of the Church in the sense of supporting its weight in the days of crisis, and shepherding its members until his call to martyrdom. How inevitable: Matthew, the converted scribe, sees the significance in terms of authority; Luke, the historian, in terms of pastoral support. And how inevitable that the Catholic wing of the Church, concerned about authority, should follow Matthew; and that the Protestant wing of the Church, concerned about pastoral ministering, should follow Luke.

(34) The Transfiguration 17.1–13

Hanukkah coincides with the old Canaanite feast of mid-winter.[34] The winter solstice, when the unconquered sun resumes his empire, was not observed, or not observed officially in biblical Israel; but the rededication of the Temple by Judas Maccabaeus on 25th Chislev 164 B.C., enabled Judaism to baptize the festival into the historical faith, and to celebrate it for eight days on the model of Tabernacles. The letters prefixed to 2 Maccabees make it clear that that work was applied to the celebration of Ḥanukkah,[35] and the adaptation of the light symbolism is made plain in them: Jeremiah 'went forth into the mountain where Moses went up and beheld the heritage of God . . .'. and hid the tabernacle and the ark and the altar of incense 'until God

---

[34] On the possible pagan origins of Ḥanukkah, see O. S. Rankin, *The Origins of the Festival of Ḥanukkah* (Edinburgh 1930), and 'The Festival of Ḥanukkah', in *The Labyrinth*, ed. S. H. Hooke (London 1935), pp. 159–209; F.-M. Abel, 'La Fête de la Hanoucca', in *RB* LIII (1946), pp. 538–46; J. Morgenstern, 'The Chanukkah Festival and the Calendar of Ancient Israel', in *HUCA*. xx (1947), pp. 1–136; XXI (1948), pp. 365–496. Whether or not the midwinter solstice had been unofficially celebrated from early times in Israel, the influence of the 'lights' motif once it was established is indisputable.

[35] 1.18; 2.16.

gather the people again together, and mercy come; and then shall the
Lord disclose these things, and the glory of the Lord shall be seen,
and the cloud, as also it was shewed with Moses . . .' (2 Macc. 2.4–8).
The midwinter sun is thus perhaps aligned with the glory-cloud of
Exod. 40 that suffused the Tabernacle after Moses' vision on Horeb.
When Nehemiah refounds the Temple (2 Macc. 1.22, 32 writes), 'the
sun shone out . . . there was kindled a marvellous blaze . . . when
light from the altar shone over against it, [the sacrifice] was consumed.'
And in due course Judas also, cleansing the sanctuary, strikes fire
from the stones for the sacrifice and the lighting of the lamps (10.3).
The old calendrical basis for the festival is thus exorcized.

Hanukkah means 'Dedication', and the *sidrāh* that has come down
to us is from Num. 7,[36] when the princes offer the bowls for the
Tabernacle the noun *hᵃnukkāh* occurs for the only time in the Torah.
It is probable, however, that the original *sidrāh* continued further.
The opening verses of Num. 8 ordain the lighting of the lamps, and
Num. 9 records the rearing of the Tabernacle and the descent of the
glory-cloud, a duplicate to Exod. 40. The *haphtārāh* in the Talmud[37]
is Zech. 3—4.7, where Joshua the high-priest is cleansed from his
defiled garments, and the prophet sees the candlestick vision. We can
well understand therefore the development of the Transfiguration
story as the NT fulfilment of Hanukkah. Jesus' ascent of the mountain
follows that of Moses with his three companions, Nadab, Hur, and
Abihu, in Exod. 24, to his first vision of the Shekinah; like Jesus, he
heard the voice of God after six days. His transfiguring is closer to
Moses' second vision in Exod. 34, when the skin of Moses' face shone.
The garments made white follow both Num. 8 and Zechariah. In the
former the Levites were cleansed of their impurities and washed their
ἱμάτια, in the latter Jesus son of Josadak had his filthy ἱμάτια taken
away, and the angel clothed him with rich apparel:[38] now (in Mark)
Jesus the son of God has his ἱμάτια made shining white, so as no fuller
on earth can white them. Elijah is drawn in from the theophany on
Horeb, so similar to Moses'; as are the tabernacles, and the whole
overshadowing cloud symbolism of Exodus–Numbers. For the
greater part Matthew is content to transcribe this. He expands Mark's,

[36] M Meg. 3.6 merely specifies 'Princes', which is interpreted by Danby to mean
Num. 7.1–89, in line with modern practice. But in rabbinic practice the title
merely refers to the first unit of a perhaps extended reading, and there was
certainly a tendency to abbreviate Jewish readings over time.
[37] B Meg. 31a.
[38] cf. also the opening word of God in the passage, 'The Lord rebuke thee
(ἐπιτιμήσαι), O Satan' with Jesus' word to Peter at Mark 8.33; Matt. 16.22f;
and perhaps Zech. 3.9, 'Behold the stone that I have set before Jesus' with Matt.
16.16ff, 23.

'and he was transfigured before them' with further Horeb symbols. 'And his face shone' echoes the shining of Moses' face at Exod. 34: 'like the sun' takes up the old midwinter symbolism which we have seen exploited in 2 Maccabees, in the dedication legends. Christ's garments become white 'as light', and the cloud a cloud 'of light' (AT) for the same reason. The Church since Paul had seen in Christ the fulfilment of Tabernacle and Temple, of God's glory on earth: Matthew has merely reinforced the Marcan symbols of Transfiguration with touches from the traditional liturgy, and sited the pericope on the opening day of his church's celebration of Hanukkah.[39]

(35) *The Lunatic 17.14–23*

The story is much abbreviated from the Marcan account. This is in part due to Matthew's general tendency to shorten, but it should be noted (*a*) that the exorcistic words of power, 'You deaf and dumb spirit, I command you, come out of him, and never enter him again', have already been developed into the Return of the Evil Spirit following the similar story in 12; and (*b*) that the theme of the faith of the father interceding for his son has been fully used in Matthew's own Centurion's Boy.[40] Verse 20, which lacks a Marcan parallel, is a clear case of Matthew's own hand. 'Why could we not cast it out?' Mark had the unsatisfactory, 'This kind cannot be driven out by anything but prayer'. Well, but had not the apostles been praying? The reason will be that their prayer had lacked depth: ὀλιγοπιστία. Faith that God or Jesus will do the work, and its converse, little-faith, are Matthaean themes;[41] the mustard-seed, as the symbol of power within the smallest, is in the Marcan tradition; 'this mountain' comes from the context, and from Mark 11.23. μεταβαίνω (2) is Matthaean as well as ὀλιγοπιστία; ἀμὴν λέγω ὑμῖν, ὡς = like, ἐρῶ, ἐάν, and ἐκεῖ are semi-Matthaean—10 characteristic words out of 31. ἀδυνατέω is used with reference to the similar promise to Abraham in Gen. 18.14.

(36) *The Didrachma 17.24–end*

Upon Moses' descent from Sinai, he took up a freewill offering for the furnishing of the Temple (Exod. 35). The dedication of these offerings is the subject of the Hanukkah *sidrāh* in Num. 7. The divine command

---

[39] Mark has it on the 6th day of Ḥanukkah, perhaps even more aptly; see above, ch. 9, appendix B.
[40] See pp. 319–21 above.　　　　[41] G. Barth, *TIM*, pp. 112ff, 118ff.

ordaining them is given in Exod. 30—31, and of these chapters the paragraph which became most familiar to later generations was the section *Sheqalim* (Exod. 30.11–16), which provided for a levy, later interpreted as an annual levy, of a half-shekel per head. The passage was read each year as a special lection on the seventh sabbath before Passover. Three things suggest taking the Didrachma pericope here rather than on sabbath *Sheqalim*: first, the theme of Dedication is now in the Church's mind, and the question of gifts for the earthly Temple is exactly apposite; second, the main point of doctrine which Matthew wishes to instil is the avoidance of scandal, which is the theme of the following Marcan discourse; third, the payment of the Temple tax was already touched on in a saying of the Lord read in Adar, 'Render to God the things that are God's.' But at all events the topic must be included. Matthew's church is struggling to maintain its position within Judaism despite its heterodox Christology, and the first question to be asked of any religious community near the borders of heresy is, 'Do they pay?' Just as Paul was anxious to commend his radical Christianity by the collection, so is Matthew determined to give no handle to the enemies of his radical Judaism by ceasing to contribute.

Is the pericope a traditional floating unit which Matthew has anchored here, or is it one more instance of Matthaean midrash? The answer must depend on the interpretation of v. 27. The view taken by nearly all commentators is that Matthew intends to suggest a miracle. He does not actually say that Peter went and took fish and stater, but that is what is implied. If this is so, unquestionably the passage is pre-Matthaean. We have no instance elsewhere in Matthew of the evangelist adopting traditional Greek wonder-stories into the Gospel. Despite an earlier view, we have seen that Matthew does very little to heighten the miraculous: the only new miracles in the whole book are the Centurion's Boy, which is a development of Mark's Paralytic and other matter, and the Virginal Conception, which is a development of Isa. 7.[42] It would be, so far as I am able to gauge, quite out of character for him to have invented a wonder-tale on the basis of Polycrates' Ring.[43] However, by the same token, why should he insert material of such a plainly legendary kind once only in his Gospel? Precisely the same arguments apply. If this wonder-legend was in circulation, surely others were too: why did Homer nod only the once? And why, furthermore, having brought us to the brink of the marvel, does he

---

[42] Peter's Walking the Water could be added, a development of Jesus'.

[43] The Polycrates' Ring story must, of course, have been familiar to the evangelist in some form. For its currency among the rabbis see H. W. Montefiore, 'Jesus and the Temple Tax', *NTS* xi, (1964), p. 70.

not recount it? It will not do to reply that the Slaughter of the Innocents and the Temptations are equally legendary; for the whole point is that these are biblical midrash, and not Greek thaumatography.

Perhaps I may venture another suggestion. The teaching of Jesus in Mark is mainly in the form of epigrams, direct, telling, and literal. If Jesus says better that a millstone were hanged about one's neck, then better it were. A feature which is rare in Mark and L is hyperbole, a trait which is, however, not uncommon in Matthew. People do not have planks in their eyes, or swallow camels, and the dead cannot bury their dead. When Jesus says, 'If you had faith . . .', nobody supposed that he should attempt to move Mt Tabor into the Lake of Galilee;[44] or that Peter was intended to count 490 acts of forgiveness. So, I submit, here we have another instance of Matthaean hyperbole. We must pay, says the evangelist, or they will resent it; and where is the money to come from? Why, the good Lord will provide: go and try with your rod, and the first fish you catch will have enough for two of us in its mouth! The suggestion is not meant to be taken literally.

Other considerations favour this view, since there is so much else Matthaean about the section. 'When they came to Capernaum' comes straight from the next verse in Mark, 9.33, and so does the conversation 'in the house'; not scandalizing is the subject of Mark 9.42ff so that we have here the customary traces of a Marcan foundation for midrash. The concern for Christian observance of the Torah is Matthaean, and so is the giving of laws to Peter, and the firm belief in divine providence. The notion that the Church is God's sons, and that the Jews are no more the kingdom but foreigners is basic to Matthew.[45] προσῆλθον, τί σοι δοκεῖ, are Matthaean. λέγει Ναί, λαμβάνω (3), ἤ (2), λέγων, κῆνσος, ἔφη, ἐκεῖνος, ἐλθών (2), πορεύομαι, ἄραγε, ἀνοίγω, στόμα, γῆ, are semi-Matthaean—23 characteristic words out of 100. οἱ βασιλεῖς τῆς γῆς is from the Psalter.[46] προφθάνω, ἀλλότριος, ἐλεύθερος are only here; but the style remains predominantly Matthaean.[47] No doubt the problem of paying poll-tax arose before A.D. 70, and was settled on the wise Pauline basis of not scandalizing. The situation after the War was complicated by the Romans' enforcing of the tax for the Temple of Jupiter; but here as elsewhere[48] Matthew, like the rabbis, assumes that the Temple will soon be rebuilt. In a word, the pericope is as Matthaean as anything else in the Gospel, and should be ascribed to the evangelist.

[44] Mark 11.23 is a similar instance outside Matthew.
[45] cf. Trilling, *WI*, Pt I; see esp. Matt. 21.41,43.
[46] Ps. 2.2.   [47] So Kilpatrick, *Origins*, p. 41.
[48] 5.23f; 23.16f.

(37) The Great and the Little 18.1–10

Mark's revealing account of the ambitions, rivalries, and humiliation of the Twelve is subtly rephrased: in place of the Lord's reproachful 'What were you discussing on the way?', Matthew has the apostles ask Jesus, 'Who is the greatest?' The account in Mark of the taking of the child is famously unclear, and Matthew rewrites the omitted Mark 10.35, 'If anyone wants to be first, he shall be last of all and servant of all', to illuminate the matter. Taken with reference to the child this means, 'Ambition is of the devil: childlike humility is the condition of entering heaven.' 'Will never enter the Kingdom' is probably taken over from the other 'children' pericope, Mark 10.15. The rest of the phrasing is characteristic: the kingdom of heaven (2), resumptive οὗτος, to become as. With the rhythm, 'Unless you turn . . . you will never enter the kingdom of heaven', cf. Matthew's. 'Unless your righteousness exceed . . . you will never enter the kingdom of heaven' (5.20).[49]

The matter of Mark 9.38–41 has been handled elsewhere (Matt. 12.30; 10.40, 42), and Matthew can move on from the apostle's duty to be humble as a child to his duty (Mark 9.42–8) to care for the little ones. The wordy Marcan section is abbreviated, the point being underlined in two *inclusio* verses. 'Woe to that man by whom . . .' (18.7), the first, is closely similar to Jesus' word to Judas (Mark 14.21), 'Woe to that man by whom the Son of man is betrayed', and signs off the 'Better dead' theme. 18.10, the second, draws together the whole paragraph. Any of you who scandalizes one of these little ones were better dead . . . See that you do not despise one of these little ones or their guardian angels will report your carelessness. My father in heaven, ὅρα μή, εἰς τούτων, λέγω ὑμῖν ὅτι, οὐρανοί, and the activity of angels are all characteristic.[50]

(38) The Lost Sheep 18.12–20 (A–22)

Mark handed on the Lord's directive to care for the little ones of the Church: Matthew now expounds this directive, first with a parable, then with a series of concrete instances. The Twelve are to rule the Church with humility, taking care that the μικροί do not stumble;

---

[49] J. Jeremias, *Infant Baptism in the first four Centuries* (E.T., London 1960), claims (p. 64, n. 4) the independence of Matt. 18.3 on the ground of four Aramaisms. The claims are answered by J. Dupont in 'Matthieu 18,3 ἐὰν μὴ στράφητε καὶ γένησθε ὡς τὰ παιδία, in *Neotestamentica et Semitica*, ed. E. E. Ellis and M. Wilcox (Edinburgh 1969), p. 57, n. 31.

[50] Luke has more angels than Matthew, but their activities are more widespread in the latter. For guardian angels cf. Enoch 90.1–10; 104.1.

like a shepherd going after the stray sheep; that is, visiting the sinner, taking witnesses, examining him before the Church. The development is natural, and is paralleled in 24—25, where Matthew first transcribes the Marcan Apocalypse, then expounds it in a series of parables, and finally describes the Last Judgement.

The theme of the parable is not arbitrary. It was a secondary theme of Ḥanukkah that Israel should be gathered into the restored and rededicated Temple. In the prayer in 2 Macc. 1, in which the feast is commended to the Jews of Egypt, Jonathan prayed, 'Accept the sacrifice . . . and consecrate it. Gather together our Dispersion, and set at liberty them that are in bondage among the heathen' (26f). At the close of the introductory letter it is said, 'Seeing then that we are about to celebrate Ḥanukkah, we write to you . . . in God we have hope that he will quickly have mercy upon us and gather us together out of all the earth' (2.16ff). The Zechariah prophecy used as *haphtārāh* similarly contains the promise, 'In that day every man will invite his neighbour under his vine and under his fig-tree.' Jewish evidence for the use of Ezek. 34 is lacking, apt as it would be: but we do have Christian use of Ezek. 34 evidenced at Ḥanukkah in John 10. John may, of course, be simply elaborating the Matthaean Good Shepherd of Dedication–tide, but the evidence I have just cited makes it seem that the gathering of God's people like sheep goes back to pre-Christian tradition.

The parable is characteristic in language. τί ὑμῖν δοκεῖ and πρόβατον are Matthaean: semi-Matthaean are πλανάομαι (3), οὐχί; ἐάν, πορεύομαι, ἀμὴν λέγω ὑμῖν, οὕτως, θέλημα, ἔμπροσθεν, my father in heaven, ἐν τούτων—that is, not merely in the conclusion but in the body of the parable too, 25 words out of 65. It is characteristic in the black-and-white contrast and the standard image and the one-for-one allegory correlation and the appended interpretation; it is not even uncharacteristic in being an imperative parable, for the imperative is masked under, 'So it is not God's will . . .', and remains formally indicative, like every other parable in Matthew. The Lucan version changes the point of the parable from the apostles' duty to be pastors to the joy of heaven at repentance, a Lucan theme. 'What man of you . . .?' is a standard Lucan introduction to a parable; ἔρημος for ὄρος,[51] rejoicing, parties, ἀπόλλυμι, φίλος, γείτων, συγκαλῶ, 'in heaven' for God, ἁμαρτωλός, μετανοέω, μετανοία are all characteristic: even more typical are the colourful non-allegoric touches, 'Lays it on his shoulders', 'calls together his friends and his neighbours'; and the shepherd's words to the company which repeat and drive home the

[51] 8.29/Mark 5.5.

point in the customary Lucan way.[52] All the evidence points to
the secondariness of the Lucan version.[53]

It remains for the parable to be applied. All care must be taken,
the Lord had said in Mark, that none of these little ones be cast into
gehenna. The apostle is not to vex himself with the faithful part of his
flock, but to go and seek out the wanderer: 'If your brother sin, go
and tell him his fault.'[54] If so be that he finds it he rejoices; but
pastoral experience is not always so happy—'If he refuses to listen
even to the Church, let him be to you as a Gentile . . .'. The scene
envisaged follows closely the pattern of church discipline in 1 Corinthians and elsewhere,[55] and the wording is so close to Paul in places
that direct dependence is the most obvious solution. 'ἀδελφοί', writes
Paul, 'if a man is overtaken in any trespass, you who are spiritual
should restore him in a spirit of gentleness':[56] so first 'go and tell him
his fault, between you and him alone'. κερδαίνω, 'gain' your brother,
is a technical Pauline term.[57] But in doubtful cases Paul writes,[58]
'Any charge must be sustained by the evidence of two or three
witnesses': Matthew not only quotes the same text from Deut. 19,
but quotes it in the Pauline version.[59] In cases of obduracy Paul took

---

[52] cf. 'Father, I have sinned . . .', 'This my son was dead . . .' from the same
chapter.

[53] Jeremias (*PJ* 38ff) says that the Matthaean version and context are 'a secondary, wholly artificial, composition', but he does not see how wholly Matthaean
they are. The Semitisms which he cites (from the conclusion, v. 14) are in any case
to be expected from a Semitic Greek author (cf. p. 116f above), but are also
instanced as Matthaean. His conjectural Aramaic *raʿawa*, which he takes to lie
behind Matthew's θέλημα and Luke's χαρά (following Manson, *SJ*, p. 208) is
weak. 'The Matthaean tradition has altered the tradition somewhat . . . the
correct rendering should be εὐδοκία' (l. 1, p. 29n). How can we trust Aramaic
conjectures that do not even fit the text as it is? Eta Linnemann (*Parables of
Jesus* (E.T., London 1960), pp. 65–73), says correctly that the introduction in
Luke (15.1f) is, a 'theological utterance', and that the conclusion (15.7) 'cannot
come from Jesus', as it would be 'over the heads of his hearers' (p. 70): Luke,
she claims, has reset the parable in its proper context as comment on Jesus' eating
with sinners. Neither Linnemann nor Jeremias notes how Lucan the Lucan
version is: Luke has reset the *Matthaean* parable in a *Lucan* form with a *Lucan*
context as comment on Jesus' eating with sinners. We have no evidence that Jesus
taught a Good Shepherd parable as such. Bultmann, *HST* 171, as so often, is
half-way to the heart of the matter: 'Matt. 18.12–14 is essentially more
original . . . but admittedly the application in Matt. 18.14 is also secondary.'
But even Bultmann's scepticism did not test Matt. 18.12f for Matthaean
characteristics.

[54] ἁμαρτήσῃ B fam. 1 Or; Nestle–Aland, BFBS, NEB: ἁμαρτήσῃ εἰς σέ DW.,
etc.; RSV, by assimilation to 18.21.

[55] cf. p. 154 above and p. 163 above.

[56] Gal. 6.1.

[57] Five times in 1 Cor. 9.

[58] 2 Cor. 13.1.

[59] See p. 169 above.

the matter to the Church, as in 1 Cor. 5, and excommunicated. He says, 'deliver this man to Satan', Matthew says, 'Let him be to you as a Gentile and a tax collector': but the meaning is the same in both cases, exclusion from the fellowship of grace. It is the concluding verse which most clearly shows Pauline influence. Paul writes, 'I have given judgment on the man who has done this, in the name of the Lord Jesus, you being gathered together and my spirit . . .' (ἐν τῷ ὀνόματι τοῦ Κυρίου ἡμῶν Ἰησοῦ Χριστοῦ, συναχθέντων ὑμῶν καὶ τοῦ ἐμοῦ πνεύματος).[60] Matthew writes this in a more Jewish form, 'For where two or three are gathered in my name (συνηγμένοι εἰς τὸ ἐμὸν ὄνομα), there am I in the midst of them'. The rabbinic epigram, 'Where two sit and there are between them words of the Torah, there the Shekinah rests between them',[61] has clearly been influential here. It is hardly to be believed that Jesus rephrased the rabbis' words to speak of his spiritual guidance of his Church in judgement and intercession after his death. The doctrine is the Pauline teaching of the Body and Spirit of Christ, and the words in Matthew read like an adaptation of the Pirqe Aboth saying to familiar words from 1 Corinthians.

Pauline influence is important because of the consistency of our picture of Matthew. We have found him at every point hitherto a *darshān*, not an innovator: developing the text of Mark out of other texts of Mark or OT texts, or by standard rabbinic devices, parables, and the like. The paragraph is highly Matthaean in language, interest, and rhythm: it is not easy to think that it developed in the anonymous church and was taken over by Matthew as tradition. I should be most unwilling to think that Matthew had inserted the matter out of his own head: such a procedure would not be in character. But the strong evidence we have of reliance on Pauline authority leaves our picture of the evangelist consistent: this is apostolic practice, sanctioned in apostolic correspondence now reverenced by the Church. In part it goes back to Deuteronomy; and in part no doubt (Matthew might think) Paul had it from the Lord.

The interest in church order is nearly confined to Matthew among the evangelists, cf. the Temple Tax, fasting, mourning, and alms rules. Characteristic language includes: ἀδελφός (2), παραλαμβάνω, ἐκκλησία (2), ἔστω, ὥσπερ, Gentile and publican, ἐάν (6), κερδαίνω, ὅσος ἐάν (2), heaven-and-earth (2), (binding-and-) loosing (2), δύο (3), ἤ (2), ἀμὴν λέγω ὑμῖν (2), συμφωνέω, my-father-in-heaven, συνάγω, εἰς τὸ ὄνομα, ἔμος, ἐκεῖ—52 words out of 120. ἐλέγχω is a technical term from the LXX (e.g. Lev. 19.17). The triple climax,[62] 'If he does

---

[60] 1 Cor. 5.3f (AT). [61] Pirqe Aboth 3.2,6,8.
[62] See scandalics, p. 81 above.

not listen . . . if he refuses to listen . . . if he refuses to listen . . .'
is standard Matthaean rhetoric: cf. 'He who is angry . . . says
Raqa . . . says Fool'. The authority to bind and loose is given in the
same rhythm, and virtually the same words, as the authority to Peter.
'For where two or three . . .' is a paragraph-closer of the aetic form
like 'Wherever the body is . . .' or 'For where your treasure is . . .'.[63]

(39) *The Unmerciful Servant 18.21–end (A23–)*

'Be at peace with one another': so Mark had ended his ninth chapter.
Matthew stopped short of this at 18.9, and he takes it up now, and
amplifies it, drawing in the theme of 'Forgive that you may be forgiven' from Mark 11.25. How shall we ensure peace in the Church?
A brother sinning calls for tact and firmness from the apostolic
pastor: but if the offence is against himself the response must be
unending forgiveness. 'If your brother sin . . .' is followed naturally
by 'How often shall my brother sin against me . . .?' The image of
brother sinning against brother carries the expositor's imagination
back to Cain and Abel, and the unending forgiveness demanded of
the Christian apostle is set in contrast to the unending vengefulness
of the Gen. 4 story. Lamech said to his wives, 'Because vengeance has
been exacted seven times (ἑπτάκις) on Cain's behalf, on Lamech's it
shall be seventy times seven (ἑβδομηκοντάκις ἕπτα) (Gen. 4.24, LXX).
The combination of numbers makes the reference almost certain,
and points to midrash in the Greek church, as the Hebrew has 'seventy-
seven times'. The giving of church law to Peter is again typical of
Matthew; and of the language τότε, προσελθών, ἀδελφός, κύριε,
ἀφίημι, anarthrous λέγει, and prepositional ἕως are all characteristic—
8 words out of 32.

The parable with which Jesus expounds the duty of forgiveness is
to the Pauline teaching, 'Be kind, forgiving one another, as God in
Christ forgave you' (Eph. 4.32): but the exposition is in every respect
Matthaean.

(a) The parable is indicative in form, not imperative. It describes
what God will do to the unforgiving, and the Christian's duty is
left unexpressed.

(b) It is a personal, not a nature parable.

(c) It offers a black-and-white contrast, the Merciful King and the
Unmerciful Servant, like all Matthew's other long parables. This
contrast is made specially plain by the repetition of phrases such
as, 'Have patience with me and I will pay you', 'till he should pay

[63] See p. 78 above.

the debt'—a feature of other Matthaean parables such as the Two Builders or the Talents.[64]

(*d*) The king is the stock rabbinic image for God, and the 'servant', here the satrap, is a stock rabbinic image for man.

(*e*) The allegory content of the parable includes eleven points out of sixteen, which is quite high for a long parable. The selling of the servant and his wife and children are just parabolic colour, as is the threat of prison to the fellow-servant, and the grief of the σύνδουλοι, and the final paying up. None of these points has a 'meaning', but the remainder have obvious allegorical correspondence: the king is God, the account is judgement, the servant is the apostle/Christian, the king's patience and remission of debt are God's grace, the fellow-servant is the ἀδελφός, the 100d. owed are his offence, taking him by the throat is unforgiveness, mercy is forgiveness, the king's wrath is God's wrath, and the tormentors are the powers of gehenna. The parable thus approximates to the Matthaean allegorical ideal.

(*f*) There is an appended interpretation in the rabbinic/Matthaean manner: 'So also my father in heaven will do . . .'.

(*g*) The scale is in the fabulous: the vast sum, the despotic aura, and oriental torture-chamber are all in the Matthaean mode, unknown to Mark and Luke.

(*h*) The doctrine of hell is Matthaean, and so also is the teaching that our forgiveness by God depends on our forgiveness of others— this comes in the Lord's Prayer, and is powerfully underscored by the converse, 'For if you forgive men their trespasses . . .' (6.14f) at its close. This is a development of Mark 11.25, and is not found elsewhere in Mark or L.

(*i*) Of the images: kings, debtors for sinners, taking account, talents, prison, and payment in full are all typical of Matthew.

(*j*) Of the language διὰ τοῦτο, ὡμοιώθη, the kingdom of heaven, ἄνθρωπος with a noun, εἷς = τις, ἀποδίδωμι (6), κελεύω, προσκυνῶ, σύνδουλος (4), ten nominative aorist participles, σφόδρα, τότε, λυπέομαι, my heavenly father, are all Matthaean: semi-Matthaean are θέλω (2), ὀφείλω (4), συναίρω λόγον, πιπράσκω, πάντα ὅσα, ἐάν, ἕως (2), ἐπεί, λέγων (3), ἐλθόντες, βάλλω, φυλακή, πεσών, οὖν (3), κύριος/δοῦλος (4), ἀφίημι (3), pleonastic ἐκεῖνος (3), δοῦλε πονηρέ,[65] ἐλεῶ (2), κἀγώ, οὕτως, ἀδελφός, nouns in -της

---

[64] Contrast the Lucan versions at 6.46ff; 19.16ff, where such repetition is studiously avoided. Luke uses repetition, but in a different way from Matthew: not to give higher relief to a contrast, but to drive home a teaching: cf. above, p. 400, n. 52.

[65] cf. 25.26.

(βασανιστής)—79 words in all out of 214. The only words not occurring elsewhere in the Gospel are προσάγω, μακροθυμέω (2), πνίγω.[66] The conclusion of Matthaean authorship of the parable appears to be compelling.[67]

(40) Marriage and Divorce 19.1–15

Matt. 18 was an exposition of the passage on not scandalizing at the end of Mark 9: he follows on now with the next pericope from Mark 10. We have already noted the tendencies of the Matthaean redaction,[68] assimilating the teaching of Jesus to that of the House of Shammai, and so saving the Deut. 24 text: our concern is now with the three 'eunuch' verses at the end.

Matthew elsewhere, alone of the evangelists, introduces the notion of the second best. We are not to be angry: well, but if we have been angry we are to be reconciled. The apostle is to 'gain' his brother: and if he cannot, he must excommunicate him. A further example is to follow in the next story, the Rich Ruler. Mark: 'One thing you lack.' Matthew: 'If you would be perfect . . .'. Perhaps there may be a second-best way, but if you want perfection, this is the path. Now that we are speaking of marriage, does not the same thing apply? Did not Paul teach the Corinthians not to marry as the ideal, but give them permission rather than that they should burn? 'If you marry you do not sin . . . yet those who marry will have worldly troubles, and I would spare you that' (1 Cor. 7.28). This note is missing from the Marcan tradition on marriage, and Matthew proceeds to supply it in his own words: 'If such is the case of a man with his wife'— Matthaean οὕτως ἐστὶν, i.e. worries over divorce, etc.—'it is not expedient to marry'—Matthaean οὐ συμφέρει. To which his Jesus echoes the Pauline doctrine, 'I wish that all were as I myself am: but each has his own gift, one of one kind, one of another' (1 Cor. 7.7): 'Not everyone goes this word, but those to whom it is given' (AT), and the *inclusio*, 'He who can go it, let him go it' (AT). For the rhythms

---

[66] But such methods of extracting repayment are evidenced in Jewish sources: 'If a man seized a debtor by the throat in the street . . .' M Baba Bathra 10.8.
[67] Manson (*SJ*, p. 213) drives a wedge between the parable and its introduction: 'The point of v. 22 is not merely that one should be ready to forgive, but . . . to forgive again and again. . . . There is nothing in the parable about repeated forgiveness.' So also Jeremias (*PJ*, pp. 80, 210ff). But the question is whether such consistency-tests prove anything. Many of the rabbinic parables do not pass them, when they have apparently been constructed to elucidate given texts; most congregations do not apply them, and are impatient with preachers who do; Matthew regularly fails them (cf. Labourers in the Vineyard, Virgins), and would seem content to illustrate a part of his preamble.
[68] pp. 18f above.

of these two logia, cf. 'Not everyone who says to me, Lord, Lord . . .
but he who does the will . . .', and 'He who has ears, let him hear.'
The crisp four-word Matthaean form of the last (11.15; 13.9) with
participle subject is the exact model for the *inclusio*. The idiomatic
use of χωρέω is found here only, but the word is inserted in a Marcan
context at 15.17. The eunuch logion is a typical Matthaean epigram.
The point is the renunciation of marriage for God: Matthew makes
of it a three-bar climax[69]—like the misthics, only the last line is not
from Mark. There are 8 logia of this, scandalic,[70] rhythm in Matthew,
2 in Mark, 4 in Luke (3Q). The threefold εἰσὶν εὐνοῦχοι οἵτινες is
similar to the threefold ὅς ἄν εἴπῃ . . . ἔνοχος ἔσται . . . at 5.22.
ὅστις (3), λέγουσιν, οὕτως (2), εἰ, ἄνθρωποι = men, αἰτία, γεννάω,
συμφέρει the Kingdom of Heaven, are characteristic language—16
words out of 62. For the strong metaphor, to make oneself a
eunuch for to renounce marriage, cf. Matthew's 'hunger and thirst'
for to fast, 'mourn' for to repent, 'beggars in spirit' for men of prayer.

(41) The Rich Young Man 19.16–30

Matthew again follows Mark on: his redactional touches are noted
in the commentaries; our only concern is with the Q logion at 19.28.

Jesus makes to Peter in Mark 10.28 a promise which has all the
stress on the earthly rewards of discipleship: houses and family and
lands a hundredfold in this present age, with persecutions, and eternal
life hereafter thrown in. Now Matthew has already devoted the Beatitudes and much of the Sermon to the earthly reward of a disciple.
Blessed in Matt. 5 are those who like Peter in Matt. 4 have left all;
blessed are the persecuted, the πραεῖς; they shall inherit the land, they
shall be filled, all these things shall be added unto them, your Father
who sees in secret shall reward you. This story is about a young man
who came asking how to inherit eternal life, and Matthew goes lightly
on the earthly side of the reward (19.29), and concentrates on the
heavenward side. Now in Mark Peter draws Jesus' attention to the
faithfulness of the apostles—'Lo, *we* have left everything . . .'—but
the Lord's promise is a general one—'There is no one who has left
house . . .'. Matthew supplies the apostles' own reward at the
Resurrection. As in Matt. 10 the apostles' ministry is to the lost sheep
of the house of Israel, so here: their very twelvefoldness shows that
this was to be their concern by Jesus' own intention. So in the age to
come their calling will be to judge the Twelve Tribes, as now they have

---

[69] The distinction between a eunuch born (*seris ḥāmāh*) and made (*seris
'ādhām*) is rabbinic; S–B I, pp. 805ff.
[70] See p. 81 above.

evangelized them. If need be, Matthew could have drawn the same idea of sharing in the future judgement from Paul: 'Do you not know that the saints will judge the world?' (1 Cor. 6.2). For the language: οἱ ἀκολουθήσαντές μοι picks up ἠκολουθήσαμέν σοι of v. 27; ἀμὴν λέγω ὑμῖν ὅτι, the throne of glory of the Son of Man (25.31), κάθημαι, Ἰσραήλ, are all characteristic. παλιγγενεσία is here only in the Gospels.[71]

The Rich Young Man brings Matthew's week of Hanukkah to a close. The Jewish festival commemorating the Rededication of the Temple has already been transformed in Mark into a Feast of the Church, with the church law of 9 following on the Transfiguration: the glory-cloud that once suffused the Temple, and should again when the prayers of Hanukkah are granted, is now upon the Lord and his community. Matthew has developed this strongly, as one for whom Christ perfectly fulfils the Jewish Year. He sets the Transfiguration on the first instead of the sixth day of the week; he turns the Marcan logia into a full church-law discourse in 18, with further teaching material in 17.24ff, and 19. In his church, far more than in Mark's, there is a governing body, an apostolic sanhedrin, to whom authority is clearly committed. In 16 Peter is declared the foundation-stone of the Church, in 18 his powers are shared with the Twelve, at 19.28 they are given authority in the age to come. Concern with apostolic powers is concentrated and limited to this section of the book. Once more we have found no passage that does not respond to our tests of Matthaean authorship in exposition of Mark: in theology, in rhythm, in imagery, in language, in parabolic manner, all display the unity of the evangelist's own midrashic mind.

[71] Luke keeps to Mark in the Ruler pericope, and introduces Matthew's logion with other material on the apostles' future at the Last Supper. He removes the first δώδεκα to save the Semitic repetition; and puts Matthew's θρόνους into the better Greek genitive. His postponement of κρίνοντες for style ends by clumsily dividing 'the twelve tribes' from 'of Israel'. Matthew's future καθήσεσθε draws the second half of Luke 22.30 out of its natural subjunctive following διατίθεμαι.

19

GOING UP TO PASSOVER (20—23)

When Ḥanukkah is past, the year moves on to Passover: and the Matthaean church went up to Passover, week by week, in the steps of her Lord. Jesus turns to go to Jerusalem in 16, at the first Passion prediction, as Ḥanukkah begins; he leaves Galilee at 19.1, as Ḥanukkah draws to its end: each pericope, each week, brings him closer to the Feast, and to his Passion. Purim is the only minor feast between, and Matthew has a suitable passage to insert for that. Having taken the Transfiguration five days earlier than Mark, he has still one or two sabbath-readings in hand, and he proceeds to use one of them now.

(42) The Labourers in the Vineyard 20.1–16

One of Matthew's commonest uses of parables is to expound a difficult Marcan epigram. 'For to him who has will more be given; and from him who has not, even what he has will be taken away.' Concentration may extract a Christian meaning, or yield honest despair at Mark 4.25: but Matthew has provided an interpretation in the parable of the Talents for his hearers' edification; and he appends the epigram to the parable at 25.29. Similarly, 'There is nothing hid except that it may be made manifest' is expounded in the parable of the Treasure; or 'Watch therefore, for you do not know when the Master of the house will come' in the Virgins. So here we have the difficult, 'But many that are first will be last, and last first.' The context gives the line to the first century as to the modern commentator. Christ has exclaimed how hard it is for the wealthy to enter the kingdom, but has promised the judgment-thrones of heaven to his simple followers: many wealthy, or 'first', will find themselves at the end of the queue, and some (ἔσχατοι, Matt., οἱ ἔσχατοι, Mark) of the simple 'last' will be in authority.

Now Matthew, as a good *sôphēr*, was not in the habit of composing his own parables, but of adapting, or copying, from the traditional stock. Parables about masters, workmen, and pay were very much in the Jewish tradition, and it may be well to cite one or two of the *genre*. Sifra to Lev. 26.9, 'And I will have respect unto you'. 'Unto what may this matter be likened? Unto a king who had many labourers, and among them was one who had done work for him for many days. When the labourers came in to receive their wages, that workman came in with them. Whereupon the king said to that workman, My son, I will have respect unto you, and deal with you at my leisure.[1] These others, though greater in numbers, have done but little work for me, and to them I give but small wages; but as for you, I have a large reckoning to make with you. Even so did Israel in this world claim their reward from God . . .'.[2] Midrash to Ps. 4.7: 'And to what was David like? To a labourer who all his life was working with the king, who had not yet given him his wages. And the labourer was very grieved, saying, "Perhaps I shall receive nothing." The king then hired another labourer. He had only worked with him one day, and the king gave him food and drink and his wages in full. Then the life-time labourer said, "If this is done for him who has worked for one day only, how much more will be done for me, who have worked all the days of my life." Even so said David . . .'.[3] Midrash to Eccles. 5.11 (R. Abun died at the age of twenty-eight): 'To what might the case of R. Abun b. R. Hiyya be likened? To a king who owned a vineyard and hired many labourers to tend it. Among these was one labourer who greatly excelled all the rest. What did the king do? He took him by the hand and walked all over the vineyard. At evening the labourers came to receive their wages, and that workman too came with them. The king paid him his wages in full. At this the labourers began to complain, saying, "We have toiled through the whole day, and he toiled only two hours, and yet the king gave him his pay in full." Then the king said to them, "Why do you complain? This man by his diligence has done more in two hours than you in the whole day." Even so did R. Abun . . .'.[4]

These parables, like all rabbinic writings, are post–Matthaean: but we can hardly credit such widespread influence to a Nazarene heretic. Rather they are to be seen as parables developed from the same stock on which Matthew himself was drawing. In that case he was taking something very like the R. Abun parable, with the labourers in the vineyard, the evening pay-line, the grumbling workers, and the master's justification for his paradox. Such a tale, with its inbuilt image of the queue, is a natural complement to the Marcan Last-and-First logion: and if they are crossed, the story writes itself. The virtuous Pharisees, seeing their wealth and position as an earnest of God's approval, expect to be paid first; and first or not, to be paid more. The simple Christian apostle, who has left all, instead takes the first place, and is paid in full.

Now, as the evangelist himself says, 'Wheresoever the carcase is,

---

[1] *ûphānîthî*, 'and I shall turn' is connected with *pn'i*, Leisure.
[2] Feldman, *PSR*, p. 49.
[3] Shoher Tob, 37.3; Feldman, *PSR*, p. 48.
[4] Eccl. R. 5.11; Feldman, *PSR*, pp. 48f.

there will the vultures be gathered together'; and the scent of inconsistency draws the form–critic as the smell of death the vulture. You
cannot take a suit off the peg at Montagu Burton's, let down the
sleeves, and pass it off as tailor-made in Savile Row; nor can Matthew
adapt a parable from the rabbinic stock to his Marcan text without
the seams showing. Of course there are inconsistencies. The difference
of places in the queue is of fiddling importance; Jewish jealousy is
a different point; the Pharisee *receives* his wage, i.e. he enters the
kingdom, according to the parable, but he is 'last', i.e. outside,
according to the text. But Matthew's central point of comparison
comes through clearly: the Christian, for his faithful discipleship, is
given the kingdom, and the thrones of judgement in it, while the
wealthy and pious stand waiting and rebuked. We may compare
21.31, 'The publicans and harlots go before you into God's kingdom'
(AT): precedence here too is made to stand for inclusion and exclusion.
But I am not disposed to apologize for the evangelist. The image of
first and last, of the pay-line, is what he is given, and he has illuminated
it.

The parable-plot, we have said, Matthew drew from Jewish
tradition. But could it not be from dominical tradition? Many
commentators, most famously Jeremias,[5] have indulged this speculation, indeed have assumed that it was a fact: but alas, there is no basis
for it in the text. We are at liberty to cut away the parable from its
context; to take the Last-and-First saying as an independent catch-
word originally meaning, 'How easily fortunes change overnight';[6]
to conjecture that the parable was originally spoken by Jesus to his
opponents with the point, 'God in his mercy will admit sinners to his
kingdom; are you jealous because he is good?'; and to build up an
impressive history of misinterpretation, through scribal interpolators
to the Roman Catholic and Lutheran Churches. But where is the
evidence for this theory, whose scholarly foundation and imaginative
structure have so impressed the critics? It is nothing but a series of
axioms, for which no justification is provided. 'This, says Jesus, is
how God deals with men':[7] but what, other than pious conservatism,
leads us to suppose that we have an original parable of Jesus here?
'None of the detailed parables of Jesus consists of mere teaching':[8]
but how does Jeremias know this, other than by assuming that all the
parables are Jesus', and applying the canon that whatever is 'mere

---

[5] *PJ*, pp. 33–8.
[6] ibid., pp. 36n, 47; cf. J. Schniewind, *NTD*, on Mark 10.31.
[7] ibid. p. 37.
[8] *PJ* (e.1), p. 25. The generalization is omitted, but still assumed, in the later
edition.

teaching' is a later insertion? 'In all double-edged parables the emphasis lies on the second point':[9] but what indicates that this axiom is
true, other than that Jeremias applies it three times, none too convincingly, elsewhere? The only evidence for dominical authorship
would be if the parable were in its language and manner uncharacteristic of Matthew. Jeremias applies these tests to the introduction and
conclusion, and finds them typical of the evangelist: it is for us to
complete his work, and try them on the parable itself.

In 20.1–15 the following phrases are Matthaean: ὁμοία ἐστίν, the
kingdom of heaven, ἄνθρωπος with a noun, ἀποδίδωμι, μισθός, ἀπό...
ἕως, ἀγαθός/πονηρός, and nine nominative aorist participles. In
addition semi-Matthaean words are οἰκοδεσπότης (2), ὅστις, ἐργάτης
(3), ἀμπελών (5), ἑστώς (2), ἐλθών (2), ἀργός (2), δίκαιος, ὧδε, κατὰ +
gen., κύριος with a gen., λαμβάνω (4), νομίζω, ἕταιρε coldly, ἀποκριθεὶς
εἶπεν, ἐκεῖνος, ἔσχατος (5), συμφωνέω (2), οὐχί; τὸ σόν/τὰ ἐμά, θέλω (2)
ὁ ὀφθαλμὸς πονηρός = jealousy, meanness, λέγοντες, anarthrous
λέγουσι, λέγει—62 characteristic words out of 239 in all. Non-
Matthaean words are ἐκ of price, distributive ἀνά, ἐπίτροπος,
γογγύζω, ἴσος, καύσων. Since the latter are for the most part words
and idioms we should not expect to find more than rarely in the
Gospel, the linguistic evidence is in favour of Matthaean authorship.

In other ways the parable is not quite of the usual Matthaean stamp.
The scale is comfortable—perhaps there are a dozen workers—but
nothing that would be out of place in the other Gospels. The allegory-
content is the second lowest in the Gospel. The householder is God,
the labourers the people, the vineyard Israel, those hired early the
Pharisees, those hired at the eleventh hour the Christians, evening is
judgement day, the pay is eternal life, the murmuring is Pharisaic
resentment, their expecting more is Jewish presumption, the burden
and heat is the Law, the Lord's generosity is God's grace: but there is
no equivalent for the third, sixth and ninth hours, idleness, the
market-place, or the steward, which are parabolic colour. Eleven
points out of seventeen thus have allegoric significance, 0.65: higher
than any L parable, but low for Matthew. Nevertheless there are other
characteristics of the parable which indicate Matthaean authorship.
The characters and plot are from the rabbinic stock, like those of other
Matthaean parables.[10] There is a strong black-and-white contrast
between the good 'last' and the bad 'first'.[11] It is an indicative and
not an imperative parable,[12] a personal parable.[13] There is plenty of
Matthaean repetitiveness. 'And going out about the third/sixth and
ninth/eleventh hour (vv. 3,5,6) . . . You go into the vineyard too

[9] *PJ*, p. 38.   [10] p. 55 above.   [11] pp. 53f above.
[12] pp. 48ff above.   [13] pp. 51ff above.

(vv. 4,7) . . . He saw/found others standing (vv. 3,6) . . . and coming . . . they received each man a/the dinar (AT, vv. 6,10)".[14] So even if the parable is less markedly characteristic than some, it is still characteristic. The evidence for dominical authorship is thus negligible. Matthew has adapted a standard Jewish parable to expound an enigmatic dominical epigram.

(43) Third Passion Prediction, and the Sons of Zebedee 20.17–28 (A20–28)

This follows Mark, with the apologetic introduction of the mother of James and John to save the apostles' good name.

(44) The Two Blind Men 20.29–end

For the second time Matthew puts together the two Marcan blind men, the Bethsaidan and Bartimaeus, in a compendium miracle.[15] Bartimaeus belongs at Jericho, and needs to be taken here; the second man is pleonastic, so far as the healing scheme is concerned.[16] But from at least Mark's time it had been customary to see the opening of the eyes of the blind as symbolic of the opening of Christians' eyes.[17] The Bethsaidan comes gradually to sight after the disciples in the boat have been asked, 'Having eyes, do you not see?', and before Peter sees Jesus to be the Christ (Mark 8.14–30). Bartimaeus' faith is contrasted with James' and John's unspiritual ambition (10.35–52). Matthew underlines the symbolism. There are two blind apostles, and two healed blind men. We may compare Matthew's working out of spiritual dumbness, blindness, and possession at the healing of the blind and dumb demoniac.[18]

---

[14] Contrast Mark 4.1–9, where the only repetition is 'And other(s) fell . . .' (vv. 5,7,8), and Mark 12.1–12, 'And he sent (another) (slave)' (vv. 2,4,5). For Luke's eschewing of repetition compare especially his Two Builders and Two Sons with Matthew's: and *passim*.

[15] cf. pp. 44f above.   [16] pp. 317f above.

[17] cf. D. E. Nineham, *St Mark* (London 1963): 'All this Mark teaches . . . by capping [the conversation in the boat] with the incident of Jesus . . . giving sight to a blind man, and that incident by the story of how he gradually opened the disciples' eyes . . .' (p. 214); 'We are reminded of the point of view from which the preceding section [James and John] is to be understood, and are also perhaps led to contrast Bartimaeus with the disciples, who "though they see are blind." ' (p. 282; cf. p. 283).

[18] pp. 331ff above.

(45) The Entry into Jerusalem 21.1–9 (A–13)

Jesus' entry into Jerusalem upon the colt (πῶλος always in Mark) is further assimilated in Matthew to the Zechariah prophecy, which is now cited. The first part of the citation is straightforward. 'Rejoice greatly, daughter of Sion' (Zech. 9.9a, LXX) recalls the similar 'Tell ye the daughter of Sion, Behold thy saviour comes to thee . . .' (Isa. 62.11, LXX), and the opening phrase of Isaiah displaces Zechariah. 'Behold your king is coming to you . . . humble and mounted . . .' follows the Greek Zechariah, but omitting 'just and saving' for brevity. The interest is concentrated upon the last line where Matthew deserts the Greek, 'on a beast of burden and a new colt' (ἐπὶ ὑποζύγιον καὶ πῶλον νέον)for the Hebrew, 'on an ass and on a colt the son of a beast of burden' (*'al hāmôr weʿal ʿāîr ben ʾaʾthōnôth*). Matthew's second ἐπὶ and the υἱόν show that he is giving a literal version, presumably his own, of the Hebrew.

Why does Matthew thus move over to the Hebrew? Is it because tradition told him there were two animals, and the Hebrew with its second 'and on' makes this more plain?[19] Hardly: the Greek already gives two animals, one a ὑποζύγιον, one a πῶλον νέον, not yet a ὑποζύγιον;[20] the Hebrew puts the matter beyond question. So Matthew gives two animals in the story, an ὄνος and her πῶλος, and justifies himself with a literal version of the Hebrew. For a similar literal reading of a *parallelismus membrorum*, compare John 19.33f, where the soldiers both part Jesus' garments and cast lots for his clothing.[21]

(46) The Cleansing of the Temple 21.10–17 (A14–)

At the end of the previous section Mark had the crowds crying (ἔκραζον), 'Hosanna . . . blessed is the kingdom of our father David that is coming' (11.10), a clause which Matthew suppresses, that he may, as usual, expound it more fully. Two associations spring to his mind from scripture. First, when David entered Jerusalem, he was defied by the blind and the lame (τυφλοὶ καὶ χωλοί),[22] whom he smote with the sword: so Matthew, for whom the coming of the kingdom is so often symbolized by healings, introduces the blind and the lame,

[19] So Stendahl, *SSM*, pp. 118–20, 200; Gundry, *UOTSM*, pp. 120ff; O. Michel, *TWNT* v, pp. 284ff.

[20] Stendahl writes somewhat cryptically, 'A secondary reason for Matthew's form of the quotation might have been that he had pondered upon the virginity of the foal, cf. Mark 11.2': Mark reads, 'a colt on which no one has ever sat'. Stendahl does not explain why such pondering, which is the presupposition of his book, should be secondary.

[21] See further pp. 21–3 above.   [22] 2 Sam. 5.6ff.

whom, by contrast, the son of David makes well. Second, the phrase, 'our father David', suggests the salute of his children, and it is from the psalms of David, Ps. 118, that their Hosanna is taken. The mind of the *darshān* is drawn to Ps. 8 by the wording. Ps. 118 is cited, 'Blessed is he who comes ἐν ὀνόματι Κυρίου.' Ps. 8 opens, 'κύριε, our κύριος, how excellent is thy ὄνομα in all the earth. Out of the mouth of babes . . .'. Matthew cites the verse in the Greek version, which alone gives the sense he needs, and styles the story of the children accordingly. κράζοντας, Hosanna, and David are carried over from Mark 11.9f: προσῆλθον, θεραπεύω, children as a group, ναί, have you never read?, are characteristic. θαυμάσια which is non-Matthaean, is perhaps taken from Ps. 118.23, θαυμαστή, cited at 21.42: the scribes are included in a surprising way (since Matthew commonly exculpates the *sôphᵉrîm*),[23] because it is they who might be expected to know the scriptures.[24]

(47) The Withered Fig-Tree 21.18–22

The two halves of the Marcan story are taken together, not to increase the impressiveness of the Withering as an instant miracle, but for liturgical convenience. The Fig-Tree can now be read all on one day: while the symbolism of the fruitless Temple-worship and its rejection can be fully worked out in the Wicked Husbandmen, and other parables to come.

(48) The Question about Authority 21.23–7

The pericope follows Mark almost verbatim, but is amplified by

(49) The Two Sons 21.28–32

The phrase, 'You did not believe in him', in the former (21.25), is repeated after the parable, and is contrasted with, 'the tax collectors and harlots believed in him' (21.32), so it is clearly Matthew's intention to expound the disbelief of the authorities in first John and then Jesus. Indeed the phrase, 'For John came' (21.32) is identical with the opening words of 11.18, where the same theme of the rejection of John and Jesus by this generation is worked out: and 21.32 is, by common consent, full of Matthaeanisms. The question at issue is whether the parable is Matthew's own also, or if it was received by him from earlier, perhaps dominical, tradition.

[23] cf. pp. 13ff above.
[24] cf. 12.38, where scribes are similarly introduced into a Marcan context, not to their advantage: but Matthew is also inserting a midrash on Jonah, which they would be needed to appreciate.

The parable is Matthaean in almost every way. It is an indicative parable, with or without the reference to John Baptist, explaining that sinners now achieve entry into the kingdom while the righteous wait. It is a personal, contrast parable, with the two sons set against each other in the starkest terms. They are entirely stock characters, unrelieved by any personal colour; doing and not doing their father's will. The rabbinic mode is followed: cf. R. Simeon b. Lakish, 'God may be likened to a king who had two sons. He became enraged against the first of them, took a stick and thrashed him so that he writhed in agony and died; and the father began to lament over him. He later became enraged against the second son, took a stick and thrashed him so that he writhed in agony and died; and the father then exclaimed, "No longer have I strength to lament over him." '[25] Matthew is similarly repetitive, and gives a similar black-and-white caricature, though with a happier theology: 'He went to the first/ second and said (vv. 28,30) . . . He answered, I will/will not, but (afterwards) went/did not go' (vv. 29,30b). The allegory-content is 100 per cent. The father is God, the vineyard is Israel, the first son is the sinners, work is the will of God, refusal is sinning, change of mind is repentance, the second son is the Jewish authorities, their 'I, sir', is their keeping of the Law, their disobedience is not repenting at John's preaching. Publicans and harlots are a male-and-female pair.[26] The theme of working in the vineyard is carried on from 20.1–16,[27] and goes back to the Wicked Husbandmen, which comes next, and ultimately to Isaiah's parable: and precedence—'they go before you'—as a euphemism for their entry and your exclusion also follows the pattern of the Labourers in the Vineyard. For language, not only τί ὑμῖν δοκεῖ in the introduction, and in the conclusion δικαιοσύνη, ὕστερον, μεταμελοῦμαι, and theological ἦλθον, are characteristic: but δύο (2), προσελθών (2), ἐργάζομαι, ὕστερον, to do the will of the father,[28] which are Matthaean, and θέλω, ἀμπελών, ἀποκριθεὶς εἶπεν (2), anarthrous λέγει, λέγουσιν, μεταμελοῦμαι, κύριε, and ἀμὴν λέγω ὑμῖν, which are semi-Matthaean, in the body of the parable—31 characteristic words in all out of 104. The suggestion that ἡ βασιλεία τοῦ θεοῦ is un-Matthaean is an error. The expression is used by Matthew emphatically, *God's* Kingdom, to show the equivalence, God = the father of the parable, just as it is inserted editorially by Matthew at 21.43 to show the equivalence, God = the owner of the vineyard.[29]

There seems to be no ground for postulating non-Matthaean authorship. Matthew had a reading in hand, and has inserted the not

---

[25] Lam. R., Proem II.   [26] cf. p. 98 above.
[27] cf. Matthew's use of dominant images within a discourse, pp. 98ff above.
[28] cf. pp. 299, 399 above.   [29] See above, p. 332, n. 64.

very striking parable of his own composition, on the lines of the other vineyard parables, to keep level with the calendar, and for the sake of his own view of the importance of John in the new dispensation.

(50) *The Wicked Husbandmen 21.33–end*

following Mark, brings him to the first Saturday in Adar.

(51) *The Marriage Feast 22.1–14*

The second week in Adar, on a date varying between 11th and 14th, comes the feast of Purim,[30] celebrating the deliverance of Israel under Esther. Purim will not have been celebrated in the Pauline churches, for whom the very nationalist sentiment of the Book of Esther had no appeal, and if Matthew is to emulate the Jewish synagogues in orthodoxy, he must write his own fulfilment of the theme of the Festival. And this is precisely what he has done, in a masterpiece of midrash. The Marriage-Feast parable is nothing but a second version of the Wicked Husbandmen[31] in terms of the Esther story, with suitable Christian glosses, and in the Matthaean manner. Esther is a book about King Ahasuerus who marries Esther, and the book describes a series of banquets: so the vineyard-owner becomes a king, and the plot of the parable a marriage-banquet. Since Jesus has described himself as the bridegroom (Mark 2.19f), and his disciples as wedding-guests, the situation is changed from being the king's wedding to being the king's son's wedding: only too suitably, since the king is always God in Jewish parables and Jesus is God's Son. Matthew refers to the banquet-hall as the νυμφών[32] (22.10; Mark 2.19),and the attending guests are, as in Mark 2, the Christians. 'He sent his servants . . . again he sent other servants' (vv. 3,4), repeats the words of the Wicked Husbandmen (21.34,36); the refusal of the invitation answers to the refusal of rent; and as before, the envoys are insulted and killed (v. 6; 21.35): Matthew's soaring allegory has now transcended the reality of the story situation, but, as elsewhere in his Gospel, allegory is his stock-in-trade, and never mind the tale.[33] In the Husbandmen God was wretchedly to destroy those wretches, and in the Marriage-Feast he does so, with Titus' armies and the burning of Jerusalem making their presence felt through the thread-

---

[30] M Meg. 1.1–2.

[31] So Jeremias, *PJ*, p. 69, n. 77, somewhat tentatively.

[32] There are many references in Bauer, s.v., for νυμφών = bridal chamber, and the Marcan υἱοὶ νυμφῶνος = the rabbinic *b^enei huppāh* (S–B, I pp. 500ff): but this is the only instance of νυμφών = marriage reception hall. Maybe Matthew is stretching the Marcan word to his purpose.

[33] See pp. 56ff above.

bare story; then God's kingdom was to be taken from the Jews and given to the Church,[34] now the banquet is opened to all on the street-corners, bad and good.

But what of the final phrase of the Husbandmen, 'other tenants, who will give him the fruits in their seasons'? Matthew believed that the Church was a *corpus mixtum*,[35] and that the kingdom was not for all and sundry, but for those who paid the fruits, who did the Father's will, who kept Christ's Law: and the image that he uses for this is the wearing of a wedding garment. Doubtless he is thinking of the provision of such garments for the occasion as Jehu made at 2 Kings 10.22f, or Samson at Timnah: but the point is not who provided them but if they were worn. R. Johanan b. Zakkai commented on Eccles. 9.8 ('Let thy garments be always white') 'Lo, it means [keeping] precepts, good deeds, and Torah',[36] and R. Judah the Prince expounded the text in the following parable: 'To what may the matter be likened? To a king who made a banquet to which he invited guests. He said to them, Go wash yourselves, brush up your clothes, anoint yourselves with oil, wash your garments and prepare for the banquet; but he fixed no time when they were to come to it. The wise among them walked about by the entrance of the palace saying, Does the palace lack anything? The foolish among them paid no regard or attention to the king's command. They said, We will in due course notice when the king's banquet is to take place; for can there be a banquet without labour and company? So the plasterer went to his plaster, the potter to his clay, the smith to his charcoal, the washer to his laundry. Suddenly the king ordered, Let them all come to the banquet. They hurried the guests so that some came in their splendid attire, and others came in their dirty clothes. The king was pleased with the wise ones who had obeyed his command, and also because they had shown honour to the palace. The king said, Let those who have prepared for the banquet come and eat of the king's meal, but those who have not prepared themselves shall not partake of it. You might suppose that the latter were simply to depart, but the king continued, No: but the former shall recline and eat and drink, while these shall remain standing, be punished and look on and be grieved.'[37] Similarly, in Rev. 19.8, the Bride is clothed in fine linen, bright and pure, 'for the fine linen is the righteous deeds of the saints.' Now the Esther story has to some extent kept pace with Matthew's parable, apart from

[34] Not to the Gentiles; cf. Trilling, *WI*, pp. 55ff.

[35] cf. 13.47ff; 25.1ff, 14ff.   [36] Eccles. R. 9.8.

[37] ibid.: the parable also occurs at B Shab. 153a, where the white garments are interpreted as repentance, cf. Jeremias, *PJ*, p. 188. Note the king, and the wise-and-foolish, as rabbinic traits common to Matthew: and also the appendix, which is *not* where the stress of the parable falls.

providing the setting: for Esther also prepared (ἡτοίμασεν, 6.14) a reception, and sent out her eunuchs to summon the guest. But the guest was the unworthy (οὐκ ἄξιος, 7.4) Haman, who was cast out by the angry king, and hanged on his own gallows; so now Matthew glosses the traditional parable with the Haman theme—the unworthy wedding guest is bound and cast into the scarcely parabolized hell-fire. 'For', Matthew ends with a pardic epigram (AT), 'many are invited' to the marriage-feast of the Lamb—the Jews, the baptized but faithless, all and sundry—'but the elect are few', only those who accept God's invitation to baptism and actually do 'put on' the Lord Jesus Christ. Only such can be the genuine worshippers at the Christian Purim.

Not only is the parable thus perfectly adapted to Matthew's calendar, but it shows evident traces of its author in numerous ways. It is an indicative parable—it describes the Jews' refusal of the kingdom, and the events of A.D. 70, and the Church's call, and God's demand for δικαιοσύνη, and the fate of the unrighteous. It is a personal parable, and a contrast-parable—two contrasts, the Jews and the Church, the good and the bad within the Church: overall, the bidden and the elect. The figures are caricatures: angry king, rude guests, Christians good and bad. The excuses are stock, one in the country and one in the town; the menu is stock, oxen and fatlings; the punishment is stock, darkness and weeping. The allegory is notorious: it has a content of 1.0, since the only points without meaning are the oxen and fatlings, and the field and merchandise, and these are outbalanced by Titus' armies and the burning of Jerusalem, and the hell-fire at the end, which do not fit the story. The scale is grand: a king, a royal wedding, no expense too much, armies, cohorts of servants, the slain all of whom are immediately replaced, wedding garments for all, a private hell. The doctrine repeats the Matthaean glosses on the Husbandmen: the miserable destruction of the Jews, and the transmission of the kingdom to a righteous Church. The appendix especially stresses the Matthaean *corpus mixtum* view. Marriage is a favourite Matthaean image. Linguistically Matthaean are: the kingdom of heaven is likened, ἄνθρωπος + a noun, δεῦτε, τότε (2), ὅσος ἄν, πονηρός/ἀγαθός, συνάγω, ἔνδυμα (2), outer darkness: there shall be weeping and gnashing of teeth, and six nom. aor. participles. Semi-Matthaean are: ὅστις, ἰδού, ἀποκριθεὶς εἶπεν, introductory ὁ Ἰησοῦς, λέγων (2), θέλω, ἕτοιμος (2), . . . μὲν . . . δὲ (2), οὖν, πάντες, ἀγρός, pleonastic ἐκεῖνος (2), γάμος (7), δοῦλος (5), πορεύομαι, ἄξιος, ἀνακεῖμαι (2), θεάομαι, ἐκεῖ, cold ἑταῖρε, ὧδε, πολύς/ὀλίγος. Not elsewhere in Matthew are ἄριστον, ἀμελῶ, ὑβρίζω, στράτευμα, ἐμπρήθω, διέξοδος. In all there are 71 characteristic words out of 223.

I have already shown[38] how many tendencies of Matthew's are reversed by Luke, and there are few better illustrations of this than his Great Supper (14.16–24), whose secondariness is made certain by the added allegory of the Gentile Mission. The scale is smaller: it is a commoner, no wedding, 'many' guests but only three excuse themselves, one servant suffices for all, and for two further round-ups— he must have been exhausted. The two latter anomalies both suggest that a grander-scale parable has been reduced to the level of Luke's middle class. The people are alive, as is usual with Luke: there is *oratio recta*, and the excuses are different and colourful. The allegory is much reduced overall, 0.64, despite the introduction of the additional allegory of the Gentile Mission. The point in Luke is unclear,[39] but the proximity of 'When you give a feast, invite the poor, the maimed, the lame, the blind',[40] suggests that Luke saw it as at least partly an imperative parable. The common assumption that Luke's form of the parable, without the second mission, is earlier than Matthew's depends upon the graph fallacy.[41] There is no substance to the belief that allegorization, embellishment, scale, etc., increase with time on a neatly ascending graph. Luke diminishes the allegory and the scale in Marcan parables, and in the Matthaean ones too.[42] Nor is there any basis for the common assertion that the Marriage Feast was originally two parables.[43] The opening phrase ἐν παραβολαῖς cannot be pressed to mean two parables:[44] it is used generally before the single parable at Mark 12.1, and very likely that is where Matthew has taken it from. διάκονος is used for servant at v. 13 in the appendix, and δοῦλος in the main part of the parable, because the δοῦλοι stand for the prophets and apostles, and the διάκονοι for angels. Luke omitted the appendix because he believed in grace, not merit.[45]

---

[38] pp. 59f, and 62 above.   [39] cf. Jeremias, *PJ*, p. 64.

[40] 14.13f, cf. 21.

[41] See my article, 'Characteristics of the Parables in the Several Gospels', *JTS* XIX, Pt I (April 1968), esp. pp. 60f, 66.

[42] Although Luke's interest in his stories results in a deallegorizing of Mark and Matthew, he does on two occasions add an allegorical twist to a parable: the second mission here, and going to receive a kingdom in the Pounds.

[43] e.g. Jeremias, *PJ*, p. 65, but maintained by almost all commentators: an exception is K. H. Rengstorf, 'Die Stadt der Mörder (Mt. 22,7)' in Festschrift J. Jeremias, *BZNW* 26 (1960), pp. 106–29.

[44] cf. Kilpatrick, *Origins*, p. 30.

[45] Thomas, 64, gives a bastardized version of the Lucan parable (a man, δεῖπνον (4), his servant, παραιτεῖσθαι (4)) with four *oratio recta* excuses—the recovery of debts, the purchase of a house, to be best man at a wedding, the purchase of a village. As Thomas' moral is 'The buyers and merchants shall not come into my Father's place', he omits subsequent round-ups of the poor. The wedding does not fit the moral, and shows Thomas to be secondary to Luke.

The remaining pericopae (52)–(55), down to the end of 22, follow Mark to the end of the year.

Passover increased in importance over the centuries, from being an attachment to Unleavened Bread to becoming the second feast of the Jewish Year. Already in Ezekiel preparations are ordained for it, cleansing the sanctuary on the 1st and 7th Nisan:[46] and in Joshua, events, probably of a cultic nature, are described on 3rd and 10th Nisan.[47] In rabbinic times these preparations were multiplied. The sabbath *Sheqalim* was the fifth from the end of the year,[48] and marked the beginning of extensive preparations to bring the poll-tax into the Treasury by Passover. On 15th Adar the graves were chalked so that no one should contract uncleanness before the feast.[49] The sabbath *Pārāh*, the second from the end of the year, symbolized cleansing before Passover:[50] proselytes were circumcised either then, according to Beth Hillel, or just before Passover (Beth Shammai).[51] On the last sabbath in the old year, *Ha-Ḥodesh*, the Exod. 12 story was read, to warn the people of the coming need to take a lamb (12.3) and to take the leaven out of their houses (12.15). The first sabbath in the New Year the Genesis story began,[52] with Creation, and the temptation of Eve by the serpent: the story of Cain and Abel fore-shadowed God's acceptance of the offering of a lamb, and the oppression of the pastoral by the agricultural peoples. Thereafter the preparations were transferred to the home.

The reading which Matthew inherited from Mark for the first Saturday of the new year was brief, and in two parts: three and a half verses warning the crowd against the scribes, with their robes and greetings and chief places—and rapacity on widows; four verses on the Widow's Mites. The former of these he makes into a discourse of ten times the length, expanding it with pre-Passover themes and other matter: the latter cannot be worked in, and for once is omitted.[53] But for the structure of the Discourse he turns back to an earlier part of

---

[46] Ezek. 45.18–20. [47] Josh. 1.11; 3.2; 4.19.

[48] B Meg. 30a. [49] M Shek. I.1.

[50] Moore, *Judaism* I, p. 298.

[51] According to M Eduyoth 5.2, B Pes. 91b–92, the Shammaites said, 'If a man became a proselyte the day before Passover he may immerse himself and eat Pesah in the evening', but the Hillelites said, 'He that separates himself from uncircumcision is as one who separates himself from the grave', requiring a week of intermission. The law of separation from the grave, here referred to, is Num. 19.14ff, 'Whoever touches . . . a grave shall be unclean seven days . . . and on the seventh day he shall cleanse himself.' Num. 19 is the *Pārāh* lesson. Hence it would seem that proselytes, on the stricter view, separated themselves from death at *Pārāh*, and were baptized on *Ha-Ḥodesh* sabbath—cf. Exod. 12.48.

[52] See pp. 227ff above. [53] There are no spare liturgical days now.

his own Gospel. The Sermon on the Mount proclaimed blessing upon the disciples of the new kingdom: as a Pentecostal celebration this was right, for the ritual of Pentecost had from primaeval times included the blessing and the curse on Mts Ebal and Gerizim,[54] but the curse seemed out of place to Matthew in the opening of the Lord's teaching.[55] The curse he has held over till the rejection of Jesus is complete: now, by the opening of his last discourse, the authorities have with their repeated malice shown their colours, and the Marcan warning can be made the text for a parallel series of Woes. The flow of the story and the Marcan text alike thus make a Woe-chapter apposite: and the liturgical season is appropriate too. In 16.6,11f Matthew elucidated the Marcan warning against the leaven of the Pharisees and of Herod: 'Then they understood that he did not tell them to beware of the leaven of bread, but of the teaching of the Pharisees and Sadducees.' The Pharisees and Herodians had tempted Jesus over the tax-money, the Sadducees over the Resurrection, and Matthew broadened the warning from the Pharisees and Herod to include both the major groups in the Jewish hierarchy whose hypocrisy was to be instanced in 22. Thereafter comes the Paschal season, when the old leaven of malice and wickedness is to be purged out of the Church, and the teaching of the Pharisaic scribe in all its sophistry should be put away. Just as Israel was warned on the last sabbath in Adar to put away the leaven from its houses before Passover, so the Church must be taught from the beginning of Nisan to beware of a more deadly leaven.

The analysis of the Discourse shows the same elegant composition which marks the Matthaean teaching blocks, and distinguishes them from the rambles in the other evangelists. It has an Introduction (vv. 2–12), seven Woes, each opening with the same formula (vv. 13–31), and a peroration (vv. 32–9). Its nearest OT type is Isa. 5, where the vineyard-parable forms a proem to a series of οὐαὶ τοῖς formulas (vv. 8–23) with a peroration to the end of the chapter: Isaiah's parable is the subject of dominical midrash in Mark 12/Matt. 21, and might well be still in the evangelist's mind. But the substance and wording of the Discourse are marked by strong affinities with the Sermon on the Mount, and the conscious influence of the latter is made certain by the parallel development of the Woes to the Beatitudes *in order*.

[54] The association of the blessing and cursing with Pentecost is made by the Qumran sectaries; cf. B. Noack, art. cit.; G. Vermes, *The Dead Sea Scrolls in English*, p. 44.
[55] Not so to Luke, who has set the two in antithesis from the beginning of his Sermon on the Plain.

Matthew's introduction elaborates the Marcan warning against the scribes. For Mark's στολαί he is able to give true local colour, phylacteries and fringes; and the greetings in the market-place he expounds with real-life instances, Rabbi, Father, Teacher. But before he comes to such details, he states the fundamental theological position, exactly as in 5.17–20. The whole Law is valid, written and oral, and the Church is to keep it all: anyone who relaxes one of the least of these commandments will be least in the Kingdom (5.19; 23.2–3a). But the Church is to follow the Pharisaic scribes' teaching, not their example: for unless your righteousness exceeds that of the Pharisaic scribes, you will never enter the Kingdom (5.20; 23.3). They do everything to be seen of men: for example, their almsgiving, their prayers, and their fasting (6.1–18; 23.5).

The Woes now form a series of contrasts to the Beatitudes,[56] and the material expounding them in the Sermon. The reward of the eighth blessed and first expounded was, 'For yours is the kingdom of heaven': contrast the Pharisaic scribes, who shut the kingdom of heaven before men. They do not go in themselves, and those wishing to go in they obstruct (5.10; 23.13). The reward of the seventh blessed and second expounded was that they should be called the sons of God. Contrast the Pharisaic scribes, who are the sons of gehenna, and proselytize to make others the same (5.9; 23.15). The sixth blessed and third expounded were the pure in heart, who, so far from swearing falsely, do not swear at all. Contrast the Pharisaic scribes, who permit any sophistry in swearing (5.33–7; 23.16–22). Whereas the Christian will see God, they are blind guides (5.8; 23.16,19). Oaths by heaven and him who sits thereon as his throne, are similarly suggested by, 'Do not swear at all, either by heaven, for it is the throne of God' (5.34; 23.22). The offering on the altar (23.18f) follows from 'Leave your offering before the altar' (5.23). The fifth blessed and fourth expounded are the merciful, who love their enemies and give their 'mercy' in secret. Contrast the Pharisaic scribes, so scrupulous in paying their tithes, but neglectful of justice and *mercy* and faithfulness (5.7; 6.2–4; 23.23f). Next blessed are those who hunger and thirst after righteousness; and, taken with them (since the Woes are one shorter than the Beatitudes), the meek who give generously, and trust God for food and drink. Contrast the Pharisaic scribes, with their *cup* and *plate* full of extortion and rapacity (5.5f; 6.25ff; 23.25). Next blessed are the mourners for their sins, who look to the log in their own eye, and not, like the hypocrite, to the speck in their brother's.

[56] There were eight Beatitudes for the eight watches of Pentecost, but seven is the suitable number for a week's lection; cf. the seven parables in 13, or the seven observations on swearing, 23.16–22.

Contrast the Pharisaic scribe, who is like a whited sepulchre, full of hypocrisy and iniquity (5.4; 7.3–5; 23.27f). Finally Christ blessed the persecuted, to rejoice and be glad, for so men persecuted the prophets who were before them: and Matthew finally contrasts the Pharisaic scribes who build the tombs of the prophets and protest their innocence—but sons of those who slew the prophets they are, they persecute and kill the Church's prophets, and the blood of all the martyred prophets in history shall be visited upon them (5.10–12; 23.29–39).[57] In each case the Woe picks up a key word or phrase in the series of Beatitudes, or their exposition, taken in order. In the case of the Introduction, the Swearing, and the persecution of the prophets, the relevant passages in the Sermon are given detailed and verbal contrasts.

23.1–4

The structure of 23 is Matthew's own then: but has he drawn on traditional material for the substance, or is this his own midrash also? Let us apply our normal tests. Verses 2–4—Mark had warned against 'the scribes': Matthew, a scribe himself, adds 'and the Pharisees', which, in view of the position they are credited with, must mean 'the Pharisaic scribes'. The doctrine of the Church's subjection to the authority of Jamnia is the view of a very Jewish church indeed. Matthew in 15 skilfully evades the frontal attack which the Marcan Jesus makes on the Oral Torah: the point there made against the Pharisaic tradition is exactly the same as in the present chapter—that it frustrates the spirit, and often the letter, of the Law. Since there is no other comparable attitude in the NT, it is natural to attribute it to Matthew. Moses' seat, *qāthedhrā'de-Mōsheh* is a rabbinic expression.[58] The contradiction between v. 3 'Practise and observe whatever they tell you', and 16.11f, 'Beware of the teaching of the Pharisees' is purely formal.[59] The distinction is between formally promulgated

---

[57] There is a slight, but understandable, muddle here. In 23 Matthew has been following the order of the Sermon, and so the reverse order of the Beatitudes. He should therefore close with the first Beatitude, the Poor in Spirit. But the Poor in Spirit are with the Persecuted in that theirs is the Kingdom of Heaven, and whether by oversight or intention Matthew takes up the theme of the Persecuted and the prophets, which is so much to the point.

[58] P. de R.K. 7b.

[59] E. Haenchen ('Matthäus 23', *Zeitschrift fur Theologie und Kirche* (1951), pp. 38–63), finds a series of inconsistencies in the chapter: for example, in v. 4 the scribes are accused of laying heavy burdens on men, whereas in vv. 2f the weight is immaterial; or in vv. 8–10 the rabbis' habit of title-claiming is disapproved, whereas it is accepted in vv. 2f that they sit on Moses' seat. Haenchen carves the chapter up into four strands, as do most exegetes: the Marcan matter is there for all to see; the Q material is usually taken to be original in the Lucan

rulings, which to Matthew are binding, and the sophistries of the normal scribe, which are abomination: just as high Anglican clergy used to use the Roman rite and hang portraits of His Holiness in their studies, and still warn their congregations against Roman Catholic error. The notion of the Law as a load comes also in Matt. 11.29f, where the πεφορτισμένοι are bidden to take the yoke of Christ's law on them, for his φόρτιον is light. πάντα ὅσα, ἐάν, τηρῶ are Matthaean: οὖν, οἱ ἄνθρωποι, θέλω are semi-Matthaean. δεσμεύω is found here only, but δέσμη in the Tares. The saying-and-doing contrast comes also in 'Not everyone who says to me, Lord, Lord', the Builders, and the Two Sons.

23.5–12

The view that Pharisaic piety is done to be seen by men is the theme of 6.1–18, and is Matthaean: the phrase πρὸς τὸ θεαθῆναι comes also in 6.1. Thereafter Matthew is simply expanding Mark. Mark's scribes walk about in στολαί, long robes—showing off, no doubt, but not religiously: Matthew's enlarge their prayer-boxes and tassels, so that their piety is visible to all. Mark's want greetings in the market-places: Matthew adds for the parallelism, 'and being called Rabbi by men'. The business of public salutation comes also at 5.47 and 10.12, and not elsewhere in the NT. Matthew has nine names of different religious classes, of which rabbi and καθηγητής are two. The triple repetitive parallelism, or scandalic, is a Matthaean rhythm, cf. 'There were eunuchs who were born so . . .'. The equality of all Christians as brothers in contrast to Pharisaic pretensions recalls the words of the greatness disputes at 20.26f, and 18.4: the former is virtually quoted, 'Whoever would be great among you must be your servant', the latter is turned into an elegant caesaric epigram (exalt, humble, humble, exalt). The whole passage is a lattice-work of parallelisms and antitheses. The religious technicalities are all Matthaean. ἀδελφός, heaven-and-earth, μείζων, ἔσται, ὅστις (2), πρὸς τὸ + infin., θεάομαι, οἱ ἄνθρωποι = men (2), φιλέω, μὴ + aor. subj. (3), ὁ πατὴρ ὁ οὐράνιος, χριστός, are characteristic words.

---

form since there are so many Matthaeanisms in the Matthaean form (logic!); and the consistency game can be played to find 'seams' between the evangelist and his Sondergut. The article has much insight to contribute, but it never occurs to Haenchen that Matthew's consistency might not reach his exacting standard: the evangelist is treated like a candidate for Ph.D., and needless to say his thesis is referred.

23.13

The first Woe is because the Jewish authorities not only reject the Kingdom themselves, but prevent the simple-hearted from accepting it too. It comes first because of the first and eighth Beatitudes, 'Yours is the kingdom of heaven', and it may be that there is also a reference to the temptation story in Genesis. The scribes and Pharisees are called serpents (ὄφεις, v. 33) in this chapter only, and ὁ ὄφις is the name for Satan in Gen. 3: Satan fell from God's kingdom, and enticed Adam and Eve to their exclusion from Eden. The kingdom of heaven, ἔμπροσθεν, οἱ ἄνθρωποι = men, κλείω are characteristic. Luke (11.52) adapts the verse with his Greek νομικοί, and his characteristic κωλύω and αὐτός = himself; Matthew's 'you shut' (κλείετε) becomes 'you have taken away the key (κλεῖδα) of knowledge (γνώσεως'—cf. Luke 10.22, 'No one γινώσκει who the Son is').

23.15

The second Woe turns on the contrast, sons of God/sons of Gehenna: but the reference to proselytism is seasonal. It was the custom to receive and to circumcise proselytes in time for Passover.[60] The school of Shammai permitted lustration of the circumcised the day before Passover; the school of Hillel insisted on circumcision earlier, probably on sabbath *Pārāh*, the third in Adar, and lustration before 7th Nisan. Indeed the Exodus liturgy suggests the same: 'When a προσήλυτος . . . would keep the Passover to the Lord, let all his males be circumcised, that he may come near and keep it.'[61] Similarly there is circumcision directly before the first Passover in the land in Josh. 5. We hear of Roman soldiers being baptized and eating their lambs in the evening.[62] The sea and the dry land are a pair, and occur in Gen. 1.10: περιάγω, γέεννα, and the Hebraic use of υἱός are characteristic. διπλότερον is non-Matthaean.

23.16–22

The parallels to 5.33–7 are striking and intended: but the phraseology is almost exclusively Matthaean besides. Metaphorical τυφλός, ὄμνυμι, χρυσός, μωρός, θυσιαστήριον, δῶρον are on Hawkins' list: semi-Matthaean are ναός, ὀφείλω, μείζων, ὁδηγός, ἁγιάζω, ἐπάνω, κάθημαι, κατοικῶ, θρόνος. The formulas 'It is nothing/he is liable' are close to the rabbis.[63] The rhythm is again a triple repetitive antithesis, more elaborate, more formal, and more Matthaean than vv. 8–10. The details of Matthew's gravamen are not supported or contradicted

[60] See above, p. 419.
[61] Exod. 12.48, LXX, part of the *Ha-ḥodesh* reading.
[62] J Pes. viii.8.   [63] S–B i, p. 932.

by rabbinic writings, but we have something very close in a Baraita, 'Whoever vows by the Torah has said nothing: but whoever vows by what is written in it, is liable'.[64] The passage is too Jewish to edify Luke's congregation: and demands a *Sitz-im-Leben* within the world of Jewish lore such as Matthew provides. The concern with such detailed sophistries transcends the single instance of Korban in Mark, and is unparalleled in Luke.

23.23–4

The tithe reference is also seasonal. 'On the eve of the first Festival-day of Passover in the fourth and seventh years . . . Terumah and Terumah of tithe were given to whom they were due, and the First Tithe was given to whom it was due, and Poorman's Tithe was given to whom it was due, and Second Tithe and Firstfruits everywhere were removed.'[65] Dill and cummin were liable to tithe according to the Mishnah:[66] the leaf of mint was liable to the Fallow Year law, which is close enough for Matthew's rhetoric.[67] The three minimal tithes are set against the three weightier matters,[68] with ἔλεος in the middle place. It is Matthaean–rabbinic doctrine that the tithing rules should be kept as well as the weightier matters. For v. 24, the abusive vocative ὁδηγοὶ τυφλοί, the animal images of camels and gnats, the hyperbole of swallowing a camel, and the neatly condensed pardic rhythm are all evidence of Matthaean authorship. Luke (11.42), mindful that in his previous chapter he has taught that to love God and our neighbour is the essential commandment, substitutes 'the love of God' for Matthew's 'mercy and faith', and balances this with 'mint and rue' and every herb. Rue was a more familiar plant than dill or cummin, and was grown as a border in Greek gardens.[69] As so often, Luke's changes show his ignorance of Jewish law: rue was not tithable,[70] still less every herb. For the vague 'and every herb', cf. Luke 21.29, 'the fig-tree and all the trees'.

23.25–6

Again the Matthaean version shows familiarity with Jewish casuistry: the whole tractate *Kelim* in the Mishnah is devoted to the cleansing

[64] B Ned. 14b; S–B I, p. 932.
[65] M M.Sh. 5.6. 'Removed' signifies either consumed (the Second Tithe and Firstfruits were eaten by the producer in Jerusalem) or thrown away. Terumah and Cattle tithe were paid out on 1st Nisan, as well as on 29th Elul and before Pentecost (M Shek. 3.1; Bekh. 9.5).
[66] M Maas. 4.5; Dem. 2.1.   [67] M Sheb. 7.1.
[68] There is assonance between *dīnā'*, judgement, and *dandannā'*, mint, in Aramaic, but this must be coincidence, unless a similar assonance can be found for *shebheth*, dill, and *kammōnah*, cummin.
[69] Ar. *Vesp.* 480.   [70] M Sheb. 9.1.

of vessels, and ch. 25 is given to the distinction in cleanness between the inner and outer surface. It was said, for example, 'If the outer part contracts uncleanness, the inner part remains clean.'[71] Matthew has in mind his Marcan text, 'They devour widows' houses', and points to the weightier matter of where the money for the food came from. The obvious antitheses, inside and outside, within and without, cup and dish, are typical of Matthew, as are τυφλός, the abusive vocative, and καθαρός. We may well have a Paschal reference here also: παροψίς properly means a side-dish, as opposed to τρύβλιον, πίναξ, an achete. Side-dishes were an essential part of the Passover meal, as was the ποτήριον.[72]

Luke (11.39) supplies the commoner πίναξ for παροψίς. Lacking the rabbinic background, he takes ἔξωθεν to be the surface (outer and inner) of the vessels, while ἔσωθεν becomes the inward disposition of the Pharisee: rabbinic subtlety is too recherché for Luke himself, let alone his congregation. ἄφρων comes also of the Rich Fool, and is only in Luke. With 'But (πλὴν) as for what is within . . .' (AT), cf. Luke 19.27, 'But (πλὴν) as for these enemies of mine . . .'. Luke is fond of phrases with τά: τὰ ὑπάρχοντα, τὰ πρὸς, τὰ κατὰ, τὰ περὶ, etc. δότε ἐλεημοσύνην (for the commoner ποιεῖτε) comes again at Luke 12.33, where it explains another Matthaean epigram, 'Do not lay up for yourselves . . .'. The emphasis on giving money away in alms in common in Luke–Acts—Zacchaeus, Cornelius, Dorcas, Paul, as well as purses that wax not old. Zacchaeus is an especially apt Lucan instance of one who gave away ill-gotten gain, and all was pure to him. Wellhausen's theory[73] that behind the Lucan reading stands an Aramaic *dakko*, cleanse, which Luke misread as *zakko*, give alms, thus explains what requires no explanation: Luke misinterprets Matthew's rabbinic niceties, as he usually does, and explains Matthew's poetic indirectness in plain prose, as he often does, with a phrase and language that he uses elsewhere, and a doctrine on which he constantly harps.[74]

---

[71] M Kel. 25.3. [72] Jeremias, *EWJ*, pp. 85f.
[73] *Einleitung in die drei ersten Evangelien* (Berlin 1911), p. 27.
[74] Black writes (*AAGA*, p. 2), 'The genesis of Luke's reading is quite certainly to be found in a wrong understanding of Aramaic *dakko*.' Such confidence is remarkable. It assumes (*a*) a written Aramaic document (since the error is supposed to arise from the similarity of letters ⁊ and ⁊), in addition to the Greek document Q which Black takes to lie before Luke and Matthew; (*b*) an interpreter who was prepared to give a literal translation of his misreading of the words 'Cleanse the inside', and let the rest go hang—Matthew's 'first . . . of the cup, that the outside also . . .' are not rendered. As so often, the Aramaic theory rests upon a documentary hypothesis which is not argued for: and the alleged mistranslation accounts for only half the evidence.

23.27–8

The seasonal nature of the sixth and seventh Woes is well-known. All graves had to be whitewashed on 15th Adar, a month before Passover as part of the separation from death (Num. 19.16) at the time of *Pārāh*, and to prevent accidental incurring of uncleanness before Passover.[75] This will have included the reputed graves of Israel's saints, which were popularly reverenced according to Josephus.[76] The inside/outside contrast, and γέμω are carried on from the previous Woe. τάφος, φαίνομαι (2), ὅστις, . . . μὲν . . . δὲ (2), οὕτως, οἱ ἄνθρωποι = men, δίκαιος, ἀνομία are characteristic: ὡραῖος and μεστός are non-Matthaean. The Matthaean version turns upon a knowledge of Jewish custom which would not be easily available to the Greek churches. Luke (11.44) therefore interprets, somewhat adjusting the meaning, 'You are like graves which are not seen'—this loses Matthew's inward–outward contrast which runs through his discourse, and places the emphasis on the contagion of Pharisaic impurity—cf. Luke's, 'Beware of the leaven of the Pharisees, which is hypocrisy' (12.1).

23.29–36

The seventh Woe follows from the sixth, prophets' graves from whitened graves, and moves into a rhetorical peroration. We note the Matthaean balance, 'You build the tombs of the prophets, and adorn the monuments of the righteous': prophets and saints are a Matthaean pair (10.41; 13.17). The Matthaean version of the next two verses makes sense: 'You say, Our fathers killed the prophets; we should never have: so you admit you are their sons, do you? And true sons you are.' It turns upon the double sense of the Hebrew *ben*, meaning first a literal descendant, and second one of the same nature. This is a semi-Matthaean use,[77] which Luke attempts to put into prose, and lands himself in a *non sequitur*: by building a prophet's tomb we do *not* witness and consent to the deeds of our fathers who killed him. τάφος, αἷμα = life taken, φονεύω, δίκαιος, εἰ . . . ἄν, are characteristic: in the Lucan version μάρτυς εἰμί, συνευδοκῶ, are characteristic of Luke.

For his peroration Matthew draws on traditional invective against the Jews. In 1 Thess. 2.15f,[78] Paul makes five points against the Jews: (a) they killed the Lord Jesus and the prophets; (b) they persecuted us out and displease God; (c) and oppose all men, hindering us from

---

[75] M Shek. 1.1   [76] *Ant.* 16. 7.1; *Bell. Jud.* 4. 9.7.
[77] cf. sons of the kingdom, by whom do your sons. . . .
[78] cf. p. 165 above. 1 Thess. 4. 13—5.11 is similarly developed in Matt. 24—25.

speaking to the Gentiles; (*d*) so as always to fill up the measure of their sins (ἀναπληρῶσαι αὐτῶν τὰς ἁμαρτίας; (*e*) wrath has come upon them at last. Matthew has opened his Woes with the charge that the Pharisees shut the kingdom against men (*c*), and completed them with the charge that they continue the work of killing the prophets (*a*). Now he throws in the three remaining counts: (*d*) 'Fill up then the measure of your fathers!' The doctrine of a set measure of sins to be filled up is found only here in Paul and only here in the Gospels; πληρόω is Matthaean. Verse 33 which caps it is a catena of Matthaean-isms, the echidnic rhythm, offspring of vipers, κρίσις, γέεννα.[79] (*b*) 'Therefore I send you prophets and wise men and scribes . . . you will persecute them.' The σοφοί and γραμματεῖς are *ḥᵃkhāmîm* and *sôphᵉrîm*, higher and lower grades of rabbinic teacher, and part of the hierarchy of Jewish religious officers so familiar to Matthew: he has them in threes also at 10.41f, prophet, saint, disciple, and at 23.8ff, rabbi, father, teacher. Luke (11.49) takes the prophets from the context to be OT prophets, and sets them with NT apostles, since grades of rabbi are not for him: then, as Jesus did not send the OT prophets, he needs God for subject, and supplies a periphrasis as usual, this time in the form, 'The wisdom of God', taking on the σοφία from Matthew's σοφούς.[80] Luke also takes over the Matthaean διὰ τοῦτο, διώκω; but ἀπόστολος is Lucan. σταυρώσετε in Matthew is for the rhetorical balance:[81] kill and crucify, flog and persecute. 'Some of them you will scourge in your synagogues' repeats 10.17, 'In their synagogues they will scourge you': 'You will persecute from town to town' resumes 10.23, 'When they persecute you in one town flee to the next'. (*e*) 'Wrath has come upon them': 'That upon you may come all the righteous blood . . .'. Matthew sees the disaster of A.D. 70 as the wrath of God for all the martyrs of both covenants. The blood of the prophets suggests at once Zechariah of 2 Chronicles, the only prophet in scripture martyred by the people; and the Chronicler himself shapes the Zechariah story on the model of Abel, with his 'May the Lord see and avenge!'[82] continuing the cry of Abel's

---

[79] cf. Mark 12.40, from Matthew's text for 23: 'they shall receive the greater κρῖμα'.

[80] cf. 8.14/Mark 4.19; 21.13/Mark 13.9f; 21.20/Mark 13.14; 24.6/Mark 16.7, for instances of Luke taking over a word but changing the meaning. There are also a number of examples in Luke's use of Matthew.

[81] E. Bammel ('Crucifixion as a punishment in Palestine', in *The Trial of Jesus* (London 1970), pp. 162–5) shows that the Jews punished political insurgency with crucifixion, but there is no evidence of such barbarism against Christians: Hare, p. 89, translates 'have them crucified', but, as he says, there is no evidence of that either.

[82] 2 Chron. 24.22.

blood from the ground. But Abel is in any case an apt reference, for Gen. 1—5 is the reading for the first sabbath in Nisan. The rabbis used the Zechariah story in *aggadah:* 'When Nebuzaradan came up against Israel [Zechariah's] blood began to seethe . . .'. He forced from them the confession of what they had done, and slew in turn the Great and Minor Sanhedrin, youths and maidens, schoolchildren and 80,000 priestly novitiates. To R. Judan in the second century it seemed as if this was not enough: 'Zechariah, Zechariah, all the choicest of them have I destroyed. Is it your pleasure that I exterminate them all?'[83] Matthew teaches the same doctrine. Like many rabbis he equates Zechariah the martyr with Zechariah the minor prophet, the son of Barachiah,[84] a 'mistake' omitted by Luke. ὅπως, αἷμα = life taken, φονεύω, θυσιαστήριον are Matthaean: ἀμὴν λέγω ὑμῖν, ἀπὸ . . . ἕως, ναός, γῆ, δίκαιος are semi-Matthaean. Verse 36 gives a Matthaean *inclusio.*

23.37–9

Killing/stoning, prophets/those sent are Matthew's customary balanced rhetoric: killing and stoning are a pair at 21.35 also. The doubled Jerusalem is a rabbinic device, cf. 'Zechariah, Zechariah' above: or in Matthew, 'Yea, Yea, Nay, Nay', 'Not everyone who says to me, Lord, Lord'. Animal imagery is Matthaean: the image is suggested by the use of ἐπισυνάγω in Mark 13.27. There the Temple is to be destroyed, and Christ's angels will gather in the elect: but Christ did not wish it so. He would have gathered Israel as a hen gathers her chicks,[85] but no: your house is left to you. θέλω (2), ἰδού, are characteristic: with 'your house', cf. 'your/their synagogues'. In the whole chapter there are 646 words, of which 180 are characteristic of Matthew.

Sometimes Matthew felt that Israel's disobedience was so monstrous as to shut them permanently out of salvation:[86] but at other times the softer, Pauline doctrine triumphed. The gifts and call of God are irrevocable: a hardening and wrath has come upon them now, but at the eleventh hour all Israel will be saved (Rom. 11.25–32).

[83] Lam. R. Proem XXIII.
[84] Gundry, *UOTSM,* pp. 86f: 'The utmost confusion'.
[85] 2 Esdras 1.30, where the passage occurs in a close parallel, is part of 2 Esdras 1—2, a Christian V-Ezra; cf. O. Eissfeldt, *The Old Testament* (E.T., Oxford 1966), p. 625.
[86] 8.12.

The words of v. 39 *must* mean Israel's cry of welcome to her returning Saviour.[87] The children hailed the kingdom of our father David in the words of Ps. 118 at the triumphal Entry: and so will all Israel hail him in faith at his coming in ultimate Triumph.

[87] οὐ μὴ . . . ἕως ἄν and ἄρτι are characteristic of Matthew, and here, as elsewhere, avoided by Luke.

20

PASSOVER (24—28)

Matthew inherited from Mark a liturgical use which already provided a skeleton for Holy Week.[1] On the sabbath before Passover the Apocalyptic Discourse was read: how suitably, R. H. Lightfoot has demonstrated, with the Church's passion-to-be the shadow of her Lord's.[2] The verses on Watching, and the opening of ch. 14 were read 'two days before the Passover', on 13th Nisan; Jesus' anointing 'beforehand for burying' at Simon's supper were read on 14th Nisan, and wherever the gospel was preached in the whole world what the woman had done was told in memory of her (14.3–9). There were two readings, if we may trust the old Ms. divisions, on Passover night: one at the beginning of the meal (14.10–17), Judas' treachery and the Passover preparation story; one at the end (14.18–65), the Last Supper, Gethsemane, and the Sanhedrin Trial. Peter's denial and the Passion are given in one unit, read presumably during the day of 15th Nisan: the Burial and the Resurrection are also one unit (15.42—16.8), and would be used on Easter Day. As we are not now concerned with Mark, I leave open the question whether we should assume further liturgical divisions according to the notes of time in the text.

Matthew elaborated this skeleton into a full Holy Week use. He retained the Apocalyptic Discourse on the Saturday before Passover, but provided a lesson for each week-day up to Passover by a series of midrashic expansions of the little Marcan Door-keeper parable, and by references to the Noah and Exodus stories which are the *sidrôt* for the season. There are three additional readings thus provided, the Virgins, the Talents, and the Sheep and Goats. If Passover fell on a Friday there was one lesson per day through the seven days: if it fell earlier, two or more lessons could be telescoped together. There are five actual Passover readings in the Ms. divisions of Matthew, and they correspond to the watches of the night: evening for the beginning of the Supper, 9.00 p.m. for its end, and the three-hour watch in Gethsemane, midnight for the Arrest, cockcrow for Peter's Denial, and morning for the Passion. It is very difficult to think that these divisions were not in the evangelist's mind, and in the tradition before him. The Burial and Resurrection are still one unit, the Gospel for

---

[1] See ch. 9, appendix B.
[2] *The Gospel Message of St Mark* (Oxford 1950), pp. 48–59.

Easter Day. The Passover-tide readings in Mark and Matthew (following A) may thus be tabulated as follows:

	MARK			MATTHEW
Sat. before Passover	(42) 13.1–31	Apocalyptic Discourse	(57) 24.1–35	
Sunday		Burglar, Servants	(58) 24.36–end	
to		Ten Virgins	(59) 25.1–13	
12th Nisan		Talents	(60) 25.14–30	
13th Nisan	(43) 13.32—14.2	Doorkeeper/Assize	(61) 25.31—26.	
14th Nisan	(44) 14.3–11	Anointing with Myrrh	(62) 26.6–16	
15th Nisan, 6 p.m.	(45) 14.12–17	Passover Meal	(63) 26.17–25	
9 p.m.	(46) 14.18–65	Gethsemane	(64) 26.26–46	
midnight		Arrest	(65) 26.47–68	
3 a.m.		Peter's Denial	(66) 26.69—27.2	
day	(47) 14.66—15.41	Passion	(67) 27.3–56	
Sat. after Passover	(48) 15.42—16.8	Burial, Resurrection	(68) 27.57—28	

Both the provision of lessons through a Festal Week, and the practice of vigils marked by three-hourly liturgical readings, were familiar from Judaism. The Mishnah sets Lev. 23 for the first day of Tabernacles, and the respective paragraphs for each following day from Num. 29.[3] The Talmudic tradition is less concerned with a defensive stress on ritual, and sets more varied lessons for several days in all the feasts.[4] For the use of vigils, we have seen that Pentecost has been celebrated among the Jews as a vigil from ancient times,[5] and the 119th Psalm is ancient evidence of three-hourly watches through the night and into the day.

Our earliest surviving lectionaries all show strong traces of the Matthaean pattern. I cite four sources: the early Syriac,[6] dating from A.D. 480; the Armenian,[7] from 690, but going back in tradition to Cyril of Jerusalem; Etheria at Jerusalem about 380; and the Greek lectionary,[8] which is ancient, though only preserved in ninth-century Mss.

[3] M Meg. 3.5.
[4] B Meg. 31a.   [5] See pp. 185f above.
[6] F. C. Burkitt, 'The Early Syriac Lectionary System', *Proc. B.A.*, vol. XI (1923). Burkitt takes B.M. Add. 14528 as the earliest evidence we have: the date is given by the colophon, and checked by the simplicity of the Church's Year, before the sixth-century innovations.
[7] F. C. Conybeare, *Rituale Armenorum* (Oxford 1905), pp. 507ff. The lections are from an eighth to ninth-century Ms., AF 20, but they agree closely with the divisions commented on by Gregory Asharuni about 690. Gregory believed the lectionary to come from Cyril of Jerusalem, and to him from Peter of Alexandria (martyred 311).
[8] This is conveniently set out in F. Scrivener, *A Plain Introduction to the Text of the NT* (4e., 1894), pp. 80ff.

	SYRIAC	ARMENIAN	ETHERIA	GREEK (Liturgy)
Palm S.	Matt. 21.1–17	Matt. 21.1–11	incl. Matt. 21.8f	John 12.1–18
M.	Luke 12.35–50	No Gospel	Suitable lections	Matt. 24.5–35
T.	Matt. 24.3–14	Matt. 24.3—26.3	Matt. 24—25	Matt. 24.36—26.2
W.	Matt. 26.14–16	Matt. 26.14–16	incl. Matt. 26.14	Matt. 26.6–16
Th.	Matt. 26.17–35	Matt. 26.20–39	Suitable lections	Matt. 26.1–20
Vigil	Matt. 26.36–75	Matt. 26.36—27.2, etc.	Suitable lections	John 13.3–17; Matt. 26.21—27.2, etc.
F.	Matt. 27.3–26, etc.	Matt. 27.3–53, etc.	Matt. 27.2, etc.	Matt. 27.1–38, etc.
S.	Matt. 27.62–6	Matt. 27.62–6		Matt. 28
Easter	Matt. 28.1–7; John 20	Matt. 28; John 20, etc.	'Resurrection'	John 1.1–17

It will be seen that both in the Jerusalem[9] tradition, represented by the Syriac and Armenian uses and Etheria, and in the Greek tradition: (*a*) a continuous, or nearly continuous, reading of Matt. 24—28 is kept up through the week; (*b*) the reading of the Apocalyptic Discourse is observed in the week-day(s) before Wednesday; (*c*) a vigil is kept on Thursday night, and usually through Friday, with Matthew as the backbone of the lections; (*d*) the Matthaean burial and resurrection stories are used through Saturday night to dawn on Easter Day. We can see in these lectionaries the adaptation of Matthew's Passover Week to the developed Holy Week of the fourth century.

(57) *The Consummation 24.1–36 (A 3–35)*

For the greater part Matthew transcribes Mark with minor changes. Mark 13.9–12 has already been used at Matt. 10.17–21, so he rewrites this paragraph:[10] v. 9 from Mark 13.13a, v. 10 from Mark 13.12, v. 11 from Mark 13.22, v. 13 from Mark 13.13b, v. 14 from Mark 13.10. Verse 12, 'And because lawlessness (AT) is multiplied, most men's love will grow cold' forms an introductory antithesis[11] to the following Marcan, 'But he who endures to the end will be saved.' Matthew's bogies—ἀνομία (the non-observance of the Torah)[12] and the false prophets who advocate this, the weaker members of the Church being scandalized and led astray and cooling off—all feature. The false prophets are sufficiently warned against in vv. 11 and 24; but the false Christs, the long line from Judas of Gaulonitis which was to end with Bar-Kochba, might do with some amplification, which Matthew gives them (vv. 26–8). All three verses are in Matthaean rhythm. The balanced antithesis of 'So, if they say to you, Lo, he is in the wilderness, do not go out; Lo, in the inner rooms, do not believe it', is an expanded version of v. 23, 'Then if anyone says to

[9] cf. R. Zerfass, *Die Schriftlesung in Kathedraloffizium Jerusalems* (Münster 1967).
[10] cf. Kilpatrick, *Origins*, p. 32.
[11] Like the thesaurics, p. 79 above, and the misthics, p. 83 above.
[12] Cf. G. Barth, 'Matthew's Understanding of the Law', *TIM*, pp. 159ff.

you, Lo Christ here or there, do not believe it' (AT). Verses 27 and 28 are both aetics, 'For as . . . so shall be . . .', 'Wherever . . . there shall be . . .'. Astronomical and animal imagery, especially the latter, are frequent in Matthew. ταμ(ι)εῖον comes also at 6.6, east and west at 8.11; 'so shall be the *parousia* of the Son of Man', ὥσπερ, φαίνομαι, συνάγω are Matthaean. The simile of the lightning covering the whole sky signifies the simultaneous vision by the whole world of Christ coming on the clouds, as opposed to the secret appearance to the few in desert or hide-hole: it is in fact due to the astronomical matter following. The vultures are similarly said (originally in Job)[13] to be ubiquitous: no corpse can escape them, nor can any eye fail to see Christ at his coming. The picture of the Parousia is touched up with further use of the Marcan prophetic passages. Isaiah's vision of the darkening of sun and moon and stars at the Day of the Lord opens with the setting up of a standard, σημεῖον, which Matthew introduces as the standard of the Son of Man.[14] Zechariah yields the mourning of the tribes.[15]

(58) *Watch! 24.37–end (A 36–)*

No one knows the day or the hour, says Jesus in Mark: and Matthew begins his midrash with a reference to the *sidrāh*. The second sabbath in Nisan, Gen. 6.9—11 was read, the whole Noah cycle and Babel: and one may suspect that the Apocalyptic Discourse was partly sited on this sabbath before Mark because the themes fit in so well together —it was natural to repeat Christ's words on the cataclysm coming when the cataclysm of old was read. Noah is the subject of a three-verse simile, and a few words are quoted from Genesis: 'in those days' (Gen. 6.4), 'Noah entered the ark' (Gen. 7.7). The illustration is sewn into the context by the words 'until the day', following Mark's 'no one knows the day'; and 'they did not know (ἔγνωσαν)', following Mark's 'know (γινώσκετε) that he is near'; and by the repeated 'So shall be the *parousia* of the Son of Man', from v. 27. 'For as . . . so shall . . .' is the aetic form again. Matthew deliberately uses the coarse word τρώγοντες for his normal ἐσθίοντες: the Nephilim were on the earth in those days, and unnatural unions and violent behaviour were the norm.[16]

Noah goes with Lot as a pair of 'righteous' men saved from heaven-sent catastrophe, and is so found in 2 Pet. 2.5–8, and Josephus *Ant.* I. 2.3: indeed the influence of the Lot story is there from the beginning

[13] 39.30. cf. Lam. R. I.42, where Job's 'Where the slain are, there is he' is interpreted of the Shekinah at the death of Nadab and Abihu.
[14] Isa. 13.1,10.   [15] Zech. 12.12ff, LXX.
[16] The subject was a popular outlet for rabbinic feelings: cf. S–B I, pp. 961ff.

in 'Let them flee to the mountains' (Mark 13.14; Gen. 19.17). Now as Lot and his wife fled over the open country from Sodom, the angels warned him, 'Do not look back; escape to the mountains lest you be taken with them (συμπαραλήφθῃς)' (Gen. 19.17): Lot escaped, but his wife was taken. So Matthew appends to his Noah simile, 'Then shall be two (AT) in the field; one is taken (παραλαμβάνεται) and one is left.' But in the second week of Nisan a third case of divine catastrophe is in men's minds, the angel of destruction who killed all the first-born of Egypt, 'from the first-born of Pharaoh who sits upon his throne, even to the first-born of the maidservant who is behind the mill' (Exod. 11.5, παρὰ τὸν μύλον). Matthew styles the second line to the first, to form a characteristic mylic[17] couplet. Since it is normal for men to be in the 'field' and women to be grinding, he has a natural and typical male–female pair, and leaves by the complications of Lot's wife and the grinders' children. The language is of the evangelist. ὥσπερ, τότε, and 'Thus shall be the *parousia* of the Son of Man' (2) are Matthaean. Semi-Matthaean are: pleonastic ἐκεῖνος, ἕως + ind., ἔσονται, ἀγρός, παραλαμβάνω (2), δύο (2), and the somewhat obvious pairs, 'chewing and drinking', 'marrying and giving in marriage'. ἄχρι, τρώγω, ἀλήθω, are not found elsewhere in Matthew.

Luke (17.20–37) adapts and expands the Matthaean version: καθώς and ἀπόλλυμι in the Noah unit are his language; and the four-point catalogue, 'they ate, drank, married, were wed', for Matthew's two pairs, is Lucan. He avoids Matthew's *parousia* as usual. But what is somewhat surprising is that he then takes Matthew's Lot reference, and works it up into an antistrophe. This is achieved largely by repetition: 'As it was in the days of Noah . . . Likewise as it was in the days of Lot . . .'; 'They ate, drank, married, were wed . . . They ate, drank, bought, sold, planted, built.' Marriage was not what Sodom was famous for: the planting of Noah's vineyard and the building of Babel were more the sort of things happening then. Similarly: 'Noah entered the ark . . . Lot went out from Sodom'; 'The flood came and destroyed them all . . . Fire and brimstone rained from heaven and destroyed them all.' ὁμοίως, καθώς, κατὰ τὰ αὐτά are typical of Luke. Luke retains most of Matthew's crinics, but this is the only occasion where he works up an antistrophe to form one of his own. His handling of Matt. 24.40 is less happy. Having expounded Lot and his wife to the full, he replaces the two in the field with two in one bed, since the destruction of Sodom came at the end of the night, and the Parousia is often spoken of in nocturnal images: the phrasing is clumsy if a married pair is intended, and in any case women do not grind in the dark, a characteristic Lucan failure of adjustment.

[17] See p. 77 above.

24.42–4

Matthew resumes with an adaptation of Mark 13.35, 'So watch; for you do not know when the master of the house is coming', and the four watches are given. Now Matthew has already glossed the Marcan apocalypse with details from the similar Pauline teaching in 1 Thess. 4: for the use of the word παρουσία is peculiar to Thessalonians and Matthew, and the divine trumpet at Christ's coming[18] likewise. He now proceeds to expand the Pauline simile, 'The Day of the Lord is coming (AT) like a thief in the night' (1 Thess. 5.2). Paul's simile becomes Matthew's allegory: the thief now stands for the Lord, instead of the Day of the Lord, the householder for the Christian, the unknown watch for the unknown day. ἡμέρα, κύριος, κλεπτής, ἔρχεται, γρηγορῶ are in the Thessalonian passage: the unknown watch is indicated in Mark. Thieves dig through in Matt. 6.19f also: ἐκεῖνος, εἰ . . . ἄν, διὰ τοῦτο, ἕτοιμος, οἰκοδεσπότης, and 'the Son of Man is coming' are Matthaean. So is the *inclusio*. What is not normal in a Matthaean parable is a disreputable comparison for God or Christ. The rabbis, and Matthew elsewhere, favour kings, rich householders, bridegrooms, etc. Unjust judges and stewards, and the general 'how much the more God' approach are Lucan; Matthew would never have introduced the suggestion that Christ was like a thief if Paul had not put it in his head.[19]

24.45–51

Mark's Doorkeeper began, 'It is like a man going on a journey, when he leaves home, and puts his servants in charge (δοὺς τὴν ἐξουσίαν), each with his work . . .'. Mark's householder is a village gentleman, away for the evening: he speaks to each of the domestics and gives him his job, and to the nightwatchman to stay up. But ἐξουσία means something bigger to Matthew: his householder has a large staff and a major-domo with ἐξουσία over the others, and he is away for days, perhaps weeks—'he will come on a *day* which he does not expect'. As usual the grand scale is where Matthew is at home: and it is natural to him also to develop his similitude as a contrast, a faithful and sensible servant (Matthew's standard adjectives of praise) and a

---

[18] μετὰ σάλπιγγος μεγάλης, 24.31: ἐν σάλπιγγι θεοῦ, 1 Thess. 4.16.

[19] Dodd claims (*Parables of the Kingdom*, pp. 167ff) that Jesus had a particular case of burglary in mind, on the basis of 'If *the* householder had known . . .'. Wishful thinking, alas: Matthew is full of Semitic concreteness, cf. 5.25f, 'the way, the judge, the warder, the last farthing'; 5.40, 'the cloak'; 5.1, 'the mountain', etc.

bad servant: stock characters as usual. Thessalonians again helps him on his way: immediately after the thief, Paul charges to wakefulness and sobriety—'For those who get drunk get drunk (μεθύουσιν) at night'.²⁰ So Matthew's bad servant eats and drinks with the μεθύοντες. The reward of faithfulness is to be put in charge of more affairs, just like the servants in Matthew's Talents. The doctrine of hell with which the parable ends is Matthaean, and so is the allegory which breaks the story up: for when an earthly master has cut his servant in half, it is too late to appoint his portion with the hypocrites. Anxiety about the postponement of the Parousia—'My master is delayed'—is also found in Matthew's Bridesmaids—'As the bridegroom was delayed' —and Talents—'Now after a long time . . .'. The language is characteristic. Matthaean are: φρόνιμος, τροφή,²¹ σύνδουλος, ὑποκριτής, and 'there shall be weeping and gnashing of teeth': with ὃν ἐλθὼν ὁ κύριος cf. ὃν λαβὼν ἄνθρωπος (13.31,33,44). Semi-Matthaean are: ἄρα²², δοῦλος/κύριος, καθίστημι, ἐάν, ἐλθών, οὕτως, λέγω ὑμῖν ὅτι, pleonastic ἐκεῖνος, the day and the hour. οἰκετεία, μεθύω, διχοτομέω are not found elsewhere in the Gospel. There are 161 words between the two parables, of which 52 are characteristic.

Luke copies the paragraph closely (12.42–6) with some characteristic alterations. A senior servant of this kind is called in Luke a steward, οἰκονόμος,²³ which he substitutes at first, but lethargy causes him to leave Matthew's δοῦλος at 12.43,45,46,47; ἀληθῶς is Lucan for ἀμήν (cf. 9.27; 21.3), and τε is Lucan. ἀπιστῶν is an improvement on Matthew's hypocrites: 'Who then is the *faithful* steward . . .? He will put him with the *unfaithful*.'²⁴

²⁰ 1 Thess. 5.7.
²¹ cf. Ps. 104.27, δοῦναι τὴν τροφὴν αὐτοῖς εὔκαιρον.
²² P. Joüon suggests plausibly that the rhetorical τίς clause is an Aramaic conditional, *Notes philologiques*, xviii (1928), p. 349. There is a similar example at Matt. 12.11; cf. Black, *AAGA*, p. 118: testifying to Matthew's Semitic Greek.
²³ 16.1ff; cf. 1 Cor. 4.2, 'It is required in stewards that a man be found πιστός.'
²⁴ Jeremias, *PJ*, pp. 55f, n. 31, argues for a double misunderstanding of a hypothetical Aramaic original. (a) διχοτομέω is translated in the Syriac versions by *pallegh* (divide, share, distribute). The Aramaic form, using this root, would be *yᵉphallegh leh*, which originally meant, 'He will give him (dat., sc. blows, or his portion)', but was misunderstood as, 'He will divide him (acc.)'. (b) τὸ μέρος τινὸς τίθεναι μετά means 'to treat anyone as', and is a Semitism. Luke has the right meaning, 'he will treat him as a profligate', for the second half: the right meaning for the first half, 'he will beat him' has disappeared. This will hardly do. For (a) *pallegh* in Syriac means to divide, and translates μερίζω, σχίζω, δι—: it is used of distributing when dividing is part of distribution, as with the loaves of John 6.11. 'He will distribute him (sc. blows)' requires some substantiation as a translation. For (b) Jeremias cites no evidence: the phrase does not occur in LXX.

But we do not need such explanations: the text is self-explanatory from the established manner of writing of the two evangelists.

(59) The Ten Virgins 25.1–13

When Mark had finished the Doorkeeper parable (13.34), he concluded, 'Watch therefore—for you do not know when the master of
the house will come, in the evening, or at midnight, or at cockcrow,
or in the morning—lest he come suddenly and find you asleep.'
Matthew virtually quotes the opening of this at the end of the Bridesmaids: 'Watch therefore, for you know neither the day nor the hour'
—a Matthaeanized shorter version. The master-and-servants theme
he has now dealt with, but has done nothing to expound in it the theme
of sleeping and waking, which is not only Marcan, but in Thessalonians also, 'So then, let us not sleep, as others do, but let us watch'
(5.6). It is the Matthaean manner to pair the female with the male, so
to the wise and bad servants he supplies the wise and foolish bridesmaids. The bridegroom image, already in Mark 2 and used a number
of times by Matthew, provides the necessary setting: for just as the
Christians in Mark were the sons of the bridechamber, so now they
can be its daughters. The bride, here as there, has no allegorical
standing left, and is unmentioned.[25]

For the scene to be nocturnal Matthew has to make free with
marriage customs.[26] Bridegrooms did not normally arrive to claim
their brides in the early hours, but the night is required by the waking/
sleeping theme. The Jews believed that Messiah would come in the
night,[27] and this tradition agrees with the Exodus type which Matthew
has already referred to with the women grinding at the mill: now he
writes, 'At midnight there was a cry (μέσης δὲ νυκτὸς κραυγὴ γέγονεν)',
just as in Egypt at midnight there was a great cry (μεσούσης τῆς
νυκτὸς . . . ἐγενήθη κραυγὴ μεγάλη, Exod. 12.29). The Israelites were
watching then, their loins girt, while Pharaoh and his servants were
asleep.[28] When the community of the saved was in the ark, too, God
shut them in (ἔκλεισε, Gen. 7.16); and so now does the bridegroom
shut the door (ἐκλείσθη ἡ θύρα) on the wedding-party. Jewish weddings
took place in the bridegroom's home, but it is natural to read Matthew's
text as if it was at the bride's in this case.[29] There are scriptural

[25] She is introduced by a number of Western, Syriac, and other Mss., no doubt
from the feeling that the Church is the bride of Christ, and the wedding would be
incomplete without her. Paul's teaching is not taken into the Church's imaginative
thinking until the Apocalypse.

[26] See S–B I, pp. 500ff for Jewish marriage customs.

[27] Jerome says, 'Traditio Judaeorum est Christum media nocte venturum, in
similitudinem Aegypti temporis quando Pascha celebratum est', cited by
McNeile, p. 358.

[28] 'And Pharaoh rose up in the night, he and all his servants . . .' (Exod. 12.30).

[29] McNeile supposes that after v. 10a the bridal party go to the bridegroom's
house: but this seems forced.

precedents for this in the case of Jacob, Samson, and Tobit, all for special reasons, but the dominant influence on Matthew is undoubtedly the allegory. As Christ will come to earth and find the Christian wedding-attendants ready or otherwise, so must the bridegroom come to the bride's home in the parable.

It is unfortunate that so telling a parable should have an inbuilt contradiction. Matthew inherited the waking/sleeping image, which in the case of the bridesmaids should have involved some in keeping awake and some in sleeping, and so missing the bridegroom's coming. But then his parable would have been laughable: for the foolish virgins must be heavy sleepers indeed to nod on through the arrival of the groom's cavalcade, and the wise must be lacking in charity to let them! No, the point of the γρηγορεῖτε theme is not literal staying awake, since Christians like pagans must rest: it is in being prepared (ἕτοιμος v.10; 24.44). This is easily represented by the wise virgins providing enough oil for the night, and so being ready for the groom's arrival, while their ill-provided sisters are away. It means that Matthew must put up with the superior smiles of twentieth-century scholars, who note that the quotation of Mark, 'Watch therefore . . .' (v.13) does not fit the parable, since the wise slept too: but he might well feel that such a price was worth paying. There is a similar failure to fit in the Labourers in the Vineyard, for a similar reason. There is no basis for allegations of muddle over the purchase of oil in the night: sales at all hours are still normal in the East, where money is precious, and Luke testifies to a man even going borrowing at the same hour, though this is less popular.

What is remarkable is the modern clinging to the idea that the parable, or a part of it, is dominical: for if ever a pericope was stamped with the Matthaean hallmark in every part, this is it. The stock figures, wise and foolish like the Matthaean Builders; the black-and-white contrast, five in the feast, five excluded, like the Matthaean Servants, or Talents, or Wheat and Tares; the bridal imagery, like the Matthaean wedding-feast; the harsh theology in the exclusion of the unready from the messianic feast and kingdom, a version of the Matthaean hell; the view of the Church as a mixed body, some of whom may not be saved, as in the Matthaean Net and Marriage-Feast—all are typical of the evangelist, and against the manner of the Marcan and Lucan Jesus. The preconceptions of the 70s are writ large—the delay of the Parousia and the centrality of preparedness for it. Of the language, the following expressions are Matthaean: τότε (2), ὁμοιόω, the kingdom of heaven, three nominative aorist participles, μωρός (3)/φρόνιμος (4), γάμος, ὕστερον; semi-Matthaean are παρθένος (3), ὅστις, λαμβάνω (4), ἐγείρομαι, νύμφιος (3), pleonastic ἐκεῖνος, πέντε (2), πᾶσαι (2), νύξ, ἰδού, λέγουσαι (2), ἕτοιμος, γάμος, κλείω, ἀρκέω, πορεύομαι, κύριε κύριε (cf. 7.21), ἀνοίγω, ἀποκριθεὶς εἶπεν, ἀμὴν λέγω ὑμῖν, οὖν, the day and the hour. With ἀγγείοις cf. ἄγγη (13.48); slumber-and-sleep occurs in 2 Kings 4.6, and approximations elsewhere. ἀπάντησις, if that is the right reading, is only here in Matthew. Of 168 words 53 are characteristic.

Luke does not give the parable as it stands, but twice gives a shorter version. At 12.35ff, 'Let your loins be girded' is clearly under the influence of the Exodus story; '. . . and your lamps burning' recalls the Virgins: here too there is a marriage, but the similitude is with servants waiting up for their master who has been a guest at it. The thief, and the faithful, wise steward, follow immediately. At 13.24 Luke has, 'Strive to enter by the narrow door' for Matthew's gate, and this leads on to the householder rising and shutting the door. The disappointed stand knocking and say, 'κύριε, ἄνοιξον ἡμῖν', and the reply is, 'I do not know you where you come from'. The situation envisaged by Luke is irrational—gatecrashers are welcome if they push hard. It arises from an attempt to combine Matthew's two rational pictures, the exclusion of those who fail to find the narrow gate, and of the bridesmaids who were not ready.

(60) The Talents 25.14–30

There is still one aspect of Mark's Doorkeeper which has been neglected. The Thief and the Virgins took up the theme of waking, and the watches of the night; the Servants took up the notion of the master going away and giving ἐξουσία to one of his staff; but Mark says that he gives his servants the authority, to each (ἑκαστῷ) his work. There remains the implication of a master giving responsibility to a number of his men. Further Mark uses the adjective ἀπόδημος. The context shows that the journey is a short one, but the word, especially the verb ἀποδημέω, implies a journey out of the country (cf. 21.33 and parallels). Matthew accordingly elaborates a fourth parable, beginning, 'For it will be as when a man ἀποδημῶν called his own δοῦλοι and entrusted to them his property, . . . to each (ἑκαστῷ) according to his ability . . .'. Matthew being the parabolist, the property is large, a talent being, on the basis of one day's wage as a denarion then and £4 in England in 1970, something around £40,000. As a Matthaean parable, the contrast is of the essence, and being, like all Matthaean parables, an allegory, it turns upon the contrast between the faithful servant who has fulfilled his trust, and the faithless one who has disregarded it. Matthew's eyes are again upon the backsliders in the Church, and of course on the Lord's return in judgement. The business milieu is congenial to the evangelist. The figures are as much caricatures as ever, good and faithful, wicked and slothful servants. They are diversified only by there being two of the good and one of the bad, a clever psychological touch (cf. 99 : 1 sheep): but the two good servants are plaster replicas of each other. Verse 22 repeats v. 20, v. 23 v. 21, almost verbatim; and the master's reply to the bad servant in v. 26 nearly repeats the servant's own words in v. 24. We thus have a strong element of Matthaean repetitiveness. The rewards of the good servants take up the reward of the Faithful and Wise Servant in 24. His lord was to set him over all his property, as they are now set over much. Note the repeated, slightly obvious, Matthaean antithesis 'Over a little were you faithful, over much will I set you' (AT). The bad servant speaks in pardics, 'reaping where you did not sow, and gathering where you did not winnow'. For the settlement of the money position, Matthew has recourse to the riddle of Mark 4.25, 'To him who has will more be given . . .', which he quotes in a Matthaeanized form at v. 29.[30] He who has (the money and the faith to use it), Matthew glosses, he shall have more; he who has not (the faith to fulfil his responsibility) shall lose it. So the extra talent goes to the man with ten. As for the settlement of the fate of the faithless, that is no problem: there is the standard Matthaean outer darkness, with attendant weeping and gnashing of teeth.

Linguistically Matthaean are: ὥσπερ, nine nominative aorist participles, κερδαίνω (4), ἐργάζομαι, φημί (2), ἀγαθός/πονηρός, προσέρχομαι (3), συνάγω (2), προσφέρω, τὰ ἀργύρια, and the last two clauses. Semi-Matthaean are: κύριος (7), δοῦλος (5), . . . μὲν . . . δὲ, πέντε (5), δύο (5), εὐθέως, πορεύομαι, λαβών (3), γῆ (2), κρύπτω (2), ἐκεῖνος, συναίρω λόγον, λέγων, κύριε (3), ὀλίγος/πολύς (3), καθίστημι (2), λαμβάνω, γινώσκω of people, ὅθεν (2), σός, ἐμός, ἀποκριθεὶς εἶπεν, οὖν (2), βάλλω, ἐλθών, ἄν, περισσεύω. 93 words out of 302 are characteristic of Matthew. Only here in Matthew are ὀκνηρός, τόκος, κομίζομαι, ἀχρεῖος.

The secondariness of the Lucan Pounds is obvious:

(a) Luke begins with ten servants, but in the story they are described as the first, the second, the other: nor is the tell-tale ὁ ἕτερος accidental. The parable has become in its plot a tale of three servants under the attraction of the Talents.

(b) Luke has grafted a political allegory on to a business parable, with disastrous results. The bad servant now resents the king not doing his own farming, which is irrational; the governor of ten

---

[30] καὶ περισσευθήσεται is added as at 13.12 (redactional): added παντί, and participles for relative clauses, are regular in Matthew's redaction.

cities is tipped a *mna*, which is ridiculous; and the king's enemies are then slaughtered, which is irrelevant.

(*c*) In the second half of the parable, as so often, fatigue operates, and the Matthaean wording is increasingly used, including such non-Lucan expressions as πονηρὲ δοῦλε, παντὶ τῷ ἔχοντι.[31]

(*61*) *The Last Judgement 25.31—26.5*

It is noticeable how closely 24—25 correspond to J. Mann's *schema* for a rabbinic sermon.[32] Mann sets out five points:

(*a*) *Yelammedenu Rabbenu*.   The disciples approach with a question ('Let our Rabbi teach us . . .'), to which the Master gives his answer (*Hᵃlākāh*).

(*b*) *Petihta* text, taken from the Writings, to open the subject up.

(*c*) *Aggada*.

(*d*) Peroration.

(*e*) Text from the Torah, taken from the *sidrāh* for the day, to which the whole sermon has been aimed, forming a kind of *inclusio*.

So

(*a*), 24.1–3, Jesus' disciples show him the Temple and ask the signs of the End, followed by 24.4–36, *Hᵃlākāh* (Take heed . . . see that you are not alarmed . . . flee to the mountains . . . do not believe it . . . know that he is near), forming the Marcan Discourse;

(*b*), 24.37–41, *Petihta* texts (but from Noah, Lot, the Exodus, in place of the Writings);

(*c*), 24.42—25.30, *Aggada*, the four Parables;

(*d*), 25.31–end, Peroration, The Last Judgement. Mann notes of the Sermon on Seder I in the Tanhuma, what would be true of many others, 'The Sermon is concluded with a peroration as to the respective lot of the sinner and the well-deserved.'[33]

---

[31] Jeremias (*PJ*, pp. 58ff) concedes the secondariness of the Lucan version, but claims that both versions are embellished forms of the original: (*a*) 'With regard to the amounts, the lesser must be original' (p. 60, n.41)—an instance of Jeremias' graph fallacy: why should we think that steady increase of scale is the invariable rule? Luke *reduces* Mark's scale in the Wicked Husbandmen, cutting the later delegations of 'many servants', and the murders. (*b*) He pictures the original as spoken to the leaders of the people—see p. 409 above. Black, *AAGA*, p. 2, justifies Nestle's claim that behind Matthew's 'talents' lies an Aramaic *kkrin* which Luke's source has misread as *krkin*: but then cities are as suitable a reward from the Lucan king as talents are from the Matthaean millionaire.

[32] *BRPOS*, p. 14.

[33] ibid., p. 27.

(e), the peroration, 'When the Son of Man comes . . .' takes up the dominical text, 'They will see the Son of Man coming . . .' (24.30): as Mann says, 'In this manner the circle was repeated by returning to the starting point.'[34]

Matthew develops his peroration in three ways. He begins from his version of Mark 8.38c (Matt. 16.27), 'For the Son of Man is to come with his angels in the glory of his Father, and then he will repay every man for what he has done', of which the last clause is from Ps. 62.12. The glory is the Son's own glory here, as in 24.30, but the Psalms text is the substance of what follows, and does not occur in 24. 'Every man' means the whole world, all the *gôîm*, as is invariable in Jewish pictures of the final Judgement. Second, he draws in the shepherd image from Ezek. 34, which he has already deployed in the parable of the Lost Sheep. The prophecy foretells the establishing of David as the one shepherd over God's sheep in a reign of peace and plenty (vv. 23–31); and it is said, 'Behold, I will distinguish (διακρινῶ) between sheep and sheep (προβάτου), rams and he-goats.' It is for the sheep that God is concerned in Ezekiel, so they are, as is natural to Matthew, symbolic of the saved; and the goats draw the shorter straw. The left-and-right situation is rabbinic: for example, 'This you learn from Micaiah, who said, "I saw the Lord seated on his throne, and all the host of heaven on His right and left". Is there a physical right and left in heaven? Right means "inclining to the right, or acquitting", and left must mean "inclining to the left, or condemning." '[35]

The stage thus set, the King pronounces judgement on the basis of men's attitude to the Church. Four considerations rule out the popular view that it is men's attitude to the poor which is the criterion:

(a) 'These my brethren' are a group apart, among neither the acquitted nor the condemned, but at the King's side in judgement.[36] The apostles' share in the Final Judgement is Matthaean (19.28).

(b) The phrase, 'my brethren', elsewhere in Matthew (12.50; 28.10) means the Christians, and the ἐλάχιστοι (v. 40, and especially v. 45) may well be a synonym for the μικροί, the humble Christians of ch. 10 and ch. 18.

(c) Jesus speaks of himself elsewhere in Matthew as being 'in the midst of' (18.20), and 'with' (28.20) the Church, so that the equivalence of Christ and his Church would be natural here: and

---

[34] ibid., p. 14.   [35] Tanḥuma B Shemot, 4b.
[36] I am grateful to the Reverend R. Kempthorne for drawing my attention to this point.

it is part of the Son of Man concept in Daniel and generally that leader and community are one.

(*d*) In Matt. 10.41 eschatological reward is promised to whoever gives 'one of these little ones', a Christian layman, a cup of cold water. The gospel is to be preached to 'all nations', fish 'of every kind' will be gathered in; and by how they have treated the preachers shall 'all nations' be judged. The Christian evangelist is Christ present in weakness: a sixfold weakness, as Paul expresses it, 'πεινῶμεν καὶ διψῶμεν καὶ γυμνητεύομεν καὶ κολαφιζόμεθα καὶ ἀστατοῦμεν καὶ κοπιῶμεν' (1 Cor. 4.11). Hungering and thirsting Matthew takes over as they stand. Homeless makes a pair with garmentless—he puts ξένος for ἀστατέω. κολαφίζω would naturally be associated with prison beatings, but Paul uses it also of the messenger of Satan, his illness (ἀσθένεια, 2 Cor. 12.7ff):Matthew puts the two in a third pair, sick and in prison.[37] The three pairs form a triple balance, or typhlic, which is then repeated three further times, with a repetitiveness typical of Matthew and effective to its theme.

Hell is Matthaean, as is the following language: the Son of Man comes, sits on the throne of his glory (19.28), τότε (6), συνάγω (4), ὥσπερ, πρόβατα (2), δεῦτε, my Father, hunger-and-thirst (4), εὐώνυμος (2), ξένος (4), γυμνός (4). Semi-Matthaean are: angels of judgement, ἔμπροσθεν, ἔθνη, πάντες (2), ἀφορίζω, τὰ μὲν . . . τὰ δὲ . . ., ἱστάναι, the foundation of the world, περιβάλλω (3), φυλακή (4), ἐρεῖ (2), κληρονομέω, ποτίζω (3), λέγων (2), κύριε (2), ἤ (8), ἀποκριθείς, ἀμὴν λέγω ὑμῖν (2), δίκαιος (2), εἷς τούτων (2), ἐλάχιστος (2), ἀδελφός, ἐφ'ὅσον (2), πορεύομαι, διάβολος, eternal fire (18.8). Non-Matthaean are ἔριφος, –ιον, καταράομαι, κόλασις. More than 100 out of 279 words are characteristic.

A fittingly Matthaean climax to the evangelist's teaching labours.

For the greater part of the Passion story Matthew follows Mark closely. His occasional departures from his *Vorlage* appear to be for easily interpretable reasons.

1. He feels the need to explain Jesus' attitude in places where it is liable to misunderstanding. 26.28, 'This is my blood which is poured out for many'—but how can it affect 'many'? It is 'for the forgiveness

---

[37] cf. also Isa. 58.7: 'Break your bread to the hungry (πεινῶντι), and bring (εἴσαγε) the unsheltered poor into your house: if you see the naked (γυμνόν), clothe him, and you shall not disregard the relations of your own seed.' I have said enough to indicate how Matthew would have interpreted the 'poor' of this text.

of sins'. Matthew suppressed the phrase from his account of the Baptism of John,[38] because, he believed, John's baptism could accomplish no such thing: it is the Christian sacraments alone that can achieve this. 26.50, Judas hails Jesus and kisses him: and in Mark the arrest follows without a word. But what was Jesus' attitude—did he resent the treachery? No: ἑταῖρε, ἐφ' ὃ πάρει—Jesus accepted it without resentment. As at 3.15, where Matthew inserts Jesus' attitude to his being baptized with a laconic ἄφες ἄρτι, so brief as to be vague, so here: the cold ἑταῖρε is Matthaean, ἐπί of purpose comes also at 9.9 (= Mark) and 22.5, and there are suppressed main verbs followed by relatives at 19.11 and 20.24 (Mark), though nothing as drastic as the presumed omission of ποίει here.[39] πάρειμι is non-Matthaean. 26.52 similarly forestalls the question of Jesus' attitude to the wounding of the High Priest's servant, left open by Mark. Jesus disapproved: (*a*) violence was not his way, cf. Matt. 5.38ff on retaliation and loving your enemies; (*b*) divine power was always available to him, cf. Matt. 13.58, where Mark's limitation, 'He *could* do no mighty work', is removed; (*c*) the scriptures must be fulfilled, cf. Matt. *passim*. The epigram, 'All who take the sword . . .' is developed from the law of God to Noah in the *sidrāh* (Gen. 9.6), 'Whoever sheds the blood of man, by man shall his blood be shed.' The machaeric rhythm is typical of Matthew, as are the words ἄρτι, my Father, and fulfil (the scriptures). Semi-Matthaean are δοκέω, πάντες, λαμβάνω, angels, οὖν, and οὕτως. λεγίων and παρίστημι are non-Matthaean.

2.   There is a marked interest in Judas. This is supplied partly from the Marcan text, as at 26.25, where Judas repeats the apostles' question, 'Is it I, Master?', and gets the Matthaean answer, σὺ εἶπας; or 26.50 (see above): but principally from scripture. Mark's 'they promised to give him silver' (AT) recalls a complex of scriptures, most notably Zechariah's, 'They weighed my wage, thirty shekels of silver' (11.12, LXX). Matthew is master of both Greek and Hebrew, and there is no doubt which text is closer to the Gospel event: where the Greek has the innocuous 'as I was proved for their sake', the Hebrew has 'the glory of the price at which I was priced by them'. At 26.15 he inserts the LXX words ἔστησαν . . . τριάκοντα, with ἀργύρια, the normal form in Matthew, for LXX ἀργυροῦς: in 27.3ff he follows the Hebrew when it diverges. Now the Hebrew Zechariah says that the shekels were cast both to the potter and in the house of the Lord, and to elucidate this riddle Matthew turns to other scriptures, linked

---

[38] Mark 1.4.
[39] This seems the best view available, though the ellipse is extremely difficult. For other attempts, cf. Lohmeyer, p. 364.

by word-association, as midrash is done. At Jer. 18—19.13 (LXX), the prophet went to the potter's house (κεραμεύς, 18.1), bought a flask, and broke it at the burial ground as a prophetic sign—the kings have filled Jerusalem with innocent blood (αἱμάτων ἀθῴων), so this place shall be called the burial-place of slaughter (19.6). At Jer. 32. (LXX 39.)7ff, the prophet bought a field and weighed (ἔστησα) seventeen shekels of silver for it; he gave (ἔδωκα) the deed to Baruch and commanded (συνέταξα) him—so the Lord (κύριος) had said. These passages are linked by several word-associations. ἔστησα(ν). . . ἀργυροῦς(–ίου) is common to Zech. 11.11 and Jer. 39.9; 'I knew this to be the word of the Lord' to Zech. 11.11 and Jer. 39.8. 'The Lord said to me, Buy' comes in Jer. 19.1 and 39.6, and the potter is in Zech. 11.12f and Jer. 19.1. But neither of these Jeremiah prophecies, nor Zech. 11, reveals how Judas died. That must be inferred from the story of David, for often in the Psalms David complains of his enemies and of traitors within his house, and Ps. 55 in particular, 'It is not an enemy who taunts me . . . but it is you, my equal, my companion, my familiar friend . . . let death come upon them . . .'. Now Ps. 55 was interpreted by the rabbis with reference to David and Ahitophel, who betrayed David and went over to Absalom;[40] and in 2 Sam. 17.23 Ahitophel set his house in order and hanged himself (ἀπήγξατο) and was buried (ἐτάφη). Finally we should add the passage in Gen. 37, where it is Judah who persuades the sons of Jacob to sell Joseph for twenty shekels of silver.

These passages give Matthew what happened. The Psalms are prophecy as well as lament on David's woes of old: Judas will have hanged himself, like Ahitophel, and, like him, from remorse. So he will have set his affairs in order by returning the thirty shekels—as Zechariah says, 'I cast them into the Lord's house.' Judas' confession, 'I have betrayed αἷμα ἀθῷον', draws in Jer. 19.4. Now unclean money would defile the Temple treasury, so we have a natural explanation for both the potter and the house of the Lord in Zechariah. The Temple authorities will have passed it on to the potter, and the field and the burial-ground, both in Jeremiah, supply the purchase: indeed the name of the well-known charity cemetery, Akeldamach, tells the same tale. The story is crowned with a combined citation of the passages used: since two are from Jeremiah and he is the senior prophet, he gets the credit. Matthew moves from the LXX to his own version of the Hebrew when the latter is more to the point, and this affects the story as well as the quotation. ῥίψας, hurling the money, is more attuned to Judas' despair than the LXX ἐνέβαλον (Zech. 11.13): the Hebrew *hashlîkhēhû, wā'ashlîkh*, give the option on a stronger

⁴⁰ Ps. R. and Yalqut, ad loc.; Feldman, PSR, p. 76, n.1.

word. κορβανᾶς has no place in the scriptures used: the high-priests merely say the money cannot go there as it is blood-money. The first words of the citation are from the Greek Zechariah, 'And they took the thirty pieces of silver'. Matthew gives his own rendering of the Hebrew 'pricing' passage, with 'the price of him that was priced' for the first person. For 'by them', Matthew glosses 'by the sons of Israel', with an eye on the pricing of Joseph by the sons of Israel at Judah's behest in Genesis. The remaining words occur in the Greek Jeremiah passages which I have noted.[41]

3.   There is a tendency to fix the blame on the Jews and to exonerate Pilate; by the Matthaean device of a dream-warning[42] through the latter's wife; by the hand-washing, drawn from Deut. 21.6ff; and by a number of small touches such as the whole people's cry, 'His blood be on us, and on our children.' These have been shown by Trilling[43] and others to be of a piece with Matthew's theology, and to be Matthaean in language, and there is no need to repeat the evidence.

4.   Mark's account of the Resurrection is highly defective, and Matthew does his best to correct its weaknesses.

(*a*) Mark does not describe the event at all: the women arrive to a *fait accompli*. Matthew takes the two points of Mark's angel sitting (καθήμενον) and wearing white (λευκήν, Mark 16.5), and adds a great earthquake, as at the crucifixion (27.51) and the storm on the Lake (8.24): since the women found the stone rolled away (ἀνακεκύλισται ὁ λίθος) Matthew's angel rolls it away. His face is like lightning, following the angel's face at Dan. 10.6; his garment is white as snow, like the Ancient of Days in Dan. 7.9 (Theodotion καὶ τὸ ἔνδυμα αὐτοῦ ὥσει χιὼν λευκόν); his effect upon the guards is to turn them as to corpses from fear, like the angel in Dan. 10.7–9.

(*b*) Mark leaves the Church open to the now current Jewish slander (28.15b) that the disciples stole the Lord's body. Now we ought to beware of the suggestion that legends such as the guards' tale 'arose' in the Church to answer an apologetic need. We have found no other instance in Matthew where the evangelist has either invented or accepted legends without basis in tradition or scripture. If we cannot believe that the guards' story was current in early tradition, can we find scriptures which might have seemed prophetic to a Christian scribe? Truly we can: for we have just seen how Matthew draws on the Book of Daniel, and Mark before him draws on Josh. 10. Dan. 7, which Matthew has just quoted to describe the angel, and to which he will

---

[41] See the full discussion in Stendahl, *SSM*, pp. 120ff.
[42] cf. p. 236 above.   [43] *WI*, Pt. I.

return for Christ's authority, tells of the wearing out of the Son of Man before his exaltation to God's side; but the earlier parts of the book have given concrete instances of the saints of Israel travelling the same road. And in particular, most famously of all, Daniel himself had so suffered and gone his way to glory: condemned under malicious calumny against the King's will, and sent down to the lions of death, with a stone brought and laid against the mouth of the den. 'And the king sealed it (ἐσφραγίσατο, Dan. 6.17) with his own signet', and at break of day to his amazement received Daniel alive from the pit. The parallel is natural, and impressed the Fathers: it suggests to Matthew that the stone of Christ's tomb was sealed against Christian stealing of his body. But if this parallel is natural, how much more Josh. 10. The Book of Joshua was read in the ancient synagogue as a second lesson to Genesis:[44] 7—10 on the third sabbath in Nisan. In ch. 10 Jesus son of Nave captures the king of Jerusalem and other kings, and immures them in a cave: 'Roll great stones against the mouth of the cave, and set men by it to guard them.' Later he brings them alive out of the cave, 'and smote them and put them to death, and he hung them on five trees. And they hung upon the trees until evening; but at the time of the going down of the sun, Jesus commanded, and they took them down from the trees, and threw them into the cave where they had hidden themselves, and they set great stones against the mouth of the cave.' (Josh. 10.26f). This passage has had a profound effect upon the formation of the Marcan tradition. Matthew takes from it an additional detail, the guards. His story now tells itself, and in Matthaean form. συνάγω (2), the last shall be worse than the first, κελεύω, τάφος (2), κλέπτω (2), seven nominative aorist participles, ἰδού followed by gen. abs. part., take counsel, ἀργύρια, ὁ ἡγέμων, are all Matthaean. Semi-Matthaean are: pleonastic ἐκεῖνος, πλαν– (2), ἔσται, ἐγείρομαι, οὖν, prep. ἕως, νυκτός, πορεύομαι, μέχρι τῆς σήμερον (11.23). Only here in Matthew are ἐπαύριον, κουστωδία.

(c) The weak Marcan ending, with the women terrified and silent, demands amendment. Matthew retains their φόβος, but interprets their ecstasy and trembling into great joy (cf. 2.10). Mark, it is true, reads that they said nothing to anyone, but this cannot be so, for the angel had bid them tell the disciples and Peter, and this they surely will have done: 'nothing to anyone' else. Matthew leaves out Mark's 'and Peter': whether because he is included in the disciples, or because Peter was the first of all to see the Lord, and would not need telling. Matthew knew from Pauline tradition that the Lord had appeared to a number of Christians on Easter Day, and he wishes to indicate this as an important part of the primitive tradition, as well as finishing

[44] See pp. 215–17, 222 above.

with the promised Galilean appearance. He can hardly describe the appearance to Peter, of which tradition tells him nothing, so he contents himself with an innocuous account of an appearance to the women. Jesus says 'Hail', as the Matthaean Judas did at 26.49; they worship him (Matthaean), grasping his feet like the traditional suppliant (cf. 2 Kings 4.27): for the rest Jesus repeats the angel's words almost verbatim, except that the Lord summons the whole Christian community ('my brethren'), not just the Twelve.

(*d*) Mark implies a Galilean appearance, which Matthew supplies, and makes the climax of his book. Paul had told of a mass gathering of some 500 Christians who saw the Lord, and this gives him licence for his final scene. The Eleven go to Mark's Galilee, to the place where Jesus had appointed—a mountain is so natural to Matthew as the locus of revelation that he slips it in. They believe and worship at his appearing, while others doubt, and give the opportunity for his final words of authority and command. Matthew begins with the exalted Son of Man of Dan. 7.14 to whom authority was given (ἐδόθη αὐτῷ ἐξουσία, LXX), as God had authority over all in heaven and on the earth (πάντων τῶν ἐν τῷ οὐρανῷ καὶ ἐπὶ τῆς γῆς, Dan. 4.17, LXX). The preaching of the gospel to the world was likewise implied in Mark (13.10/Matt. 24.14) and is a Matthaean concern: it is expressed in Matthew's own wording—πορεύομαι, a nominative aorist part., οὖν, μαθητεύω, are all typical Matthaean language, as are τηρῶ, πάντα ὅσα, prep. ἕως, and 'the close of the age', likewise from 24. (3). There is no justification for omitting the baptismal formula, which is in all the Greek Mss., the *Didache* and Justin, beside 1 Pet. 1.2. This is Easter Day, and the catechumens are waiting to be baptized: what could be more suitable than that the authority of the risen Jesus should be cited for the occasion? It agrees well with Matthew's ecclesiastical concern, and his habit of justifying established church procedure with a word of the Lord. Matthew completes his book with an *inclusio*. He has brought the Son of Man to his exaltation; the authority the devil tempted him with in 4 is now given him by God; the disciples he then first gathered by the mountain are to be extended to all nations; the baptism promised by John in 3 is to be administered in the threefold name; Jesus' commands, given from 5 on, are to be taught to the world; and his presence, promised in 1, Emmanuel, God-with-us, is to be with his Church for ever.

NOTE ON PROFESSOR N. A. DAHL'S
Die Passionsgeschichte bei Matthäus

Perhaps the most influential writing on the Passion story in Matthew in recent years is the article by Professor Dahl with the above title in *NTS* 2.1 (September 1955): and deservedly so, for it is a compound of minute accuracy and balanced judgement. I am in agreement with much of the article, and am indebted to it, but I would dissent from that portion in which Dahl deals with the non-Marcan traditions behind Matthew. Dahl maintains five positions in this respect: (*a*) Matthaean dependence on Mark; (*b*) an oral tradition behind the Matthaean special matter, at least in 27.3ff; (*c*) an oral development of Mark which accounts for the thirty-seven minor details which Matthew and Luke have in common against him; (*d*) a common pre-Matthaean, pre-Johannine source for the considerable elements which Matthew and John have in common; and (*e*) probable historical accuracy, against Mark, in the names Caiaphas and Jesus Barabbas, in the red cloak at the mocking, and in Eli, Eli.

Point (*a*) is common ground, and so in part is point (*e*)—Caiaphas at least is tradition. For (*b*) Dahl bases his belief in 'eine lange Geschichte hinter' 27.3–10 in part on the development of different texts of Zech. 11 alleged by Kilpatrick and Stendahl, and in part on the aetiology of Akeldamach, which 'muss auf jerusalemische Lokalüberlieferung zurückgehen'. We have seen that it is possible to understand the story of Judas' death without recourse to a development in the use of Zech. 11 over time; and Akeldamach requires no more local knowledge than would be acquired by any pilgrim to Jerusalem, such as Matthew must have been in earlier years.

But the serious matter is point (*c*). Dahl rejects Lucan knowledge of Matthew because all agreement stops at the point where Mark ends, and Luke has none of Matthew's non-Marcan material. This, however, is simply accounted for: Luke takes long sections of Mark and follows them consecutively, in 4.31—6.19, in 8.4—9.50, and in 18.15—24.12—in the former two sections there is no Matthaean material introduced, in the last there is very little. Luke follows one source at a time, and (as Dahl says) the Matthaean insertions are historically unconvincing and full of Matthaean theological tendency. We should therefore hardly expect him to introduce considerable Matthaean units.

Dahl explains the minor agreements of Matthew and Luke against Mark as oral developments of Mark which reached the later evangelists independently: i.e. a form of the Deutero–Marcus hypothesis, only a more problematic one, since we have to suppose Matthew and

Luke as both following the written Mark and adjusting it to the oral Deutero–Marcus. Now the problem with Deutero–Marcus is that his changes are so often in line with Matthew's vocabulary and thought. Among the thirty-seven points credited to the reviser of Mark by Dahl are the following expressions, all characteristic of Matthew: ἀπ'ἄρτι, πρὸς τοὺς μαθητάς, γενηθήτω τὸ θέλημά σου, gen. abs. + ἰδού, ἐκάθητο (5/2/2), ὁ υἱὸς τοῦ Θεοῦ (8/4/6), ἄλλος, λέγοντες, ἐξέρχεσθαι ἔξω (3/1/1), officers τοῦ λαοῦ, ἔφη, οὗτός ἐστιν ὁ, εἰ . . . εἰ (5/0/5 (4 Q)), ἑκατόνταρχος, προσελθών, ἀπαγγέλλω. In some of these Luke has a *Lucan* expression in place of the Matthaean one—ἕτερος for ἄλλος, ἀπὸ τοῦ νῦν for ἀπ'ἄρτι both times: in others (θέλημα, ἐκάθητο, ἐξέρχεσθαι ἔξω, gen. abs. + ἰδού) he takes over a definitely *non-Lucan* expression. These points amount to nearly half of the thirty-seven details isolated by Dahl! The simple solution seems to be, Deutero–Marcus = Matthew.

For (*d*), John writes so much more freely than the Synoptics that this kind of detailed criticism is more difficult: and since the sources of John are a large question, suffice it to say that there is no reason why John should not have had the common matter, directly or indirectly, from Matthew rather than a pre-Matthaean source.

21

LUKE'S USE OF MARK AND MATTHEW

No solution to the problem of Matthew can be proposed without involving the whole problem of Luke. If Matthew had Q, then Luke had Q: if we foreswear Q and do not explain Matthew by reference to Luke, then we must maintain that Luke knew Matthew, and explain the whole Third Gospel in the light of such knowledge. This is the solution which I am adopting, that Matthew knew Mark, and that Luke knew Mark and Matthew, and it has the great virtue of simplicity. But it has also many notorious difficulties, for, as Streeter wrote long since, '(i) Sometimes it is Matthew, sometimes it is Luke who gives a saying in what is clearly the more original form; (ii) subsequent to the Temptation story, there is not a single case in which Matthew and Luke agree in inserting the same saying at the same point in the Marcan outline . . . A theory which would make an author capable of [so destroying the appropriate Matthaean contexts] would only be tenable if, on other grounds, we had reason to believe he was a crank'.[1] Streeter's first point I have contested seriatim in the last ten chapters: I have given reasons for thinking that at all points the Lucan form is secondary, carrying over Matthaean expressions and theology, and adapting them with Lucan expressions and theology. Streeter, like many exegetes since, settled the question of originality on criteria such as Matthew's church interest and Luke's 'primitive' message, which we have seen to be oversimplifications; nor could it have occurred to him in 1924 that the obviously Matthaean nature of much of Matthew was due to midrashic development by the evangelist. But the problem of Luke's rearrangements we have not considered, and it is to the general structure of the Lucan Gospel that I now turn. If Luke knew Matthew, we must ask (a) why did he select the Q material out of Matthew, (b) on what principle did he order his Gospel, and (c) why did he omit, or substitute for, much of M material such as the Infancy narratives, or the M parables?

To answer these questions I shall assume the following,[2] from the stock of current hypotheses on Luke:

(a) Luke was the companion of Paul and author of Acts.
(b) He wrote the Gospel soon after A.D. 85. As he joined Paul at

[1] FG, p. 183.
[2] I assume them because I think they are true, and I cannot argue the case here. A much later date, and the separation of the evangelist from Paul's companion, do not greatly affect the argument following.

Troas in A.D. 50 as a qualified man, he is likely to have been born in the early 20s, and to have been writing the Gospel in his middle 60s. A later date makes him improbably old; an earlier date does not allow time for the circulation of Matthew and his preaching by Luke. Further, Luke shows evidence of the break with Judaism which took place with the institution of the Birkath-ha-Minim, usually dated about A.D. 85.

(c) Luke was an ἐπίσκοπος of the church at Philippi, or another of the major Greek churches.

If we make these assumptions, then how should we expect Luke to have reacted to the Gospels of Mark and Matthew? Mark he has known and used in church for a dozen years. It is a document of the very highest authority. It comes (so we may believe) from Rome, where Peter and Paul gave their lives for the faith. It carries (if Papias' account is either true or current) the preaching message of Peter. Its simple and detailed narrative is self-authenticating. On any question of comparison in Luke's eyes, Mark is bound to hold priority. On the other hand Matthew had attempted to rewrite Mark because liturgically Mark was unsatisfactory. The readings he provided were for only the half-year from New Year to Passover: and of what use is a six and a half month lectionary book? Luke's church needed what Matthew professed to supply, serial readings for the entire year. Furthermore, Matthew is a highly attractive work of art. It contains many epigrammatic sayings which are immediately memorable, and invaluable preaching material. If Mark has priority, it is plain that Matthew, once known, cannot be neglected.[3]

Matthew, however, must seem to a Greek Christian preacher an ambivalent work. It is so Jewish. It is the readings for a *Jewish–* Christian church, with a twenty-four hour Pentecost and eight-days Tabernacles and Hanukkah, with mourning on 9th Ab, and Purim the second week in Adar. But we cannot suppose that these feasts were celebrated like that in the Pauline churches. Paul wrote to the Galatians (4.10), 'You observe days', for example Ninth Ab, 'and months', i.e. New Moon, 'and seasons', like Tabernacles and Hanukkah, 'and years', i.e. the entire Jewish calendar. The Pauline Christian went to church on Saturday night, and he celebrated Passover and Pentecost, no doubt for a day apiece. We do not know that he celebrated Tabernacles and Atonement even, though as biblical feasts

---

[3] The minor agreements, as instanced in the note to ch. 20, would suggest that Luke used Mark till a copy of Matthew reached his church, and thereafter Matthew. The unsatisfactoriness of the latter would cause a return to Mark, now amplified by Luke from Matthew, and from his own 'treasure-chest': but reminiscences of Matthew would keep creeping into the Marcan stories.

they might die hard. He would hardly have put his heart into Ninth Ab and Purim. Matthew is therefore liturgically of no use to him. It is likely that the Pauline churches retained the traditional sabbath readings of Law and Prophets in some form, but it is these which are neglected by Matthew, except for his midrash on Genesis. Matthew provides a Festal cycle which the Greek church does not observe, and broadly neglects the sabbath cycle which they do.[4]

Furthermore Matthew is doctrinally a highly unsatisfactory book for a Philippian Christian. Paul had taught a radical attitude to the Law, and so had the Marcan Jesus: yet here is a constant reaction in favour of the Torah, written and oral, with authority for the rabbis in Jerusalem and a running battle with the Pharisaic scribes. All this Luke did not wish his church to absorb: and here precisely is the answer to our first question. The common feature of the Q material is, as Farrer said, its Luke-pleasingness.[5] The open sayings, the memorable epigrams, the striking similes: that is the Q material—in its full antithetical form in Matthew, abbreviated and Lucanized in Luke. The Jewish piety of prayer, fasting, and almsgiving, wise men and scribes, fringes and phylacteries: that is the M material, which Luke rejects along with many points of Jewish law and controversy—these matters did not concern the thriving churches of Greece. But between M and Q there is much material which, I should claim, Luke felt he could rewrite—the parables of the Talents and the Great Dinner, or of the Father and his Two Sons, or the whole Infancy complex. And this will account for the third of our questions. The Jewish and controversial material Luke omits as not edifying his church: the remainder of the M material he rewrites to make it more edifying. For the licence to midrash which we have given to Matthew we cannot deny to Luke altogether. He was not a scribe as Matthew was, but he had sat at the feet of Jewish preachers many a year: ten years at Paul's feet, perhaps as long before his conversion. Only occasionally does he attempt the epigrammatic midrash of which Matthew was the master; here he relays or amends the Gospel tradition. But Luke's gift is to be the Church's mythographer: he can turn Matthew's black-and-white allegories into living parables, and Matthew's fairy-story infancy legends into the homely and persuasive tale of Luke 1—2. The

[4] Luke believed that every jot of the OT would be fulfilled (16.16); he knew the Greek OT himself intimately; a knowledge of it, and the Church's appropriation of it (1 Cor. 10.1), is frequently assumed by Paul; its reading is familiar to Luke's readers as Jewish practice (4.16ff; 16.29ff; Acts 15.21); and was insisted upon in the Deutero–Pauline churches (1 Tim. 4.13); and was practised in Justin's church (I *Apol.* 67).

[5] 'On Dispensing with Q', in *Studies in the Gospels*, ed. D. E. Nineham (Oxford 1954), pp. 179–99.

omission of the 'M' material is not a problem: the irrelevant is omitted because it is irrelevant, the relevant is rewritten to make it more so.

This leaves us with the second and hardest of our questions, the ordering of the Marcan and Matthaean material in Luke. The picture which I have sketched of the Lucan church's reaction to the two earlier Gospels would lead us to expect any third Gospel to be written on two principles: (*a*) wherever possible Mark should have priority over Matthew; (*b*) readings should be provided, as in Matthew, for a Christian Year, but following the sabbath-cycle and not the festal cycle. The second principle seems the inescapable corollary of our conclusions on Matthew: if this is what a Gospel was in Matthew's case, surely Luke will be the same. It is in the light of this, I shall go on to suggest, that the riddle of Luke's order is to be resolved. But it is immediately clear that the first principle has been followed. There are three great blocks of Mark in Luke: from Mark 1.16, the call of Simon and the others, to Mark 3.19, the call of the Twelve; from Mark 3.35, Christ's real brethren, to 6.44, the Five Thousand, and 8.27, Peter's Confession, to 9.41, the Strange Exorcist, taken together; and Mark 10.13, the Children, to the end. Throughout these blocks Mark's order is followed with only trifling adjustments: only a few Marcan paragraphs, such as the cursing of the Fig-Tree, the call of Simon, or the Woman who Anointed Jesus, are seriously rewritten. The only places where Matthew is preferred to Mark are those, like the Baptist's Preaching, the Temptations, or the Beelzebul Controversy, where Matthew gives a much fuller account. There is the Long Omission of Mark 6.45 to 8.26, and one or two short omissions, on which I will reserve comment.

The key to the sub-division of Matthew into calendrical lections was the system of numbering in the A group of Mss., and I have suggested that the numbering of Mark in the same Mss. is suggestive of a similar conclusion. The existence of such systems is an invaluable independent check upon our theorizing, and it is proper for us to turn to them in attempting to reconstruct any lectionary basis for Luke. A gives Luke 83 κεφαλαῖα plus a proem,[6] a large number for a year: but then 68 κεφαλαῖα plus a proem seemed *prima facie* a lot for Matthew's year. Two facts make us wary of trusting the A divisions as completely as we did with Matthew.

---

[6] The Bodmer papyrus, p[75], has a system of divisions similar to Alexandrinus, and the breaks are on occasion more logical. But (*a*) the beginning and end of the Gospel is missing; (*b*) the κεφαλαῖα are marked by edentation without numbers, so that we cannot reconstruct the early divisions; (*c*) while the divisions seem trustworthy up to 9.50, there are a number of very short and illogical divisions (e.g. the Woes in 11) during the Journey. Nevertheless, the papyrus is second-century evidence for lectionary use of the Gospel.

1. There are a number of clearly irrational divisions. There is a one-verse lection, for example, 19.12, the Nobleman who went to a Far Country, divided from 19.13–28, the Pounds.

2. Judaizing Christians in the East, who still celebrated the full Jewish festal year in the time of John Chrysostom, would use Matthew and keep the Matthaean subdivisions marked in their Mss.: but if Luke was based on an annual sabbath-cycle in line with the serial reading of the Torah, what congregation would still be reading the Torah in series by even the second century in the Greek church, its Jewish roots now cut? Luke was in any case less widely used in church than Matthew, and we could not have the same confidence that the author's structure, noted in dispensable marginal numbers, would stand the same chance of surviving intact.

We shall therefore attend to the A divisions, but warily. Happily Luke is given to writing something in the nature of rubrics in his text, which provide a reliable check both on A and on the critic's imagination.

Luke's exordium sets the book in the milieu of respectable Greek histories, with a flowery introduction and a dedication. They were read publicly at dinner-parties and occasions: Luke is to be read in church at the Lord's Supper, as the things which have come to fulfilment among us religiously. Mark, Matthew, no doubt others elsewhere, have put their hand to such a task: in Mark's case, drawing on apostolic eye-witness, in both as the last of a series of 'ministers of the word' expounding and developing the παράδοσις. But Luke has carefully been through this work in detail, and has decided to rewrite the Gospel-story καθεξῆς, that the aspiring Christian, whether a distinguished Beloved-of-God under a pseudonym, or no, may have certain knowledge of his faith. Now καθεξῆς cannot mean 'in chronological order'. I hope that no strictures of mine upon the extravagances of form-criticism will have caused any wavering of faith in the great demolition of the biographical view accomplished by Schmidt and Dibelius in 1919. Yet καθεξῆς means 'in order': why should it not mean 'in liturgical order'? There is in fact no satisfactory alternative interpretation.[7] Luke from his first paragraph authorizes the lectionary theory. The proem is couched in vague and high-sounding phrases; but the atmosphere of the book, especially of Luke 1—2, is not that of Polybius and Arrian, and ἀσφαλεία is to be had, as

---

[7] RSV's translation, 'orderly', is a counsel of despair: I do not know what evidence there is for such a rendering.

Justin said,[8] more from the word of God than from fallible human witnesses. Attempts to press the words into claims of chronological order end by making Luke a liar: all Luke is advertising is order and the genuine gospel, and these are goods which he can deliver.

As soon as Luke begins his tale we have a pastiche of the LXX, and above all the LXX of Genesis: the first story brings to fulfilment without question the story of Abraham and the birth of Isaac. Abraham and Sarah were well advanced in days and had no child because Sarah was barren; and so are Zechariah and Elizabeth. An angel visits Abraham and promises him the birth of a son: first the patriarch asks, 'How shall I know?', later he disbelieves: the angel's words are, 'Sarah your wife shall conceive and bear you a son, and you shall call his name Isaac', and he reassures him, 'No word shall be impossible with God.' An angel announces John's birth to Zechariah, 'Your wife Elizabeth will bear you a son, and you shall call his name John'; he asks, 'How shall I know this?', and is punished for his disbelief; and it is said of Elizabeth's pregnancy, 'No word shall be impossible with God.' Other OT texts are woven in midrashically —Malachi, Zechariah, Daniel, Chronicles, Samson: but the Torah text of the first story in Luke (1.1–25) is Abraham and Isaac. Now nothing could be more encouraging to the liturgical hypothesis which we are testing than this. Luke begins where Matthew begins. The subject is different, John's conception instead of Jesus', but the OT passage on which the story is based is the same. In the synagogue the Abraham–Isaac cycle was read on the three sabbaths after Passover. Matthew began with Abraham–Isaac on the fifth sabbath of the year, after the Easter Octave, and it looks as if Luke were doing the same.

Lection 5 of the Jewish annual cycle closed with Abraham's death (Gen. 25.18).[9] Lection 6 told of the story of Isaac's twins. Now there is one quite striking parallel with the following story in Luke, in that the babes leaped in Rebecca's womb in foreshadowing of their future, and the babe leaps in Elizabeth's womb in salutation to his embryo Lord. Rebecca's marvellous conception is thus seen as a second type of the divine conceiving of Christ, and the Sarah/Rebecca parallel suggests an opening diptych: Lections 3–5 the annunciation of Isaac, Lection 6 the annunciation of Jacob; Luke 1.5–25 the annunciation of John, Luke 1.26–56, the annunciation of Jesus. This is re-emphasized in the Magnificat: God has helped his servant Israel, as he spoke to our fathers, Abraham and on. Luke draws in the oracles of mothers likewise blessed in scripture: Hannah with her Song, and Leah from

---

[8] I *Apol.* 30.
[9] I have set out the *sidrôt* in parallel with the Lucan κεφαλαῖα in an appendix to the chapter.

the next section of Genesis. At the birth of Jacob's first child Leah named the boy Reuben, 'For the Lord has looked on my ταπείνωσις': at the birth of her last, she named him Asher, 'For henceforth all women shall call me happy.' Mary opens her Song as Hannah does, but turns at once to the Reuben and Asher oracles, 'He has looked upon the lowliness of his handmaid: for behold from henceforth all generations shall call me happy' (AT). The theme of God's mercy promised to our forefathers is further celebrated in Zechariah's canticle, 'Blessed be the Lord God of Israel', of which the greater part is given to the fulfilment of the patriarchal covenant: the deliverance from enemies, and the rejoicing over the birth of the boy John and his naming, are all themes well adapted to stand opposite Lection 7, which described Jacob's double escape from Esau, and from Laban, and the birth and naming of his sons.

The Matthaean tradition told Luke that Jesus, fulfilling scripture, had been born at Bethlehem. Now the last son of Israel of old had also been born at Bethlehem in Gen. 35, in Lection 8, when Jacob came to the Tower of Flocks driving his herds before him. Jacob had come from Penuel, at the beginning of the *sidrāh*, where he had seen the face of God and lived. So now Jesus' birth at Bethlehem is hailed by shepherds, and by Symeon and Anna the daughter of Penuel: Symeon's eyes have seen God's salvation, now prepared before the face of all people. Lection 9 told of the dreams of Joseph's greatness, and how Jacob kept these things and pondered them in his heart; the boy's loss nearly sends his father sorrowing to the grave, but he is safe in Egypt. The story of Jesus aged twelve foreshadows his future: his questioning with the doctors in the Temple and recovery after three days. His parents seek him sorrowing, and Mary 'kept all these sayings in her heart'.

We have thus a continuous thread, sometimes impressive, at times slight, of fulfilments of the Genesis story week by week in Luke. The division into five is guaranteed both by the subject matter and by the Lucan rubrics. We have the two annunciations, the two birth-and-presentation stories, and Jesus aged twelve. The first story ends with Elizabeth hiding five months, and her brief oracle (1.25). The second starts, 'In the sixth month . . .', and ends with Mary's oracle and her three-months visit and return home. The third ends with Zechariah's oracle, and 'And the child grew . . .'. The fourth ends with Symeon's oracle, the family's return home, and 'And the child grew . . .'. The fifth ends with the family's return home, and 'And Jesus increased . . .'. We have thus a double internal check against A, which likewise gives five units to the two chapters, but ascribes the whole of Luke 1 to the Proem. The remarkable thing is that each of the five sections thus marked out by Luke contains both general and detailed verbal correspondences with the five Lections 5–9 taken one by one. There is thus ample grounds for continuing to examine the lectionary hypothesis.

What more general view is implied then by such a construction? Luke knew Matt. 1—2, we are supposing, and knew it to be midrash. The basic texts which Matthew used, Luke uses also: Gen. 17, the annunciation and marvellous birth of Isaac; Isa. 7, the virginal conception; Mic. 5, Christ's birth at Bethlehem; Mal. 3, John the forerunner; Judg. 13, he shall be a Nazir. To these Luke adds from his own rich knowledge of the LXX: Zechariah with Malachi, Hannah and Samuel with Manoah and Samson, Daniel's angel Gabriel and his dumbfounding, Isa. 8, the writing of the child's name on the tablet, Isa. 9 the son of David, and much else. The need for a new story is not due to Luke's following the weekly cycle, because we have seen that in Matt. 1—2 Matthew was doing the same. It is that Matthew's midrash is seen by Luke as only one attempt to draw history from scripture. It suffers from a certain fairy-tale atmosphere—magi and the royal slaughter of infants, dreams and the constant appearance of an angel *ex machina*: Luke's manner throughout his Gospel is more domestic, and nothing could be more homely than his picture of family devotion in 1—2. It is also true that Matthew's story drifts away from Genesis quite soon, and takes Joseph too quickly. The language of the chapters is Lucan and the theology is his with its blessing of the poor and overthrow of the rich, its doctrine of the Holy Spirit and prophecy, its view of Elijah, etc. Luke has simply written another and highly characteristic midrash of his own: and who will say that he has not written a better one?

Luke now turns to the Baptist's ministry, and naturally prefers the fuller Matthaean account of his preaching, to which he adds. The crowd with their pretensions to being the children of Abraham, and their need to repent, might serve as an antitype to Joseph's brothers in Gen. 41—44; but the real parallel is with Pentecost. Pentecost falls in the tenth week of the year, and to the author of Acts is the feast of the Holy Spirit. The Gospel of the preaching of John foretells this very event: 'I baptize you with water . . . he will baptize you with the Holy Spirit and with fire.' Matthew had written of the fire as of judgement: to Luke the fire is rather the tongued flame of inspiration. At 3.10 the crowds ask John, 'What then shall we do?'; at Acts 2.37 the crowd ask Peter and the Twelve, 'Brethren, what shall we do?' Luke has deliberately set John's preaching of the baptism with the Spirit for a Greek church's Pentecost, and written it up accordingly. Matthew's new Torah is by-passed: the Spirit, not the Law, is the Pentecostal gift of the new dispensation, and the Greek church has no need of special Jewish Pentecost readings from Exodus, or twenty-four-hour feasts. The Pharisaic Shabu'oth on the fifty-first day after Passover becomes the Greek Pentecost, the seventh Sunday after Easter.

It was normal to finish reading Genesis in eleven weeks:[10] the concluding chapters describe the settlement of the sons of Jacob in Egypt. They and their children are named in a Genealogy in Gen. 46, and blessings are pronounced upon them, and especially upon the sons of Joseph, Ephraim and Manasseh. It is to the story of Jesus' baptism that Luke glosses his Genealogy: Jesus is God's Son through the line, as was supposed, of Joseph, and in the next chapter the Lucan crowd, amending the previous tradition, ask, 'Is not this Joseph's son?' The long list of names is clearly composed in part from the list of patriarchs: Jesus is descended, at some distance, from Levi the son of Simeon the son of Judah the son of Joseph; there are three Josephs and a Josech, two Levis, two Judahs and a Joda, a Simeon and a Semein. A gives two units to Luke 3, the Preaching of John and the Baptism-and-Genealogy, but divides after 3.9: our division after 3.20 is more logical in giving the whole of John's Preaching to the former lection, and stopping at the natural break. It also enables the Pentecostal lesson to be read on the correct day, and thus provides a proper reading for each Sunday for the whole Genesis section.

Lection 7 in A is given as Luke 4.1–30, both the Matthaean Temptation story and the Rejection at Nazareth, and the similarity of the themes makes this possible as Luke's intention. Very likely they could be divided in those years when Genesis was read in twelve weeks. It was inevitable that Luke should prefer the full Matthaean Temptations to the brief Marcan note: the puzzle to commentators has been the reversing of Matthew's second and third Temptations, and the promotion of the Rejection to such an early place in the Gospel. Now our liturgical hypothesis would suggest that Luke has in mind here the opening *pārāshāh* of Exodus, Exod. 1—5. In Stephen's speech in Acts 7 we have an insight into Luke's reading of the passage, and into its importance for him, for he devotes nineteen verses to it (7.17–35). Moses, mighty in words and deeds, defended an oppressed Israelite, supposing that his brethren understood that God was giving them deliverance by his hand; but they did not understand, they thrust him aside, they refused him. He spent forty years in Midian and was sent

---

[10] There are 54 *sidrôt* to be covered in 50/51 sabbaths in a normal year. But Lev. 16—18, the Atonement *sidrāh*, is no. 29, and the 186 days before Atonement include either 26 or 27 sabbaths. Therefore one or two sabbaths in the first half of the year will have had two *sidrôt* read together: the end of Genesis, or the end of Exodus, to judge by traditional synagogue practice, or both.

by God in the wilderness to deliver the people; but the fathers continually refused to obey him, and resisted the Holy Spirit. The Matthaean Temptation story turns upon the forty years that Israel wandered in the desert: Luke's narrative brings him to the same point at an earlier forty years in Moses' life, when he was tested alone. He went to Midian unprovided, and Jethro said, 'Call him that he may eat bread' (Exod. 2.20); he went to Horeb the mount of God, and was told, 'When you have brought the people out of Egypt you shall serve God upon this mountain' (Exod. 3.12). It would seem proper, therefore, against this background, to retain the bread temptation in the first place, but to promote the worship of God alone on the mountain to the second. Moses was present later in life when the people tempted God, and he called the Rock of Horeb πειρασμός, so that may well stand last. The Rejection theme is provided by the transfer, and elaboration, of Mark 6.1–6. Christ, full of the Spirit, in the power of the Spirit, proclaims his inspiration in a full citation of Isa. 61: since Isaiah is itself a prophecy of the new Exodus, the words are well suited to a new Moses, 'He has sent me to proclaim release to the captives . . . to set at liberty those who are oppressed, to proclaim the acceptable year of the Lord.' Elijah at Zarephath, Elisha with Naaman, are only prophetic examples of those in whom the people have resisted the Holy Spirit from the days of Moses on. Temptation and Rejection of God's anointed have been the pattern since the Exodus began.

From Exod. 6 begins the record of God's mighty works, to which Christ's great acts of healing might well be seen as fulfilments. Now after Jesus' baptism and temptations he had performed a series of healings in Mark, and since Mark is Luke's preferred authority, it is natural for him to leave Matthew at this point; and having turned, to follow Mark consistently. A gives nine Marcan lections in a row, and nine *sidrôth* would bring us to the end of Exodus in years when Exodus was read in ten weeks. The A divisions are all natural breaks, except that the Ears of Corn is taken with the Call of Levi and the Eating and Fasting controversies. As an eating controversy itself, it belongs: if Exodus were read in the full eleven weeks, it could be taken separately. The sections are in the Marcan order, except that the call of the first apostles is described in an expanded form as Lection 11, being delayed by three units. There is a ready explanation for this. In Exod. 6—9 Moses does wonders, as it is said, 'by the finger of God' (Exod. 8.19). Luke records (11.20) Jesus as saying, 'But if it is by the finger of God that I cast out demons . . .': so it is apt for Luke's wonders to begin at Lection 8 with the casting out of the demon in the synagogue, the first Marcan miracle. On the other hand Matthew had recorded the Call of the Four as an antitype to the call by Moses of the

Seventy, and Luke follows him in setting the call of Peter, James, and John against Exod. 18, when this incident occurred (*Sidrāh* 17). For the rest Mark is followed in order. It is true that this means in part neglecting Exodus as a source of inspiration; but no servant can serve two masters. Nor is Exodus forgotten. Christ goes up the mountain to pray alone as Moses went up Sinai alone in Exod. 24. The call of Levi recalls to the Christian preacher Moses' call of the Levites in Exod. 32, and the law of the Shewbread Table is in Exod. 25. There is the supersession of sabbath law, and the last pericope tells of Christ's all-night prayer on the mountain and choice of his Twelve Apostles, as Moses prayed on the mountain and came down to ordain Aaron and the old priesthood.

Leviticus presents some problems to the Christian expositor, and Luke is not the last preacher to survey the sacrificial laws and then turn elsewhere for inspiration. It was read in the old synagogue in the months of Elul and Tishri, with ch. 16ff falling on Atonement, and 21—24 on Tabernacles;[11] and with New Year besides much of the time was given to Festal themes. The great text to Christians was 19.18, the second of Jesus' great commandments, and this had been developed in Matthew's Sermon on the Mount at the end of 5: 'You have heard that it was said, You shall love your neighbour . . . But I say to you, Love your enemies . . .'. Matthew had glossed the Tenth Commandment, not to covet our neighbour's goods, with Leviticus,[12] and it is to this that Luke now turns. His Sermon on the Plain is a gutting of Matthew's great edifice. He does not want an antithesis to the Exodus law-giving, so all the 'You have heard . . . but I say . . .' element goes. All he wants basically is the 'Love your enemies' section with which the Lord has transcended Leviticus, and it is this which forms the backbone of his Sermon. He prefaces it with a cut-down version of Matthew's Beatitudes culminating in 'when men hate you', as an introduction to 'Love your enemies, do good to those who hate you'. He sites the Sermon at the foot of the mountain, where Moses had delivered the Levitical laws. He adds such further texts from Matthew's Sermon as may fit the same theme: the 'eye for an eye' section, as being mercy to our enemies; the opening verses of Matt. 7 as not judging or reproaching our enemies. Much of the wording too is styled by Lev. 19. His 'Be merciful even as your Father is merciful' recalls Lev. 19.1, 'You shall be holy, for I the Lord your God am holy'. His 'To him who strikes you on the cheek . . .' recalls Lev. 19.18, 'Your hand shall not avenge you'. His 'Figs are not picked from thorns nor are grapes gathered from bramble' uses the two verbs

---

[11] See p. 223 above.   [12] cf. p. 271 above.

συλλέγω and τρυγάω in the law of the vineyard in Lev. 19.10. Lection 17, Luke's Sermon, is thus the 'Love your enemies' section of Matt. 5, with other allied texts, seen in the light of Lev. 19.

The same chapter closes with the warning, 'If there should come to you a προσήλυτος . . . he shall be among you as the native, and you shall love him as yourself' (19.33f). Matthew's Sermon had been followed shortly by the healing of the centurion's παῖ ς, and Luke takes this over (v. 18) as an instance in life of loving the Gentile as yourself: he elaborates Matthew's Gentile into an ideal proselyte, one who has built a synagogue, with details from Cornelius, the proselyte centurion of Acts. Leviticus is much concerned with the perils of uncleanness, and in ch. 22 is given the repeated prohibition of touching the dead. Luke gives as his third Levitical pericope (19) the story of Jesus touching the dead youth at Nain, and restoring him to life as did Elijah of old.

The Festal Season now begins. New Year falls in the week following the twenty-fifth Sunday of the year, i.e. Lection 20. Mark had written his Gospel (I have suggested) as a series of readings starting at New Year with the Mission of John Baptist, preaching the New Year themes of repentance and the advent of God's Kingdom. This Luke cannot give, because he has already described the Baptist's mission in ch. 3; but what he can give, and does, is the expanded Matthaean version from Matt. 11, Matthew's New Year reading, citing the Malachi prophecy that goes back to Mark 1.2, and exposing the failure of 'this generation' to repent, though the people and the tax-collectors do; the mighty works of Jesus are the guarantee that God's kingdom has indeed begun, and the reference to Isa. 35, the New Year *haphtārāh*, carries the same point. The following Sunday precedes the Atonement, and provides an interesting insight into the fade-out of the Jewish Calendar in the Greek church. There is no longer a week-day celebration with a special Lection, and parallels with Jonah are therefore beside the point: but the theme of forgiveness is a Christian theme, and needs full exposition. Luke transfers the story of the woman who anointed Jesus at Simon the leper's dinner from Mark 14, and gives (21) a full version with all the emphasis on the forgiveness of sins in relation to love and faith. Lection 22 brings us to Tabernacles: the Harvest Festival with the traditional Christian harvest lesson from Mark and Matthew, the Parable of the Sower and its Interpretation, and the sayings affixed in Mark. It is the correct landfall of the Sower on Tabernacles which assures us both that the A numbering is significant, and that the liturgical hypothesis is well-grounded. The provision of suitable lessons for New Year and Atonement is impressive, of the proper lesson for Tabernacles is decisive. Once again we observe the moribundity of the Jewish Year: Mark's and Matthew's eight-day celebrations are done with; Harvest Festival Sunday is of universal significance, and survives alone.

From the Sower on, Luke is back with Mark, and he follows Mark in order for ten lections. There are some changes which the liturgy would require, but the general faithfulness to Mark is obvious. The changes are:

1. The Mother and Brothers pericope is appended to the Sower, whereas it precedes it in Mark. Luke has amended Jesus' words to 'My mother and brothers are those who hear the word of God and do it', which fits the 'hear and bear fruit' theme of the parable. It so happens that the Mother and Brothers pericope was a detachable unit in Matthew, which could be used as an independent Gospel if required by the vagaries of the calendar. In a year such as I have dated, with the first Sunday on 2nd Iyyar,[13] Tabernacles falls within the Sower week: in other years, when the first Sunday fell earlier, the pericope could be detached and read earlier, in the Marcan order, so as to leave the Sower on the Sunday before 15th Tishri.

2. Mark celebrated an eight-day Hanukkah with the Transfiguration on the sixth day, the Demoniac Boy on the seventh and the remainder of Mark 9 on the final day. Now not only is Hanukkah of no concern to the Greek church as an eight-day festival: it is not even a biblical feast, and is therefore of no concern at all. Luke is left then with an *embarras de richesse* in the form of seven surplus lections, the whole Marcan provision for Hanukkah, and it is this that lies behind the celebrated Long Omission. He records the great works of Mark 4.35 —5 with fidelity, one per week. He omits the Nazareth scene which he has already described in 4, and the Baptist's death, which is inessential, and all the incidents between the Five Thousand and Peter's Confession, and is left with exactly the correct number of lections to carry him through to Hanukkah. It is often commented that the Omission is skilfully done: several of the incidents left out are 'doublets' of ones left in. Luke does not, however, forget the material which his shorter calendar compelled him to put by: parts of it are taken over and expanded where they are needed, in the scantily provided period after the Resurrection.

Luke is following Mark over the same period of the year, between Tabernacles and Hanukkah, when the Book of Numbers was read; and he is naturally able to take advantage of the fulfilments of Numbers which lay behind this section of Mark. The healing of the woman

[13] cf. p. 189 above.

with flux would be read alongside Num. 5, where those with sexual flux or contact with the dead were ordered out of the camp. Uncleanness through touching the dead is again treated in Num. 9, where the reading would coincide with Jairus' daughter. The Sending of the Twelve on Mission would be read the same week as Moses' sending of the Twelve Spies in Num. 13. The Feeding of the Multitude takes up Moses' Feeding of the Multitude the previous week in Num. 11. The stern sayings that whoever would save his life shall lose it well fulfil the stories around Num. 20 of the death of the old generation who tried to save their lives by refusing to enter the land: only Caleb and Jesus son of Nave were willing to lose their lives in obedience, and only they survived the desert. The descent of the glory-cloud to cover the σκήνη is recorded in Num. 9.15—10.11: Luke changes Mark's now meaningless 'After six days . . .' to 'About eight days after . . .', i.e. the week later. The refusal of Jesus to forbid the exorcist follows the refusal of Moses to forbid the uncovenanted prophesying of Eldad and Medad. The last two passages belong with the Hannukah lesson, Num. 7—11, in Mark, and are really too late in the Lucan story, but they retain the Numbers atmosphere. All told, we cannot help feeling, Luke has provided a very workmanlike Numerical section. More than half the pericopae can draw on Numbers fulfilments from their own *sidrāh* or near; Hanukkah is dispensed with, and no important section of Mark is lost for good.

Hitherto Luke has covered four books of Torah, and he has drawn twice apiece on his two source-documents. In rough terms, he has rewritten Matt. 1—3 for his Genesis, he has transcribed Mark 1.16—3.19 for his Exodus; he has quarried Matthew for his Leviticus, and transcribed Mark 4—9, with some considerable omissions, for Tabernacles and Numbers. Hitherto we have found that the Ms. divisions in the A group have been a reliable guide, apart from the opening units. They have corresponded with common sense, and have provided us with impressive landfalls for eight months of the year. It is clear, however, that a difficulty now faces us, for there is a major imbalance in what remains. We have covered eight months in nine chapters: fifteen chapters remain for the last four. We might expect, on analogy with Mark and Matthew, that the Apocalyptic Discourse in Luke 21 and the Passion story in Luke 22—24 would account for Holy Week, but even so eleven chapters remain for the three months in which the Book of Deuteronomy was read. Up to now we have covered the Proem and 32 lections in A; there are 42 more units to the end of Luke 20, and 9 for Holy Week.

The correspondence of the Lucan Journey with the Book of Deuteronomy was expounded in a brilliant article by Professor C. F.

Evans in the essays in memory of R. H. Lightfoot in 1954.[14] Two criticisms might be made of Evans' article: (a) perhaps for the sake of completeness he includes a number of parallels that are verbal rather than substantial; and (b) he suggests no motive for such an apparently quixotic procedure. The motive we are in a position to supply: Luke was providing a year's readings for a Greek church which was loosening its Jewish roots but retaining its Jewish Bible. The verbal parallels we are in a position to neglect. But Evans' perspicacity was remarkable, and for details which I have no leisure for now I must refer the reader to him.

But what are we to make of the imbalance? I can only hazard a conjecture. Baptism in the Church was from the first century at Easter. In later centuries the habit was evolved of a forty-day period of instruction before Easter. The first surviving instance we possess of such an instruction is the Catecheses of St Cyril of Jerusalem, given in A.D. 348, of which eighteen were delivered in the six weeks before Easter. Now the habit of giving an annual short course of instruction before Baptism/Confirmation is one which has endured to the present day, and it is very hard to see how any church baptizing or confirming adults can dispense with it. It is only that the ancient Church gave its course of catechesis at the rate of three lectures per week where we are content with one. Nor is the pattern of thrice-weekly instruction for the devout a Christian invention: pious Jews went to synagogue three times a week, Saturday evening, Monday, and Thursday, to hear the *sidrāh* of the coming sabbath read in shorter sections. Now Cyril treats of such subjects as Faith and Repentance, which are the themes of sections of the Lucan Journey, before turning to the Creed; and Deuteronomy, with its strong paraenetic note, would be the ideal basis for a Christian catechesis on the Way. Catechumens would need to be registered by the end of the civil year, and by Easter they would have a competent knowledge of Christian morals and of the Passion story. They would hear in three short week-day sections what the whole church would have as its Gospel the next Sunday. The full narrative of the Eucharist, and of the Lord's death and resurrection, would be reserved till Passover night. Indeed, Luke himself seems to encourage us to think that this is so: for does he not promise Theophilus after Easter that he will now know the full truth of the things in which he has been *catechized?*

There is a fine brash hypothesis, as Professor A. N. Flew would say: all that remains is to test it. Deuteronomy consists of eleven *pārāshiyyôt*, of which the last four are short, for telescoping when the

---

[14] 'Deuteronomy and the Central Section of Luke', in *Studies in the Gospels*, ed. D. E. Nineham.

calendar requires; but as Luke's provisions for the other books have been on the short side, he will need the full eleven. We are to expect therefore a series of thirty-three pericopae, subdivided into eleven topics of instruction in such a way that each provides a fulfilment of the relevant *pārāshāh* of Deuteronomy. We are fortunate that frequently during the Journey Luke marks off one section from another by such a formula as, 'When the crowds were increasing he began to say . . .': whenever there is such a change of audience or of scene, we shall take it that a new pericope is being marked off by rubric by the evangelist. These rubrics do not coincide with the divisions in A, which appear often to be irrational. The first 32 divisions, which we have broadly followed, require some adjustment according to the vagaries of the calendar. If followed strictly, they would leave 18 further Sundays, of which 4 would fall in Nisan: 14 weeks with 3 lections apiece would require 42 lections, which is what A supplies.

Such an independent criterion would yield the following division:

Topic 1:
Discipleship is a hard life but blessed

Deut. 1—3.22 describes the hard life that the people had in the desert, and the blessings awaiting Jesus ben-Nave and the new generation going with him. (a) Luke 9.51–end. Jesus sets out on his journey, is repulsed, and warns three aspiring disciples; (b) Luke 10.1–16 Jesus sends out the Seventy before his face; (c) Luke 10.17–24. The Seventy return, and there is rejoicing. All three sections have strong Deuteronomic parallels, and the topic is ideal for beginning a course of catechesis.

Topic 2:
The Two Great Commandments

Deut. 3.23—7.11 recapitulates the Law given at Horeb, most famously the Shema'. (a) Luke 10.25–37. Moses warned (Deut. 6.16), 'You shall not tempt (ἐκπειράσεις) the Lord your God', but a lawyer does tempt (ἐκπειράζων) the Lord. To inherit the land (κληρονομήσῃς, Deut. 6.18, etc.), and to live (ζῶμεν, Deut. 6.24, etc.) were the rewards of keeping the Law. Jesus' reply is to cite the Shema' (Deut. 6.5). For the story as a whole, Luke has only to reproduce the account in Matt. 22, but the first three touches are his own; as is the Good Samaritan. (b) Luke 10.38–end. The Good Samaritan shows what it means to love our neighbour as ourselves: the scene at Mary and Martha's shows what it means to love the Lord with all our heart, soul, strength, and mind. Jesus is repeatedly called the Lord, and

Mary obeys the word, 'Draw near and hear all that the Lord our God shall say' (Deut. 5.27). (c) Luke 11.1–13. But the love of God is shown principally in prayer, and Luke goes to Matthew both for the Lord's Prayer and Ask, Seek, Knock. The first petition in the Lord's Prayer is for God's name to be hallowed, as in the Third Commandment (Deut. 5.11). The petition for daily bread is no longer for one day at a time, but regularly, as from the land which God undertakes to give (Deut. 6.3,10).

Topic 3:
Pharisaic Hypocrisy

Deut. 7.12—11.25 instils the warning, Do not repeat the disobedience of the wilderness, but Luke 11.14–end shows how they do it still. (a) Luke 11.14–28. The classic instance is Matthew's Beelzebul Controversy with the Return of the Spirit appended to it in Matt. 12. (b) Luke 11.29–36. The Matt. 12 passage continues with the Ninevites and the Queen of the South witnessing against this generation for their unrepentance, and the following verses adapted from Matt. 5f testify to their darkness. (c) Luke 11.37–end. Above all there are the Woes of Matt. 23, which Luke takes over as a climax to the theme, dividing the Woes into two halves as he does the Beatitudes. Deut. 11.26 sets out before Israel the blessing and the curse: the Woes are the curse.

Topic 4:
The Perils of Apostasy and Prosperity

Deut. 11.26—16.17 consists of various laws in which the themes of apostasy and prosperity recur. (a) Luke 12.1–12. Deut. 13 is a warning of apostasy, and this is taken up in the Matt. 10 exhortation not to deny Christ. (b) Luke 12.13–40 describes the dangers of money, and speaks of Christian detachment from riches. Deut. 12.20 warns, 'If the Lord your God shall enlarge your borders . . . and you say, I will eat meat, if your soul desires . . .', which is taken up in the Rich Fool. Deut. 15 is given to the duty of Alms as the following passage is to making purses that wax not old. (c) Luke 12.41—13.9. The slave-laws of Deut. 15 are then taken up with Matthew's faithful and wise slave, and Matthew's bridesmaids become slaves awaiting their master's return from the wedding, followed by some comments on the beating God's disobedient slaves may expect. Deut. 14.28 had promised Israel that they should eat all the tithes of their fruits after three years: but Jesus' experience of Israel had been as of an unfruitful fig-tree, and Luke turns Mark's (somewhat scandalous) miracle into a parable.

Topic 5:
The Rejection of Israel and Invitation to the Gentiles

Deut. 16.18—21.9 give the laws which Israel broke under Manasseh, and earned her rejection and exile. (*a*) Luke 13.10–21 gives another form of Matthew's Withered Hand, modified in the light of Deut. 15.12ff. The Israelite slave was to serve for six years only, and be released in the sabbath year: Satan has exacted three times his due from the daughter of Abraham, bending her double like the animals —shall she not be released on the sabbath day? 'So' (13.18) the kingdom will grow into a great tree full of Gentile birds: the Gentiles will share Israel's heritage. (*b*) Luke 13.22–end draws in the rejection verses from the Sermon on the Mount: the narrow gate suggests the shut door of the Bridesmaids and the rejection of the wicked in Matt. 25.41, whose weeping and wailing in turn recall the replacement of Israel by many from East and West in Matt. 8.11f, and the lament over Jerusalem in Matt. 23. (*c*) Luke 14.1–24 takes up the theme of humility from Deut. 17.12 (cf. Prov. 25.6f), and develops the Israel/ Gentiles theme with a rewriting of Matthew's Dinner-Party parable: the excuses the Jewish guests offer are brought into line with those allowed in Deut. 20—a new farm, oxen, wife for a new house, vineyard, wife.

Topic 6:
Repentance and Money

Deut. 21.10—25 consists of assorted laws, of which Luke gives a Christian version as it seems fit. (*a*) Luke 14.25–end. As Deut. 20.10ff commanded the offering of peace to an enemy city, so will the provident Christian count the cost of his faith, like a king suing for peace with a more powerful foe. There follows (*b*) Luke 15.1–32, three parables on repentance. Deut. 22.1 is the law of the lost sheep, which recalls Matthew's parable: Deut. 21.18ff is the law of the disobedient son, recalling Matthew's parable of the Two Sons. Luke writes his own version, contrasting Christian mercy with OT judgement. (*c*) Luke 16.1–13. Deut. 23.19 is the law against usury, especially with food, and Luke's Unjust Steward provides a commentary on that.

Topic 7:
Pistis

Deut. 26—29.9 set out the blessings promised for obedience, and the curses that will reward disobedience. Luke teaches (*a*) that hypocrisy will be abased, that the law will be fulfilled, and that the rich and oppressive will suffer in hell (Luke 16.14—17.4; cf. the laws of rich and poor in Deut. 24.12ff); (b) that we must serve God faithfully and will be rewarded by grace (Luke 17.5–10); (c) remembering the thankfulness of the Samaritan leper, who was saved by his faith (Luke 17.11-19).

Topic 8:
Judgement

Deut. 29.22–end predicts that future generations will find the land like Sodom and Gomorrah for the people's disobedience, and in (a) Luke 17.20–end Luke brings in the passage from Matt. 24 on the Coming of the Day of the Son of Man, as in the days of Noah and Lot. (b) Luke 18.1–8, the Unjust Judge, tells the Church that the ἐκδίκησις threatened in Deut. 28ff is at hand: their faithfulness will need to exceed Israel's (Deut. 32.20; cf. 24.19 for the judging of widows). (c) Luke 18.9–14, the Pharisee and Publican, develops the Lucan image of faithful prayer.

Topic 9:
Across the Jordan

In Deut. 31 Moses commands Joshua to lead the people across the Jordan, and to inherit the land. Luke now returns to Mark, who provides him with three pericopae: (a) 18.15–17, only those who become as children will enter the kingdom; (b) 18.18–34, how hard it is for the wealthy to enter the kingdom; (c) 18.35–end, over the Jordan to Jericho where the blind man is healed.

Topic 10:
Destruction at Hand

Deut. 32 renews the threat of destruction on disobedient Israel, to which Luke responds with a typical contrast between the saved publican of (a) Luke 19.1–10, Zacchaeus, and (b) Luke 19.11–28, the Pounds, in which the king slaughters the citizens (i.e. the Jews), who do not wish him to reign over them. Thereafter Luke follows the Marcan pericopae home.

To analyse the whole Gospel of Luke in a single chapter is a rash venture: I have attempted a fuller exposition in the extension of my tenure of the Speaker's Lecturership, which I hope to publish in due course. But at least I hope that I may have persuaded the reader that the lectionary hypothesis provides a striking series of parallels with the OT *sidrôt*, and so a credible motive for Luke to have rearranged Matthew. The lectionary view explains so many of the standing problems of Luke: the 'Genesis-type' infancy narrative that is Lucan and yet un-Lucan, that contradicts Matthew yet does not seem to be historical; the change in order in the Temptations, the Rejection, and the Call of Simon; the structure of the Sermon on the Plain; the function and arrangement of the Journey; and the Long Omission, to name a selection. The whole theory cannot be argued here in detail: what I hope to have shown is the possibility that Luke re-ordered the Matthaean material, and yet was not a crank.

APPENDIX

THE LUCAN YEAR

Agreement with Mark's order is underlined

SIDRAH		DATE	LUCAN LECTION			CF.
5.	Gen. 23—25.18	2 Iyyar	0a	1.5–25	John's Annunciation	Gen. 17—18
6.	25.19—28.9	9	0b	1.26–56	Jesus' Annunciation	25.25
7.	28.10—32.3	16	0c	1.57–80	John's Birth	29—30
8.	32.4—36	23	1–4a	2.1–40	Jesus' Birth	35.16ff
9.	37—40	1 Sivan	4b	2.41–52	Jesus Aged 12	37.11
10.	41—44.17	Pentecost	5a	3.1–20	John's Preaching	Acts 2
11.	44.18—47.28	15 Sivan	5b–6	3.21–38	Baptism, Genealogy	Gen. 46
12.	47.29—50		(7a	4.1–13	Temptations)	
13.	Exod. 1—6.1	22	7b	4.14–30	Rejection at Nazareth	Exod. 2ff
14.	6.2—9	29	8.	4.31–37	Demoniac in Synagogue	8.19
15.	10—13.16	6 Tammuz	9.	4.38–39	Simon's Wife's Mother	
16.	13.17—17	13	10.	4.40–end	Sick at Evening	
17.	18—20	20	11.	5.1–11	Call of First Apostles	18
18.	21—24	27	12.	5.12–16	Leper	24.15
19.	25—27.19	5 Ab	13.	5.17–26	Paralytic	
20.	27.20—30.10	12	14a	5.27–end	Levi, Fasting	32
21.	30.11—34	19	14b	6.1–5	Cornfield	25.23
22.	35—38.20	26	15.	6.6–11	Withered Hand	20.8
23.	38.21—40	3 Elul	16.	6.12–19	Call of Twelve	
24.	Lev. 1—5	10	17.	6.20–end	Sermon on Plain	Lev. 19
25.	6—8	17	18.	7.1–10	Centurion's Slave	19.34
26.	9—11	24	19.	7.11–17	Widow at Nain	10.1–5
27.	12—13	New Year	20.	7.18–35	John from Prison	Isa. 35.5–6
28.	14—15	9 Tishri	21.	7.36–end	Sinner Forgiven	Lev. 16
29.	16—18	Atonement				
30.	19—20	16 Tishri	22a	8.1–18	Sower, etc.	
		Tabernacles				
31.	21—24	23 Tishri	(22b	8.19–21	Mother and Brothers)	
32/33	25—27	30	23.	8.22–25	Storm on Lake	
34.	Num. 1—4.20	7 Cheshvan	24.	8.26–39	Gerasene Demoniac	
35.	4.21—7	14	25.	8.40–48	Woman with Issue	Num. 5.1ff
36.	8—12	21	26.	8.49–end	Ruler's Daughter	9
37.	13—15	28	27.	9.1–9	Mission of Twelve	13
38.	16—18	6 Kislev	28.	9.10–17	Feeding of 5000	11
39.	19—22.1	13	29.	9.18–27	Peter's Confession	20, etc.
40.	22.2—25.9	20	30.	9.28–36	Transfiguration	9.15
41.	25.10—30.1	27	31.	9.37–43a	Demoniac Boy	

SIDRAH		DATE	LUCAN LECTION			CF.
42/43	30.2—36	4 Tebeth	32a	9.43b–50	The Greatest, Exorcist	11.26
44.	Deut. 1—3.22	11	32b–33	9.51–end	Samaritan Village, Disciples	Deut. 1.6ff
			34a	10.1–16	Mission of Seventy	1.9ff,21
			34b	10.17–24	Return and Joy	1.13; 8.15
45.	3.23—7.11	18	35–6	10.25–37	Lawyer, Good Samaritan	6.5,16,18
			37.	10.38–end	Mary and Martha	
			38.	11.1–13	Prayer	
46.	7.12—11.25	25	39–40	11.14–28	Beelzebul	
			41.	11.29–36	Jonah, Light	
			42–3	11.37–end	Woes on Pharisees	11.26
47.	11.26—16.17	3 Shebat	44.	12.1–12	Fearless Confession	13
			45–46a	12.13–40	Fool, Anxiety, Servants	12.20; 15.1ff
			46b–47	12.41—13.9	Repent!	13.12; 14.2
48.	16.18—21.9	10	48–9	13.10–21	Bent Woman, Mustard	15.12ff
			50–1	13.22–end	Israel Rejected	
			52–4	14.1–24	Dropsy, Humility Dinner	17.12; 20.1f
49.	21.10—25	17	55.	14.25–end	Tower, Embassy, Salt	20.10ff
			56–7	15	Sheep, Coin, Son	22.1; 21.18
			58a	16.1–13	Unjust Steward	23.19
50.	26—29.8	24	58b–59a	16.14—17.4		
					Law, Divorce, Dives	24.3; 18.18
			59b	17.5–10	Servant Ploughing	28.1
			60a	17.11–19	Ten Lepers	
51.	29.9—30	1 Adar	60b	17.20–37	Day of the Son of Man	29.23; 28.49
			61.	18.1–8	Unjust Judge	24.19; 32.20
			62a	18.9–14	Pharisee and Publican	26.13
52.	31	8	62b	18.15–17	Children	
			63.	18.18–34	Rich Ruler	5.16–20
			64.	18.35–end	Blind Man at Jericho	31.2,7,14
53.	32	15	65.	19.1–10	Zacchaeus	
			66–7	19.11–28	Pounds	
			68a	19.29–38	Approach to Jerusalem	
54.	33—34	22	68b	19.39–end	Lament for Jerusalem	32.28ff
			69.	20.1–8	Authority	
			70.	20.9–18	Wicked Husbandmen	
1.	Gen. 1—6.8	29	71.	20.19–26	Tribute-Money	
			72–3	20.27–44	Sadducees, David's Son	
			74.	20.45—21.4	Widows, Widow's Mite	
2.	6.9—11	7 Nisan Passover	75.	21.5–end	Apocalypse	Gen. 7
			76–81	22—23.49	Passion	
3.	12—17	21 Nisan	82.	23.50—24.12	Burial, Resurrection	
4.	18—22	28	83.	24.13–end	Emmaus, Ascension	

22

CONCLUSION

I have accepted the common conclusion that Matthew was over-writing Mark. I have found no considerable passage in the Gospel which seemed to require a written or an oral source, and I have suggested reasons for thinking it to be unlikely that there were many non-Marcan traditions in Matthew's ambit in the 70s. Does this mean that there was no non-Marcan tradition in the Matthaean community? Not none. The names of Joseph, Mary's husband, and Caiaphas the high priest, were not in Mark; and Chorazin and Barabbas' name Jesus may be due to tradition also. Other features for which an entirely satisfactory explanation has not been forthcoming include Pilate's wife, and the fish and stater, and the reader may add his own hesitations. The more closely a passage corresponds to the liturgical structure of the Gospel and the Matthaean manner, in so far as they can be established, the more heavily does the burden of proof rest upon those who claim underlying non-Marcan traditions.

During the Speaker's Lectures I was asked a number of times, 'Since Matthew writes a Matthaeanized version of Mark in the agreed redactional passages, how do you know that the Matthaean features to which you point in the non-redactional passages do not cover another source or sources—perhaps Q and M?' At the time I could only urge probabilities: now I have what seems to be statistical proof. About half of the Gospel consists of passages generally acknowledged to be Marcan, 9,280 words, on my computation, of which 5,334 are the actual Marcan words, (or very nearly the actual Marcan words) or LXX words, and 3,946 are new words, Matthew's redactional words. Of the words in Marcan passages 1,668 words are characteristic, 18 per cent; 1,129 of these occur among the new words, making $28\frac{1}{2}$ per cent of the new words. If Matthew is overwriting other alien sources (Q, M, etc.), therefore, we should expect the percentage of characteristic words in the Q-passages, M-passages, etc., to be around 18 per cent as they are in the Marcan passages overall: while if the midrashic theory is correct, we should expect an incidence of around $28\frac{1}{2}$ per cent, since that is the figure in Matthew's own words when redacting Mark. In the Infancy Narratives, if we omit the Genealogies (because of the difficulty whether to count γεννάω or not), there are 561 words from 1.18—2.23, of which 157 are characteristic—28 per cent: therefore the Infancy Narratives are Matthew's midrash. In the Q-passages there are, on my computation, 3,561 words, of which

965 are characteristic—27 per cent. In the M-passages there are 4,346 words, of which 1,351 are characteristic—31 per cent. Since in my selection of characteristic words one of the criteria was that there should be more instances in Matthew than in Luke, any use of Matthaean words by Luke (in Q-passages) will tend to diminish the number of characteristic words in Q-passages: so it is inevitable that the Q-passages figure should be less than the M-passages figure. Despite this, the overall percentage in non-Marcan passages is 29 per cent: therefore the non-Marcan passages are, over all, Matthew's midrash.

Luke says that many had taken in hand to write a Gospel. Once Mark was available, every church in Christendom must have been engaged in a process of adaptation to answer the need for the edification of the faithful round the year. But there were not many *ḥ^akhāmîm* in the Church: if there had been, Matthew would not have been the only Jewish–Christian Gospel to survive. Matthew's being a *sôphēr* enabled him to excel all the other churches' attempts: he had the tradition of the elders at his finger-tips. But this would not have sufficed had he not also been an artist, and, the presupposition of art, a man of profound conviction. Matthew provided a liturgical work of art which will not be transcended, and he provided it by adapting Mark in a cataract of epigram, poetry, and parable which has been the dominant influence in forming the Church's image of Jesus. He was the Church's liturgist and the Church's poet, adapting Mark by midrash and through lection.

23
MATTHEW'S VOCABULARY

An essential tool for the study of the Gospels is a vocabulary of characteristic words for each of the evangelists. I have made some comments on Hawkins' classic work in ch. 6 above; and for the need for a clear criterion in wider claims of characteristic language. The following list will not be exhaustive even on its own criteria, for the noticing of combinations and inflexions of words as being characteristic, and of words in particular meanings, is a sophisticated exercise.

Hawkins' criteria were (i) that a word should occur at least four times; and (ii) that it come either twice as often in Matthew as in Mark and Luke together, or not at all in one of them. These words, and a number which Hawkins included as coming close to his criteria, and a few expressions which meet them but are not on his list, I have called Matthaean in the text: Hawkins' own words are marked *, my additions (*). Where a word on Hawkins' list is found in only one context I have put it in parenthesis. The words without asterisks are those which I have called semi-Matthaean, and they meet one of two criteria. Either they occur twice as often in Matthew as in Mark *and* more often than in Luke; or they are inserted redactionally by Matthew into an agreed Marcan context or OT citation. I have included some words and expressions that come only three times. Many of my semi-Matthaean words meet both criteria, in which case I have given a single instance of a redactional insertion in the right-hand column: where the word is included on the redactional criterion, two instances are given.

The figures are, where possible, from R. Morgenthaler, *Statistik des neutestamentlichen Wortschatzes* (Zürich 1958).

	NUMBER OF OCCURRENCES			REDACTIONAL INSERTION BY MATTHEW
	MATT.	MARK	LUKE	
(*)ἀγαθὸς/πονηρός	8	0	4	
(*)ἄγγελος κυρίου	5	0	2	28.2
ἁγιάζω	3	0	1	
ἀγρός	16	7	9	13.31
(*)ἀδελφός (in transferred sense only)	14	0	5	
αἷμα = life taken	10	1	5	27.24
αἰτία	3	1	1	27.37
ἀμὴν λέγω σοι (ὑμῖν)	31	13	6	19.23
(*)ἄλλην παραβολήν	4	0	0	13.31
ἀμπελών	10	5	7	
ἄν	40	20	32	21.44
ἀναγινώσκω	7	4	3	19.4
* ἀνέγνωτε, οὐκ/οὐδέποτε	4	1	1	19.4
ἀνάκειμαι	5	1	2	9.10
* ἀνατολή	5	0	2	
* ἀναχωρέω	10	1	0	4.12
(*)ἄνθρωπος (ἄνηρ) with noun	7	0	1	21.33
ἄνθρωποι, οἱ = men	27	5	10	9.8
ἀνοίγω	11	1	7	20.33
* ἀνομία	4	0	0	24.12
ἄξιος	9	0	8	10.11
ἀπαγγέλλω	8	4	11	12.8, 28.8
* ἀποδίδωμι	18	1	8	21.41
(*)ἀπὸ . . . ἕως	8	1	1	27.45
ἀποκριθεὶς εἶπεν	45	14	34	13.11
ἀπολύω = divorce	9	4	1	
ἄρα (+ ἄραγε 2/0/0)	7	2	6	18.1
ἀργός	3	0	0	
* ἀργύρια	8	0	0	26.15
ἀρκέω	3	0	1	
ἁρπάζω	3	0	0	12.29, 13.19
* ἄρτι	7	0	0	9.18
(*)αὐτῶν = the Jews'	7	2	1	9.35
ἀφίημι = forgive	17	8	14	12.31
ἀφορίζω	3	0	1	
βάλλω	34	18	18	18.8,9, 26.12
βάλλομαι	11	5	5	9.2
βαπτιστής	7	2	3	14.2
(*)βασιλεία, absolutely	4	0	1	9.35
* βασιλεία τῶν οὐρανῶν	32	0	0	3.2
* βρυγμὸς τῶν ὀδόντων	6	0	1	

| | NUMBER OF OCCURRENCES | | | REDACTIONAL INSERTION BY MATTHEW |
	MATT.	MARK	LUKE	
* γάμος	8	0	2	
γάρ	124	64	97	3.2
γέγραπται γάρ	3	0	1	26.31
γέεννα	7	3	1	
* γενηθήτω	5	0	0	26.42
(*)(γεννάω	45	1	4)	
γεννήματα	3	0	1	
γῆ	43	19	25	
(*)γῆ with a name	8	1	0	4.15
γινώσκω of people	3	0	1	
(*)γραμματεῖς καὶ Φαρισαῖοι	10	0	3	12.38
δαιμονίζομαι	7	4	1	9.32
δένδρον	12	1	7	21.8
δέξιος (adj.)	3	0	2	
* δεῦτε	6	3	0	28.6
δηνάριον	6	3	3	
διά + gen.	26	11	13	
(*)διὰ τοῦ προφήτου	11	0	1	3.3
* διὰ τοῦτο	11	2	4	13.13
διάβολος	6	0	5	4.1
διαφέρω	3	1	2	
δίκαιος	17	2	11	
* δικαιοσύνη	7	0	1[1]	
* διψάω	5	0	0	
* διώκω	6	0	3[2]	
δοκέω	10	2	10	22.17, 42
δοῦλος	30	5	26	
δύναμις = miracle	7	3	2	
δύο	40	19	28	22.40
* δῶρον	9	1	2	8.4
ἐάν	56	29	26	21.21
ἐγείρομαι	30	10	14	9.25
* ἐγερθείς	8	0	1	9.19
* ἐθνικός	3	0	0	
ἔθνος	15	6	13	21.43
εἰ	35	13	31	8.31
εἰ . . . εἰ	5	0	5	27.40
* εἷς = τις	4	1	0	21.19
(*)εἷς τούτων	7	1	2	10.42
(*)ἐκ of parenthood	7	0	0	

[1] + 4 Acts [2] + 9 Acts

	NUMBER OF OCCURRENCES			REDACTIONAL INSERTION BY
	MATT.	MARK	LUKE	MATTHEW
ἑκατόνταρχος	4	0	3	27.54
(*)ἐκβάλλω = bring out	5	0	2	12.20
ἐκεῖ	28	11	16	14.23
ἐκεῖθεν (* in narrative)	12	5	3	9.9
ἐκεῖνος	54	23	33	14.1
ἐκκλησία	3	0	0	
ἐκκόπτω	4	0	3	18.8
ἐκτείνω τὴν χεῖρα	5	2	3	12.48
ἐλάχιστος	5	0	4	2.6
ἐλεέω	8	3	4	15.22
ἐλθών, –όντες	30	11	11	4.13
ἐμός	5	2	3	
ἔμπροσθεν	18	2	10	27.11
* ἔνδυμα	7	0	1	28.3
ἕνεκεν ἐμοῦ	4	1	1	16.25
(*)ἐνθυμέομαι, –ησις	4	0	0	9.4
* ἔνοχος	5	2	0	
ἐντέλλομαι	4	2	1	17.9
ἐξώτερος	3	0	0	
ἐπάνω	8	1	5	27.37
ἐπεί	3	1	1	21.46
ἐπιδείκνυμι	3	0	1	16.1
* ἐργάζομαι	4	1	1	
ἐργάτης	6	0	4	
* ἐρρέθη	6	0	0	
ἐρῶ	30	12	19	21.4
ἔσται/ἔσονται	38	10	33	19.27
ἑστώς	7	0	4	16.28
ἔσχατος	10	5	6	
(*)ἑταῖρε	3	0	0	26.50
ἕτοιμος	4	1	3	
εὐθέως	11	0	6	4.20
* εὐώνυμος				
(cf. ἀρίστερος 1/1/1)	5	2	0	20.21
ἐφ' ὅσον	9	1	5	9.15
ἔχιδνα	3	0	1	
ἕως	48	15	28	17.9
ἕως as preposition	28	10	13	22.26
ἕως with indicative	4	0	2	
(* ζιζάνια	8	0	0)	
ζυμή	4	2	2	

| | NUMBER OF OCCURRENCES | | | REDACTIONAL INSERTION BY MATTHEW |
	MATT.	MARK	LUKE	
ἤ = or	59	28	36	27.17
* ἡγέμων	10	1	2	27.11
ἦλθον theological	9	3	4	
(*)ἡμέρα/ὥρα	4	1	1	
* ἡμέρα κρισέως	4	0	0	
'Ησαΐας	6	2	2	8.17
θάπτω (cf. τάφος)	3	0	3	14.12
θεάομαι	4	2	3	
θέλω	42	24	28	15.28, 17.4
(*)θέλημα = God's will	6	1	1	26.42
θεραπεύω	16	5	14	4.23
θερισμός, –τής	8	1	3	
θησαυρός	9	1	4	
θρόνος	5	0	3	19.28
* θυσιαστήριον	6	0	2	
ἰδού	62	17	57	9.2
* ἰδού after gen. abs.	11	0	1	9.18
'Ιερεμίας	3	0	0	16.14
(*)'Ιεροσόλυμα, πᾶσα/πᾶσα πόλις	4	0	0	8.34
(*)'Ιησοῦς Χριστός	6	1	0	16.21
(*)'Ιησοῦς, ὁ introductory	38	11	2	8.14
ἴσθι/ἔστω	4	1	2	
'Ισραήλ	12	2	12	15.31
ἴστημι, active	4	1	2	26.15
'Ιωνᾶς	5	0	4	16.4
'Ιωσήφ	11	2	8	
κἀγώ	9	0	6	21.24
καθαρός	3	0	1	27.59
κάθημαι	19	11	13	26.29, 27.61
καθίστημι	4	0	3	
κἀκεῖ	3	1	0	10.11
κάλαμος	5	2	1	
καλός, epithet	15	4	8	
καρπός	19	5	12	21.34
καρπὸν ποιέω	9	0	5	21.43
* κατὰ + gen.	16	7	6	12.32
κατακαίω	3	0	1	
(*)κατοικέω	4	0	2	4.13
* κελεύω	7	0	1	14.9

	NUMBER OF OCCURRENCES			REDACTIONAL INSERTION BY
	MATT.	MARK	LUKE	MATTHEW
* κερδαίνω	6	1	1	
κῆνσος	3	1	0	22.19
* κλαυθμός	7	0	1	
κλείω (+ κλεῖς 1/0/1)	3	0	1	
* κλέπτω	5	1	1	
κληρονομέω	3	1	2	
κληθήσομαι	5	1	4	2.23
κόπτω (cf. ἐκκόπτω)	3	1	2	24.30
* κόσμος	8	3	3	18.7
κράσπεδον	3	1	1	9.20
* κρίσις	12	0	4	
* κρύπτω	7	0	3	13.35
κρυπτός	5	1	2	
κυλλός	3	1	0	15.30
κύριε	29	1	28	8.2
κύριος of a man	32	3	24	15.27
κύριος with gen.	25	5	18	15.27
κωφός	7	3	4	15.30
λαμβάνω	57	21	22	16.7
λαβών	22	7	8	13.31
(⁽*⁾λάμπας	5	0	0)	
λάμπω	3	0	1	17.2
⁽*⁾λαοῦ, officers τοῦ λ.	5	0	0	21.23
⁽*⁾λέγει –ουσι, anarthrous	21	2	0	26.64
* λεγόμενος, with names	13	1	2	
λέγω ὑμῖν ὅτι	21	4	12	
λέγων, –οντες	114	42	96	8.3
λόγοι οὗτοι, οἱ	5	0	3	7.28
* λυπέω	6	2	0	14.9
⁽*⁾λύω (of commandments)	5	0	0	
(* μάγος	4	0	0)	
* μαθητεύω	3	0	0	27.57
* μαλακία	3	0	0	4.23
μανθάνω	3	1	0	9.13
μαστιγόω	3	1	1	10.17
μάχαιρα	7	3	5	26.52
μείζων	10	3	7	20.31
μέλλω	10	2	12	12.32, 17.32
μὲν . . . δὲ	20	6	10	20.23
μέρη, εἰς τὰ	3	1	0	15.21

	NUMBER OF OCCURRENCES			REDACTIONAL INSERTION BY
	MATT.	MARK	LUKE	MATTHEW
μεριμνάω	7	0	5	10.19
* μεταβαίνω	5	0	1	15.29
μεταμελέομαι	3	0	0	
(* μετοικεσία	4	0	0)	
μή with aor. subj.	28	9	18	24.23
μήτι	4	2	2	26.25
* μισθός (μισθόομαι 2/0/0)	10	1	3	
* μόνον, adverb	7	2	1[1]	9.21
* μωρός	6	0	0	
ναί	9	1	4	9.28
ναός	9	3	4	
νομίζω	3	0	2	
νόμος	8	0	9	12.5, 22.36
νόσος	5	1	4	4.23
νύμφιος	6	3	2	
νύξ	9	4	7	26.31
* ξένος	5	0	0	
ὁδηγός	3	0	0	15.14
(*)ὁδούς	8	1	1	
* ὅθεν	4	0	1	14.7
οἰκοδεσπότης	7	1	4	21.33
* ὀλιγόπιστος, –ία	5	0	1	8.26
* ὀμνύω	13	2	1	
(*)ὁμοία ἐστί	8	0	3	13.31
* ὁμοιόω	8	1	3	
* ὁμολογέω	4	0	2	14.7
* ὄναρ, κατ'	6	0	0	27.19
(*)ὄνομα, εἰς	5	0	0	10.42
* ὅπως	17	1	7	8.34
* ὅρκος	4	1	1	14.7
(*)ὅρα μή	4	1	0	24.6
* ὅσος ἄν/ἐάν	6	2	1	21.22
ὅστις	29	4	21	12.50
οὐ μή . . . ἕως ἄν	6	1	3	24.34
οὐκ . . . εἰ μή	14	12	9	12.24, 39
οὖν	57	5	31	14.15
οὐρανός/γῆ	15	1	6	
οὐρανός, –οί	82	18	34	28.2

[1] + 8 Acts

	NUMBER OF OCCURRENCES			REDACTIONAL INSERTION BY
	MATT.	MARK	LUKE	MATTHEW
οὗτος resumptive	6	3	2	13.20
οὕτως	32	10	21	19.8
(*)οὕτως εἶναι	12	2	2	
οὐχί;	5	0	4	13.56
ὀφείλω	6	0	5	
ὀφθαλμός	24	7	17	17.8
* οἱ ὄχλοί	33	2	15	7.28
(*)ὄχλοί πολλοί	5	0	2	4.25
παῖς = child	7	0	4	17.18
πάντα ὅσα	8	2	3	
παραλαμβάνω	16	6	6	27.27
* παρθένος	4	0	2	
* παρουσία				
(τοῦ υἱοῦ τοῦ ἀνθρώπου)	4	0	0	24.3
* πατὴρ ἡμῶν, etc., ὁ	20	1	3	26.29
* πατὴρ ὁ ἐν τοῖς οὐρανοῖς, ὁ	13	1	0	12.50
* πατὴρ ὁ οὐράνιος	7	0	0	6.14
πεινάω	9	2	5	12.1
πέντε	12	3	9	
περιάγω	3	1	0	4.23
περιβάλλω	5	2	2	
περισσεύω	5	1	4	14.20
πέτρα	5	1	3	27.51
πιπράσκω	3	1	0	
πλανάω –η –ος	10	4	1	24.24
πλὴν λέγω ὑμῖν	3	0	0	26.64
* πληρόω, of scripture	12	1	2	8.17
πολύς/ὀλίγος	4	0	3	
* πονηρός, ὁ	5	0	0	13.19
* πονηρός	26	2	13	16.4
πορεύομαι	29	3	51	26.14, 28.7
πορνεία	3	1	0	19.9
ποτίζω	5	2	1	
πραΰς	3	0	0	
* πρόβατον	11	2	2	15.24
* πρὸς τὸ with inf.	5	1	1	26.12
* προσέρχομαι	52	5	10	8.2
προσέχω	6	0	4	10.17
* προσκυνέω	13	2	2	15.25
προσκυνέω . . . πεσών	3	0	0	
* προσφέρω	14	3	4	4.24
προφητεύω	4	2	2	
πύλη	4	0	1	
πῦρ	12	4	7	3.11

	NUMBER OF OCCURRENCES			REDACTIONAL INSERTION BY
	MATT.	MARK	LUKE	MATTHEW
* ῥηθείς	13	0	0	3.3
* Σαδδουκαῖοι	7	1	1	16.6
* σαπρός	5	0	2	
* σεισμός	4	1	1	28.2
* σείω	3	0	0	21.10
* σκανδαλίζομαι ἐν	4	1	1	26.31
σκάνδαλον	5	0	1	18.7
σκότος	6	1	4	
Σόδομα	3	0	2	
Σολομών	5	0	3	
σός	8	2	4	24.3
στόμα	11	0	9	15.11
* συλλέγω	7	0	1	
* συμβούλιον λαμβάνω	5	0	0	27.1
* συμφέρει	4	0	0	18.6
συμφωνέω	3	0	1	
* συνάγω	24	5	6	26.57
συναίρω λόγον	3	0	0	
* σύνδουλος	5	0	0	
συνίημι	9	5	4	13.19, 23
συντάσσω	3	0	0	21.6
* συντελεία (τοῦ) αἰῶνος	5	0	0	24.3
* σφόδρα	7	1	1	17.6
(*)σῶμα/ψυχή	4	0	2	
* τάλαντον	14	0	0	
* τάφος (and ταφή 27.7)	6	1	1	28.1
τάχυ	3	1	1	28.7
τελευτάω	4	2	1	9.18
τελέω	7	0	4	7.28
* τηρέω	6	1	0	19.17
* τί σοι/ὑμῖν δοκεῖ;	6	0	0	22.42
* τότε	90	6	14	9.6
τοῦτο δὲ (ὅλον) γέγονεν ἵνα	3	0	0	21.14
* τροφή	4	0	1	3.4
* τυφλός, metaphorical	6	0	0	
τυφλός	17	5	8	15.30
ὕδατα, τά	3	1	0	8.32
υἱὸς Δαυίδ	8	3	3	15.22
υἱὸς τοῦ ἀνθρώπου ἔρχεται, ὁ	7	2	3	16.28

| | NUMBER OF OCCURRENCES | | | REDACTIONAL INSERTION BY |
	MATT.	MARK	LUKE	MATTHEW
(*)ὑπὲρ with acc.	4	0	2	
* ὑποκριτής	13	1	3	22.18
* ὕστερον	7	0	1	21.37
* φαίνομαι	13	1	2	9.33
* φημί	17	6	8	14.8
φιλέω	5	1	2	
* φονεύω (and φονεύς 1/0/0)	5	1	1	
* φρόνιμος	7	0	2	
φυλακή = prison	8	2	6	
χριστός	17	7	12	24.5
* χρυσός	5	0	0	10.9
χωλός	5	1	3	15.30
ὧδε	17	10	16	8.29, 17.4
* ὥρα ἐκείνη in narrative	6	0	1	9.22
* ὥσπερ	10	0	2	20.28
ὡς = like	40	20	25	17.2

Bibliography
Indexes

BIBLIOGRAPHY

Abel, F.-M., 'La Fête de la Hanoucca', *RB* LIII (1946), pp. 538ff.

Allen, W. C., *A Critical and Exegetical Commentary on the Gospel according to St Matthew* [Allen]. Edinburgh 1907.

Amstütz, J., ΑΠΛΟΤΗΣ. Bonn 1968.

Anderson, G. W., 'Canonical and Non-Canonical', *Cambridge History of the Bible* (Cambridge 1970) I, pp. 113ff.

Anderson, H., ed. with W. Barclay, *The New Testament in historical and contemporary perspective: essays in memory of G. H. C. MacGregor*. Oxford 1965.

Arndt-Gingrich, see Bauer.

Bacon, B. W., *Studies in Matthew*. London 1931

Bammel, E , 'Crucifixion as a punishment in Palestine', in his *The Trial of Jesus*. London 1970.

Barth, G., 'Matthew's Understanding of the Law', *TIM* (1960), ed. G. Bornkamm, G. Barth, and H. J. Held. E.T., London 1963.

Bartlett, J. R., 'Zadok and his Successors at Jerusalem', *JTS* XIX, pt. 1 (April 1968), pp. 1ff.

Bauer, W., *A Greek-English Lexicon of the New Testament and other earlier Christian Literature*, tr. and ed. W. F. Arndt and F. W. Gingrich [Bauer]. 4e., Cambridge 1957.

Berakot (*Die Mischna*), ed. O. Holtzmann. Giessen 1912.

Billerbeck, see Strack.

Black, M., *An Aramaic Approach to the Gospels and Acts* [*AAGA*]. 3e., Oxford 1967.

—, ed. with H. H. Rowley, *Peake's Commentary on the Bible*. London 1962.

—, 'The Festival of Encaenia Ecclesiae', *JEH* V, no. 1 (April 1954), pp. 78ff.

Bloch, Mlle. R., 'Midrash', *Dictionnaire de la Bible*, Supplément V, cols. 1263–81.

Borgen, P., 'Observations on the Targumic Character of the Prologue of John', *NTS* XVI, no. 3 (April 1970), pp. 288ff.

Bornkamm, G., *Jesus of Nazareth*. E. T., London 1960.

—, ed. with G. Barth and H. J. Held, *Tradition and Interpretation in Matthew* [*TIM*]. E.T., London 1963.

Bowker, J., *The Targums and Rabbinic Literature*. London 1969.

Brock, S., Review of *An Aramaic Approach to the Gospels and Acts* (M. Black), *JTS* XX, pt. 1 (April 1969), pp. 274ff.

Brown, R. E., *The Gospel according to John* I. New York 1966.

Brownlee, W. H., 'Biblical Interpretation among the Sectaries of the Dead Sea Scrolls', *The Biblical Archaeologist* XIV, no. 3 (September 1951), pp. 54ff.

Bruce, F. F., ed., *Promise and Fulfilment*, essays presented to S. H. Hooke. Edinburgh 1963.

Büchler, A., 'The Reading of the Law and the Prophets in a Triennial Cycle', *JQR* V (1893), pp. 420ff and VI (1894), pp. 1ff.

Bultmann, R., *The History of the Synoptic Tradition*. Göttingen 1931; 2e., E.T., London 1968.

—, *Theology of the New Testament* I. E.T., London 1952.

Burkitt, F. C., 'The Early Syriac Lectionary System', *Proc. B.A.* X (1923), pp. 301ff.

Burney, C. F., *The Poetry of Our Lord*. Oxford 1925.

Butler, B. C., *The Originality of St Matthew*. Cambridge 1951.

Cadbury, H. J., 'The Single Eye', *HTR* XLVII, no. 2 (April 1954), pp. 69ff.

Carmignac, J., *Recherches sur le 'Notre Père'*. Paris 1969.

Carrington, P., *The Primitive Christian Calendar*. Cambridge 1952.

Casey, R. P., ed. with others, *Quantulacumque*, Studies presented to Kirsopp Lake. London 1937.

—, 'St Mark's Gospel', *Theology* LV, no. 388 (October 1952), pp. 362ff.

Cerfaux, L., *Christ in the Theology of St Paul*. 1951; E.T., New York 1959.

Clark, K. W., 'Worship in the Jerusalem Temple after A.D. 70', *NTS* VI, pt. 2 (July 1960), pp. 269ff.

Clemen, W. H., *Development of Shakespeare's Imagery*. London 1951.

Conybeare, F. C., *Rituale Armenorum*. Oxford 1905.

Creed, J. M., *The Gospel according to St Luke*. London 1930.

Crockett, L., 'Luke iv. 16–30 and the Jewish Lectionary Cycle', *JJS* XVII (1966), pp. 13ff.

Cullmann, O., *Early Christian Worship*. E.T., London 1953.

—, *Peter, Disciple, Apostle, Martyr*. 2e., E.T., London 1962.

Dahl, N. A., 'Die Passionsgeschichte bei Matthäus', *NTS* II, no. 1 (September 1955), pp. 17ff.

Daily Prayer Book, ed. S. Singer. Cambridge 1914.

Dalman, G., *Arbeit und Sitte in Palästina* IV. Gütersloh 1935.

—, *Jesus-Jeshua*. Leipzig 1922.

—, *The Words of Jesus*. E.T., Edinburgh 1902.

Daniélou, J., *The Bible and The Liturgy*. 1956; E.T., London 1960.

Daube, D., *New Testament and Rabbinic Judaism* [*NTRJ*]. London 1956.

Davey, F. N., Review of *A Study in St Mark* (A. Farrer), *JTS* III, pt. 2 (October 1952), pp. 239ff.

Davies, J. G., 'The Genesis of Belief in an Imminent Parousia', *JTS* XIV, pt. 1 (April 1963), pp. 104ff.

Davies, W. D., *Setting of the Sermon on the Mount* [*Setting*]. Cambridge 1964.

—, ed. with D. Daube, *The Background of the New Testament and its Eschatology*, in honour of C. H. Dodd. Cambridge 1956.

—, 'Matthew v. 18', *Mélanges Bibliques rédigés en l'honneur de André Robert*. Paris 1957.

Delling, D. G., *Worship in the New Testament*. Göttingen 1952; E.T., 1962.

Dibelius, M., *An die Thessalonicher*. 3e., Tübingen 1937.

—, *From Tradition to Gospel*. 2e., E.T., London 1934.

Didier, M., ed., *L'Evangile selon Matthieu*. Bibl. Ephemer. Theol. Lovan. 29, Gembloux, 1972.

Dobschütz, E. von, 'Matthäus als Rabbi und Katachet', *ZNW* 27 (1928), pp. 338ff.

Dodd, C. H., *Parables of the Kingdom*. 3e., London 1936.

—, "Εννομος Χριστοῦ, *Studia Paulina* (in hon. J. de Zwaan, Haarlem 1953), reprinted in his *More New Testament Studies*. Manchester 1968.

—, 'Matthew and Paul', *New Testament Studies*. Manchester 1953.

Drazin, N., *History of Jewish Education from 515 B.C. to 220 C.E.* 1940.

Dugmore, C. W., *The Influence of the Synagogue upon the Divine Office*. 2e., London 1964.

Dupont, J., 'Matthieu 18.3 ἐὰν μὴ στραφῆτε καὶ γένησθε ὡς τὰ παιδια', *Neotestamentica et Semitica*, ed. E. E. Ellis and M. Wilcox. Edinburgh 1969.

Ebner, E., *Elementary Education in Ancient Israel*. 1956.

Edgar, C. C., *A new group of Zenon papyri*. Manchester 1934.

Eissfeldt, O., *The Old Testament*. E.T., Oxford 1965.

Elbogen, I., *Der Jüdische Gottesdienst*. 3e., Frankfurt 1931.

Ellis, E. E., *Paul's Use of the Old Testament*. Edinburgh 1957.

—, ed. with M. Wilcox, *Neotestamentica et Semitica*. Edinburgh 1969.

Ellis, I. P., 'But Some Doubted', *NTS* XIV, no. 4 (July 1968), pp. 574ff.

Emmet, D. M., *Function, Purpose, Powers*. London 1958.

Evans, C. F., 'The New Testament in the Making', *The Cambridge History of the Bible* I, pp. 232ff.

Evans, C. F., 'Deuteronomy and the Central Section of Luke', *Studies in the Gospels*, ed. D. E. Nineham. Oxford 1954.

Farmer, W. R., *The Synoptic Problem*. New York, Macmillan, 1964.

Farrer, A. M., *Materials on St Mark*. Posthumous, unpublished.

—, *The Revelation of St John the Divine*. Oxford 1964.

—, *St Matthew and St Mark*. 2e., London 1966.

—, *A Study in St Mark*. London 1951.

—, *The Triple Victory*. London 1965.

—, 'On Dispensing with Q', *Studies in the Gospels*, ed. D. E. Nineham. Oxford 1954.

Feldman, A., *The Parables and Similes of the Rabbis* [*PSR*]. Cambridge 1927.

Fenton, J. C., *The Gospel of St Matthew*. London 1963.

Fiebig, P., *Altjüdische Gleichnisse und die Gleichnisse Jesu*. Tübingen 1904.

Forster, W., and G. Quell, *Lord*. E.T., London 1958.

Frame, J. E., *The Epistles of St Paul to the Thessalonians*. I.C.C. 1912.

Fuchs, A., *Sprachliche Untersuchungen zu Matthäus und Lukas*. Rome 1971.

Gardner, H., *The Limits of Literary Criticism*. London 1956.

Gerhardsson, B., *Memory and Manuscript* [*MM*]. Uppsala 1964.

—, 'The Parable of the Sower and its Interpretation', *NTS* xiv, no. 2 (January 1968), pp. 165ff.

—, 'The Seven Parables in Matthew xiii', *NTS* xix, no. 1 (October 1972), pp. 16ff.

Goguel, M., *The Primitive Church*. 1947; E.T., London 1964.

Goppelt, L., *Christentum und Judentum im ersten und zweiten Jahrhundert*. Gütersloh 1954.

Goudoever, J. van, *Biblical Calendars*. Leiden 1959.

Goulder, M. D., *Type and History in Acts*. London 1964.

—, 'Characteristics of the Parables in the Several Gospels', *JTS* xix, pt. 1 (April 1968), pp. 51ff.

—, 'The Composition of the Lord's Prayer', *JTS* xiv, pt. 1 (April 1963), pp. 32ff.

—, with M. L. Sanderson, 'St. Luke's Genesis', *JTS* viii, pt. 1 (April 1957), pp. 12ff.

—, Review of *The Parables of Jesus in Matthew 13* (J. D. Kingsbury), *JTS*. xxi, pt. 1 (April 1970), pp. 164ff.

Grant, F. C., *The Gospels: Their Origin and Their Growth*. London 1957.

Grant, R. M., 'The New Testament Canon', *The Cambridge History of the Bible* i, pp. 284ff.

Green, F. W., *St Matthew*. Oxford 1963.

Guilding, A., *The Fourth Gospel and Jewish Worship*. Oxford 1960.

Gundry, R. H., *The Use of the Old Testament in St Matthew's Gospel* [*UOTSM*]. Leiden 1967.

Haenchen, E., *The Acts of the Apostles*. E.T., Oxford 1971.

—, 'Matthäus 23', *Zeitschrift für Theologie und Kirche*. 1951.

Hare, D. R. A., *The Theme of Jewish Persecution of Christians in the Gospel according to St Matthew*. Cambridge 1967.

Hawkins, Sir J. C., *Horae Synopticae*. 2e., Oxford 1909.

Heinemann, J., 'The Triennial Lectionary Cycle', *JJS* XIX (1968), pp. 41ff.

Hengel, M., 'Die Ursprünge der christlichen Mission', *NTS* XV, no. 1, pp. 15ff.

Higgins, A. J. B., ed., *New Testament Essays*, Studies in memory of T. W. Manson. Manchester 1959.

Holtzmann, H. J., *Hand-Kommentar zum NT*. 3e., Tübingen 1901.

—, *Theologie des NT* I. Tübingen 1911.

—, ed., *Berakot* (*Die Mischna*). Giessen 1912.

Hooke, S. H., ed., *The Labyrinth*. London 1935.

Hummel, R., *Die Auseinandersetzung zwischen Kirche und Judentum im Matthäusevangelium*. Munich 1963.

Jeremias, J., *The Eucharistic Words of Jesus* [*EWJ*]. E.T., London 1966.

—, *Infant Baptism in the first four Centuries*. E.T., London 1960.

—, *Jerusalem in the Time of Jesus*. E.T., London 1969.

—, *Jesus als Weltvollender*. Gütersloh 1930.

—, *Jesus' Promise to the Nations* [*JPN*]. E.T., London 1958.

—, *The Parables of Jesus* [*PJ*]. 6e., 1962; 2e., E.T., London 1963.

—, *The Prayers of Jesus*. London 1967; *SBT* ii.6.

—, *The Sermon on the Mount*. E.T., London 1961.

—, *Unknown Sayings of Jesus*. E.T., London 1957; 2e., E.T., London 1964.

—, γραμματεύς, *TWNT* II, pp. 740ff.

Jewish Encyclopaedia.

Jewish Year Book, 1970.

Johnson, M. D., *The Purpose of the Biblical Genealogies*. Cambridge 1969.

Jones, C. P. M., *Bampton Lectures 1970*. Unpublished.

Joüon, P., Notes Philologiques, xviii (1928), pp. 349ff.

Juster, J., *Les Juifs dans L'Empire Romain*. Paris 1914.

Kenyon, F. J., *Handbook to the Textual Criticism of the New Testament*. 2e., London 1912.

Kilpatrick, G. D., *The Origins of the Gospel according to St Matthew* [*Origins*]. Oxford 1946.

Kilpatrick, G. D., 'Galatians 1.18', *New Testament Essays*, Studies in memory of T. W. Manson, ed. A. J. B. Higgins. Manchester 1959.

Kilpatrick, G. D., 'The Greek New Testament Text of Today and the *Textus Receptus*', *The New Testament in historical and contemporary perspective: essays in honour of G. H. C. MacGregor*, ed. H. Anderson and W. Barclay. Oxford 1965.

Kingsbury, J. D., *The Parables of Jesus in Matthew 13*. London 1969.

Kosmala, H., 'Matthew xxvi. 52—a Quotation from the Targum', *Novum Testamentum* 4 (1960), pp. 3ff.

Kraus, H.-J., *Worship in Israel*. E.T., Oxford 1966.

Lagrange, M.-J., *L'Évangile selon S. Matthieu*. 3e., Paris 1927.

Léon-Dufour, X., *Études d'Évangile*. Paris 1965.

Lightfoot, R. H., *The Gospel Message of St Mark*. Oxford 1950.

Lindars, B., *The New Testament Apologetic*. London 1961.

Lohmeyer, E., *Das Evangelium des Matthäus* [*Lohmeyer*], ed. W. Smauch. 3e., Göttingen 1962.

—, *The Lord's Prayer*. E.T., London 1965.

Lohse, E., *Das Passafest der Quartadecimaner*. Gütersloh 1953.

McConnell, R. S., *Law and Prophecy in Matthew's Gospel*. Basle 1969.

McKelvey, R. J., *The New Temple and the Church in the New Testament*. Oxford 1969.

McNeile, A. H., *The Gospel according to St Matthew* [*McNeile*]. London 1915.

Mann, J., *The Bible as Read and Preached in the Old Synagogue* [*BRPOS*] I. Cincinnati 1940.

Manson, T. W., *The Sayings of Jesus* [*SJ*]. London 1937.

—, *The Teaching of Jesus*. Cambridge 1931.

—, 'The Lord's Prayer', *BJRL* 38 (1955–6), pp. 99ff, 436ff.

Massaux, E., *L'Influence de l'Évangile selon S. Matthieu*. Louvain 1950.

Merkel, H., 'Jesus und die Pharisäer', *NTS* xiv, no. 2 (January 1968), pp. 194ff.

Metzger, B. M., *The Text of the New Testament*. 2e., Oxford 1968.

Montefiore, H. W., 'Jesus and the Temple Tax', *NTS* xi, no. 1 (October 1964), pp. 60ff.

Moore, G. F., *Judaism*. Cambridge, Mass., 1927.

Morgenstern, J., 'The Chanukkah Festival and the Calendar of Ancient Israel', *HUCA* xx (1947), pp. 1ff; xxi (1948), pp. 365ff.

Morgenthaler, R., *Statistik des neutestamentlichen Wortschatzes*. Zürich 1958.

Morris, L., *The New Testament and the Jewish Lectionaries*. London 1964.

Morris, N., *The Jewish School*. London 1937.

Mowinckel, S., *Psalmenstudien* II. Kristiana 1922.

—, *The Psalms in Israel's Worship* I. E.T., Oxford 1967.

Munck, J., *Paul and the Salvation of Mankind*. E.T., London 1959.

Myers, J. M., *I and II Chronicles*. Anchor Bible. New York 1965.

Neil, W., in *Peake's Commentary*, ed. M. Black and H. H. Rowley, p. 999. London 1962.

Nepper-Christensen, P., *Das Matthäusevangelium—ein judenchristliches Evangelium?* Aarhus 1958.

Nestle-Aland, *Novum Testamentum* [*Nestle-Aland*]. 25e., 1963.

New Testament Apocrypha I, ed. R. McL. Wilson and W. Schneemelcher. London 1963.

Nineham, D. E., *St Mark*. London 1963.

—, ed., *Studies in the Gospels*. Oxford 1954.

Noack, B., 'The Day of Pentecost in Jubilees, Qumran and Acts', *Annual of the Swedish Theological Institute* I (1962), pp. 73ff.

Oepke, A., 'Der Herrenspruch über die Kirche: Mt. 16, 17–19 in der neuesten Forschung', *Studia Theologica* II, Fasc. I–II (Lund 1949–50), pp. 110ff.

Otto, R., *The Kingdom of God and the Son of Man*. E.T., London 1938.

Peake's Commentary, ed. M. Black and H. H. Rowley. London 1962.

Porter, J. R., 'The Pentateuch and the Triennial Lectionary Cycle', *Promise and Fulfilment*, essays presented to S. H. Hooke, ed. F. F. Bruce. Edinburgh 1963.

Quell, see Forster.

Rad, G. von, 'The Levitical Sermon in I and II Chronicles', *The Problem of the Hexateuch and Other Essays*. E.T., Edinburgh 1966.

Rankin, O. S., *The Origins of the Festival of Ḥanukkah*. Edinburgh 1930.

—, 'The Festival of Ḥanukkah', *The Labyrinth*, ed. S. H. Hooke. London 1935.

Rengstorf, K. H., 'Die Stadt der Mörder (Mt. 22, 7)', *BZNW* 26 (1960), pp. 106ff.

Richards, H. J., 'Christ on Divorce', *Scripture* 11 (1959).

Riesenfeld, H., 'Sabbat et Jour du Seigneur', *New Testament Essays*, Studies in memory of T. W. Manson, ed. A. J. B. Higgins. Manchester 1959.

Rigaux, I. B., *Les Epîtres aux Thessaloniciens*. Paris 1956.

Rordorf, W., *Sunday*. E.T., London 1968.

Rothfuchs, W., *Die Erfüllungszitate des Matthäusevangeliums*. Stuttgart 1969.

Rudolph, W., *Chronikbücher.* Tübingen 1955.

Sanday, W., *Sacred Sites of the Gospels.* Oxford 1903.

Sanders, E. P., *The Tendencies of the Synoptic Tradition.* Cambridge 1969.

Schlatter, A., *Der Evangelist Matthäus.* Stuttgart 1929.

—, *Die Kirche des Matthäus.* Gütersloh 1929.

Schmid, J., 'Markus und der aramäische Matthäus', in his *Synoptische Studien.* Munich 1953.

Schneider, H. H., μαστιγόω *TWNT* IV, pp. 521ff.

—, Ναζαρῆνος/ωραῖος, *TWNT* IV, pp. 879ff.

Schniewind, J., *Das Evangelium nach Matthäus, NTD.* 11e., Göttingen 1964.

Schrenk, G., δικαιοσύνη, *TWNT* II, pp. 199ff.

Schürmann, H., *Das Gebet des Herrn.* Leipzig 1957.

Schweitzer, A., *The Quest of the Historical Jesus.* 2e., E.T., London 1911.

Scrivener, F. H. A., *A Plain Introduction to the Criticism of the New Testament.* 4e., London 1894.

Segbroek, F. van, 'Les citations d'accomplissement dans l'Evangile selon Matthieu d'après trois ouvrages récents', *L'Evangile selon Matthieu*, ed. M. Didier. Bibl. Ephemer. Theol. Lovan. 29, Gembloux 1972.

Selwyn, E. G., *The First Epistle of Peter.* London 1947.

Singer, S., ed., *Daily Prayer Book.* Cambridge 1914.

Soden, H. von, *Die Schriften des Neuen Testaments* I. Berlin 1911.

Sparks, H. D. F., 'Some Observations on the Semitic Background of the NT', *Bulletin of the SNTS* II (1951), pp. 39ff.

Spurgeon, C., *Shakespeare's Imagery.* Cambridge 1935.

Stendahl, K., *The School of St Matthew* [*SSM*]. Uppsala 1954.

Stenning, J. F., *The Targum of Isaiah.* Oxford 1949.

Strack, H. L., and Billerbeck, P., *Kommentar zum NT aus Talmud und Midrash* [*S-B*] I. 4e., Munich 1926.

Strecker, G., *Der Weg der Gerechtigkeit* [*WG*]. Bonn 1966.

Streeter, B. H., *The Four Gospels* [*FG*]. London 1924.

—, 'Codices 157, 1071 and the Caesarean Text', *Quantulacumque*, Studies presented to Kirsopp Lake, ed. R. P. Casey and others. London 1937.

Taylor, V., *The Formation of the Gospel Tradition.* London 1935.

—, *The Gospel according to St Mark.* London 1952.

Tödt, H. E., *The Son of Man in the Synoptic Tradition.* E.T., London 1935.

Torrey, C. C., 'The Biblical Quotations in Matthew', in his *Documents of the Primitive Church.* New York, London 1941.

Torrey, C. C., 'The Foundry of the Second Temple at Jerusalem', *JBL* LV, pt. IV (1936), pp. 247ff.

Trilling, W., *Das Wahre Israel [WI]*. 3e., Munich 1964.

Vaux, R. de, *Ancient Israel*. 2e., E.T., London 1965.

Vermes, G., *The Dead Sea Scrolls in English*. London 1962.

—, 'Bible and Midrash: Early Old Testament Exegesis', *The Cambridge History of the Bible* (Cambridge 1970) I, pp. 199ff.

Vögtle, A., 'Das christologische und ekklesiologische Anliegen von Mt. 28. 18–20', *Studia Evangelica*, II (Berlin 1964), pp. 266ff.

Weiss, B., *Das Matthäusevangelium und seine Lukas-Parallelen*. Halle 1876.

Wellhausen, J., *Das Evangelium Matthaei*. 2e., Berlin 1914.

—, *Einleitung in die drei ersten Evangelien*. Berlin 1911.

—, *Prolegomena zur Geschichte Israels*. 3e., Berlin 1886.

Westminster Historical Atlas to the Bible, ed. G. E. Wright and F. V. Filson. London 1945.

Wilcken, U., *Urkunden der Ptolemäerzeit*. Berlin 1923–57.

Wilcox, M., *The Semitisms of Acts*. Oxford 1965.

Willis, G. G., ed., *St Augustine's Lectionary*. London 1962.

Wilson, R. McL., ed. with W. Schneemelcher, *New Testament Apocrypha*. London 1963.

Windisch, H., *Der Sinn der Bergpredikt*. 2e., Leipzig 1937.

Wrege, H. T., *Die Überlieferungsgeschichte der Bergpredikt*. Tübingen 1968.

Zahn, T., *Das Evangelium des Matthäus*. 3e., Leipzig 1910.

Zerfass, R., *Die Schriftlesung im Kathedraloffizium Jerusalems*. Münster 1967.

Ziegler, I., *Königsgleichnissen*. Breslau 1903.

INDEX OF BIBLICAL PASSAGES

OLD TESTAMENT

NEW TESTAMENT

INDEX OF EXTRA-BIBLICAL PASSAGES

APOCRYPHA AND PSEUDEPIGRAPHA

RABBINICA

(See also index of rabbinic parables on pp. 66–9)

GENERAL INDEX